Capital and labour in South Africa

Monographs from the African Studies Centre, Leiden

Capital and labour in South Africa

Class struggle in the 1970s

D. du Toit

Kegan Paul International Ltd
London and Boston

First published in 1981
by Kegan Paul International Ltd
39 Store Street,
London WC1E 7DD and
9 Park Street,
Boston, Mass. 02108, USA
Set in Press Roman by
Hope Services,
Abingdon, Oxon
and printed in Great Britain by
Redwood Burn Ltd
Trowbridge & Esher

British Library Cataloguing in Publication Data

Du Toit, D

Capital and labour in South Africa.
1. South Africa – Economic conditions
I. Title
330.9'68   HC517.S7   80-41576

ISBN 0-7103-0001-8

Contents

Contents

Tables

Tables

Introduction

This study was begun in Cape Town in 1974 and published as a legal thesis (somewhat lengthier than the present edition) at the University of Leiden, the Netherlands, in 1979.

The limitations of this work should be noted at the outset. It does not pretend to provide a definitive, all-round analysis of social relations in South Africa. Its chief aim is to examine the *class* nature of the social struggle in South Africa and, in particular, to illustrate the nature that this struggle has taken on in practice.

As such, it concentrates on certain aspects of this vast and complex subject that were pushed to the fore in practice and appeared to be most in need of discussion and clarification. Other questions, including some of great importance, are treated in less detail. The position of South Africa within the world capitalist system, for instance, and the implications of the South African revolution for Southern Africa as a whole, are dealt with only briefly. Yet these two questions, above all, are fundamental to any understanding of South African society. For this reason the passages concerned (pp. 8-9, 23-4, 247-9, etc.) deserve to be given all the more attention.

The main focus of the book is the concrete unfolding of the class struggle in South Africa in the course of the 1970s. It was written in the course of a period of momentous social change in Southern Africa and on a world scale. Different chapters reflect different stages in a rapidly developing situation. The historical chapters in particular were written at a time when much of the analysis of South Africa that has been stimulated by the events of recent years had not yet appeared in print, in the light of which a clearer, more incisive treatment would have been possible. Nevertheless, to preserve the completeness of the work as a whole, these chapters could not be omitted.

Introduction

Inevitably, in a number of respects, this account has already been overtaken by events. Nevertheless its main conclusions – especially in regard to the *class* foundations of racial conflict in South Africa, and the crucial but contradictory role of the traditional black nationalist leadership within the movement of the working class – have been abundantly confirmed. The struggles of the workers and the youth have risen to new heights; the strike movement of 1979–80 has surpassed even the struggles of 1973. Conversely, the crisis of the Botha government has become even more acute than that of its predecessor. On the one hand it is driven by irrestistible mass pressure to change its methods of rule; on the other hand it is threatened with destruction by those same forces if it should yield one centimetre or lose its basis of white support. Confusion and division are rife within its ranks and in those of the capitalist class as a whole, which remains completely unable to meet the demands of the black masses. In this situation the question stands forth more sharply than ever before: what must take the place of the white capitalist regime when it crumbles, as sooner or later it must? What alternatives are at hand?

Here, too, events have confirmed that the strongest potential forces among the oppressed population remain the traditional mass organisations, in particular the African National Congress. This has remained so despite their continued lack of involvement in the struggles erupting on the ground. At the same time it is clear that the contradictions within the ANC and the South African Congress of Trade Unions – in essence, the conflict between middle-class leaders in exile (supported by the SA Communist Party) and the pressures of the proletarian masses at home – have by no means been resolved. On the contrary, over the recent period they have crystallised into a struggle for or against Marxism, for or against the task of organising the working-class following of the ANC on the basis of its own revolutionary programme that must become the programme of the movement as a whole.

Everything indicates that this struggle will be resolved only in practice, in the approaching situation where the SA state will no longer be able to prevent the presently illegal organisations, and tendencies within organisations, from competing openly for mass support. Under these conditions the alternatives to the existing regime will at last present themselves concretely to the black working-class population, and indeed to workers of all races – on the one hand, the utopian programme of *'national democracy' within the framework of capitalism*, on the other hand the fight for the *simultaneous abolition of national oppression and capitalist exploitation*. Thus the class contradictions in South

x

African society, as well as in the national liberation movement, are moving towards resolution in one and the same process in the period that has been opened up by the mass struggles of the 1970s.

Such contribution as this study can make to the discussion among those engaged in the struggle has only been possible on the foundations established by those in the labour movement in Britain, the Netherlands and elsewhere, and in the South African liberation movement, who have consistently, over the years, explained events from a working-class point of view. Their practical example has been an indispensable source of education and inspiration in carrying out this study. At the same time, its shortcomings are entirely my own responsibility.

Translations from Afrikaans and Dutch sources, unless otherwise stated, are by the author.

London   D. d. T.
September 1980

Abbreviations

AC	*The African Communist* (London)
AIM	Agency for Industrial Mission
CNV	Christelijk Nationaal Vakverbond
CIS	Counter Information Services
F	*Focus* (International Defence and Aid Fund, London)
FM	*Financial Mail* (Johannesburg)
FTF	*Forward to Freedom: Strategy and Tactics of the African National Congress*, Morogoro, Tanzania, no date
IIE	Institute for Industrial Education
OHSA	M. Wilson and L. Thompson (eds), *The Oxford History of South Africa*, Oxford, 1969, 1971
PCP	South African Communist Party, *The Road to South African Freedom*, Programme of the South African Communist Party, *The African Communist*, January–March 1963
SABRA	South African Bureau of Racial Affairs
SACTU	South African Congress of Trade Unions
SRR	South African Institute of Race Relations, *A Survey of Race Relations in South Africa*, Johannesburg, annual
Star IAW	*The Star*, International Airmail Weekly edition, Johannesburg

Part I

Historical background

Chapter 1

The industrial revolution in South Africa

A diamond was found near the Orange River in 1867, and gold was discovered on the Witwatersrand in 1884. The transformation of South Africa from a backward agrarian country into a modern industrial state dates from this period. A hundred years later, the full implications of South Africa's industrial revolution are only beginning to be realised.

At the beginning of the mining period the substructure for industrial society was almost entirely absent. Transport was primitive, markets were undeveloped, the population of the country as a whole was poor and thinly scattered. South Africa was fragmented into three British colonies, two Boer republics, several African chiefdoms and other independent communities. In the main urban centre, Cape Town, there were only seventy manufacturing concerns in 1860. Of the half-million inhabitants of the Cape Colony, only 20,000 were employed in manufacturing and commerce (*OHSA*, vol. 2, p. 2). The major export was wool. Labour relations centred upon the labour requirements of the landowners. Social and political relations centred on the landowners' relations on the one hand with British imperial power, on the other hand with the African tribal and semi-tribal population.

One vital condition for urban and industrial growth, however, did exist. Out of the African tribal peoples, the landowners had created an abundant supply of labour. Already at the close of the eighteenth century, the once-independent tribal population of the Western Cape had been reduced to a 'landless proletariat' (Marais, 1939, p. 109). Over the following hundred years the same process was repeated on an ever-widening scale in the interior of South Africa. De Kiewiet (1941, p. 74) describes this process as 'the keen competition of two groups, with very similar agricultural and pastoral habits, for the possession of

3

the most fertile and best-watered stretches of land'. But it was violent
and bloody competition, marked by innumerable wars and battles. The
effects of the struggle, de Kiewiet (1941, p. 75) observes, also reveal its
causes:

> They can be seen in the loss of native land, in the growing
> inability of the natives to maintain themselves in the more
> restricted and less fertile areas, and in the diminishing means
> of independent livelihood of the tribes.

For the surplus population thus created in the remaining pockets of
African settlement, survival meant work on the farms. No alternative
remained. All rebellion was defeated. The break-up of tribal society
was hastened by other means. Forced labour was an early institution
at the Cape, and later in the north. Innumerable African men, women
and children were transported to the farms as 'apprentices'. At the
same time traders developed markets in African areas for manufactured
commodities ranging from alcohol to clothes, soap and spades. Taxation,
direct as well as indirect, was increasingly imposed on the remnants of
the tribal population, the aim being 'not to provide revenue, but to
compel labour' (Hobson, 1938, p. 268). The missionaries played an
important role in undermining the ideological independence of the
African peoples and preaching the gospel of wage labour. These burdens
were more than the weakened tribal economies could bear. New sources
of wealth had to be found: 'The tribes had only one thing to sell which
was in steady demand,' writes the historian. 'It was their labour' (*OHSA*,
vol. 2, p. 281).

This was the beginning of the *reserve system*, which would later be
developed methodically to meet the enormous labour requirements of
industry and mining. Together with this system developed its inevitable
concomitant, the *pass laws*. This process was more than military conquest. It was the transition from one social order to another. For all
the surface resemblance between the pastoralism of the landowners
and that of the tribes, the systems were fundamentally different. In
general, tribal society was based on communal land ownership and
communal division of labour: 'The worth of . . . possessions lay in
their utility rather than in accumulation' (Glass, n.d., p. 7). Surplus
was divided in prescribed ways and 'the profit motive was unknown'
(*ibid*., p. 8).

The order imposed by the landowners and later the British army,
on the other hand, was a capitalist order. Established by Dutch merchant capital in the seventeenth century, it remained at the primitive

level of a merchant system for the better part of two centuries to come. The very backwardness of capitalism in pre-industrial South Africa has led some authors to regard it as 'pre-capitalistic'. Of course this was not so. The productive system of the landowners was based on the private ownership of capital and land. The labour they employed was wage labour, even though wages were often so low as to be almost non-existent, and were paid in kind as often as in cash. Despite severe limitations on the market, production was for profit, and sharp differences in wealth developed among the farmers. At no stage did they abandon the exchange of commodities. At all stages they remained linked to the trade routes with Europe to obtain commodities, such as rifles, on which their survival depended.

Indeed, during the last phase of the pre-industrial period capitalism in South Africa finally entered a period of growth. With the conquest of the Cape by industrial Britain, the worst restrictions of the merchants' order were abolished and South Africa was opened to world trade. From 1806 to 1831 the Cape wine industry experienced an unprecedented boom. In the interior wool production increased sharply from the 1840s onwards. 'The native wars', it has been concluded, 'were merely spectacular phases in a social and economic revolution' (de Kiewiet, 1941, p. 78). Although brought about by military conquest and not by popular struggle, this revolution transformed South Africa no less fundamentally. This was the form that South Africa's 'bourgeois revolution' took historically. Tribalism as a living system was broken beyond repair. In the wake of military conquest a new possessing class established the basis of a capitalist system, while growing sections of the African population were reduced to a rural proletariat.

The industrial revolution, therefore, did not change South Africa from a pre-capitalist into a capitalist society. Within the existing capitalist system it ended the dominance of primitive agrarian production and established that of industry and mining. It created an urban working class next to the rural working class and a layer of skilled workers on top of the unskilled. It finally welded the different parts of the subcontinent into a single economic system. It subjected South Africa to the interests of finance capital, in the first instance British finance capital. In this entire process it shifted the focal point of South African society – and with it that of industrial relations – from the countryside to the towns.

The social and industrial system that now developed in South Africa was fundamentally no different from the more advanced systems of America or Western Europe. This is reflected in the fact that investment, labour and commodities are readily interchangeable among these different areas. In essence industrial relations in South Africa can be studied no differently from industrial relations in other capitalist countries. South Africa does not have a new and unique system to which new and unique criteria should be applied. It has industrial workers and employers standing in the same fundamental relationship to one another as industrial workers and employers elsewhere. The forms are inevitably different, but the substance is the same.

The impact of diamond mining on backward South Africa was explosive and the march of events ever since has been rapid, ruthless, violent, anything but moderate or gradual (*OHSA*, vol. 2, p. 12):

> Diamond-mining provided a new source of wealth which
> dramatically altered the pattern of economic life . . . the lure
> of diamonds attracted both capital and immigrants; the
> concentration of people on the diggings required food, and a
> new market was opened to the farmer; new forms of transport
> became essential, and the revenue from diamonds helped to
> finance railway construction.

Then, in 1886, the Witwatersrand was proclaimed a gold-mining area, 'and the whole of Southern Africa was drawn into the new mining boom which exceeded anything yet experienced' (*ibid.*, p.13).

In itself the South African economy was completely unable to cope with development on this scale. It had neither the capital nor the skilled labour with which to exploit its fabulous mineral wealth. In medieval and post-medieval Europe capital had been formed gradually out of agricultural surplus and commercial profit. In South Africa these sources were hopelessly inadequate. Instead capital came pouring in from overseas, especially from Britain, in fully developed forms, drawn by the promise of rich and easy profits. Investment in diamond mining by 1881 totalled an estimated R16 million. In gold mining, from 1887 to 1905, some R208 million was invested. Of the R400 million invested on the Witwatersrand up to 1932, an estimated R240 million had come from overseas (Frankel, 1938; Houghton, 1973, p. 39). By 1973 a total of some R1,300 million of foreign capital was invested in the South African mining industry (*Financial Mail*, 15 April 1976).

In gold as well as in diamond mining the early developments laid the basis for future industrial relations. Individual diggers and small operators were soon eliminated. As mining proceeded to deeper levels, ever larger operations and investment were required. Corporations developed and rapidly merged or combined into huge monopolies, like the de Beers Consolidated Mines in Kimberley and the Chamber of Mines in Johannesburg. Operating in a relative vacuum the mammoth corporations wielded tremendous power. At the same time this power rested very much in the hands of foreign bankers and investors. Even the administration of Griqualand West, we are told, 'was so poor and its income so insufficient, that its solvency was at the mercy of banking interests' (de Kiewiet, 1941, p. 92). This administration reflected, in an extreme form, the future South African state in its relationship to foreign capital. South African employers were at the same time the managers of overseas interests and heavily dependent on the latter. The weakness of South African capital in relation to world capitalism would be of decisive importance in shaping the development of the future industrial state.

The skilled men needed to work in the mines were imported together with the capital required. According to the principle of supply and demand, labour is hired at the lowest price for which it can be obtained. Higher wages, and working conditions equivalent to what they were used to, had to be offered to British artisans and miners to bring them to a far and backward country. This included the right of trade-union organisation and a certain degree of social and political freedom. In the case of the impoverished survivors of disintegrating tribal society, on the other hand, supply and demand had a very different meaning. Lacking any prospects on the land, they were generally forced to accept employment on whichever terms it was offered. The main alternative to mine labour, with wages ranging from ten to thirty shillings a week, was farm labour for as little as ten or seven shillings a month (*OHSA*, vol. 2, pp. 121-2; van der Horst, 1942, p. 80). Some 10,000 Africans flocked to the diamond fields each year (de Kiewiet, 1941, p. 91).

With unskilled workers available in vast numbers and at low wages, without any form of organisation, the demand for immigrant workers was limited to an absolute minimum. This is one important reason why South Africa never attracted European immigrants on the same scale as Australia, America or Canada. The vast majority of the people who flowed to the diamond fields were Africans looking for work as unskilled manual workers:

> For every little clerk, deserting sailor, drought-stricken farmer
> or turn-collar parson who came to the fields, there came two,
> three and four Zulus, Basuto, Bechuana and Xosas. . . . They

7

were evidence of the disruption of tribal life and economy. Henceforth the native problem was urban and industrial as well and no longer simply rural. The first step was taken towards the later detribalized and landless urban proletariat of the South African industrial towns (*ibid*.).

Thus from the outset sharp differences marked the conditions of white immigrant and black South African workers, of skilled and unskilled labour. From the standpoint of later development, the first two centuries of capitalism in South Africa can be summarised very briefly. In satisfying their own hunger for land and labour, the land-owners had at the same time created a vast potential supply of cheap industrial labour. But they lacked the means to harness it. Now British capital appeared on the scene and began exploiting these conditions to the full.

On the Kimberley diamond fields employers discovered an extremely favourable situation as far as unskilled labour was concerned. African unskilled workers were available in practically limitless numbers, willing to work for negligible wages and lacking the organisation to drive their wages up. At the same time the danger existed that this favourable situation might not last for long. The conditions which employers found at Kimberley reflected a certain stage in the collapse of tribalism and the development of capitalism. Left unmanaged, they might tend to disappear, giving way to industrial relations that would grow progressively less favourable from the employer's point of view. Supply and demand, however, obeys no mechanical law. They are created by active competition, and are not passively obeyed. Market forces can be controlled. The market 'always operates within politically defined parameters' (IIE, 1974, p. 136). A party enjoying a favourable market position is free to try and preserve it, and normally will do so. Where labour is available freely and cheaply, employers will do their utmost to ensure that it remains so.

Capitalism, moreover, is an international system; competition takes place not only nationally but internationally. Despite the lucrative earnings of the mine-owners and for all its industrial growth, the South African economy as a whole remained weak in relation to the world economy. Industry appeared late on the scene, at a stage when murderous competition between the major industrial powers had already led to the First World War. Capital invested in South Africa – except in gold and diamond mining – was unable to conquer a significant share of the world market. Even the internal market was largely a playground of foreign interests. This placed severe limits on the ability of the South African economy to develop on a capitalist basis. These limits have been expressed most clearly in the level of wage rates. South African capital, deprived of adequate markets, could only expand at the cost of the working class. South African capital in general has remained dependent on a low average rate of wages.

These pressures have been of decisive importance in shaping South African social relations. History reflects this very clearly. The pragmatic experience of employers gave rise to deliberate policy. By 1903 it was explicitly recognised by the gold mine owners that any economic independence on the part of the African population meant an interruption in their flow of labour (Reports of the Transvaal Labour Commission, 1904). For a labour market that would remain satisfactory from the employers' point of view, certain conditions had to be maintained. A large part of the African population would have to remain tied to limited pieces of land, on which they would be unable to support themselves.[1] Only then would they be forced to continue offering themselves for employment in large numbers and for whatever wages they could get. Once systematic legal control is established over this flow of labour, any change in the relationship is theoretically ruled out. One effect of the reserve system is that for many urban Africans it is illegal to be unemployed. Thus many workers must stay with their jobs, regardless of wages or working conditions.[2] It takes no great insight to realise that employers would safeguard these conditions very jealously indeed.

The destructive effects of the reserve system on African family life have been widely recognised. Also, from the point of view of the reserves themselves, the system is a vicious circle. The more men are driven by poverty to work in the towns, the more the reserves will tend to stagnate into even greater poverty through the drain of manpower. This process – the proletarianisation of the rural African population – may be compared with the process that took place in Britain between the sixteenth and the nineteenth centuries, i.e. the expropriation of the peasants and small independent farmers by the landlord class. Marx (1974, p. 676) describes the essence of what happened:

> Even in the last decade of the 17th century, the yeomanry, the
> class of independent peasants, were more numerous than the class
> of the farmers. . . . About 1750, the yeomanry had disappeared,
> and so had, in the last decade of the 18th century, the last trace of
> the common land of the agricultural labourer.

This development came to a climax in the eighteenth century with the creation of legal instruments for destroying the independence of the peasantry: the Acts for enclosures of commons. The effect is described by a contemporary observer (*ibid.*, p. 679):

> When this land gets into the hands of a few great farmers, the consequence must be that the little farmers will be converted into a body of men who earn their subsistence by working for others, and who will be under a necessity of going to market for all they want... Towns and manufactures will increase, because more will be driven to them in quest of places and employment.

If in Britain the transformation of the independent rural population into a proletariat was carried through without interruption, in South Africa it has been retarded. By means of legislation it has been deliberately attempted to slow down the movement of rural people to the cities, thus prolonging the period of forced migration, and with it the cheapness of labour power that is characteristic of this period. The reconstitution of the dislocated rural people into a coherent urban proletariat has been fought with might and main. Comparable with South African state policy is the 'migrant worker' system that has been operated on a large scale in the advanced industrial countries since the Second World War. What is said of foreign workers in the Netherlands by Harmsen and Reinalda (1975, p. 406) might equally well have been said of the black migrant workers of South Africa:

> Unskilled and with a weak legal position, they form an extremely mobile section of the labour force, one that can be freely reduced or expanded. When employment is reduced they can be discarded and fall back into the industrial reserve army, when employment is increased this reservoir can once again be drawn upon. The [foreign workers'] wages remain lower than the wages of [Dutch workers], and exercise a downward pressure on the latter.

In South Africa the labour market found on the diamond fields thus became a precedent for the industrial economy as a whole. Few employers are prepared to hire labour on worse terms than their competitors. Where the precedent is set by employers as immense and powerful as the mining companies, its effect becomes all-pervading. It becomes a basic condition for competitive investment: 'The servile tradition of the farm', as de Kiewiet (1941, p. 91) puts it, 'was introduced into industry. It was a crude political economy that exploited the ignorance and poverty of the natives, and at the same time perpetuated these defects.'

The overwhelming power of the first large-scale employers in South Africa was exerted in different ways. Characteristic of their power was the compound system, and this has remained so to the present day. Even in the eyes of the moderate Douwes-Dekker (Coetzee, 1976, p. 188), the compound system is the most rational form of labour exploitation yet devised. Again, it may be noted, such a system is not unique. In the Dutch pottery industry in Maastricht, for instance, comparable methods were used in the early years of this century (Harmsen and Reinalda, 1975, p. 97):

Poverty forces the parents to send their children to the factory. But if the parents are reluctant to do so because of the miserable working conditions, they are dismissed. . . . [The children] are housed at the factory and separated from their parents for three months at a time. They escape from the workplace in groups. The prison stands opposite the factory. To make escape impossible, a tunnel has been dug from the sleeping quarters to the factory. On Sundays the children are taken to and from church under escort, but then they go through the tunnel to the factory again.

It is commonly alleged that the compounds on the South African diamond mines were established to prevent (black) workers from appropriating diamonds and selling them independently. This explanation, however, is insufficient. It does not tell us why compounds were also established on the gold fields, where the chances of finding an ingot of pure gold were remote, and later even at large factories and elsewhere. It does not even explain properly why the Kimberley compounds were 'closed'. Also, the mine-owners of Johannesburg, we are told (*OHSA*, vol. 2, p. 180), 'would have preferred closed compounds as a measure against desertions [but] it was impossible to establish them, owing to the strong opposition of the traders'.

The economist Wilson (1972a, pp. 6-7) suggests a number of further explanations. The men were drawn from far afield and had to be assured of a place to stay; neighbouring governments might be unwilling to let thousands of men leave permanently with their families; compound housing was cheaper. None of these factors could have been decisive. Other South African employers, faced with the same considerations, did not respond by building compounds. Whether or not compound housing is available, African people have streamed to the towns in search of work. This explains the shanty towns which even today are sprawled around towns and cities and which, from the employers' viewpoint, are also the cheapest of all. There is even a tendency for workers to abandon their bachelor quarters and drift to the shanty towns where they can live with their families, even though precariously and mostly illegally. Wilson (1972b, p. 2) further suggests that closed compounds may have provided the workers with some stability and security. But there is no evidence that this factor weighed heavily with the mine-owners who established the compound system.

Notwithstanding all this speculation, a more fundamental explanation for the compound system is not difficult to find. It is clear that such a system must affect industrial relations profoundly. It limits the worker's independence, isolating him from other workers and placing him more completely under the employer's influence and control. Employer and landlord become one. Coupled with the reserve system, a closed circuit is formed to which the employer in theory holds the key. In the mining industry, with its vast capital outlay, calling for maximum assurance of stable industrial relations, such a consideration must weigh very heavily indeed. In the existing system, Wilson acknowledges (1972a, p. 135), employers see the following benefits: 'Low wages, less leave and absenteeism, better control, less risk of the men getting silicosis, and greater output in jobs involving hard physical work.' From the employer's point of view, it is basically the fact of control that justified the establishment of the system and, later, its maintenance in the face of severe public criticism and unrest among the inmates of the compounds.

Nor could the effects of the compound system remain limited to the mines alone. Capitalist production takes place on the basis of competitive investment. Market forces drive investors in the non-mining sector to seek equally favourable conditions for themselves. In practice this could only mean restrictive legislation. Within the framework of the reserve system the mine-owners could effectively control their workers. Other employers could only rely on the state to place them in an equally strong position. The outcome has been a complex of laws and regulations by which, in effect, African workers in general are prevented from reaching a stronger bargaining position than those inside the compounds. Legislation has kept the reserve system in existence. It has placed crippling disabilities on those Africans who managed to break free of the migratory cycle and settled themselves permanently in the towns. In this way the conditions of the colonial labour market have been prolonged into the modern industrial state – a policy that has been bound to call for increasing rigour as the historical incongruities which it sought to maintain became greater.

The enormous power over their workers wielded by the original employers thus became a characteristic of, and indeed a condition for, the further development of the capitalist economy, and with it of the legal order. The explosive tensions created by this policy have led to a great deal of discussion on how the explosiveness can be eased away. From the side of the government and its supporters, it is argued with child-like logic that if the urban African population forms a danger to law and order, then this population should be eliminated or reduced. Many statements have been put out to the effect that 'the government is therefore determined to abolish the old laissez-faire approach to Bantu labour and limit such labour to the necessary and inevitable minimum' (Rhoodie, 1965, p. 133).

But the expanding industrial economy has come to depend on more, not less, African labour. Among employers who recognise this fact some degree of reform is generally considered to be essential as a means of minimising conflict. It is stated with great regularity that the conditions of the African workers ought to be improved. 'Liberalism' of this nature is dictated not so much by progressive instincts as by ordinary business interests. Even an avowed anti-liberal such as van Rensburg (1965, p. 206) has no quarrel with liberalism on this score:

> happy and contented employees are an investment [for the employer] yielding its dividends in the form of higher productivity, less turnover, better quality work, less absenteeism, longer lasting machinery ... and greater continuity. For the Bantu worker a healthier attitude towards his work brings more confidence in his employer and greater diligence.

Certain 'liberals' go further and argue that every increase in the wages of African workers means an expansion of the market. Through sharp wage increases the idle capacity of the South African economy could be taken up and real income could rise without inflation setting in. There are further reasons also, Doxey (1961, p. 186) suggests, why the existing wage structure might be disadvantageous to employers:

> The apparent savings made as a result of the comparatively low wage-rates for non-whites are very likely to be at least partly offset by their low productivity, while any net saving may be more than negated by a failure on the part of whites to match their high wages with compensatingly high standards of work performance.

These ideas are a thinly veiled attack on the wages and working conditions of free labour. As the Institute for Industrial Education (1974, p. 152) more openly declares, 'if Black wages are meaningfully increased the present high rate [of] saving and of growth can be maintained, but only by cutting in to the level of consumption of property owners and White salary and wage earners'. The deep-rooted conflict between 'liberal' capitalism and the existence of free labour in South Africa will be considered more fully in due course. For the moment it need only be noted that even from a capitalist point of view the 'liberal' argument is inconclusive.

Doxey (1961, p. 183) uses the term 'productivity' in its most general sense as referring to the average standard of output per worker. On this basis it is not clear how he reaches his conclusions as to the productivity of specific groups of workers. More generally, the 'liberal' argument implies that employers would benefit from an increase in the wage rate of African workers. In fact, employers have always been free to increase wages, collectively as well as individually, to any level that they wished. In industries such as the mining industry, wages for African workers are unilaterally determined by employers, without dictation by any interest other than their own. In general, however, they have shown no desire to increase wages of their own accord. If anything, wage strikes by African workers bring out the clear determination of a large cross-section of employers to resist increases in the wage rate. Even a government highly concerned with increasing productivity has shown no practical recognition of increased wages as a means of achieving this.[3] In the circumstances the remarkable reluctance of employers to reap the benefits of paying their workers higher wages, despite having these benefits repeatedly pointed out to them, needs to be explained.

The basic explanation is that Doxey's line of reasoning is false. Professor Steenkamp (1962, p. 107) no doubt speaks for a great many employers when he answers that

> no one has yet succeeded in proving that a large general rise in Bantu wages would exert a net favourable effect upon the economy. It is true that an increase in consumption would have a stimulating effect and that the existence of idle capacity would tend to reduce what inflationary pressures there might be. But it must not be concluded that an increase in consumption purchased at the expense of a *direct increase in business expenditures* would not, on balance, raise our cost structure or create unemployment, or do both of these things.

Proponents of the theory of higher consumption, it is pointed out, argue from a generalised ('macroeconomic') standpoint, disregarding the short-term implications of a sharply rising wage rate in the case of particular industries or firms. Industries such as brick-making, for example, where the rate of profit is relatively low and the proportion of African workers relatively high, would not remain profitable in the event of a significant wage increase. The alleged benefits of increased consumption would be limited to employers who produce for the internal consumer market. To employers producing for the export market, higher wages would be an unmitigated disaster. Thus a general rise in the wages of African workers would have a 'deleterious net effect' (Steenkamp, 1962, p. 103) by

> causing a profit deflation and hence further inhibiting investment both from local and overseas sources; raising unit costs of production and thus reducing our net foreign earnings by, on the one hand, reducing export earnings and, on the other hand, stimulating imports; and disturbing the balance of payments.

A number of factors thus help to explain the strong unwillingness among South African employers to permit a significant increase in the wages of African workers and hence in the overall cost of labour. In the first place the general laws of competition in South Africa tend to keep wages from rising. Lower wages tend to mean higher profits, and capital will generally seek out situations where the return on investment is high. In South Africa, as in other countries, the rate of wages is an important factor in determining the rate of profit. Existing investment has taken place on the basis of existing wage rates and the existing rates of profit. Any significant increase in the average rate of wages will create an entirely new situation. It will tend, in the absence of some compensating factor, to make investment less profitable. Compensation in the form of a larger consumer market, Steenkamp argues, might prove more illusory than real. A decline in the profitability of investment will give rise to a tendency for capital to withdraw to more favourable situations. Certain employers, Steenkamp points out, would literally be ruined by a higher rate of wages. Employers with few reserves, who operate on the fringes of profitability even in the present situation, would be instantly wiped out by a sharp rise in the cost of labour.

'Reform', in the sense of a meaningful increase in the living standards of African workers, would thus be more or less catastrophic to the capitalist system in South Africa. Large-scale bankruptcy among small employers, coupled with an outflow of foreign investment, would mean serious economic dislocation and untold further consequences. Wage reform can be considered a viable proposition only as the lesser of two evils, when even greater catastrophe is impending. These considerations, notwithstanding all academic arguments to the contrary, are second nature to South African employers. General Smuts, many years ago, made this absolutely clear:[4]

> You cannot, as our industries are today here in South Africa, pay the black man a wage which will be a subsistence wage for the white man and still continue to run these industries. Many of these industries will be closed, unemployment will be accentuated, great confusion and dislocation will result.

This answers the question of why, though in Europe it has proved possible to mitigate or abolish practices such as migrant labour and the compound system, in South Africa they have remained an integral part of the economy. Nothing has happened since the time of General Smuts to lessen the dependence of South African employers on a low rate of wages. Indeed, investment on the basis of cheap labour has multiplied; the 'dislocation' resulting from a change in the wage rate would be all the greater.

'Liberal' theorists tend to shrink from these conclusions and suggest instead that the wages earned by white workers – which are 'normal' by the standards of Western capital – are the cause of the abnormally low wages earned by African workers. As de Kiewiet (1941, p. 213) puts it, 'because it was possible to give high rates of pay to only a small proportion of the population, it inevitably followed that the remuneration of the rest of the population was unusually low'. This conclusion, however, is by no means inevitable, nor does it even remotely follow. Rather, it can be said that it proved impossible to *avoid* giving 'high rates of pay' to certain sections of the working class, and possible to avoid it in the case of others. In this process a low average rate of wages combined with sharp differentials undoubtedly became a feature of the South African economy. It is the result, however, of no necessity other than the functioning of the capitalist labour market. Marred by contradictions and *non sequiturs* of this nature, the 'liberal' analysis obscures rather than illuminates the nature of the South African economy; and Steenkamp (1962, p. 108) must be agreed with when he observes that some liberal economists, 'in their anxiety about the social and political aspects, are inclined to overlook the economic side'.

By the early 1890s gold mining had taken precedence over diamond mining as South Africa's major export industry. Its role in relation to the growth of manufacturing industry was not a simple one. On the one hand, it created the urban markets which both agriculture and secondary industry needed for their development. On the other hand, de Kiewiet observed (1941, p. 163):

> diamonds and gold did much to restrict industrial development. They absorbed skilled and unskilled labour alike. They paid such high wages that other employers could hardly compete with them for the services of skilled labour. They brought such an increase in prosperity to the land that the protection of local industries did not become an imperative issue.

With the growth of local industries new contradictions arose. Manufacturing industry in South Africa could only develop behind walls of tariff protection. To the mining industry, however, tariffs meant cost increases. Only gradually was this conflict lessened by the growing merger of mining and industrial capital. In the early stages the state had a crucial role to play in overcoming these contradictions. State intervention was needed not only to secure a labour supply for the factories, but to render manufacturing at all competitive. A government report of 1948 (Houghton, 1973, p. 112) explained:

> Many agricultural products and a large number of secondary industries receive protection from the State in the form of tariffs, subsidies, . . . etc., and this cost must ultimately be borne by those economic activities which receive no protection, of which gold mining is one of the most important.

In an economy where the scales were tilted heavily in favour of the mining industry, the state thus acted to even the balance and create a more uniform rate of profit for the economy as a whole. It created the social and legal conditions under which industrial capital found it possible to coexist with mining capital, and it diverted part of the enormous mining profits to new industries. This points at a conclusion that will present itself again and again: in the final analysis the interests of employers in general must prevail over those of one particular section of employers; and an important function of the state is to manage the general interest of employers.

The industrial revolution brought political upheaval in its wake. Before the advent of diamond mining South Africa was only loosely held together. Isolated pockets of tribal resistance remained. The primitive agricultural order developed under Dutch merchant rule still survived in the interior of the country. In the Orange Free State and the Transvaal the landowners were still politically independent. Only the coastal areas were under direct control of British industrial capitalism. Diamonds and gold, however, were found in the remote interior. Modern industrial growth exploded precisely in the most backward parts of the country. It was overwhelmingly British capital that found its way to these new sources of wealth and profited from their exploitation. German imperialism, however, was hovering in the wings. The extension of British political control over the interior was the inevitable next step. The annexation of the diamond fields was carried through in the face of relatively weak opposition. In the case of the gold fields a full-scale war was required to wrest power from a more solidly established Boer state.

The Anglo–Boer war marked a major turning-point in South African history. It involved a struggle between the urban and the rural sections of the possessing and employing classes in South Africa, and it led to the clear triumph of finance and mining capital. As far as urban industrial relations were concerned, it brought about a shift in the balance of power. In Kruger's republic the state had given the mine-owners only qualified support. Under the British crown the mine-owners were immediately in a far more powerful position.

The Anglo–Boer war paved the way to a politically and economically unified South Africa. With the political independence of the landowners destroyed, their dependence on urban capital was complete. Electoral arrangements would continue to give them a strong voice in government, always subject, however, to the dominant interests of industry and mining. This relationship was foreshadowed with remarkable clearness by the friendship between Cecil John Rhodes, archetypal imperialist, and Jan Hendrik Hofmeyr, leader of the Afrikaner Bond (*OHSA*, vol. 2, pp. 306–7):

As acquaintance ripened into friendship, they found that their political attitudes had a great deal in common. They agreed that the British government should not be permitted to interfere in the internal affairs of South Africa. They agreed that the future of South Africa depended on the co-operation of Boer and Briton. They agreed in regarding the African tribesmen as 'barbarous' people who should be prevented from obtaining a foothold in the political systems of the colonies and republics. In general terms, too, they agreed that South African union, and British imperial co-operation for trade and defence, were both desirable objectives.

During the same period the last opposition by the African tribes was crushed. The 1906 rebellion among rural Zulus against the imposition of new taxes was suppressed at the cost of some 4,000 African lives (Roux, 1964, pp. 89-96). For the rural African people there could be no further independent role. Their future would be governed by urban industrial society. In all essentials the South African political economy in this period took on its modern shape. The Union of 1910 was merely the formal seal.

The reserve system likewise was legally enshrined in this period. In 1913 the Native Land Act was passed. Not only did this Act prohibit Africans from buying any further land outside the reserves, it also prohibited them from holding such land as the tenants or partners of white farmers. The effect was to dispossess large numbers of settled African farmers and turn them into a landless proletariat. At the same time, it was ensured that the mounting pressure on land would find little further relief. To the existing reserves or 'scheduled areas' the Bantu Trust and Land Act of 1936 added certain further 'released areas'. But 'scheduled' and 'released' areas together amounted to little more than one-eighth of the area of South Africa and, according to one government commission, could not support more than one-half of the total African population, even when fully developed (*OHSA*, vol. 2, p. 409). Henceforth a large part of the black population would have absolutely no alternative but to seek a living in the towns.

At the same time, the conditions under which people could leave the reserves and enter paid employment became more rigidly circumscribed. The administration of the reserve system depends completely on the pass laws, as a means of exercising the necessary control over the movement of each individual African. In general, wage labour is the African's only real passport for leaving the reserve. A pass may be defined as a document stating whether or not an African is employed. In one form or another pass laws have existed in South Africa since 1760. The classical pass law was promulgated by Sir John Craddock in 1809. The industrial revolution gave the system a new lease on life. 'Mining pressure,' we read, resulted in the passing of [Transvaal] law 31 of 1896 whose aim was 'to have a hold on the native whom we have brought down . . . at a considerable outlay to ourselves (*ibid*., p. 197).

The policy that now took shape was contradictory only on the surface. It is this contradictory appearance by which van der Horst (1942, p. 123) was struck: 'While all these efforts were being made to increase the supply of labour, restrictions on movement were at the same time tending to make the search for employment a hazardous undertaking which might end in imprisonment for the would-be labourer'. In fact, by these very means South African employers have gained an iron grip on the majority of their workers. A survey published in 1970 is revealing. Of the 150 African workers interviewed, only 15 per cent were in their jobs because they liked them. The remainder were 'forced into it, so to speak', by 'the need to obtain employment as soon as possible in order not to lose the right of residence' (IIE, 1974, p. 143).

With the growth of manufacturing industry a uniform pass law was extended to the country as a whole. The basic instrument was the Native (Urban Areas) Act of 1923, as amended on numerous occasions, consolidated in 1945 and amended yet again. Even in its final form the thrust of this measure was simple. Section 10(1) prohibited all people classified as 'Bantu' from remaining in any urban area for more than seventy-two hours unless they were born there or unless, in effect, they worked there. Unless their labour-power is required, Africans coming to town are subject to immediate removal or imprisonment. In 1952 the administrative side of the system was placed on a more methodical footing with the statute misleadingly known as the Bantu (Abolition of Passes and Co-ordination of Documents) Act. In fact, only the word 'pass' was abolished; the term 'reference book' was now introduced in its place. These legal provisions will be discussed more fully below. The point to be noted here is that the basic instruments of state control over the mass of the working class, the reserve system and the pass laws, grew to their full stature as the industrial revolution developed. Social oppression and economic development have never been opposed to each other, as liberal spokesmen allege. They have manifestly gone hand in hand.

In this light the nature and significance of social oppression in South Africa can be more precisely understood. By means of the processes that have been described, there took place the creation and maintenance of 'a supply of cheap docile labour' (Doxey, 1961, p. 109). With this commodity available, employers inevitably made extensive use of it. 'You can deal with the Kaffir very much as you like,' explained an employer in the early years of this century, 'but you cannot deal with the white man as you like' (Johnstone, 1976, p. 60). The powerful position enjoyed by the first major employers were extended by law to employers as a class. Conversely, the disadvantages imposed by history on the first unskilled workers in the towns were imposed by law on African workers in general. In 1976 the press (*Cape Times*, 3 April 1976) would still be able to speak of 'the use of the baton charge as a weapon in industrial disputes'. The conclusion can be drawn at this stage already that, under these conditions, political democracy and free collective bargaining were ruled out in advance.

In the same process the racialistic division of the working class became an entrenched feature of South African industrial relations. As the *Oxford History* (vol. 2, p. 22) observes: 'The wage structure in mining tended to be carried over to other industrial activities. One might have expected that this disparity would have tended to disappear in the course of time as unskilled workers acquired new skills. This has not been the case.' The reasons for this peculiar development, the *Oxford History* finds, were partly customary and partly legislative. But what were the reasons for such legislation and the maintenance of such custom? In the 'liberal' view it is the white working class, rather than the interests of employers and state, that is basically responsible for racialism in South Africa. According to van der Horst (1942, p. 186), it was the 'social policy characterised by the social bar' which influenced 'both the living conditions and the organisation and payment of the Native labour force', and not vice versa. According to this mode of reasoning, employers and black workers are fellow victims of the white workers in that 'employers . . . are prevented from making full use of the capacities of the native' (*OHSA*, vol. 2, p. 191).

A different side of the matter is reflected in the finding of a government commission (van der Horst, 1942, pp. 177–8) that 'the pass laws made the employment of Natives more attractive than the employment of Europeans', and 'the conditions which made coloured labour more attractive than white were "almost entirely conditions created by legislation and administration" '. Elsewhere, indeed, van der Horst herself (1942, p. 157) concedes that 'the predominant European attitude [during the late nineteenth century] was that of an employer class concerned to increase the supply of labour without increasing its cost.'

It is precisely this inconsistency on the part of eminent authorities, and the resultant confusion of ideas, that will compel us to return to a question that may have appeared fairly obvious at first.

The industrial transformation of South Africa shifted the basis of social, political and legal development from the countryside to the towns. 'After 1870,' according to the *Oxford History* (vol. 2, p. 174), 'the main area of conflict was the industrial labour market.' The classes and groupings of agrarian colonial society gave way to those of the modern industrial state. 'If cultural homogeneity *between* [racial] groups increased,' as the *Oxford History* (*ibid*., p. 242) puts it, 'differentiation *within* each group increased as well.' By the end of the nineteenth century this process had become marked within the erstwhile Afrikaner community (*ibid*., p. 339):

> As a result of the closing of the frontiers of white settlement and the growth of the market economy, many families were being reduced to landlessness and becoming either *bywoners* (clients of landowners with squatting rights) or unskilled urban workers. At the same time, more capable men were exploiting the opportunities presented by the growth of urban markets to become progressive, capitalist farmers and a few, after higher education in the Cape Colony and in Britain or the Netherlands, were practising as lawyers or journalists.

This process of class differentiation gathered momentum with the onset of the industrial revolution. The twentieth century saw the further growth not only of the politically influential Afrikaner middle class but also of 'a prosperous and assertive entrepreneurial class, greatly assisted after 1948 by an Afrikaner nationalist government' (*ibid*., p. 207).

The degree of urbanisation of the white population as a whole increased from 51.6 per cent in 1911 to 65.2 per cent in 1936 and 86.7 per cent in 1970 (*South African Statistics*, 1974). The division between Afrikaans and English-speaking whites, though still stressed in some quarters, lost most of its original sharpness. Political and economic divisions could no longer be identified with language divisions alone. Emerging instead to overshadow all sectional interest of this nature we find the more clear-cut interests of employers, of the middle classes and of an urban working class. 'White unity' as a front of these different social classes was symbolised by the Republic of 1961.

A similar process had been taking place since the eighteenth century among the 'coloured' working people of the Cape, and was to repeat itself among the African and Indian population of Natal and the interior. The social formations of the agricultural period were breaking down. Classes of wage workers, traders, professional men and a few employers of industrial labour were emerging in their place. Compared with the history of the Afrikaners, however, there was one important difference. The thrust of state policy was to force the black population of South Africa to yield its labour power cheaply. Within the framework of this policy, at that stage, a black middle class had little role to play. It was feared in particular by sections of the white middle classes whom it threatened to compete out of existence. Certainly, political rights for

Africans had no place within this system. The franchise could not be extended to the mass of African workers without radical social change taking place and setbacks or ruin to many employers. Nor, by implication, could political rights be allowed even to the black elite beyond a certain point. The danger was only too clear that the pressure and demands of the black workers might sooner or later find expression by this means.

Politically as well as economically the framework of modern social relations had thus emerged by the early years of this century. On the one hand, the workers were sharply divided, while on the other hand employers were increasingly united. The majority of workers were subject to the greatest insecurity and rigid state control; state policy was firmly based on the interests of urban employers. Tensions were already arising from the racialistic form in which this policy was cast, as if on the assumption that all black South Africans were destined to be labourers and all white South Africans were destined to be employers. While this may have reflected the prejudice or the naïve belief of many people, objectively it was false from the start and increasingly it has been experienced as such. Large numbers of white people were manual workers, whose position could hardly be confused with that of their employers. Similarly, a growing number of black people were emerging as small or medium proprietors and employers. On the one hand, the latter could not but share in the material, political and cultural aspirations of employers and the middle class in general, while on the other hand they found themselves isolated from the remainder of their class and in many ways reduced to the same insecurity and rightlessness as the mass of workers. From the ranks of these relatively educated, articulate and politically active people many of the spokesmen for black South African workers would emerge.

South African social relations did not remain confined within the boundaries of South Africa itself. As early as the 1880s the mining magnate Rhodes 'determined that northward expansion should take place under the aegis, not of the British government, but of the colonial' (*OHSA*, vol. 2, p.306). The gold-mining industry made the Witwatersrand into a centre of employment, trade and transport for an area that included not only the present-day Lesotho, Botswana and Swaziland, but to a greater or lesser extent drew Rhodesia, Zambia, Mozambique, Malawi and Angola into its orbit. From the start, extensive recruiting by the mining companies resulted in a flow of labour to the South. In the period 1896 to 1898 some 40,000 African workers (representing 75.7 per cent of all African workers employed by the Chamber of

Mines) were recruited outside South Africa. By 1936 this number had risen to more than 150,000 (47.9 per cent) and in 1972 to almost 300,000 (78.8 per cent) (Wilson, 1972b, p. 4).

In itself the political independence of most of the countries concerned did not affect the situation very much. On the basis of continuing economic imbalance, South African capital and manufactured goods have flowed increasingly to the North. South African exports to the rest of Africa grew from R5 million in 1938 to R153 million in 1957. Trade declined somewhat during the great upsurge of African nationalism and independence struggle, but recovered to R264 million in 1970, or 17 per cent of South Africa's total exports (Houghton, 1973, p. 176). Even more significantly, South African capital investment in the rest of Africa had risen to R771 million by 1973 (*Financial Mail*, 15 April 1976). This flow of capital, commodities and labour was accompanied by the construction of a transport network knitting the sub-continent together. The railway from Cape Town reached the Zambian copper belt and beyond, while the present-day Maputo has served the Rand as a seaport since 1894. The most concrete evidence of the unification of the Southern African economy, however, remains the growing integration of its labour force, the physical drawing together in South African cities of men and women from the furthest reaches of the sub-continent. Wilson's comment in this regard (1975, p. 541) is apt:

> The fact that a decision by Dr Banda in Zomba regarding labour on the Witwatersrand has repercussions rapidly felt by apple farmers in Grabouw and sugar farmers in Mandini, who find it increasingly difficult to get labour from the Transkei, does drive home the extent to which in the economy of Southern Africa we have, over the past 50–100 years, all become members of one another.

Just as the dominant mining industry had far-reaching consequences for South African society in general, so the dominant South African economy continues to have unmistakable implications for social development in the surrounding countries. In general, it imposes severe limitations on the actual independence that the politically independent states of Southern Africa are able to attain. To a large extent their development must depend on the course of events in the common industrial heartland, and their progress on the sources of wealth in South Africa. In this sense South African social relations are decisive for the future of the entire sub-continent.

Manufacturing industry, for reasons that have been noted, did not develop far during the first stages of the mining boom. It required the impulse of the First World War to establish manufacturing on any significant scale. By this time room for the development of new industry had become relatively limited. World markets were being dominated by the major industrial powers and competition among them, as the war itself testified, had become murderous and extreme. South African industry was confined very largely to the role of substituting various imports. It never overcame its historical handicap. Instead, its growth would depend on the supply of 'cheap docile labour' and on the measures needed to maintain and expand this supply.

By 1918 a total of 124,000 workers were employed by private manufacturers, compared with 291,000 in the mines (*OHSA*, vol. 2, p. 21). But the real growth of industry dates from the mid-1920s, when the Nationalist–Labour coalition government embarked on a deliberate policy of industrialisation. One aim was to reduce the dependence of the economy on gold, another was to provide work for the large numbers of landless whites who were pouring into the towns. Tariff protection was extended in 1925. An iron and steel industry was established in 1928 under state control. The Great Depression interrupted this development. Then, at the end of 1932, the gold standard was abandoned and the South African pound was devalued. Earnings from gold immediately soared and state income from the gold mines trebled from £4,587 million in 1932 to £14,915 million in 1933 (Horwitz, 1967, statistical appendix to ch. 4). Capital now poured back into the country, and under these conditions industrialisation went forward by great strides. The number of manufacturing establishments increased from 6,543 in 1932-3 to 8,614 in 1938-9, while the number of people employed rose from 133,000 to 236,000 (Houghton, 1973, p. 122).

Industrial growth continued more or less uninterrupted during the Second World War and for thirty years to follow. By 1970, 1,164,000 people were employed in the manufacturing sector, compared with 676,140 employed in mining and quarrying. The number of workers per establishment had increased from an average of twenty-eight in 1938-9 to eighty in 1967-8 (*ibid.*, pp. 124-5). After this long period of growth, the recession of the mid-1970s was felt all the more acutely. Anxiety and uncertainty became widespread in business circles in place of earlier self-confidence. Among workers of all races a new note of persistent discontent appeared. Conditions were made all the more volatile by sweeping political and social changes elsewhere in Africa and the world, and by the return of political violence to the streets

of the cities in June 1976. Capitalism in South Africa, having transformed the economy and created a class of wage workers several
millions strong, for the first time entered a period of serious instability.

The basic tendencies that characterised South African industrial
relations from the outset have continued to make themselves felt.
Foreign capital has remained a pillar of the economy. A huge inflow
took place immediately after the Second World War and continued
at a rate of well over R100 million per year until 1954 (*OHSA*, vol. 2,
p. 40). Only the political upheavals of 1960-1 brought about a significant reverse. By 1965 the confidence of investors had been restored
and the inflow of capital resumed. In 1970 the capital inflow amounted
to R403 million (Houghton, 1973, p. 277). In general, the return on
investment in South Africa has been extremely high. In the case of
American investment in the period 1958-61 it averaged 17.1 per cent
per year, before taxation (Spence, 1965, pp. 53-4). As late as 1974
the average profit on all foreign investment in South Africa amounted
to 6 per cent after taxation (*Financial Mail*, 15 April 1976).

With worsening economic conditions in the major industrial countries,
European and American capital may be expected to seek out the
relatively more favourable conditions of the colonial and semi-colonial
world, or other countries where the working class is poorly organised.
At the end of 1973 total foreign investment in South Africa stood at
R10,400 million, yielding R619 million in dividends, interest and profit
to be remitted overseas. Of this total R3,600 million was invested in
manufacturing industry and R1,300 million in mining. Some 60 per
cent of investment was accompanied by control (*ibid.*). During 1974
further capital to the value of R741 million flowed into the country
(*Financial Mail*, 27 March 1975). Only the political upheavals of
the Soweto period, coming on top of a declining rate of profit (see
Chapter 7), brought about a change in this development (see Table
1.1).

Table 1.1 *The decline in foreign investment 1975-7 (Rm.)*

	1975	1976	1977
Long-term capital movements	1,746	989	211
Short-term capital (not related to reserves)	−238	−415	−1,086

Source: *Financial Mail*, 14 April 1978.

Side by side with the flow of capital from overseas, the volume of domestic capital formation increased dramatically in the post-war period. This reflected a growth in the size and importance of the national capitalist class. R284 million of the domestic product was converted into capital in 1945. By 1960 this amount had increased to R1,061 million and by 1970 to R3,061 million (Houghton, 1973, pp. 40, 261). 'It would thus appear,' Houghton observes (1973, pp. 40-1), 'that South Africa is now becoming a mature economy, increasingly capable of maintaining a high rate of capital formation from within itself.' This view, however, is too one-sided; it disregards the tendency towards crisis that is inherent in the capitalist system. In reality the South African economy remained weak and dependent in relation to the world economy. The limits on its development imposed by the predominance of the major industrial countries had by no means been broken through. Within these limits the South African economy is capable of expanding when the world economy expands, while absorbing and incorporating all the contradictions of capitalist growth. During a period of contraction on the world market the South African economy is subjected to inexorable pressures and forced into decline.

What has been the significance of this pattern of development as far as industrial relations are concerned? We have already encountered the argument that, with expansion, the capitalist economy would tend to change itself, in particular by eliminating racial discrimination: '[A] partheid in the industrial and commercial spheres cannot be reconciled with an increasing demand for skilled labour which white immigration alone cannot supply', Spence (1965, p. 50) declares, 'and a *political* settlement will have to be made with the "new men" thrown up by the twin processes of industrialisation and economic integration.' Horwitz, a leading exponent of this theory, concludes his treatise (1967, p. 427) on the following optimistic note: 'The South African economy is inescapably integrated in the pursuit of productivity. Economic rationality urges the polity (i.e. the system of political relations) forward beyond its ideology (i.e. of racial discrimination).' More recently this argument has been revived in qualified terms by M. Lipton and the *South African Labour Bulletin* (vol. 3, no. 3, October 1976). Yet for all its distinguished apologists, the 'liberal' theory is overwhelmingly contradicted by the actual course of events. This is recognised by 'liberal' spokesmen such as the columnist Gerald Shaw (*Cape Times*, 3 April 1976): 'Whatever Mr Pik Botha might say at the United Nations about moving away from race discrimination, the apartheid juggernaut goes rolling on.'

A more serious analysis would have to draw one unavoidable conclusion from modern South African history: investment and growth in South Africa have *depended* to a large extent on oppressive industrial relations. From the investor's point of view this system has created a disciplined and economical work-force, and 'to businessmen generally, the continuance of a supply of cheap docile labour appeared important' (Doxey, 1961, p. 109). Legassick (1974, pp. 6, 9) points out that South Africa's growth rate in the 1960s was exceeded by that of Japan alone, and defines apartheid as 'the application of the cheap forced labour system established under segregationism . . . to secondary industry rather than to mining and farming alone'. Whatever further developments the industrial revolution might bring, it is most unlikely that change will be freely permitted by employers, let alone sought, in the 'polity' by which this growth has been made possible. More rational from the standpoint of 'economic rationality' is the effort to accommodate all necessary changes *within* the 'polity' of pass laws, reserves and low wages. While certain disadvantages may result – for example, restrictions on the internal market and on the mobility of labour – history leaves us in no doubt that at the level of 'economic rationality' these drawbacks are far outweighed by the fundamental advantage of keeping strict control over a majority of workers and preventing their effective organisation.

Foreign investment and economic growth are thus the reverse side of an oppressive system of industrial relations within a relatively weak industrial economy. In terms of this analysis it follows that oppression would tend to *increase* with economic growth, and the 'apartheid juggernaut' would tend to go 'rolling on'. Other aspects of the 'liberal' theory may likewise be criticised on this basis. Liberals frequently point out that in a developing economy increasing supplies of skilled labour are required. Liberal theory assumes that workers performing more skilled work will be paid significantly higher wages and enjoy significant freedom. South African practice has shown this assumption to be groundless.

Seen in this light there is no basis for regarding the year 1948 as a fundamental turning-point in South African history. In that year the National Party obtained a majority in Parliament. The main distinction between this government and its predecessor was the closer link between the National Party and the rising Afrikaner business class. If anything, Nationalist policy reflected more truly the interests of the national capitalist class. It extended racial discrimination and cut down even more drastically on the freedom of political activity.

Yet the sequence of events forms a single consistent whole. The 1940s, and especially the late 1940s, was a period of tremendous economic expansion in South Africa. The number of manufacturing establishments increased from 8,505 in 1939–40 to 12,517 in 1949–50. Industrial employment doubled in this period from 245,457 to 497,887 (*Union Statistics for Fifty Years*). From 1936 to 1951 the urbanised part of the South African population rose from 31.4 to 42.6 per cent. Of the African people 17.3 per cent were officially resident in the towns in 1936. This figure had increased to 27.2 per cent in 1951 (*South African Statistics*, 1974). The number of African workers in private industry more than doubled, from 126,067 in 1938–9 to 345,928 in 1950–1 (*Union Statistics for Fifty Years*). By 1951 there were 827,851 African workers officially employed in mining and secondary industry alone (Doxey, 1961, p. 105). What all these figures reflect is a multiplication of the urban working class as a result of increasing industrialisation. With only one-third of the white population, one-third of the 'Asian' and fewer than half of the 'coloured' population left in the rural areas by 1936 (Suid-Afrikaanse Buro vir Rasse-Aangeleenthede, 1951, pp. 104–5) this meant in particular the rapid increase of the urban African population. Even at this tempo, however, economic growth brought about no general prosperity. South African capitalism has depended not merely on African labour in general but on African labour at an extremely low rate of wages, hence subject to strict control to prevent collective action that would drive the wage rate up. The massive growth of the African working class called for reinforcement of the measures designed to control it. Official theoreticians, awed by the black proletariat, reflected a fearful mood (*ibid.*, p. 106):

1. The Council of SABRA has noted with concern the large measure of the integration of natives into the white economy, and is convinced that if this situation is allowed to continue and develop further, it must necessarily have disastrous consequences for the whites as well as the natives.
2. The Council therefore pleads for the consistent application of the policy of separate development as the only satisfactory measure.

The growth of the African working class has thus been the key to the policy of apartheid. The connection between state policy and industrial relations is explicitly recognised by Rhoodie (1965, p. 126):

The fact that the worsening of the so-called Native problem has run parallel to the process of urbanisation and industrialisation in South Africa, shows irrefutably that Bantu policy has implications extending beyond the limits of pure economic relations. . . . The involvement of Bantu in the labour pattern of the Whites has within two decades created a conflict of interest between Whites and Non-Whites which has found its characteristic form and situation in our urban areas par excellence.

The suggestion that a United Party government would have carried out a basically different and more liberal policy after 1948 should therefore be treated with great caution. Rather, given the objective situation, what needs to be shown is how any policy aimed at maintaining the existing labour supply could have taken a different form in practice. The demand for cheap labour ruled out the prospect of general prosperity and stability. The consequent enforcement of the pass laws and the reserve system ruled out the prospect of political democracy. The repeal of these measures, on the other hand, would have caused insoluble problems for large numbers of employers and, most likely, a massive withdrawal of foreign capital. The entire course of South African history before and after 1948 bears out this conclusion.

Of all aspects of South African society the numerous laws imposing racial discrimination have excited the broadest controversy. At first sight the so-called 'petty' forms of discrimination may seem irrelevant to the exploitation of African workers. Employers do not grow richer, after all, by making black and white people use separate ends of the counter at a railway station. Yet the connection is real and fundamental. Apartheid has little objective basis outside economic exploitation. At the industrial level oppression of the mass of workers and the division of workers along racial lines were consolidated in the post-war period. Severe disabilities were placed by law on those workers classified as 'Bantu' and, to a lesser extent, on those classified as 'coloured' and 'Asian'. At the same time, different categories of workers were placed in still more competitive or hostile relationships to one another. The net result is that a large supply of cheap and unfree labour, comprising some 70 per cent of the total work-force, has remained a feature of the modern South African economy.

Workers subject to hardship and oppression sooner or later turn to political action to alter their position. This is shown, for example, by the history of the labour movement in Europe during the nineteenth and early twentieth centuries. This tendency became marked in South

Africa from the end of the Second World War onwards. The state reacted to the workers' movement by struggling to suppress it. In the first place it attempted to stifle any form of independent organisation among the African working class. More than this, it took increasingly rigorous action against political organisation in general. Objectively it needed to seal off all channels by which the pressure of the African working class might find indirect expression. Severe measures were taken against the political organisations of the black middle classes, in particular the African National Congress, which in growing frustration were turning to the masses. Laws enacted in this process included the Suppression of Communism Act of 1950, the Public Safety Act of 1953, the Unlawful Organisations Act of 1960, the 'Sabotage Act' of 1962, and the Terrorism Act of 1967. The coloured voters were disenfranchised by the South Africa Act Amendment Act of 1956. The final possibility of indirect participation by black people in parliamentary politics through 'mixed' political parties was sealed off by the Prevention of Political Interference Act of 1968.

Racial discrimination in South Africa can thus be defined as the *extension* of class oppression. To secure the existing supply of labour at the existing rates of wages it proved necessary to take certain measures against the black population in general. Concessions to *any* section of Africans, the state has evidently reasoned, may be 'abused' by radicals and fall into the hands of the masses. On every level of society, divisions had to be consolidated: developments that threatened the status quo had to be nipped in the bud. The basic priority was always to regulate the conditions under which African people could leave the reserves and enter the urban working class.

The liberal theory is thus applicable only in reverse. Once established at this fundamental level the extension of racial discrimination to every other level of social activity must follow. This tendency has been reflected in the Prohibition of Mixed Marriages Act of 1949, the Immorality Act Amendment Act, the Population Registration Act, the Group Areas Act (all of 1950), the Bantu Education Act, the Reservation of Separate Amenities Act of 1953, and further measures too numerous to mention here. Amidst the tensions, emotions and violent conflicts called up by this process, the objective link between racialism and economic relations has often been lost sight of. Incorrect impressions (for example 'The entire system rests upon an irrational criterion of biological differentiation' (Mathews, 1971, p. 298) are found side by side with correct interpretations (for example: 'the laws and machinery of government in South Africa are being used to consolidate the economic and social advantages, and the political power, of a minority section of the population (*ibid.*, p. 298)). Consolidating profits, privilege and power - this, it is submitted, is the opposite of 'irrationality'. Objectively the relationship between apartheid and economic exploitation has remained unambiguous at all stages. A clear understanding of this relationship is needed to grasp the significance of racial discrimination.

The industrial revolution in South Africa has been carried through at a feverish tempo. The latest achievements of world technology were put to use in South Africa, regardless of social consequences. Modern industrial society was imposed in sharp contradiction to the backwardness of the country in the pre-industrial period. Old institutions that stood in the way were ruthlessly broken down. This explains the convulsive nature of the industrial revolution in South Africa and the harshness of its forms. Today, extreme contrast remains typical of almost every aspect of social life, from the urban to the rural, from the material to the ideological. Intermediate forms, which might have been the basis for a more gradual process of change, scarcely came into existence. This alone indicates that future development in South Africa will be no less rapid and convulsive than in the past.

The mid-1970s have seen prolonged economic growth change into recession. After increasing by 10.5 per cent in 1974, private investment fell by 2.9 per cent in 1975 (*Financial Mail*, 3 January 1976). As in other capitalist countries, the slowdown in the economy was preceded by high rates of inflation and led to rising unemployment. This has made harsher the already harsh conditions to which the majority of African workers are subject, and the shell of industrial peace began to crack. Underneath racial contradictions the class contradictions of industrial society have been locked away in an especially explosive form. After a whole period of almost exclusive preoccupation with racism in itself, these more fundamental relationships are today becoming more clearly visible and more widely understood.

It may be argued that by world standards the industrial revolution in South Africa has not yet been carried to its logical conclusion and, hence, that the capitalist system still has a progressive role to play. Such arguments are academic, taking no account of the real unfolding of events. Whatever prospects might exist in theory, in reality world capitalism has entered a period of instability and decline. In Southern Africa sweeping political and social changes have already taken place. There is little visible basis on which the South African system of social and industrial relations can continue beyond the immediate future in its existing form. Indeed, the elements of revolutionary struggle and change – on the one hand, radical demands; on the other, compulsive resistance – have been present for decades. Looking at labour policy in 1942, van der Horst (1942, p. 325) remarked:

> Are not all such restrictive measures short-sighted? They
> involve the creation and maintenance in South Africa of a
> caste system dependent upon authoritarian action. In the
> economic environment of the twentieth century a caste system
> can be maintained only by the exercise of force. It is a highly
> unstable condition, promising racial and social strife.

In our survey of present-day South Africa we discover the same contradictions, greatly sharpened by thirty-five years of deepening repression. Closer examination is needed of certain aspects of the process that has been outlined. Thereafter we shall return to our main subject – the historical relationship between capital and labour in South Africa, as manifested in the struggles of the present time.

Chapter 2

Divisions in the working class

As in all industrial countries divisions exist among the workers of South Africa. Such divisions, indeed, are a condition for the existence of capitalist society. Had the workers been united, their power would have been overwhelming and employers could not have maintained themselves in existence.

Contrasts are found between urban and rural, skilled and unskilled, organised and unorganised, enfranchised and unenfranchised, free and unfree workers. South Africa is unique, however, in that the state has superimposed on all these material differences a series of *legal* divisions on lines of colour or race. To the extent that they are enforced the legal divisions are always in the foreground. At the same time, we must not lose sight of the material differences to which the legal distinction may relate in any given context. In general it can be said that white workers are relatively organised, skilled and free, while black workers are in an opposite position. But this is only a generalisation. The only respect in which the real and the legal distinctions are entirely at one is that white workers have the right to vote in parliamentary elections, while all other workers are denied this right.

The racial division of the working class is a key feature of South African social relations. In one way or another it has preoccupied politicians and writers of every description for generations. Yet to this day it cannot be said that the question has been fully resolved. There has never been much difficulty in identifying the different social origins of different groups of workers. On this there is general agreement. Uncertainty exists, however, as to the causes that have kept the original differences alive. The *Oxford History* writes (vol. 2, p. 22):

Initially skilled workers were mostly white, and unskilled were Coloured or African, and for a variety of reasons this racial division has been perpetuated. Various obstacles, some legislative, but up to 1918 mainly customary, made it difficult for any but white people to acquire skills. In the nineteen-twenties, however, the customary barriers were reinforced by legislation.

This may broadly describe events, but it offers us no explanation. Racialism in South Africa tends to be treated as something so self-evident that no explanation is needed. Racialism 'always' existed, it is implied, and 'naturally' perpetuates itself. Such assumptions, however, do not stand up to closer scrutiny. The industrial order was established in South Africa by a harsh and violent process in which no part of the old society, except its reservoir of labour, was spared. In crushing the resistance of the landowners and the tribes war itself was used as an instrument. Having asserted their power in this totally uncompromising way, the new rulers of South Africa can scarcely be said to have had the norms of the old society in any way thrust on them. Having crushed the Afrikaner landowners, British imperialism did not become their instrument. The root causes of racialism in the modern industrial state must be sought not in the interests or prejudices of the defeated farmers but in the modern state itself. If racialism remained entrenched in South Africa, we can only conclude that it was in the interests of industrial capital to maintain it.

To a whole school of writers the conclusion is different. The white workers enforced segregation. This idea is given substance by the racist attitudes that have been so prevalent among white workers from earliest times. The South African Labour Party officially declared in 1917 (Cope, n.d., p. 180) that it was 'entirely against equal rights for White and Black'. In 1975 A. Paulus, secretary of the Mineworkers' Union, declared that the black miner must always remain subservient to the white miner (*Financial Mail*, 25 July 1975). Taking this attitude in itself van der Horst's explanation (1942, p. 157) appears to be conclusive:

> In the twentieth century a cleavage of interest appeared between the European employee, on the one hand, and, on the other, the European employer and Native labourer . . . . Some of the Native labourers began to acquire skill and to compete for work with European-skilled artisans . . . . At the same time . . . some of the Europeans who had no land were losing such means of support as were hitherto available to them. They had consequently to compete with Natives and other non-Europeans for unskilled work.

35

In both cases Natives and Europeans became competing factors of production, and it was in the sectional interest of groups of Europeans to exclude Native competitors. The attempt of such groups to maintain or create a privileged position for themselves has been one of the dominating forces in the labour market of South Africa.

Many later authorities have explicitly or implicitly accepted this line of reasoning. Not surprisingly, it has proved especially popular among employers, who are thereby divested of responsibility for racial discrimination. Recently it was endorsed once again by a research centre for investment responsibility in Washington, D.C. In response to the accusation that American corporations, by investing in South Africa, are helping to maintain the policy of apartheid, responsibility for apartheid was placed on the shoulders of the white South African workers. Among the findings of this body, according to a press report (*Rapport*, 23 May 1976), was the following:

> The white worker is lazy, overpaid, unproductive, resigns over the smallest reason or grievance, promotes inflation and uses every possible device to maintain the shortage of white workers and the exclusive privileges of the white. And the white consumer public encourages this conduct.

At the same time, a different aspect of the matter was admitted by which the entire question is placed in a different light (*ibid.*): 'Equal wages are beyond the reach of most companies, even if they want to pay it.' The contradiction between these two lines of argument is fundamental. Notwithstanding this, the employers' case against white labour has over the years been supported by numerous academics and theoreticians. It has even found credence among opponents of apartheid. Webster (1974) gave the following reasons for the 'parting of the ways' between black and white labour organisations which, according to him, became decisive in 1922:

1. The fact that the white worker had access to political power opened the door to economic privilege and this economic privilege gave the white worker a vested interest in the perpetuation of the system.
2. The relatively easy embourgeoisement of the white artisan, who could move out of his class to set up as a master on his own and employ his own cheap African labour. The 'caste-like' barrier to upward social mobility blocked a similar process for Africans.

3. The structure of the labour market on the mines was such that white miners could have a gang of African miners contracted to them These men were under the arbitrary control of the white miner, subject to his discipline and ultimately with the power of dismissal in the hands of the white miner.

4. The work situation cannot be considered in isolation, as even if interests in friendship did emerge in the workplace, the battery of racial discriminatory custom and law in the overall structure of society militated against common political action . . . .

5. Most important of all was the system of migrant labour itself, which prevented at that time full proletarianisation from taking place – the necessary condition for effective trade unions.

In itself this reasoning is plausible, and most of the points are correct. Yet it shows a lack of perspective amounting to fundamental error. In effect, it overlooks the fact that South Africa is a capitalist state. For all their political influence the white workers never held power. During the formative stages of the modern economy their influence was negligible. By no stretch of the imagination can the white workers be held accountable for what Webster himself calls the most important factor of all: the system of migrant labour. Political parties have spoken almost unanimously from the employers' point of view. Until well into the twentieth century employers and landowners (who were themselves employers) had a more or less free hand in determining national policy. What *is* true is that white workers have tended overwhelmingly to support the policy of racial oppression developed by employers and the state. Undoubtedly their support was one of the factors, and a highly important factor, that contributed towards the maintenance of this policy. Yet this remains a fundamentally different proposition from the theory that the white workers are primarily responsible for the divisions in the South African working class.

From 1907 onwards white labour began emerging as a political factor. In 1909, anticipating Union by a year, the South African Labour Party was formed. Even this process, however, leads us to conclusions different from those of Webster. In 1913, in 1914 and again in 1922, the state did not scruple to use armed force against white workers. The struggle of 1922 was on the scale of a minor civil war and ended in crushing defeat for the organisations of enfranchised labour. The suggestion that the white workers purely and simply compelled successive governments to impose segregation in their favour is thus, at best, one-sided. It is true that the demand for segregation has consistently gone out from the organisations of free labour. Had this demand been unacceptable, however, it would no doubt have been dealt with by the capitalist class in the same uncompromising way that other unacceptable demands were dealt with. The fact that segregation was a feature of industrial relations before white workers were in a position to demand it, let alone enforce it, indicates that there were other, more basic influences at work. The white workers could not have been the prime mover in this process. Their limited emancipation took place on terms dictated by employers and the state. If their demands could not have been decisive, it remains to be established which *were* the decisive factors.

Those who hold the white workers responsible for racial segregation imply that the state has been their ally and the opponent of employers. This theory has been given a superficial plausibility by the existence of a Nationalist–Labour coalition government from 1924 to 1933 which, verbally at least, was critical of the Chamber of Mines. In fact, the policies of that government and of every other government during the present century can leave us in no doubt that an absolute priority at all times was to maintain the supply of 'cheap docile labour' for the benefit of employers. Compared with the enormous growth of the industrial economy, especially since 1939, the white workers' 'vested interest in the perpetuation of the system' has been relatively slight.[1] The industrial revolution has primarily meant a huge growth of investment and production, and a spectacular increase in the power and wealth of the capitalist class. To approach it from the point of view of the living standards of white workers shows an utter lack of perspective. To even suggest that such improvement has been the basic object of state policy is absurd.

The weakness of Webster's and van der Horst's approach is precisely its one-sided preoccupation with the role and position of the non-African minority of workers. To understand the racial division of the South African working class it is necessary to start with the relationship between capital and the mass of workers. In the words of Morris and Kaplan (1976, pp. 17–18), the tendency 'to view the racial stratification of labour primarily from the point of view of its protective function for White labour' is 'a fundamentally incorrect approach . . . . For the words capital and profit are absent as the principal forces or as the main beneficiaries of this process.'

Seen in a broader perspective the situation becomes clearer. In no case where the divisive forces of competition are at work does solidarity among workers arise spontaneously. Often, divisions are only overcome by the pressure of major events, and then only while the pressure continues. For more enduring unity deliberate organisation is required, often taking long periods before it is established. In South Africa the pressure of events in the past has tended to separate workers rather than bring them together. Organisation with the serious intention of uniting workers across the colour bar has functioned only briefly and sporadically. The suggestion that immigrant artisans should have spontaneously overcome racial barriers, in the face of tremendous opposing forces, is idealistic. To hold them primarily responsible for the entire historical situation is only slightly less absurd than accusing African workers of rejecting solidarity with white workers by agreeing to work for lower wages.

Against this background some writers have gone further and raised the question of whether white workers belong to the working class at all. In recent years attempts have been made to show that white workers, because of their relative freedom and the higher level of earnings which is a consequence of this, are not workers at all but a 'new middle class' who 'appropriate surplus value produced by African workers' (Wolpe, 1976, p. 206). The conclusion following from this is that 'no alliance either in the trade union or in the political sphere is possible between the African working class and the "white working class"' (*ibid.*, 1976, p. 197).

A major difficulty in explaining the class position of white workers, as Wolpe points out, stems from 'the confusion and conflation of the economic, political and ideological levels of analysis' (*ibid.*). Under South African conditions, given the all-pervading emphasis on differences of colour, such confusion is to some extent inherent. If we accept racial differences as constituting fundamental divisions in society, then we can hardly conceive of any fundamental unity of interest between workers who are white and black, nor can we imagine any fundamental division between workers and employers who are white. This appears to be the basic explanation for the line of reasoning in question. Although often couched in Marxist terminology, it is non-Marxist in content in that the relations of production are either ignored or treated as a secondary factor. On the level of theory this has inescapable consequences. If social classes are not to be defined in terms of the relations of production, then other criteria must be found. Most common, on the part of the state as well as the majority of its liberal and radical critics, is the impressionistic conclusion that race is the decisive determinant of 'class'. This leads to observations, such as those of the IIE (1974, p. 70), that white South Africans 'are nearly all what might be described as "middle class"'. Other arguments, while more sophisticated, in the end amount to much the same. Rex, for example, uses as his criterion the 'structure of constraints' (quoted in Wolpe, 1976, p. 202); Davies uses the criterion of income – if white miners as a group receive a higher than average *per capita* share in the net output of the mining industry minus depreciation, then this supposedly proves that white miners 'indirectly share in the exploitation of blacks' (quoted by Wolpe, 1976, p. 208). That is to say, employers and white workers share between them the surplus produced by black workers.[2]

Wolpe easily disposes of these arguments. The nature of an economic relationship, he writes (1976, p. 209), 'cannot . . . be derived from the size of the pay packet'. Only in a metaphorical sense can it be said that the higher-paid worker shares in the exploitation of the lower-paid worker. The moment we take this metaphor literally, its limitations become obvious. Any random distinction we draw between different groups of workers (e.g. manual and non-manual; underground or surface; older or younger) will yield precisely the same result, i.e. that one group earns more and the other earns less than the average *per capita* share of output. To interpret this in the way that Davies does must lead to the absurd conclusion that nearly every worker is both exploited and exploiting, thus robbing the term 'exploitation' of all meaning. As it stands, Davies's approach is essentially no different from the openly impressionistic approach which looks no further than differences of colour. Starting with the racial distinction he merely reformulates it in pseudo-Marxist terms.

Wolpe, on the other hand, sets out to define the position of the white workers in South Africa from the standpoint of the relationship between capital and labour in general. On the one hand, there is the 'collective labourer' – i.e. all workers engaged in the productive process – and on the other hand, capital with its dual function of co-ordination and control. The function of capital, Wolpe argues, need not be performed by capitalists in person. It may also be performed by workers employed for that purpose alone, or by workers who partly perform the function of capital and partly engage in productive labour. These workers are regarded as forming a 'new middle class'. Wolpe then turns to the question of income and concludes (1976, p. 221):

> insofar as it [the 'new middle class'] carries out the productive functions of the collective worker it is paid out of variable capital

a wage which is determined by the value of labour-power; insofar as this class performs the global function of capital it is paid out of revenue and its income represents a share in the surplus.

The non-productive worker, Wolpe concedes, is also exploited: 'not however, through the production of surplus value (which it does not produce) but through the appropriation of surplus labour'. The wage of unproductive workers is also determined by the value of labour-power. Marx himself put the matter more simply: the same labour-power may be productive or unproductive, depending on whether the capitalist buys it in the capacity of producer or consumer (*Marx–Engels Werke*, vol. 26.1, p. 135). Every worker, productive or unproductive, thus belongs to the proletariat in the sense that he must sell his labour-power for a living. The non-productive worker, standing outside the productive process, is paid out of the revenue as opposed to the capital of his employer. Only the source of his income is different. His relationship to the means of production is fundamentally the same. The theory of the 'new middle class', on the other hand, sets out not from the ownership of the means of production but from the 'global' division of labour between capital and labour. This abstraction is used as the basis for class analysis, a method fundamentally different from that of Marx and Engels.

Nor does the distinction between productive and unproductive, supervisory and non-supervisory labour help us to explain wage differentials. Even assuming (as some writers do) that white workers are by definition supervisors, we cannot dispose of the huge differential between the wages of black and white workers in South Africa by dismissing it as 'a share of profits' which is added on to 'wages'. This would fail to explain the differentials between different categories of productive labour. It would also leave us with those unproductive workers who are earning no more, or less, than their productive counterparts. As such, wage differentials may be purely the result of market forces. They may also be the result of political manipulation. It does not help us, indeed it confuses the issue, to seek the origins of wage differentials exclusively in the relations of production.

The merit of Wolpe's approach is its criticism of the traditional racial analysis of the South African working class. What are the implications of this? In the first place it means that the 'privileged' position of free labour is a secondary, not a fundamental characteristic of the social system. Black and white workers are not irreconcilably opposed to each other, as the racial analysis would have it. On the contrary, they stand in fundamentally the same relationship to the capitalist class. In the second place it means that state protection of the free working class is by no means an immutable policy. As Wolpe points out, this policy has already been modified significantly, notably in respect of job reservation and maintenance of white workers' living standards. Wolpe refrains from drawing more concrete conclusions. A possible development, he indicates (1976, p. 237), may be 'shifting class alliances and conflicts within the white group' which may 'weaken the political unity of the classes within the white group' and thus 'be of considerable importance in the struggle of the African working class against the existing state'. This very important proposition will be considered more fully in due course.

A further observation should be added: no mechanical conclusions can be drawn as to the political role of white workers who are employed in non-productive or supervisory capacities. In certain cases – though this has nothing to do with either race or franchise – the nature of his work or the size of his income may set a particular wage-earner aside from workers as a class (for example, a policeman or factory foreman). In general, however, the use to which his services are put has no fundamental bearing on a worker's social position. From his own point of view his condition is in the first place propertyless and proletarian. The work that he happens to do at any given moment is primarily a consequence of this.

In pre-industrial South Africa urban production and industrial wage labour had been concentrated mainly in Cape Town. Industrial relations in the Cape up to the early part of this century showed a mixture of racial integration and racial segregation. Market forces unerringly sought out the weaknesses in the social position of black workers and held back their advance. Some, however, overcame these obstacles, at least to the extent of working on equal terms with whites. If we believe that historical conditions perpetuate themselves more or less mechanically, then we would expect these elements of racial integration to have likewise projected themselves on to the later industrial economy. This, however, did not happen. The paradox can be explained by contrasting conditions in nineteenth-century Cape Town with those on the booming Witwatersrand. So poor were the prizes of the former – in terms of profits or work opportunities – that a policy of large-scale and systematic industrial segregation was uncalled for from any quarter. Only in the mining industry did the conditions for such segregation finally arise. Only with the welding together of the industrial economy around its new centre of gravity, Johannesburg, did segregation as an essential feature of industrial relations extend itself over the country as a whole.

What were the conditions that called forth segregation in this form? In the first place there was a wide gulf between the immigrant workers, who came to South Africa in large numbers, and the still larger African proletariat. Similar contrasts in language, background, race and skills had been unknown within the urban work-force at the Cape (which had also been a fraction of the size and relatively unimportant to the economy as a whole). On the Rand, for the first time, great issues depended on the use to which urban labour was put.

With the destruction of the tribal system the African peoples were reduced to poverty and impotence. They were dispersed, divided by language and historical differences, almost uniformly unskilled. A proletariat with less power to assert itself cannot be imagined. At the opposite extreme in terms of skill and working-class development were the artisans and miners recruited from abroad. Thus, in the late nineteenth century employers found themselves able to hire unskilled African workers on virtually their own terms. They found it impossible, on the other hand, to recruit skilled labour except on terms vastly less favourable to themselves. Since they required both these forms of labour, early industrial relations were characterised by a wage and social differential between skilled and unskilled workers that coincided with differences of race.

The unfolding of the industrial economy brought growing conflict among the diverse interests that were concentrated in the South African gold-mining industry. Skilled labour tended to become less scarce. Unskilled workers tended to become more skilled and at the same time better organised. The employers' obvious interest in such a situation is to drive skilled wages down, while preventing unskilled wages from rising. The latter objective, as we have seen, was realised by means of state policy. In this way, through the enforcement of employers' interests by the state, the South African labour market was given its characteristic form. By this policy the racial divisions in the working class were maintained, even after their original causes had disappeared.

What, then, has the notorious racialism among white South African workers consisted of? If the state-controlled labour market has any inherent tendency to close the gap between white and black labour in South Africa, then it is the tendency to drive down the standards of all workers to the level of the basic labour force – the landless proletariat of the reserves. Racialism is the form historically given by

South African conditions to the struggle by free labour to preserve its existing standards.

Prejudice and rationalisation developed at an early stage among white workers to cloak and mystify the concrete driving-forces of working-class division. Propaganda and indoctrination from childhood onwards extended the same racialist ideas to each new generation. To most observers, and even to most workers themselves, these ideological overtones have tended to be more visible than their underlying causes. This was illustrated in a meeting between Joseph Chamberlain, British Colonial Secretary, and a delegation of the Johannesburg Trades and Labour Council in 1902. The Labour men, we read (Cope, n.d. p. 67):

> launched into a long complaint against the influx of Indians. The Indians, they said, were insanitary; their filthy living conditions were a breeding-ground for epidemics such as the small-pox which was prevalent in the town. Strict segregation should be imposed on them in the public interest. Chamberlain intervened laconically:
> 'What you mean, gentlemen', he said, 'is that the Indians have a low living standard, and you fear the effect of their labour competition on your wages'.
> The delegation glanced at one another and agreed. Chamberlain had put their unspoken thoughts into words.

The conflict between 'liberal' employers and conservative white workers is nearly as old as the mining industry itself. As early as 1913 a campaign of 'fair play to the Natives' was launched by the Chamber of Mines. The Chamber, Cope (n.d., p. 149) wrote:

> attacked the 'colour bar' as being an unfair discrimination which was holding back the development of the Natives . . . . Nothing was more calculated to exacerbate the already bitter feelings of the White workers. They needed no theorist to tell them that when the magnates started talking about removal of the colour bar they meant one thing – an attack on wage standards by the use of the cheapest labour available . . . . After the lapse of time, it appears on the surface that the stand taken by White workers in relation to their Coloured and Black fellow-workers was thoroughly reactionary. They were, however, constantly harassed by the capitalists with threats of depressing their wage standards, and their racial and colour prejudices were exploited to the utmost. In the face of such provocations, they tended to concentrate on a defence of their own standards above all else.

From the point of view of the mass of workers 'removal of the colour bar' has an entirely different meaning than that ascribed to it by 'liberal' employers. To the workers it means their own emancipation. Some commentators may have this in mind when they speak about a 'free labour market'. But market forces in South Africa, it has been argued, in themselves have an opposite tendency. The liberation of the unfree working class implies the destruction of the capitalist labour market. It implies a struggle by free labour for the maintenance of their conditions, linked to the struggle of the unfree workers for the extension of these conditions to themselves. This, in turn, presupposes the united organisation of workers of all races. From the employers' point of view the immediate result would be a colossal rise in costs and a disastrous decline in profits. In the longer term it would call for a complete transformation of the economy, which may not be possible on a profitable basis, and hence spell the end of capitalist production. These are the broad alternatives to continued racial segregation among workers – the abolition of free labour, or the abolition of unfree labour. This conclusion has never been lost on the organised labour movement (at least its left wing) or on the capitalist class. It is against this background that the divisions in the working class have been maintained, and it is in this light that the question should be viewed.

If overwhelming political power rested with the mining magnates, at least in the early years of the industrial revolution, then events should be looked at from their point of view in order to understand the labour policy that was developed in this period. From the employers' point of view an obvious aim was to reduce the cost of skilled labour. For a number of reasons this proved impossible in the short term. The employers accordingly settled for the less of two evils. If the skilled workers' wages and freedom of organisation could not be levelled out at once, then these could at least be confined to white workers and prevented from 'spreading' to Africans. If the colour bar could not be abolished by doing away with free labour, then at least the status quo could be preserved. And if free workers could be led to see maintenance of the status quo as the sole alternative to their own immediate ruin, then this was a major political advantage.

The policy of racial segregation among workers may thus be regarded as a form of deadlock between the pressures exerted on the one hand by capital, and on the other hand by labour. A line has been drawn, as it were, at the lowest level at which labour-power can be obtained – the level of unfree migrant labour. Had it been left to employers, this level would tend to become the norm. In practice, through the combination of objective political conditions and resistance by the unions of free workers, free labour has succeeded in maintaining itself above the minimum or 'economic' level: the level of 'cheap docile labour'.

Webster treats 1922 as the 'parting of the ways' between white and African workers. To be precise it was the stage at which the capitalists and their political representatives found it more advisable to compromise with free labour nationally than to fight it into the ground. The aim of the compromise was to defeat the emerging movement of the black masses; the compromise could only exist on the basis of their continued subjugation and super-exploitation. Doxey (1961, p. 122), attempting to rationalise the capitalist position, only succeeds in exposing its true nature:

> Thus, in order to maintain a level of full employment for all whites, at a given standard, it would be necessary to seek some means of subsidising the marginally inefficient and uneconomic members of this group. Failing this, the inefficient white labour elements would either swell the ranks of the unemployed or compete with Africans in the unskilled field . . . . Under such circumstances the inner privileged society was only possible if subsidised by surpluses created by the low-paid non-whites, and if the non-white wage-rate remained below the white wage-rate.

'Possible' and 'necessary', in this amazing argument, apparently mean nothing more than 'in accordance with employers' given rates of profit'; 'inefficient' is used in the same sense as 'better-paid'; and 'inner privileged society' refers to workers earning more than bare subsistence. It is generally known that employers will tend to prefer a policy of low wages to a policy of high wages. According to Doxey, however, it is the existence of a small proportion of relatively highly paid workers that leads South African employers to this elementary conclusion. To Doxey, 'marginal efficiency' happens to coincide with the lowest level to which the combined power of employers and the state is able to force down the wages of migrant workers. Workers who gain the 'privilege' of rising above this level supposedly need to be 'subsidised'. Similarly, there is no visible reason why the freedom of some workers should only be 'possible' at the expense of the lack of freedom of others. Again, the answer is provided by the vested interests of employers and the state.

The question remains why the organisations of free labour accepted the compromise of an industrial colour bar which leaves them in precisely the same exposed and isolated position as before. On the one hand, the state has acted decisively against all trade unionists who took a different view. By 1956 seventy-five trade unionists (thirty-five 'White', twenty-one African, twelve 'coloured' and seven 'Asian') had been listed in terms of the Suppression of Communism Act. Fifty-six had been ordered to resign from their unions. 'Since then,' wrote Muriel Horrell in 1969 (p. 14), 'hundreds of trade unionists who were never members of the Communist Party have been banned on the ground that the Minister considered them to be furthering one or more of the aims of communism as broadly defined in the Act'. Walker and Weinbren (1961, p. 241) comment as follows:

> The Suppression of Communism Act has proved to be the most effective weapon used by the Government in the campaign to smash the free trade unions. Not only has this law been freely used to ban and remove from office those trade union officials who were most active in defending the rights and furthering the interests of South Africa's most depressed classes of workers, but it has had the effect also of filleting a number of trade union leaders.... It is this instrument, more than any other action of the Government's, which is responsible for the lack of unity in the trade union movement which is less effective today than ever before.

Even so, the labour movement has developed a vision broader than that of 'liberal' employers and their academic apologists. The full liberation of unfree labour has always been a subject studiously avoided by employers in their exhortations to 'abolish the colour bar'. An eloquent statement is that of the Director of Native Labour to the Low Grade Mines Commission of 1919–20: 'To make him [The African worker] an entirely free agent as labourer . . . would certainly cause industrial dislocation and jeopardise the economic prosperity of the country' (Johnstone, 1976, p. 35). In contrast, the Statement of European Miners to the Mining Industry Board in 1922 boldly drew an opposite conclusion (*ibid.*, p. 74): 'If they [the employers] abolish the colour bar, then they must abolish the indentured labour system and give every man full facilities to earn the full amount.' Yet in practice the majority of non-African workers have acquiesced in the oppression of the African masses even though, objectively, this goes counter to their own interests. In itself the advance of the African workers would strengthen the position of free labour. Every reduction in the wage gap would lessen the competitive downward pressure on their wages. The answer lies in the fact that the oppression of the African masses is an indispensable condition for capitalist production in South Africa. On the basis of capitalism, free labour in South Africa is not an 'economic' proposition. As the IIE (1974, p. 137) put it, the 'White rate is not an economic rate at all, and it would be economically impossible to simply move the Blacks up on to the "White" wage curve as it exists at the moment.'

To employers, therefore, 'abolition of the colour bar' has remained synonymous with destruction of the conditions of free labour. This is reflected in Wilson's assumption (1972a, pp. 141-2) that a rise in the wages of African miners must mean a fall in the wages of white miners. Job reservation, Wilson argues further, keeps the supply of skilled labour artificially small and pushes wages up. But since 1945 the supply of labour in general has grown smaller. Today, Wilson concludes (1972a, p. 114), echoing van der Horst:

> the interests of management and black labour have come closer
> and closer together in favouring the abolition of the colour bar.
> For not only would this lower the costs to industry, but it would
> raise the wage of those blacks who could go straight into skilled
> jobs as well as raising the wages of the unskilled by reducing the
> number available to do these unskilled jobs.

Taking on skilled African workers at the same wages paid to other skilled workers, however, would hardly be specifically in 'the interests of management'. Nor would costs be lowered, unless skilled African workers were employed at a wage rate lower than that of their white colleagues. This implies that the average wage rate would come down and, in the language of the trade unions, cheap black labour would be used to drive out white. This much is openly conceded by Coetzee (1976, p. 141): 'It needs emphasising, however, that in presenting this new approach of job-structuring (on a non-racial basis) it is not the intention to ask that the Blacks replacing the Whites in the phasing-over process be paid the wages previously paid to Whites.'

The inevitable converse of the 'liberal' approach is hostility and defensiveness on the part of white labour. This is clearly reflected in the statement by A. Nieuwoudt, President of the South African Confederation of Labour, that job reservation 'will remain necessary for as long as there are differences in the standards of living and in the standards of remuneration' (*Financial Mail*, 10 January 1975). Under existing conditions he cannot see that minimum wage rates would protect the higher-paid workers. Such rates, he assumes, would lie well below the rates that free labour is at present able to command. The state would proclaim the rate for 'cheap docile labour' as the official minimum. Similarly, collusion between employers and the state is taken for granted by another conservative trade-union leader, C. P. Grobler, General Secretary of the Artisan Staff Association (Coetzee, 1976, pp. 169–70):

On examination it will be found that the rate for the job is the published or gazetted rate for the job . . . . Invariably it is found that this rate is such that, by today's economic standards, no White worker can exist thereon. Non-Whites, by virtue of a lower economic standard, can, however, and almost automatically and virtually overnight the work is relegated to Non-Whites.

Similar arguments are found in what purports to be a scientific treatise: 'Support of equal pay for equal work has led to a rate for the job,' according to M. A. du Toit (1976, p. 134), 'which simply cannot protect the White worker against the competition of cheap labour.' If this means anything at all, it means that workers cannot be paid equally as long as they are paid unequally. The writer goes on to explain (1976, pp. 133–4) why wage rates must of necessity be unequal in South Africa: 'Blacks, as a result of cheap subsidised housing, transport and a traditional way of living completely different to that of the whites, are prepared to accept lower wages.' It is the existence of cheap labour in this form, the writer concludes, that would drive down higher wages if 'free competition' took place. Therefore, 'equal pay cannot be applied strictly' (*ibid.*, p. 134).

It is a devastating criticism of the leadership of the free labour movement that no effective answer has so far been given to these crude, upside-down arguments. White workers see no possibility of employers undergoing a change of heart and willingly bearing the cost of reform. They realise that tremendous struggle would be called for to change the situation. In such a struggle the existing security of free labour would be destroyed, while the outcome is wrapped in uncertainty. A cautious and conservative attitude on the part of free workers in general is the result.

These questions are implicitly answered by the call for common organisation. What free workers cannot achieve alone, they might well be able to achieve in common struggle with the unfree working class. Why has the alternative of common organisation gained so little support among free workers in the past? The general answer can only be that, in the eyes of the majority, it never seemed feasible. Maintenance of the status quo appeared to be the only realistic course, and one which excluded co-operation with the mass of workers. Opposed to this, the exponents of common organisation were rarely clear or consistent. Thus the predominance of racist ideology among the free workers remained effectively unchallenged.

With the influx of landless Afrikaners into the ranks of the working class, the influence of racist ideology became stronger and more overt. From 1907 onwards the white working class began to change its original composition. The majority of foreign-born men with trade-union experience gave way to a majority of local men, often from a rural background. From the start the ranks of the immigrant miners had been thinned by miner's phthisis. 'By 1907,' Cope records (p. 90), 'it was estimated that a man operating a drill could count on an average working life of five years.' In 1907 the white miners' strike was defeated. Hundreds of strikers were dismissed and replaced by unemployed Afrikaners at lower rates of pay. By 1960, 70 per cent of white miners were Afrikaans-speaking. Landless Afrikaners also made up a large part of the work-force in the new manufacturing industries that were established after 1924.

The Afrikaner workers, coming from the land, lacked the industrial experience and trade-union background that the immigrant workers had possessed. To a greater or lesser extent they were steeped in the primitive racialism of the class they had so recently left. Ideologically, the low level of the white working class went backward even further as the industrial revolution advanced. The ignorance, caution and prejudice that stood in the way of common organisation were significantly strengthened. Among white workers the idea of common organisation was thus driven further into the background at the very time that the development of the African working class was making it more feasible in practice.

The change in the composition of the white working class had another, more tangible result. Afrikaans-speaking workers tended to remain within the orbit of Afrikaner nationalism, while Afrikaner nationalism became more and more closely linked to the interests of the capitalist class. The Labour Party, built up by British immigrant workers, failed to win general support among the section of white workers that in due course became the majority. Through the medium of Afrikaner nationalism white workers as a group became highly susceptible to the pressure of employers and the state. From the 1930s onwards Afrikaner nationalist politicians deliberately and systematically intervened in the labour movement with the purpose of breaking down the existing organisations and building Christian-National organisations in their place. In this way white workers were inhibited even further in developing their class consciousness and the movement towards common organisation was even more retarded. As a result of all these pressures, organised labour has continued on separate roads for an entire historical period. The tradition of segregation has become entrenched to a point where today, after generations of common labour on the shop floor, only the barest theoretical foundation of common organisation has been laid.

Out of the contradictory relationship between capital and free labour some extremely contradictory attitudes have emerged. Compared with the views of Wilson or Doxey, the following extract from the Statement of European Mine Workers to the Mining Industry Board in 1922 is a model of clear insight (Johnstone, 1976, p. 74):

> Our reply . . . is that we are not responsible for the policy which makes the employers continually less dependent on our aid and leads to our position constantly being assailed; and that in the circumstances as they exist, we are entitled to such temporary protection as can be devised, however imperfect.

'Temporary protection', however, has hardened into established practice. Fifty years later similar arguments would be used. According to A. Nieuwoudt, President of the South African Confederation of Labour, it is not the advancement of black workers that the registered unions oppose but the 'attitude of certain employers' (*Financial Mail*, 10 January 1975). White workers have nothing to fear from such advancement, it is stated, provided it proceeds according to actual labour requirements, 'so that the White employee is not ousted or the White labour market flooded'. These conditions, however, are said to rule out the unionisation of black workers, for then the question arises of 'what protection do White workers have against Black?' (*ibid.*).

Yet this question by no means arises from the considerations that have been stated. It can only be explained on the basis of compromise with employers and the state. It is employers, and not the white workers, who would need 'protection' against the organisation of African workers and in due course against a common rate of pay. All that threatens the free worker is the likely reaction by employers in such a situation, of attempting to 'recover their losses' and cut off the advance of unfree labour by forcing down the standards of free labour.

Similarly, the attitudes of employers and the state towards the white working class reflect the contradictory nature of their relationship. On the one hand, white workers are regarded with hostility and misgivings, while on the other hand they are seen as a social force whose support or tolerance is essential. The early industrial and political struggles between free labour on the one hand, and employers and the state on the other, made clear the intensity of the underlying conflict. Yet the danger of allowing this conflict to remain unchecked was equally apparent. To refuse any compromise with free labour would have driven them into the arms of the African working class. It would have created the basis for common organisation, combining the industrial experience and political assertiveness of the white workers with the numbers, the demands and the power of the unfree. This danger was warned against by the Carnegie Commission during the interwar period. It found that the poorest sections of the white proletariat, exposed to the pressures of the ordinary labour market, were becoming fundamentally alienated from the existing order (Joubert, 1972, pp. 39–40):

> Prolonged economic equality between poor whites and the vast majority of coloureds, and the closeness of their dwellings to each other, tend to cause social equality between them. This weakens the tradition that counter-acts racial mixing. The weakening of the social colour bar is taking place at present in a partially visible way.

The fact that this refers to Afrikaners, who are considered inveterate racists, lends force to these conclusions. The notion of a 'parting of the ways' in 1922 is seen to be an extreme simplification. Coetzee describes what actually took place (1976, pp. 12-13):

> The State seemed to argue that the inevitable direct confrontations resulting from violent repression might eventually become the vehicle by which the majority of White workers would come under the influence of those self-confessed communist labour-leaders who were already identifying their members' problems with the Black workers' aspirations and struggles which, it was claimed, indicated common grounds for the general feeling of insecurity.

Johnstone more systematically explains the reliance of capital in South Africa on a divided working class. The colour bar in industry, he says, maintained and reinforced the general division among workers. This division was – certainly by the 1920s – recognised by employers in general as being an essential condition for the maintenance of the supply of unfree labour on which the economy had grown dependent (Johnstone, 1976, pp. 81, 85–6):

> The last thing the [mining] companies wanted was an end to these divisions, for instance by white workers incorporating non-white workers into the ranks of unionised labour . . . . Without the protection of the job colour bar, the white workers might have been inclined to take more radical protectionist measures, to act towards eliminating the enormous differential between the wages and the cost of white and non-white labour. But the job colour bar reduced the likelihood of this, thereby serving to stabilise the labour status quo.

Thus, from the employers' point of view, nothing less than their own survival was bound up with the fragmentation of the working class. Employers, in contrast to the white workers, were in a position to translate their interests directly into state policy. In essence the division of the South African working class thus amounts to a policy of divide and rule carried on in the interests of employers, in terms of which the conditions of free labour received a qualified guarantee, while the white workers carried the odium of 'enforcing' racial segregation.

The same divisive forces have been extended to those workers classified as 'coloured' and 'Asian'. These categories of the population did not form the primary sources of cheap industrial labour and were not subject to the same intense pressures as the African population.[3] At the same time, the majority of people in these categories never gained sufficient economic and political influence to advance or consolidate their position very far. In an intensely competitive society, with racial oppression called into existence by the relationship between employers and the mass of workers, the weaker intermediate groupings fell victim to similar oppression. Politically they were reduced to much the same position as the African population. Economically they remained in a somewhat better position. Being relatively free, and entitled to form recognised trade unions, workers of these categories have certain rights in common with the white workers. In the printing and building industries of the Western Cape especially many artisans are 'coloured'.

Though placed in a separate legal category, 'coloured' and 'Asian' workers as such have played no independent role in South African industrial relations. Within their own ranks they reflect the same basic division that characterises the working class as a whole. 'Coloured' and

'Asian' craftsmen share in many of the benefits that free labour in general enjoys; unskilled 'coloured' and 'Asian' workers find themselves in much the same position as the unfree working class. Due to the pressure of competition and their lack of political rights they cannot advance beyond this level. 'Cheap docile labour' remains the keystone of the existing South African economy. Within this economy the basic division of workers is that between 'free' and 'unfree' or 'African' and 'non-African'. The entire system of industrial relations stands or falls with the maintenance or abolition of this contrast.

What, then, is the basis for these 'intermediate' legal categories? Apart from historical differences that have lost much of their relevance, why have these categories not been legislated out of existence as so many other historical survivals have been? Thus far there has been no need to take such a step. The advantages of increasing the already massive supply of unfree labour by some 16 per cent do not weigh up against the tremendous struggles that such a step would lead to. Conversely, the existence of some 900,000 relatively free 'coloured' and 'Asian' workers is not sufficiently objectionable from the capitalist point of view to call for urgent action. At the same time, by maintaining these categories, a further element of division is injected among free as well as unfree workers. The question of coloured membership, for example, has long kept the registered trade unions divided. Similarly, divisions are created among black workers by the degree of preference enjoyed by those workers classified as 'coloured' or 'Asian', especially in the Western Cape. The maintenance of these intermediate categories thus has a contradictory effect. On the one hand it is divisive, while on the other it forms a 'bridge' between the two main groups of workers, the 'free' and the 'unfree'.

The main object of South African labour policy is to maintain a supply of 'cheap docile labour'. This implies a low level of wages at which African skilled and semi-skilled labour, unorganised and strictly controlled, can be employed. To this level employers will ultimately seek to depress the wage rates for skilled and semi-skilled labour. This pressure by employers runs counter to the interests of free and unfree workers alike. Apart from the pressure by workers in general to improve their standards of living, in South Africa pressure is exercised by the mass of African workers to abolish the gap between their own poverty and the wealth of the surrounding society. They aspire to precisely those conditions of free labour that employers would prefer to destroy. At the same time, pressure is exercised by free labour to prevent the wage gap from being closed by the downward movement of their own wages. These pressures by free and unfree labour respectively can be reconciled only through the upward movement of the lower rates of wages to the level of free labour. Objectively such a tendency is called forth by the struggles of free and unfree labour alike, even when starting in complete isolation from each other. The same applies in respect of the freedom to organise, and working conditions in general.

If we view these general tendencies in their concrete social form, our analysis becomes clearer. Under conditions of rapid economic growth – such as South Africa has experienced almost continuously for approximately forty years – adjustments to the wage rate are possible. Wages may be increased 'normally' – i.e. at least on a par with inflation – or sharper increases can be afforded in the event of sharp or sudden pressure. This has been seen in practice. For the coming period, on the other hand, the outlook is very different. The general prospect is one of recession and political instability, alternating with periods of weak recovery. These conditions call forth greater struggles on the part of workers to maintain their living standards, but at the same time rule out constant wage increases in response to pressure. In the case of the higher-paid workers real income is already decreasing. The effect of the official wage policy adopted in 1975 was that wage increases for these workers were limited to 70 per cent of the rise in consumer prices.

Under these conditions the tendencies described above may be expected to take on a more concrete form. Pressure by workers of all categories, whether for improvement or mere maintenance of their position, must call forth increasing counterpressures from employers and the state. Sharp confrontations may be anticipated, leading to sharper adjustments and changes than before. The conditions of free labour are likely to suffer to some extent; unfree workers are likely to press for improvement on an ever-growing scale. These struggles are likely to lessen the contrast between the conditions of free and unfree labour.

The relationship between different sections of workers must be tested in the final analysis at the level of practical interaction: the level of the work-place. On the one hand, state policy must tend to pull workers apart. On the other hand, the growing uniformity in the experience and consciousness of workers of all races is a unifying force. In the work-place this leads to complex and contradictory relations between workers of different races. Data collected from 4,500 black workers in eleven countries in 1959 led to the following conclusion (Glass, n.d., p. 52):

the black industrial worker, born into the traditional society
and emerging into Western economic society . . . nevertheless,
within the span of a short industrial lifetime, assumes the work
patterns, the job attitudes and the occupational expectations
of Western industrial man.

In secondary industry it was found that black South African workers
in their behaviour and attitudes do not differ significantly from other
South African workers, nor from workers in other countries. In a
comparison between the job attitudes of American and black South
African workers, only one noteworthy contrast came to light. The
American workers tended to rate 'opportunities of advancement' far
higher than black South African workers. But this has an obvious and
non-biological explanation (Glass, p. 50): 'Since there are practically no
opportunities for advancement for [black South African] workers, they
do not perceive this as an industrial expectation.'

Differences among the various categories of South African workers
should thus be interpreted in the light of material conditions. But it is
precisely the material differences among workers that are constantly
being reduced by the process of industrialisation. It forces the tribal
or peasant farmer into the life pattern and the experience of the urban
industrial worker. Wage labour, according to another survey, becomes
regarded as 'a normal and inevitable situation' (Leistner, 1968, p. 10).
This change is fundamental. From this point onward, differences in
attitudes and behaviour are secondary and destined to be worn away
by the pressures of common experience. Precisely the same could be
said of white workers with a rural background, and Afrikaner workers
in particular.

State policy, on the other hand, creates new differences between
workers of different races, and hence in their experience and attitudes.
African and non-African workers are forced into competition with each
other, and the former made subordinate to the latter in almost every
way that can be legally devised. In the work-place, however, absolute
barriers cannot be maintained. Men working shoulder to shoulder form
personal relationships which no law can entirely prevent. This was
shown by a study carried out among the employees of an urban bus
company in 1966. The general characteristics of white–black worker
relations were found to be 'ambivalence, ambiguity, and the involvement of participants in a dilemma' (Hahlo, 1969, p. 14). But relations
varied greatly according to the categories of workers concerned.
Relations between white supervisors and unskilled black labourers are

described as joking and paternalistic. These men had no contact with each other outside the place of work. Relations between 'middle-level Africans' (e.g. drivers, electricians' assistants or clerks) and white section heads, on the other hand, were of a different nature. A certain measure of 'informal equality' was acknowledged on both sides. It was found that these African workers 'are able to have discussions with Europeans in which they freely express their opinions' (*ibid*., p. 21). They are also able 'to make jokes at the expense of their European colleagues in front of other European staff' without giving offence. Both groups are aware that 'neither of them has the power to alter their present situation'. Significantly enough, 'all the staff, European and African, can see management as a separate group, which consists of the Bus Company directors and outsiders who are also involved in the transport business'. Among themselves, on the other hand, workers of both races accept that they 'share the same ambitions'.[4]

Divisions among workers of different races are thus at their weakest in the place of work itself. Especially under conditions of struggle, divisions – even racial divisions – are open to serious question. Referring to a strike, a black miner asks: 'Why did the white miners not stand with us when the police were molesting us unfairly [with truncheons, dogs and tear-gas]? Some miners are eager to know' (AIM, 1976, p. 24). Contact built up at this level, however, is stunted and distorted by social relations in general. While divisive tendencies must predominate under these conditions, a basis also exists out of which an opposite tendency could grow. It may be concluded that common organisation among workers of all races is likely to emerge at the industrial level sooner than at other levels. The 'mixed' trade unions of white and coloured workers already provide a certain precedent. Common industrial organisation could, under certain conditions, provide a foundation for common political action.

Seen in its historical context the South African State has at every stage shown an unmistakable identity of interest with the capitalist class. Its functions have included managing and reconciling the interests of employers as a class and, later, enacting a legal compromise between employers and organised labour. In this the state has been guided by direct influences, such as the sources of its income, not to mention the close relations between men in power and leading businessmen.

The role of the state is revealed most clearly in its policy towards working-class organisation. In 1924 the Smuts government, after years of bitter hostility, was finally obliged to recognise the unions of free workers. The mass of African workers, however, were excluded from the recognised unions. Subsequent governments have maintained this exclusion and made it absolute. From the viewpoint of employers the need for such a policy is clear. Were African workers to be given full union rights, they would play a decisive role in collective bargaining. The existing wage structure would collapse. Even if trade unions were to remain formally segregated (as the registered unions are today), unions of free workers would be forced to come to terms with the unions of unfree workers. Common organisation would take shape, in substance if not in form, bringing with it the need for economic and social change on a scale undreamed of at present. Against such a prospect the state has inevitably set its face. As the Minister of Labour explained in 1953 (quoted by Hepple, 1966, p. 133): 'It is obvious that the stronger the native union movement should become, the more dangerous it would be to the Europeans in South Africa . . . we would probably be committing race suicide if we gave them that incentive.' Nor has this hostility diminished over the years. M. A. du Toit, writing in 1976, found some truth in the belief that the recognition of separate trade unions for African workers 'will result in claims for full recognition' (p. 123). He goes on to explain, in his own bigoted terms, why this is an intolerable prospect for the state (*ibid*., p. 124):

> The stronger these unions become, the more dangerous the position will be for the whites. Most of their members cannot even read the constitution of a trade union and know nothing about negotiation and the industrial structure of South Africa. It would only mean racial suicide.

In particular, according to this writer, one cannot ignore the danger 'that White supremacy will be challenged by powerful Black trade unions, which can paralyse the country through strikes' (*ibid*.).

The compromise between employers and white miners was first given legal force in 1893, when the first mining law of the Transvaal Republic was enacted. Employers had begun to question the wisdom of paying a white man £5 a month for work that a black man would do for £2. Immigrant miners, on the other hand, were concerned with preserving their livelihood. The Boer state feared the growing power of the mining corporations, and intervened with the uneasy compromise of a legal colour bar. Certain work was reserved for white workers only, while employers remained free to use African workers for all remaining work. To craftsmen and immigrant miners racial discrimination was thus presented as a simple solution to their problems, if not the only condition on which employers would continue to employ them. The presence of black men in occupations where white men worked began to be seen as the 'thin end of the wedge'. In 1896 the Ironmoulders Union was formed and resolved that 'no Coloured members be permitted to work as moulders' (Walker and Weinbren, 1961, pp. 6-7).

While by the turn of the century the pressures that drove the immigrant workers to seek refuge in racism were more or less fully developed, the countervailing pressure towards common organisation had not yet properly begun to manifest itself. Neither the small craft unions, nor the unorganised African workers, were capable of resisting the forces of competition except to a very limited extent. After 1902 it became even clearer that industrial segregation was rooted in South African social relations rather than in mere ideology. Ideologically, no clearer difference can be imagined than that between the Kruger Republican government and the post-war British administration. Yet the British administration maintained the previous system in all its essentials, including the pass laws and the industrial colour bar. Indeed, it was during the last four years of the Crown colony, from 1904 to 1907, that the colour bar took on a more drastic form than ever before or since.

The 'Chinese labour' dispute provides us with a clear illustration of the forces that hold the industrial colour bar in existence. Through wage reductions the Chamber of Mines had created a shortage of African miners after the Anglo-Boer war. This problem the Chamber proposed to solve by importing Chinese labourers on contract. The alternative of importing unskilled labourers from Europe, though strongly argued by the mine manager F. H. P. Cresswell and others, was never acceptable to the Chamber. Its objections arose from the fact that European workers would be more likely to organise, would form links with existing unions, could not be reduced to the level of compound labour, and would command a higher wage. In 1904, after a political campaign in which the enormous influence of the Chamber was exerted to the full, the Transvaal legislature duly passed the enabling ordinance (no. 17 of 1904). *Inter alia*, it provided that Chinese workers would be imported for fixed periods only, would work a sixty-hour week and earn a minimum wage of 2s a day. The minimum wage for African miners at this time was 2s 6d a day (Transvaal Labour Commission, 1904, Exhibit no. 1). Such a policy could hardly enjoy lasting popularity among an enfranchised public consisting largely of workers and farmers. In 1907 Ordinance no. 17 was repealed by the first independent government of the Transvaal, subject to the guarantee, offered by General Smuts to the mining companies, that 'no Chinese would be allowed to leave unless proper substitutes have previously been found' (Coetzee, 1976, p. 7). The Chamber accordingly turned its attention to the African reserves once more. The last of the Chinese workers were shipped out in 1910.

The precarious position of free labour at this time was revealed by the wage rates in categories of work in which white as well as black men were employed. Work done by free workers at an average cost of 9s 10d a shift was done by unfree workers at 2s 4d a shift (Transvaal Labour Commission, 1904, Exhibits 'A' to 'G'). How was the opposition of the white workers to the large-scale importation of even cheaper Chinese labour overcome? Ordinance no. 17 provided that the Chinese workers would only be used for 'such labour as is usually performed in the Witwatersrand district by persons belonging to the aboriginal races or tribes (van der Horst, 1942, p. 171). They were specifically excluded from all skilled trades, including some outside the mining industry. This arrangement unmistakably embodied a compromise between employers and free labour, recognised and regulated by the state. Employers would refrain from using their power, based on the abundance of 'cheap docile labour', to attack the position of the free minority of workers. In return, the latter were called on to support the cheap labour policy, or at least refrain from opposing it. Their role was passive or at most defensive; the initiative rested with the employers.

From these events it is also clear to what extent the immigrant miners had outserved their purpose and grown dispensable. The insecurity of free labour was growing greater. As Coetzee observes, 'the higher their wages became in relation to unskilled workers, the more economical it became for employers to introduce mechanised technology needing less, or sometimes unskilled, labour' (1976, p. 6). By virtue of the laws of supply and demand African workers were fast gaining title to every job in the country. The reserve system and the pass laws placed them in an unassailable 'competitive' position. No worker would henceforth be able to work in South Africa on any better terms, except when protected by some special agreement or arrangement. As the position of the free workers became less secure, their dependence on a policy of industrial segregation increased. This dependence was destined to continue, until a viable alternative could be provided by common organisation.

In 1907 the accumulated grievances of the white miners led to a general strike. Although defeated, the strike drew attention to the potentially explosive situation in the mines. Two government commissions were appointed to investigate the mining industry. One of these was the Mining Regulations Commission under the chairmanship of F. E. T. Krause, former Deputy Attorney General of the Transvaal Republic and a known supporter of racial discrimination. The next important instrument of industrial segregation, the regulations framed under the Mines and Works Act of 1911, was based on the report of this commission.

In itself the Mines and Works Act neither contained nor authorised a colour bar. It empowered the Governor General to make regulations in respect of 'the grant, cancellation, and suspension of certificates of competency' for all occupations where he deemed it expedient to do so. In the regulations, however, it was laid down that certificates of competency should not be granted to 'coloured persons' in the Transvaal or Orange Free State. A total of fifty-one occupations were reserved by this means for white workers in the period up to 1920. In the strike of 1922 the organisations of white labour suffered a crushing defeat and the Chamber of Mines went to court to attack the industrial colour bar. The Supreme Court found in 1923 that the regulation in question 'discriminated against coloured persons . . . on the ground of their colour, and as no power was conferred either in express terms or by necessary implication to make this discrimination the regulation was *ultra vires* the enabling Act' (R. *v*. Hildick-Smith, 1924, Transvaal Provincial Division 69). We have seen, however, that employers refrained from pressing home their advantage too far. Enabling legislation was passed afresh in 1926 to provide explicitly for racial discrimination in the issue of certificates. In practice, the colour bar continued in force without any interruption.

Although the Mines and Works Act remained the only statutory colour bar until 1951, further steps were taken in the 1920s to regulate the status quo between employers and white workers. With the Rand revolt of 1922 this issue came to a head. Thousands of white miners, supported by most of the white population of the Reef, rose up in arms against the threat of being replaced by African compound labour. Although their isolated resistance was broken by the superior power of the state, the full significance of the issue was finally understood both by the employers and the state. Van der Horst describes the one side of the matter (1942, p. 182):

Although the strikers failed [in their demands] the influence of
the Rand 'revolution' has been very great. Alarmed by the previous

strikes in 1913 and 1914, the Government had begun before
the war to embark on social legislation. The 1922 strike showed
the lengths to which European labour was prepared to go in
the endeavour to protect its position, and there is no doubt
that memories of the strike have been behind subsequent
industrial legislation, much of which has been designed to
protect Europeans from Native competition.

During this same period, however, a vastly more significant development was taking place. For the first time organised African labour was
coming to the fore. Its power drove home to employers and the state
the importance of gaining the political support of the white working
class, rather than driving it into irreconcilable opposition. Division of
the working class, and support for state policy by the free minority,
became understood as necessary conditions for the continued exploitation of South Africa's 'black gold', the mass of unfree workers.

To this period of 'reform' belongs the Apprenticeship Act of 1922.
Although this Act contained no reference to race, it laid down the
requirement of education to Standard VI level for all apprentices in
the skilled trades. Due to poverty and the meagre educational facilities
available to them, this requirement was, and is, beyond the reach of
the great majority of the African population. At the same time, the
Mining Industry Board recommended 'the creation of permanent
machinery of conciliation for the gold and coal-mines' (de Kiewiet,
1941, p. 271). The result was the Industrial Conciliation Act of 1924,
by which the unions of non-African workers, and those alone, were
recognised by law. The government of Smuts, having violently beaten
down the white workers' movement, now extended the hand of friendship by reinforcing the colour bar.[5]

For the Smuts government it was too late. As in 1914, large numbers
of voters were thoroughly alienated by the bloody action that the
government had taken on behalf of the Chamber of Mines. This time,
however, no war intervened and no 'khaki election' could be held. The
Nationalist and Labour Parties had given the strike at least token
support and were seen as opposing the Chamber of Mines. The two
parties formed an electoral pact and were returned to power in 1924.
By this time racial discrimination as the keynote of industrial relations
was established state policy. It was no longer the property of any single
party. The Pact government, however, was more crudely overt than its
predecessor in carrying this policy out. Forever associated with its
name is the so-called 'civilised labour policy'. In fact, this policy had

already been implemented by the colonial governments prior to 1910. The role of the Pact government was to extend it to employment by the state. Two years later the Pact government restored the legal status of the colour bar in mining.

If the immigrant miners had grown partly dispensable as early as 1907, this was even more true of the impoverished, unskilled white men who were drifting to the cities from the land. With the 'civilised labour policy' the Pact government set out to place them in sheltered employment, and thereby win their votes. This policy, in the words of van der Horst (1942), amounted to 'the employment of European unskilled labourers at wage-rates above those generally prevailing for unskilled work'. By definition, such labour was 'uneconomic'. Yet within an expanding economy, given the massive and increasing employment of unfree labour at strictly 'economic' rates, it was a worthwhile investment that yielded rich dividends in political stability. The alternative, in the words of the Carnegie Commission, was poverty and a 'demoralising' effect on the white labourer (Joubert, 1972, pp. 39–40).

'Civilised labour' was defined by the government as 'the labour rendered by persons whose standard of living conforms to the standard generally recognised as tolerable from the usual European standpoint' (van der Horst, 1942, p. 250). Strictly speaking such a definition excluded large numbers of the 'poor white' population itself, whose standards of living could not have been described as 'tolerable' in this sense. However, the definition appears to have been no more than a formality. Inspectors of the Department of Labour went so far as to state that 'under no circumstances would Natives be regarded as "civilised labourers"' (*ibid.*). This, it is submitted, was the policy's underlying intention as well as its effect. Whatever measures might be taken in regard to free labour, it is always the maintenance and control of South Africa's 'black gold', its supply of unfree labour, that is implicitly at stake.

In the post-war period these simple measures for maintaining the status quo became inadequate. Given the growth in employment and the huge expansion of the African working class, more sophisticated means were called for to maintain control of the situation and to neutralise African 'competition' as far as white workers were concerned. In 1951 the Bantu Building Workers Act was passed. Its aims were (i) to provide for the training of African building artisans in order to help meet the acute shortage of manpower in the building industry,

and (ii) 'to protect building workers other than Bantu against competition from Bantu building at lower wage rates' (de Kock, 1973,
p. 328A). What lower wage rates? How are they determined? In terms
of section 13 of the Act they are determined by the Minister of Labour.
It is also provided that African building workers (as defined by the Act)
may not be employed in urban areas except in 'Bantu areas'. African
building apprentices are excluded from the Apprenticeship Act. The
underlying aim of the Act thus emerges clearly. Skilled African building
workers, already excluded from the normal processes of collective
bargaining, are now explicitly obliged to work under worse conditions
than other building workers.[6] Having thus transformed them into a
'danger' to their fellow building workers, the legislature sets about
protecting the latter from this danger.

In 1956 industrial segregation was taken to its logical conclusion.
An instrument was finally created whereby any form of work in any
industry could be regulated and all or any occupations could be reserved according to race. This took the form of amendments to the
Industrial Conciliation Act. First introduced in 1954 these proposed
amendments eventually resulted, after much debate and revision, in
a new consolidating Act that was promulgated in 1956. 'Full consultation with organised industry and the trade unions', it is said, had
taken place (de Kock, 1973, p. 502). Although a number of registered
trade-union officials had belonged to the ministerial committee involved,
their role was controversial and dubious. The proposed new measures
had far-reaching aims: to extend racial segregation among trade unions
and their members, and to empower the Minister of Labour to decree
the reservation of all or any work in terms of race. Yet, according to
Walker and Weinbren, 'the rank and file of the unions were not made
acquainted by their representatives with the contents of the successive
drafts of the Bill' (1961, p. 245). It is alleged that the government
imposed a duty of secrecy on the trade-union officials concerned. In
view of the fact that many trade unionists were directly affected by
these changes, the question presents itself as to how meaningful the
'consultation' with the unions had been, or what the outcome would
have been of an open and general discussion. Even so, a certain amount
of trade-union opposition to the measures took place, though in a form
that was completely ineffectual.

The law of 'job reservation' was embodied in section 77 of the new
Industrial Conciliation Act. Entitled 'Safeguard against inter-racial
competition', it provided that the Minister of Labour may order an
investigation by a specially created organ, the *industrial tribunal*, into

any industry or categories of employment. The tribunal then submits a report to the Minister, containing its recommendations. Such recommendations may relate to the 'prohibition of the replacement by an employer of employees of a specified race by employees of another race', or to the reservation of work according to race, as provided for in detail. The Minister may then make a determination in accordance with the recommendation. Contravention of such a determination is a criminal offence. Determinations were made in respect of numerous categories of work. In 1975 it was reported that twenty-seven categories were reserved, of which sixteen were being enforced.

During this same period a new and contradictory tendency began to manifest itself. With the growth of industry and the shortages of manpower that arose during the Second World War, the old 'civilised labour policy' had begun to fall away. Industrialisation in the post-war period increasingly broke down the traditional barriers of craft and skill among workers and expanded the layer of semi-skilled operatives among all racial categories.

With the return of the National Party to power in 1948, the 'civilised labour policy' was to some extent reintroduced. But one of the conditions for this policy, a reservoir of unemployed white labourers, no longer existed, and with it the need to protect these workers from African 'competition' was, for the time being, gone. On the contrary, employers were now forced to draw increasingly on the reserves of African labour. The inadequacy of the existing skilled labour force called for an adaptation of state policy. Unfree labour now had to be channelled into skilled as well as unskilled jobs. The Bantu Building Workers Act was the precursor of this development. In practice, skilled African labour would remain subject to the same fundamental disabilities as unskilled. The compromise with free labour was 'amended' to provide for the 'fragmentation' of skilled work and its division between free and unfree workers. What Doxey would call the 'inner privileged society' would no longer encompass skilled labour as a whole; it became further limited to certain categories only.

The effect has been a superficial liberalisation of employment policy. 'It is impossible to escape the conclusion,' wrote Professor Steenkamp in 1971, 'that, if we want growth, we shall have to make better use of our black labour resources, quantitatively as well as qualitatively, outside as well as inside the established industrial areas' (p. 104). 'Better use' in this sense need mean no better conditions as far as black workers are concerned. In practice, 'better use' means the more extensive use of cheap labour. For doing more skilled work the unfree worker need be paid no more than for doing unskilled work. His wage is in any event a fraction of that of the free artisan. In 1976 a survey in Natal revealed that the average wage of the African labourer was R24 per week. For machine operators the average was R29.30, though 25 per cent earned no more than R24. For more skilled men the average wage was R41.89, though even of these 14 per cent earned less than R20 to R24. The average earnings of the African 'artisan aides' ranged from R34.74 to R55.64, depending on length of service. Of white fitters, by way of comparison, 41 per cent were paid from R100 to R112 per week (*Financial Mail*, 21 May 1976).

Officially, more skilled African workers are employed in a 'caretaker' capacity, and higher unemployment among free workers may slow this tendency down. In the 1976 industrial agreement for the engineering industry, for example, it was once again provided that registered trade-union members will enjoy preference in the event of unemployment. Opposed to this there is the cost factor. If economies are to be effected, the logic of replacing expensive labour with cheap is more compelling than ever. In any event the racial integration of the industrial labour force has gone too far to be reversed. In the secondary sector alone the number of black workers had reached nearly one million by 1967, or 70.3 per cent of the total work-force, compared with 178,487 (57.6 per cent) in 1936 (Steenkamp, 1971, pp. 105–6). Even on the railways, the stronghold of 'civilised labour', 3,500 (vacant) 'white' jobs were given to African workers in 1974 alone (*Financial Mail*, 28 February 1975). Depression would have to reach massive proportions indeed before this situation could be significantly changed.

Like the 'civilised labour policy', formal job reservation was gradually undermined by the growing demand for skilled and semi-skilled labour. No new determinations were made after 1971. In January 1975 a new determination for the building industry opened up skilled work in the Transvaal and the Orange Free State to coloured artisans, as in the Cape Province and Natal, subject to the condition that no such worker may supervise a white worker. In rural areas and in Kimberley, Queenstown and Grahamstown, job reservation in the building industry was scrapped. These measures were prompted by a shortage of building artisans, reaching 3,000 on the Reef.[7] In the Transvaal clothing industry, where job reservation has been in force for many years, the number of white workers decreased from 7,500 in 1954 to 734 in 1975 and the number of coloured workers from 6,500 to roughly 700. The number of African workers increased from 2,000 to 18,000 (*Financial Mail*, 29 August 1975). Similarly, though the job of truck-driver in various industries on the Reef has been reserved for whites, it is conceded by officials of the Department of Labour that in practice 'you seldom see a white man driving a lorry'. It is alleged that employers disregard the relevant determinations very widely (*Financial Mail*, 27 February 1976).

Besides its official and legal forms, the compromise between employers and free labour continues to exist in its original informal character. To young Africans wanting to learn skilled trades, even if they do obtain the necessary schooling, this remains a serious obstacle. Most white journeymen will refuse to train black apprentices and, for precisely the same reason, coloured journeymen often refuse to train Africans. In general, the 'conventional colour bar' amounts to this: employers will refrain from employing black workers who in any way directly threaten the position of white employees, while the latter will refuse to work with any black worker who is thus employed. As a means of negating the forces of competition, however, such practices have been no more effective than the legal forms of racial discrimination. The tide of African labour into every branch of industry has been irresistible, and employers in general have made no attempt to resist it. In the process the craft-protectionist position of the registered trade unions has grown hopelessly outmoded and outflanked.

In the gold-mining industry this has been especially apparent. The procedure has been for the wages and working conditions of white workers to be improved, in return for which African workers take over a portion of their work. Agreements to this effect were reached between the Chamber of Mines and the Mineworkers' Union in 1967 and again in 1975–6. In the manufacturing sector a similar tendency has been at work over a long period of time. Here it has mainly been African labour that was taken up into the new 'operative' categories of work. In many cases the work of the artisan has been reduced to a number of 'semi-skilled' jobs, which can then be given to African workers at lower rates of pay. During the years of full employment white workers did not resist this tendency to any great extent. Today, from the point of view of restoring their position, it has become too late. Any significant change in the system of industrial relations must tend towards either the emancipation of unfree labour or the abolition of free labour. Such are the pressures on the system today that its maintenance beyond the immediate future is speculative. Even more remote is the possibility of turning the clock back to the position of the 1960s.

Two conclusions re-emerge from the above with renewed insistence. First, the basic demand of capitalist production is for labour-power in general, not for the labour-power of any racial group as such. As a result, in terms of race the working class has become inextricably intermingled. What remains at issue are the relations of workers with each other, with employers and with the state. Second, the compromise between employers and free labour is only one aspect of the overall system of industrial relations. It is brought about not so much by the demands of white workers as by the pressure of the mass of workers. To resist this pressure and prevent the unification of the working class, employers and the state have resorted to compromise with free labour. By this means free labour is kept from the arena and the state is allowed a relatively free hand to deal with the African masses.

The essential function of the industrial colour bar is to regulate the supply of 'cheap docile labour' which is now required in a growing variety of functions. The demands of the white workers cannot be considered the basic reason for the racial division of the working class. The causes must ultimately be sought in the forces of *competition* which are inherent in the capitalist system. The statement, for example, that 'the true rate for the job . . . cannot be applied in South Africa' (M. A. du Toit, 1976, p. 133) would be incomprehensible on any other basis. It can be said only of a South Africa in which employers are dependent on cheap labour, where the state enforces employers' interests, and where workers must compete with one another for work. The demands of the white workers are basically no different from the demands of other workers. In itself the demand for the maintenance of an existing standard of living by no means implies the victimisation of any other group of workers. Yet in South Africa it has precisely this ostensible effect.

The answer to this riddle is provided by the traditional policy followed by employers and the state to maintain a supply of 'cheap docile labour' by means of the reserve system and the pass laws. As a result of this system African workers are placed in an unassailably 'competitive' position. In terms of 'normal' competition the tendency must be for free labour to disappear. From the employers' point of view the only question is whether or not this tendency should be enforced. At a certain stage, as we have seen, the question was answered in the negative, and the state turned all its attention to the task of holding in check the masses of African workers.

Thus the function of the industrial colour bar, contrary to appearances, is not so much to keep free labour *above* a certain level; essentially, it is to keep the mass of workers *below* a certain level. In the capitalist analysis a completely spurious link is created between the lower wages of black workers and the higher wages of white workers, the one being presented as an 'inevitable' consequence of the other. In fact, there is no causal link. If the African worker is paid less than the white worker for doing similar work, then only the employer and his need to maximise profits can be held responsible for this. If African workers are maintained as 'cheap docile labour' with whom free workers cannot compete without sacrificing their freedom, then demands by the latter for 'protection' are scarcely to be wondered at. The official analysis of the industrial colour bar focuses exclusively on these demands. The interests of employers and the state are made to appear unrelated.

Another conclusion is implicit in this entire situation. The maintenance or the removal of racial divisions in the working class depends, in the final analysis, on the balance of power between employers and workers in general. In times of economic crisis and political upheaval it is all but unthinkable that the existing relationships will continue unaffected. With political crisis looming, it is equally unlikely that the compromise with the white workers will easily be broken. As long as the latter remain on the defensive, the prime mover in the process of change can only be the African workers. On their movement depends the continued division or the future unity of the South African working class, and with it the survival of the present social system.

Chapter 3

Working-class organisation

Working-class organisation may take different forms, depending on prevailing conditions and on the purpose of the organisation. This seemingly straightforward proposition, it will be seen, is contradicted by certain well-established opinions on the subject.

The main distinction that must be drawn is that between industrial (or economic) organisation, and political organisation. Trade unions are the typical and most general form of industrial organisation. In South Africa legislation has also created the system of works committees and liaison committees, which are designed to represent African workers only on the basis of a single place of work. Political organisation in general means political parties in one form or another. Workers' organisation may also be spontaneous and informal. In South Africa, due to the restrictive conditions under which open organisation must take place, spontaneous organisation will often mean *secret* organisation. Such organisation may be industrial or political in character, or a combination of both.

Counterposed to workers' organisation at every level are employers' organisations. These may likewise be registered in terms of the Industrial Conciliation Act and likewise take part in the official system of collective bargaining. Historically preceding the registered employers' bodies were chambers of commerce, mining and industry, and other unregistered though frequently powerful and very influential bodies. Another form of capitalist combination has been the merging of individual employers into corporations, and of corporations into still larger trusts or monopolies, often carrying on business in several different countries, either directly or through subsidiary companies. Finally, political parties have been formed to safeguard the interests of the capitalist class.

In theory joint organisations of workers and employers reconcile the interests of the classes and might therefore be expected to supersede their separate organisations. In practice, this has not happened, nor is it likely to happen in the absence of state compulsion. Joint organisation in South Africa refers mainly to Industrial Councils registered in terms of the Industrial Conciliation Act. Significantly enough, there had been little tendency towards joint organisation before the original statutory framework was created in 1924. Since then Industrial Councils have attended to collective bargaining, while the basic and more general differences between workers and employers have continued undiminished. This ongoing contradiction is reflected in manifold forms. One example must suffice: in May 1976, after decades of industrial peace, negotiations between the Master Diamond Cutters' Association and the Diamond Workers' Union over a new industrial agreement broke down and a lengthy strike ensued.

The significance of the industrial council system is interpreted in different ways. On the one hand, it is described as an 'admirable' system which has helped to give South Africa 'a remarkable degree of industrial peace and freedom from strikes' (*OHSA*, vol. 2, p. 30). Past and present co-operation between registered organisations of employers and employees is accepted without question as the basis for continuing co-operation in future. Opposed to this, it will be argued that past co-operation has been based on certain peculiar conditions, and that the continuing divisions between workers and employers will be decisive in the end. Within capitalist society the interests of workers and employers are fundamentally opposed. Legally and economically, the employer has always been the ruler. Historically, employers' combinations have enjoyed every advantage over workers' organisations, the more so where the latter have been actively suppressed. Adam Smith's observations of two hundred years ago remain valid to the present day (quoted by Gitlow, 1963, pp. 22-3):

> The masters, being fewer in number can combine much more easily . . . . Masters are always and everywhere in a sort of tacit, but constant and uniform combination, not to raise the wages of labour above their actual rate . . . . Masters too sometimes enter into particular combinations to sink the wages of labour even below this rate.

If the fundamental contradictions between capital and labour became less visible in Western Europe and North America after 1945, in South Africa it has remained unmistakable at every stage of modern history. In the advanced states the working class has gained a great deal in size and influence. At the same time, combinations of employers remain (by definition) the bodies where the dominant economic and legal power is located. In the eyes of the employer 'Industrial relations arrangements must leave unimpaired management's prerogatives and freedom' (Reynolds, 1974, p. 431). Far from asserting themselves *over* the employers, the historical achievement of the workers' unions thus far has been to challenge the once unlimited freedom and prerogatives of management and to exercise some control thereover. Unions have succeeded in reducing the degree of power wielded by employers over workers. They have never succeeded in ending this power, or even matching it for any length of time. To do so would mean, in effect, taking over and abolishing the function of management that is vested in the employer, thus ending the system of private enterprise. In countries where this system has been ended it has not been the result of a simple expansion of workers' industrial organisation. Long before it reaches a decisive point, any conflict between workers and employers will be transferred on to the political or even the military stage.

No mechanical rule can be laid down as to the relationship between the trade unions and the political organisations of the workers. In the case of Britain the Labour Party was 'the by-product of trade union activity' (Attlee, 1937, p. 36), while in the Netherlands, for example, social democracy was partly responsible for the birth of industrial unionism. What has been the position in South Africa? All working-class organisation, in the first place, has tended to develop on a basis of racial fragmentation. Among all groups of workers industrial organisation preceded political organisation. At an early stage, however, racist or nationalist tendencies began establishing their predominance among different sections of the working class. By the early 1950s this process was complete. Not a single independent working-class party of any consequence remained. A peculiar and contradictory situation had arisen. At the industrial level workers were increasingly becoming organised on the basis of their own independent class interests. Yet at the political level workers were largely under the sway of nationalist parties proclaiming the unity of the workers with other classes and the non-independence of the workers. Only the industrial and political upheavals of the 1970s, to which the rapid industrialisation of the 1950s and the 1960s formed the prelude, would provide even the beginnings of a resolution.

The original form of economic organisation in South Africa, long preceding the industrial revolution, was the organisation of employers.

In one respect the Cape of the seventeenth and eighteenth centuries had been extremely 'modern': economic and political power lay overwhelmingly in the hands of a single multinational monopoly. The Dutch East Indies Company, having founded an outpost of its empire at the Cape in 1652, maintained its predominance as employer, its monopoly of foreign trade and its restrictions on internal trade until the first British occupation of 1795. To rising British industrialism colonies had different uses than to the merchants of Amsterdam. Trade restrictions were relaxed and private enterprise could develop more freely. In 1804 the first attempt was made 'to put private business on an organised footing' (*OHSA*, vol. 1, p. 294) with the establishment of a *Kamer van Commercie*. This body collapsed but by 1822 its place had been taken by a Commercial Exchange 'with its own impressive building'.

From this time onwards the common interests of employers would increasingly be managed by common organisations. In 1861 the Commercial Exchange was renamed the Cape Chamber of Commerce. As capitalist enterprise spread to the remainder of South Africa it was followed almost immediately by similar organisations. Chambers of Commerce were established in Port Elizabeth in 1864, in East London in 1873, in Pretoria and Pietermaritzburg in 1884, and in Johannesburg in 1890. A Commercial Exchange of Southern Africa was established in 1905 with 101 member firms. By 1974 the Association of Chambers of Commerce had a membership of 144 local Chambers. In addition, an *Afrikaanse Handelsinstituut* was formed in 1942.

With the growth of urban production on a large scale, the basis for large-scale industrial organisation came into existence. Unlike workers, employers were in a favourable position from the outset to reap the advantages of combination. From the outset, too, combination meant the merger of companies. In the mining industry colossal structures arose whose power would be enormous and would remain so to the present day. Two new names gained world currency in this process, reflecting the growth of a new ruling class in South Africa: *Rhodes*, whose De Beers Corporation by 1891 had a virtual monopoly of diamond production and marketing, and '*the Randlords*', of whom Hobson wrote in 1926 (quoted by Wilson, 1972a, p. 32): 'nowhere in the world has there ever existed so concentrated a form of capitalism as that represented by the financial power of the mining houses in South Africa, and nowhere else does that power so completely realise and enforce the need for controlling politics'.

Massive investment was demanded by the gold-mining industry in particular. This led to the development of finance houses, which from an early stage took over the function of channelling capital from Europe to South Africa, while at the same time controlling individual mines. Today, 'the reins of power rest in the hands of the parent group whose officials possess, in effect, a monopoly of financial and mining expertise and it would be well-nigh impossible for any body of shareholders to wrest them away' (*ibid*., p. 28).

The first of the finance houses, Consolidated Gold Fields of South Africa, was formed as early as 1887. Johannesburg Consolidated Investment Company followed in 1889, Rand Mines in 1893, the General Mining and Finance Company in 1895, the Union Corporation in 1897. In 1917 Ernest Oppenheimer launched what was to become the biggest of them all: the Anglo-American Corporation of South Africa. By 1969 these corporations owned forty-five gold mines among them and accounted for 93 per cent of all gold production in South Africa. The Anglo-Transvaal Consolidated Investment Company, formed in 1933, accounted for a further 6 per cent (*ibid*., pp. 23-6).

Co-operation among the mining houses was simple from the start, 'partly because the individual units were large and also because many of the financiers controlling the mines were interested in several properties' (van der Horst, 1942, p. 129). Steps towards formal combination were taken as early as 1887. A major object in combining was to reduce the wages paid to workers. In the case of the skilled workers, in the early years at least, scarcity made reductions impossible. The position in relation to unskilled workers, given their abundant numbers and their lack of organisation, was different. Effective agreement among employers was all that was needed to reduce the unfree workers' bargaining power virtually to nil. In 1889 the Chamber of Mines was established: 'It immediately directed its attention,' van der Horst writes, 'to the cost and supply of Native labour . . . to reducing the money-wages paid to Natives, to establishing a fixed scale of wages on all the mines, and to reduce the cost of recruiting' (*ibid*., pp. 129, 130).

The recruiting side of the Chamber's activities eventually grew out into the Witwatersrand Native Labour Association, operating in Mozambique and the tropical areas, and the Native Recruiting Corporation, operating in the former Bechuanaland, Basutuland and Swaziland. In 1960 a total of 195,809 men would be brought to the mines by these two agencies (Owen, 1964, p. 9). Wage-cutting activities were no less successful. By 1896 the number of unfree miners had risen to 70,000 and their average wage to 60s 10d per month. The Chamber then ordered a reduction to a maximum average of 3*s* 0*d* per day and a minimum wage of 1*s* 9*d* per day. The result was a drop in the average wage to 48*s* 7*d* per month in 1897, when the maximum average was further reduced to 2*s* 6*d* per day. In 1901 yet a further reduction was imposed to a maximum average of 35*s* 0*d* per month and a minimum fixed wage of 30*s* 0*d*. Only with the number of unfree miners plummeting from 96,704 in 1899 to 42,587 in 1902 – wartime disruption was to a large extent responsible for this – was the wage rate of 1897 restored.[1]

For the following seventy years real wages of African miners were prevented from increasing despite the enormous growth of productivity and of the economy in this period (see Table 3.1).

Table 3.1 *Real wages of African miners 1905–69*

Year	Wage (R)	Index
1905	54	—
1911	57	100
1921	66	69
1936	68	100
1946	87	92
1961	146	89
1969	199	99

Source: Wilson (1972a, pp. 45–6).

In recent years limits have appeared for the first time on the supply of labour from the politically independent states of Southern Africa. Unlike 1960, when a similar threat was in the offing, the present curtailment of the labour supply coincided with a rise in the price of gold. Under these conditions the Chamber of Mines decided to increase the wages of African miners in order to compete with manufacturing industry. The average annual earnings of the African miner rose to R636 in 1974 and R852 in 1975 (*Financial Mail*, 9 January 1976). The subsequent instability in the price of gold placed a question-mark over this policy. Thus the annual increases for African miners laid down by the Chamber in June 1976 were considerably lower than the 37.5 per cent increase of 1975. They ranged from 13.5 per cent for underground workers to 10.7 per cent for surface workers, approximately equal to the increase in the cost of living. Monthly minimum wages were thereby raised to R65 and R40.30 for underground and surface workers respectively, figures which were far below the average wage of R115 earned by African industrial workers during the period December 1975 to January 1976 (*Financial Mail*, 4 June 1976).

Two general conclusions emerge from this brief look at employers' organisation in the mining sector. Overwhelming power over 90 per cent of the work-force, reflected in the power to determine wages unilaterally, has remained with the Chamber of Mines. This flows from the exceptional degree of management centralisation and the exceptional lack of organisation among the mass of miners. This weakness, in turn, can be traced directly to the policy of the state, to the system of migratory labour. Workers are recruited from different areas, housed in compounds under strict supervision, and kept in constant rotation. Any trade union that may be formed under these forbidding conditions is excluded from legal recognition. Thus in the final analysis, as Albeda has observed, the position of the mining companies depends on the support provided by the state (Kooy, Albeda and Kwant, 1969, p. 152): 'It is clear that the entire gold mining industry in South Africa stands or falls with the availability of an extremely cheap work force, which is connected with the system of migratory labour.'

In the manufacturing sector, similarly, employer organisation developed at an early stage. The South African Federated Chamber of Industries was formed in 1917. Production, and therefore power, are less concentrated than in the mining sector. As in the mining sector, however, the combination of employers must inevitably strengthen their position as against their workers. A similar development has taken place more gradually in the farming sector, where capital is least concentrated of all. Only with the pressure of industrial development and the sharpening of competition was the backwardness of the landowners partly overcome. The isolation of individual producers was broken through by improved communications, by the centralisation of production in the cities, and the growing integration of agriculture into the industrial economy. With the Co-operative Societies Act of 1922 the formal structure for the combination of rural employers was created.

The significance of employers' organisation emerged very clearly in the course of the general strike by black workers in Namibia in the summer of 1971-2. The strikes were aimed against the system of contract labour. Under this system a single company, the South-West Africa Native Labour Association (Pty) Ltd (SWANLA), acted as the agent of employers in general in hiring African labour. Workers were then distributed among the individual employers. The result, as the strikers pointed out, was to rule out any remaining possibility of free contract between worker and employer (Kane-Berman, 1972, p. xi). The strike resulted in a tactical retreat on the part of employers and the state: 'SWANLA has indeed been abolished, but its functions are to be carried out by other means' (*ibid*., p. 9). One such means is the system of state labour bureaux, another was the formation of new organisations of employers. The Divisional Inspector of Labour was 'active in encouraging employers to fix uniform wage rates and working conditions' (*ibid*.). A meeting was held in Windhoek in February 1972 with the aim of eliminating wage competition among employers in commerce and industry. Represented at this meeting were the Chamber of Commerce, the Windhoek Municipality, the *Afrikaanse Sakekamer*, the South African Railways and Harbours, the Department of Posts and Telegraphs, the Master Builders' Association and the civil engineering and hotel industries. Similarly, a month later, a Farmers Employers' Association was formed 'to handle the recruiting of labour and to ensure uniformity of pay to all Ovambo and Kavango workers' (*ibid*., p. 10). The contract system was revised in such a way that contract workers would henceforth be employed by a group of employers rather than by single employers.

Thus resistance by workers against a particular form of employer combination led to the further consolidation and extension of employer combination. Such an outcome is entirely logical. One aim of industrial organisation, explicit or implicit, is to strengthen one side against the other. Where combined action on the part of workers has reached the level of a general strike, it is inevitable that employers will take urgent steps to recover their own position.

In general, the road of workers' organisation is infinitely harder and more beset with obstacles than that of employers' organisation. In South Africa, though the industrial revolution is already a hundred years old, workers' organisation is still nowhere near the level that employers' organisation had reached with the establishment of the Chamber of Mines in 1887.

In theory as well as in practice, the different forms of working-class organisation are closely interrelated. There is no absolute division between working-class organisation at the industrial and political levels. At the same time, trade unions and political parties are distinct types of organisation with distinct traditions and methods. Each is adapted to its given function. What are the functions of the working-class party and the trade union respectively? In general, it can be said

77

that both have the function of furthering working-class interests. Yet in practice trade unions and workers' parties direct their efforts more specifically, taking up different aspects of working-class interests in general. Trade unions are based primarily on the workers in a given trade or industry. The workers' party, on the other hand, is based primarily on a given programme reflecting more or less accurately the interests of the working class as a whole.

The trade union sets out to organise all workers in a particular trade or industry regardless of political or religious differences among them. It bases itself on the immediate interests of the workers concerned, such as wages, working conditions and security of employment. Through organisation it provides a school of learning for the workers. For most workers it is their first experience of organisation on the basis of class interests. The result is, in general, demands and struggles relating in the first place to the industry concerned and addressed to employers in that industry. At the same time, it does not follow that trade-union action is limited to this. The moment it engages in collective bargaining, indeed, the union is confronted with issues of national policy.

The workers' political party stands in contrast to the union on nearly all these points. Its task is to bring together the demands and interests of the working class as a whole and translate these into a programme that provides an alternative to the policy of the employers. Its demands are directed at the state and relate to the structure of society as a whole. Both the trade union and the party must have some overall social perspective; in practice, the task of formulating this rests very largely with the party. While unions may tend to initiate action in matters of direct concern to their members, in matters of general working-class concern this is the function of the party.

All these differences are reflected in the difference in membership between the union and the party. Members of the workers' party, in general, have reached a certain level of political awareness. They will have drawn certain political conclusions from their day-to-day social and industrial experience. This applies regardless of the social origin of the individuals concerned. In this sense the workers' party may be defined as a distillation of working-class experience, much of which is gained through organs such as the trade unions.

In practice, different parties and tendencies within parties appeal to the workers for support on the basis of different social analyses and different political programmes. Every party and tendency is constantly in the process of developing or modifying its position and adapting itself to changing social conditions. The success or failure of a workers' party at any given stage will depend on a number of factors. The *history* of the organisation will determine the section of workers that see it as their 'own' organisation. The *leadership* of the organisation may be decisive in the short term. It may dominate the organisation, suppress opposing views, become identified with the organisation and shape its further history. In the long term, however, the leadership has no independent role. The judgment of the workers is in the last resort decisive. Their criterion will be the success or the failure of the party in furthering their interests. The policical understanding achieved by the workers will determine the sharpness of their judgment. Explaining events and creating political clarity, on the other hand, is itself a function that workers will expect their party to perform. Political education is a means to this end, but experience, once again, will have the final say. The ultimate determining factor of the success or failure of a workers' organisation will be the extent to which workers experience its theory and practice as being correct or being false.

Trade unions and political parties, it should be emphasised once again, are only two general forms that working-class organisation has historically taken. In addition to these many other forms of organisation may arise. In the final analysis, however, all working-class organisation is born from the needs and demands of the workers, and these, in turn, are the product of their social position: their need to work for others, their lack of property or security, apart from their ability to work. Modern social reform – itself very largely the consequence of working-class organisation – has softened, not abolished this condition. The link between social conditions and working-class organisation is aptly expressed in the following observation (Banks, 1974, p. 51): 'the original organiser of the trade union movement is the shop, the factory, the mine and the industry. The agitator or the labour leader merely announces the already-existing fact.' This insight may be extended to the political level as well. The slum, the housing estate, the overcrowded schools, hospital queues and the defeated strike are the original organisers of the workers' political party. It goes without saying that the precise form of organisation and the precise demands it raises will be determined by the issues involved and by other prevailing conditions. It is only afterwards that classifications such as 'political' or 'industrial', 'reformist' or 'revolutionary', can be applied to the organisation.

A totally different approach must be noted at this stage: selecting one type of organisation, treating it as the norm, and considering all organisations in relation to this norm. In respect of trade unions there is a widespread tendency in academic, business and government circles to regard what has been termed 'bread-and-butter (or "business") unionism' as 'mature', 'responsible' or 'correct' trade unionism. Other types of organisation are, by definition, 'immature', 'irresponsible' or 'incorrect'. 'Business unionism' is described as being 'generally temperate and co-operative'. Its main aims, according to the American professor Hoxie, are (Gitlow, 1963, pp. 36-7):

> to improve the wages, hours, and working conditions of the immediate group. Viewing itself as a bargaining institution, its goal is a collective bargaining agreement beneficial to it. It tends to develop strong leadership, which maintains itself so long as it delivers higher wages and greater security.

'Mature' trade unionism thus means trade unionism in the *narrowest* sense of the word. Theoretically, this approach lacks even the semblance of consistency. It can be understood only as a one-sided reflection of the economic boom in America and Western Europe during the 1950s and 1960s. High and increasing levels of production were taken for granted by the proponents of 'mature' trade unionism. This would make possible, in theory, an end to poverty, the gradual creation of security for all and an equally gradual extension of prosperity to the poorer countries of the world. The basic condition for such a development is the constant growth of the capitalist economy. It follows that trade unions should stay within the limits of the capitalist system. They must show their maturity by co-operating with employers and the state; they must turn their backs on the struggles of a by-gone epoch. Above all they must respect the interests of employers, on whose welfare all welfare depends.

According to this analysis, therefore, the employer and the union leadership are 'partners'. In return for the concessions extended to its members the union is expected to render services of its own. Union-employer collaboration becomes an institution, part of the 'control system of management' (Hyman, 1971, p. 22). Not only from the viewpoint of the capitalist class, but also from that of the pro-capitalist trade-union leadership, union-employer collaboration appears preferable to the disruption caused by struggle. 'Security for the top hierarchy and the good life on a sizeable salary,' it was observed of British trade-union leaders in 1958, 'may be part of a group of corrupting influences' (*ibid.*, p. 21). Material privilege and conservative attitudes, indeed, go hand in hand among trade-union leaders. 'Let there be no mistake,' asserts T. S. Neethling, General Secretary of the Amalgamated Engineering Union of South Africa, 'we do not deny the right of the employer to seek the highest possible profit; in fact, we recognise this as a healthy aspect of our capitalist society' (Coetzee, 1976, p. 164). The only proviso is that employers must not 'neglect their moral responsibilities to their employees'. P. J. Paulus, General Secretary of the Mineworkers' Union, argues in the same vein (*ibid*., p. 213): 'Therefore I believe that only a strong trade union is able to ensure the continued existence of the capitalist system, because only a strong trade union can protect the employer against his own weakness.'

At the political level this attitude is taken to its logical conclusion. 'Partnership' between the unions and the state, Coetzee argues (*ibid*., p. 26), 'is essential to the survival and development of democracy in the modern technological world.' In the interests of partnership, to avoid placing too much pressure on employers and the state, *limiting* the workers' political influence becomes an important task of the 'mature' trade-union leader. In South Africa, as in the USA, according to M. A. du Toit (1976, pp. 92–3), 'union leaders agree that the unions should not have direct representation in Parliament by way of a workers' party.'

These characteristic relationships of the post-war boom years are then projected on to history in general (quoted by Hyman, 1971, p. 24):

> Contrary to Marx, industrial conflict peaks early, not late, in the
> process of industrialisation. Rather than facing greater and greater
> conflict ending in revolution, industrialising societies face more
> and more peace once the early period of industrial unrest has been
> passed. Problems get solved, attitudes get changed, mechanisms get
> developed.

Economic boom, and with it conservative attitudes on the part of working-class organisations, are thus elevated to a status of supra-historical permanence. On this basis 'bread-and-butter trade unionism' is ascribed an absolute validity and logic. It becomes the overriding criterion by which to judge workers' organisation in general.

In South Africa 'maturity' on the part of the trade unions has been further encouraged by state action against trade unionists who take a different view. The South African Trades and Labour Council (1930–54) was considered a 'left-wing organisation' by the National Party government 'and it was largely due to this body', M. A. du Toit informs us, 'that the Suppression of Communism Act which aimed at ridding the trade union movement of unwanted elements was implemented'.[2] Coetzee explains more fully the connection between this measure and the 'maturity' of the recognised trade unions (1976, pp. 43-4):

> During the ten years following the passing of the Suppression
> of Communism Act in 1950 there were no major industrial
> disputes. This calm may also have been partly due to the
> residual effects of the economic paralysis which had set in
> after the Wall Street panic of the early 1930s . . . but it was
> most certainly also due to fear of the powers of the Act.
> Trade unions were aware that the right to strike, and especially
> the right to strike on a large scale, was hedged about with
> perilous restrictions and they were reluctant in the face of
> 'a hostile Government' to take the risks involved.

Also among the African workers, who are subject to infinitely
stricter state control, the Industrial Legislation Commission in 1951
found a number of trade unions that were 'well organised and . . .
conducted on correct lines'. By this the following was meant (*ibid.*,
p. 28):

> The leaders of some of these unions have in the past rendered
> considerable assistance by advising against, and restraining their
> members from taking drastic action; they are able to place the
> case for the workers before wage-fixing bodies, and some of them
> have shown indications of a measure of ability to negotiate with
> employers.

In the turbulent 1970s 'correct' trade unionism for African workers
was rediscovered. Among employers and liberal academics, not to
mention the leaders of registered unions, it was increasingly regarded
as an essential means of stabilising the capitalist system in South
Africa: 'A conflict of interest can only be contained within the social
fabric if some institutionalised way of resolving the conflict can be
designed,' wrote the Institute for Industrial Education in the aftermath
of the Durban strikes, and went on to draw the following conclusion
(IIE, 1974, p. 154): 'It is necessary to analyse the part which could be
played by trade unions in institutionalising conflict so as to permit a
process of orderly negotiation between powers, replacing a far more
unstable process of negotiation by strike and demonstration.' The
works committee system is inadequate for this purpose. Trade unionism
of this type, it is repeated with tautological emphasis, is 'the precon-
dition for stable industrial peace in South Africa' (*ibid.*, p. 180).

The same approach leads to a distinction between 'moderate' (or
'responsible') and 'radical' (or 'irresponsible') political positions. One

set of demands and one strategy, it is implicitly assumed, must be adhered to under all and any circumstances. We need not belabour the point. It is evident that this entire approach is unscientific and that the standard of 'maturity' or 'correctness' is arbitrary. Its weaknesses are glaring. The requirements of the capitalist economy are taken entirely for granted. This reflects a fundamental disregard for the course of historical development. An even more serious error is the assumption that boom is a permanent condition of the capitalist economy. Even though the post-war boom was unusually long and sustained, at a certain stage, inevitably, it turned into recession. Together with the boom, the conditions for 'mature' trade unionism began to fall away. Trade-union leaders are no longer able to 'deliver higher wages and greater security'. Today the opposite is true: 'So long as our economic system continues to produce ever higher living standards,' the American professor Gitlow wrote confidently in 1963, 'our trade unions are happy to work within the framework of that system' (1963, p. 15). Today, even the mighty American economy is in a state of decline. According to Gitlow's own reasoning, the 'mature' trade unions of yesterday must grow increasingly restive and find themselves in growing conflict with the capitalist system.

In South Africa, too, the onset of recession brought immediate strain to the previously 'mature' relationship between employers and registered union leaders. 'In fact', as a trade-union leader observed in the mid-1970s, 'it requires considerable expertise from trade unionists these days to confine themselves to bread-and-butter politics' (Coetzee, 1976, pp. 170–1). An appeal for wage restraint by the Prime Minister in March 1975 was criticised even by conservative trade-union leaders. The producers continue to raise prices, complained C. P. Grobler of the Artisan Staff Association: 'Thus we as unions cannot be concerned about appeals' (*Financial Mail*, 25 April 1975). The Trade Union Council of South Africa put forward a view, initially at least, that probably reflected the mood of the majority of workers: 'No matter what the Prime Minister says [TUCSA] cannot advise restraint from its unions below the 15% increase in the cost of living' (*ibid.*). In the months that followed Vorster's appeal, the 'maturity' of the registered trade-union leaders was increasingly put to the test. In October 1975 the government persuaded most registered union leaders to subscribe to the 'Collective Campaign Against Inflation' in terms of which they accepted certain reductions in the living standards of their members. In return, producers were supposed to limit price rises. Coetzee describes the situation which had developed by the mid-1970s (1976, p. 96):

Inflation, as it is exhibiting itself now, inevitably poses an insidious threat to social and, if left unchecked, political stability. It would therefore be in the national interest to control it. The achievement of this ideal, however, demands a very high and refined degree of co-operation, inconvenient as it might be, to supersede the self-interest which has always been the driving force of the free enterprise system. One cannot help but feel that what is happening now is the reassertion of this jealously-guarded self-interest by all concerned – the Government, employers and employees – with the circumstantially-phrased agreement between them to readjust their monetary demands consequently subject to enormous stresses and strains.

The theory of a one-way evolution towards 'bread-and-butter trade unionism' and political moderation has thus been exploded by events. In every industrial country the conditions that produced conservatism have given way to conditions that are arousing the workers to new militance. This development confirms our original thesis: the form and the demands of working-class organisation are determined in the first place by material conditions.

Whatever view workers may have of employers' combination, they are seldom in a position to oppose its creation effectively. Employers, on the other hand, have always been in a strong position to hold back organisation among their employees. In South Africa working-class organisation has furthermore been impeded by state-imposed divisions among workers, by workers' lesser access to the skills and resources required for effective organisation, and by the far-reaching legal restrictions imposed on the majority of workers.

Webster describes the migrant labour system as something 'which prevented at that time full proletarianisation from taking place' (see above, p. 37). In fact, the growth of a class of Africans totally dependent on wage labour was not prevented by the policy of discouraging them from settling permanently at their place of work. At most it was retarded. Many African workers were indeed turned into 'temporary sojourners' by this means. A growing number, however, became proletarianised in the full sense of the word, while remaining subject to great insecurity in the event of losing their employment. According to a survey among African workers in Pretoria, wage labour is generally considered 'normal and inevitable'.[3] Insecurity and repression, it is submitted, hold back organisation among urban African workers far more than limits on their number.

Working-class organisation in South Africa originally took place at the industrial level and rapidly took on political significance. The character of the labour movement was determined at a relatively early stage; to study its formative period is to gain the clearest insight into the processes that are at work today. The racial segregation imposed among organised workers will compel us to deal separately with the history of separate organisations. Our overall point of departure, however, must be the opposite of this. Working-class organisation must ultimately correspond to the working class itself. Where the working class consists of different racial groups, no genuine class-based organisation can be limited to one of these groups. Working-class organisation means non-racial organisation. Historically, it is the segregated nature of the South African labour movement that forms an aberration, and the incipient forms of non-racial organisation that should be regarded as the norm. To the extent that segregated unions and parties have in fact followed separate paths, we are obliged to examine them separately, but always with the broader perspective in mind; and hence we have the task of discovering the process by which the different sections of the South African labour movement can ultimately come together.

The growth of the registered trade unions

In South Africa, as in other industrial countries, it was the skilled workers who were first able to organise themselves. During the early decades of the industrial revolution, when the pattern of modern industrial relations was in the process of emerging, the mass of workers played no conscious role. The dividing-line between skilled and unskilled never coincided entirely with race. In the Cape the original artisan class was 'coloured'; in Natal men of Indian extraction learned trades. They were never considered a threat or an independent force, and were accepted as trade-union members in due course. The dominant role in these unions, however, was to belong to the white workers, with their overwhelming political weight. Organisationally, as in every other respect, the greatest contrast in the working class lay between the white enfranchised workers and the mass of unfree Africans.

From 1838 onwards the first attempts were made by Cape printers to organise themselves. In 1881 a Typographical Society was formed in Cape Town that was destined to survive, and in the same year a Cape Town branch of the (British) Amalgamated Society of Carpenters

85

and Joiners was formed. By the 1890s the main concentration of labour had shifted to the Witwatersrand. For several decades to follow, the Reef would be the centre of gravity of the organised labour movement.

In 1892 the grievances of the immigrant gold miners led to the formation of the Witwatersrand Mine Employees' and Mechanics' Union (known as the 'Labour Union'). At this time a working week of fifty-six hours was common on the Rand. Skilled wages ranged from 18*s* 4*d* to 20*s* 0*d* a day. The work was dangerous and unhealthy. The main grievance, however, was the threat by the Chamber of Mines to step up white immigration, thus driving down wages and creating unemployment. The 'Labour Union' did not last long. Here, too, adventurers and scoundrels were among the first to make a bid for office. Weakened by corruption among its officials and by confusion as to aims and tactics, it had collapsed by 1895.

But in the fertile environment of the industrial revolution labour organisation could not be held back for long. A branch of the (British) Amalgamated Society of Engineers, which was formed in Durban in 1892, survived. By 1906 this union had built itself into a national organisation. This was the forerunner of the Amalgamated Engineering Union, established in 1920, and it served as a model for unions that followed. A Trades Council had been set up in Johannesburg in 1894, consisting of the 'Labour Union' and five of the eight existing craft societies. Although this pioneering body was swept aside by the war of 1899, a United Trades Council emerged again from the anti-piecework strike of the skilled miners in 1902. Out of this Council the Johannesburg Trades and Labour Council was formed, while also in 1902 the Transvaal Miners' Association was established. The functions of the Trades and Labour Council were taken over in 1911 by the Transvaal Federation of Trades, which in turn was succeeded in 1914 by the South African Industrial Federation. In 1909 the South African Labour Party was formed. At this stage trade unions in the Cape were organised separately in the Federation of Labour Unions. Trade-union membership rose from 3,836 in 1900 to 11,941 in 1914.

The early period of trade unionism, leading up to the legal recognition of the unions of free workers, was marked by the miners' strikes of 1907, 1913, 1914 and 1922. Most writers emphasise the element of racial contradiction in these struggles. In fact, more than this was involved. Generally speaking, the white workers found themselves struggling over two basic issues: preservation of their jobs, and trade-union recognition. Furthermore, numerous 'industrial' issues arose.

Little or no attempt, however, was made to join forces with the mass of African workers. Racial hostility towards the African workers was fanned from an early stage. Thus the struggles remained isolated and ended in defeat for the unions. Even so they were militant, and a number of concessions were won. But these were concessions on the terms of the employers, extended by the victors to the vanquished. The basic interest of the employers, their access to 'cheap docile labour', remained unaffected. The role of the white workers and their unions as an independent factor in South African industrial relations was ended for a whole period with the crushing of the strike of 1922.

In 1907 the chief issue was the proposal by mine-owners to cut rates of pay, while increasing from two to three the number of drills to be supervised by each skilled miner. This would have the effect of increasing the number of African miners in relation to white miners (it is this aspect of the matter that catches the eye of most writers). Coupled with this was the issue of health. There was general dissatisfaction at the ravages of miners' phthisis, which threatened to grow worse under the new arrangements: 'The extent to which this dreadful disease was destroying miners at this period,' write Walker and Weinbren (1961, p. 22), 'can be judged from the fact that by 1913 there were alive only four of the 18 men who constituted the miners' strike committee of 1907. Thirteen of these men had died of phthisis. One was killed in an accident and the four survivors were all phthisis sufferers.'

The 1907 strike was totally defeated. For the first time unemployed Afrikaners from the country were recruited on a large scale, and for lower wages, to do the strikers' work. African and Chinese workers were also used as 'scabs', thus demonstrating, incidentally, the extent to which the immigrant miners' skills had grown generalised by this time. Imperial troops were called out to keep pickets from the mines and escort the strike-breakers to and from work. Afterwards hundreds of strikers were dismissed, including the executive of the Transvaal Miners' Association.

Yet it was precisely the experience of defeat that now boosted trade unionism among the white workers on the Reef. The issue of trade-union recognition, to the limited extent that unions existed, was pushed directly to the fore. As late as 1913 gold-mining companies were refusing to deal with the unions. It was against this background that the general strike of white miners broke out in 1913. 'All the evidence,' write Walker and Weinbren (*ibid*., p. 32), 'indicated that the Chamber of Mines had decided upon a trial of strength as the Miners' Union was becoming stronger and had the support of the Federation of Trades, to which most of the unions were affiliated.'

The high-handed dismissal of two mechanics was the incident that sparked off the strike. Despite attempts by the union to limit the dispute, 18,000 men stopped work within three days. As in 1907, strike-breaking was organised on massive scale by the employers. British troops again assisted by preventing the pickets from intervening. Violence by police and soldiers against unarmed workers became a feature of the strike. This culminated in the 'Battle of the Rand Club', when strikers attempted to march on the stronghold of the 'Randlords'. At least twenty people were killed in a day of demonstrations. Significantly, the strikers responded by beginning to arm themselves, though on this occasion no organised militia was formed. The strike ended when the prime minister, General Botha, together with General Smuts, met with armed strike leaders to negotiate a settlement. This amounted to *de facto* recognition of the workers' organisation, in a very remarkable form.

Yet the strike leaders did not press home their demands, 'because of the extreme seriousness of the situation' (Cope, n.d. p. 141). The settlement, not surprisingly, was unsatisfactory to the majority of the strikers. Besides reinstating the striking workers, employers conceded only a promise that the government could inquire into the grievances of the men. In practice, little came of this. Trade-union membership increased by several thousands, while attempts to form company unions failed. It was clear that the conflict was unresolved. Having been allowed to escape from a difficult position, employers began to prepare systematically for the following trial of strength. In December 1913 riot insurance rates for the Witwatersrand began rising steeply in London. The Government Printer started turning out proclamations of martial law. High security fences were built around mining property. Every trade unionist who experienced the events of 1913 and 1914, according to Walker and Weinbren, 'was – and still is – convinced that the Government, smarting at the humiliating position in which the authorities had found themselves during the previous July, had decided "to teach Labour a lesson"' (1961, p. 47).

On Christmas Eve 1913 events were set in motion when the government announced the dismissal of a large number of skilled workers on the railways. Troops were almost immediately mobilised and martial law declared. Numerous workers' leaders were arrested, including Labour MPs and the entire executive of the Amalgamated Society of Engineers. The Minister of Railways at that time is reported to have said that he was not prepared to meet the workers 'as he was out to smash syndicalism and trade unionism' (*ibid*., p. 48). On 12 January 1914 – twelve days after the declaration of martial law – rank-and-file railwaymen at Pretoria struck work. This prompted the executive of the Federation of Trades to declare a general strike.

Tremendous force was used by the state in suppressing the 1914 strike. Some 60,000 commandos and troops were mobilised. At one stage 4,000 soldiers surrounded the Johannesburg Trades Hall, training a field gun on the door, to demand the 'surrender' of eleven members of the Federation executive and thirty-two pickets who were in the building. All along the Reef apparently indiscriminate violence was unleashed by the army against strikers and their families, in their homes as well as on the streets. Routed by this onslaught, the strike was called off on 17 January. Yet the state offensive continued. A climax was reached on 27 January, when nine strike leaders were removed from their cells in Johannesburg and (illegally) deported to Britain. A special indemnity Act was passed to legalise the actions by the state and a Peace Preservation Bill was tabled that would give the government sweeping new powers. Under pressure of the opinion of the voting public, the latter was withdrawn. In its place, however, the Riotous Assemblies and Criminal Law Amendment Act was passed, designed to 'make peaceful picketing illegal' (Davies, 1966, p. 56).

The defeat of the 1914 strike was followed by 'an unparalleled campaign of victimisation' (Walker and Weinbren, 1961, p. 57). Many strikers were blacklisted and forced to leave the country in order to find work. General Botha could boast that he had 'killed trade unionism on the Witwatersrand' (*ibid*., p. 55). The organisations of white workers, when faced with a serious challenge, had been found seriously wanting. Craft divisions persisted, and there was extreme unclarity in realising the political dimension of the struggle. While employers used every form of official, political and legal attack, the Federation confined itself to the 'purely industrial' field. Even here it addressed itself only to a small fraction of workers. Under these conditions its stand against the government was doomed to failure from the start.

Yet it was the political repercussions of the strike that rallied the white labour movement. The indignation of the enfranchised public at the actions of the Botha government was expressed in the 'Red Flag' elections of 1914 to the Transvaal Provincial Council and in subsequent parliamentary by-elections, where Labour made sweeping gains. At this point, however, the First World War broke out, and the whole situation was changed. The government revised its labour policy.

The 1914 Economic Commission of Enquiry had already recommended that the unions of white workers should be recognised. Hostility to the trade unions turned into conciliation. The nine deported leaders were allowed to return. The Labour Party, having changed its position twice, ended up in 1915 by supporting the war. What remained of the South African Industrial Federation was drawn closely into the orbit of the Chamber of Mines and the government. The Chamber decided on *de facto* recognition of their enfranchised workers' unions. Many of the craft unions adopted a policy of 'no strikes for the duration of the war', in return for which they were 'recognised' by employers. Amid world-wide slaughter, trade-union rights were being won 'bloodlessly'.

The wartime experience of the white trade unions was in many ways the opposite of that before and after. But the conditions for a return to 'normal' industrial relations were steadily maturing. The war brought with it an expansion of industry and an increase in the number of workers. By 1916 the rising cost of living was driving workers back to their unions in unprecedented numbers.

As the war drew to a close, industrial peace was already something of the past. Walker and Weinbren (1961, ch. 9) refer to this period as one of 'strikes galore'. An event that cast its shadow over the whole world at this time was the Russian Revolution. Its dramatic impact was felt by conservatives and socialists alike. In Johannesburg in March 1919, and in Durban in January 1920, strikes by white municipal workers led to the temporary suspension of the municipal authorities and their replacement by Boards of Control formed by the striking workers. These Boards have been referred to as 'soviets'. Writing about the Johannesburg Board of Control, S. P. Bunting explained why the term 'soviet' was inappropriate (Roux, 1944, pp. 40–4). The Board regarded itself as a temporary institution only; it confined itself to Johannesburg; it did not represent workers outside the municipal service; and above all it made no attempt to involve the majority of municipal workers themselves – the Africans. These features of the Johannesburg Board of Control reflected quite accurately the mood of the white working class in general. These features, in particular racial exclusiveness and preoccupation with isolated issues, would repeat themselves to disastrous effect in the events of 1922.

It was under these conditions of unrest at the close of the First World War that the white miners became 'strong enough to oblige the Chamber of Mines to sign a *Status Quo* Agreement' (Walker, 1957, p. 586) in terms of which the existing ratio of black to white miners would be left unchanged. This agreement, though of brief duration, was to acquire great significance. In 1920 the Low Grade Mines Commission recommended 'an increase in native employment and the removal of the legal colour bar in order to open up to cheaper native labour certain activities formerly closed' (de Kiewiet, 1941, p. 170). In 1921 the gold price began to fall. A return by sterling to the gold standard at the pre-war parity was announced. This would reduce the (sterling) price of gold by 35 per cent. In December 1921 the Chamber of Mines gave notice of its intention to terminate the status quo agreement. The alternative, it said, was to close down the low-grade mines. The wages of white miners were reduced on the coal mines by 5s 0d a shift. Arrangements were also being made between the Chamber of Mines and the government, though the precise details may never become known. 'The cry ran through all the ranks of white labour,' as de Kiewiet puts it (*ibid.*), 'that the Chamber of Mines was debasing white men to the level of black men.' The action by the Chamber, according to Walker and Weinbren, and the government's support of it, 'was responsible for all the terrible happenings which followed' (1961, p. 93).

The events on the Rand in 1922, known variously as the 'Rand rebellion', the 'Rand revolt' and even the 'Rand revolution', have been recorded very amply and need no detailed description here. In these events the conflict between employers and white labour reached a bloody climax; but no resolution followed. Existing tensions were merely covered over, and the previous status quo was restored.

On 10 January 1922 some 20,000 white workers on the gold mines followed the coal miners out on strike. The role of the state at this stage consisted of urging the strikers to go back 'on any terms'. The prime minister, General Smuts, achieved notoriety for his statement that the government intended 'letting things develop'. The strikers themselves had learned from the experiences of 1913 and 1914. An important development was the organisation of workers' commandos, at first unarmed, later arming themselves in an atmosphere of mounting tension. A clearer understanding of the political issues was revealed. A mass meeting of strikers demanded of Nationalist and Labour MPs that they proclaim a Republic and form a provisional government. But the basic weaknesses of 1914 had not been overcome.

As always, violence arose from the use of 'scab' labour. There followed arrests, prohibitions of meetings and increasingly violent incidents. The turning-point came on 28 February, when police opened fire on unarmed members of the Putfontein commando unit who had gathered outside Boksburg gaol to sing *The Red Flag* to their comrades in the cells. On 4 March the Chamber contemptuously rejected an attempt by the Federation to re-open negotiations. Martial law was proclaimed on 10 March. For some days the strikers were in control of most of the Witwatersrand, enjoying general support among the white population. But the odds against them were overwhelming. Although the strike had formally been declared general, it was barely carried beyond the Reef. According to official figures, 153 people were killed in the fighting, including seventy-two soldiers and policemen, thirty-nine strikers and forty-two others, of whom eighteen were white and twenty-four black. 534 people were wounded, including 219 on the government side and 118 strikers. The Legal Defence Committee of the strikers, on the other hand, estimated the casualties at 250 killed and over 1,000 wounded. According to the historian Walker (1957, p. 591), 230 people were killed. Four strikers were convicted of murder and hanged.

Besides the battles between strikers and government forces, clashes also occurred between strikers and African miners. These clashes must be seen in the light of the racist spirit that pervaded the commandos and their leadership in particular. It is not unlikely, however, that police provocation was involved. Certainly these clashes stood the government in good stead. The effect was to divert attention from the causes of the strike and make it appear an anti-African pogrom. It also created divisions among the strikers. If any doubts existed as to the issues behind the strike, however, these should have been dispelled by the aftermath. The number of white miners was reduced from 21,607 in 1921 to 14,681 in 1922, and machine stopers' average earnings per day fell from 33*s* 5*d* to 21*s* 0*d*. In an atmosphere of defeat and demoralisation trade-union membership collapsed from 108,242 in 1921 to 81,861 in the period following the strike (*Union Statistics for Fifty Years*, 1960).

From all accounts confusion and lack of direction among the strikers were apparent. A great deal of light is shed on the nature of the white workers' movement by the tendencies that emerged among them in the heat of struggle. In the first place there was the existing leadership of the Industrial Federation – which might be described as 'reformist'. On 7 March 1922 thousands of strikers surrounded the building where the Federation executive was discussing whether or not to terminate the strike. Either inspired or frightened by this pressure from the ranks, the leaders declared the strike 'general'. They then disappeared completely from the scene of action. Leadership passed to the militant wing of the movement, which had formed itself into a Council of Action. The Council, however, proved unable to take the place of the national leadership, at least on such short notice. It was a product of the strike, and like the strike it remained local. Next to these tendencies there were the strikers' commandos. These consisted mainly of Afrikaner workers and the leadership was solidly Afrikaner Nationalist. Although the Council of Action and the commando leaders were in constant contact, the latter remained aloof and no unified organisation developed.

A major issue dividing the strikers was their attitude towards the black miners. From the Afrikaner nationalist side, African workers were considered hostile, an attitude that accorded with state policy and with the prejudices in which the great majority of white workers had been steeped. Opposed to this, the Council of Action attempted to explain the class contradictions involved. In practice, however, little conviction was shown. The resultant ideological confusion is accurately reflected in the well-known slogan of the strikers: 'Workers of the world, fight and unite for a White South Africa!'

All things considered, it is at first sight remarkable that a relatively small group of militants could have played such a leading part in the struggle of 1922. For all their failings, however, these militants came closest to meeting the requirements and the mood of a combative rank and file. The unfolding of events confirmed them in their position. For all the racism of the Afrikaner nationalists, the real situation was that the strikers were fighting not against black miners but against white soldiers and policemen and white mine-owners. Afrikaner nationalism failed completely to explain this situation, while the ideas of the militants were to a large extent confirmed. Despite their better understanding, however, the militants had no concrete alternative to propose. Their arguments as to the solidarity of labour turned out to mean nothing more in practice than the unity of the white miners, which had in any case developed under the pressure of events. When clashes took place between white and black workers, the militants could only call verbally for African miners to be left alone as the mine-owners and the government were the real enemies. No counter-action was organised. While a working relationship was kept up with the racist commando leaders, little or nothing was done even at this critical stage to build up links with the African miners. One result was a rising tide of hostility on the part of black middle-class leaders against the white working class in general. Within the trade unions the racist ideology now became entrenched. Racism, having gone unchallenged and untested at its time of greatest crisis, became virtually unchallengeable.

This was the 'end to an epoch in South African trade union history' (Cope, n.d., p. 284). In defeat the militants lost their position and the mass of white workers, beaten and demoralised, picked up the pieces as best they could. They had found themselves unable to make an independent stand against employers and the state. Henceforth they would be doubly cautious and doubly inclined to accept any compromise that offered them even a semblance of security in their work.

Such a compromise was not long in coming. From the employers' point of view the crushing of union power in 1922 removed one major objection to union recognition. At the same time, they were awakened to the dangers of allowing confrontation on such a scale to develop a second time. The state now embarked on a systematic policy of controlling industrial relations. The political sequel to the strike of 1922 was the return of a Nationalist–Labour coalition to power in 1924. Its programme was one of protecting the white workers while allowing the use of 'cheap docile labour' to continue undiminished. But the new dispensation had already been heralded by the Apprenticeship Act of 1922 and the Industrial Conciliation Act of 1924, passed by the Smuts government shortly before its fall. In effect, this measure 'practically forced the parties [employers and unions] to co-operate' (M. A. du Toit, 1976, p. 156). Africans subject to the pass laws – i.e. the mass of workers – were excluded from recognised union membership.[4] This necessarily had the effect of maintaining African workers in their 'competitive' position and placing non-African workers in need of continued protection against such competition. The gulf between free and unfree workers was deepened even further.

The machinery for state control over industrial relations was completed with the enactment of the Wage Act in 1925. This Act provided for the unilateral determination of wages and working conditions by the state in any trade where no agreement in terms of the Industrial Conciliation Act was in force. It applied to African workers as well. Its primary object was clear. The procedures laid down by the Industrial Conciliation Act were by definition limited in their application, and left large areas at the mercy of 'free collective bargaining'. The Wage Act enabled the state to make binding orders in respect of these areas as well. The power of the state could henceforth be used to overrule all differences between workers and employers. The mining, agricultural and domestic sectors, it may be noted, were excluded from the Wage Act; the latter two sectors were also excluded from the Industrial Conciliation Act. In precisely those sectors where unfree labour is at its weakest and most unorganised, state control is deemed superfluous.

This, as much as anything else, makes clear the function of these measures. By these same measures trade-union freedom was largely curtailed. From the moment of applying for registration unions would operate under strict control and scrutiny by the state. The right to strike, in particular, was now severely limited.

The effect of the 'reforms' of the early 1920s can thus be briefly summarised. On the one hand, they legally laid down the compromise between employers and the 'labour aristocracy'. On the other hand, they closed the door against organisation and self-improvement by the mass of workers. Other changes were also set in motion. Stable occupations became possible in the unions. Salaried officials began taking the place of the popular, radical leaders. Coetzee describes this development from a sociological point of view (1976, p. 22):

> A leader was in close daily contact with the workers he
> represented and his life was identical with theirs; so, providing
> he spoke what was in their minds and remained loyal to their
> interests, he fulfilled his function admirably. With the advent
> of the 'official trade-union representative', a leader's role
> changed dramatically - he now saw himself primarily as the
> person concerned with conducting negotiations through
> established machinery, with avoiding disputes as far as possible,
> and with guarding against breaches of agreements . . . . Weber
> states that the authority of this type of leader does not
> necessarily express the 'will' of his followers, and 'majorities',
> if employed at all, are given authority only because they are
> thought to have the correct solution, and not because a greater
> number have, as such, a greater right to prevail.

In essence, the chief demands of the left wing had been conceded: union recognition had been gained, and white workers' living standards had been safeguarded, at least for the time being. This victory in defeat was only made possible by the limited nature of the programme that the left wing put forward. By campaigning for nothing more than that which employers were prepared to concede out of pure self-interest, they rendered themselves redundant at the point when the employers finally complied. For the following period the left played little part in the registered trade-union movement. Some left-wingers went on to hold high positions under the new order. For men accustomed to struggle and persecution, the change in their relationship with the state was sudden and dramatic. This is reflected by Walker and Weinbren; the change in their own position is naively ascribed to Smuts (1961, pp. 184, 186): 'Gone was the ruthless tyrant of the 1907-1922 period and in his stead was a patient, kindly man, full of understanding and tolerance . . . there is little doubt that after 1922 Smuts was a radically changed man who loved his people and his country.'

The growing industrialisation of South Africa from the mid-1920s onwards brought new growth to the membership of the unions. The year 1922 had brought the collapse of the South African Industrial Federation. In 1924, however, F. H. P. Cresswell, now Labour Party leader and newly appointed Minister of Labour, encouraged the formation of a new co-ordinating body of registered trade unions. In March 1925 the South African Association of Employees' Organisations was established (a year later it changed its name to the South African Trade Union Congress). To Cresswell's dismay, the respected Communist Party leader W. H. Andrews was elected secretary of the new organisation and held this position until his retirement in 1932. But this reflected no revival of militance within the registered trade unions. On the contrary, the pendulum was still swinging to the right. Left-wingers like Andrews were being absorbed into the new, conservative apparatus of 'white labour'. Andrews himself was one of the signatories of the memorandum by the South African Trades Union Co-ordinating Committee (a body representing the South African Trade Union Congress and the Cape Federation of Labour Unions) which recommended that the application for affiliation by the Industrial and Commercial Workers' Union, the general union of African workers, be rejected: 'The first objection,' it was recorded, 'is that the 100,000 members claimed by the ICU would on a card vote in any Congress out-vote all the other unions put together if a division took place, as is possible, on racial lines' (Kadalie, 1970, p. 150). More important, however, were the fears and the prejudices of 'important sections of organised labour'. It was the 'considered opinion' of the Committee that 'whilst keeping in view the soundness of the principle that all *bona fide* trade unions . . . should be linked up in a national co-ordinating body, and through the national body to the international organisation . . . a considerable amount of propaganda is needed among the Union membership before affiliation can take place with benefit to all concerned' (*ibid.*, p. 151).

There is no evidence, however, that a 'considerable amount of propaganda' was carried on among the members of the registered unions in the period that followed. The left wing succumbed with hardly a struggle to the existing situation. Turning their backs on the mass of the working class precisely at the time of its awakening to organised activity, they confined themselves to the narrow, arid movement of the labour aristocracy in the period of its *rapprochement* with the ruling class. Under these conditions the initiative to struggle for change in the system of industrial relations passed definitively to the African masses. Just as the black proletariat had mainly been onlookers during the early battles between free labour and capital, so the white proletariat now became bystanders in the mounting struggles launched by the unskilled and semi-skilled masses. As before, divisions among the workers weakened the active vanguard. In the early period African workers had been used as strike-breakers against white workers. In the later period these roles were reversed. White workers were mobilised politically and even militarily in defence of capitalist interests.

The shift of initiative from themselves to the African workers was recognised implicitly, but clearly, by the registered trade-union leadership. The most burning issue facing them henceforth would be not so much their own role, which had become one of defensive passivity. More pressing would be the question of their relationship with the active vanguard of the working class – the organisation of African workers.

The rise of the African trade-union movement

If workers in general encounter greater problems than employers in the effort to organise themselves, then among workers it is the unskilled who experience the greatest difficulties of all. In Britain, the Netherlands and other industrial countries, unions of unskilled workers were formed in the aftermath of the pioneering struggles by craftsmen. In South Africa this development was held back still further by the lack of freedom of the mass of unskilled workers, the Africans. It has been state policy to oppose the organisation of African workers since the time that such organisation first began to manifest itself. To men and women who cannot vote, who cannot move freely in search of work, whose right to remain in the town where they live may depend on their remaining in a given job, the added danger of dismissal or arrest for engaging in trade-union activities is a formidable deterrent. Despite all these obstacles, the movement towards organisation of the African working class has continued for more than half a century.

The African trade-union movement dates from the same period that the compromise between free labour and employers took on its modern form. This fact is by no means coincidental. Employers as well as the state had reason to fear the emergence of a united labour movement. The beginnings of organisation among the previously unorganised African labourers made this possibility real. Connections between unions of black and white workers, according to M. A. du Toit, 'would eventually result in mixed unions, something which cannot be allowed'. He goes on to explain (1976, p. 124): 'Although the Government believes in a sound trade union movement, it also believes that Black unionists will mean the end of the present movement if they are allowed as members of existing unions.' If the 'present movement' means the registered unions only, the government is correct. The alternative, which it rejects, is the growing together of this narrow-based, conservative movement with the movement of the African masses, and the submersion of the former's moderate ideas in the revolutionary demands of the latter. As early as 1917 tentative links had been formed between the two wings of the labour movement. From the state's point of view the need to prevent these links from growing into bridgeheads was obvious. The growth of organisation among the African workers was the catalyst that brought into being the compromise between the capitalist class and the leaders of free labour.

Among the compound workers on the gold and diamond mines, organisation was all but excluded in the early period. The workers lacked industrial experience and were subject to the employers' constant scrutiny and control. Under the contract system they were shuttled back and forth between the work-place and the reserve. 'Trouble-makers' could easily be eliminated in the process. The growth of a core of class-conscious workers was thus severely stunted. Only during and after the First World War, with the rise of manufacturing industry, did stable concentrations of African workers begin to gather on the outskirts of the major towns. By the end of the First World War the experience of these workers had matured to the point where the first significant organisations of the African working class came into existence.

African workers were unable to join the existing unions. Initially they had entered industry in the capacity of unskilled labour; for them there was no room in the craft unions. They were handicapped in various ways in learning industrial skills. A deliberate policy of racial discrimination was brought to bear on them. African labour was regarded as unskilled labour. Thus African workers were forced to organise separately from whites. Being without recognised skills, they could not organise on the basis of craft. Organisationally, there was little reason for African workers in any industry – and sometimes in separate industries – to differentiate among themselves. The unions of African workers thus tended to take the form of industrial or general ('all-in') unions, as opposed to trade unions in the strict sense of the word.

A certain pattern has emerged in the development of the unions of African workers. Periods of upsurge have alternated with periods of decline. The growth of the African working class and the harsh conditions to which they are subject have created classical conditions for organisation and struggle. The pressure of the workers, however, has been met with relentless counter-pressure from the state. At times this has led to the semi-paralysis of the African trade-union movement. The pressure of the masses, however, coupled with their accumulated experience and demands, inevitably sets the same process in motion again on a higher level than before. We can trace the development of the African trade unions through several cycles of upsurge and repression, followed by the upsurge of the present period, of which the end is not in sight. The first upsurge started after the First World War. In this period the nature and significance of the African trade-union movement emerged perhaps more clearly than at any later stage.

A further characteristic of the African trade unions was crucial from the outset. In the advanced industrial countries today trade-union aims can be realised at least partly through negotiations with employers and or the state. This, rather than 'political' activity, has come to be accepted as 'normal' trade-union activity. In South Africa, on the other hand, 'trade-union' and 'political' activities are much more closely interwoven from the black worker's point of view. The freedom to negotiate does not exist, nor does the economic structure of the country permit it to exist. Lack of freedom, apart from poverty, is precisely the condition that weighs most heavily on the worker. His struggle for self-improvement cannot be confined to those issues that are formally termed 'industrial'.

'Experience has shown,' it is now lamented in some quarters, 'that Black trade unions are extremely susceptible to political influences' (M. A. du Toit, 1976, p. 123). Coetzee (1976, p. 18) provides a more accurate formulation: 'In order to discharge their duties and to achieve the aims of any conventional trade union, [African trade unions] are inevitably drawn on to the political platform.' African unions are under pressure to reflect the demands of their members in relation to the pass laws, job reservation, influx control and other 'political' issues, all of which are inseparably bound up with the 'purely economic' situation of the worker. Any attempt by the African union to dissociate itself from 'politics' is doomed to failure in the long run, or else the union will fail. The result is, once again, to bring the African trade-union movement into conflict with the state. The hostility between the organisations of African labour and a state that is committed to a policy of 'cheap docile labour' is fundamental and irreconcilable.

The earliest struggles of the African workers, which became significant in the aftermath of the Boer War, gave rise to no lasting organisation. The first significant African unions were formed at the end of the First World War. Industrial unrest was sharpened to a new edge by the impact of the Russian Revolution. As in other industrial countries, socialists and members of craft unions took the initiative in organising the unskilled. The Industrial Workers of Africa (IWA) was the result of a series of classes for African workers which the International Socialist League (ISL) held in the Johannesburg Trades Hall during 1917. The first class was addressed by Charles Dones, a white miner, who asked the black workers what they wanted. The answer was: '*Sifuna zonke!*' ('We want everything!'). This became the slogan of the IWA. The union was almost immediately caught up in the struggles of the African workers that rose to a climax during 1918. As a result it bore the full burden of government reprisal. In the years that followed the black labour movement was swept to new heights by the growth of the Industrial and Commercial Workers' Union (ICWU, later ICU). The IWA was thus the forerunner of a larger movement and it was superseded in the developments that ensued.

In February 1918 the rising cost of living led to a boycott by African miners on the East Rand of company concession stores. The police broke the boycott by arresting pickets. The government, supported by the press, unleashed an attack on African trade unionism - an attack which has continued to the present day. Then followed the 'bucket strike' in Johannesburg in May and June of 1918. Encouraged by a successful strike of white mechanics at the power station, African workers in the municipal sanitary service demanded an increase from 1*s* 8*d* to 2*s* 6*d* a day. This was refused. Fifty men came out on strike and were arrested. Thirty-five were convicted in terms of the Masters and Servants legislation. Another 152 men joined the strike. Water-borne sewage was not yet general at that time. African policemen were drafted as strike-breakers but could not keep up with the work. 'The growing stench in the city,' Roux reports (1964, p. 130), 'assailed the noses of all citizens.' All strikers were arrested on charges of breach of contract and sentenced to two months' imprisonment with hard labour. In passing sentence McFie, the Chief Magistrate of Johannesburg, added the following remarks from the 'impartial' judicial bench (*ibid.*, pp. 130–1):

> While in gaol they [the strikers] would have to do the same work as they had been doing, and would carry out that employment with an armed escort, including a guard of Zulus armed with assegais and white men with guns. If they attempted to escape and if it were necessary they would be shot down. If they refused to obey orders they would receive lashes as often as might be necessary to make them understand they had to do what they were told.

A year later, the strikers' demands were to be met by a Labour-controlled city council. But the matter did not end there. In the turbulent climate of the times industrial struggle set political struggle in motion. The African National Congress (ANC) launched a campaign for the prisoners' release. Despite the opposition of the ANC leadership, a general strike was called for 1 July 1918. The ISL warned the African workers that they were insufficiently prepared. Magistrate McFie again came to the fore, urging the South African Industrial Federation to organise a 'defence force' against the strike. Crawford and Forrester Brown (two former left-wingers, now leaders of the Federation) agreed. The press and the authorities, however, began to take fright at the extent of the looming confrontation. The government called for the release of the strikers and the Supreme Court suspended their sentences on 28 June 1918. J. B. Moffatt, Chief Magistrate of the Transkei, was appointed government commissioner to investigate the grievances of the Africans in Johannesburg. The general strike was called off. Talbot Williams, Transvaal leader of the African Peoples Organisation and organiser of the IWA, went so far as to make a 'signed confession' of his activities to the Johannesburg Chief Magistrate, and undertook 'to do all he could to stop the movement he had initiated' (Walker and Weinbren, 1961, p. 278).

But events could no longer be turned back so easily. 15,000 African workers employed at three mines refused to go to work on 1 July. Police and troops were rushed to the compounds to drive them down the shafts. Serious clashes developed. The workers fought back with axes and pickhandles before their resistance was broken. The police then proceeded to round up some leading critics of state policy who had allegedly been involved in the events of May and June. The charge brought against them was 'incitement to violence'. Eight men were brought before the Magistrate's court for preparatory examination: three members of the IWA, three members of the ISL, and two members of the ANC. The socialists were held responsible for causing not only the bucket strike and the miners' strike but various other strikes and demonstrations as well. Their defence was that 'They were concerned to propagate the doctrines of socialism and trade unionism. They believed in strike action, but only when it was prepared by adequate trade union organisation. They had considered that the Natives were not well enough organised for strike action and had advised accordingly' (Roux, 1964, p. 131).

J. B. Moffatt pronounced the official point of view. Their activity, he said, was like 'teaching children to play with matches round an open barrel of gunpowder' (*ibid*.). Some indication of official machinations against the IWA emerged in the course of the hearing. Several detectives and police informers had been sent into the organisation. One of these had become secretary, another had been elected to the committee. A third, who was to have served as chief witness for the prosecution, broke down under cross-examination and admitted that he had made a perjured affidavit at the request of the authorities. The Attorney General thereafter felt unable to proceed.

Despite the blows suffered by the IWA, the growth of organisation among the African workers in this period of strikes and unrest was irrepressible. The next great impetus was the upsurge of the Industrial and Commercial Workers' Union. The ICU was formed in Cape Town in January 1919. It was the result of a chance encounter between Clements Kadalie, an educated immigrant from Nyassaland, and A. F. Batty, a member of the Labour Party. Batty, it appears, had his own reasons for promoting the formation of an African trade union. Known as a 'prominent office-seeker', he was at that time contesting a parliamentary by-election and was interested in the African and coloured vote. At the first meeting called by Kadalie and Batty, twenty-four workers joined the new union. Batty associated himself with the organisation only as an 'adviser'. He 'made it plain that he wanted this to be a purely non-European trade union' (*ibid*., p. 154). J. Paulsen, a foreman in Table Bay docks, became the first chairman of the ICU. During the middle of 1919 the ICU began to organise the African and coloured work-force in the docks. A branch of the IWA, established in competition with the ICU, was absorbed into the latter during the December dock strike.

About the same time Selby Msimang, a member of the ANC, had started to organise the African workers of Bloemfontein. A campaign for a general wage increase from 2s 0d to 4s 6d a day, which included a washerwomen's strike, led to his arrest in March 1919 in terms of the

Riotous Assemblies Act. At this stage Clements Kadalie started to communicate with him. The African Peoples Organisation, too, was active at this time in promoting trade unionism among the coloured workers of Cape Town. Its object, however, was to prevent these workers from joining open unions together with white workers. In Durban large sections of the Asian working class had been organised by the end of 1919, but here, as elsewhere, African workers were excluded. It was the ICU that answered the demand for organisation among the African workers and reflected their growing critical awareness.

In July 1920 a conference was called in Bloemfontein of all the existing organisations of African workers. The aim was to set up a country-wide organisation. The president of the ANC, S. K. Makgatho, refused to participate on the grounds that the workers should not be organised independently. Kadalie and Msimang agreed on a constitution for the new organisation, which was to be called the Industrial and Commercial Workers' Union. In the election of office-bearers Msimang was chosen as president. Despite the support of Msimang, Kadalie was defeated as general secretary. Kadalie and the Cape delegation thereupon walked out of the meeting taking with them all conference papers. Msimang and the remaining delegates proceeded to set up the ICWU, while the ICU continued in Cape Town under the leadership of Kadalie. Msimang subsequently concluded that 'we could not run two parallel organisations, it would confuse the issue' (Msimang, 1977, p. 6). When it became clear that Kadalie refused to co-operate with him, he resigned from the organisation. At the end of 1921 the ICWU was absorbed into the ICU. The unified organisation was known by the initials ICU and Kadalie was, for the time being, its undisputed leader.

One or two incidents from the early years of the ICU will suffice to show the storm-tossed nature of its development. On 4 December 1919 the Cape Federation of Trades, in protest against the rising cost of living, called on all workers to refuse to handle food for export. On 17 December the ICU and the Cape Town branch of the IWA responded by calling out their members in Table Bay docks. They also used the occasion to demand a pay rise for African and coloured dockers from 4s 0d to 8s 6d a day. Their strike enjoyed the moral support of the union of free workers in the docks, and the National Union of Railways and Harbours Servants (NURAHS). Estimates of the number of men on strike range from 400 to 8,000. The first reaction of the state was to move in police and troops, to eject the unfree workers from their quarters in the docks, and to prosecute many for breach of contract under the Masters and Servants Act. Then it yielded on the demand regarding food exports and prohibited the further export of food except on permit. This had the effect of dividing the workers. NURAHS withdrew its support of the strike. White railwaymen scabbed and after two weeks the strike was called off. The ISL accused the white workers of treachery and the Cape Federation of Trades of not ensuring sufficient support among its members before calling on the African workers to strike. The secretary of the railwaymen could only retort that workers had been called on to refuse to handle food for export, not to strike. In August 1920 the stevedoring companies agreed to a minimum wage of 8*s* 0*d* a day for African as well as coloured dockers. According to some the strike was a failure, while according to others it was a success.

Riots, strikes and mass meetings were taking place among African people in different parts of the country. A massive strike involving some 70,000 African miners on the Reef in February 1920 was broken by the police. In Port Elizabeth Samual Masabalala, employed by Lennon's wholesale chemists, had established a Native Labour Union in February 1920. Masabalala attended the July conference of the ICWU in Bloemfontein. On his return the local organisation was renamed the ICWU. A campaign for higher wages was started and a mass meeting was announced, which Masabalala would address. Dr Rubusana, an African leader from East London, was invited by the Port Elizabeth City Council to come to Port Elizabeth and use his influence against Masabalala. Rubusana agreed; but at his first meeting he was assaulted by followers of Masabalala. Masabalala was thereupon arrested. No charge was laid and bail was refused. On 23 October 1920 a crowd of indignant workers gathered outside the police station where he was held. Stones were thrown. A shot was fired, the crowd retreated; then police and armed civilians opened fire. Twenty demonstrators and three white bystanders were killed, and 126 people were wounded. The state denied liability for damages arising from the shooting, even though an official commission of inquiry found that the shooting had been unjustified. An amount of £2,857 1*s* 0*d* was eventually paid out *ex gratia* to the claimants. Of this, £2,327 11*s* 0*d* went to the dependants of the three whites who had been killed and twelve who had been injured. A further £377 7*s* 6*d* was paid to the dependants of three coloured victims. £152 2*s* 6*d* remained for the mass of African victims.

Masabalala was subsequently tried on a charge of 'public violence' and acquitted. The funeral of the dead workers was attended by a crowd of 30,000 people. In July 1921 the black municipal workers of Port Elizabeth finally secured a cost-of-living allowance. In April 1925 another serious clash took place in the Bloemfontein area. Five Africans were killed and twenty-four wounded by the police. 'In this atmosphere of dissatisfaction,' writes Roux (1964, p. 156), 'the newly formed ICU spread from Cape Town like a veld fire over the Union of South Africa.' In London *The Times* reported (*ibid.*):

> The genuine grievances of the South African Natives provided
> the hotbed in which the ICU flourished. Rack-rented Natives
> in the urban locations, underpaid Natives in Government employ,
> badly treated Natives on European farms, flocked to join the
> movement.

By 1923 the ICU had spread to the country districts and to the northern provinces. It found support not only among African workers but also among coloured labourers in the Cape. By 1925 it claimed 50,000 members and in 1927 100,000. 'Whatever its paid-up membership,' Coetzee observes (1976, p. 19), 'it had an enormous following and, in view of its general policy, was tremendously popular.'

In the mid-1920s the ICU reached its zenith, eclipsing the ANC. As a mass working-class movement it had grown into the focal point for the demands of the African people. It became, in the plaintive words of M. A. du Toit (1976, p. 35), 'nothing more than a political organisation'. The secret of the massive basis of the ICU, Coetzee suggests (1976, p. 17), lay in its appeal to coloured and Asian workers as well as to African workers. A glance at the relatively small number of the coloured and Asian workers, however, will show that this is incorrect. The key to the massive nature of the ICU was its appeal to the *working class* as opposed to the African middle class or even the middle-class elements of all black groups combined. Nor did the ICU deliberately confine itself to black labour. In 1919 it applied for affiliation to the South African Industrial Federation and in 1927 to the South African Trade Union Congress. In this way it raised the perspective of common working-class organisation more concretely than had ever been done at that stage. However, on both occasions its application was refused.

From this powerful position the ICU rapidly slid into decline and disintegration. The causes were various but not unrelated: 'Persecution helped to kill it,' Roux writes (1964, p. 196), 'but the forces of internal disruption were a more fundamental cause of its collapse.' Undoubtedly the hostility of employers and the state promoted internal disruption. Kept under constant attack the ICU was severely handicapped in the process of outgrowing its problems. Different observers, speaking from different points of view, arrive at different interpretations of its decline and fall. M. A. du Toit, an avowed enemy of independent African trade unionism, points triumphantly at 'the influence of leftist elements' and the supposedly disastrous effects of radical statements by Kadalie. He does not explain how this factor destroyed the organisation. Indeed, he goes on to list as a further cause of decline the expulsion of Communist Party members from the ICU. In doing so, we now learn, 'Kadalie lost people with organisational ability' (1976, p. 35). This contradictory argument is then taken to its logical conclusion. Black trade-union leaders with ability, in the view of M. A. du Toit, were often 'of the wrong type, trying to use the unions to their own advantage'. Conversely, by a strange coincidence, 'Those who were serious did not have the necessary education and experience (*ibid.*, p. 39). Moreover the shift of the ICU headquarters to Johannesburg meant that the influence of the 'more responsible and experienced Coloureds' was lost (*ibid.*, p. 35). Coetzee, too, refers to the 'organisational immaturity' of the ICU (1976, p. 19). Also Walker and Weinbren (1961, pp. 279–80) draw attention to Kadalie's personal ambition. Yet these observations are one-sided. The decline of the ICU should be seen against the background of class struggle and industrial relations as a whole. Today, with the African trade-union movement once again in the ascendant, it is more important than ever to understand its nature, its relationship with the rest of society and the forces that threaten it with destruction.

Throughout its existence the ICU was confronted with intense hostility on the part of employers and the state: 'The Government', Roux explains (1964, p. 161), 'had grown alarmed at the rapid growth of the movement.' Detectives and informers were sent into the organisation. In November 1920 Kadalie was served with a deportation order. Pressure from different quarters, however, led the government to withdraw it. In August 1926 Kadalie was declared subject to the pass laws. Soon afterwards he was convicted for entering Natal without a permit, the authorities having refused to issue him with one. Also, the workers who went into action under the banner of the ICU were met with repression. In October 1928, at the Onderstepoort government laboratory near Pretoria, the ICU led a campaign for higher wages. The government refused to negotiate with the union and the workers' spokesmen were dismissed. A protest strike then broke out, which was ended with the dismissal and arrest of seventy-one workers.

In Natal hostility against the ICU reached a high pitch of intensity in 1928 and 1929. The ICU *yase* Natal ('ICU in Natal') had come out in support of a boycott of the new municipal beer canteens. In Grey-town and in Weenen mobs of white men attacked the offices of the ICU. In Durban in June 1929 two white men were killed in an attempt to storm the ICU hall. African workers from the Point dock area were met with police gunfire when they attempted to relieve the hall. Six of them were killed. The defenders of the hall eventually surrendered to the police. Champion, leader of the ICU *yase* Natal, was banned from the province in 1930 for a period of three years. Finally, during the early months of 1931, the ICU *yase* Natal was largely broken up with the arrest and deportation of many of its members.

The last strike to be organised by Kadalie's 'Independent ICU' was the strike of railway and harbour workers in East London in January 1930. It was called in support of a demand for a wage increase from 3*s* 0*d* to 6*s* 6*d* a day. Without a strike fund the workers were unable to hold out much longer than a week. Kadalie and eight other leaders were arrested. From prison Kadalie ordered the workers to return to work. He was convicted on a charge of incitement to public violence.

Also by means of legislation the government reacted to the rise of organisation among the African workers. By the mid-1920s the Communist Party had begun to direct its attention towards the African population. Tielman Roos, the Nationalist Minister of Justice and subsequently a Judge of Appeal, threatened to bring in a 'Sedition Bill' to make an end to agitation. The result was the so-called 'hostility clause' of 1927 (section 29, Act no. 38 of 1927), which read:

> Any person who utters any words or does any other act or thing
> whatever with intent to promote any feeling of hostility between
> Natives and Europeans, shall be guilty of an offence and liable
> on conviction to imprisonment not exceeding one year or to a
> fine of one hundred pounds or both.

To any organisation of African workers, an inescapable point of reference is the superior conditions reserved by law, in racial terms, for workers of European descent. By prohibiting, in effect, any agitation in relation to these inequalities, the government was striking directly at the organisation of African workers. Roux explains (1964, p. 203):

> There was no intention of using the law against whites who
> incited race hatred against blacks. Such incitement is an almost
> daily occurrence in South Africa, but in no instance has anyone
> been charged with such an offence. On the other hand, the law
> was used against persons who protested against the unfair
> treatment of blacks.

107

Within six months of its proclamation in September 1927 five members of the ICU and four members of the Communist Party had been arrested in terms of section 29. In 1929 the Riotous Assemblies Act was amended in the same spirit. The Minister of Justice now received the power to order any individual to leave any part of the country if the Minister considered that his presence might lead to the creation of feelings of hostility between the different racial groups. This measure was used almost immediately to ban Champion from Natal.

Having rallied large numbers of unfree, impoverished workers for the purpose of improving their condition, the ICU could scarcely help reflecting demands and attitudes that were explosive in the context of South African society. It could scarcely help adopting a militant attitude which 'put fear into the hearts of the authorities' (Roux, 1964, p. 196). Kadalie himself, in the early years, often pledged that he would not rest until Lenin's victory had been repeated in South Africa. In his May Day message of 1926 he called on the ICU members to fight for the overthrow of capitalism and the establishment of a workers' commonwealth. Besides all attempts at physically crushing this danger, the capitalist class could resort to other, more subtle means of neutralising or destroying the ICU. The greatest success in this direction was enjoyed by a seemingly insignificant group of white liberals who had formed the so-called Joint Councils of European and Bantu. Prominent among them were Mrs Ethelreda Lewis, a novelist, and Miss Margaret Hodgson, later known as Mrs Ballinger, Liberal MP. This group liaised with British Labour circles and enjoyed the support of 'moderates' such as Lord Olivier within the British Labour movement. It was this group that persuaded Kadalie to abandon the workers' demands and steer a 'middle course'. These 'humanitarian representatives of the ruling race', Roux (1964, p. 162) informs us,

> told him that Government hostility could be attributed only to the presence of certain communists and agitators among the leaders of the ICU. They told him that if only he would get rid of these 'reds' all would be well with the ICU. The Government would tolerate – nay, even recognise – the organisation. The ICU, thus freed of its red incubus, could affiliate to the International Federation of Trade Unions . . . and this improved status would lead ultimately to recognition from the white trade union movement in South Africa.

Kadalie concedes that he received advice and help from 'distinguished' white women 'behind the scenes' (Kadalie, 1970, p. 85). Their advice was put into practice at the ICU national council meeting in December 1926. Amidst disorderly scenes, a motion to the effect that 'no member of the ICU shall be a member of the Communist Party' was adopted by six votes to five. Kadalie, having swung round from his May Day call for a workers' commonwealth, thus became the first trade-union leader in South Africa to impose anti-communist proscriptions. The expulsion of Communist Party members by various ICU branches followed. Opposition also arose. The Port Elizabeth branch called for the unconditional reinstatement of the members who had been expelled. In Johannesburg a stormy meeting called for a review of the national council decision by the congress of the ICU. At the seventh annual congress held in Durban in April 1927 the national council decision was endorsed, with five delegates voting against.

These developments should be seen in the light of the general situation within the ICU, in particular the relationship between the leaders and the rank and file.[5] The general state of the organisation can be characterised as undemocratic and unco-ordinated. The leadership was entrenched and autocratic. Except at annual congresses discussion with the rank and file scarcely took place. Control by the members over the leadership apparently did not exist. Kadalie himself, a man of considerable energy and flair, was extremely powerful in the organisation as its founder and national leader. To thousands of workers the names of Kadalie and the ICU were synonymous. As with workers everywhere, their loyalty to their movement would remain unshakeable until events had shown them that their trust had been abused. Their reaction would be one of bitter disappointment. In Natal, Champion had likewise achieved a position of great personal influence. The same was true, to a lesser extent, of other local leaders.

African intellectuals, including conservatives such as A. M. Jabavu, flocked to join the ICU; and they were admitted. Most of the ICU officials, Kadalie states (1970, p. 222), were former teachers who were drawn to the ICU because it offered them higher pay. It was these people, together with Kadalie and a few other charismatic figures, who formed the leadership of the ICU. The leadership, personified by Kadalie, gave no sign of serious commitment to the workers' aspirations and struggle; it failed completely to base itself on the objective situation of the workers, or to submit to their control. The irresponsible use made of union resources was only one symptom of this rampant bureaucratisation. Money was spent freely. In Natal one legal firm collected £3,334 11s 0d in fees from the ICU in a period of only four

months. Worse than this, corrupt individuals were able to rise unchecked
to responsible positions. The acting provincial secretary in Natal was
convicted of stealing £865 belonging to the union. Champion himself
had the habit of paying union money into his personal banking account.
The result was a growing chasm between the leadership and the
members. Kadalie himself preferred addressing mass audiences to
dealing with the workers' more humdrum problems. In June 1927 he
went to the International Labour Organisation conference in Geneva
as an unofficial delegate from South Africa. From there he set off on
a lecture tour of Europe. He returned to South Africa more moderate
and more intent than ever on becoming a respectable trade-union
leader. The fact that no more than a handful of white liberals supported
him in this role apparently made no difference. Kadalie showed no sign
of grasping the real nature of the relationship between the working
class and the state. Employers and the state, on the other hand, could
clearly see the glaring contrast between the postures of the ICU leaders
and the relentless demands of the masses. Under no circumstances were
they prepared to recognise an independent African trade union. Not for
a moment did they believe that the moderating influence of the 'distinguished' liberal ladies extended very far beyond Kadalie and his
circle. Nor did the ICU members uncritically accept their leader's
change of heart. At Kimberley Kadalie was told that he had gone to
Europe a black man and come back a white man. Indeed, even the
manner of his going to Europe might have caused raised eyebrows
among his followers. He travelled in a first-class suite on the mailboat.
In Europe, according to his own account, Kadalie was no stranger to
'first-class' hotels and formal dinner-parties. On his return Kadalie
travelled from Cape Town to Johannesburg in a 'luxurious' express
train. Small wonder that, in Kadalie's own words, 'the majority of
ICU members . . . did not realise that the mission to Geneva . . . was
not merely a waste of money on a pleasurable adventure' (1970,
p. 111).

In November 1928 the *Workers' Herald*, organ of the ICU, boasted
that the ICU had used the strike weapon on only three occasions in
ten years. In every other dispute where the union had intervened it
was to try and persuade the workers to return to work. On occasion,
however, the workers would refuse. Roux describes the position as
follows (1964, p. 160):

Two schools of thought emerged: the left-wing believed in direct
action, strikes, the burning of passes, refusal to pay taxes, etc.;

the right wing was all for a policy of *hamba kahle* (go carefully).
In practice, the believers in *hamba kahle* were not able or
willing to produce any concrete plans. Nothing was done.
Disillusionment spread among the rank and file. But as people
grew disillusioned in one district, as their enthusiasm waned
and they ceased to pay their subscriptions, the ICU moved on to
new, untouched districts.

Communist Party members had been the most active in criticising the
inefficiency of the right wing, as well as their failure to fight for the
workers' interests. This undoubtedly contributed to their explusion.

The basic reason for the inconsistency of the ICU leadership, according to Bonner (quoted in Coetzee, 1976, pp. 73-4), was its poor understanding of the nature of South African society:

> What the ICU leaders seem to have lacked was any systematic
> theory of how economy and society functioned in South Africa,
> and this in turn prevented them from evolving any adequate
> strategy to promote change. As a result, for the best part of a
> decade, they mistook protest for pressure and numbers for
> strength, ignoring all the while that there had to be some way for
> pressure to be brought to bear for it to have any effect.

This lack of perspective is apparent from the leadership's effortless
switching from radical to conservative postures and back. One or two
further instances may be noted. In March 1922 the ICU supported the
government in its suppression of the Rand strike. This was no doubt a
reaction to the violence against Africans committed by certain strikers
and the racial overtones in which the strike as a whole was presented.
None the less it shows a remarkable misunderstanding of social relations
and the role of the state in South Africa. Related to this were attempts
by the ICU leaders to deny or evade the political implications of the
workers' struggle. As Johns observes, even a modest programme of
minimum wages and similar demands 'held the potential for a fundamental challenge of the *status quo* of white South Africa' (1967, p. 191).
Yet in 1921 the ICU specifically dissociated itself from any political
perspectives. At its conference of 1923 this commitment was repeated.
The ICU resolved 'unreservedly to dissociate itself from any political
body whatever, and declares that its objectives are solely to propagate
the industrial, economic and social advancement of all the African
workers through industrial organisation on constitutional lines' (Kadalie,
1970, p. 56). Assurances of this nature, needless to say, did not deceive

the state for a moment. At most the effect may have been to deceive a section of workers into thinking that their demands could be realised by refraining from political involvement.

Failure to adapt organisational methods to the demands made by the workers, Simons and Simons suggest (1969, p. 356), was the basic weakness of the ICU. A further conclusion is drawn by Bonner: the 'negligence' of the ICU leaders 'can be traced to their elite or bourgeois background' (Coetzee, 1976, p. 74). Although in themselves both these statements are incomplete, they are not hard to reconcile. What needs to be explained is the connection between an 'elite or bourgeois background' and failure in leading a workers' organisation. In the case of Kadalie himself, as the personification of the ICU leadership, this connection meets the eye. Personal ambition is a leading trait of elitism or the bourgeois philosophy in general, and personal ambition, according to contemporaries, dominated Kadalie's conduct to a very large extent. The other side of personal ambition in a workers' leader is irresponsibility as far as the interests of the workers are concerned. Kadalie, apparently, was incorrigible. Msimang's words, aimed very likely at Kadalie, deserve to be quoted in this regard (Johns, 1967, p. 185):

> As he [Msimang] had said before, it was only destructive to engage
> in wild phrases and flowery words which only served to stir the
> passions of the people who were at present not well organised for
> anything. A wise leader should think more of the dangers that
> might befall his people if he did not lead them safely and wisely.
> He should scarcely allow personal ambitions to come before the
> sacred duty and the sacred cause he is out to win, not for himself,
> but for the helpless.

Kadalie's approach to working-class organisation, on the other hand, is best expressed in his own words. It was not long after his appointment as paid secretary of the ICU, he recorded, that 'it dawned on me that I had a big part to play in the trade union movement' (Kadalie, 1970, p. 44). An admirer of Kadalie could find no better apology than the following: 'If Clements Kadalie is a great egoist, so were Tshaka, and Kruger and Rhodes. So are all of us' (*ibid*., p. 28).

Sound working-class organisation, on the other hand, presupposes internal democracy, precisely to ensure that the interests and demands of the members come clearly and decisively to the fore, and to check abuse by officials. This means more than proclaiming democratic procedures; the membership needs to be instructed and encouraged in their use until the tradition of democratic discussion and decision-making has become indestructible. Such a tradition, in turn, presupposes complete dedication by the leaders to the interests of the workers, and collides head-on with personal ambition. The failure of Kadalie may thus be said to lie not so much in his 'elite or bourgeois background' in itself but more precisely in his failure to overcome certain aspects of this background which are incompatible with working-class organisation. This also explains the failure of the ICU leadership in general, its bureaucratisation and its failure to develop clear perspectives. It is only when working-class interests are fought for single-mindedly that a consistent programme is essential. Mere personal ambition can be served only on the basis of short-term, haphazard manoeuvres.

In South Africa the irreconcilable conflict between the interests of unfree labour and capital completely excludes 'respectability' on the part of a genuine workers' leader in the eyes of employers and the state. A leader such as Kadalie who has set his heart on 'respectability' can only gain this by ignoring his mandate and taking up, instead, a position that the capitalist class can accept. Democratic control by the workers would rule out such a course of action. Within the African labour movement, therefore, political 'moderation' and bureaucratisation go firmly hand in hand.

From his early period of militance, Kadalie, and with him the ICU, lurched violently to the right in 1926. From echoing the militant feelings of the workers, the leaders now veered to demanding moderation and inactivity in no less irresponsible a way. From the workers' point of view the organisation became even less effective in carrying their struggle forward. While new members continued to be recruited in new areas, in effect on false pretences, in older branches the seeds of disillusionment and dissent were rapidly taking root. In a nutshell, Roux explains, 'members were tired of paying subscriptions and getting nothing for their money' (1964, p. 161). In the event it was the rival ambitions of Champion that set off the final collapse. Champion, sooner than face an inquiry into his handling of union funds, persuaded the Natal branches of the ICU to split off. Early in 1928 the ICU *yase* Natal was formed as an independent organisation with Champion in control.

Other local leaders followed Champion's example. A 'moderate' trade-union adviser, W. G. Ballinger, was sent out from Britain to come to Kadalie's aid. He arrived in mid-1928 but was unable to save the situation. Organisational improvements could be of no avail against political disintegration, feeding on a loss of confidence among the rank and file. Ballinger, no more than Kadalie, could alter the relationship

113

between capital and labour in South Africa. To employers and the State, if not to Kadalie and Ballinger, it was clear that African workers have radical demands. A 'moderate' African union is one that is isolated from the workers. But even a 'moderate' African union, suppressing the demands of the members by bureaucratic methods, had its dangers. On the one hand, it might become militant through a process of internal democratisation. On the other hand, it might pave the way for other, more representative unions. Ballinger's hopes of being reasonable and negotiating with employers were thus misguided from the start. The main result of his intervention was growing resentment on Kadalie's part. Ballinger was trespassing on his prerogatives as leader. A rupture became inevitable. In January 1929 Kadalie broke with Ballinger, taking with him most of the remaining members of the ICU. At Easter he formed his followers into the Independent ICU, based mainly in East London. Ballinger's section of the ICU very soon ceased to function. Champion reverted to a policy of extreme *hamba kahle* and used his power 'to hold back the Africans from action' (Roux, 1964, p. 193). Even this could not save him from deportation. In the wave of arrests and deportation that followed the pass-burning campaign of 1930, the ICU *yase* Natal suffered important losses. In April 1931 the Department of Justice could report (quoted by Roux, 1964, p. 251):

> The ICU *yase* Natal has dwindled in numbers and influence until its strength to-day is described as of little consequence. Since the deportation of Champion, the leading officers and organisers have quarrelled frequently for supreme power, resulting in undercurrents being revealed to the masses which alienated the bulk of the ICU following. The attendance at open-air meetings has fallen from approximately 2,000 to some 250, and most of the latter are not members. Practically no fees are being paid into the coffers of the organisations by members.

In 1933 Champion was allowed to return to Natal on the understanding that he should 'behave himself' (*ibid.*, p. 194). Champion behaved himself. The ICU *yase* Natal, once the most vigorous section of the ICU, slowly wasted away. Champion eventually set up as a trader.

Kadalie continued his erratic career of opportunistic adaptations. We have seen how, in 1926, he swung round from left to right. On a platform of moderation the ICU duly affiliated to the International Federation of Trade Unions and even applied for registration in terms of the Industrial Conciliation Act. Less than three years later the break with Ballinger became the occasion for a new and dramatic about-face.

From Kadalie's point of view Ballinger probably stood in the way of a continued relationship with the British Trades Union Council, the International Federation of Trade Unions and white South African liberaldom. 'Having broken with that section of white nigrophilists whose advice had led to his expulsion of the communists in 1926,' Roux records (*ibid.*, p. 187), 'he now returned to his earlier policy of co-operation with the "reds". But he found that now the communists were much less willing to help him.' In May 1929 Kadalie's Independent ICU applied for affiliation to the League Against Imperialism (which two years earlier he had denounced as a tool of Moscow). All responsibility for the ICU's conservatism of the preceding period was laid at Ballinger's door. Ballinger, Kadalie said, 'fraternised with the boss class' and 'desired us to worship at the shrine of capitalism' (*ibid.*, pp. 187-8). Kadalie's application, together with his request for £200, was refused.

At East London his 'dying candle gave one last revolutionary flicker' (*ibid.*, p. 194) during the strike of the railway and harbour workers early in 1930. Little was heard of Kadalie for some months afterwards. Then, in December, it appeared that he had once more swung around. Repulsed by the League Against Imperialism, he rediscovered his anti-communist convictions. At the height of the anti-pass law campaign of 1930 Kadalie appeared at a public meeting in Bloemfontein. He warned his listeners to have nothing to do with the Communist Party and declared himself an opponent of the campaign for burning passes on Dingaan's Day. No doubt this contributed to the failure of the campaign. At this stage the disintegration of the ICU was more or less complete, with the exception of Durban, where Champion's organisation still struggled on. Twenty years later the Industrial Legislation Commission would discover that only the East London branch was still in existence but 'had degenerated into a sort of social club' (Horrell, 1961, p. 67).[6]

The rise and fall of the ICU was of lasting significance for the labour movement in South Africa. It brought out unmistakably the enormous potential for organisation and struggle within the African working class. In Kadalie, Champion and others, the workers found men willing to lead, and their response was overwhelming. Few of their demands were taken up; in the sense of improving the material position of the workers the ICU achieved very little. But then, significant changes within a system of social relations as armoured and unyielding as that in South Africa could scarcely be brought about by a handful of leaders without clear perspectives and without a consistent strategy, acting in isolation from the workers. The ICU was significant, rather, in establishing the possibility of mass organisation among the black workers as a historical fact. Several leading trade-union organisers of the 1930s (Thomas Mbeki, Gana Makabeni and Moses Kotane among them) received their basic training in the ICU. In particular, the ICU created a precedent of common organisation by African and coloured workers.

The fall of the ICU was a complex process, demonstrating the pressures and pitfalls to which an African workers' organisation in South Africa is exposed. The responsibility of leadership under such conditions is enormous. There can be no doubt that Kadalie and his lieutenants, 'drunk with the heady wine of success' (Roux, 1964, p. 197), failed to carry out their task. Their policies were marked by confusion and inconsistency. They did not learn from experience, let alone theory, to any visible extent. They advanced from error to needless error. The result was to deal a heavy blow to the African workers' movement (Roux, *ibid.*):

> The mounting wave crashed, but not against the barriers that held the Bantu in misery. It fell amidst the rocks and pools of intrigue, incompetence, mismanagement and dishonesty. Kadalie, failing to take the current when it served, had lost the venture. The masses sank back into sullen suspicion. But of this tragic tale of Kadalie, the most tragic feature is that the opportunity he thus squandered was unique in the history of the black man's struggle for freedom in this country. . . . No single mass movement of the black workers in South Africa has ever even remotely approached the power that was in the ICU.

These conclusions are too pessimistic, and not entirely accurate. New generations of African workers would arise who had not tasted the bitter experiences of the 1920s. In 1945, the Council of Non-European Trade Unions could claim 119 affiliated unions with a total of 158,000 members. At the end of the 1950s African trade-union membership numbered nearly 60,000. From 1973 onwards African trade unionism would undergo a new period of meteoric growth. At every stage, however, African trade unions would be subject to the same fundamental pressures and conditions. Then, as now, their course lay between the Scylla of state repression and the Charybdis of 'liberal' seduction. From the point of view of the African unions today it is vital that the history of the ICU be well learned.

Part II

South Africa at the beginning of the
1970s

Chapter 4

Legal regulation

The fundamental legal condition for the existence of capitalist society is the protection of private ownership of the means of production. In South Africa the doctrine of *dominium*, or absolute ownership, has proved adequate to safeguard also the specifically capitalist forms of property without mentioning them by name. Ownership in South African law means 'the right which a person has in a thing to possess it, to use it and take the fruits, to destroy it, and to alienate it' (Gibson, 1970, p. 198). In this sense the entire body of law described as the 'law of things' provides the legal basis for capitalist production, while various other laws - notably the law of letting and hiring - create further essential conditions. The legal framework of capitalism is inherent in the South African legal system as a whole.

'Co-operation' between capital and state is the material foundation of this system. In practice, this has far-reaching implications: 'Since the private sector is predominant in the South African economy,' the South Africa Foundation explains (1962, p. 51), 'its soundness is of major concern to the State.' Thus 'public interest' is identified to a large extent with the interests of private capital. Not only the capitalist system in general, but *the form which it has taken in South Africa*, is an integral part of the 'public order' which the state has the function of maintaining. In this light terms such as 'state security', 'public order' and 'public interest', which in themselves are vague, take on a more concrete meaning. 'State interest' as well as 'public interest', in their legal definition, must show a definite correlation with the interests of employers. In this sense South African 'security' legislation forms a perfectly consistent whole and distinctions such as that drawn by Mathews (1971, pp. 299-301) between the 'security' and 'non-security' functions of these laws reflect an unclear understanding of the function

of the state. Capital and state are mutually interdependent in South
Africa. Employers depend on a supply of 'cheap docile labour'. To
maintain this supply an oppressive legal system is required. Thus the
'political' and 'security' laws which are dealt with below form an
integral part of the system of industrial relations.

If the historical basis for the unfreedom of the African working class
is the reserve system, then its legal cornerstone is section 10(1) of the
Bantu (Urban Areas) Consolidation Act. The operative part reads as
follows:

> No Bantu shall remain for more than 72 hours in a prescribed
> area[1] unless he produces proof in the manner prescribed that
>
> (a) he has, since birth, resided continuously in such area; or
> (b) he has worked continuously in such area for one employer
>   for a period of not less than ten years or has lawfully resided
>   in such area for a period of not less than fifteen years, and
>   has thereafter continued to reside in such area and is not
>   employed outside such area and has not during either
>   period or thereafter been sentenced to a fine exceeding one
>   hundred rand or to imprisonment for a period exceeding
>   six months; or
> (c) such Bantu is the wife, unmarried daughter or son under
>   the age at which he would become liable for payment of
>   general tax under the Bantu Taxation and Development Act,
>   1925 (Act No. 41 of 1925), of any Bantu mentioned in
>   paragraph (a) or (b) of this sub-section and after lawful entry
>   into such prescribed area, ordinarily resides with that Bantu
>   in such area; or
> (d) in the case of any other Bantu permission so to remain has
>   been granted by an officer appointed to manage a labour
>   bureau in terms of the provisions of paragraph (a) of section
>   *twenty-one ter* of the Bantu Labour Regulation Act, 1911
>   (Act No. 15 of 1911), due regard being had to the
>   availability of accommodation in a Bantu residential area.

Exempted from these provisions are Africans recruited to work in the
mining industry, or other industries specified by the state, in terms of
a contract of employment – i.e. 'contract labour' (section 13). The
logical corollary of section 10(1) is contained in section 10 *bis*, which
lays down that no person shall take any African into his employment

in a prescribed area unless permission to take up employment has been granted to such African by the state labour officer for the area concerned. Numerous grounds are provided on which the labour officer may refuse permission.

By these simple measures an iron hold is established over some 70 per cent of the South African working class. To all intents and purposes survival for the propertyless black masses means wage labour in the cities. Exclusion from the 'prescribed areas' generally means confinement to the reserves, where low productivity, increasing poverty and pressure of population render the prospects of survival bleak in the extreme. Yet, in effect, the African worker may only remain in the city – and only in one urban area at that – for as long as he is employed. The number of Africans who can remain in the city in terms of section 10(1) without performing wage labour is thus extremely low.

Contravening section 10(1) is a criminal offence. To prove an African guilty in terms of this sub-section the state need merely *allege* his guilt. Thereupon 'it shall be presumed until the contrary is proved that such Bantu remained in the area in question for a period longer than 72 hours and that such Bantu is not permitted under sub-section (1) to be in such area' (section 10(5)). Africans who cannot prove their innocence may be 'removed'. More than this, any African considered to be 'idle' or 'undesirable' by the Bantu Affairs Commissioner may be 'removed' to a place determined by that official. By 'idle Bantu' is meant, *inter alia*, the unemployed (section 29). Africans who are 'normally unemployed' may be arrested without warrant and 'removed'.

Provision is also made for the large-scale 'removal of redundant Bantu from urban areas' in cases where 'the number of Bantu within that area is in excess of the reasonable labour requirements of that area' (section 28). Yet further provisions ensure that the African working class will enjoy the least possible economic independence. No African worker can acquire land or any interest in land in any urban area, even if he could afford it, without the approval of the State President (section 6). With few exceptions, urban Africans are required to live in a 'location, Bantu village or Bantu hostel' (section 9). The terms and conditions for residence in these townships are laid down by the local authority or by the state. Africans who disobey such regulations may, once again, be 'removed' (section 38 *bis*).

The right of remaining in town, where the jobs are to be found, is thus precarious from the African worker's point of view. 'Removal' is an ever-present threat. To the worker 'removal' is likely to be disastrous, to the employer no more than a passing inconvenience. Almost any worker can be replaced by one of the hundreds of thousands of unemployed Africans in South Africa, while the worker himself, by the same token, is likely to remain unemployed.

To regulate the movement of millions of workers an elaborate control system is needed. Such a system was created by the so-called Bantu (Abolition of Passes and Co-ordination of Documents) Act of 1952 by which the traditional 'pass' was given the new name of 'reference book'. Every African was required to apply for a reference book on reaching the age of 16 years. The function of the reference book is explained by section 8:

(1) Any person who enters into a contract of service or employment with a Bantu . . . shall . . . lodge . . . with the labour bureau . . . having jurisdiction in the area . . . and record in the reference book issued to such Bantu, prescribed particulars relating to such contract or to such employment.

(2) Any person shall if such Bantu deserts from his service or if such contract is terminated advise such labour bureau . . . of the date of such termination or desertion and in the event of termination . . . also record the date thereof in such Bantu's reference book.

If wage labour is the African's real passport to survival, then his reference book provides the legal proof, and his status can be checked at a glance. The effect is to tie the African worker to his job, subject to the will of his employer. This is reflected by section 8 *ter* (1): 'No person shall employ any Bantu if it appears from such Bantu's reference book . . . that he entered into a contract of employment with some other person and such other person has not recorded in such book . . . the fact that such contract has been terminated.'

Nor are employers confined to the means of controlling their workers that Parliament has placed at their disposal. In May 1971 the Black Sash Advice Office issued a report about the 'unnecessary disasters' that were caused by the 'thoughtlessness, sometimes even the deliberate malice of employers' (SRR, 1972, p. 165):

In many cases, employers made no effort to register their employees in accordance with pass law requirements. Worse than this omission, however, were the troubles caused by deliberate actions on the part of employers, who threaten to 'spoil' pass books, or refuse to allow employees to leave jobs, knowing that if the 'F' card is not sent in, registration in new employment will be refused. There were also employers who 'used the pass laws in order to exploit a worker'. If a man hoping to qualify for permanent urban residence rights in terms of Section 10(1)(b) of the Act after ten years' continuous employment with one employer leaves the employer in under ten years, he is endorsed out and forced to work on yearly contracts for the rest of his life. Men in this position have no bargaining power, and the Black Sash reported that some employers took advantage of the situation.

Any authorised officer may at any time call upon any African to produce his reference book (section 13). In addition, a Bantu Reference Bureau is provided for where information concerning each individual black South African can be stored up, including fingerprints. Theoretically, the surveillance of African workers is complete. The effect of section 10(1), coupled with the 'pass laws' and other supplementary measures, is to exclude the vast majority of workers from the areas where work is to be found, and to admit them only on such conditions as employers and the state may lay down. Official sources are ambivalent about the functions of 'influx control'. Its purpose, in the words of the Transkeian authorities, is to bring about 'an orderly flow of labour to the industrial centres and . . . to ensure that people seeking work in the cities are assured that there will be work and suitable housing' (Kotze, 1975, p. 167). On the other hand, a municipal labour officer explains the essence of the system in somewhat different terms (Kingsley, 1950, p. 6): 'The labour bureau official is daily acquainted by commerce, industry, government departments . . . etc. of their needs, and consequently it is possible to regulate supply in accordance with demand.'

In the development of the pass-law system, the aim of catering for the labour requirements of employers has clearly been the keynote. If the African worker may not freely present himself on the labour market, how does the employer obtain his labour-power? As far as the African working class is concerned, the place of a labour market has been taken by a system of state-run labour bureaux. In terms of the Bantu Labour Act of 1964 labour bureaux were established throughout 'white' South Africa at the local, district, regional and national levels. Employers must acquire special licences or permits if they personally want to 'recruit Bantu for employment'. The alternative is to employ black workers at a labour bureau. The rules that govern this 'labour market' have been laid down by the state. They are contained in two decrees, the first entitled the 'Bantu Labour Relations' (BLR) of 1965 and the second entitled 'Regulations for Labour Bureaux at Bantu Authorities' (RLBBA) of 1968. The BLR prescribes in detail every step involved in the employment of African workers from the issue of reference books onwards. Labour bureaux in the 'white' areas are provided for in chapter VIII. The RLBBA of 1968 is concerned exclusively with the labour bureau system in the reserves. It is clear, however, that the state envisages the two sets of labour bureaux as a single, interlocking system.

In the reserves, labour bureaux have been created at the 'tribal', 'district' and 'territorial' levels. The functions of the rural and urban bureaux are fundamentally the same. Their task is to place Africans in employment according to the requirements of employers. The method is simple. Every unemployed African male is compelled to register as a work-seeker at the local labour bureau. Every employer is required to register his vacancies. The labour officer then 'places' workers in 'suitable' employment.

The labour bureau system is based on the function of the reserves as labour reservoirs. Africans required to register for employment at the 'tribal' labour bureaux are defined as those who are 'unemployed but . . . dependent on employment for [their] livelihood' (RLBBA, regulation 6(1)). 'Requisitions for labour' are forwarded to the 'territorial' labour officer, from where they are then referred to the appropriate 'district' and 'tribal' bureaux. Finally, it is provided that the 'tribal' labour officer may 'place' work-seekers in employment outside as well as inside the area of the 'tribal' authority concerned.

Once the work-seeker at the 'tribal' bureau has been 'placed', a written contract of employment must be completed in the prescribed form. The employer need not be a party to the contract; he may be represented by an official of the labour bureau. From the worker's point of view, state and employer are merged into one. After attestation of the contract, the worker's reference book is endorsed with the following stamp (RLBBA, regulation 17): 'Permitted to proceed to . . . for the purpose of taking up employment as . . . with . . . under attested contract of employment.' Finally, the circuit is closed and the legal unfreedom of the African worker is made complete by the following provisions (*ibid.*, regulation 21(1)):

> No Bantu shall leave and no person shall cause a Bantu to leave the area of a tribal labour bureau for employment outside [the reserves] save when such Bantu has been registered with that tribal bureau and his contract of employment has been attested as required by these regulations.

The result is that the unemployed in the reserves must accept such work as they are offered, on the terms that employers lay down, or else remain unemployed.

In the cities the state is confronted with the existence of Africans who have 'Section 10 rights' and thus enjoy the relative freedom to remain within a particular town and there to seek employment in the manner of free workers. To the state this limited freedom represents an anarchic element in an otherwise perfectly ordered system. Over this section of Africans the grip of employers is less than absolute. The BLR, however, sets out to remedy the matter and subjects 'Section 10' Africans to the same criterion as all others – the requirement for their labour-power. For as long as they are working, their presence is accepted. It is when they become unemployed that their freedom is substantially reduced.

Within three days of becoming unemployed the BLR provides, an African with 'Section 10 rights' must register at the local labour bureau. His reference book is then endorsed: 'Permitted to reside at . . . and to seek work as . . . within the prescribed area of . . . until . . .' (BLR, Regulation 12). If he fails to find employment in the time that he is given or refuses such 'suitable' employment as the labour bureau might offer, he may be arrested without warrant as an 'idle Bantu' and 're-moved'. His 'freedom' has come to an end. It may be argued that at least for a limited period of time the unemployed African can compete freely on the (local) labour market. But competition is a two-edged weapon. Employers have the option of 'requisitioning' labour from the reserves – or alternatively employing a registered work-seeker who is compelled to accept whatever 'suitable' work he is offered. Thus the 'free' work-seeker derives little benefit from his 'freedom'. In all probability he will have to accept work on precisely the same terms as if he had been employed through a 'tribal' or municipal labour bureau.

In this way the social value of labour-power in South Africa is fixed at a low level. This general analysis was confirmed by the Deputy Minister of Bantu Administration and Development when he explained to Parliament in 1964 that urban Africans would not be 'forbidden to walk around looking for work; but the practice is to be discouraged. The correct method for an African wanting work is to apply at a labour bureau' (SRR, 1964, p. 178).

As in Act 25 of 1945, it is laid down in the BLR that no person may employ an African in a prescribed area unless permission to be so employed has been granted to the African in terms of the Regulations. Upon employing an African the employer must sign his reference book and inform the municipal labour officer. The latter may then endorse the worker's pass as follows: 'Permitted to remain in the prescribed area of . . . while employed by . . . as . . .' (BLR, regulation 16). To ensure that no loophole remains for the worker – for example, to escape from a harsh employer – it is provided that the employer must sign his reference book each month. Failure to register as a work-seeker, in towns or in reserves, is a criminal offence. Legally and practically, the black South African is treated as a unit of labour-power to be utilised in the most profitable way. Any other conclusion would be euphemistic.

The history of personal hardship arising under these conditions, of people spending 'many months going from one office to another in one area after another living in permanent danger of arrest and able to earn nothing' (SRR, 1972, p. 165) is long. Less vivid but more comprehensive are the official statistics describing the massive use made by the state of the 'pass laws' in the period with which we are concerned (see Table 4.1).

Table 4.1 *Prosecutions and removals in terms of the pass laws 1969–70*

Prosecutions	
July 1969 – June 1970	621,380
July 1970 – June 1971	615,075

Africans removed from the Witwatersrand, the Cape Peninsula, Pretoria, Durban and Port Elizabeth	
1969	33,257
1970	33,851

Sources: SRR (1969, p. 164); *ibid.* (1971, p. 142); *ibid.* (1972, p. 161).

If we turn to the place of production, we find that effective organisation by African workers has been held back for many years by the simple device of excluding them from the registered trade unions, and hence from the system of collective bargaining provided for in the Industrial Conciliation Act. The legal cornerstone of this policy was the definition of 'employee' in section 1 of the Act, by which 'Bantu' were excluded. In itself, the absence of legal recognition of trade unions is by no means an insuperable obstacle to working-class advancement. In South Africa restrictions on trade-union organisation form yet another burden on the mass of workers. It is part of an overall political system that is designed to prevent any form of organisation among the working class by which the existing social order would be threatened.

Parliament is the 'sovereign legislative authority in and over the Republic', with 'full power to make laws for the peace, order and good government of the Republic' (section 59, Republic of South Africa Constitution Act, 1961). The right to vote in elections to Parliament and Provincial Councils, however, is limited to white South African nationals over the age of 18 years (section 3, Electoral Consolidation Act, 1946). By this simple provision some 70 per cent of workers are disenfranchised and excluded from the constitutional political process, certainly as far as the areas are concerned where the majority must spend their working lives. Over these areas the 'Bantu authorities' and 'homeland governments' have no jurisdiction, and will acquire none. For practical purposes the African worker is appointed to the sphere of extra-parliamentary politics, an area which, as we shall see, is fraught with the greatest dangers. The effect of the applicable laws can be stated very simply. It is to prevent the unfree working class from organising in such a way as to change its position materially. Whatever else may be the effect of these laws, this very important proposition must be our point of departure.

Materially, the South African state has formidable means at its disposal. The police have built up a tradition of ruthlessly dealing with radical opponents of the government in power. As early as the 1950s, the security police were said to be 'drunk with power' (Forman and Sachs, 1957, p. 108). Twenty years ago L. Forman, a lawyer with personal experience of the 'Branch', described its methods as follows (*ibid.*, p. 111):

> It is not surprising that, once hell-bent on intimidation, the
> Branch should find the law a hindrance to it, and should then,
> regularly, go beyond the limits of the law to achieve its purpose.
> In search raids they seize books and material beyond the scope
> of their warrants. They secretly tap telephones without legal
> authority. They order local town councils to prohibit meetings as
> a 'threat to the peace'. They invade meetings, illegally photograph
> all present for their files, press people for details . . . to which the
> law does not entitle them. Microphones are hidden in hall ceilings
> to record the proceedings of conferences; spies and informers
> are sent into organisations. Gradually, in the eyes of the Government
> and in their [own] eyes, they have risen to be above the law.

Since the Emergency of 1960 the power of the state has been increased by leaps and bounds. Military spending rose sharply from this time onwards, the staff of the security police was trebled during 1963 and in the same year a (white) police reserve was established. Illegal methods have increasingly characterised the activities of the police. Torture was frequently alleged by political detainees and more and more often death was the result. One of the most notorious cases on record is that of the Imam Haroun, an elderly Moslem leader in the Cape, who died in 1969 after four months in detention. The *Cape Times* published the findings of the inquest (10 July 1977):

> He had 28 bruises all over his body, some fresher than others, haematoma on his back and a broken rib. The cause of death [was] described as a disturbance of the bloodclotting mechanism and blood circulation due in part to trauma superimposed on severe narrowing of a coronary artery.

The inquest magistrate found that a 'substantial part of the said trauma was caused by an accidental fall down a flight of stone stairs [which police witnesses alleged was the cause of death]. On the available evidence I am unable to determine how the balance thereof was caused.'

Legal development has kept pace with the physical struggle of the state against its political opponents. As the common law rules became inadequate for fettering political organisation, statutory instruments were multiplied. What is known as 'security' legislation has thus undergone a vigorous and grim development in South Africa. A milestone in this process was the Treason Trial. Its significance is explained by the former Judge of Appeal, H. H. W. de Villiers, in his account of the Rivonia trial (1964, pp. 28-9):

> I asked Dr Yutar [the Deputy Attorney General for the Transvaal] why they had indicted the accused in the main counts under the Sabotage Act and not for high treason under the Common Law. His reply was that in view of the previous abortive marathon treason trial of 1956-1961, in which all the accused were acquitted, and the stricter proof required by law, it was considered wiser to charge the accused under the Sabotage Act, and not for common law high treason.

The crime of high treason with which the 156 original accused were charged 'is committed by those who with a hostile intention disturb, impair or endanger the independence or safety of the State, or attempt or actively prepare to do so' (Karis, 1965, p. 2). The 'key document in the Prosecution's case' was the Freedom Charter, adopted by the Congress of the People in 1955, with which the accused had been associated (*ibid.*, p. 6). The defence contended that (Sampson, 1958, pp. 17-18): 'the ideas and beliefs which are expressed in this charter, although repugnant to the policy of the present government, are such as are shared by the overwhelming majority of mankind . . . and also by the overwhelming majority of the citizens of this country'. Of the ideas contained in the Freedom Charter, the judge in his summing-up singled out the following for special mention (Karis, 1965, p. 70):

1. Every man and woman shall have the right to vote for and to stand as candidate for all bodies which make laws.
2. The national wealth of our country, the heritage of all South Africans, shall be restored to the people.
3. The mineral wealth beneath the soil, the banks and monopoly industry, shall be transferred to the ownership of the people as a whole.
4. Restriction of land ownership on a racial basis shall be ended, and all the land redivided amongst those who work it, to banish famine and land hunger.

The state was concerned not so much to deny that these ideas were shared by the overwhelming majority of South Africans as to show that they amounted to high treason. Hostile intent, explained Pirow, the chief prosecutor, 'was evident in the demands of the accused for equality'. They knew that 'to achieve the demands of the Freedom Charter' in their lifetime would 'necessarily involve the overthrow of the State by violence'; alternatively they must have known that 'the course of action pursued by them would inevitably result in a violent collision with the State resulting in its subversion' (*ibid.*, p. 17). Such a collision, added another member of the prosecution team, would have come 'at least from the side of the State' (*ibid.*, p. 75).

This reasoning failed to persuade the court and all the accused were eventually discharged. What the Treason Trial did establish, however, was that attempting to put the demands of the 'overwhelming majority' of South Africans into practice is regarded by the state as a capital offence. The will of the majority is not binding on the state; it is high treason against the state. Thus the Treason Trial reflected in a very concrete way the relationship between the South African state and the mass of the population. If the state finds the will of the masses intolerable, it follows that the mass of the people must find the state intolerable. The effect of the acquittals in the Treason Trial was to make inevitable the enactment of new laws under which popular spokesmen and leaders could be convicted with relative ease. These laws were to lay down the death penalty as the ultimate sanction.

The uncompromising attitude on the part of the state is entirely in accordance with the objective situation. The existing state, which is based on existing property relations, is indeed incompatible with the realisation of equal political rights and a redistribution of wealth. The powers conferred on the state by the various 'security' laws can be summarised as follows: the power to prohibit political activity; the power to prohibit organisations; the power to prohibit publications; the power to prohibit meetings; the power to restrict and detain individuals. The keynote of all these powers is the element of *discretion* on which they are based. In measure after measure we shall find that the State President, the Minister concerned, or various subordinate officials down to non-commissioned officers of police are entitled to take the most far-reaching steps if they are 'satisfied', if in their 'opinion' or if it 'appears' to them that certain conditions are present. The effect of this element of discretion is to give the state well-nigh absolute power to act as it wishes against persons and organisations. Two examples will suffice.

In R. *v.* Sachs (1953(1) S.A. 392 (A.D.)) the meaning of section 9 of the Suppression of Communism Act was at issue. This section authorised the Minister of Justice to take certain action whenever 'in [his] opinion . . . there is reason to believe that the achievement of any of the objects of communism would be furthered'. This means, Chief Justice Centlivres found, that 'it is the opinion of the Minister that is the decisive factor and, as long as there is no attack on the bona fides of the Minister, that opinion must prevail'. Similarly, regulation 4(1) of the Emergency Regulations proclaimed on 30 March 1960 authorised commissioned officers of police to arrest and detain any person whose arrest and detention is 'in the opinion of such . . . commissioned officer desirable in the interest of public order and safety'. In Stanton *v.* Minister of Justice and Others (1960(3) S.A. 353 (T)) a detained person attempted to prove the unlawfulness of her arrest. 'How can she do this . . .?', the court asked, and found: 'It would appear that the only manner in which the applicant can establish the unlawfulness of her arrest and detention is to show that Captain Cilliers acted *mala fide.*' In fact, bad faith is precisely what the applicant alleged. The court found that it was impossible in the circumstances to infer any improbability of the arresting officer having a genuine opinion that it would be desirable to detain the applicant in the interest of public order or safety, and added: 'It must again be emphasised that the inquiry is not whether he was justified in his opinion, but whether he held that opinion.'

It follows that the state is perfectly clear as to its role and as to the nature of its powers. Appeals to the conscience of the government, which are frequently uttered from religious and liberal quarters, are fundamentally misplaced. Any doubts on this point are dispelled by the government itself. The following, for example, was B. J. Vorster's understanding of his task as Minister of Justice (D'Oliveira, 1977, p. 158):

> If I see a man or a woman as a threat to the State and if there
> are valid reasons for not bringing that person to trial, then I must
> take them out of circulation one way or another. That is my
> responsibility as Minister of Justice, and if I cannot take that
> responsibility, I must leave my job.

The liberation of the African working class is a prospect unconditionally rejected by the state. In 1947 the National Party had made its position quite clear (Kruger, 1960, p. 405): 'The Bantu in the urban areas should be regarded as migratory citizens not entitled to political or social rights equal to those of whites.' This position completely excludes the realisation of working-class freedom and equality. From this position the party has never wavered. Nor did the parliamentary opposition offer any radically different alternative. The opposition, no less than the government, based itself on the interests of the capitalist class. The aim of the most 'radical' parliamentary opposition, the Progressive Party, was 'the energetic development of a modern economy based on free enterprise' (*ibid.*, p. 107).

The essential demands of free enterprise in South Africa, it has been argued, are already contained very adequately in the policies of the existing government. In any event, within the existing legal order the position of the government was practically unassailable. By the mid-1960s it had consolidated its position in Parliament to the extent, as Thompson puts it, 'that it could only be dislodged by some major catastrophe' (1966, p. 93). Its parliamentary opponents were completely powerless. They had made, in Thompson's view, 'an impressive diagnosis of the malady affecting South Africa, but they cannot agree among themselves which remedy to prescribe and they lack the means to apply any remedy at all' (*ibid.*, p. 176).

Being unenfranchised, the vast majority of workers are excluded from constitutional procedures for changing the legal conditions by which their lives are governed. Extra-constitutional methods are the only alternative remaining. Their struggle against particular laws thus brings them into conflict with law and order itself. This was well understood by the state; its attitude towards extra-constitutional activity was relentless and uncompromising (B. J. Vorster, quoted in *South African Digest*, 22 October 1976):

> No person had the right to overthrow or to subvert a sovereign state from outside Parliament. South Africa had a constitution and in South Africa, as anywhere else in the world, if a person wished to overthrow the constitution, he was committing a crime. Wherever this was attempted the state would do its duty and take the necessary action, irrespective of the people or bodies involved.

This is the background against which the powers of the state for dealing with extra-parliamentary opposition should be seen. In general, political activity in South Africa since 1950 has been narrowly circumscribed by the Suppression of Communism Act and, later, the Terrorism Act. (In 1976 the Suppression of Communism Act was renamed the Internal Security Act and the powers of the state were extended even further.) In terms of the Suppression of Communism Act, 'communism' was defined as

> the doctrine of Marxian socialism as expounded by Lenin or Trotsky, the Third Communist International (the Comintern) or the Communist Information Bureau (the Cominform) or any related form of that doctrine expounded or advocated in the Republic for the promotion of the fundamental principles of that doctrine and includes, in particular, any doctrine or scheme –
>
> (a) which aims at the establishment of a despotic system of government based on the dictatorship of the proletariat under which one political organisation only is recognised and all other political organisations are suppressed or eliminated; or
>
> (b) which aims at bringing about any political, industrial, social or economic change within the Republic by the promotion of disturbance or disorder, by unlawful acts or omissions or by the threat of any such acts or omissions or by means which include the promotion of disturbance or disorder, or such acts or omissions or threats;
>
> (c) which aims at bringing about any political, industrial, social or economic change within the Republic in accordance with the directions or under the guidance of or in co-operation with any foreign government or any foreign or international

institution whose purpose or one of whose purposes (professed or otherwise) is to promote the establishment within the Republic of any political, industrial, social or economic system identical with or similar to any system in operation in any country which has adopted a system of government such as is described in paragraph (a); or

(d) which aims at the encouragement of feelings of hostility between the European and non-European races of the Republic the consequences of which are calculated to further the achievement of any object referred to in paragraph (a), or (b).

'Communist' includes any person *deemed by the State President* to be a communist. The South African Communist Party was legally defined as a 'Marxian socialist organisation' (Mathews, 1971, p. 100) and dissolved by section 2(1) of the Act. The State President was given the power of declaring unlawful any other organisation *if he is satisfied* that one of its purposes is to promote any of the objects of communism (as defined). Statutory communism need in no way be related to Marxian socialism. Even attempts at legal reform may amount to statutory communism in terms of the above definition. This has been confirmed by the Supreme Court (R. *v.* Njongwe, 1953(2) S.A. 848 (E)):

> The features which characterise our policy are largely enshrined in statutes such as the Suppression of Communism Act, 44 of 1950, the Group Areas Act, 41 of 1950, and the Establishment of a Bantu Authorities Act, 68 of 1951, and their appeal must involve a change of the sort contemplated by section 1(1)(ii)(b) of Act 44 of 1950.

In terms of section 2 of the Terrorism Act a person is *prima facie* guilty of terrorism if

(a) with intent to endanger the maintenance of law and order in the Republic . . . [he] commits any act . . . (or attempts, advises or conspires to do so); or

(b) [he undergoes] any training which could be of use to any person intending to endanger the maintenance of law and order (or attempts, advises or consents to do so); or

(c) [he] possesses any explosive, ammunition, firearms or weapon.

'Intent' as referred to in paragraph (a) will be presumed if the act in question was *likely* to have had any of the various results that are set out in the section. The effect of these provisions was explained as follows in S. *v*. Moumbaris (1974(1) S.A. 681 (T)):

> As far as the counts based on Section 2(1) (a) are concerned . . .
> the State has to establish not only that the accused committed,
> attempted to commit or conspired to commit the acts alleged
> as the case may be, but also that he acted with the intention to
> endanger the maintenance of law and order in the Republic . . . .
> The prosecution is assisted in this regard by the presumption
> referred to in Section 2(2), which arises when the act alleged in
> the charge had or was likely to have had any of the results
> enumerated in paragraphs (a) to (1).

The 'results' referred to are extremely general. They range from
'deter[ring] any person from assisting in the maintenance of law and
order' to 'embarrass[ing] the administration of the affairs of the State'.
Thus an accused who is shown to have committed *any act* which,
according to the state, endangered the maintenance of law and order
can only escape conviction if he can prove beyond reasonable doubt
that such an act was unlikely to have had any untoward or embarrassing
result from the viewpoint of the state. Upon conviction as a 'terrorist'
in this sense, a minimum penalty of five years' imprisonment is laid
down. The maximum penalty is death.

These provisions form a menace to any organisation based on the
mass of workers. The dividing-line between 'changing the existing law
and order by extra-parliamentary means' and 'endangering the maintenance of law and order' is tenuous and thin. The avowed intention of the
state is to prevent the urban African population from changing the
existing social order by any *lawful* means. Lawful means of change do
not exist from the African workers' point of view; unlawful means are
equated with communism or even terrorism, and constitute a capital
offence.

Yet another weapon at the disposal of the state is the so-called
'hostility clause' (see p. 107 above). A high degree of 'hostility between
Bantu and Europeans' is inevitably created by the law itself, which
imposes the most explosive social differences in purely racial terms. To
explain the situation and call for the abolition of legal inequalities, a
workers' organisation must not only touch on the most sensitive causes
of 'hostility' but must mobilise support on that basis. To do so would
inevitably strengthen the feeling of resentment among people classified
as 'Bantu' towards certain persons classified as 'white', while promoting
fear and hostility on the part of certain 'whites' towards 'Bantu'. However objectively it may express itself, a workers' party could scarcely

avoid falling foul of the 'hostility clause' sooner or later if it seriously campaigns for the abolition of racial discrimination. The alternative is evasion, mystification, euphemism or untruth.

Legally, therefore, impenetrable barriers to meaningful political discussion have been created. The provisions outlined above were swords hanging over the head of every working-class organisation, whichever way it might turn. Should it voice its demands in the same racial terms that Parliament has laid down, the 'hostility clause' confronted it. Should it deal with class relations, it was threatened by the Suppression of Communism Act. In any event the more progress it made, the more it was exposed to the omnibus provisions of the Terrorism Act. This should not surprise us. It is the *content* of the workers' demands that the state is fundamentally opposed to. It is therefore entirely consistent that the road to realising these demands should be blocked by every legal means, and that the scope for lawful and effective activity by a workers' organisation should be narrow and uncertain.

Once an organisation has been declared unlawful in terms of the Suppression of Communism Act, a list may be compiled of all former office-bearers, members and active supporters of such an organisation. This also applies in respect of any other organisation if the Minister of Justice *suspects* that it *ought* to be declared unlawful. Listed persons may be prohibited by the Minister from belonging to any organisation. They may not be quoted in any way and, in general, may take no further part in public life. These powers were extended even further by the Unlawful Organisations Act of 1960. By this Act the State President was explicitly authorised to declare unlawful the African National Congress and the Pan-African Congress, or any other organisation which *in his opinion* directly or indirectly carries on the activities of the African National Congress or the Pan-African Congress, or proposes to carry on such activities *or like activities*. The penalty provisions of the Suppression of Communism Act were extended to organisations declared unlawful in terms of the Unlawful Organisations Act. Also prohibited were acts furthering objects 'similar to the objects' of an unlawful organisation. Here it need only be considered that the objects of the African National Congress as laid down in the Freedom Charter are so comprehensive as to include most demands that a party of workers would raise. The government thus has ample power to declare a workers' organisation unlawful whenever it chooses to do so; and against such a decision there can be no legal recourse.

For practical purposes we may conclude that the stronger and more effective a working-class organisation becomes, the greater is the likelihood of suppression by the state. Historically the chief target of the state has been those organisations with significant African working-class support, in particular the African National Congress and the Pan-African Congress. Both were declared unlawful during the Emergency of 1960. Other organisations which the state identified with these two organisations were likewise declared unlawful. Thus *Umkonto we Sizwe* and Spear of the Nation were proclaimed under section 1(3) of the Unlawful Organisations Act to be the African National Congress, and *Poqo*, The Dance Association, the SAA Football League, the Football League and the Football Club were proclaimed to be the Pan-African Congress. In addition, the Congress of Democrats was declared an unlawful organisation in 1962, the African Resistance Movement in 1964 and the South African Defence and Aid Fund in 1966. As at 31 July 1970, 568 former members of the South African Communist Party and the Congress of Democrats were listed in terms of the Suppression of Communism Act (SRR, 1970, p. 39).

Nor is legal activity exempt from state repression. Any political activity can be suppressed by the state on a basis of discretion, whether or not it forms part of the activities of an organisation, and whether or not it is lawful in itself. Through the exercise of these powers, individuals can be prevented from speaking, writing or meeting, and lawful organisations can be prevented from functioning. Here it will be attempted to show briefly the nature of these powers in relation to the forms of activity that an organisation of the working class might be expected to undertake.

In terms of the Riotous Assemblies Act and the Suppression of Communism Act, the state had 'broad powers to control and prohibit public gatherings' (Mathews, 1971, p. 234). Prior to 1974, the Riotous Assemblies Act dealt exclusively with meetings of more than twelve persons held in an open space, while the Suppression of Communism Act dealt with any gathering of any number of people held in any place. If these measures were read together, Mathews pointed out, 'it becomes plain that the Minister is unrestricted in his power to control meetings of all kinds' (*ibid.*, p. 235). Since the time that Mathews wrote, these powers have been expanded even further. 'Gathering' in the Riotous Assemblies Act has been redefined in the same general terms as in the Suppression of Communism Act. In some areas open-air meetings have been totally forbidden. Not only can the state decide whether a meeting shall be held and who may be present at that meeting, it also has extensive powers to decide what may be said there. The police are entitled to be present at any meeting, including a private meeting, if they *consider* that any law is *likely* to be contravened. Similarly, no 'procession' may be held without the permission of the magistrate as well as the local authority for the area concerned. The magistrate may withhold permission *if he has reason to believe* that such procession will endanger the maintenance of law and order.

State control over publications was equally extensive and sufficient to make it impossible for a working-class organisation to publicise its views. In terms of the Suppression of Communism Act the State President could prohibit the printing or distribution of any publication which *in his opinion* expresses, *inter alia*, the aims of an unlawful organisation or furthers any of the objects of communism. In practice, very many publications have been prohibited in terms of this provision. A subsequent provision went further still. Section 6 *bis* of the Suppression of Communism Act – inserted in 1962 – prohibited the registration of any newspaper (i.e. a periodical published at intervals of not more than one month) unless its owner has deposited an amount of up to R20,000 with the Minister of the Interior. An exemption could only be made if the Minister of Justice certifies that he has no reason to believe that prohibition in terms of section 6 will be necessary. If prohibition does take place in terms of section 6, the money deposited may be forfeited to the state. The effect, as Mathews put it, was that 'The establishment of an anti-government newspaper is now almost entirely in the discretion of the Minister' (*ibid.*, p. 75).

For a working-class organisation, therefore, the publication of a newspaper at less than monthly intervals was hardly feasible in practice. Other forms of publication were subject to the sweeping powers of censorship that the state possessed apart from section 6. Prior to 1974 these powers were regulated by the Publications and Entertainments Act of 1963 and the Customs and Excise Act of 1964. In terms of these laws it was an offence to distribute, display or keep for sale any publication which had been declared 'undesirable' by the Publications Control Board or 'objectionable' in terms of the Customs and Excise Act. (In 1974 the power of censorship became more sweeping still.) These powers have been very widely used. In 1972 the Minister of the Interior announced that 11,938 publications and sixteen other objects were on the list of 'banned' material (SRR, 1972, p. 80). Mathews summarises the position (1971, p. 213):

While the great majority of these [publications] have been banned under the obscenity provision of the laws, an appreciable

number consists of political and sociological publications. Up to
the present, restrictions upon the free flow of political information
and opinion have been brought about by the banning of publications
under the [Publications and Entertainments] Act rather than by
the prosecution of persons for printing or publishing undesirable
material.

In terms of the Riotous Assemblies Act the State President had the
discretionary power to prohibit the circulation of any 'documentary
information' in an area or to prohibit articles or pictures in the local
press. Furthermore, it was an offence to publish or disseminate any
statement by a listed person. 'Banned' persons could not be quoted
except with the permission of the state. Yet listed and 'banned' persons
by definition will tend to include the leading spokesmen for the mass
of the working class. In effect, the state can prevent an organisation
from making known its views in any 'lawful' way. In the case of a party
of workers, with views that are by definition intolerable to the state,
there can be little doubt that the scope for lawful publication would
be negligible.

Most sweeping and formidable of all, however, were the powers
reserved by the state for action against individuals. In general, state
action could take the form of 'banning orders' or of imprisonment
without trial. Against Africans, special powers were available of
'banishment' or 'removal' from urban areas. These powers were of an
entirely discretionary nature. If the Minister *was satisfied* that a person
was engaging in activities furthering the objects of statutory communism,
he could prohibit that person from attending gatherings, confine him
to a given area, even to his own home, or exclude him from any area or
place, prohibit him from performing any act or communicating with
any person, or require him to report to a police station at stated intervals. This list is not complete; it only includes those powers that are
most frequently used in practice. The ' "standard" banning order',
Mathews notes, is 'usually a combination of the majority of the permitted restrictions' (*ibid.*, p. 77). The effect is to confine a person to
the district where he lives, forbid him to be in the company of more
than one other person at a time, and prohibit him from entering a wide
variety of places. Such places usually include 'Bantu areas', factory and
newspaper premises, schools and universities, and the premises of
various organisations, including trade unions and student organisations.
'House arrest', while more severe, is officially regarded as being a
'humane' alternative to prison (D'Oliveira, 1977, pp. 133-4).

A 'banned' person could be prohibited from taking part in the activities of any organisation. This provided the government with a simple, theoretically infallible means of crippling an organisation without declaring it unlawful. Every leader, every spokesman, every active member could successively be 'banned' until there was no one left to carry on the work. Legally, a 'banned' person has virtually no right of recourse against the opinion of the Minister of Justice. In practice, 'banning' has been one of the major weapons used by the government against its opponents. During the period 1954 to January 1960, 173 people were placed under restrictions of this kind, including at least thirty-six trade-union officials. As at 23 July 1971, a total of 274 people were subject to restrictions (SRR, 1971, p. 67). Not only 'banning orders' but also the threat of 'banning orders' could be used by the government as a means of intimidating and neutralising its opponents. Thus we read that during 1963 nine persons were 'warned that they might be served with orders of house arrest unless they abandoned their political activities' (SRR, 1963, p. 44); in 1972 the Minister of Justice told Parliament that one person had been 'warned by a magistrate to refrain from activities considered to be furthering the aims of communism' (SRR, 1972, p. 74).

At the same time, from the point of view of the state, 'banning orders' can provide no final solution to the problem of political opposition. A limited freedom of action remains, and determined individuals may use this freedom to continue their activity clandestinely. To achieve complete neutralisation nothing less than imprisonment will suffice. To allow an opponent no loophole for escape, imprisonment must be completely at the discretion of the state. If, subsequently, some infringement is discovered for which a court of law might convict, the prisoner can also be brought to trial. That this is the general approach of the government was revealed by the Minister of Justice in 1971. The power of imprisonment without trial, he explained in Parliament, is used whenever a person is suspected of being a terrorist or of having contact with or information about terrorists (SRR, 1971, p. 85): 'Wide investigations were often necessary before a case could be made out for presentation to a court of law. Communism could not be fought by the use of democratic methods, the Minister declared.'

This material need of the state for 'undemocratic' powers has been provided for by statute. The so-called '180 days' detention' - which took the place of '90 days' detention' in 1965 - was provided for in the following terms (section 215 *bis*, Criminal Procedure Act of 1955, as amended):

> Whenever in the opinion of the Attorney General there is any
> danger of tampering with or intimidation of any person likely to
> give material evidence for the State in any criminal proceedings in
> respect of any offence referred to in Part II *bis* of the Second
> Schedule or that any such person may abscond, or whenever he
> deems it to be in the interests of such person or of the
> administration of justice, he may issue a warrant for the arrest
> and detention of such person.

In sub-section (3) the period of detention was limited to six months.
On expiry of this period the prisoner could be re-arrested. No person
other than certain state officials could have access to a person in
detention. The conditions under which the prisoner is held were
determined by the Minister of Justice.

Even more sweeping were the powers of the state in terms of the
Terrorism Act. Section 6(1) provides, *inter alia*, the following:

> Any commissioned officer [of Police] of or above the rank of
> Lieutenant-Colonel may, if he has reason to believe that any person
> ... is a terrorist or is withholding from the South African Police
> information relating to terrorists or to offences under this Act,
> arrest such person or cause him to be arrested, without warrant.

In this case no limit was placed on the period of imprisonment. The
prisoner could be held at such place and subject to such conditions as
the Commissioner of Police may determine. No person other than
certain state officials could have access to or information concerning
any detainee. In the light of this section, Mathews concludes (1971,
p. 151):

> it is now certainly possible for persons to disappear without trace
> into detention and to remain there until they die. Even the fact
> of the detention itself may be suppressed, so that parents, children,
> husbands or wives are denied information. 'Disappearance in the
> night', that dreaded phenomenon of the police state, is made a
> reality by this law.

Because of the secrecy provided for in the section, little is known of
the extent to which it is being used. During 1972, for example, the
Minister disclosed that sixteen persons had been detained in terms of
the Criminal Procedure Act. Asked about detentions under the Terrorism
Act, the Minister replied (SRR, 1973, p. 78): 'Except to confirm that
a number of persons were arrested ... during 1972, I consider it not to
be in the public interest to disclose the required information.'

All these measures could be used at will against the members of a workers' organisation. Moreover, against persons classified as 'Bantu' yet further powers were available to the state. In terms of section 1 of the Bantu Administration Act of 1927 the State President may order the detention of any African if he is satisfied that such African is a danger to the public peace. In terms of section 25(1) of the same Act, the State President may legislate by proclamation in respect of the reserves. Thus, it has generally been declared illegal throughout the African areas for any person, without official permission, to hold or address any gathering at which more than ten Africans are present. Furthermore, any African (or even whole 'tribes') may be 'banished' by the State President from any part of the country to another. In the period 1948 to 1958, eighty-one Africans were 'banished' in terms of this section. By July 1962 the number had risen to 126 (SRR, 1959-60, pp. 36-7; SRR, 1962, p. 19).

Of special importance to the question of working-class organisation are the powers of the state to 'remove' Africans from urban areas on account of their political or trade-union activity. We have already seen that, in terms of the Bantu (Urban Areas) Act, 'idle' or 'undesirable Bantu' could be summarily arrested and 'removed' to a place decided by the Bantu Affairs Commissioner. 'Undesirable Bantu' included any African who has been convicted either under sections 10-13 of the Riotous Assemblies Act or under the Unlawful Organisations Act. Thus an African trade unionist or political organiser who had managed to escape conviction under these laws could not be declared 'undesirable'. To remedy this defect the following provision was added to the Act in 1964 (section 29 *bis* (1)):

If in the opinion of an urban local authority the presence of any Bantu in a prescribed area . . . is detrimental to the maintenance of peace and order in any such area . . . the urban local authority may order such Bantu to depart from any such area within a specified period.

Activities 'detrimental' to 'peace and order' are, presumably, even more inclusive than activities 'endangering' such order. Any active member of a workers' party, it is submitted, could be dealt with under this provision without hope of legal recourse. A possible loophole appears to be created by the reference to 'urban local authority' in section 29 *bis* (1) rather than to the Minister or the Police. It was also provided, however, that if an urban local authority fails to give effect to the 'objects and purposes' of the Act, the Minister of Bantu

141

Administration and Development may step in and either compel the local authority to act in accordance with his directions or exercise its powers himself.

The list of further measures by which the state could suppress opposition in general, and working-class opposition in particular, could be extended almost indefinitely. The right of workers to organise strikes, for example, was severely limited. In terms of the Industrial Conciliation Act, strikes and lock-outs were prohibited, *inter alia*, during the currency of any agreement, award or determination which is binding under the Act or for one year after publication of a determination in terms of the Wage Act. Strikes were also forbidden unless the statutory procedure for conciliation had been followed. Strikes not directly connected with the conditions of employment of the workers in question were totally illegal. Also, workers providing 'essential services' – such as municipal workers – were completely forbidden to strike. Similar prohibitions were applied in 1973 to workers classified as 'Bantu'.

Even on the rare occasion that a strike may lawfully be called, the workers' freedom of action was drastically curtailed and employers enjoyed every legal safeguard in their use of strike-breaking labour. The Riotous Assemblies Act prohibited any person from trying to compel another person to do something or to prevent him from doing something, whether by violence, by threat of violence, by 'jeers, jibes or like conduct', or merely by remaining 'near' the other person. Any attempt to put pressure on another person to stop work was an offence. Even pamphlets or statements attacking strike-breakers were prohibited. Picketing, in short, has been all but excluded in South Africa. The effect of chapter II of the Riotous Assemblies Act, Mathews wrote, 'is to prevent employees from using their position as workers to secure an improvement in their conditions. If they take any action that is likely to be effective they run the risk of drastic criminal punishment' (1971, p. 195). Even the 'Sabotage Act' could be brought to bear on major industrial disputes. The crime of 'sabotage' includes wrongfully and wilfully damaging or destroying any property of any person or the state, or attempting or conspiring to do so. It also includes illegally entering any land or building. To escape conviction, an accused person needs to prove that his action was non-political, not aimed at causing disorder or substantial financial loss, nor culpable in terms of the Act in any other way. Upon conviction the minimum penalty is imprisonment for a period of five years. The maximum penalty is death.

'Emergency powers' were yet another weapon available to the state for dealing with resistance on any major scale. By declaring a State of Emergency the State President entitles the state to legislate by proclamation. Regulations may then be made by the executive – also retrospectively – to provide for any circumstance arising from the emergency. Penalties of up to five years' imprisonment or a fine of R1,000 may be laid down in this way. The State of Emergency that was declared in 1960 gives us some idea of what these powers mean in practice. During the 156 days of the Emergency, 11,503 people were imprisoned without trial in terms of emergency regulations. Of these, only 152 were subsequently found guilty of any breach of law (Mathews, 1971, p. 224). In effect, the proclamation of a State of Emergency is the proclamation of state dictatorship: 'Whenever a court judgment has demonstrated that some shred of judicial control remained,' Mathews writes, 'the regulations have immediately been altered to exclude the jurisdiction of the courts' (*ibid.*, p. 229). In the final analysis, we must conclude, if a workers' party comes close to realising its demands, the situation will by definition amount to a State of Emergency from the government's point of view. When the existing legal system no longer serves its purpose of regulating the existing status quo, it can be suspended and the will of the executive can openly take its place. This is the ultimate factor to be borne in mind when considering the question of working-class organisation within the existing legal order.

If we view the measures that are outlined above, certain conclusions are inescapable. By 1970 the state was entitled to outlaw any organisation, to prohibit any activity and restrict or imprison any individual of whom it disapproved. In all of this the discretion of the Minister or other officials concerned was all but absolute. Of course, it may be inexpedient, or even physically impossible, to 'ban' each and every organisation to which African workers belong and each and every individual who calls for social change. On this point, however, we should have no illusions. If any organisation or individual is permitted to continue with political activity, it is only because the state has not yet found it necessary or advisable to intervene. Its implacable suspicion and hostility towards organised mass-based opposition has been demonstrated time and again. Even clearer than decades of official statements has been the actual development of the law in relation to the freedom of organisation. The tendency has been to close all loopholes in the blanket of state control. Two examples will suffice. In R. *v.* Ngwevela (1954 (1) S.A. 123 (A.D.)) the court upheld the defence of the accused,

a 'banned' person, to a charge in terms of the Suppression of Communism Act of having attended a gathering in contravention of his 'banning
order'. It was held that the 'banning order' was invalid because the
accused had not been heard prior to the order being issued. The result
was an amendment to the Act abolishing any right of persons to be
heard prior to being 'banned'. In S. *v*. Nokwe and Others (1962(3) S.A.
71 (T)) the accused had been acquitted on charges in terms of the
Unlawful Organisations Act of having performed acts 'calculated' to
further the achievement of any of the objects of the African National
Congress. The prohibition, the court found, did not extend to acts
carried out independently of the African National Congress. The reply
of the legislature was to amend the Unlawful Organisations Act and
prohibit, in addition, objects 'similar to' the objects of an unlawful
organisation.

Not only Parliament, the police and the executive play their part in
enforcing the network of 'security' laws, but so does the judiciary. It
is frequently argued that 'the South African judiciary is independent
and . . . its judges are not amenable to pressure from government,
public or any source' (de Villiers, 1964, Foreword). This may be true
in the formal sense that judges and magistrates generally require no
pressure to deliver the verdicts that are demanded by the state. Generally,
the outcome of political trials is assured by the wording of the law
itself. The independence of the judiciary consists of applying the law
free from pressures other than their duty to abide by the letter of the
law. Within the narrow limits that remain, it has been possible for
liberal judges occasionally to reach a decision that is in conflict with
state policy. The best-known example of this – on which, indeed, a
great deal of the 'independent' reputation of the South African judiciary
has been built – was the case of Harris *v*. Minister of the Interior (1952
(4) S.A. 769 (A.D.)), where the first attempt by the government to
disenfranchise coloured voters was held to be unlawful. The limits of
this 'independence', however, were quickly demonstrated. In a subsequent case the government's second attempt at striking coloured
voters from the roll was challenged. The same court found that on this
occasion all the requirements of the law had been duly met.

On the other hand, the self-same 'independence' of the judiciary
makes it possible for judges and magistrates to be outspoken supporters
of state policy, and encourages them to adopt at least a neutral or
uncritical attitude. This appears to be the only basis on which a former
judge of appeal, in full knowledge of the measures that are dealt with
above, could come to the following conclusion (de Villiers, 1964,

p. 58): 'It is clear, and it should be emphatically stated, that South
Africa is a democratic country where free speech prevails in its entire
ambit and spirit.'

It is entirely possible that a person charged with political offences
may be tried before a judge or magistrate sharing this astonishing belief.
Legally he is not entitled to object. He is presumed to receive a fair
trial before an independent court. Yet in reality the views of the
judge must inevitably affect the exercise of his discretion, not least in
the matter of sentence. In particular, it should be noted that in the
1950s the government deliberately resorted to a policy of political
appointments to the Appellate Division bench. As a result of its
experience in the case of Harris *v*. Minister of the Interior the government decided to create for itself a majority in the court of appeal. The
number of Appellate Division judges was increased from six to eleven,
and this was done, a visiting British barrister observed (quoted in
Forman and Sachs, 1957, p. 178):

(a) after [the] Minister of the Interior, Dr Donges, had said,
    'Unless Parliament can be assured that its Acts will not be
    declared invalid, it will be compelled to use the American
    expedient of appointing Judges who share its views.'
(b) in circumstances in which the Leader of the Opposition had
    said, 'The new Judges have been appointed in a manner which
    will result in making them focal points of political controversy
    and this will undermine the respect in which the judiciary has
    always been held.'
(c) in the face of a resolution by a majority of the members of
    the Johannesburg Bar, 'We are forced to conclude that
    the Government is moved solely by the hope that it will
    obtain the decision it desires from the new 11-Judge Court.
    This conclusion is confirmed by the fact that there are
    several Judges whose eminence, ability and experience are
    such that it is incredible that all of them should be passed
    over in any genuine attempt to strengthen the Appeal
    Court. Political considerations alone can account for their
    exclusion.'

For a workers' political party no legal protection could exist in
South Africa. Its activities, even its existence, would be subject to the
virtually unfettered hostility of the state. The available evidence leaves
us in no doubt as to how the state would act. Hudson, Jacobs and
Biesheuvel have stated the position concisely (1966, p. 126):

As Marx stated, 'A landless, rootless proletariat constitutes the
spearhead of the revolution.' More fertile breeding ground for
the development of Communism [than the aspirations of the
African working class in South Africa] is hardly imaginable.
The fact is that only by steadily developing the apparatus of a
police state can those aspirations be controlled.

The political system in South Africa, Mathews concludes, 'is best
described as authoritarian, [though] it is not without totalitarian
features' (1971, p. 297). The 'close and intensive system of control'
over the African population, 'which may be styled legal-bureaucratic
domination, makes it possible to keep direct coercion in the background' (*ibid.*, p. 298). The laws and machinery of government 'are
being used to consolidate the economic and social advantages, and the
political power, of a minority section of the population', while the
security system 'also serves the function of suppressing threats directed
against the political order itself' (*ibid.*, p. 299). The author goes on to
explain (*ibid.*):

There will necessarily be a confusion between attempts to
introduce political change and assaults against the basic order
when government is committed to securing the interests of a
group and to a policy of blocking social change. Such a
government is bound to regard pressure for change as an attack
upon society as well as a challenge to its own policies.

These views reflect a serious and deeply rooted error which is the
quintessence of liberal theory in South Africa. The crux of the error
is the distinction that Mathews draws between the 'economic and social
advantages . . . of a minority section of the population' on the one
hand, and 'the political order itself' on the other. 'Attempts to introduce
political change', we read, are *confused by the government* with 'assaults
against the basic order'. In terms of our own analysis, such a distinction
is false. In identifying the political order with the 'basic order', the
government hits the nail precisely on the head. Confusion lies not with
the government but rather in the 'liberal' assessment of the matter.
This becomes apparent when we look more closely at the reason that
Mathews gives for the repressive political system in South Africa. It
is used, he says, in the interest of a 'minority section of the population'.
Which 'minority section'? It is clear from the context that Mathews is
referring to the 'white' group; 'non-whites' are the victims of the
system (*ibid.*, p. 302). Even as a *description* of the situation this is an
over-simplification. To mention only one inconsistency, it leaves out of

account the administration of the reserve system in which not merely a few individual 'non-whites' are involved but an entire bureaucratic caste. As an *analysis* it fails completely. It offers us no explanation of the *nature* of 'white self-interest', which is said to be the reason for the system of 'legal-bureaucratic domination'. We are left with the impression that 'self-interest' refers to something that is common to the white population as a whole, shared by the gold-mining magnate and the motor mechanic alike. As such it becomes completely vague and abstract, without any definite content or definite demands.

At this point, therefore, the 'liberal' approach falls down. In order to become intelligible the notion of 'white self-interest' needs to be explained. Precisely which interests are the rulers of South Africa defending? We have attempted above to answer this question. We have proceeded from the fact that South African society is based on a capitalist system of production in which the capitalist class – for historical reasons consisting very largely of whites – has made itself dependent on unfree labour drawn from the black population of South Africa. The 'minority section', the 'group' whose interests are protected by the political and legal system, is essentially the capitalist class. Whites falling outside this class have at best a secondary function in the system and the protection of *their* interests (which are completely distinct from the interests of the capitalist class) is only incidental. The essential relationship in South African society around which all other relationships revolve is that between capital and the unfree working class.

The moment that we look at the notion of 'white self-interest' from which the 'liberal' analysis proceeds, therefore, this analysis is seen to be false. The distinction that it draws between the political and economic aspects of South African society is no more than an illusion. In reality the economic and political system in South Africa forms a single, consistent whole. The 'basic order' that Mathews refers to is a capitalist order with concrete, identifiable demands. It is this order, existing in a given historical setting, that has called forth the laws against freedom of movement and freedom of organisation which Mathews treats in isolation as the product of an abstract and amorphous 'white self-interest' and 'white fear'.

The weakness and inconsistency of the 'liberal' approach arise precisely from its failure to identify the 'basic order' of South Africa as a capitalist order, and to analyse the requirements of this order under the historical conditions prevailing in South Africa. Mathews thus ends by presenting the security laws as a more or less inexplicable anomaly. In contrast, we have tried to explain these laws as an integral part of the social system as a whole. The law, we have argued, does not distort, it accurately reflects the function of the state in South Africa. At the same time, the legal order is the outcome of a complex process of historical development. The state does not of itself enforce the interests of employers. It will only do so where capitalists as a class have established their political supremacy over workers as a class. The question of the law thus raises the question of political organisation. The nature of the existing state is explained by the political relationship of capital and labour to each other. By examining the nature of the political parties that base themselves on capitalist interests, we shall gain a more concrete understanding of the functions of the state. Conversely, when we turn to the organisations through which workers' demands are expressed, we shall gain some idea as to the alternatives that are available to the existing order in South Africa.

Chapter 5

Political organisation

In South Africa there has been little formal unity between the industrial and political organisations of the working class. Informal connections, however, have existed since early times. The ideas that have guided the working class, or sections of it, have generally been developed and expounded by political organisations. Leading trade unionists, as members or supporters of political organisations, introduced their ideas into the unions as well.

During the late 1930s and early 1940s this process was particularly marked. The struggle of the National Party to gain control of various registered unions was then at its height. Unregistered unions were affected by the split in the world communist movement between the followers of Stalin and Trotsky. African unions on the Rand, according to Roux, could at that time be divided into (i) unions controlled by the Communist Party, (ii) unions controlled by the Workers' International League (Trotskyist), (iii) a group of originally independent unions, led by Gana Makabeni (expelled from the Communist Party in the 1930s), and (iv) a group of unions led by D. Koza, originally with Trotskyist leanings, but claiming, in 1945, to be without political affiliations (Roux, 1964, pp. 333-4).

Since 1950, with the growing suppression of political debate, political tendencies within the working class have been forced into the background. The exception has been white racism, which received every encouragement. But political differences did not for this reason become any less definite or real. Traditionally, the major *ideological* contradiction in South Africa has been that between white racism and South African nationalism as expounded by the African nationalist movement. 'Liberalism' has vacillated in between these two positions, on the one hand upholding the material basis of white racism - the system of 'cheap docile labour' - while in words agreeing with certain democratic demands of the African nationalist movement. In *real* terms, on the other hand, class distinctions that cut across racial distinctions have always existed and are coming increasingly to the fore: 'The races,' writes Kuper, 'do not confront each other as solid antagonistic blocs' (1965, pp. 5-6). Property-owners of different races are discovering their common interests, while contrasts between the working and possessing classes within each racial group are becoming more and more pronounced. The theory of nationalism, however formulated, offers us no explanation for this historical development. It denies the fundamental nature of class divisions within the different racial groups. The theory of national identity as a basis for political unity, and the existence of social classes with fundamentally different interests, are irreconcilable.

Class divisions are explained by the theory of socialism. In this sense the major ideological conflict of the future lies between nationalism and socialism. Historical development will undoubtedly resolve this conflict in a decisive and concrete way. Here we are faced with it at the level of theory.

The South African Labour Party

Long before the 1970s the Labour Party was defunct. Yet the causes for its disappearance, foreshadowed in the development of the registered trade unions, shed light on the political relations of the present period.

The mass of workers in South Africa are unenfranchised. Thus parliamentary struggle is only of indirect significance as far as the South African working class is concerned. In 1971 less than one-third of workers outside the agricultural sector were enfranchised. No working-class parties existed that they could vote for. The South African Labour Party had collapsed precisely because of its failure to become what its name implied: a party of South African labour. Its policies at the best of times reflected the prejudice and conservatism of a narrow upper layer of workers, intent on preserving their own relative 'privilege' rather than on the advancement of the working class as a whole. Membership of the party was limited to whites. After the Second World War even these tenuous links with the working class rapidly dwindled away. The party increasingly reflected a middle-class, 'liberal' outlook. By 1953 it was left with 722 active members and two affiliated trade unions with a total membership of 1,200. In 1958 all its candidates were resoundingly defeated in the parliamentary elections, and the Labour Party disappeared.

Among the objects of the Labour Party had been listed a 'democratic and socialist commonwealth', qualified, however, as an 'ultimate achievement' (Carter, 1958, p. 475). The failure of the Labour Party can be traced directly to its equivocation as to its aims and principles. Historically the final parting of the ways between the Labour Party and the struggle for socialism took place as early as 1915. Confronted with the issue of supporting or opposing the British war effort, the party was put to the test. A choice had to be made between imperial loyalties on the one hand, and the lives and interests of the workers on the other. As in most other social-democratic parties, a pro-war majority was found. Adherents of the cause of working-class internationalism broke away and established the International Socialist League. From this stage onwards the socialist objective would be no more than a platitude as far as the Labour Party was concerned: 'There is no socialist party in South Africa,' wrote Marquard in the 1950s. 'The Labour Party had gradually become more liberal after the Nationalists had come to power; but it could not be called socialist' (1962, p. 182).

The inconsistent nature of the Labour Party was not limited to the level of ideology; it also revealed itself in practice. In the general election of 1920 Labour had claimed 13.3 per cent of the vote and returned twenty-one representatives to parliament (Walker and Weinbren, 1961, p. 330). Yet by 1924 the Labour Party had transformed itself into the junior partner of Hertzog's National Party. In this capacity it retained a semblance of political influence until 1933. Once sacrificed, however, political independence was never regained. In 1943 the Labour Party 'changed horses' and attached itself to the ruling United Party. With the tacit or active support of the United Party it retained a token delegation in Parliament until 1958. In that year the United Party withdrew its patronage and the Labour Party finally and ignominiously collapsed.

The significance of this collapse should be clearly understood. The allies on which Labour had depended for so long were pro-capitalist parties, making little pretence of upholding working-class interests. For a time the National Party appeared to take up an 'anti-imperialist' position. The Nationalist–Labour Pact of 1923 had been based on a platform of common opposition to 'big finance'. Reflected in this platform, however, were the fears and ambitions of the farmers and the urban middle classes, rather than the struggle of the workers. The opposition of the Pact to 'big finance' was little more than an election cry. From the point of view of 'big finance' itself, the change of government in 1924 was scarcely noticeable. Such basis as might have existed for a coalition with the National Party *against* the party of 'big finance', however, only brings out more sharply the role of the Labour Party from 1943 to 1958. Its new election pact was entered into *with* the party of 'big finance', the United Party. In this alliance the original role and position of the Labour Party were finally buried and forgotten. The history of the South African Labour Party can therefore be briefly typified, and its lessons are unmistakable. Turning its back on the mass of workers, the Labour Party aligned itself first with the small employers, then with 'big finance', until it was rejected by both. Sooner than reorientate itself towards the mass of workers even at this late stage, the party chose extinction.

The National Party

If the Labour Party lost its function as the vehicle of 'white labourism', what took its place?

By the 1930s, Carter writes, 'the Hertzog–Smuts policies and prosperity were satisfying white labour's needs and aspirations, [and] the Labour Party found very little on which it could make a distinctive and attractive appeal' (1958, p. 352). The Hertzog–Smuts government, and later the National Party, promised white workers the same advantages, on the same terms of racial protectionism, that the Labour Party offered. But these were bigger parties, hence more attractive than the Labour Party with its appeal very largely confined to English-speaking artisans. Thus the Labour Party became obsolete. The white workers, having been led into a pact with the Afrikaner middle class in 1923, to all intents and purposes remained there even when their leaders were expelled. It was this leadership without a following that formed an alliance with the United Party in 1943. The policy of 'white labourism' was appropriated by the National Party and carried into the Fusion government in 1934. It was continued by the Nationalist government after 1948.

Although there is little precise information on this point, surveys suggest that a majority of white workers vote for the National Party. Certainly the National Party depends on the urban working-class vote for its majority in Parliament. This support it has gained through a long, systematic campaign to separate Afrikaner workers from the

liberal and socialist tendencies that existed in the labour movement. A
leading role in 'white-anting' the established trade unions was played
by Nationalist politicians such as Dr A. Hertzog, later to be leader of
the Herstigte Nasionale Party, and Dr N. Diedrichs, later to be State
President. By 1948 the once-radical Mineworkers' Union had been
brought under Christian–National control. Immediately afterwards
a split was forced in the South African Trades and Labour Council.
In itself, none of this need have been decisive. Coinciding with the
political self-liquidation of the Labour Party, however, the Nationalist
onslaught effectively filled the vacuum which the failure of the Labour
Party had created.

The appeal of the National Party was not limited to workers, nor to
Afrikaners. Its more fundamental policy is reflected in its programme.
The party declares itself to be 'definitely opposed to any politics or
policy which is calculated or which has the tendency to promote class
struggle' (National Party, 1960, p. 15). It is pledged to (*ibid.*):

(a) inspire a feeling of common interest and mutual friendship
between employer and employee . . .
(b) in general to protect the civilised worker effectively against
expulsion by uncivilised labour and in particular the white
worker against expulsion from the area to which, by virtue
of his position and the living standard that is expected of him,
he is entitled.

The main thrust of this policy has been to maintain, under the style of
'Bantu homelands', the system of labour reserves on which South
African capitalism depends, and within this system to preserve a truce
with free labour on the basis of racial protectionism. This policy seeks
its theoretical justification in violent anti-communism. At the same
time, the National Party, as a coalition between capital and labour, is
fundamentally unstable. The growth of a capitalist class within the
Afrikaner population meant a shift in the balance of forces within
the Nationalist 'popular front'. Differences between the so-called
'verligte' and 'verkrampte' (bourgeois and petit-bourgeois) wings of
the party came to the surface from the mid-1960s onwards. By 1969
it was openly being said among white workers that the National Party
was no longer concerned with the interests of the worker and the
small man; it had become a party of capitalists. The National Party
ruled the country, it was said, but Harry Oppenheimer ruled the party
(Mackintosh, 1970, pp. 68–9). The division in the National Party has
been explained as follows (CIS, 1977, p. 54):

The 'verkramptes' represent mainly farming interests, and the 'verligtes' represent industrial interests with links with international capital. The interests of the verkramptes lie in keeping black wages as low as possible . . . . The verligtes, on the other hand, are more aware of the need to boost productivity and stabilise the black workforce by raising wages and granting concessions over job reservation and trade union rights. They also see the black worker as a means of limiting the power of the white trade unions and reducing the overall costs by upgrading Blacks into Whites' jobs, while continuing to pay Blacks at their traditional lower rates.

The conflict between 'verligtes' and 'verkramptes' is thus one of social class. The banker, the doctor or professor might have sufficient resources to survive the abolition of racial discrimination without personal discomfort. The less well-off farmer, the worker or small employer, on the other hand, sees little alternative to his present way of life. He has come to rely, materially and psychologically, on the existing system of social and industrial relations. Yet more fundamentally, as social crisis began to emerge out of the relative stability of the 1960s, the divergence between the 'verligte' and 'verkrampte' tendencies reflected the increasing perplexity of the capitalist class as a whole. Neither the traditional forms of national oppression, nor the reforms proposed by the 'verligtes', offered a clear and convincing solution to the problems facing the system. Under these conditions mutual mistrust could only harden into open hostility among the different classes of the white population. The conflict between 'verligte' and 'verkrampte' is reflected also in the 'outward-looking policy' or '*détente*' with certain African governments that the South African government has engaged in since the late 1960s. By the mid-1970s a considerable volume of trade – much of it furtive and unrecorded – was being carried on between South African producers and a number of African countries. Commercial goodwill, in a relationship of traditional hostility, or at least suspicion, called for the creation of political goodwill. South African businessmen and politicians who sought an improved relationship with their black African counterparts were encouraged to adopt a 'softer' position on racial discrimination at home. This tendency was not lost on the 'verkramptes', and tensions in the National Party became exacerbated.

The Herstigte Nasionale Party (HNP), emerging out of the 'verkrampte' tendency, tried to harness white working-class dissatisfaction on a platform of hard-line racism combined with opposition to big business, criticism of 'wealthy cabinet ministers', and a call for the nationalisation of the gold mines. Although the HNP gained an average 10.7 per cent of the vote in Afrikaans-speaking working-class areas in the 1970 general election, compared with 5.8 per cent in an upper-middle-class Afrikaans-speaking area, its support in the cities on the whole was minimal (Molteno, 1970, pp. 103–4). By 1970, we may conclude, events had not yet convinced the mass of white workers that the policy of the National Party ought to be abandoned. The dominance of the ideas of white racism among white workers depended on two conditions: in the first place, continued protection of their living standards on a racist basis; and in the second place, the absence of viable alternatives. In the 1970s, as we shall see, these conditions were to be seriously challenged for the first time in living memory.

Liberalism

The dominant attitudes of the international capitalist class towards South Africa are shared, to a greater or lesser extent, among the upper layer of the South African capitalist class and expressed in the form of 'liberal' parties and tendencies, as embodied at one stage by the 'left wing' of the United Party and, later, by the Liberal and Progressive Parties. At the same time, South African 'liberalism' has little in common with the classical liberalism of the rising European capitalist class. Under the twilight conditions of capitalism in South Africa it stands, not for national unity and parliamentary democracy, but for continuing national oppression in a form only slightly more sophisticated than at present. Its policies are based on the continuing fragmentation of the country. Its main resemblance to classical liberalism lies in its verbal appeal to liberal tradition. The term 'liberalism' is used in these pages because of the currency it has been given in South Africa; it is used, however, in a purely descriptive sense.

From the white workers' point of view there was little formal difference between the programme of the National Party and that of the 'liberal' parties. The United Party had always been pledged to maintain the 'civilised labour policy'. The Progressive Party likewise declared: 'No undercutting of wage rates by workers prepared to subsist at lower standards will be permitted' (Kruger, 1960, p. 108). The predominance of the National Party, however, is explained by historical development rather than by formal demands. By 1934, when the United Party was formed, Afrikaner nationalism had already established its credentials in the eyes of the white workers. The United Party and the Progressive Party have always been correctly identified as the parties of big business. By the early 1970s neither the United Party nor the Progressive Party could hope for a substantial following among white workers. On grounds of pure language prejudice a section of English-speaking workers supported the United Party, but not enough to give it a majority in Parliament.

After 1959, with the establishment of the Progressive Party, differences between the social bases as well as the political positions of the United Party and the National Party had grown relatively slight. From this stage onwards the Progressive Party was the major representative of business interests in South Africa and, as such, the leading exponent of a liberal alternative to the policy of the Nationalist government. Increasingly the Progressive Party found an echo in the 'verligte' or bourgeois wings of the United and National Parties; yet it remained the Progressive Party that embodied liberalism in South Africa in its most authentic form.

If the direct influence of liberalism among the white workers was small, its implications for the working class in general are great. Two key elements of liberal policy were concisely stated in the Progressive Party programme. One of the aims of the party was the development of 'a responsible urban non-white middle class'. Another aim was (Kruger, 1960, p. 108):

> the inclusion of skilled and semi-skilled Africans in the definition
> of 'employee' in the Industrial Conciliation Act; and the
> recognition of Trade Unions established for unskilled African
> workers under the control and guidance of the Department of
> Labour, until such workers have learned to undertake the
> responsibilities of collective bargaining.

Read together, these two objects call for the emancipation of the black middle classes and an upper layer of black workers. In terms of the franchise proposals of the Progressive Party these layers would be entitled to vote or have the prospect of becoming so entitled. If such a policy were to be carried through, an important realignment of forces would, at least in theory, result. A certain section of the black population, including a minority of workers, would be offered advancement within the capitalist system. It is less clear what would be offered to the masses. Any significant concession to them must involve first and foremost a substantial rise in their wages. In the absence of a corresponding rise in production this must lead to a collapse of 'white' wages or a collapse in the rate of profit or, very possibly, both. It is not difficult to see how employers, however liberal, would attempt to resolve a dilemma of this nature. One question that arises from the liberal programme, therefore, is the means by which the cost of free labour is to be cut if at the same time trade unions are to have the freedom of defending their members' living standards.

In theory, of course, a solution lies in the possibility of sharply increasing production, expanding the existing markets and making possible a rise in prosperity all round. The utopian nature of this theory, which had already been exposed by the early 1960s in the debate among capitalist economists (see pp. 13–16 above), has increasingly revealed itself in practice. Whatever the economic outlook may have seemed in 1959 when the Progressive Party programme was drafted, by the 1970s there was no prospect whatsoever of a boom of these massive proportions developing in the foreseeable future. On the contrary, the outlook was one of political and economic instability. Furthermore, even in 1959 it had been apparent that the policies of liberalism implied the abandonment of the existing constitution. By 1970 it had been established beyond any lingering doubt that electoral support for these policies was small. The dilemma of liberalism in South Africa will become clearer if we briefly examine its history in recent years.

The strategy of liberalism has been described as one of 'building bridges' between 'moderate whites' and 'moderate blacks' (Robertson, 1971, p. 115). In reality such bridges have tended to remain suspended in mid-air. J. H. Hofmeyr revealed the dilemma of liberalism when he wrote the following in 1946 in respect of hitherto 'moderate [African] intellectuals of the Professor Mathews type' (Paton, 1964, p. 435): 'We can't afford to allow them to be swept into the extremist camp, but I don't see what we can do to satisfy them, which would be tolerated by European public opinion.'

The Liberal Party, established by dissidents from the United Party in 1953, rediscovered this dilemma to its cost. Standing on a programme of moderate reform and calling for a qualified franchise, it found that this position was acceptable neither to the electorate nor to most African leaders. Increasingly the Liberal Party, shunned by the electorate, turned towards the 'moderate' black leaders. Its programme underwent a corresponding turn. By 1960 it was calling for universal adult suffrage and by 1963 it had recognised the link between political and economic reform. The party now described itself as 'social-democratic'. Its electoral support in the elections of 1961 had dwindled to 2,461 votes, while its membership had increased to between four and five thousand, of whom a majority was black. It had become a pressure group trying to keep contact with blacks who had not yet been 'swept into the extremist camp' (*ibid*., p. 217). As a result the Liberal Party incurred the growing displeasure of the state. In 1963 and 1964 a sizeable proportion of its leading members were arrested or banned; others left the country.

From this experience the Liberal Party drew certain inescapable conclusions. In 1953 it had been totally committed to parliamentary methods, explicitly confining itself to 'democratic and constitutional means' (Kruger, 1960, p. 104) to implement its programme. As it became evident that there was no possibility of doing this in practice, the Liberal Party abandoned its exclusive parliamentarism and came out in favour of extra-parliamentary forms of struggle such as boycott actions. Some members of the party went further, secretly organising themselves into the African Resistance Movement and resorting to sabotage against government installations. With the enactment of the Prohibition of Political Interference Act in 1968 the Liberal Party, given its integrated membership, was effectively disbanded. Liberalism had run a full cycle in the course of fifteen years.

In 1959 a new cycle was begun when another group of liberals split from the United Party and established the Progressive Party. Based in the wealthy urban constituencies and in the circles of big business, the 'progressives' had lost patience with United Party pandering to the fears and prejudices of the voters. The mass movement of the African people in this period put pressure on them to break with the die-hard conservatives. The Liberal Party, however, was no longer suited to their purpose. A number of right-wing Liberals likewise crossed over to the Progressives. As the Liberal Party before it had done, the Progressive Party stood on a moderate platform and called for a qualified franchise. Like the Liberal Party, it enjoyed only limited electoral support. In the election of 1970, it polled 51,760 votes (3.43 per cent of the total vote) compared with the 820,968 (54.43 per cent) cast for the National Party (Molteno, 1970, p. 100).

Yet important differences distinguished the Progressive Party from the Liberal Party. The Progressive Party enjoyed strong support in leading business circles; in the case of the Liberal Party the links had been ideological rather than material. Electoral statistics leave us in no doubt as to where the basis of the Progressive Party lay. In the wealthy urban constituencies which it contested in the 1970 election,

it gained an average 38.5 per cent of the vote. In poorer urban constituencies its average support was 20.1 per cent (*ibid.*, p. 102). Clearly
the Progressive Party was a far more serious proposition than the
Liberal Party had been. If the United Party reflected the interests of
a broad cross-section of the employing class, then the Progressive
Party was linked more exclusively to the upper layers of this class.
In a statement such as the following, Helen Suzman reveals much of
the *raison d'être* of the Progressive Party (Strangwayes-Booth, 1976,
p. 185):

> I can think of no other country in the Western world where the
> greatest employers of labour, and indeed, by far the biggest
> taxpayers and contributors to the State coffers, would be
> treated by their Government in the contemptuous and arrogant
> manner used by the Nationalist Government.

In essence the Progressive Party called for the freer use of African
labour and a programme of limited reforms which, while relieving
certain grievances of the African population, would be kept in the
bounds of 'the Rule of Law'. Alongside the reformist proposals approved by the first congress of the Progressive Party was 'the strong
emphasis placed by many of the delegates on the importance of not
upsetting the existing structure of South African society, reflecting the
deeply held views of Lawrence and Eglin on the necessity for gradualism'
(*ibid.*, p. 172). The Emergency of 1960 was the occasion for Helen
Suzman to make clear her party's ideas on the struggle against radical
change (*ibid.*, p. 182):

> the lesson this country should learn [is] that greater force,
> greater banning and greater disabilities lead to greater revolutions
> and greater counter-measures. Putting down a movement which
> is devoted to non-violent measures simply means that organizations
> which are devoted to violent measures will arise. Banning people
> does not mean . . . that ideas disappear: it simply means people
> go underground, that things are more difficult to control and you
> do not stop the rebellion that goes on in people's hearts against
> genuine grievances and genuine disabilities.

When all is said and done, however, there was, and is, no prospect
of the liberals coming to power by means of parliamentary elections.
Even while supporting the Progressive Party, the businessman knows
that the National Party will remain in power. In the view of the liberal
millionaire Oppenheimer, apartheid will only have to be abandoned

'in the end' (Legum and Legum, 1964, p. 119). Despite all 'urgent' warnings, political change is only envisaged in the relatively distant future. Progressive Party policy relates entirely to the situation when National Party policy, through causes other than elections, can no longer be maintained in existence.

This explanation is consistent with our conclusion that the policy of the National Party is to serve the interests of the existing capitalist class. The programme of the Progressive Party, in contrast, may be described as an emergency plan for the exclusive salvation of 'big business' at a stage when the interests of employers in general can no longer be preserved intact. 'Survival of the fittest' becomes the watchword at that stage. The 'non-white urban middle class' which has featured so largely in liberal policies since 1953 will then be called on to display its 'moderation' and 'responsibility' by rallying to the side of the bourgeoisie. They are expected to calm down unrest and to restore the Rule of Law in order to benefit from the concessions that are offered to them in return. The support of the white workers and even a section of the white middle class could, in such a situation, become dispensable – at least, according to 'liberal' theory.

The Progressive Party, however, has followed a far more 'gradual' course than the Liberal Party had done. Whereas the Liberal Party had adopted the demand for universal suffrage within a few years of its foundation, the Progressive Party would not begin to reconsider its qualified franchise proposals until the middle of the 1970s. The Liberal Party was a party of intellectuals rather than businessmen. It had been swayed by idealism and impatience to set the pace of change. The Progressive Party has been more conscientious in serving the interests which it represents. It has made no attempt to hasten the downfall of the existing political order; it has scrupulously kept itself in reserve against the day when through other, unavoidable causes this order will be threatened. Faithful to this function it did not disband in 1968 but continued 'under protest and compulsion' (Strangwayes-Booth, 1976, p. 222) as an all-white party. It has remained in existence for the purpose of 'building a bridge' to 'moderate blacks' at a time when this can be done. And if in the meantime it has remained suspended in mid-air in much the same way as the Liberal Party had been, it has done so with much greater self-assurance. The criticism and even the outright rejection which its programme encountered among the more militant black groups dismayed it very little. 'Although the ANC publicly demanded universal franchise', it was reasoned in Progressive Party circles, 'it might be willing to accept less if it could be convinced of the sincerity and good faith of the Whites' (*ibid.*, p. 169). After the banning of the African National Congress and the Pan-Africanist Congress in 1960, constraints on liberal aplomb grew even less. This is shown by the absurd claim that after 1961 Helen Suzman, as the only parliamentary representative of the Progressive Party, was 'the sole focus of the unenfranchised millions' (*ibid.*, p. 199). This, too, is explained in the light of the powerful interests that the Progressive Party represents, and the confidence springing from power.

The differences between the Liberal Party and the Progressive Party were therefore differences of degree. The one might be described as premature, the other well-considered. Both belong to the same political tradition and both were subject to the same laws of historical development. The Progressive Party, just like the Liberal Party, cannot hope to take power by means of parliamentary elections. Its basis of support is too narrow to permit it to govern except in coalition with a party enjoying popular support. A lasting coalition between the liberals and the present National Party is inherently unlikely. The mass basis for a Progressive Party coalition must be looked for beyond the existing electorate, i.e. among the black population. The key to such a basis, clearly, would be a close alliance with the 'responsible urban non-white middle class'. Liberalism, like Oppenheimer, must 'put [its] faith in winning over black and white moderates to join in a common front' (Legum and Legum, 1964, p. 118).

This perspective presupposes radical changes in the existing constitution and, inevitably, extra-parliamentary struggle as the instrument of such change. Just as the Liberal Party, the Progressive Party has no function in the absence of such a struggle. Whereas the Liberal Party had allowed itself to be drawn into the struggle prematurely, the Progressive Party chose the pragmatical role of cautiously awaiting developments. Its programme cannot be put into practice until such time as the existing constitution has been overthrown. Until such time capitalist interests are served by existing state policy. There is no cause for impatience except, as Progressive Party spokesmen so frequently point out, the radicalising effect of delay and frustration on potentially 'responsible' leaders of the 'urban non-white middle class'. This danger was confirmed by a 'responsible' member of the African middle class as early as 1961 (Mkele, 1961, p. 18):

It is true that the [African] middle class will act as a bridge
between the black masses and the whites, as in fact it is already
doing, but this will hold only for so long as the middle class still

clings to the view that it can still make an impact by reasoned appeals to the white man's own self-interest. That this is becoming increasingly difficult to achieve is evident enough. Already, the middle class is identifying itself with the African masses with whom it shares common disabilities in its fight against white domination.

Liberalism in South Africa thus corresponds to the position of the international capitalist class and Western governments. This is reflected in the viewpoint of 'British interests' in relation to the future of South Africa (Austin, 1966, p. 23):

> Disaster may sweep through the Republic: but in the end –
> however long it may be in coming – there would have to be a
> slow and painful period of reconstruction. It is then that the small
> number of South Africans who now try to preserve a belief in
> the values of a free society may be of inestimable value. They
> are there in South Arica today, and the West ought not to
> abandon them.

The words 'preserv[ing] a belief in the values of a free society' (*sic*) explain the otherwise futile role of a solitary Progressive Party Member of Parliament during the period 1961 to 1974 that has been so widely acclaimed in bourgeois circles both at home and overseas. At the time there was little urgency involved. 'Western democracy', as long as national oppression was effective, was at peace with the South African state.

To the working class, liberalism offers a programme of petty reform as opposed to the programme that a working-class party might be expected to advance. In essence it is hostile to independent working-class organisation. Proceeding from the principle that 'if moderate leaders are silenced, they will be replaced by extremists' (Strangwayes-Booth, 1976, p. 211), it sets out to cultivate the 'moderate leaders' and win them to liberal ideas. For such an exercise to have any object, it is essential that the 'moderate leaders' must control the mass of workers and sway them to support a programme endorsed by big business. In this process the workers' independent demands, to the extent that they differ from those of their employers, would have to be defeated, and their own spokesmen, to the extent that they challenge the 'moderate leaders', would have to be thrust aside.

It is inherently unlikely that the liberal programme will appeal to white workers. This programme relates to a situation where the existing security of free labour will largely have been destroyed; it represents an alternative which the majority of free workers regard with suspicion or fear. Liberalism in South Africa must stand or fall with the response of the black workers. This, in turn, must depend very largely on the extent to which the workers' own demands are translated into a coherent and viable programme. In the trade unions, as we shall see, the conflict between liberal and working-class tendencies is relatively far advanced. Politically, the conflict is less visible, since organisations reflecting the demands of the African workers tend to be suppressed. What remained of legal political activity among the black population at the beginning of the 1970s was dominated by groupings that operated in terms of state policy among the different 'ethnic groups' into which the South African population is legally divided. On the one hand, these groupings were an obvious area for 'moderate blacks' to work in, offering lucrative careers and protection from left-wing opposition. At the same time, they were areas of prime importance for liberals to explore and cultivate. A question that needs to be answered, therefore, is the extent to which these legal groupings had been able to take the place of the banned organisations and gain a significant following among the black working class.

Bureaucratic groupings

In terms of the Bantu Authorities Act of 1951 an elaborate bureaucratic structure was created for the administration of the African reserves. The Act made provision for the establishment of 'authorities' at the 'tribal', 'community', 'regional' and 'territorial' levels. The state was given the power to constitute 'tribal authorities' or to replace an existing customary authority where it found it 'expedient' to do so. The functions of the 'Bantu authorities' can be laid down by the state and provision is made for Parliament to finance them. The earlier 'Native Representative Council' which had been set up to represent urban Africans generally was abolished. The new bureaucracy was based on the policy of maintaining absolute 'ethnic' divisions within the African population.

Over the years this bureaucracy has been strengthened and the administrative fragmentation of the African people intensified. Only a few of the relevant measures can be mentioned here. In 1959 the 'Bantu peoples' of South Africa were proclaimed 'separate national units on the basis of language and colour' (Preamble, Promotion of Bantu Self-Government Act). Eight 'national units' were created. The 'territorial authorities' of 1951 were to be turned into 'governments' of 'national units' through the simple device of delegating more capacities to them. At the same time, 'commissioners-general' would be appointed in respect of the 'national units' to supervise local officials and watch over state interests.

A serious problem connected with this policy was the fact that only a minority of Africans live in the reserves; a majority live in the 'white areas'. Only a minority of Africans could effectively be segregated into 'tribal' or 'national' units; the majority must tend to coalesce into an undifferentiated proletarian mass. The reaction of the government was to try and create machinery for extending the rural divisions to the towns. Thus 'territorial authorities' or 'self-governing territories' were given the right to appoint urban representatives. In 1961 'Bantu Advisory Boards' were abolished in favour of 'Urban Bantu Councils'. Like the Advisory Boards, the Urban Bantu Councils were administrative bodies under control of the local municipal authorities, carrying out certain functions assigned to them by the latter. Unlike the Advisory Boards, however, the Urban Bantu Councils were not established purely and simply in respect of residential areas. They could also be established in respect of 'Bantu belonging to any national unit . . . and resident in any urban Bantu residential area' (section 2(1)(b), Urban Bantu Councils Act of 1961).

Efforts to involve urban Africans in the rural administrative machinery have continued undiminished over the years. In 1963, when the Transkei was proclaimed a 'self-governing territory within the Republic of South Africa', its 'citizens' were defined to include 'every Xhosa-speaking Bantu person in the Republic, including every Bantu person belonging to any associated linguistic group who normally uses any dialects of the languages spoken by what is commonly known as the Cape Nguni' (section 7(2), Transkei Constitution Act of 1963). In this way language differences were turned into national differences, though only as far as the Africans were concerned. In 1970 this policy was taken to its logical conclusion. The Bantu Homelands Citizenship Act laid down that 'every Bantu person in the Republic shall, if he is not a citizen of any self-governing Bantu territory in the Republic . . . be a citizen of one or other territorial authority area' (section 2(2)). Once again, in the case of urban-born Africans, language or dialect became a criterion of 'citizenship'. To formalise the position it was provided that every 'citizen' of a 'self-governing Bantu territory' or a 'territorial authority' shall be entitled to a 'certificate of citizenship' (section 5).

Finally, in 1971 the Bantu Homelands Constitution Act was passed as a *pro forma* framework for the establishment of 'executive councils' and 'legislative assemblies' in place of 'territorial authorities', and the transition of reserves to the status of 'self-governing territories'. By this time, it is interesting to note, the term 'national unit' had given way to 'nation' (Preamble). By 1972 'territorial authorities' or 'legislative assemblies' had been established in all the reserves except the Swazi, in each case with a minority of elected members and a majority of nominated members. In general, the nominated members of the legislative assemblies were state-appointed chiefs. The preponderance of chiefs over elected members was by no means accidental. In 1961 Prime Minister Verwoerd had opposed the institution of a majority of chiefs in the legislative assemblies. It is recorded that Chief Kaiser Matanzima corrected him on this. Matanzima 'contrasted the conservatism and stability of the chiefs against the Transkeian disturbances of 1960, and so won his argument in favour of a minority of elected members' (Kotze, 1975, p. 28). From a bureaucratic point of view, this argument was obviously sound.

In the case of those South Africans who are classified as 'coloured' and 'Asian' identical measures were impossible. No separate areas exist to which they could be legally assigned. At most they could be treated as separate groupings with segregated social institutions wherever this was deemed feasible. At the level of government, however, Parliament is sovereign in South Africa. Any institutions that may be created for the 'separate government' of any group of people in the country, no matter what they are called, must in fact be subordinate legislative bodies comparable with municipal or provincial councils.

This position was confirmed by the legislation providing for a 'Coloured Persons' Representative Council' (CRC) (1964) and a 'South African Indian Council' (SAIC) (1968). Like the 'Bantu authorities', these bodies would nominally represent important sections of the urban working class; like the 'Bantu authorities', however, they were in essence bureaucratic organs existing for the purpose of carrying out lesser administrative functions in respect of a given population group. The subordination of the CRC to the state was provided for in several ways. Of the sixty members of the council, forty were elected; the remaining twenty were to be nominated by the State President. No proposed law could be introduced into the council without the approval of the Minister of Coloured Affairs. Every member of the council, before taking up his duties, had to take the following oath (section 11(1), Coloured Persons' Representative Council Act of 1964): 'I . . . do hereby swear to be faithful to the Republic of South Africa and

165

solemnly undertake to perform my duties as a member of the Coloured Persons' Representative Council of the Republic of South Africa to the best of my ability. So help me God.' All 'laws' made by the CRC required the assent of the State President before they could be valid. The Minister of Coloured Affairs was authorised to make regulations in respect of the proceedings of the CRC and 'any other matter which he considers it necessary or expedient to prescribe in order that the purposes of this Act may be achieved' (*ibid.*, section 26). Finally, in 1975 it was added that whenever the executive or the council fails to carry out any of its powers or duties – apart from the power of legislation – the Minister of Coloured Affairs may carry out such power or duty in its place and in its name.

The SAIC occupied a similar position, except that it was given no power of legislation. The general function of this body was advisory and consultative. Its administrative function, relating in particular to education and community welfare, was concentrated in the hands of its executive committee.

If we look at the various organs of 'ethnic self-government' in the context of South African society, it is clear that we are dealing with *bureaucratic* organs of the South African state, as opposed to government structures existing independently of that state. We are dealing with the same bureaucratic organs that had been created in 1951, though in a somewhat changed appearance. In 1976 formal independence would be granted to the bureaucracy in the Transkei, and in 1977 to their colleagues in Bophuthatswana. Despite this, the reserves and all their 'citizens' would remain entirely immersed in the South African political economy. Power, as in every modern society, is concentrated in the hands of a central authority – the state. Nothing prevents the state from delegating any of its powers – even a limited legislative power – to subordinate bodies. Such delegation is indeed inevitable in a country as developed as South Africa. But does this objectively exclude the ultimate power of the state? In the examples of 'ethnic self-government' that we have considered the answer to this question is quite clear. Nothing has happened to change the fundamental nature of the South African political economy. Sections of the state apparatus have been given legislative powers that may *in theory* be unlimited, but which are in practice narrowly defined by their material position as subordinate elements of the overall social system. The role of the 'ethnic' bureaucracies is explained by Adam as follows (quoted by Buthelezi, 1974, p. 9):

Less important political decisions and bureaucratic functions
are delegated to various non-White local and regional self-
governing bodies, whose members work under White supervision.
Apart from the propaganda effect, these institutions prove useful
to the central authority in at least [three] respects: first,
upwardly mobile and politically ambitious individuals are
absorbed into its administration; second, immediate discontent
of non-Whites is directed towards members of their own groups
... and third, the real authorities are freed from burdensome
and tedious spadework and thus ... confine themselves to
'advisory' functions without losing factual control.

As far as the urban workers are concerned, the position is not open to
the slightest doubt. In theory as well as in practice the power that they
are directly faced with is the power of the South African state.

All that is significant about the sections of the bureaucracy that we
are here concerned with is the fact that their rule-making bodies are
partially elected. The result is that the principle of representation is
thrust into the foreground. This in itself is not unusual; elections also
take place, for example, in the case of municipal councils. It has never
been suggested, however, that municipal councils are in any way
independent, nor that municipal councils, as opposed to Parliament,
represent the people. Furthermore, elections to municipal and provincial councils are generally contested by the same parties that compete
for power in Parliament. Also politically, municipal or provincial
elections are a *subordinate* arena of struggle.

The Bantu authorities and the CRC, on the other hand, are totally
confined to the subordinate or bureaucratic level. Yet in their case the
fiction is created that they wield independent power. What, then, is
the significance of elections to the ethnic legislative bodies? Wherever
there are elections, there is some form of political competition. Within
the context of the 'Bantu authorities' and the CRC rival factions have
sprung up, competing for seats in the legislative councils. Even this
would scarcely have interested us had it not been for the peculiar
situation in South Africa. With the suppression of the mass organisations, a certain political vacuum was created. In this vacuum it became
possible for bureaucratic functionaries to advance on to the political
stage: 'The demise of the ANC and the PAC', as Professor Kotze
puts it, 'was simultaneous with the rise of new opportunities for
political action as a result of the clearer definition of the political
aspects of the policy of separate development' (1975, p. 22). The

question that we are thus faced with is the extent to which bureaucratic 'parties' have developed as political organisations of the working class.

Objectively, it is clear that no bureaucratic grouping can serve as a workers' political party. The organs within which they function - the 'Bantu authorities' and the CRC - lack the capacity to deal with the workers' demands. What remains to be clarified is the extent to which these groupings were *seen* by the workers as authentic organisations through which to express their interests, as genuine pressure groups and vehicles of change. In dealing with this question it will be convenient to limit ourselves to those groupings which claimed to oppose state policy. This refers in particular to the Transkeian Democratic Party, the majority in the Kwazulu legislative assembly led by Chief Gatsha Buthelezi, and the ('Coloured') Labour Party. In South Africa, every grouping that hopes to find a following among the black people is compelled to give at least verbal support to the workers' most serious grievances. Thus in the Transkeian legislative assembly a number of motions in support of democratic reforms have been unanimously accepted. They were supported, in other words, not only by the Democratic Party but also by the party of Chief Kaiser Matanzima and the nominated chiefs. Included among these motions were demands for the abolition of influx control and reference books, revision of the contract labour system, and higher wages for African workers. Even more general is the rejection of job reservation and the demand of equal pay for equal work. Given this substantial uniformity of demands, a better test of the different groupings is their objective relationship with the state. Given the fundamental conflict between the state and the interests of the workers, this question is decisive.

From this point of view, too, there is general uniformity among the bureaucratic groupings, but in a different sense. The basic feature of all groups is that, regardless of their policy on paper, in fact they participate in carrying out the functions of the state. This material relationship has inevitable ideological consequences. In 1973, for example, the Democratic Party supported military training for black South Africans on the grounds that the 'security of the State knew no colour bar' (Kotze, 1975, p. 72). For the state official, no matter in what capacity he serves, the 'security of the State' is of paramount importance. The moment he turns to the mass of the people, however, it is necessary to argue the opposite. Chief Gatsha Buthelezi demonstrates the impossibility of reconciling this contradiction. It is not true, he says in an attempt to justify his position, 'that all of us working

within Separate Development, *out of no choice whatsoever*, are necessarily enemies of either SASO or the Black People's Convention' (*ibid.*,
p. x). The gist of the argument lies in the words that are here emphasised. Not only does the very policy of 'working within Separate
Development' immediately imply the alternative of working outside
Separate Development, but Buthelezi is also compelled to acknowledge
the existence of organisations that are doing precisely that. Buthelezi
and his colleagues have voluntarily assumed responsibility for carrying
out the policy of 'separate development'. 'Working within Separate
Development', instead of outside it, is a clear political choice. Its
consequence cannot be evaded by denying that the choice exists.

As far as the political groupings of the 'homelands' bureaucracy are
concerned, the consequence of their choice is political weakness and
hostility to the independent movement of the workers. Political
insignificance is the natural attribute of the bureaucrat far removed
from the instruments of power. Lack of credibility is inevitable if he
tries to combine democratic slogans with service of an undemocratic
state. We must therefore expect the influence of bureaucratic groupings
to be limited among the urban workers; and in general this is the
position. For a number of reasons, Kotze indicates, most urban Africans
have no wish to involve themselves with 'homeland politics'. Many
regard membership of the 'homeland parties' as a 'waste of time'
(*ibid.*, pp. 112-13). The general nature of these parties can be gathered
from the following (*ibid.*, p. 74): 'The recruitment policy of the homeland parties is deliberately directed, in the first place, at traditional
communities in the homelands, and secondly at elite groups in the
homelands, with homeland citizens in White areas relatively poorly
attended to.' Even the turn-out to vote in elections to the legislative
assemblies is, in the cities, 'extremely low' (*ibid.*, p. 200).

Despite the priceless asset of legality, therefore, even the most
pretentious bureaucratic groupings could make relatively little impact
on the urban African workers. Impotence, conservatism and lack of
real support have further consequences as far as organisation is concerned. Kotze's study shows that 'homeland' parties are characterised
by authoritarian leadership and organisational confusion. They are
precluded by their very position from taking up a consistent position
in support of working-class demands, let alone waging an effective
struggle. For this reason we cannot regard them as significant political
organisations of the workers.

Chief Gatsha Buthelezi, chief minister of Kwazulu, is sometimes
regarded as a notable exception to this rule. Besides carrying out his

administrative function, he uses his position as a platform from which to criticise government policy. The liberal press in particular has discovered in Buthelezi an important spokesman of 'black opinion'. He has been credited with the insight that 'the difference between extreme poverty and extreme wealth could result in revolution' (Kotze, 1975, p. 167), and this, as we shall see, explains a great deal about his stand. We further learn of the 'great personal popularity' that Buthelezi, on account of his verbal opposition to state policy, has gained in urban areas. Fundamentally, however, there was nothing to distinguish Buthelezi from other 'ethnic leaders' who, like him, expressed disapproval of apartheid. Kotze, in describing the general characteristics of the ethnic bureaucracies and their leaders, found no reason to make an exception of Buthelezi: 'The approach of all homeland governments,' wrote Kotze (whose scholarship, according to Buthelezi, is 'in no doubt' (*ibid*., p. ix)) 'is utterly pragmatic, almost to the point of being devoid of any ideological content' (*ibid*., p. 111). In all the reserves 'the chiefs form a majority in the Legislative Assembly, and without exception they have been wooed by every aspiring candidate for chief ministership' (*ibid*., pp. 120–1). In Kwazulu this was unmistakably the case: Buthelezi's 'government' in the early 1970s had no party organisation behind it but depended directly on the support it received from a majority of chiefs.

Prior to 1973, therefore, the distinction between Buthelezi and the 'homeland' bureaucracy in general consisted very largely of intangibles such as the 'great personal popularity' of Buthelezi in the cities. Popularity and ideas, however, are of little account in the absence of political organisation. Buthelezi's tactics did not resolve the contradiction between democratic pretensions and service of an undemocratic state, between popular demands and carrying out an unpopular policy; on the contrary, they heightened it. By repeating popular demands he was bound to strike a sympathetic echo; at the same time, he drew attention to his own anti-popular function. It was only in the period after 1973 that Buthelezi would come partly into the open and embody his principles in the form of an organisation: Inkatha.

A position very similar to that of Buthelezi was held by the dominant group in the CRC, the 'South African Labour Party' (SALP). We should note at the outset that this title is misleading. The SALP is not 'South African'; it is confined to the 'coloured' section of the population. Likewise its connections with labour are obscure. Like the corresponding 'homeland' groupings, the SALP suffered from impotence and ambivalence: impotence, because it had no hope of access to the instruments of power; ambivalence, in calling for rejection of the CRC while at the same time calling for support in elections to that body. The SALP was formed in 1965, soon after the Act for the establishment of the CRC was passed. Its first leader was Dr R. E. van der Ross, an educationalist who later became principal of the University College of the Western Cape. In September 1969 the first elections to the CRC took place. Although some 570,000 people were qualified to vote, only 293,348 votes were cast. The SALP gained 135,202 votes and twenty-six out of forty elected seats. The more conservative Federal Party, generally regarded as being pro-government, received 90,025 votes and twelve elected seats. The twenty nominated members of the CRC, however, were all appointed from among the defeated 'pro-government' candidates, thus giving the Federal Party a majority of two. Among those appointed in this way was T. Swartz, leader of the Federal Party and defeated candidate in the Kasselsvlei constituency, who then became chairman of the executive of the CRC.

The tactics of the SALP consisted mainly of criticising government policy and boycotting certain parts of the proceedings of the CRC, for example official openings and the committee stage of budget debates. In 1971 the SALP proposed a motion for the 'total abolition' of the CRC and the transfer of its forty elected members to Parliament. Since that time the SALP has gained an absolute majority in the CRC. While friction with the government increased, the CRC has continued to function in the same way as before. No evidence can be found of the SALP campaigning on a programme of working-class demands, let alone organising workers into a cohesive and politically conscious force. Its chosen role of working in the state bureaucracy leaves it little or no scope for taking part in the extra-parliamentary mobilisation of the workers.

In general the role of the various bureaucratic groupings may be characterised as one of 'opposition within the system'. They had isolated themselves from the workers, whose demands challenge the existence of this system. All the different bureaucratic groupings may oppose the Nationalist government in a number of respects; none of them oppose the capitalist state. They support the system of free enterprise and within it they call for a number of reforms. In this their position is no different from that of the liberal opposition in Parliament. All that was lacking at the beginning of the 1970s was the getting together of like-minded groupings and their agreement on a common programme. At that time, however, no immediate pressure to do so existed, and fear of government disapproval no doubt played a part. As we shall see, it was the course of events from 1973 onwards that would provide the necessary impetus. Caution would be overcome, and the building of bridges between black and white 'moderates' would recommence in all earnest.

The Black Consciousness movement

Organisationally, the Black Consciousness movement began when African students broke away from the National Union of South African Students in 1968 to form a new body for black students only, the South African Student Organisation (SASO). According to Adam (1973, p. 150) there were two main reasons for the split. In the first place it was caused by the 'objective status differences' between black and white in South Africa, a difference that tends to reproduce itself in integrated organisations, giving a superior position to whites and an inferior position to blacks. In the second place it was caused by the 'different problems and perceptions of Africans' who had been studying for some years in segregated, ethnic universities.

The split was significant in that it stimulated the ideology of 'black consciousness' and led to further organisations being formed. Inevitably the question arose as to whether the Black Consciousness movement would take the place that the African National Congress and the Pan-Africanist Congress had occupied prior to their banning in 1960. Defining the role of the Black People's Convention – together with SASO the leading organisation of the movement – the secretary of the organising committee of the Black Renaissance Convention of December 1974 declared (*Reality*, May 1975):

> We refer here particularly to the political leadership vacuum
> which was left by the demise of the ANC and the PAC. None of
> the existing ethnically-based organizations have bridged the gap.
> Instead, they have absolutely thrown the Black people into
> political confusion. BPC the only non-tribal political organization
> needs to treble its efforts before it can even begin to give a
> semblance of being a people's mass movement. So far, it looks
> as if the choice lies between Bantustan politics and the BPC.

In judging the Black Consciousness movement by this criterion – the extent to which it became a 'people's mass movement' – we immediately come to the question with which we are more directly concerned: to what extent was the Black Consciousness movement in the process of becoming a significant tendency among the urban working class?

According to Kotze, the Black Consciousness movement was 'essentially a middle-class movement' (1975, p. 97). According to Adam, writing in 1973, black consciousness had not yet emerged from the circles of 'esoteric intellectual elites' where it had been born (p. 161). The Black Renaissance Convention of December 1974 had been attended by churches, church associations, chambers of commerce, leading figures in education, students and 'homeland' politicians. Membership, however, is not the only criterion of the nature of an organisation. No less important is its political orientation. In order to discover the social nature of the Black Consciousness movement we need to examine not only its membership but also its ideology, its programme and its strategy. We must discover the nature of the interests that are embodied in this ideology and programme; we must see whether these are the interests of the urban working class.

'Black Consciousness' may be defined, in general terms, as a reflection of the struggle of the black individual against domination and oppression by whites. The theory of Black Consciousness was defined as follows by Steve Biko (1972a, p. 5): 'The *thesis* is . . . a strong White racism and therefore, *ipso facto*, the antithesis to this must be a strong solidarity amongst the Blacks on whom this racism seeks to prey.' Its 'unadulterated quintessence', according to Biko, is 'the realisation by the Black man of the need to rally together with his brothers around the cause of their oppression – the blackness of their skin – and to operate as a group in order to rid themselves of the shackles that bind them to perpetual servitude' (*ibid.*, p. 6). Likewise, Adam defines Black Consciousness as a means of strengthening 'group cohesion' in the face of 'white imposed fragmentation', and ridding the 'colonized' of their 'slave mentality' (1973, pp. 154-5).

In the first place, therefore, Black Consciousness had the function of calling for unity as a condition for political struggle. Further questions now arise: unity by whom, struggle against what, on which demands and programme? Black Consciousness proceeded from the assumption that society is basically divided into racial groups. Society, according to Ndebele, contains three kinds of 'significant' groups: ethnic, racial and national. In South Africa, however, 'there is no nation . . . the greatest conflict is between the races' (Biko, 1972b, pp. 13-14). Conflict *within* racial groups is acknowledged by Ndebele but only, apparently, 'on the level of simple human relations'. The black racial group, according to this analysis, includes those South Africans who are officially classified as 'Bantu', 'coloured' and 'Asian'. These, it is assumed, form a culturally and/or politically homogeneous block by reason of the social discrimination that is practised against them in common. The conclusion is that black people, thus defined, should combine into a popular front in order to resist the popular front of whites by which they are oppressed on account of 'the blackness of their skin'.

The political programme of the Black Consciousness movement was unclear. It was acknowledged that South African society is capitalist and that racism was originally introduced by whites as a means of rationalising their power and position, though today they have come to 'actually believe that Black is inferior and bad' (Biko, 1972a, p. 4). Thus 'only economic equality can ultimately solve the racial problem' (Adam, 1973, pp. 157–8). Bennie A. Khoapa explained the economic implications of Black Consciousness as follows (quoted by Adam, 1973, p. 158):

> Racial integration requires economic integration, and this in turn, requires a recognition that the race problem cannot be solved without profound structural modification in the country, without real changes in the tax structure and the relations between the private and public sectors; without a redefinition of all values and a redistribution of income and power.

In December 1974 the Black Renaissance Convention defined the general object of 'black solidarity' in South Africa (*Reality*, May 1975, p. 10):

i. A totally united and democratic South Africa, free from all forms of oppression and exploitation.
ii. A society in which all people participate fully in the Government of the country through the medium of one man, one vote.
iii. A society in which there is an equitable distribution of wealth.
iv. An anti-racist society.

Demands of this general nature may have a profoundly revolutionary significance; on the other hand, they may equally be interpreted in a limited, liberal sense. This ambiguity may be seen as a result of the divergent interests that were gathered together under the umbrella of Black Consciousness. As to the abolition of racial discrimination in itself, there will be little disagreement among black South Africans. As to the precise and concrete meaning of 'economic integration', on the other hand, it is hard to imagine a programme of specific demands that would satisfy all sections of the black community: workers, students, businessmen, clergymen, teachers, and so on. Ndebele's argument that 'labour' and 'black person' in South Africa are synonymous (Biko, 1972b, p. 20) is clearly incorrect. A common economic programme of groups with divergent economic interests must of necessity be ambiguous if it is to avoid bringing out into the open those conflicts within the black population that Ndebele refers to in passing.

Besides its call for unity on a racial basis, the most outstanding feature of the Black Consciousness movement was its militance. The 'new black generation', writes Adam, 'expects that a ruling group does not give up its privileges voluntarily, unless pressured into doing so by the strength of its opponent' (1973, p. 155). According to the SASO policy manifesto, the efforts of white liberals 'are directed merely at relaxing certain oppressive legislations and to allow Blacks into a white-type society' (Wolfson, 1976, p. 50). Co-operation with white liberals was therefore rejected, while co-operation with whites in general was regarded as being tactically undesirable. The 'message and cry' of Black Consciousness was: *'Black man, you are on your own!'* (Biko, 1972a, p. 5).

In practice, therefore, Black Consciousness proceeded from the theoretical and political standpoint of analysing society primarily in terms of race, thereby obscuring the nature and significance of class. In the light of our own analysis such a standpoint must be rejected. The cause of black people's oppression is not, as Biko says, 'the colour of their skin'. The criticism levelled by Ndebele at white liberals, that their ideas are 'in essence intended to hoodwink the black man into believing that his only problem is the racial one' (Biko, 1972b, p. 20), might equally have been levelled at the theoreticians of Black Consciousness themselves.

If we reject the theoretical cornerstone of Black Consciousness, its further conclusions must likewise be called into question. The strategy of racial exclusivism flows directly from the theory of race. It may well be that there is a tendency in mixed organisations for whites to displace blacks by reason of 'objective status differences'. A tendency, however, is not a law. The internal regime of an organisation depends entirely on the organisation itself. To 'pre-empt' discrimination by excluding whites may be an understandable reaction; politically, it goes counter to the building of working-class organisation. A further implication of the theory of race is that black liberals have little in common with white liberals because they belong to different racial groups. Common economic interests, upon which the liberal policy is built, are in effect denied. If consistently adhered to, therefore, the theory of Black Consciousness must lead to serious miscalculations. Its programme and its strategy will not correspond to the developments that actually take place.

The strategy of the Black Consciousness movement necessarily excludes collaboration with the state. On the other hand, the amorphous programme of Black Consciousness is supported by figures 'within Separate Development' such as Gatsha Buthelezi. Such support is officially repudiated. In 1972 the president of SASO, T. Sono, was expelled from the organisation for arguing in favour of co-operating with supporters of Black Consciousness inside the state bureaucracy. In 1974, on the other hand, Buthelezi would allege that 'There is a lot of behind-the-scenes contact despite the differences in tactics. In principle, we believe in the same things and have the same goals which we are trying to accomplish in different ways' (Kotze, 1975, p. x).

In general, where there is political agreement, organisational links will sooner or later develop. It is difficult to see how the division between individuals inside and outside the state bureaucracy who agree on the 'minimum programme' of 'Black Consciousness' can remain absolute. It is thus to be expected that those who reject an alliance of this nature will be forced to define the political reasons for their tactical differences more clearly. A programme of Black Consciousness that can be furthered by collaboration with the state is by definition a relatively limited programme. Those who reject such collaboration in advance, on the other hand, can only be impelled by a more radical interpretation of Black Consciousness and the knowledge that their unspoken demands will meet with outright rejection in official circles. Thus there emerged in broad outline a 'right wing' of the Black Consciousness movement, tending towards limited demands of a liberal or middle-class nature, and a 'left wing' with more radical ideas, capable of reflecting the demands of the black workers, and ultimately, indeed, with no possible basis of support outside the black working class. In 1972, however, these differences were as yet unclear. The 'left wing' deferred to the 'right wing', apparently in the belief that political uniformity must be maintained in the interests of organisational unity. The position that the movement as a whole put forward was thus essentially reformist.

To what extent did the Black Consciousness movement succeed in winning working-class support? In 1972 SASO decided to establish organisations of black workers, and in 1971 had already launched a scheme 'to put students in employment to experience working conditions that will enable SASO to advise workers on their problems' (Kotze, 1975, p. 184). A pilot scheme, however, failed. The workers' organisation eventually launched under the auspices of the Black Consciousness movement was known as the Black Allied Workers' Union (BAWU). Of this body, little trace would be found in the history of working-class struggle from 1973 onwards. Its general secretary was D. Koka, a founder member of the BPC and former member of the Liberal Party. While described as a 'nascent umbrella organisation', BAWU had no more than 'several hundred members' at a time when tens of thousands of African workers were streaming to join trade unions (M. A. du Toit, 1976, pp. 43-4).

The reasons for the relative obscurity of BAWU should be sought, in the final analysis, in its social and political orientation. It developed out of a white-collar organisation, the Sales and Allied Workers' Association. While this in itself need not have been decisive, BAWU turned for inspiration not to the industrial masses but to the ideas of the black intelligentsia. Adhering to the same abstract position as the Black Consciousness movement in general, it functioned as a subordinate organ of this movement. It approached the workers as blacks with general 'black problems', rather than as workers with specific interests and demands distinct from those of other classes in the black community. Thus BAWU, according to the *Review of African Political Economy* (September–December 1976, p. 111), 'does not organise and operate at shop-floor or industry level. Unlike SACTU . . . it has not striven to make the link between economic and political struggle; it has also stressed productivity and pride rather than class struggle.' Refracted through the Black Consciousness movement, the intention of SASO to join hands with the workers has resulted, instead, in BAWU – an organisation for, rather than of, the workers.

The contradictory position of the Black Consciousness movement in relation to the workers' movement is further explained by Ndebele. The black middle class, he states, is 'obsessed with capitalist values' and has 'no political commitment' (Biko, 1972b, p. 22). At the same time, surprisingly, Ndebele asserts that 'This is a group that should be in the forefront of a black renaissance in South Africa' (*ibid.*, p. 23). It must 'come nearer' to the workers, since the workers can give them 'genuine support', as opposed to white liberals who can give them no 'genuine support'. As for the black workers, Ndebele on the eve of the Durban strikes found them 'to some extent conscious' but with their dissatisfaction 'only feebly and vaguely expressed' and lacking in effective leadership. On the basis of such an analysis Ndebele's conclusion is inescapable (*ibid*): 'It is the educated middle class who can explain to the workers the workings of the system they live in, in order to channel this vast wealth of initiative towards the destruction of the system.'

It is difficult to see, however, in which way the ideas of Black Consciousness would have the effect of explaining to the workers 'the workings of the system they live in'. Rather, the incorrectness of its analysis and the ambivalence of its programme must create confusion. Also, at the concrete level of organising workers, the Black Consciousness movement had serious limitations. Its ideas and mode of explanation were highly intellectual. The essence of 'Black Consciousness', we are told, is a form of individual rebellion, 'an attitude of mind and a way of life' (Biko, 1972a, p. 6). 'I have to assert my *being* as a person', Pityana exclaims. While this feeling may be shared by black people in general, it provides no basis from which to address the problems of working-class organisation. Appeals for unity and common struggle are bound to meet with approval among workers, but in South Africa, as elsewhere, workers do not need to be told what they already know. The black man who has lately been led by racial discrimination to discover, in the words of Biko, 'the need to rally together', is likely to belong to the intelligentsia or the middle classes. The worker discovered this long ago through his experience of wage labour.

In general, intellectuals in the labour movement have the function of making available to the working class certain specialised skills and knowledge to which workers themselves have little access. This, however, must either take place on the terms desired by the workers, or it must lead to conflict. The leadership function claimed by Ndebele for the black middle class in general – a class 'obsessed with capitalist values' – is clearly unrealistic. On the contrary, it is becoming increasingly clear that the roles should be precisely reversed: the workers, who provide the basic strength of the mass movement as a whole, must also provide the leadership and direction.

Criticism of the Black Consciousness movement has been voiced from different sides. In the absence of political clarity, Adam argues, 'Black Consciousness' seeks to build up unity on the basis of cultural or abstract values. Such methods tend to be 'artificial' – for example, trying to introduce African cultural symbols among South Africans of Indian descent. Unity in this sense is a 'remote utopia'. Adam draws the following conclusion (1973, p. 161): 'If an alliance between Africans, Coloureds and Indians is ever to receive mass support, as compared with the mutual flirtations of esoteric intellectual elites, it can only be on the basis of a common *political* cause and not *cultural* unity.'

Kotze describes the Black Consciousness movement as a 'middle-class intellectual movement with strong emotional appeal to the masses' and goes on to mention certain limitations arising from this background: 'Relevant to its middle-class nature,' according to Kotze, 'is SASO's failure to instil Black Consciousness ideals among peasants through literacy programmes' (1975, p. 98). He adds that 'the broad ideal and philosophical content of Black Consciousness is often regarded by [African workers and rural people] with little comprehension'; indeed, where a more 'parochial orientation' prevails, it may even be regarded as 'a sell-out to other ethnic groups'. Finally, he observes that (*ibid.*, p. 115):

> Failure to offer simpler explanations retards expansion of BPC as well as SASO. Both organisations have their origins among intellectuals and their roots in idealism, and in consequence are regarded as snobbish, elitist and exclusive not only by homeland leaders but by an increasing number of potential supporters, especially among the less well educated.

The Black Consciousness movement, we may conclude, was poorly fitted for the part of organising the workers moving into struggle. Its attempt to embrace different sections of the black population within a single 'black identity' has met with limited success. According to a survey (February, 1976), for example, only 2 per cent of 'coloured' people consider themselves 'black'; the majority think of themselves as 'South African'. Even among the youth of Soweto, according to a survey of 1970–1, only 13 per cent preferred to be called 'Black'; 64 per cent thought of themselves as Africans (Edelstein, 1972, p. 112). The gap between the spokesmen of Black Consciousness and the workers was particularly marked. While the general slogans of 'unity' and 'struggle' are bound to find an echo among workers, Black Consciousness offers the workers no basis on which to organise themselves. Under these conditions even the creation of BAWU can be regarded as little more than a gesture, an attempt at including black workers at least nominally in a movement that is not of the working class.

These weaknesses were the result of internal contradictions. On the one hand, the Black Consciousness movement displayed an essentially liberal programme, implying the tactics of moderation and conciliation; on the other hand, it followed uncompromising tactics, presupposing much more radical demands. This gave it the worst of both worlds. By its programme it was separated from the mass of workers, by its tactics from the mainstream of the liberal tendency. For the right wing of the movement, future progress was bound up with finding a road to the liberal bourgeoisie; for the left wing, with the black workers. It was essentially to the left wing that Adam referred in his perspectives for the movement – perspectives that have since been overtaken by events (1973, p. 163):

> Above all, what would appear decisive, is the only weapon which Blacks share,[1] their withdrawal of labour and its potential effects. A mobilization or pacification by nationally recognized leaders could make the difference in the degree of success of spontaneous strikes. In the absence of African union negotiators, official African spokesmen are likely to be called upon to play a mediating role. The potential mobilizing strength of Black Consciousness in effecting real change of the fossilized South African structure would seem to lie first and foremost in such eventualities. The test of the most appropriate Black tactics and strategies is yet to come.

Illegal organisation

Of the various organisations that were legally permitted to exist in South Africa at the beginning of the 1970s not one could be regarded as capable of leading the mass of workers towards the realisation of their demands. Even those organisations that were critical of state policy lacked the programme, the strategy and the orientation that are required for such a role. This is in accordance with our finding that the state will tend to suppress any political organisation that sets out to mobilise the mass of workers on the basis of their own interests. By the 1970s a working-class party could only exist in a potential or embryonic form, that is to say, underground or in exile. Underground organisation during the period in question was very largely absent. Potential working-class parties existed principally in the form of exiled leaderships. This presents us with obvious difficulties in establishing the nature and significance of the organisations concerned. Our analysis must be based mainly on the anticipation of future events. In each case the question is whether the leadership, once it returns to South Africa, would be capable of attracting working-class support. Two factors in particular must be taken into account in dealing with this question: in the first place, the history and tradition of the organisation concerned; in the second place, its programme and orientation. In general those organisations that are *known* to have struggled against the state can expect to attract large numbers of workers to their banner in the first hour of a revolutionary situation. Thereafter, their ability to retain and expand this support will depend on a large variety of factors, not least on their own conduct.

Different organisations exist in exile which, quite apart from the correctness of their methods, have established their credentials in the past as organs of struggle against the state. Of these the most important, historically and organisationally, was the African National Congress (ANC). Others were the South African Communist Party (SACP), the Pan-Africanist Congress (PAC) and the Unity Movement of South Africa (UMSA, previously the Non-European Unity Movement). Only the SACP explicitly claimed to be an organisation of the working class. Yet given the nature of South African society the slogans of 'national liberation' and 'armed struggle' that were common to all these organisations, were likely to find a response among the urban working class.

In terms of numbers the ANC in the late 1950s was said to have had approximately 120,000 members and the PAC in March 1960 about 30,000 members. The SACP was always a much smaller organisation, but distinguished itself by its relative stability and also by its name, which would always, regardless of its policy, be associated by workers as well as the state with socialist revolution. The PAC was characterised by a militant activism that inevitably found an echo among the urban masses. Especially younger men, according to a survey, 'believed that its brand of militancy would be most effective in shaking and perhaps even in overthrowing the government' (Feit, 1971, p. 88). The Unity Movement, on paper, took up the most leftward position of all. Yet its actual policy did not differ fundamentally from that of the other organisations, and its influence remained limited very largely to parts of the Cape Province.[2] The ANC stood closest to the line of political development among the unfree masses. It enjoyed a reputation and tradition of long standing. Its increasing militance from the late 1940s onwards, according to Kotze, 'resulted in a phenomenal increase of paying members' (1975, p. 9). Politically conscious workers, together with the radical petite-bourgeoisie, increasingly accepted the ANC as the major organisation to turn to in their struggle for social change.

By 1960 the ANC and the PAC, regardless of their differences and shortcomings from the working-class point of view, had conclusively revealed their nature as far as the state was concerned. The government feared, according to Feit, that radical African movements could 'always conjure up some sort of support, and this support could come in impressive numbers' (1971, p. 49). The ANC and the PAC had shown themselves capable of rallying tens of thousands of Africans in the cities. Potentially they had become organisations that the mass of the workers might seize as the instruments of their own liberation: 'The government,' Feit continues, 'seems to have believed that there was only one way it could cope with the threat: to physically remove the leaders' (1971, p. 49). This culminated in the prohibition of the ANC and the PAC on 8 April 1960.

Despite their prohibition, the SACP, the ANC and the PAC have not been disbanded.[3] Nor have they been effectively replaced. They have set themselves the task of continuing their work illegally and returning to open activity as soon as conditions permit. They have continued to carry on propagandist and other activities abroad. At the present time there is no reason to doubt that as and when they return to open political activity, each of the exiled organisations will regain a following similar to or – allowing for changed conditions – more substantial than their following of 1950 or 1960.

Activity inside the country by the banned organisations has continued, albeit at a very low level, throughout the 1960s and 1970s. This has been shown by recurrent prosecutions in terms of the 'security' laws. There can be no doubt that the state takes the banned organisations very seriously indeed. By their continuing existence, and by the practical impossibility of new organisations arising in their place, the SACP, the ANC and, to a lesser extent, the PAC and the UMSA, remain obvious rallying-points for black workers as and when open political activity becomes possible once again. In particular the SACP and the ANC must, therefore be looked at as potential mass organisations of the urban working class. How consistent were their programmes as a whole; how well, in terms of analysis, demands and strategy, did they answer to the workers' purpose? This question must lead us to consider more concretely the meaning of 'nationalism' and 'socialism' in South Africa. To what extent, in other words, was the working class regarded as an independent force, or as a subordinate part of the 'nation'? Was it proposed to mobilise the workers *as a class*, or as *part of a racial group*? Which demands and strategies were raised? These are the questions that must concern us – as they will concern the workers in due course.

The South African Communist Party

The SACP regards itself as the party of the South African working class. It is the only organisation that claims to have this function. Having existed since 1921, it has a certain reputation and tradition. The very name 'Communist Party' is accepted by many – including politically conscious workers – as being synonymous with revolutionary Marxist organisation. As such, regardless of anything else, the SACP must occupy an important place in our study.

In general the programme of the SACP contains two parallel and mutually contradictory lines of reasoning. On the one hand, the programme proceeds from the class structure of South African society and the role of the workers as a class. On the other hand, it proceeds from the racial structure of South African society and the role of the African people as a race. This leads, quite naturally, to two distinct and separate conclusions. On the one hand, it is concluded that South Africa must become a socialist state in which the working class will hold power. On the other hand, it is concluded that South Africa must become a non-socialist democracy, in which the African (or black) people as majority will hold power. The SACP then attempts to reconcile these conclusions by separating them in time. Non-socialist democracy is put forward as the immediate objective; socialism is relegated to an undefined future (PCP, pp. 26, 58). In effect, therefore, the SACP relegates its socialist or working-class character to the background and campaigns on the basis of 'nationalism' or race. This course of action it attempts to justify by its analysis of South Africa. This, its programme implicitly asserts, is the course that politically conscious workers in general should follow.

Historically, the ambivalent position of the CP is by no means new or unique. On the contrary, the questions to which it gives rise have been debated perhaps more thoroughly than any other in the past. In particular, we are reminded of the conflicting theories as to the nature of the Russian revolution, on the one hand what might be termed the 'social-democratic' theory of revolution in separate stages, on the other hand the Bolshevik theory of permanent or socialist revolution. To a remarkable extent this debate has anticipated the problems of the South African freedom struggle and helps to place these in historical perspective (Sills, 1968, p. 155):

> The differences between the Bolsheviks and the Mensheviks
> centered at that time on the question of which social class, the

183

bourgeoisie or the workers, should exercise leadership in the revolution. The Mensheviks maintained that since the revolution was bourgeois, the bourgeoisie should lead it, while the workers should lend the bourgeoisie their critical support. Lenin argued that the Russian bourgeoisie was frightened of revolution and willing to compromise with tsardom; consequently, only the working class, with the support of the peasantry, could accomplish this bourgeois revolution – despite and against the bourgeoisie. Trotsky agreed with Lenin's view that the industrial workers were the chief motive power of the upheaval, but he pointed out that precisely because of this the revolution could not remain bourgeois. He asserted that it would be driven by its own momentum beyond the limits set to it *a priori* by the traditionalist theory and that it would present a peculiar combination of two revolutions, a bourgeois one and a socialist one. Once the proletariat has assumed the leading role, it would be compelled by the logic of its own class interest to turn against the capitalists as well as against tsardom and the landlords; and it would proceed to establish its own dictatorship and to socialize the means of production. Russia, Trotsky predicted, would be the first country to set up a proletarian dictatorship. This was a startling and hotly contested conclusion. Shortly before 1917 Lenin arrived independently at the same conclusion, and this induced Trotsky to join the Bolshevik party. The idea of permanent revolution was embodied in the programmatic statements of the Communist International during the time that Lenin and Trotsky were its leading lights.

The SACP does not embrace the theory of permanent revolution. Theoretically it may be said to occupy a position in between Lenin's and that of the Mensheviks, on the one hand upholding a 'two-stage' theory, on the other hand asserting that even during the non-socialist stage it is the working people, urban and rural, who will lead society. It will be evident that the issues involved here are by no means 'academic'. We are dealing with the concrete strategy and programme that is being proposed for the labour movement of South Africa by an important group within it. Our task is to test the programme of the SACP on its merits. As a starting-point we need to consider the analysis of South Africa on which the programme of the SACP is based, and in terms of which it justifies itself.

The ambivalence in the aims of the CP can be traced directly to the ambivalence in its concept of South African society. On the one hand, it is characterised as a *capitalist* society, on the other hand as a system of 'internal colonialism' or *colonialism of a special type*. The question immediately arises of what 'internal colonialism' means. Our own analysis of the South African political economy has indicated nothing that fell beyond the framework of capitalism in the ordinary meaning of the word. What, then, does the SACP have in mind when it speaks of 'colonialism of a special type'? If we examine the SACP programme, we must conclude that the expression essentially refers to racial oppression within the capitalist state. The oppression of the black peoples of Southern Africa is regarded as the essential feature of colonialism. Since black South Africans remain the victims of oppression, it is said that 'colonialism' has continued. The economic transformation of South Africa into a modern industrial state is treated as secondary in analysing its social nature. The political fact that racism has been used as an instrument for the reproduction of cheap labour power by the early colonial masters and the modern state alike is taken as the real point of departure.

As such, the expression 'internal colonialism' is no more than a descriptive phrase. 'If this refers to the outrages which capital perpetrates against the mass of workers,' observes Williams, 'then it can only be added that the term colonialism itself loses all historic significance, and we may just as easily look upon Britain in the 19th century or even Germany under Hitler as a colony of a special type' (1975, p. 2). In the programme of the SACP, however, the notion of 'internal colonialism' is a vital element without which its conclusions would be left hanging in mid-air. Attempts have accordingly been made to place it on firmer foundations. In the end the only decisive basis for distinguishing 'internal colonialism' from capitalism in general would be to show that the *economic* relationship between capital and labour in South Africa is different from that between capital and labour in general. The programme of the SACP gives no hint of such a difference. Yet this economic distinction is precisely what Wolpe attempted to discover.

In its original form the theory of 'internal colonialism' assumed the existence of two (or more) 'nations' - the colonising and the colonised - existing side by side in South Africa. The fact that vast numbers of the 'colonised' people are employed as wage workers by (white) capitalists, and that this is the basis for the system as a whole, does not lead the SACP to recognise that South African society is fundamentally and unambiguously capitalist. Rather, the worker-employer relationship is treated – as far as *black* workers and *white* employers are concerned – as an aspect of 'colonialism'. Of course, this places the SACP at a loss in explaining the position of white workers. Thus it is said within the space of a single paragraph that the white workers share in the super-profits made by the capitalists out of the exploitation of non-whites, but also that the white worker, like the non-white worker, is subjected to exploitation by the same employers (PCP, p. 46).

Wolpe attempts to resolve this confusion by explaining the colonial element in which might otherwise have appeared a classical capitalist relationship between black workers and white employers. Not one, but two economies, he says, have existed in South Africa (1972, p. 432). These are the capitalist economy of the colonising nation, and the pre-capitalist economy of the colonised people. The pre-capitalist economy has the function of producing part of the subsistence of the African wage worker. The employer thus pays his workers less than a full wage, i.e. less than their subsistence. To this extent the African worker is only semi-proletarian, and South African society is only semi-capitalist. Wolpe's argument continues (*ibid.*, p. 425):

> The dominant capitalist mode of production tends to dissolve
> the pre-capitalist mode, thus threatening the conditions of
> reproduction of cheap migrant labour-power and thereby
> generating intense conflict against the system of Segregation. In
> these conditions Segregation gives way to Apartheid which provides
> the specific mechanism for maintaining labour-power cheap through
> the elaboration of the entire system of domination and control
> and the transformation of the function of the pre-capitalist
> societies.

Wolpe's conclusion is that South Africa does not yet constitute a unified capitalist economy. The major contradiction in South Africa, he says, lies between the capitalist mode of production and African pre-capitalist economies; this contradiction is still in the process of 'giving way to a dominant contradiction *within* the capitalist economy' (*ibid.*, p. 454).

This conclusion is problematical in several respects. In the first place it weakens rather than strengthens the theory of 'colonialism of a special type'. Wolpe's argument leaves out of account those workers who are classified 'coloured' and 'Asian', since the reserve system does not apply to them; yet according to the programme of the SACP these workers belong to 'oppressed nations' in the same sense as Africans do. Indeed, as the programme of the SACP makes clear, Wolpe's argument can only apply to one section of the African working class itself – the migrant workers. In terms of Wolpe's argument 'internal colonialism' is reduced to a relatively limited phenomenon that cannot explain the oppression of the black population as a whole.

Williams subjects Wolpe's theory to a more fundamental critique. He concludes that South Africa is a capitalist country and that racial discrimination is 'a reaction to the inner contradiction of capital and not to conditions of production in the reserves' (1975, p. 28). In political terms this must lead to a perspective of class struggle as opposed to racial struggle forming the basic conflict in South Africa. Slovo, in an essay on the nature of the South African revolution published in 1976, makes no mention of Wolpe's theory, nor does he acknowledge the contribution by Williams. Instead, he reverts to a characterisation of 'internal colonialism' as 'predicated on the purely superstructural features of the system' and, indeed, all but waves it away. According to Slovo, the concept of 'internal colonialism' is no more than a useful shorthand, and then only (with emphasis added) at one level (1976, p. 135). As we shall see, there was good reason for this shift. The more unmistakably the African working class emerged as an independent force and not merely as part of a 'colonised nation', and the more unambiguously the capitalist nature of South African society was manifested, the less convincing the theory of 'internal colonialism' became. As long as it is formally maintained, however, the theory of 'internal colonialism' can only serve to shroud in ambiguity the nature of South African society and all its elements. Are we dealing with a capitalist society, in which the workers must lead the struggle for the establishment of socialism? Or are we dealing with a colonial society, where the colonised people as a whole are engaged in a struggle for national independence, and the working class forms a subordinate part, albeit an important part, of the nation?

On the one hand, the programme of the SACP describes South Africa as an independent state; on the other hand, it says that an independent state of National Democracy will only be established by a National Democratic revolution (PCP, pp. 43, 61). Also, the nature of the working class, and the question of working-class organis- ations, are mystified rather than explained. It is not clear to the SACP whether the white workers of South Africa belong to the working class or not. (Slovo is inclined to regard them as part of the ruling class (1976, p. 122).) At the same time, it is said that the fundamental interest of all South African workers would be served by their unity with each other (PCP, p. 47). (Slovo, more consistently, dismisses this

as a nonsensical perspective, at least for the time being (1976, p. 120).)
Nor do racial divisions among workers, in the SACP perspective of
working-class organisation, end with the division between white and
black. It appears to be accepted that African, coloured and Asian
workers must also organise separately from one another, not necessarily
as workers, but together with other classes of their respective racial
groups.[4] The ANC is defined as the representative of all classes and
strata of the African population. The South African Indian Congress
(SAIC) and the Coloured Peoples' Congress (CPC), on the other hand,
were regarded as predominantly organisations of working people and
radical intellectuals. Yet no conclusions are drawn from this. The
workers are urged to organise 'nationally'. The only explanation which
is offered is that the African middle classes are exceptionally repressed.
Their interests accordingly lie in joining the workers and rural people
in overthrowing white supremacy. The position of other sections of the
black middle class is thereby left unclear. Nor is it clear, if the SAIC
and the CPC were essentially organisations of working people, in what
relationship they stood to the SACP, which regards itself as the leading
organisation of the working class as a whole.

These questions remain unanswered. In 1955 the ANC, the SAIC
and the CPC – together with the Congress of Democrats and the South
African Congress of Trade Unions – had combined into the Congress
Alliance on the basis of the Freedom Charter. Seven years later, when
the Congress Alliance had been destroyed by the state, the SACP
contented itself with expressing unreserved support for the organisations
concerned (PCP, pp. 63-4). Its perspective of separate racially based
organisations for different sections of the working class had thus
remained unchanged. Fourteen years later still, Slovo would explain
this by stating that segregated organisations had arisen historically
in South Africa. The SAIC and the CPC, however, had effectively
ceased to exist. Therefore, Slovo upheld in principle the future unity
of all black people, and the involvement of white revolutionaries,
under the leadership of the ANC. Above all, he stated, the special
role of the working class must be recognised (1976, pp. 173-8). What
this means in practical terms as far as non-racial working-class organisation is concerned, neither Slovo nor the programme of the CP
explains.

'Colonialism of a special type', we may conclude, refers to nothing
more than capitalism in South Africa in the form that we have analysed
it. If the practical question raised by the programme of the SACP is
whether workers should organise as workers, then the political question

is whether the labour movement should struggle for socialist aims. Theoretically, the SACP comes to the conclusion that the interests of the working class, indeed of working people in general, call for the establishment of a socialist society. Capitalism is giving way to the new and higher order of socialism in which the main means of production will be under public ownership (PCP, p. 29). So far the position is quite clear. In place of the many uncertainties called up, for example, by the slogan of 'Black Consciousness', the SACP advances the slogan of socialism, a slogan implying specific demands arising from the concrete position of the workers. As we have noted, however, this clarity is created only to be destroyed. The SACP ends up in a position that is fundamentally no different from that of the Black Consciousness movement. Its socialist objective, like that of the Labour Party (out of which it originally came), is relegated to an indefinite future. The concrete objective is defined as a state 'national democracy', the nature of which is no less ambiguous than the demands of the Black Renaissance Convention.

In the world of imagination 'national democracy' may conjure up visions of post-war Western Europe. The question, however, is what this phrase means in relation to South Africa. Economically, the basic meaning of socialism is public ownership of the chief means of production. Politically, it means that supreme power is vested in the organisations of the working class. The question may therefore be put as follows: in what way does 'national democracy' depart from, or fall short of, these basic attributes of socialism?

Economically, the SACP explains, profound changes are needed to guarantee any form of democracy in South Africa. In particular, the nationalisation of the key industries is called for. Furthermore, it calls for public control of all other industry and trade. These two demands, if carried into practice, would eliminate free enterprise and the free market as these exist in the states of Western Europe. The commanding heights of the economy will be brought under public ownership and thereby the economic foundations of socialism will be laid.

Politically, the programme of the SACP calls this entire perspective into question. The basis of 'national democracy' is defined as a leading alliance of workers and rural people (PCP, pp. 37-8). Even more explicitly the SACP states that only under leadership of the working class can the full aims of the 'national democratic revolution' be achieved (*ibid.*, p. 58). In a society where the economy is publicly controlled and where political leadership is in the hands of the working people, one would have thought, socialism can no longer be regarded as a distant objective only. The order that is built up under these conditions, it would seem, can only be a socialist democracy. Slovo, indeed, agrees that the 'national democratic revolution' may have to be carried *at once* to a socialist conclusion (1976, pp. 140-1). This takes us back to the theory of permanent revolution. If the industrial workers form the 'chief motive power of the upheaval', as was the case in Russia, then the revolution cannot remain bourgeois. It becomes a 'peculiar combination of two revolutions, a bourgeois one and a socialist one'. This reconciles the contradiction between a 'national democratic' revolution on the one hand and a predominantly working-class movement on the other.

The programme of the SACP, however, draws a firm line against any such perspective. It clearly separates the socialist revolution from the so-called central and immediate objective of a democratic revolution (PCP, p. 58). The Freedom Charter, it insists, is not a programme for socialism (*ibid.*, p. 62). As opposed to the perspective of socialist democracy being created by the struggle of the workers, the SACP holds out the perspective of a 'national democratic state'. The basic attributes of this society, as defined in a declaration by eighty-one Communist Parties in 1960, may be summarised as political and economic independence, anti-militarism, anti-imperialism and general democratic freedom (*ibid.*, p. 37). Such a society, it is added, will not be capitalist. Yet at the same time it will not be socialist. It will apparently remain suspended, for an indefinite period, somewhere in between capitalism and socialism, until such time as the socialist revolution takes place and the basic contradictions in society can finally be resolved.

Important questions are raised by this remarkable perspective. What is the reason for the 'delay' in carrying the workers' revolution to what has been defined as its logical conclusion? Even more important, how is it proposed to prevent the revolution from taking on a socialist character, if capitalist society has been ended, and the working class takes the lead? No direct answers are offered by the SACP. We are told that in most parts of Africa the needs of the people will best be met at the present time by the formation of states of 'national democracy' as a transitional stage to socialism (*ibid.*). Elsewhere we learn that this stage forms an indispensable basis for the advance of South Africa along non-capitalist lines to a communist and socialist future (*ibid.*, p. 62). The key words 'best' and 'indispensable' remain unexplained, thus leaving the argument incomprehensible.

Nor does the SACP explain how the delay of the socialist revolution is to be achieved. The demands for public ownership of the major industries and public control over the remainder of the economy are accepted as being essential if any significant redistribution of wealth is to be brought about. It goes without saying that public ownership of the means of production can never become absolute, nor is there any reason why it should. In Poland, for example, a country which the SACP regards as being 'socialist', private agricultural production is an important feature of the economy. 'Public ownership of the means of production' has no other purpose than to make possible the planning of production and exchange. Hence it is the major means of production – for example, heavy industry, transport and mining – that are destined to be nationalised. What remains is small- to middle-scale production, by definition incapable of affecting the overall economy to any significant degree, moreover competing with the major public corporations as far as output, wages and working conditions are concerned. Even such industry, however, must be subject to public control; and this, too, the SACP accepts. State assistance to independent producers, it is added, should only be given in return for a state share in their undertakings. Overall development of the country should be controlled and directed by the state (PCP, pp. 65–6). At best, a narrow and dwindling area remains for private enterprise, and even then major policy decisions are taken from the hands of the remaining entrepreneurs. It is difficult to see, under such conditions, what basis remains for a non-socialist 'national democratic' state, or how the creation of a socialist superstructure can be regarded as anything but an immediate, inescapable priority.

Slovo attempts to answer this by saying that *in the economic sense* the 'national democratic' state will not be socialist, because a private sector – in the highly qualified sense that we have noted – will remain, and because small farmers may have their own plots of land (1976, p. 147). This is unconvincing. If small-scale private production controlled by public authorities is all that separates 'national democracy' from socialism, then the difference is one of words. The SACP, in any case, does not rely on arguments of this kind. We are left to draw our own conclusions. If the existence of a private sector is to hold back the establishment of socialist society for any significant period, then its influence would have to be far more substantial than the SACP has admitted. A private sector in this sense would have to operate outside the economic plan, free from control by the working-class organisations. It follows that the organisations of workers and rural people would, in reality, *not* be leading or dominant in the 'national democratic' state. Employers would be in an equally strong position. The latter would, in other words, be given state support; if it were otherwise, private investment would cease.

The programme of the SACP, while avoiding these questions, lays down the blue-print for precisely such a situation. It insists that the deadlock is not to be resolved in favour of the working class. It excludes the *immediate* establishment of socialism; it emphasises the 'future' nature of the socialist revolution, and it defines the 'national democratic state' as an intermediate stage. This has serious implications for the workers. Implicitly, but quite unmistakably, the SACP programme calls for an active struggle against socialism by the state. It follows that political leadership cannot be left in the hands of the workers' organisations. Even if they succeed in overthrowing the existing state – a prospect made doubtful by the severe limitations that a programme of this nature would impose on the workers' struggle – the workers would be asked to surrender their power to a state with the function of protecting capitalist interests.

'Public control' in such a situation would be entirely different from public control in a state where the workers are in command. The outcome of the 'national democratic' revolution itself and the ability of the workers to defeat the capitalist class would be gravely imperilled by a strategy of this nature. Exposed to this form of attack from the rear, how far can the workers advance? Finally, no indication is given of when and how this uneasy deadlock is to be broken, and under which conditions the transition to socialism can take place in the end. 'Socialism', like working-class organisation, is left an abstract phrase, with no indication of how it must come about.

As an expression of working-class interests, the programme of the SACP thus suffers from serious inconsistency. On the one hand, it calls for a socialist society as the consummation of working-class demands. On the other hand, it calls for the preservation of free enterprise in an attenuated form, for an admixture of 'obsolete' capitalism in the new society that must postpone the establishment of socialism. Slovo is unable to resolve the difficulties into which this leads. On the one hand, he recognises the prospect of a continuous process along the road to socialism, or even of proceeding at once to socialist solutions (1976, pp. 140, 148); on the other hand, he appears to accept that a number of phases are necessary along the road to socialism (*ibid.*, p. 145). If even a theorist is driven by the programme of the SACP into subtleties and indecision, the labour movement is likely to be split. The SACP tells the workers that socialism is needed but only explains to them how to reach 'national democracy'. Yet in practice a decision will have to be taken, one way or the other, whether to leave each industry or institution in the hands of private owners, whether to hand it to state officials, or whether to assert the power of the workers.

A further inconsistency in the programme of the SACP is that to all intents and purposes it relegates itself, and working organisation in general, to insignificance. Slovo may speak of the special role of the working class in South Africa, but this, too, remains an abstract phrase. No indication is given of what this special role consists of. The SACP presents itself as the party of the working class. Its precise function within the movement of the masses, however, is obscure. On the one hand, the SACP says that its central and immediate task is to *lead* the fight for the national liberation of the non-white people and the victory of the democratic revolution (PCP, p. 58). On the other hand, it says that the struggle for national liberation is led by the African National Congress and its allies, whom the SACP unreservedly *supports* (*ibid.*, pp. 63–4). Given its unqualified acceptance of the Freedom Charter, support for the ANC leadership can be seen as the actual position of the SACP. The practical advice of the SACP to the working class, therefore, is *not* to organise politically as an independent force. Organisation on a racial basis is held out as the proper course of action. The justification for the existence of the SACP itself is thereby made unclear. Its function is to organise workers for socialism; this struggle, however, is not yet on the agenda. The SACP, we must conclude, sets itself no particular function at the present stage. Its task of preparing for the socialist revolution will only arise when the 'national democratic' state has been established. Until then, workers should join or support the ANC.

The ANC, according to the SACP, represents all classes and strata of African society. The interest of the middle class, it declares, lies wholly in joining with the workers and rural people (PCP, p. 50). At the same time, the programme for this alliance, the Freedom Charter, is regarded by the SACP as being non-socialist and 'national democratic' as opposed to being a working-class programme. Concretely, therefore, it is the workers who are called upon to join with the middle classes on the basis of a non-working-class programme.

This contradiction can only be resolved by applying our analysis consistently. If the interest of the middle classes lies in joining with the workers, then it follows that this should take place on the basis of a working-class programme. Similarly, if the conflicts of the present society cannot be resolved within a capitalist framework, then the

193

demands of the black middle classes, too, can only be met through the socialist transformation of society.

The SACP, however, draws neither the practical nor the political conclusions of its own analysis. For all the important demands that the programme of the SACP contains, it does not offer the labour movement any clear way forward. It denies the need for the independent political organisation of the working class in any concrete form. It subordinates the demands of the workers to the interests of the 'nation', i.e. other classes of the same racial group. Despite theoretical protestations to the contrary, it accepts race, not class, as the basis for organisation. Finally, as the outcome of this entire position, it renounces its own function as a working-class party in favour of the ANC. South African workers, according to the SACP, should follow a non-working-class organisation on the basis of a non-socialist programme.

The African National Congress

In the course of the 1950s the ANC emerged as a major rallying-point of the urban African working class. Yet the ANC did not consider itself a working-class organisation. It regarded itself as a national liberation movement, an organisation of the people. The first question that arises is the nature of the distinction that is involved here.

In general, working-class organisation means the organisation of workers on the basis of their own demands and strategy. A 'people's organisation' presumably means an organisation not based on the working class in particular but on the people of a given race or nation irrespective of social class. Its programme and strategy cannot be determined by the workers but must equally reflect the demands of other social classes. In theory, the demands that are raised will only be those that all classes have in common. Conflicting demands, no matter how vital, must be dropped from a common programme. In practice, the programme of a front of this nature will be determined by the leadership of the organisation; the leadership, on the other hand, will be subject to the pressure of the different social classes embodied in the front.

The ANC, by the early 1970s, could be characterised as a popular front that sought its support among the black middle classes, the intelligentsia and the workers. We must therefore consider the respective situations in which these classes find themselves, and the correspondence as well as the conflict between their interests and demands. We must also consider their relative social weight. On this basis we shall be able to assess the ANC as an organisation of the workers and the implications of its strategy and programme.

Racial discrimination has been defined as the extension of class discrimination. In this process many of the restrictive measures to which the African working class is subject were imposed on the black population as a whole. Yet the position of the workers and that of the middle classes remain different in many respects. These differences have always been visible to employers and the state. Indeed, the possibility of emancipating the black middle classes without emancipating the unfree workers is the crux of liberal policy.

Kuper (1965), in his study of the African middle classes and white-collar workers, points out that a high degree of class consciousness exists among these groups. Out of seventy-two African teachers interviewed, for example, all but one asserted the existence of upper and lower classes among the African population. Only one teacher found that 'the ANC had unified all the people: they know that they are one people and their sufferings are the same, irrespective of classes' (Kuper, 1965, p. 128). Objectively, the differences are no less clear. Mkele – a 'moderate' member of the African middle class, according to his own definition – explains (1961, p. 2): 'each [social] group develops the kind of culture that meets its needs most effectively in given circumstances and this would change if circumstances changed'. The African middle classes form a group of this nature: 'Being middle class,' Mkele explains, 'means that friends must also be middle class. . . . Middle class friendships are not confined to Africans . . . . Children are brought up in middle class values' (*ibid*., pp. 11-12). Yet the African middle class finds itself in a peculiar position (*ibid*., p. 12): 'But because of inadequate contact with [middle class] values *and because neighbours are invariably working class*, it is difficult for parents to instil such values. Thus the children pick up sets of conflicting values from their homes and from the neighbours.'

Of the 5,701,948 Africans who were regarded as being 'economically active' in 1970, 357,990 were classified as employers and 5,150,572 as employees (*South African Statistics*, 1976). Traders form an important section of the African middle classes; some 16,000 African-owned retail outlets existed as early as 1960 (Kuper, 1965, p. 80). Their position in many ways exemplifies that of the black petite-bourgeoisie in general. Kuper provides us with the following analysis (*ibid*., p. 288):

A rising commercial class appears to develop a great voracity. Perhaps the explanation is that its members are recruited from strata of the population with low and regular expectations of income. Trading breaks these norms of near-subsistence living and offers endless vistas of rising standards. There are now no limits to the ambitions of the trader and, the making of money being defined as a morally praiseworthy enterprise, he acts with a ruthless disregard for the interests of others. It is to be expected that many of the African traders will not scruple to exploit racial antagonism, first for the rewards offered by apartheid, and then, as they gain the strength to set aside the burdensome restraints, for the rewards of the wider society . . . . Why should he crouch beneath a racial ceiling on his endeavours, fixed in the interests of another group? Why should he not use his numbers for the conquest of power and the enrichment of his own race by means of state power, according to the precept and example of the Afrikaner nationalists?

Similar conclusions can be drawn in respect of other sections of the black middle classes. On the one hand, they are relatively privileged in relation to the destitute mass of workers and may be concerned exclusively with their own material advancement. On the other hand, they are the victims of racism and over the years have discovered that they cannot change society by themselves. Their protests and petitions are ignored by the state. Even when organised, the pressure that they can exert is negligible. In effect they must choose between accepting the status quo or attempting to harness the power of the workers as a vehicle of social change. A tendency has built up, Kuper indicates, to turn towards the workers. This tendency found its expression in the radicalisation of the African nationalist movement during the 1940s and 1950s. The leadership of the ANC as well as the PAC, however, has remained overwhelmingly middle class, and thus 'it is under bourgeois leadership that the main African political organisations move towards racial exclusiveness and violence' (Kuper, 1965, p. 392). Inevitably, contradictions must arise between the conservative middle-class element and the workers' drive for fundamental social change. The question that we are especially concerned with is how the relationship with the middle classes embodied in the African nationalist movement presents itself from the working-class point of view.

The ANC conceives of the struggle in South Africa as the struggle of an oppressed people in which a doubly oppressed working class forms a reinforcing layer (*FTF*, pp. 3, 16–17). In this conception the relation-ship of the African working class to the African people in general is unclear. Who are the African people, and what is this people composed of? Considerable light is shed on the matter by the relevant statistics. (All figures below, unless otherwise stated, are based on the census of 1970 and the source is the Department of Statistics in Pretoria.) In the first place we see that a majority of Africans live in the 'white areas' as opposed to the 'Bantu homelands'. The effect of the migrant labour system can be seen from the preponderance of women over men in the reserves. If African workers had been permitted to take their families with them, we may conclude, the reserve population would have been still smaller. As it is, the African population in 1970 was officially distributed as shown in Table 5.1.

Table 5.1 *Distribution of the African population, 1970*

	'White areas'	*Reserves*
Total	8,201,778	7,138,000
Male	4,483,367	3,059,000
Female	3,718,411	4,079,000

Source: *South African Statistics*, 1976.

More precise conclusions can be drawn if we look at the occupations of the 5,701,948 Africans who were regarded in 1970 as being 'econ-omically active'. (Of the remainder of the African population, some 7,235,000 were children under 15 years of age.) The first division that is striking is that between town and country. Officially, 2,260,386 Africans were engaged in the agricultural sector, 636,454 of these as labourers in regular employment and a further 649,567 being casual wage labourers. The remainder were supposedly farming in the reserves. It should immediately be noted, however, that these figures are inac-curate. The government itself has conceded that the number of Africans *actually* engaged in agriculture probably deviates considerably from the official figures. In 1977 the Minister of Planning and Statistics would go so far as to admit that not much importance could be attached to them (*Star IAW*, 4 June 1977). According to a study completed in 1976, no more than 1,680,000 Africans were actually employed in the agricultural sector, of whom only 814,000 were farming in the reserves. The remainder – assumed by the government to be active in agriculture – were in reality semi- or unemployed (*Financial Mail*, 16 July 1976). Furthermore, given the system of labour bureaux, it is only those workers who are legally registered that are counted. According to a paper published in 1975, the actual number of workers migrating to the cities is much higher. Some 20 per cent of all migrant workers were estimated to be illegally employed, and hence, as far as official statistics are concerned, assumed to be farming in the reserves (*Financial Mail*, 19 September 1975).

The number of farmers in the reserves is thus considerably smaller than official figures would indicate, while the number of urban workers is considerably larger. Even so the official statistics leave no doubt as to the nature of the urban African population: 2,130,478 Africans were recorded in 1970 as wage or salaried workers in the urban sectors of the economy; of these 585,851 were employed in mining and quarrying, 567,198 in the manufacturing sector and 213,117 in construction. Also the composition of the urban working class is clear. Of the Africans employed in manufacturing, 526,909 were production workers; of those employed in construction, 211,000 were production workers. In total no more than 94,302 Africans were employed in professional or administrative positions.

From the available statistics, therefore, a reasonably concrete idea of the nature of 'the African people' can be formed. About two-thirds of the adult population were economically active. The remaining one-third were mainly women, many of whom would be housewives. Of the working population probably some 14 per cent were farming in the reserves. These comprised only a small fraction – about 11 per cent – of the (official) population of the reserves. Of the remainder some were the families and dependants of the farmers. The majority, however, were undoubtedly the families and dependants of urban migrant workers.

About 5 per cent of economically active Africans were classified as 'employers'. Self-employed individuals appear to have been included. Probably a further 12 per cent were employed as labourers on farms. Only a small fraction – some 2 per cent of the working population – belong to the professional and administrative classes; as many again (95,359 people) were classified as clerical workers. At least two-thirds of the working population (60 per cent according to official figures) are thus located in the urban sectors or looking for employment. More than half of the urban workers were migrants; their wives and families, in other words, were mainly trapped in the reserves. Of this entire population a large proportion are semi- or unemployed. The official unemployment statistics (198,273 in 1970, 366,000 in 1973) are almost meaningless; unofficial estimates put the figure closer to two million (*Financial Mail*, 16 July 1976). As a percentage of the working population, this would amount to anything from 3 to 20 per cent.

Of economically active Africans, we may conclude, at least one-half (41 per cent according to official figures) were urban manual workers. These figures are far from satisfactory. Nevertheless, we can gain some idea of the relationship in terms of size between the African proletariat and the African middle class. Using the criteria laid down by Kuper, the African petite-bourgeoisie in 1970 probably comprised some 540,000 individuals together with their families. If we assume the sizes of families to be uniform, then the middle classes constitute some 10 per cent of the African population and the urban proletariat about 60 per cent. The 'African people' can thus be defined more precisely as a (predominantly urban) proletariat, flanked on one side by a dwindling class of peasants and, on the other, by an oppressed and even smaller middle class.

What is the nature of the political relationship between the middle class and the proletariat? Without the pressure that the working class can mount, the social system in South Africa is likely to remain intact. Not only through their numbers, but also through their concentration in large masses and their experience of common exploitation, the urban workers form a potentially cohesive and tremendously powerful force. Their social and political experience is greater than that of the fragmented and relatively isolated rural population. Even from a middle-class point of view, it is essential to formulate a programme in which the workers will recognise their own interests. In view of the strength of the workers any potential conflict of interest with the middle classes may seem unimportant. Due to education and social status, however, middle-class individuals tend to find their way more readily into positions of leadership. Until an experienced leadership from the workers' own ranks has developed, the middle class is likely to exercise an influence out of all proportion to its number.

Radical sections of the middle class will thus tend to link up with the workers' movement; but from the outset the question of programme is essential. If 'freedom' may mean two completely different things to the labourer and to the lawyer, then it follows that any alliance between them should be based on a clear understanding of what precisely the aims of the alliance are. Failing such clarity, conflict becomes inevitable at a certain stage. As far as the black population of South Africa and the ANC are concerned, what is the position?

Both numerically and in terms of political power, the working class is the predominant section of the African population. Ngcobo fails to understand this when he speaks of an imperative need for the proletariat to build an alliance with the peasantry and the oppressed middle classes (1975, p. 55). This statement is justified with reference to Tsarist Russia. In pre-revolutionary Russia, however, the working class formed only a small minority of the population and the peasantry an overwhelming majority. This was why, to the Russian workers, an alliance with the peasantry was essential. In South Africa the relationship is very nearly reversed. Here it is the rural people and the middle classes who are totally dependent on an alliance with the urban workers. Under these conditions any movement of the African people must be fundamentally a movement of the working class which is likely to be supported, conditionally or unconditionally, by sections of the middle classes and the small farmers in the reserves, in so far as the latter lack the power of enforcing their own demands. The advantage of such an alliance to the working class is apparent. The middle class has technical skills to offer, and the strategic value of a movement in the reserves running parallel to the movement of the urban workers would be considerable. But from every point of view it is clear that the African workers must have the predominant role in any such alliance.

Essentially the same applies in respect of those sections of the population that are classified as 'coloured' or 'Asian'. Within the 'coloured' group 13,677 employers were recorded in 1970, compared with 690,724 employees. In the case of the 'Asian' group the corresponding figures were 17,129 and 162,560. 26,766 'coloured' people and 12,489 'Asians' were in professional or administrative positions; 26,226 'coloured' individuals and 16,331 'Asians' had incomes in excess of R2,000 (*South African Statistics*, 1976). The 'coloured' and 'Asian' middle classes discovered their dependence on the workers in much the same way that the African middle classes did, and came to similar conclusions. The outcome was the Congress Alliance, which by 1970 to all intents and purposes had been superseded by the ANC.

Ngcobo's conclusion, which ascribes equal importance to the massive proletariat and the tiny revolutionary-democratic petite-bourgeoisie, is therefore incorrect. The conclusion of the SACP that a leading role should be played by the urban and rural workers must be treated not as a phrase but as a concrete prognosis of the future development of the ANC. In this light the Freedom Charter must be considered not simply as a 'democratic programme' but as basis for a working-class movement supported by sections of the middle classes and the rural population. The Freedom Charter provides no social analysis and lays down no strategy or tactics. Much of it is extremely general. Contained within it are the principal demands of the black population in general as well as the basic demands of the African workers in particular. The former may be termed 'democratic demands' and include the following:

1 universal adult suffrage
2 abolition of racialistic restrictions, in particular
    (a) in schools and official institutions
    (b) on the ownership of land
    (c) on land occupation
    (d) on membership of the police force and the army
    (e) in sport and cultural amenities
3 free rights to trade and to enter professions
4 freedom of speech, publication and organisation
5 abolition of the pass laws
6 freedom of movement
7 free and compulsory education
8 higher education financed by the state
9 adult education financed by the state
10 free medical and hospital services provided by the state
11 the abolition of fenced locations – a national housing scheme with full social amenities.

Interwoven with the general democratic demands are a number of demands arising specifically from the position of the workers:

1 the right to enter all trades and crafts
2 full trade-union rights and the right to collective bargaining
3 full unemployment benefits for all workers
4 equal pay for equal work
5 a forty-hour working week
6 a national minimum wage
7 paid annual leave and sick leave
8 maternity leave on full pay for all working mothers
9 the abolition of child labour, compound labour, contract labour and the tot system.

From all these demands it is clear that the Freedom Charter envisages not merely formal political changes but a radical transformation of the conditions of the masses. We have already seen that any substantial rise in the wages of African workers would have a 'deleterious net effect' from the standpoint of the capitalist economy. The demands of the Freedom Charter, however, go further than wage increases. Massive state expenditure would be required for the provision of the social facilities that are called for. In periods such as the present, however, state expenditure must be limited, not increased. Also the investment climate would be radically altered by the changes that the Freedom Charter calls for. As the Sharpeville and Soweto periods have shown, a substantial outflow of capital will accompany any signs of instability in the existing order. In itself this would mean rising unemployment, falling production and falling living standards. Fundamentally, the demands of the Freedom Charter are incompatible with the capitalist economy. It is therefore impossible to raise these demands without immediately answering the question of how they can be put into practice.

To the capitalist economy, therefore, the demands of the Freedom Charter spell crisis and collapse. Like the ANC itself, they are officially dismissed as 'subversive'. Also, from the liberal point of view, the ANC, 'Like every workers' movement . . . had many obvious faults. Its demand for a universal franchise was alarming to anyone who had watched a beer-hall mob' (Sampson, 1958, p. 103). Even a left-wing liberal like Sampson dismisses the seemingly modest demand for a forty-hour week as a 'wildly wishful thought' (*ibid*., p. 109).

The approach of the ANC itself, on the other hand, must obviously be different. The ANC has the task of bridging the gap between existing conditions and the democratic society outlined in the Freedom Charter. A society of this nature is irreconcilable with the privileges and power of the capitalist class. Therefore, the ANC has concluded, the implementation of a democratic programme in South Africa must involve the destruction of the existing social and economic relationships (*FTF*, p. 14). The capitalist system must be replaced by a system that will make possible the implementation of this programme. This perspective is concretely embodied in what may be termed the socialist demands of the Freedom Charter:

1 nationalisation of the mines, the banks and monopoly industry
2 public control of all other industry and trade
3 division of the land among those who work it

In this way it is recognised that any significant redistribution of wealth calls for public control of that wealth. The major sectors of the economy, by which the bulk of wealth is produced, must in the first place be taken into ownership by the state as public authority *par excellence*. On the other hand, if the mass of the people are to share in this wealth and power in the way that the Freedom Charter calls for, then control must be exercised by the masses over the state. Thus, in addition to

the demand for universal adult suffrage, the Freedom Charter contains
the following demand:

> All bodies of minority rule, advisory boards, councils and
> authorities to be replaced by democratic organs of self-government

This is a demand with extremely far-reaching implications which
remain to be translated into concrete terms. Suffice it to note that,
according to Ngcobo, it means popular control over every section of
the state apparatus including the security forces and the courts, after
the example of the Paris commune (1975, p. 45). In Marxist terms
power is to be taken from the existing ruling class and placed *directly*
in the hands of a population that is predominantly proletarian. This,
according to the theory of permanent revolution, places on the order of
the day the further unfolding of the socialist revolution.

Thus the Freedom Charter raises the perspective of an *immediate*
transition from the democratic struggle to a socialist solution. Socialism
cannot simply be equated with state ownership of the means of production. As a prerequisite for economic planning, it involves public
ownership of the basic industries. To guard against imbalances, it also
means public control of those less important enterprises which the
community at a given stage may leave in private hands. With the mortal
blow that the private sector is dealt, a point of no return is passed; no
alternative remains now except to carry forward the socialist revolution
that has in reality been started.

To the black middle classes, this perspective holds out no prospect
of belatedly sharing the privileges that the white bourgeoisie has historically enjoyed. It offers them no perspective of developing into a bourgeoisie. On the other hand, it offers the mass of the people infinitely
greater security and dignity than at present. It is clear, however, that
a section of the black middle classes will not be satisfied with this. In
the 1950s there were differences of opinion within the ANC as to the
question of socialism. In 1956, at the time of the Treason Trial, Mandela
denied that the Freedom Charter was a programme for socialism. His
reasoning was as follows (quoted by Robertson, 1971, p. 174):

> Under socialism the workers hold state power. They and the
> peasants own the means of production, the land, the factories,
> and the mills. . . . The Charter does not contemplate such
> profound economic and political changes. Its declaration 'The
> People Shall Govern!' visualizes the transfer of power not to any
> single social class, but to all the people of this country, be they

workers, peasants, professional men, or petty-bourgeoisie. . . .
The non-European traders and businessmen are potential allies,
for in hardly any country in the world has the ruling class made
conditions so extremely difficult for the rise of a non-European
middle class.

None of this, however, contradicts the substance of what we have said.
In terms of political power the middle classes, which are here presented
as a counterbalance to the workers, are in reality heavily outweighed.
Only outside intervention could equal the scales in their favour. Failing
this it is inconceivable that middle-class demands in conflict with
working-class interests – for example, demands for wage controls or
limits on trade-union activity – could prevail under conditions of
democracy as outlined in the Freedom Charter. The middle classes
would find themselves in the position of a small minority, no doubt
an important minority, but in no sense a ruling class capable of holding
back the social transformation called for by the Freedom Charter.

If in 1956 there was pressure on Mandela to deny the socialist
implications of the Freedom Charter, it is less clear what persuaded
Mathews to do so in London in 1965 (*ibid.*, p. 173) or Ngcobo in 1975
(pp. 47–8). Like Slovo, Ngcobo does no more than point out that
private ownership of the means of production will not be immediately
and completely abolished by the measures called for in the Freedom
Charter. The question of the nature and degree of public ownership
that will be called for under given circumstances is not taken up; the
nature of the *process* that the implementation of the Freedom Charter
is likely to set in motion is not questioned. Only if the demands of the
Freedom Charter are seen as absolutely static, without social causes
or consequences, can we comprehend Ngcobo's argument. In practical
terms, short of repression of the workers' movement, limits of this
nature to the development involved in the implementation of the
Freedom Charter are difficult to imagine.

The importance of the question of socialism from the standpoint
of the working class is clear. On the answer to this question depends
the degree of freedom and power that workers will enjoy in relation
to employers and the state. From the point of view of the working
class, the socialist content of the Freedom Charter, and in particular
the demand for democratic self-government, is likely to be overwhelmingly supported. Interpretations such as those of Ngcobo, on the other
hand, are likely to be fiercely opposed. The Morogoro conference,
which approved a document on strategy and tactics in 1969, did not

attempt to define concretely the unfolding of the revolutionary process. It has left this vital question for future clarification. Directly related to the question of objectives is that of strategy. Since 1961 the strategy of the ANC has been one of armed struggle. A new organisation was created to lead this struggle: *Umkhonto we sizwe* (Spear of the Nation). Its membership was drawn from the ANC, the SACP and other sections of the Congress Alliance. Two forms of armed struggle were decided on: organised sabotage in urban areas, and guerilla warfare in rural areas, to be supplemented by guerilla activity in what was termed urban areas of a special type (*FTF*, p. 8). This strategy was confirmed by the Morogoro conference of 1969. Yet by the early 1970s neither the sabotage campaign nor the guerilla struggle had been developed very far. The sabotage campaign had been a response to the mood of frustration and militancy among the African population; its aim was to show that a new policy was seriously being followed. In this it may have succeeded (although in this case the effect of its subsequent abandonment should also be considered). It did not succeed, however, in the further strategic aims of dislocating communications or making the government seem incapable of preserving order (Feit, 1971, p. 322). With the arrest of the leadership of *Umkhonto we sizwe* at Rivonia in July 1963, the sabotage campaign was effectively ended. Similarly, the guerilla campaign made little headway during the 1960s. At least 300 men, probably many more, were sent out of South Africa for military training abroad (*ibid.*, pp. 234-5). The problem, however, lay in bringing them back and establishing a base in the country. The difficulties involved are discussed by Johns. Among those who have analysed the matter, he concludes, 'there is virtually unanimous agreement that early efforts to mount armed struggle in South Africa were doomed to failure, and that future efforts have little chance of success in the short, if not in the long run' (1973, p. 294).

The reason for this lack of success is generally seen in the material and organisational superiority of the South African government. The ANC, on the other hand, took the view that guerilla warfare is resorted to precisely because an imbalance of this nature exists, and thus the development of guerilla operations in South Africa was not impossible. It recognises that a successful guerilla war cannot be started at will. Certain objective conditions must be present. These may be summarised as follows (*FTF*, p. 5):

1 disillusionment among the people with the prospects of peaceful or traditional methods

2 willingness among the people to make the sacrifices that an armed struggle involves
3 adequate political leadership
4 favourable objective conditions both internally and internationally.

Subjective desire, it is stressed, must not predominate. The preparedness of a few heroic revolutionaries should not be confused with the preparedness of the masses. Viewed in this light, the question is whether the ANC correctly assessed the objective conditions in 1961 when it deemed them ripe for guerilla warfare. In any event no guerilla war had been started in South Africa by the early 1970s. The resurgence among the workers took place without the stimulus that guerilla operations had been intended to provide. Experience proved that this method of struggle, though it had been the vehicle of the national liberation struggle in a number of colonial countries, could not automatically be repeated in South Africa. Strategy must be determined by the nature of the society concerned. In South Africa the masses on whom the armed struggle must depend are essentially the urban working class. Thus the question of strategy is, in the final analysis, a question of what is appropriate and what is inappropriate from the point of view of working-class organisation.

This brings us back yet again to the social nature of the ANC. In so far as the ANC depends on the urban working class, it is appointed to working-class methods of struggle. Mass organisation, collective decision-taking and concerted action are, from the workers' point of view, the essential elements of any political strategy. By their very conditions of life and work a certain objective discipline is imparted to their action. Finally, by their position in society, workers – especially those in key industries – can exert a decisive power. The same cannot be said of the middle classes. The professional man, the intellectual, the trader and the peasant do not find themselves part of a large mass toiling under uniform conditions and in close proximity to each other. Their working lives consist of individual rather than collective performance. The withdrawal of their labour has little effect on the economy. The middle classes cannot have the same awareness of collective power that workers have, because in general they do not possess this power. Nor is the idea of a disciplined mass organisation self-evident to them. To the middle-class individual the alternative will always exist of small, select pressure groups or of individual advancement. In the development of strategy by an organisation as heterogeneous as the ANC it is inevitable that these different tendencies should in one way or another manifest themselves.

The pre-1949 strategies of the ANC were unmistakably middle class in nature. They were generally aimed at winning concessions through negotiation between leaders. After the Second World War this strategy increasingly came under pressure from the workers. It was the turn to the working class that provided the basis for the new radicalism in the ANC. As Robertson puts it, 'The realities of . . . "the industrial jungle" must have impinged sharply on the minds of the young men who formed the [ANC Youth] League' (1971, p. 36). Even so, middle-class ideas remained dominant in relation to overall strategy: 'Illusory hopes for the "Cape Liberal" tradition, underpinned by the Christian mission background of many African leaders,' writes Johns, 'long persisted in the ANC' (1973, p. 296). Even the decision in 1961 to resort to sabotage and guerilla warfare did not in itself mean a break with this tradition. Even then, Johns (*ibid.*) continues:

> hope persisted that in some fashion the 'demonstration effect'
> of sabotage would be sufficient to move white South Africans
> to make concessions to African opinion. In South West Africa and
> Rhodesia the Namibian and Zimbabwean leaders were also
> initially sustained by the hopes that their goals could be achieved
> through the *deus ex machina* of external intervention by the
> United Nations or Great Britain respectively.

Feit makes the same point in slightly different terms: 'The leaders of the ANC or the CP were essentially cautious men, conservative in their planning and disinclined to rash action. If there was pressure for violence, it could come only from below' (1971, p. 316).

If the middle-class strategy of bargaining for concessions was forced into the background, therefore, its place was not taken by a working-class strategy based on political mobilisation - through underground methods if needs be - of the urban masses. In 1955 the ANC found itself at the head of a massive current of resistance to the removal of Africans from the western areas of Johannesburg. By confining itself to open forms of protest, Robertson observes, the leadership rendered itself impotent (1971, pp. 155-6). Similarly, with the Alexandra bus boycott of 1956, there was a 'danger that the leadership might lose control' (Sampson, 1958, pp. 213-14). Little or no perspective emerged of an organisational structure that would be genuinely in the hands of the masses. 'Discipline' was regarded as the property of leaders; the masses were in need of 'control'. Working-class organisation, it might be said, presupposes more or less the opposite. It presupposes a firm structure built up at rank-and-file level to which the leadership is subject. Even in the 1950s such an organisation could hardly have been built in the open. In the late 1950s Mandela had the foresight to draw up a plan for underground organisation. This plan, however, was not intended to supplement legal activity; it was meant to be used if the ANC were declared illegal. In general, therefore, not only the masses had to gain experience to prepare them for new forms of struggle; the leadership had likewise to develop.

By the end of the 1950s, the ANC concluded, strikes and mass demonstrations could no longer be used as instruments of struggle because they were being suppressed by the police (*FTF*, p. 7). While this may have been true of the 1960s, it cannot be taken as a general historical conclusion in respect of the period that followed. On the contrary, as the 1970s would show, conditions would re-emerge that would call forth strikes and demonstrations on an even larger scale than those of the 1950s. In 1960 the concrete question facing the ANC was whether (and how) to develop the organisation of the workers, or whether (and how) to continue its activities independently of the workers. Guerilla warfare was seen as a synthesis of these requirements. On the one hand, it is clear that such warfare does not involve the mass of workers. It is carried on outside the working class by small groups of selected military specialists. On the other hand, it was said that guerilla struggle should be aimed at mobilising, encouraging and acti-vating broader layers of the population. Without this, it is added, the guerilla struggle is doomed (*ibid.*, pp. 8-9). Guerilla war in this sense is unknown in South Africa and thus the discussion surrounding it is largely theoretical. It does not appear, however, that the contradiction between a mainly proletarian population and a form of struggle taking place outside the working class has been adequately resolved. The ANC itself appears to expect such warfare in the first place to activate the rural population (*ibid.*, p. 9). At the same time, it is inconceivable that a guerilla struggle in the countryside would leave the workers unaffected. The effect, however, may be contradictory. It could lead to passivity as well as to militance; it could encourage workers to await liberation by invading guerilla armies. In any event the effect will be indirect, in much the same way that the war in Ethiopia had aroused the African population of South Africa in the 1930s, or the successes of Frelimo and the MPLA would do in the 1970s.

In practice, therefore, guerilla war means a form of struggle inde-pendent of the working class. It means the removal of activists from the ranks of the workers and training them to fight as guerilla soldiers, not as leaders of the working-class rank and file. This must be seen as a question of policy. On the one hand, there is the policy of preparing for the mobilisation of the workers' movement with all available means, however limited these may be at any given moment. On the other hand, there are alternative policies which, wherever they may lead in the end, do not lead to the building up of working-class organisation. In the final analysis the policy of guerillaism is of the latter kind. The new mass struggles of the workers would be left to develop independently without guidance or support from the national liberation movement.

The questions involved in the political organisation of the South African working class have thus in no sense been resolved. Independent organisation is the only means whereby the workers can realise their latent power. Also in the programme of the ANC, the objective need for working-class organisation is reflected in a number of ways. The separation of armed struggle from the political context is rejected; the primacy of political leadership is asserted; educational and agitational work throughout the country is called for; active support from the mass of people is regarded as the life-blood of the struggle (*FTF*, pp. 8-10). The urban workers form the most vital section of the masses. Employers and the state are geared to the effort of coping with the enormous, concerted power of the workers. Dealing with lesser opposition will be relatively easy. In social terms the 'political leadership' that the ANC refers to can only mean the leadership of the working class. Concretely, this leadership must be given organisational expression in order to take effect. During the early 1970s the ANC remained the most obvious instrument at the disposal of the mass of workers in the effort to assert their power.

Viewed in this light 'armed struggle' can be accorded a more definite character and function. As working-class strategy, armed struggle cannot become significant until broad sections of workers have consciously decided to carry on such a struggle from among themselves. From the working-class standpoint political mobilisation is the way to armed insurrection, rather than vice versa. One question raised by the developments of the 1970s is the explicit and concrete working-out of this relationship - the relationship between working-class organisation and armed struggle in South Africa.

Our general conclusion may be formulated thus: whatever *subjective intentions* there may exist to the contrary, *objective social relationships* in South Africa are such as to turn any democratic organisation of the black people into an organ of the urban working class. To the ANC, the relationship to working-class organisation is not an *external*, but an *internal* one. Yet in order to play its role, working-class organisation must be developed as a *politically* independent force, regardless of its links with other, lesser groupings at any point in time.

During the early 1970s the tendencies discussed in this chapter were latent. The SACP, the ANC and the PAC were banned. Officially, all three organisations were regarded as dangerous and subversive without any clear distinction being drawn between them. Only at a later stage, under conditions of relative political freedom, will each of these organisations be able to demonstrate its nature decisively in the eyes of the working class and the world at large. The resurgence of working-class activity from 1973 onwards created the early beginnings of such a situation, for the first time in more than a decade subjecting ideas and organisations to the test of mass action.

Chapter 6

Industrial organisation

If the workers' political party is a distillation of working-class experience, then industrial organisation is one form of concentration and ferment out of which the distillation takes place. Once the workers' political organisation has come into existence, leadership of the movement will tend to pass into its hands. General policies will tend to be determined by bodies that specifically set out to do so, rather than by those concerned in the first place with the problems of a single trade or industry. In South Africa this has very clearly been the case. Political tendencies have left their imprint on the industrial organisations of the working class. The political divisions that the state has drawn among workers extend to the industrial level as well.

Registered trade unions

Corresponding to the division between free and unfree labour was the division between registered and unregistered trade unions. 'A trade union' was defined by the Industrial Conciliation Act as consisting of 'employees'. An 'employee' was defined as any worker 'other than a Bantu' (section 1). 'Trade unions' of this kind could apply to the industrial registrar for registration. No union could be registered unless the registrar was satisfied that, *inter alia*, the constitution of the applicant union did not contain provisions which were calculated to hinder the attainment of the objects of any law. If the registrar considered that the applicant union was sufficiently representative in respect of the interests and the area for which it sought registration, he could register it in respect of such interests and area, or in respect of such lesser interests or area as are served, in his opinion, by the union.

Unions eligible for registration were thus limited to workers classified as 'white', 'coloured' or 'Asian'. The Act went on to create divisions between coloured and white trade unionists. Before the commencement of the Act, 'mixed' unions (of white and coloured workers) could be registered. This was now prohibited, unless the Minister of Labour considered that the number of white or coloured workers involved was too small to enable them to form an effective union by themselves. In respect of existing 'mixed' unions it was laid down that the constitutions of such unions should provide (section 8(3)(a)(i)):

(aa)   for the establishment of separate branches for white
       persons and coloured persons;
(bb)   for the holding of separate meetings by white persons and
       coloured persons; and
(cc)   that its executive body shall consist only of white persons.

Exemption from these requirements could be granted where the Minister of Labour deemed it expedient to do so. Racism was further encouraged by limiting the right of a 'mixed' union to object to the registration of a new, segregated union in respect of the same trade, area or industry. If the segregated union included more than half the workers of the racial category concerned who were employed in that trade, area or industry, then no objection by the 'mixed' union would be taken into account. Also, the splitting up of 'mixed' unions had been facilitated. New segregated unions, on splitting off from 'mixed' unions, became entitled to part of the assets of the 'mixed' union, subject to certain conditions. Employers' organisations could likewise be registered in terms of the Industrial Conciliation Act but were subject to no enforced segregation. This makes it clear that no general principle of racial, 'ethnic' or national separation was involved. 'Separation', M. A. du Toit explains, 'also means a division of worker interests' (1976, p. 122). What is involved here is purely and simply the division of the working class.

A further restriction on the registered trade unions was contained in the following provisions (section 8(b)(c)(d)):

no such union or [employers'] organization shall affiliate with
any political party or if so affiliated at the commencement of
this Act, shall continue to be so affiliated for a period exceeding
six months from the date of such commencement [and] no such
union or organization shall grant financial assistance to or incur
expenditure with the object of assisting any political party or

any candidate for election to Parliament or to any provincial
council or local authority.

These provisions, we are told, 'arose from the fact that a number of
unions had made contributions to the Communist and Labour Parties'
(M. A. du Toit, 1976, p. 24). In this way the state has attempted to
impose an absolute division between industrial organisation, which is
treated as a necessary evil, and political organisation, which is repressed.
The following explanation is offered by M. A. du Toit (*ibid.*, pp. 90-1):

> there should be no objection to the unions using politics in order
> to ensure the stability of the movement. This may merely entail
> the gaining of support in seeking certain advantages, without
> seeking affiliation to a specific political party. Such a procedure
> may be unacceptable since support for a specific party could well
> tip the scales in favour of that party. In the past, political parties
> have depended on the votes of the organised workers.

The workers should refrain, in other words, from using their full
strength in the political struggle, because if they do so they might win.
'Union leaders,' the writer goes on, 'agree that the unions should not
have direct representation in Parliament by way of a workers' party'
(*ibid.*, pp. 92-3). Having divided the working class to the greatest
possible extent, therefore, the state – with the consent of union leaders
– further tried to limit the influence of the enfranchised minority to
the purely industrial sphere. The alternative, according to the same
writer, is that 'The right to participate in political activities will be
abused by those who see it as their duty to provide the State with a
new political structure' (*ibid.*, p. 24). This attitude is perfectly consistent. As early as 1953 the Minister of Labour had explained the role
of the registered trade unions as follows (*Hansard*, 14 August 1953):

> In the past, the trade union was merely an organisation of
> individuals working in a certain industry, in order to negotiate
> with their employers and, as far as the State was concerned, to
> discuss legislation. Gradually, however, every registered trade
> union in South Africa has become a recognised part of the State
> machinery for carrying out our industrial conciliation machinery.
> Consequently, in view of the fact that the State to a large
> extent gives recognition to trade unions as part of such machinery,
> it is obvious that the State has to watch very carefully in
> composing that machinery, that it can function in a manner
> which will enable it to achieve the aim for which it was created.

The main task of the registered trade unions is to take part in the official procedure of collective bargaining. This consisted of forming an 'industrial council' together with the appropriate employers or registered employers' organisations. Such councils could be registered by the industrial registrar and should, in respect of the industry, area or trade concerned, 'endeavour by the negotiation of agreements or otherwise to prevent disputes from arising, and to settle disputes that have arisen or may arise . . . and take such steps as it may think expedient to bring about the regulation or settlement of matters of mutual interest to employers or employers' organizations and employees or trade unions' (section 23(1)). An agreement reached by an industrial council could be published by the Minister of Labour in the *Government Gazette* if he deemed it expedient to do so. The agreement thereupon became binding on the parties.

Industrial councils have the function of settling disputes between unions and employers. Where no industrial council exists an *ad hoc* 'conciliation board', consisting of workers' and employers' representatives, was the statutory instrument for resolving disputes. Strikes were prohibited in industries where no industrial council existed, unless application had been made for the establishment of a conciliation board and various further conditions had been met. Conciliation board agreements could be declared binding in the same way as industrial council agreements. Further procedures for settling disputes were 'mediation' and 'arbitration'. Arbitration could be voluntary or compulsory. It was compulsory in 'All disputes in "essential services" which are not, or are not likely to be, settled by an industrial council or a conciliation board' (de Kock, 1973, p. 575). Arbitration awards were final and binding on the parties to the dispute.

An industrial tribunal, appointed by the Minister of Labour, had the functions, *inter alia*, of hearing appeals against decisions by the industrial registrar and making job reservation determinations.

The position of the registered trade unions could thus be characterised, in two words, as 'rigidly controlled'. Upon registration the union became a corporate body capable of suing and being sued. The forms of control by the state over registered unions were too many to be listed here. Registration itself was subject to the discretion of the industrial registrar. Appeals against his decision had to be made to the industrial tribunal – a body likewise appointed by the Minister of Labour. Industrial council agreements were only made binding if the Minister found it expedient to do so. Particulars of their members as at the end of every year, financial accounts and balance-sheets, appointments of officials and particulars relating to branches had to be provided by registered unions to the industrial registrar. The registrar could further require particulars of members as at any given date, or a written explanation of any matter relating to the list of members or financial accounts. If the registrar 'has reason to believe that any provision of the constitution of a registered trade union or employers' organization has not been observed, and that as a result of such non-observance the union or organization is unable to function in accordance with its constitution' he could issue instructions 'to remedy the matter' (section 12(1)).

Without notice to the organisation concerned, the registrar could also institute an inquiry in respect of a registered organisation if he had reason to believe that it was in any way acting irregularly or 'in a manner which is unreasonable in relation to the members and which has caused serious disaffection amongst a substantial number of the members in good standing' (section 12(3)). The Minister could direct that effect be given to any recommendations resulting from such an inquiry. Ordinarily, one would have thought, 'serious disaffection' among the members of a union can be remedied by internal procedures, in particular by the election of a new leadership. The legislature, however, appears to have had a different situation in mind. If a union were 'unable to continue to function' for any reason which in the opinion of the registrar could not be remedied by an inquiry in terms of section 12(1), he could wind it up. In a variety of circumstances the registrar could also, at his discretion, cancel the registration of a trade union or an employers' organisation. Given the views of the government on what is right and proper in the field of trade-union activity – in particular its insistence on racial segregation, on 'moderation' and on abstention from political involvement – the potential use of these powers is not difficult to imagine. (See Table 6.1 for data on the membership of registered trade unions.)

Table 6.1 *Membership of registered trade unions as at 31 December 1971*

Type of union	No.	White	'Coloured'	Total
'White'	89	368,236	–	368,236
'Coloured'	50	–	71,613	71,613
'Mixed'	42	52,781	133,225	186,006
	181	421,017	204,838	625,855

Source: SRR (1973, p. 266).

215

Despite state policy, the racial segregation of an integrated working class has proved by no means a simple, one-way process. In 1971, for example, two formerly all-white unions – the Amalgamated Union of Building Trade Workers and the Amalgamated Society of Woodworkers of South Africa – decided to admit coloured members also. In the case of twelve 'mixed' unions exemptions were granted from the requirement of an all-white executive since the unions had too few white members to make this feasible. Similarly, nine 'mixed' unions were exempted from the requirement of holding separate meetings for its white and coloured members.

Prior to 1975 two major federations of registered trade unions existed. One was the Trade Union Council of South Africa (TUCSA), which at the end of 1973 consisted of sixty-three affiliated unions with a total of 233,904 members. Roughly 60 per cent of its members were coloured. The other was the South African Confederation of Labour (SACL), which at the end of 1972 consisted of twenty-five affiliated unions with a total of 179,945 members. Its affiliates included the Co-ordinating Council of South African Trade Unions, the Federal Consultative Council of South African Railways and Harbours Staff Associations, and the Federation of Mine Production Workers. A large proportion of SACL affiliates were public service unions.

The chief difference between the two federations was the fact that all registered unions could affiliate to TUCSA, whereas the SACL confined itself to unions of white workers. TUCSA's position, however, had little to do with the principle of workers' unity; on the contrary, its basic ideas were no different from those of liberal employers (M. A. du Toit, 1976, pp. 87–8):

1. It is not affiliated to any political party but is dedicated to promoting and advancing the dignity, rights, economic, social and cultural well-being of South African workers of all races, through responsible and recognized collective bargaining and free negotiation.
2. It is opposed to all forms of Communism and believes that the fundamental method of defeating communist influence in the field of labour is maintenance of free democratic trade unionism for workers of all races. It . . . actively resists all attempts by any political party to stifle or exploit the trade union movement for political ends.
3. It condemns all forms of racial discrimination which undermine the civil liberty and social justice of the individual. The right

of the individual is paramount and the State exists to serve the individual.

If the TUCSA leadership took up a liberal position, then that of the SACL was inspired by white racism. In industry as well as in politics, however, this distinction is strategical rather than fundamental. The policy of the SACL, M. A. du Toit explains, is in many respects similar to that of TUCSA. However, the SACL 'wishes to ensure that the White worker will realize that mixed unions and federations are not in their [sic] interests. It is opposed to the establishment [sic] of a working class along non-racial lines in South Africa if the White worker were to be separated from the rest of the White community' (*ibid.*, pp.88-9).

The acid test of every registered union in South Africa, however, is not so much its attitude towards the coloured minority of workers. Far more decisive is its position towards the mass of workers classified as 'Bantu'. Despite their seemingly clear-cut differences, both TUCSA and the SACL were in fact divided on this issue. On the one hand, both bodies depended on the common social basis of free labour. On the other hand, with the SACL confining itself to the white section, certain differences arose. Also in TUCSA there can be no doubt that whites have always enjoyed a dominant position. Yet the presence of a sizeable coloured membership means that there are lengths of white racism to which TUCSA cannot go. But also in the SACL different tendencies were visible. On the one hand, virulent racism was preached by a section of the leadership. A notorious spokesman for this point of view was P. J. Paulus, general secretary of the Mineworkers' Union, who justified state policy as follows (Coetzee, 1976, p.214):

It is the considered opinion [of the MWU] that the black man, as in the political field, has not been sufficiently trained in the trade union field to use the trade union weapon properly . . . . In a factory and in a country's economy a trade union in immature hands can be extremely dangerous. When the members are not mature, a trade union can easily fall into the hands of reckless leaders – and cause chaos in the workplace. It is my honest opinion that the black working masses in the Republic today are even less ready for responsible trade unionism than the white workers were even half a century ago. And where political aspirations especially in the case of the black man are so closely connected to his material aspirations, black trade unions can and will end up in the hands of left-wing political agitators overnight. Therefore I believe that the system of black works committees as applied by the Government is the appropriate means for protecting the black man's interests.

On the other hand extreme racist views were not shared by the member-ship of the SACL as a whole. Indeed, the Mineworkers' Union withdrew from the SACL in 1969 (but remained linked to it through the Feder-ation of Mine Production Workers) in protest against the statement by J. H. Liebenberg, secretary of the Artisan Staff Association, that the Confederation was the home of 'verkramptes'. As early as 1966, Liebenberg accused members of the Co-ordinating Council of using trade-union meetings 'to propagate the views of extremist right-wing Afrikaner elements' (*ibid*., p. 65). As regards job reservation, it is interesting to note, 'the union of daily-paid White railway workers, *Die Spoorbond*, never opposed the use of non-White labour ("officially on a temporary basis") in many less-skilled jobs' (*ibid*., p. 64). These differences, as we shall see, in due course resulted in a split.

TUCSA, too, was destined to split over the issue of racism under the mounting pressure of the 1970s. Its history on this issue, contrary to any expectations that its verbal commitment to 'free democratic trade unionism for workers of all races' might have aroused, was one of continuous vacillation and a series of opportunistic swings. On its formation in 1954 TUCSA confined its membership to registered trade unions. The years that followed, however, were years of unrest among African workers, culminating in the upheavals of the Sharpe-ville period. At its annual conference in 1962 TUCSA reversed its position and resolved by a vote of eighty-three to ten to allow African trade unions to affiliate. By 1963 five African unions had joined. The annual conference of that year unanimously accepted that 'all workers should have the right to membership of unions registered in terms of the Industrial Conciliation Act' (*ibid*., p. 76). Inevitably, this policy was attacked by the state. It was also attacked by the leaders of certain member unions. A few unions, such as the Motor Industry Employees' Union withdrew. The government warned TUCSA in November 1967 that it 'would not tolerate the undermining of its policy regarding Black trade unions, and if TUCSA continued to organize such unions "the Government would not hesitate to take the necessary measures" ' (*ibid*., p. 83). The TUCSA leaders yielded to this pressure. Also the leaders of six African member unions decided to submit without a struggle. The (African) National Union of Clothing Workers of South Africa, with Lucy Mvubelo as its general secretary, and the African Tobacco Workers Union issued the following joint statement (quoted by Coetzee, 1976, p. 84):

> As the only trade union co-ordinating body in South Africa
> which is dedicated to the ideals of true trade unionism, it is
> essential that TUCSA continue to prosper. Unity in the workers'
> movement is, we believe, of paramount importance and we
> could not be party to anything which would destroy this unity.
> TUCSA must continue to act as the voice of the workers in
> South Africa, irrespective of its composition, and we know that
> it will continue to do so. But in order to allow it to do this, we
> choose to remove its present source of embarrassment, and that
> is ourselves.

Six of the African unions thus voluntarily withdrew. Pressure was put on the remaining three (the African Brewery, Wines and Distillers Workers' Union, the Engineering Workers' Union of South Africa, and the African Dairy Workers' Union) to do likewise. They refused. 'Why,' asked J. Hlongwane of the Engineering Workers' Union, 'should African trade unions help to paint a positive picture of TUCSA . . . and help them avoid expelling the unions of the African people?' (*ibid.*, p. 207). In December 1967, accordingly, a special conference of TUCSA was called and decided by fifty-one votes against thirteen to expel the African unions. At the annual conference of 1968 this decision of the special conference was reconsidered and rejected by an overwhelming majority. TUCSA was once again directed to continue with the affiliation of African unions and to strive for unity in the trade-union movement. The South African Electrical Workers' Association and the Amalgamated Engineering Union thereupon withdrew. State hostility continued. 'Severe warnings' were addressed by the Minister of Labour 'to all unions who were receiving funds from abroad to organize Black unions' (*ibid.*, p. 86). By the beginning of 1969, fourteen affiliated unions with a total of 35,736 members had withdrawn from TUCSA. As a result, staff had to be reduced and projects had to be curtailed. This situation the leaders of TUCSA found intolerable. At the annual conference of February 1969 it was decided once more by seventy-seven votes against ten to terminate the affiliation of African trade unions.

This history of vacillation and right about-turns at first sight suggests that the mass of white and coloured trade unionists were completely indecisive as regards the organisation of their African fellow-workers. This is an unlikely explanation. Due weight should be given to what has

Industrial organisation

been termed 'the repressive powers inherent in the bureaucratic structure of a union' (*ibid*., p. 85). From our analysis up to this point there is no cause for doubting that the mainstream of opinion among the TUCSA rank and file was sympathetic *in a general way* to the organisation of African workers, but cautious and uncertain as to supporting it concretely. A strong minority, on the other hand – especially among the white workers – was hostile to such organisation, partly on grounds of narrow self-interest and partly, no doubt, out of fear of the state. In such a fluid situation the balance of power can easily be held by union officials. Large numbers of union members and delegates, torn between principle and expediency, could be expected to follow the lead that they were given. From the union officials' point of view, threatened with the defection of the hostile minority in 1968, their careers were directly at stake. Coetzee accounts in the following way for TUCSA's erratic career (*ibid*., p. 86):

Convinced that they are serving the best interests of the organization, leaders of labour unions use the union political apparatus to eliminate and suppress organized opposition. It may even be suggested that the power of bureaucratic organization rather than the absence of significant sources of political difference, accounts for the apparent unanimity of opinion which exists in most South African trade unions.

The tendency towards bureaucratisation, contrary to certain opinions on the subject, is not without definite social causes. No less important than racial fragmentation in determining the nature of the registered trade unions, according to the study by Lewis (1976) of registered unions in the Western Cape, is the relationship between skilled and unskilled workers. Where a union consists of skilled as well as unskilled members, the demands of the unskilled for 'job dilution' must clash with the immediate interests of the skilled. Racial segregation can only be applied where skilled and unskilled workers belong to different racial categories. Conversely, racial solidarity (or 'nationalism') in itself is insufficient to unite all workers of a given racial category. The membership of the 'mixed' and 'coloured' unions, Lewis concludes, consists very largely of skilled and semi-skilled workers. In these unions, differences between the interests of skilled and unskilled workers are 'resolved' for the time being by the dominance of the skilled workers.

The leadership not only of the craft unions but of the registered unions in general is thus based very largely on the skilled upper layer of the working class. As a result, the co-ordinating bodies of the registered trade unions 'will be dominated by the interests of the skilled workers' (*ibid.*, p. 55). Inasmuch as the better-paid skilled workers are under less pressure to fight for social change, a conservative leadership has managed to establish itself at the head of the registered unions. Subject to genuine democratic control, it would be difficult for a leadership of this nature to maintain itself for long. Under existing conditions it is all but inevitable that a tendency towards bureaucratic self-perpetuation on the part of the leadership will flourish.

One result of this state of affairs is described by a registered trade-union leader, J. R. Altman (1976). The most pressing problem, from his point of view, is the fact that 'too few younger people of the right calibre are coming to the fore in the various levels of leadership in the unions' (*ibid.*, p. 35). The reasons for this, according to Altman, are the 'distorted public image' of trade unionism resulting from government action against trade-union leaders in the past, the poor salaries and lack of security of trade-union officials, the lack of union educational facilities and, last but not least, a 'general apathy' among white workers. Having experienced a steady rise in their living standards over the past twenty years, Altman argues, white workers tend to feel 'that their obligation to their trade union ends with the payment of their subscription' (*ibid.*, p. 39). The more workers have to gain, the more enthusiastic they are about their union. Coloured workers thus tend to be more active trade unionists; 'white leadership', on the other hand, 'is an ageing leadership faced with a serious problem of succession' (*ibid.*, p. 40).

As far as the unions of white workers are concerned, Altman thus recognises a definite cleavage between the leaders and the rank and file. White workers are 'quite prepared to leave everything in the hands of paid officials', so that the latter 'have difficulties in getting quorums at meetings' (*ibid.*, p. 39). In effect, the paid officials operate in isolation from the membership. It is precisely this lack of democratic control that forms the central feature of what can be called 'bureaucratic organisation'. On behalf of the union leadership, Altman disclaims responsibility for the situation. It is the fault of state policy, he argues, and of apathy on the part of the members. C. P. Grobler, general secretary of the Artisan Staff Association of skilled railway workers, on the other hand, calls into question precisely the role of the leadership (Coetzee, 1976, p. 172):

> We can be so smug at times, but some of our existing registered
> trade unions present a rather dismal record of achievement for

their members. In fact some have no militancy whatsoever and are little more than social-security clubs, providing nothing more than sickness and funeral benefits and such like.

In the period of mass strikes by the African workers from 1973 onwards, which was also a period of falling living standards for the white workers, the registered unions would be put to a serious test. More pressing demands would be made upon them; existing policies would stand out more clearly. At the beginning of the period of mass strikes TUCSA had closed its doors against the vast majority of workers. As we shall see, the strike movement proved more powerful than the pressures of the state and white racism; following the first wave of strikes TUCSA would decide once again to admit African unions.

The committee system

The hostility of the state towards the organisation of the unfree proletariat is expressed on the one hand by the exclusion of African workers from the registered trade unions. It is also revealed in the official attitude towards African trade unions. This attitude is not confined to spokesmen of the government. It is found no less strongly among the minor officials whose task it is to carry out government policy. Thus W. F. Koch, chairman of six of the seven regional labour committees in the Transvaal, had the following to say about African trade unions (SRR, 1973, p. 275):

> African trade unions are not recognised by law. They are in a mess, with several groups of people claiming to represent black workers. I've known your [African] trade unions from the time of Kadalie, and I've never known a single one to work in the interests of the black workers.

S. S. Mahlanga, a businessman who is described as a 'veteran member' of the Johannesburg regional committee, had even more pronounced views on the subject (*ibid.*): 'We don't have the right people to run trade unions. All we have are people who will incite workers to strike. I condemn trade unions for Africans.'

This self-same point of view is reflected in the statutory framework for the organisation of the African working class. Historically, the state has been forced to acknowledge that the representation and organisation of African workers cannot be entirely suppressed. The Industrial

Legislation Commission of the early 1950s went so far as to recommend that African trade unions should be recognised subject to conditions even more stringent than those which govern the registered trade unions. The government disagreed with this finding. It argued that the recognition of African trade unions would be contrary to the interests of the country and also of the workers concerned. 'As recognition could [*sic*] not be given to their trade unions,' M. A. du Toit writes, 'alternative machinery was created which would remove the motive to organize' (1976, p. 45). Such 'alternative machinery' was the 'committee system' set up by the Bantu Labour (Settlement of Disputes) Act of 1953.

The committee system may be regarded as the industrial equivalent of the 'homelands' system. In general, any recognised organisation of African workers is likely to be given less power than the bureaucracies in the reserves. Organisation at the industrial level can only be concerned with the workers' immediate interests and could at any moment come under their control. It exists at the centre and not on the fringes of South African society. Dissatisfaction among African workers and the demand for complete emancipation are less easy to dispose of in practice than in legal theory. The reserve system may provide an abundant supply of 'cheap docile labour'; having been led to water, however, the horse must be made to drink. The African workers must be made to remain in their allotted jobs, to remain both 'cheap' and 'docile', hence without real organisation if the object of the exercise is not to be defeated. Control by the African workers over the organs created in terms of the Bantu Labour (Settlement of Disputes) Act must at all costs be excluded. The potential importance of the humblest and most obscure workers' committee is greater than that of the most celebrated 'homeland government' with all its impressive trappings.

In contrast to the bureaucracies to whom the reserves have been entrusted, it was thus laid down that the bureaucracy administering 'Bantu labour relations' must be controlled by whites. Its highest body was the 'Central Bantu Labour Board', appointed by the Minister of Labour and consisting entirely of whites. The 'Bantu Labour Officers', appointed by the Minister in respect of local areas, likewise had to be white. Africans were only permitted at the level of 'Regional Labour Committees'. These committees, too, were appointed by the Minister and had to be under the chairmanship of a (white) 'Bantu labour officer'. The main functions of the committees were to keep themselves informed about industrial relations involving African workers and to try and prevent disputes. African workers could be co-opted on to regional committees; however, the committees need include no workers. In the case of the Johannesburg regional committee in 1973, only one of its African members was himself an employee. Even a trade-union leader like Lucy Mvubelo, not particularly noted for criticising the existing system of industrial relations, was moved to comment that 'most of these people have not even worked in industry. They have no idea of the aspirations of African workers' (SRR, 1973, pp. 275-6).

Inspectors could be appointed by the Minister. Their function was mainly to gather information. The 'Central Bantu Labour Board' and the relevant regional committee had to be notified of any industrial council meeting at which an agreement would be negotiated in respect of an industry or trade in which African workers were employed. The chairman of the regional committee and the secretary of the central board – in other words, two white officials – were entitled to attend such meetings and to take part in the proceedings in so far as the interests of African workers were involved. They had no right to vote.

As for the African workers themselves, provision was made for the election of 'works committees'. In establishments where twenty or more African workers were employed, they could notify their employer that they wanted to elect a works committee. The employer was then required, 'as soon as practicable', to call a meeting of the workers under chairmanship of the 'Bantu labour officer' for the area concerned. At such a meeting a works committee, consisting of three to five members, could be elected. The functions of the works committee were vague and unimportant. It could appoint one of its members 'to maintain contact' with the regional committee or with the labour inspector. Second, 'Whenever a labour dispute occurs in any establishment in respect of which a works committee has been elected, the regional committee, or the inspector . . . shall consult such works committee in regard to such dispute' (section 7(6), Bantu Labour Relations Regulation Act of 1953). The victimisation of works committee members by employers was prohibited. Beyond this, the works committee had no capacities or functions.

According to M. A. du Toit, 'prevention of strikes' was the chief aim of the Act (1976, p. 54). This was provided for in the most direct terms possible (section 18(1)):

No employee or other person shall instigate a strike or incite any
employee or other person to take part in or to continue a strike
or take part in a strike or in the continuation of a strike and no
employer or other person shall instigate a lock-out or incite any

employer or other person to take part in or to continue a lock-out
or take part in a lock-out or the continuation of a lock-out.

On the other hand, no provision was made for any form of collective
bargaining. No machinery was created for enabling African workers to
defend their collective interests. From the point of view of 'industrial
conciliation' in the ordinary meaning of the term, such an omission is
inexplicable and baffling. From the point of view of South African
industrial relations as we have attempted to analyse the system, it is
entirely consistent. It is one thing, however, to prohibit strikes and
lock-outs, and assume that African workers will remain content with
powerless committees. It is quite another to enforce this policy. What
has been the practical significance of the rules that we have looked at?
In 1970, according to the Minister of Labour, there were twenty-seven
statutory works committees in existence. In 1971 there were twenty-
eight; in 1972, eighteen (plus 117 unofficial factory committees); and
in March 1973, thirty-one (plus 161 unofficial committees) (SRR,
passim). At this stage there were more than 30,000 registered factories
in South Africa (M. A. du Toit, 1976, p. 55). Works committees thus
led a largely nominal existence. At the same time, the period was one
of relative industrial peace. Details of strikes by black workers in these
years are shown in Table 6.2. All these strikes were by definition illegal
as far as African workers were concerned. Prosecutions followed in
only a few cases. The threat of prosecution, however, was always
present, and the risk was visible to African strikers at all times. In 1968,
sixty-six African workers were arrested for illegal striking; in 1969,
fifty-nine; in 1970, seventy; and in 1971, 250 (SRR, 1972, p. 342). The
punishment meted out to workers convicted for striking could be
severe. In November 1972, for example, four strikers from a plastic
and rubber factory in Johannesburg were sentenced to a fine of R100
or fifty days' imprisonment each (*ibid.*).

Table 6.2 *Strikes by African workers, 1968–72*

Year	Strikes	Workers involved
1968	56	1,705
1969	78	4,232
1970	76	3,303
1971	69	4,196
1972	71	8,814

Source: *South African Statistics*, 1974.

The extent to which works committees served the aim of preventing strikes was thus extremely doubtful. It cannot be seriously argued that the existence of committees in a handful of factories held millions of workers elsewhere in check. More in evidence was the strike-preventing activity of employers, the police and the criminal courts. Certainly the committee system in no sense answered the need of the African workers for industrial organisation. Trade unionists of different persuasions regarded the committees with misgivings. Even a right-winger such as C. P. Grobler, at that time Honorary Secretary of the SACL, made the following observation (Coetzee, 1976, p. 172):

> But a formula will have to be found for the urban Black and,
> in my view, that urban Black is not going to be content with
> Works and Liaison Committees. These committees are, at best, the
> equivalent of the very first line of trade-union activity, similar
> to shop stewards' and grade stewards' committees.

Nor were the regional committees capable of reflecting the demands of the African working class. This was made clear by S. S. Mahlangu, the veteran member of the Johannesburg regional committee whom we have already encountered (SRR, 1972, p. 275): 'I am a businessman. When I employ somebody, I have to calculate my costs and profits before I can decide how much to pay him. So when we go to negotiate on behalf of workers I have both sides of the question in mind.'

Supporters of the committee system were found mainly in government circles, among employers and among the minor officials responsible for administering the system. At the same time, the existence of the committee system was not seriously challenged in the period under discussion. It was only when the period of mass strikes began, and African workers were reaching for organisational weapons on a major scale, that the failure of the committee system would be shown unmistakably in practice, on the one hand as an instrument 'for preventing strikes', on the other hand as a form of industrial organisation suited to the needs of the workers.

Unregistered trade unions

Trade-union organisation among the African workers was at a low ebb at the beginning of the 1970s. The 1960s had seen the suppression of the African trade-union movement that had risen to the fore in the previous decade. In 1969, according to Horrell, the membership of the surviving African unions was 16,040 workers (1969, p. 145). By 1970, according to M. A. du Toit, all African unions except the National Union of Clothing Workers and the African Leather Workers' Union had disappeared (1976, p. 165). This, however, is incorrect. The Engineering Workers' Union, for example, has functioned continuously since 1963. Yet it is undeniable that the African trade-union movement at this stage had been reduced to a shadow of its former self.

Of the sixty African trade unions that existed in 1961, thirty-six had been affiliated to the South African Congress of Trade Unions (SACTU) and sixteen to the Federation of Free African Trade Unions of South Africa (FOFATUSA). Eight had been unaffiliated. SACTU represented 38,791 African workers at this stage and FOFATUSA some 18,000 (*ibid.*, pp. 162–4). SACTU in particular, from the state point of view, represented everything that was most dangerous about working-class organisation. It had been formed in 1955 by fourteen former affiliates of the South African Trades and Labour Council which had rejected the decision of TUCSA to restrict its membership to registered unions only. Several other unions of African and coloured workers joined SACTU. In addition, twelve new unions of African workers were formed. In 1961 SACTU could claim a total of forty-six affiliated unions with a membership of 53,323 workers. Apart from the African workers, these included 12,384 workers classified as 'coloured', 1,650 classified as 'Asian' and 498 classified as 'white' (Horrell, 1969, p. 26).

At its first conference SACTU clearly laid the link between trade-union and political activities and resolved to pursue the workers' struggle with all the means at its disposal (M. A. du Toit, 1976, p. 41):

> The South African Congress of Trade Unions is conscious of
> the fact that the organizing of the mass of the workers for higher
> wages, better conditions of life and labour, and the successful
> struggle for them, is inextricably bound up with a determined
> struggle for political rights and for liberation from all oppressive
> laws and practices. It follows that a mere struggle for the
> economic rights of the workers without participation in the
> general struggle for political emancipation would condemn the
> trade union movement to uselessness and to a betrayal of the
> interests of the workers.

On this basis SACTU joined with the ANC as part of the Congress Alliance. It helped to organise political strikes in support of demands for abolition of the pass laws and the Group Areas Act, and for a minimum wage of R2 a day. At the same time, SACTU energetically set about promoting trade-union organisation among the African workers. According to Horrell (1969, p. 26), SACTU

> arranged lectures in various subjects, and sent its organizers on tour to train union secretaries in book-keeping, the keeping of proper records, and the way to conduct meetings. It circulated ... material to the unions, for example model constitutions, model memoranda to employers, the working of the Workmen's Compensation Act, and information about statutory wages and conditions of work in the industries concerned. The books of some affiliated unions were kept in the SACTU offices.

In relation to the 'mixed' unions, SACTU argued that coloured workers had little say in the running of these unions. Rather than campaigning for democracy in the unions concerned, SACTU called on coloured workers to split off and form new unions. They would do better, SACTU argued, to be independently represented on industrial councils and the like. This strategy, based on the same reasoning that the Black Consciousness movement would follow a decade later, may indeed be effective in the short term and offer relief from the immediate burden of what might be termed 'internal' racial discrimination. Fundamentally, however, such a tactic stands in contradiction to SACTU's objective of non-racial trade-union organisation. Existing, tenuous links with white workers were to be broken; white workers were to be abandoned to white racism. To this extent SACTU's policy was adapted to the state-imposed divisions among workers.

From the state point of view, as M. A. du Toit puts it, SACTU's 'political inclination could not be tolerated' (1976, p. 42). The police moved into action: '[SACTU's] offices, the offices of its affiliated unions and the homes of its officials', Horrell records, 'were from time to time raided and searched by the police. Various leaders were served with banning orders prohibiting them from attending meetings' (1969, p. 27). Twenty-three SACTU officials were among the 156 persons arrested in 1956 on charges of high treason. Horrell gives the following account of the period that followed (1969, p. 27):

> After the 1958 'stay at home' demonstrations numbers of SACTU members were convicted and sentenced to terms of imprisonment on charges of inciting others to go on strike by way of protest against the laws of the country. Scores of them were detained during the state of emergency in 1960. During 1963, 35 of the SACTU officials or former officials were held by the police under

the 90-day detention clause, at least five of them for a second
term and six for a third term. One of them was the General
Secretary of SACTU, Mr Leon Levy, who, on his release, was
given a permanent exit permit and escorted by the police to an
aircraft leaving for overseas.

After the Suppression of Communism Act had been amended in
1962 making it possible for more restrictive banning orders to be
issued, very severe orders were served on all the leading SACTU
officials, making it impossible for them to continue trade union
activities: it was reported in March 1964 that more than 50
prominent members had been immobilized in this way, and further
orders have been issued since then.

A few of the older unions, for example the Textile Workers'
Industrial Union, ended their affiliation on the ground that it had
become impossible for SACTU to fulfil its role as a co-ordinating
body. Lacking leadership and apprehensive of further Government
action, most of the smaller, recently-established African unions
went out of existence. By about 1967, SACTU existed in name only.

The final remark is not quite accurate. Like the illegal political
organisations, SACTU had moved into exile. Like the illegal organisations, it will continue its activities in exile until such time as a return
to open operations in South Africa will be possible once again. In the
case of FOFATUSA, no concerted action by the state was needed to
dissolve it. FOFATUSA dissolved itself. It had been formed in 1959
by five African unions which disagreed with SACTU politically and
supported the PAC position. At the same time, 'somewhat inconsist-
ently', it co-operated closely with TUCSA (Horrell, 1961, p. 72). Its
formation, according to Hepple, had been largely the outcome of a
visit to South Africa in 1958 by two officials of the International
Confederation of Free Trade Unions (ICFTU) (1971, p.72). FOFATUSA
became affiliated to the ICFTU. Its policy was confusing. On the one
hand, its members were urged to 'avoid politics'. On the other hand, its
chairman was arrested in 1960 for 'having engaged in activities that
were likely to further the aims of the Pan-African Congress' (Horrell,
1969, p. 28). Mvubelo and Chitja thereafter became the 'moving spirits'
of FOFATUSA. By 1964, according to Chitja, co-operation with
SACTU was rejected because 'we are interested in industrial politics and
the welfare of the workers, and not in party politics' (*ibid.*). This
peculiar combination of Africanism with 'bread-and-butter' trade

unionism, in co-operation with conservative white trade-union officials, may be taken as further evidence of the adaptable nature of the nationalist doctrine.

In 1962 TUCSA decided to re-admit African trade unions. Several member unions of FOFATUSA thereupon drew the logical conclusion from their existing relationship with TUCSA. They left FOFATUSA and joined TUCSA. By this time, too, SACTU's activities were increasingly being disrupted by the state, and with it FOFATUSA's reason for existing disappeared. The role of promoting 'bread-and-butter' African trade unionism could henceforth be left to TUCSA. In the absence of a left alternative, the Africanistic recruiting colours – which by the early 1960s had grown embarrassing – could also be dispensed with. By the end of 1965, Horrell relates, FOFATUSA 'had only twelve affiliated unions with a membership of about 13,000 and they did not display much interest in the affairs of the organization. The organizers decided to disband. Its remaining unions were advised to affiliate to Tucsa if they had not already done so' (*ibid*.). In 1969, with the expulsion of African unions from TUCSA, these unions were left to their fate.

State policy remained unaffected by these developments. The state wanted no African unions of any description whatever. Tolerating moderate unions today might open the way to radical unions tomorrow. Also the non-affiliated unions were attacked. The following describes the history of the unaffiliated General Workers' Union in Cape Town (Horrell, 1969, pp. 56–7):

> Established in 1959, it is stated to have recruited 300 members within the first few months. Its story is typical of many of the African unions. Mainly because of the prevailing unrest and fear at the time, its organizers failed to settle any disputes between employers and employees. The Special Branch searched the founder's office, removing most of the records. He was detained during the State of Emergency in 1960, subsequently leaving the country. Most of the other committee members were detained for suspected political activities in other organizations, and members were afraid to attend such meetings as were called. The union petered out in about 1962.

The unions that managed to survive led an extremely difficult existence. The African Dairy Workers' Union may be taken as an example. Originally affiliated to SACTU, this union later got some assistance from TUCSA and the Dairy Trade Management Board. In general, however, South African industrial relations remain implacably hostile to African trade unionism. Horrell describes the conditions under which the Dairy Workers' Union existed (*ibid.*, pp. 58-9):

> There are about 250 members, scattered at various dairies on the Witwatersrand and in Pretoria, and most of them are on the road for most of the time, delivering milk. Many work at night. The secretary, himself a dairy worker, consequently works under great difficulties. He visits members early in the mornings, when they return from their rounds. He tries to clear up any misunderstandings with employers, to ensure that accidents are reported to the Workmen's Compensation Commissioner, to make certain that members receive paid leave. In most cases he has himself to collect trade union dues: these are paid irregularly, thus the union cannot afford office rent nor benefit schemes.

> There is a high turnover of labour in the dairy industry, most of the newcomers being men from country areas who know nothing about trade unions. Because of this and the other difficulties mentioned only about five per cent of the African dairy workers on the Witwatersrand and in Pretoria are members of the union.

But in the last resort, it was the reaction by employers and the state which dealt African trade unions the worst blows during the 1960s. Horrell continues (*ibid.*, pp. 59-60):

> The main difficulty is that [the African trade unions] lack official recognition and the status thus conferred. Active leaders who voice workers' grievances run the risk of finding themselves dubbed as 'agitators', being dismissed from their jobs, and then, under the pass laws, being ordered out of the town concerned, thus losing their homes. The police have raided the offices of many of the unions, confiscating the records. Some employers are understanding; but it is stated that others do not want their employees to join trade unions, and, if the organizer visits the place of work, threaten to call the police and have him arrested for disturbing the workers. Consequently, most Africans are afraid to become members of trade unions.

If the attitude of the state and that of the more conservative employers were clear, what position did the liberals take up? In 1953, Helen Suzman delivered the following criticism of the Bantu Labour (Settlement of Disputes) Act (Strangwayes-Booth, 1976, p. 78):

> It is an unrealistic measure. To refuse recognition to the Native trade unions, to hope they will die when the Natives are

becoming more and more integrated into industrial life, is
futile. We will find that these trade unions will fall into the hands
of the less responsible elements among Native leaders . . . [when
they could have] been guided and controlled and made useful
instruments of peace and order.

In the programme of the Progressive Party the demand was raised
for general trade-union recognition, subject to state control. Unions of
skilled and semi-skilled African workers should be brought within the
framework of the Industrial Conciliation Act, the Progressive Party
found, while unions of unskilled African workers should be subject to
even more rigid control.[1] In such a situation African trade unions
would be exposed more directly than at present to the bureaucracy of
the registered trade unions. Co-operation would be forced on them.
What sort of influence were the registered trade-union officials likely
to exert? Since the 1920s these officials have enjoyed an almost un-
blemished record of devotion to 'bread-and-butter' issues. They could
be relied upon, with all but absolute certainty, to impress similar
ideas on any African trade unionists who might enter their sphere of
influence. Foreshadowed by the conversion of Clements Kadalie
from militance to moderation in the 1920s, the liberal position was
further bolstered by the 'trial marriage' between TUCSA and the ex-
FOFATUSA unions in the 1960s. Informally, this relationship persisted
in the case of individual African unions such as the National Union of
Clothing Workers.

The results have strengthend the liberals' convictions. Thus Lucy
Mvubelo was 'convinced' that TUCSA, by admitting African unions,
'shows that [it] is playing a prominent and constructive role in bringing
about needed changes on the labour front' (Coetzee, 1976, p. 175).
What, however, does TUCSA's 'constructive role' in actual fact consist
of? Its role is twofold, on the one hand defending the position of free
labour within the existing social system, on the other hand combating
radical tendencies among the African workers. From its inception,
M. A. du Toit explains, TUCSA maintained contact with African
unions 'to prevent [them] from being led astray. . . . It was also pointed
out that the bargaining strength of the registered trade unions could
be undermined by the increasing number of Blacks in industries. They
could be used by employers to undermine the standard of living and
status of the other races. It was therefore in the interest of the Whites
that these unions should be controlled by Whites' (1976, p. 59). TUCSA
had always held the view, it assured the government in 1967, that 'a

responsible Black labour force should be established and that its motive had been, as in the case of the government, to educate responsible non-White leaders. This was in accordance with the policy of Separate Development and the endeavour to organize Black workers on a sound and democratic basis' (*ibid.*, p. 60).

The statutory recognition of the African trade unions, as called for by the Progressive Party, was a *sine qua non* for this 'constructive role' to be fully carried out. To give African unions the right to organise, negotiate and strike, Senator Anna Scheepers was sure, 'would be the best method possible of keeping politics out of African trade unionism' (Coetzee, 1976, p. 158). Towards the African trade unions the position of the TUCSA leadership was little or no different from that of the liberal bourgeoisie. Opposed to this position was the tendency that was resolutely determined to keep politics inside trade unionism. This tendency, though driven underground or into exile, refused to disappear and showed every sign of returning to open activity as soon as conditions permitted. Liberalism argued that state control, combined with the 'constructive role' of the existing trade-union bureaucracy, would succeed in keeping this tendency at bay. The government, with less self-assurance, acted on the opposite assumption.

Even by the early 1970s, however, it was clear that state policy and the liberal strategy were not altogether irreconcilable. All that could be stated categorically was that the government would not *voluntarily* introduce the measures called for by the liberals. A situation could be foreseen, however, where the government would be *unable*, as a result of mass upheaval, to maintain the existing system intact. In such a situation the liberal policy may prove the only remaining device for keeping any semblance of control over the organisation of the African workers. M. A. du Toit apparently has this development in mind when he puts forward the following synthesis of liberal and government policy (1976, pp. 124-5):

> One cannot ignore the dangers envisaged by the Government
> but it is also true that the present situation cannot be allowed to
> continue. The question may be asked whether non-recognition
> will not create a feeling of suppression and so stimulate the rise
> of Black nationalism, which may have even more far-reaching
> results than those foreseen by the Government. This must be
> viewed against the background of the political climate in which
> political agitators, working underground, have a great impact. . . .
> In this respect, the existing trade unions may be able to bring

the true meaning of trade unionism to the attention of the Black workers. State control will have to be applied because there are some unions which may influence them wrongly and this can only harm their cause, even under White control.

In such a situation all contradictions between liberal and government policy appear to be resolved. Yet the crucial question remained unanswered. Will it be *possible*, in a situation where the state has been forced to take 'liberal' measures, to exclude 'politics' from the black workers' organisations through a combination of state control and the 'constructive role' of the bureaucracy of TUCSA? Developments from 1973 onwards would shed more light on the matter.

Conclusions

Political tendencies in general determine the tendencies that are found among South African workers at the level of industrial organisation. As at the political level, so at the industrial level the legally tolerated tendencies provide no strong basis for working-class organisation. White racism is reflected in the position of the SACL and liberalism is reflected in TUCSA policy. Black nationalism played its part in the rise and fall of FOFATUSA; by the end of 1972, Black Consciousness was in the process of giving birth to the 'Black Allied Workers' Union'. SACTU, on the other hand, was linked to the ANC and its transition from the ideas of nationalism towards those of socialism. As for the unregistered unions existing in the early 1970s, they were forced to confine themselves largely to 'bread-and-butter' issues. Ideologically, the two major tendencies looming in front of them were represented by the pro-capitalist TUCSA and the anti-capitalist SACTU. 'Black Consciousness' offered an uncertain middle course.

Nor is it possible for two entities such as the registered and unregistered trade unions to exist side by side without a particular *historical* relationship developing between them. By the 1970s the pattern was quite clear. Defensiveness was the dominant feature of the registered trade unions; the unregistered unions, irrespective of temporary lulls, were inherently on the offensive 'There is no doubt,' Altman observed, 'that the future of the trade union movement lies in the hands of the Coloured and Black workers' (1976, p. 40). The main question facing the registered unions was that of defining their relationship to the vanguard of the labour movement, the African proletariat.

Implicit at first, this question was looming ever larger. The obvious solution it demanded was a unified labour movement based on a common programme. Squarely opposed to any such development was the existing compromise between registered unions and the state. This compromise, however, was conditional. Free labour, while it exists, remains labour. It can never grow as one with capital or the capitalist state. The relationship between them is based on conflict. As with all compromises, it was only a question of when and under which conditions it would end.

The economic changes that made themselves felt in South Africa from the early 1970s onwards created an entirely new situation. It placed the entire working class under mounting pressure. It spurred the African working class into action and opened up fissures in the alliance of free labour with employers and the state. A period of deep ferment was beginning. Employers were finding themselves less and less willing or able to maintain the compromise with free labour, at the very stage that the African workers were setting a powerful example of working-class self-defence and struggle. Such a combination of events was virtually unique in South African history. While the conflict between the state and the black proletariat grew sharper, the position of free labour was threatened with upheaval. Its relationship, on the one hand with employers and the state, on the other hand with African labour, was calling for a fundamental reappraisal. From 1973 onwards these processes, which had long remained beneath the surface, would be accelerated and increasingly break into the open.

Part III

The mass movement of the 1970s

Chapter 7

The Durban strikes

The Durban strikes began on 9 January 1973 with the strike at Coronation Brick and Tile Works, a brickworks on the outskirts of Durban. At three o'clock that morning the workers in the compound of the Number One plant were woken by a group of their fellow-workers and told to gather at the football stadium instead of reporting for work. A deputation was sent to the outlying depots and persuaded the workers there to join them at the football field. 'A high-spirited and positive response marked this early phase of the strike', the Institute for Industrial Education reports. 'Not one man from the main plant ignored the call to strike; workers from the Avoca plant marched to the stadium in two long columns . . . . When they finally surged through the stadium gates, they were chanting "Filumuntu Ufesadikiza", meaning "Man is dead but his spirit still lives"' (IIE, 1974, p. 10). In total some 1,500 to 2,000 workers joined the strike. Only one incident of 'intimidation' was reported. Five men started to leave the stadium during the mass meeting. 'Threatening gestures' were made by the workers around them, whereupon they sat down again (*ibid*.).

The original demand of the Coronation strikers was an increase in their minimum cash wage from R8.97 to R20.00 per week. The existing minimum wage had been in effect since 1967. The employers had been given at least one day's warning of the strike. Their response was stated in a note to workers put out on 8 January in which the following points were made (*ibid.*, pp. 10–11):

   (a) that the talk of a strike on the following day was the work of Communist agitators;
   (b) that loyal workers who routinely came to work would be protected from intimidation;
   (c) that the ringleaders would be severely punished.

This notice had the effect of angering the workers. Their demand was increased to R30.00 per week. Despite having threatened the 'ringleaders' with punishment, management demanded on the evening of 9 January that a committee of workers be elected to carry on negotiations. The workers refused. A request by the Durban Bantu Labour Officer to the mass meeting that they elect a committee was met with a thunderous 'No, never!' One worker explained: 'Our terms are quite clear. We don't need a committee. We need R30.00 a week' (*ibid.*, p. 11).

The strike was ended on the afternoon of the second day by the Zulu king, Goodwill Zwelethini. In an hour-long speech he appealed to the workers to return to work. Although he undertook to negotiate on their behalf, his proposal was accepted only with great reluctance. The workers felt, as one man put it, that 'You cannot extinguish fire by words, but only by action' (*ibid.*, p. 12). In the event Zwelethini took no part in the negotiations. After some argument with the Kwazulu chief minister Buthelezi he withdrew. On Sunday, 14 January the workers elected an eleven-man delegation. On 16 January an offer by management of an increase of R1.50 per week was transmitted to the workers. This was rejected. On 18 January the offer was increased to R2.07 extra per week. This time company officials, escorted by a considerable number of police, moved from plant to plant to put their offer to the workers separately. Evidently this was designed to prevent any mass meeting and full discussion among the workers. In this way each plant was separately persuaded to accept the offer. But from the outset it was clear that 'extensive dissatisfaction with the new rates remained' (*ibid.*, p. 13).

It had also become clear by this time that the Coronation strike would not remain an isolated incident, as had previously tended to be the case with strikes of African workers. On 10 January seventy African workers downed tools for forty-five minutes at the transport firm of A. J. Keeler in the Durban docks. They were protesting against a derisory offer of a wage increase of 50c per week. On 11 January 150 African workers went on strike at T. W. Becket & Co., a tea-packing firm in Durban. Their demand was a wage increase of R3.00 per week. The employers responded by calling in the police and the Department of Labour. On the advice of the latter the employers dismissed all workers who refused to return to work immediately. About 100 workers remained out. A few days later the employers offered to take back all strikers at the original rates of pay. Most of the strikers rejected this offer. Finally, on 25 January the workers' demand of

R3.00 extra per week was met and most of the strikers were taken back. The employers, however, revealed: 'We took this opportunity to weed out what we considered bad material' (*ibid*., p. 14).

Strikes by African workers were legally prohibited at this time and all those taking part were subject to arrest and imprisonment. Thus every strike was a potential trial of strength between the workers and the state in which every worker was threatened with the loss of livelihood and freedom. Nevertheless, the strikes began to spread, building up into a massive wave which the state was unable to control. Some of the biggest strikes took place in the textile factories belonging to the Frame Group. The first of these broke out on 25 January at the Frametex factory in New Germany, an industrial area near Durban. At this factory there was a long history of dissatisfaction among the workers over wages and working conditions. The IIE gives the following account (*ibid*., p. 16):

> At 8.00 a.m. that morning the workers left their machines and gathered in an open yard in the factory. They were invited by loudhailer to elect a negotiating committee, and return to work pending a settlement. They laughed at this, and refused. Their demand was for R20.00 per week, in comparison with the R5.00–R9.00 they claimed they were getting at the time . . . .
> By the following day, Friday, the strike had spread to all the other Frame Group factories in the area, and affected about 6,000 African workers, as well as many Indian workers. The workers were offered a small cost of living increase, but rejected the offer. On the Monday there was a mass meeting at which a further offer of increases, ranging from R1.75 to R3.00 was made. The workers accepted this and returned to work. Meanwhile, however, the strike had spread to workers at two other large Frame factories . . . and also to several other factories in Pinetown and New Germany.

By the end of January every single Frame Group factory in Natal was at a standstill, with some 8,000 textile workers on strike. At Consolidated Textile Mills (CTM), the headquarters of the Frame Group, the strikers were in an angry mood. Their main complaint was the low level of wages paid by the Frame Group in comparison with other employers. The workers gave examples of increases in the cost of living, especially in transport costs. They were also dissatisfied with their conditions of employment. Weavers were paid on a piece-work basis, which, they claimed, was manipulated by management so as to cancel out any increase in basic wages. The IIE continues (*ibid.*, p. 32):

> Another grievance was that they were required to arrive much earlier than the starting time so that they could oil the looms and get the yarn ready for the day's production. If a worker was slightly late, they maintained, his loom was allocated to another worker and he was told to go home, even if there was some legitimate reason for his being late. It was also said that the yarn supplied for the production of blankets was inferior, and that with frequent stoppages it was impossible to make sufficient blankets to benefit from piece rates.

The workers demanded wages of up to R30.00 per week. The demand that crystallised was for an increase of R5.00 per week. On 1 February the Frame Group made an offer of increases ranging from R1.00 to R2.50 per week. The workers held a meeting to consider the offer. It was rejected and it was resolved to continue the strike. Management, too, remained unyielding. Another mass meeting, attended by 800 workers, was held on 7 February. One speaker, who suggested that they should settle for less than R5.00, was shouted down. The general secretary of the Textile Workers' Industrial Union, who was now negotiating on the workers' behalf, obtained two further concessions: one day's strike pay would be paid to the workers; and if the workers went back the next day there would be no dismissals. The general secretary advised the workers to go back. This was eventually agreed to, apparently with reluctance.

In the Hammarsdale industrial area the strike became general. Seven thousand workers employed in twelve industries came out on strike together. Wage increases were demanded of between R3.00 and R5.00 per week. A mass assembly was formed. Employers likewise negotiated *en bloc*. While the strike movement as a whole consisted of strikes taking place either simultaneously or in short succession, at Hammarsdale it went further. Briefly, but without hesitation, workers from different factories not only struck simultaneously but came together in a single body. Organisationally, this was a development with far-reaching implications.

The period of 'the Durban strikes' lasted from January to March 1973. The present study must be confined to two main questions: the extent of the strike wave; and the general characteristics and significance of the strikes. African trade-union organisation was almost non-existent at the time. In any event it was out of the question for small, struggling unions to lead illegal strikes. The strikers thus had to manage without strike pay. At the same time, they were faced with the prospect of dismissal and arrest on a variety of charges ranging from illegal striking to 'misconduct' in terms of the Masters and Servants laws. For many workers this meant the loss of residential rights and deportation to the reserves. It is against this background that the statistics of the period 1 January to 31 March should be seen (see Table 7.1).

Table 7.1 *Statistics of the Durban strikes, 1973*

Number of stoppages and strikes	160
Number of workers involved	61,410
Nature of establishments affected	
iron, steel, engineering and metal industries	22
textile industry	21
transport industry	10
clothing industry	7
cement industry	6
local authorities	6
building industry	6
other	69
Duration of stoppages	
less than one day	32
one day	38
one to two days	24
two to three days	32
three to seven days	38
Outcome of stoppages (where known)	
wage increases granted	118 cases
work resumed on same conditions	28 cases
strikers dismissed	7 cases
negotiations proceeding	7 cases
Wage increases granted (where known)	
less than R1.00 per week	7 cases
R1.00 to R2.00 per week	71 cases
more than R2.00 per week	36 cases

Source: South African Institute of Race Relations, *A View of the 1973 Strikes*, Johannesburg, 1973, p. 1.

The Durban strikes ushered in a period of industrial unrest that would leave no part of the country unaffected. Reports by the press and by word of mouth carried news of strike successes far and wide, galvanising workers everywhere into action. The movement was unco-ordinated, yet the general uniformity of employment conditions gave it a certain consistency. The strikes were mainly in support of wage demands. Further and further from Durban they spread. On 16 January thirty transport workers at Dundee staged a brief stoppage. On 19 January a strike broke out at Consolidated Fine Spinners & Weavers in East London which involved a thousand workers. On 24 January 145 African bus drivers in Johannesburg staged a go-slow action which culminated in a two-and-a-half hour stoppage three weeks later. By the end of the month it was clear that the decade of 'law and order' and relative industrial peace that had followed Sharpeville and the Rivonia arrests was irrevocably over.

The economic crisis of the 1970s

The Durban strikes did not materialise out of thin air. Isolated strikes by African and other workers had been taking place throughout the preceding period. Some of these strikes had been hard-fought and successful. The general strike among the Namibian contract workers at the beginning of 1972 had been the most important conflict of this period. The Durban strikes, however, were of a different order of magnitude. The question that arises is what precipitated a strike wave of such unprecedented dimensions in this particular locality and at this particular time.

The conditions of the African working class in Durban were not markedly different from those of African workers elsewhere. The IIE, after comparing the average wages and cost of living of African workers in Durban with that in other cities, concludes that 'although wages in Durban are a little lower than those paid in some other centres, they are by no means the lowest in the country, and the wage differential is certainly not great enough to have precipitated the strikes of itself' (1974, p. 88). Another factor was that most African workers in Durban belong to the same language group. This, too, cannot account for the strikes in itself. The same condition is present in certain other cities. It is furthermore noted that the presence of a large 'Asian' working class in Durban limits the 'upward mobility' (access to better jobs) of African workers, thereby adding to their frustration. But again the same is true of cities such as Cape Town or Port Elizabeth where the sizeable coloured population provides an upper layer of black workers.

If anything, in Port Elizabeth the opportunities of the African working class appear to be even more limited than in Durban (*ibid*., pp. 88-9).

How does the IIE explain the strikes? It considers that 'the strikes were a series of spontaneous actions by workers, which spread by imitation' (*ibid.*, p. 99). Great importance is attached to the Coronation strike, which received a good deal of publicity and undoubtedly served as an example to workers elsewhere. Yet, to the IIE, 'What precisely sparked off the strike at Coronation Brick is not clear' (*ibid*.). A second factor which the IIE considers important is the existence in Durban of several large factories belonging to the Frame Group, where wages and working conditions were particularly bad. It is not suggested, however, that such a situation is unique in South African industry. Third, the IIE points at the rise in transport costs about the beginning of 1973 and the rumours of a transport boycott circulating among the workers. 'Once the strikes did occur,' the IIE concludes, 'the sight of large crowds of workers out on strike encouraged workers in neighbouring factories and the strikes spread geographically, road by road, starting in New Germany with the Frame Group strike on the 25th, and in Jacobs/Mobeni with the Consolidated Textile Mills strike 6 days later' (*ibid*., pp. 99-100). As to the initial or fundamental impulse, however, the IIE is silent. To explain the strikes they quote a worker with thirty-five years' experience and a wage of R9.00 a week: 'No, sir, this thing comes from God. I am not afraid, nobody told me to go on strike. This thing comes from God. How do you think that I can live on R9.00? A shirt - how much I pay for a shirt? When I get R9.00 a week how much must I save before I can buy a shirt?' (*ibid*., p. 100). This, they say, aptly described 'the spontaneity of a movement which results from the sudden release of 35 years of pent-up frustration' (*ibid*.).

The findings of the IIE, while significant, fail to answer some essential questions. The strikes are approached one-sidedly; the inquiry concentrates on the subjective motivations of the strikers rather than the objective conditions to which they were responding. To understand the Durban strikes it is vital that *both* these aspects should be clearly understood. The strikes must be seen within the context of South African social and industrial relations as a whole. The conclusions to which this broader view leads, it will be seen, are radically different from those reached by the IIE.[1]

The general reasons for the Durban strikes were clear. The African workers of South Africa were, and still are, living under barely tolerable conditions. The Durban strikes were motivated by the clear determination of the workers concerned to improve their living standards. The question 'why Durban', Maree concludes, 'needs to be turned on its head: why do workers at other centres like the Rand, East London, Port Elizabeth, Cape Town and so on *not* go on strike while they toil under the same conditions that must also create very deep feelings of resentment and frustration?' (1976, pp. 94-5). While the suggestion that the strikes remained limited to Durban is wrong, this question correctly places the situation in Durban within a more general context. The same fundamental conflict between capital and labour is inherent in the economy as a whole. In every sector and in every city African workers have much the same prospects before them. Everywhere they are faced with the tasks of organisation and struggle. The role of the state and the nature of the legal system determine that their struggle must tend to be spontaneous, secret or illegal. It is a struggle that has been carried on sporadically for half a century and more. Undoubtedly, in 1973, many African workers took it for granted that spontaneous organisation and struggle offered them the most effective means of improving their situation. Sooner or later struggles of this nature were bound to break into the open. In this sense the fact that massive strikes began in Durban and not elsewhere is incidental. The situation would have been little different if the strikes had begun in Johannesburg, Port Elizabeth or East London.

More pertinent than 'why Durban?', therefore, is the question 'why 1973?' The answers must be sought in the pressures that determined the position of the African working class, materially and ideologically, in the years leading up to this period. Subtle but important changes had taken place among the workers and in the country as a whole. African workers who had been 'afraid to join trade unions' in the late 1960s were not afraid, a few years later, to join illegal strikes. Nor, as we shall see, were they afraid to join unions in their tens of thousands. The demoralisation of the 1960s had worn off. The older workers who had suffered the crushing blows and disillusionment of the Sharpeville period had been joined every year by young workers who had not yet been 'taught a lesson' and whose morale was high. The mood of fear and pessimism that had prevailed in the 1960s had gradually given way to a mood of new confidence and determination.

The fundamental influence in this process was the course of events internationally. The former protectorates of Bechuanaland, Basutuland and Swaziland had become independent during the 1960s. Guerilla war was developing in Angola and Mozambique. The Vietnam war escalated in this period. News reports from Vietnam multiplied and left scarcely

a country in the world unaffected. The world-wide ferment among
students and intellectuals in the late 1960s found an echo in South
Africa as well. The Black Consciousness movement sent ripples of
radical protest throughout the African population. Most fundamentally,
however, the late 1960s and early 1970s saw a decisive development
in the capitalist economy on a world scale. The period of almost
uninterrupted growth that had continued since the 1940s was showing
unmistakable signs of flagging. Increasingly serious problems were
encountered, first in the sphere of exchange, then in the sphere of
production. The great boom had been fuelled increasingly by inflation.
In South Africa inflation became ominous from approximately 1964
onwards. The supply of money in circulation, as well as the creation
of credit, was increasing at a rate far outstripping the increase in the
physical volume of manufacturing production (see Table 7.2).

Table 7.2 *The inflationary process in South Africa, 1967–75*

Year	Total money (R million)	Credit* (R million)	Manufacturing production (index)†
1967	1,706,9	2,484,4	135.5
1968	2,050,9	2,765,0	140.6
1969	2,223,9	3,252,6	150.3
1970	2,261,5	3,614,2	157.2
1971	2,448,4	3,858,1	160.7
1972	2,811,8	4,306,4	165.4
1973	3,387,1	5,842,6	179.9
1974	4,019,0	6,944,0	190.5
1975	4,290,0	8,354,0	194.5

* Claims of the banking sector against the private sector.
† 1963–4 = 100.
Source: *South African Statistics,* 1976.

Internationally, the bubble of inflationary boom was pricked in
August 1971 when President Nixon announced that the USA had
suspended gold payments on the dollar and imposed a 10 per cent
duty on all imports. The resulting chaos in the world's foreign-exchange
markets, writes Houghton, 'intensified the pressure on South Africa's
current balance of payments' (1973, p. 222). Due to the smallness
of available markets and the cost of industrial expansion, the South
African economy had been characterised by a chronic balance-of-

payments deficit – in particular from the late 1960s onwards (see Table 7.3).

Table 7.3 *South African balance of payments, 1970–5* (Rm.)

	1970	*1971*	*1972*	*1973*	*1974*	*1975*
Balance of trade	−1,143	−1,381	− 634	− 998	−2,505	−3,063
Net gold output	837	922	1,161	1,769	2,565	2,540
Services (net)	− 570	− 584	− 600	− 690	−1,004	−1,224
Balance on current account	− 827	−1,003	− 11	94	− 860	−1,616
Total capital movement	541	764	407	− 158	774	1,774
Changes in gold and other foreign reserves	− 262	− 156	437	− 112	− 67	191

Source: *South African Statistics*, 1976.

Every year imports into South Africa by far exceeded exports. In addition, heavy public-sector borrowing brought increasing interest payments to creditors abroad. The effect of this has only been offset by the sale of gold (which brought in more foreign currency than ever before with the sharp rise in the price of gold from 1973 to 1974) and by the inflow of foreign capital. Houghton drew the following conclusions at the end of the 1960s (1973, pp. 222–3):

> The first lesson to be learned from the course of the boom is the basic economic principle of scarcity or limitation of resources; neither individuals nor countries can continue to live beyond their means without running into serious troubles.... The country had been consuming more than it was able to produce; hence the adverse trade balance.... One of the things that undoubtedly influenced the thinking of the government and the monetary authorities was South Africa's urgent need to maintain a high rate of growth in the real G[ross] D[omestic] P[roduct]. They were well aware of the low standard of living of the mass of the population, and the desirability of raising *per capita* incomes. They knew equally well that ... annually there were some 128,000 new entrants to the labour market.... For economic, political and humanitarian reasons it was essential to provide jobs for as many of these people as possible by maintaining a high rate of expansion in the economy as a whole. For these reasons they

were naturally reluctant to take any *premature* steps to check the rate of growth.

Since the time that Houghton wrote, the situation has grown increasingly acute. The inflation created by 'maintaining a high rate of expansion' put the poorest layers of workers in an intolerable situation and paved the way to renewed industrial unrest. At the same time, it proved impossible to maintain a high rate of growth as world recession developed. This would rebound on a working class already hard hit by rising prices in the form of growing unemployment. Under these conditions economic policy was increasingly reduced to two alternatives: limiting inflation (and promoting recession), or stimulating investment (and promoting inflation). From the workers' point of view the first alternative meant fewer jobs and a downward pressure on wages, while the second alternative meant rising prices and, once again, a downward pressure on real wages.

Up to the early 1970s the state chose to stimulate growth at the cost of rising inflation. By 1975, however, world-wide conditions of recession were making it impossible to stimulate growth by any means. The period was characterised by a decline of profits in relation to costs and investment (see Table 7.4).

Table 7.4 *Rates of profit in manufacturing industry, 1964–72* (Rm.)

Year	Capital investment*	Materials used	Wages and salaries	Profits
1964	1,291	2,404	744	405
1966	1,714	3,066	966	458
1968	2,262	3,564	1,150	465
1970†	2,593	4,352	1,392	630
1972	3,234	5,388	1,760	652

* Capital investment refers to total investment in land, buildings, machinery and other fixed assets.
† In 1970 the method of computation was altered slightly with certain industries being excluded from the category of manufacturing industry.
Source: *South African Statistics*, 1976.

The tendency for the rate of profit to fall is explained by Marx as being the fundamental contradiction of capitalist production. This tendency became even more marked in the period following 1972. In 1975 the annual capital expenditure of all manufacturing firms for the first time exceeded their total annual profit (see Table 7.5).

Table 7.5 *Manufacturing profits and capital expenditure, 1970–5 (Rm.)**

Year	Capital expenditure†	Total profits
1970	279	533
1971	330	535
1972	460	583
1973	704	811
1974	890	891
1975	1,160	1,040

* This information is based on a sample of manufacturing firms representing approximately 63 per cent of the total net output of the manufacturing sector.
† Capital expenditure refers to expenditure on building, construction, new machinery, transport and other new equipment.
Source: *South African Statistics*, 1976.

By 1973, therefore, the South African economy was rapidly approaching the stage of 'stagflation' where, despite the extensive creation of credit and inflation, profits and growth would deteriorate. Also the creation of new jobs languished (see Table 7.6).

Table 7.6 *Employment in manufacturing industry, 1970–5*

Year	Total employed	Year	Total employed
1970	1,068,921	1973	1,171,300
1971	1,107,000	1974	1,223,900
1972	1,127,500	1975	1,254,100

Source: *South African Statistics*, 1976.

Finally, the physical volume of manufacturing production began to show signs of decline. The utilisation of production capacity remained fairly constant, changing from 88.4 per cent in February 1973, to 88.6 per cent in November 1975 (*South African Statistics*, 1976). While total output continued to rise slightly in 1975, this was the result of growth in a number of strong industries. In other industries decline set in.

During the early 1970s the workers of South Africa were experiencing the combined effect of these developments mainly in the form of rising prices (see Table 7.7).

Table 7.7 *Consumer price index, 1969–75*

Year	All items	Food	Clothing and footwear	Public transport
1969	95.3	96.9	98.9	99.3
1970	100.3	101.2	100.4	100.0
1971	106.4	106.1	102.7	105.4
1972	113.3	113.6	108.0	113.7
1973	124.1	131.0	116.8	134.8
1974	138.5	150.6	133.7	148.3
1975	157.2	173.1	148.3	177.3

Source: *South African Statistics*, 1976.

It is against this background that the position of the African working class should be assessed. Different surveys during the early 1970s showed unmistakably that a majority of African workers were living in a state of dire poverty. During 1971 and 1972, for example, a survey covering the wages of some 188,000 African workers was held by the Productivity and Wage Association. It yielded, *inter alia*, the results shown in Table 7.8.

Table 7.8 *Average weekly wage for African workers: all industries (1971–2)* (R)

	Grade of skill							
	1	2	3	4	5	6	7	8
Johannesburg and Central Rand	10.53 (30.73)	12.33 (25.5)	13.98 (19.14)	16.01 (9.13)	19.52 (6.88)	24.30 (3.92)	23.84 (3.78)	32.34 (0.91)
Cape Town/ Wynberg	11.77 (33.84)	14.04 (37.67)	15.01 (10.85)	17.20 (5.54)	19.98 (3.36)	23.81 (1.02)	10.62 (7.17)	38.59 (0.55)
Port Elizabeth/ Uitenhage	12.31 (39.83)	13.35 (27.72)	14.77 (14.92)	16.87 (9.74)	18.72 (4.38)	22.28 (1.49)	19.26 (1.03)	28.25 (0.89)
Durban/ Pinetown	10.45 (26.63)	12.17 (34.64)	13.03 (17.94)	16.16 (10.18)	18.87 (4.89)	22.40 (2.43)	26.51 (2.42)	28.53 (0.87)
East London	6.57 (45.24)	8.88 (13.68)	10.20 (15.56)	11.62 (9.76)	12.88 (7.07)	13.96 (3.34)	16.38 (2.69)	19.74 (2.77)

Note: The figures in brackets are the percentages of workers in each grade of skill.
Source: IIE (1974, p. 85).

On this basis it was estimated that some 79 per cent of all African workers were earning wages lower than the 'poverty datum line', i.e.

less than the cost of bare subsistence for an average-sized family. 92 per cent were earning less than the 'minimum effective level', i.e. bare subsistence plus the cost of certain other essentials such as education, medical care, reading matter, etc. In Durban the poverty datum line for an African family of six was estimated at R69.75 per month during 1971 and the minimum effective level at R105.00. In East London the corresponding figures were R74.78 and R112.17 (SRR, 1971, p. 178). During March and April 1973 the position was as shown in Table 7.9.

Table 7.9 *Poverty datum line, March–April 1973*

Area	Average family size	Poverty datum line (Rand)
Johannesburg	6	74.68
Cape Town	6	81.80
Durban	6	78.13
Port Elizabeth	6	78.58
East London	6	76.63

Source: IIE (1974, p. 86).

In the light of these figures the conclusion must be drawn that the majority of African families could only avoid starvation if they had more than one breadwinner or some means of support in addition to their breadwinner's wage. This applies equally to migrant workers, the only difference being that the migrant worker's family must stay in the reserve. The figures also indicate that many boys and girls will be forced to start work at a very early age.

On the one hand, therefore, the majority of African working-class families were extremely poor; on the other hand, they were experiencing a continuous rise in prices, especially in the cost of food and transport. Against this steady erosion of their wages they had, in general, no remedy. They were excluded from collective bargaining and there was no question of wages being linked to the cost-of-living index. Wage levels were forced down by the huge reserve army of the unemployed to the well-nigh absolute minimum that was needed to keep the workforce physically in existence. Legal minimum wages bore little relation to the material needs of the workers. Wage rises, from the African workers' point of view, depended mainly on the discretion of the employers. Poverty and hardship were exacerbated by a general lack of security. Under these conditions it was only to be expected that sections of African workers would sooner or later take action to defend themselves. Nor will it surprise us that in many cases they demanded the doubling or trebling of their existing wages. From their point of view the situation was drastic, calling for drastic measures. Yet action, once taken, has the effect of preparing employers to deal with future action. Organising a strike involves a considerable effort, and for the African workers in South Africa there is no guarantee that this effort can be repeated at will. Once African workers take action, therefore, they must try to ensure that their action will be decisive.

In this connection we must be careful to see the 'poverty datum line' in perspective. It is a concept used by social scientists to measure the standards of living of different sections of the population. There is no evidence that this concept was generally known among the striking workers of Durban, much less that this was their goal. On the contrary, it is more likely that the workers' goals will be determined by the values and the standards of society *as a whole*. South African society, like all societies, is dominated by the values of its ruling strata. These values are ceaselessly propagated in the press and elsewhere as normal and ideal. As such they form the natural point of reference for any group of workers struggling to improve themselves. This is not to say that workers, by striking, immediately hope to achieve the life-style of the upper-middle-class white. It means that substantial improvements, that is to say, a proportionate share of what society has to offer, will tend to be the goal of workers in action, even if in that particular struggle they cannot expect to advance more than marginally. The idea that the African strikers in Durban had no greater ambition than the level of subsistence must in any event be rejected. This, too, helps to explain why they often demanded much more than bare subsistence wages, and hence went beyond what certain observers may regard as 'reasonable' or 'legitimate' demands.

The ideological contradictions

The significance of the African workers' struggle was not lost on employers. The following editorial appeared in the Johannesburg *Star* on 30 January 1973:

> Attributing the work stoppages in Natal to the activities of a few agitators is unfortunately a conditioned reflex common to some politicians and employers. But the very level of wages paid – under

R5 a week in certain categories – must surely make potential
agitators of all the workers involved as living costs inexorably
rise. These workers share a common bond of hunger and misery,
very explosive elements. If labour peace is to be restored – before
little bush fires spread into a major conflagration – employers will
have to take the initiative and raise pay at least to a survival level,
and R5 a week is not that. And this is only a first step. The next
target must be the closing of the Black–White wage gap, and . . .
[we are warned] five years is the maximum left to us if industrial
strife is to be avoided. Pay for Blacks is not the concern only of
employers of labour but of everyone; poverty breeds discontent
and provides fertile ground for real agitators to exploit for a
dangerous harvest.

A joint meeting of the Federated Chambers of Industries and the
Steel and Engineering Industries Federation of South Africa (SEIFSA)
was held early in February to discuss the strikes in Natal and the threat
of their spreading to the rest of the country. There was no agenda for
the meeting, and the head of SEIFSA found it impossible to say beforehand whether any solutions would even be suggested.

In a speech to the Johannesburg Chamber of Commerce about the
same time Dr F. Cronjé, President of Nedbank, warned that 'the real
growth rate is too low, and the inflation rate is too high' (*Star IAW*,
3 February 1973). The main remedies that he called for were the
stimulation of internal demand – meaning 'considerable increases in
the wages of the lower income group' – and an 'expansionary budget' –
in other words, greater inflation. On the other hand, the economist
Spandau argued that the pressure for higher wages in industry was
approaching 'danger levels' and therefore it was 'hardly conceivable'
that the government would try to hold back wage increases. Therefore,
the only form that state intervention could take would be a wage and
price freeze. This, too, however, offered no solution. In the words of
a British commentator, a wage and price freeze is similar to 'treating
a hysterical patient by knocking him unconscious' (*Star IAW*, 10
February 1973).

Contradiction thus piled on confusion as the South African capitalist
class attempted to grapple with the beginnings of the crisis. Outside
certain narrow limits the laws of competition rule out a general increase
in the wages of African workers. The government depended on the
support of a petite-bourgeoisie that would be ruined if wages were to
rise substantially. This prevented the government from supporting

economic reform even in a period of boom. In the period of gathering recession that followed 1973 reform along these lines was all the more excluded. The big bourgeoisie, the only section of the capitalist class that might be capable of surviving under 'liberal' conditions, had no prospect of gaining political power except in a pre-revolutionary situation. The question thus arises once again of whether it is appropriate to think in terms of *preventing* a 'major conflagration' through wage increases and other reforms. On the contrary, a 'conflagration' appears to be a necessary condition *for bringing about* any move in this direction – and there is no reason to suppose that the workers would then be halted by mere reforms.

The different tendencies within the capitalist class emerged more clearly into the open following the outbreak of the strikes. On the one hand, large employers such as Wilson-Rowntrees in East London granted wage increases of up to 40 per cent to their African employees in order to avert the danger of a strike. Also at Unilever the mere threat of a strike was enough to provoke a wage increase from R16.00 to R18.50 per week. On the other hand, the Minister of Labour, M. Viljoen, informed Parliament that the strikes 'had little to do with more money for Africans. They were caused by agitators who wanted to cause the downfall of the Government' (*Star IAW*, 10 February 1973). While some employers proposed increasing wages, other employers refused. In the long run this must cause great strains in the labour market; in the short run it caused confusion. Some employers went to the TUCSA for advice. The response of its general secretary, A. Grobbelaar, was not encouraging (*Star IAW*, 27 January 1973): 'there is nothing to stop the strikes from spreading. South African employers have been too comfortable for too long with a docile work force. They have forgotten how to handle their own employees. They have to ask us for advice.'

More detailed information emerged from a survey by the IIE of nineteen employers whose workers had gone on strike. 'Lack of communication' between workers and employers was regarded by many employers as being an important cause of the disputes. Eleven of the nineteen firms claimed to have some form of works committee: yet ten of these – and fourteen of the nineteen employers – claimed to have had no advance warning of a strike. None of them, it appears, made use of the works committee for purposes of negotiation. Once the strikes were in progress, only eight of the nineteen employers engaged in any form of negotiation with the workers. Seventeen of them claimed that 'agitators and intimidators' had been at work, but of these ten specified that they were referring to activists among their own workers, not to 'outsiders'. 'Not much evidence,' the IIE observes, 'was offered on this score' (1974, p. 80). On the other hand, twelve of the nineteen employers admitted that the police were called in during the strike. In two cases the security police were present. In fifteen cases the African foremen and office workers joined the strike. In all cases it appears that the stike was only ended when wage increases had either been given or promised.

The downward pressure of the market upon wages emerges clearly from the evidence. One employer complained that his main competitor's workers had gone back for R12.00 while his own workers had insisted on more than this. All firms claimed to have plans for further wage revisions during the coming year. Twelve said that the wage increases that had been given would not affect their long-term profitability. Six others said that the opposite was the case. Two of these added that they were operating 'in a very competitive market, and so would not be able to pass the increase on to the consumer' (*ibid*., p. 81).

Sixteen of the employers were in favour of works committees, despite their inactivity during the strikes. In contrast, seven employers opposed trade unions *in general*; only five approved (the remainder would give no answer to this question). As far as *African* trade unions were concerned, only four employers were in favour and ten opposed. Of the latter, four 'expressed fear of the power that it would give the workers'. One explained: 'It would improve the lot of the workers but the employers would be in a worse position' (*ibid*., p. 82). From its survey the IIE drew the following conclusions (*ibid*., p. 83):

> Our general impression is that, although management has been
> made aware that there are problems, they minimize the real
> extent and urgency of these problems. They do not seem to be
> in touch with the . . . urgent necessity for immediate and large-
> scale change in a number of fields, for example, in attitudes
> towards workers, wages, working conditions and training,
> promotion and communication. They seem to believe that they
> will be able to re-establish their customary total control of the
> work-force by means of a few relatively minor concession[s] .

In contrast to employers, the white working-class public appears to have felt that the strikes were justified. Only a minority appears to have been opposed to African working-class organisation. The following percentages emerged from a survey of 164 whites (IIE, 1974, p. 75):

	African wages not too low	*Strikes are fault of employers*	*Opposed to African organisation*
Professional men	5	43	30
Businessmen	17	45	17
White-collar workers	12½	53	17
Blue-collar workers	12½	60	30

It is noteworthy that, according to this survey, most white manual workers hold the employers responsible for the strikes. This, the IIE remarks, 'is at least a small indication that some of their own "class consciousness" may enter into their appreciation of the problems of fellow workers divided from them by racial barriers' (*ibid.*, p. 76). Moreover, 'in view of the fact that White workers have been among the strongest opponents of African trade unions, the fact that less than a third of those in our sample express opposition is encouraging' (*ibid.*).

What were the views of the African workers themselves? The findings of the IIE are based on interviews with ninety-five African workers. Eight questions were discussed with them. The first question was: 'What was the aim of the strike?' Ninety-three of the workers replied that the aim was to get higher wages. The second question was: 'Did the workers talk to the employers before the strikes?' The vast majority replied in the affirmative, about half of them adding that such talking was no use. This contradicts the impression created by the majority of employers who were interviewed. The third question was: 'What gave workers the idea that a strike would help them?' The answers to this question varied, but all were of a concrete nature. Among the answers were the following:

1 It was the result of poverty (26 per cent of respondents).
2 It was the only effective way (24 per cent).
3 All other methods had failed (17 per cent).
4 'It is because if the whole firm goes on strike we can't all be fired at once.'
5 'The employers would also have much to lose' (a slaughterer).
6 'We know that the work we do is important to the employer and gives him a big profit' (a laboratory assistant).
7 'Because employers are employers because of workers' (a tea-maker).

The fourth question was. 'Why did the workers go back to work?'

70 per cent of the respondents replied that they had been given or promised an increase. 20 per cent replied that they had been forced back to work by the fear of losing their jobs, fear of the police or fear of action by the state. The fifth question was: 'Did the strike help those who struck?' 43 per cent of the respondents gave an unqualified 'yes', 37 per cent gave a qualified 'yes', and 15 per cent said that the strikes had not helped at all. The remaining three questions and answers can be summarised as follows:

	Yes (%)	No (%)
Are the workers satisfied now?	10	75
Has there been any improvement at your work-place since the strikes?	10	75
Do you think the workers will strike again if they are dissatisfied?	70	20

The IIE draws the following conclusions from these interviews (1974, p. 52):

> The workers struck because of low wages and the feeling that the employer would not do anything to remedy the wage levels unless drastic action was taken. They feel that the strikes were productive, but they remain very dissatisfied. Having discovered that the strike is an effective weapon, the majority are fully prepared to use it again. It may well be, therefore, that the most significant change wrought by the strikes is not in the workers' living standards, but in their sense of their own potential power.

Another survey carried out in Durban during 1971 and 1972 shed more light on the attitudes prevailing among African workers. The survey covered 350 Africans of whom about 85 per cent were workers. Of those interviewed some two-thirds saw their poverty as having *social* causes, as being the result of discrimination, exploitation or oppression. About 70 per cent were orientated towards some form of collective action. About one-half showed awareness of the potential strength of the African working class. About 27 per cent understood collective action in clearly political terms, as involving organisation on the basis of a common programme and shared struggle. About 10 per cent understood the potential strength of the working class in clear terms of working-class action or 'broader political action' (*ibid.*, p. 56). A substantial number of African workers, we may conclude, were politically aware and capable of leading their fellow-workers ('agitators' in

the official terminology). This was undoubtedly the key to the movement of the African workers from 1973 onwards.

The Indian workers

The official breakdown of the population of Durban, according to the
census of 1970, was as follows (*South African Statistics*, 1976):

'Asian'	321,204
'White'	256,836
'Bantu'	227,717
'Coloured'	45,189
Total	850,946

To this should be added the population of a number of working-class
areas round Durban which are classified as part of the 'Bantu homeland' of Kwazulu (*ibid.*):

Umlazi	123,495
Clermont	26,125
Hammarsdale	21,657
Total	171,277

A sizeable part of the working class of Durban is thus classified as
'Asian'. By South African standards these workers are relatively free
and have the right to belong to registered trade unions. A not insignificant number of 'Asians', moreover, are themselves employers of labour.
On the other hand, all 'Asians' are disenfranchised and suffer racial discrimination and oppression in many forms. What position did the Indian
workers take up when their African fellow-workers struck? The IIE
investigated this question by speaking to the secretaries of a number of
registered trade unions and interviewing 117 workers classified as 'Asian'.
The main conclusion drawn by the IIE is the following (1974, p. 69):

> although there is still a certain amount of anti-African fear and
> prejudice among Indian workers, nevertheless the majority of
> them see Africans as fellow workers. Indian participation in the
> strikes was quite considerable, and most Indian workers are in
> favour of institutionalising their solidarity with African workers
> in combined trade unions.

Of the Indian workers interviewed, 42 per cent reported that there
had been some form of stoppage at their places of work. In about

two-thirds of the reported cases the Indian workers had joined the African workers on strike. Of the minority who did not strike and who gave reasons for not doing so, about one-third said that they were satisfied with their conditions, while about a quarter felt restrained by their membership of a trade union. Some workers, in fact, said that their union had 'specifically advised them not to strike' (*ibid.*, p. 63). From the side of the trade-union organisers it was reported that some of their Indian members had approached them because they wanted to join the strikes but were afraid of being victimised by employers. They were advised to tell their employers that they were staying away through fear of intimidation. Such a tactic, needless to say, must have the effect of presenting employers with 'evidence' of intimidation, hence with a means of discrediting the solidarity between free and unfree workers that characterised the Durban strikes. That this tactic was followed, however, was confirmed by an African strike leader (*ibid.*, p. 58): 'The Indians want to join us but they are scared of the employers. They want us to chase them out of the factory so that they will have an excuse.'

In reality, fear of intimidation appears to have played a relatively minor role as far as the Indian workers were concerned. Of those who were interviewed, 41 per cent had been worried about 'violence' during the strikes. In most cases this referred to violence at the hands of Africans. Some answers were in racist terms, such as 'You know what the natives are like' (*ibid.*, p. 62). Of those who actually took part in the strikes, about one-half said that they were afraid of the African workers; the other half said they had struck for higher wages. Fear of Africans, on the other hand, tended to be concentrated among women workers. Most of the women interviewed were young and badly paid: 42 per cent of them had been worried about 'Africans' during the strikes, compared with 15 per cent of the men. The IIE explains this discrepancy by the fact that girls in the Indian community tend to be brought up in a sheltered way. A 'fair proportion' of the women interviewed were employed in small 'all-Indian' factories, which would strengthen any tendency towards 'prejudice through ignorance' (*ibid.*, p. 69).

In practice there was no evidence of violence by African workers against Indian workers. The limited degree of hostility felt by Indian workers towards African workers is suggested by the answers to the following three questions (*ibid.*, p. 64):

	Yes (%)	No (%)
Do you think it is better if all workers in one industry belong to the same trade union . . . ?	82	9
Do you think African workers at your factory should be allowed to join your union?	74	15
If African workers of a factory go on strike, do you think that Indian workers at the factory should join them?	76	12

It may be concluded that solidarity with their African fellow-workers, rather than fear or hostility, predominated among the broad mass of Indian workers. As a 22-year-old Indian knitwear worker put it: 'They should be with us because they work with us' (*ibid.*). This is borne out by the secretaries of the registered trade unions representing the coloured (i.e. including 'Asian') workers at most of the strike-hit firms (*ibid.*, p. 59):

> None of them reported any incident in which African workers used violence against Indian workers. Most of them said that the relations between the two groups were good, and several reported instances in which Indian artisans had encouraged the African labourers to strike. In the furniture industry, artisans struck [at] several firms in support of higher wages for labourers. One significant example of this was the Indian-owned firm Trueart, where there was a particularly good relationship between Indian and African workers against the Indian employer. The one instance of potential conflict also comes from the furniture industry. At a union meeting it was reported that Indian artisans at one factory were acting as strike-breakers by bringing in their relatives to do the work of striking Africans. The mass meeting reacted furiously to this information, and the practice ceased without any intervention by the Africans being necessary.

Seen against the history of hostility between African and Indian South Africans, we must agree with the IIE that the Durban strikes have revealed 'a highly significant pattern of solidarity' (*ibid.*, p. 65). Of the large majority of Indian workers who were in favour of joining the African workers on strike, about two-thirds referred to the 'identity of interest between Indian and African workers' (*ibid.*). As a result the strikes were conducted peacefully and led to wage increases for many Indian workers. This, the IIE concludes, is 'likely to have increased the feeling of Indian–African solidarity' (*ibid.*, p. 69).

The registered trade unions

Above, we have characterised the role of the registered trade unions in the post-1922 period as one of 'defensive passivity'. This assessment was confirmed by the role of the registered unions during the Durban strikes. In the case of TUCSA, its main contribution consisted of advising not the strikers but, instead, one of the two concerns whose African workers were the first to go on strike. Only two TUCSA affiliates went so far as to negotiate between strikers and employers. For the rest, 'the registered trade union movement sat largely on the sidelines while large-scale industrial action was undertaken by the major part of the work-force (Douwes-Dekker *et al.*, 1975, p. 224).

The two registered unions that did play a role were the Garment Workers' Industrial Union (GWIU; a 'mixed' union) and the Textile Workers' Industrial Union (TWIU; a 'coloured' union).[2] The IIE gives an account of the role played by the latter. H. Bolton, secretary of the Natal branch of the union, addressed the strikers at Consolidated Woolwashing & Processing Mills (CWPM) in Pinetown, and appealed to them to negotiate through the union. In this way the leaders of the TWIU hoped to secure recognition of the union at the same time. The tactic which they then followed was to write a letter to the industrial council setting out numerous demands on the workers' behalf. In the crucial matter of wages it confines itself to the modest demand for an increase of R1.00 per week. Demands for paid holidays, a forty-two-hour week, an increase of overtime rates and equal pay for women – which had been raised during national negotiations – were dropped.

The secretary of the industrial council, replying to this letter, stated that since the existing industrial agreement had not been violated by the employers no dispute existed as far as the council was concerned. While this correspondence went on, the workers in Pinetown remained on strike. The increases offered by the employers ranged from R1.75 to R2.50 a week. On 31 January the workers of CWPM met at the factory gate with TWIU officials in attendance. The factory manager put the employers' offer to the workers. He said that the company would employ the workers who accepted this offer, and the others would be fired. The workers thereupon entered the factory. Throughout this scene the union officials were ignored. From the workers' point of view the importance of negotiating through union officials could no longer have been as clear as it might have seemed at first. By entrusting their interests to the union officials, they stood to gain an increase of

R1.00 per week. By relying on their own efforts the workers in the cotton mills had gained increases of more than twice as much.

Also, in the CTM strike, TWIU officials attempted to intervene. They 'continued to press for some response by management, but without success' (IIE, 1974, pp. 32–3). We have seen how an offer was eventually made to the workers and how the union officials advised the workers to return to work 'because it would be difficult to maintain unity much longer' (*ibid.*, p. 34). Considering that one of the primary functions of trade unions is precisely to struggle for unity among workers, it is surprising to find in the IIE account that the question is taken no further. It is not stated how the TWIU officials responded to the problem of disunity or how they attempted to mobilise the workers – workers who had struck in defiance of the law and would almost inevitably have welcomed a bold initiative.

The clearest account of an intervention by TWIU officials is given in relation to the strike at Smith & Nephews, a firm that was said to have a more progressive labour policy. The strikers demanded a basic wage of R18.00 a week for all workers. This was rejected by the employers. Union officials negotiated with management at the factory gate in the presence of the workers. The workers could thus see what was being done. The presence of the police, however, tipped the scales in the employers' favour. According to the IIE, it was a union official who proposed a settlement by which 'the total wage bill would not be increased dramatically' (*ibid.*, p. 35): in the case of workers earning less than R18.00 per week, to amalgamate their bonus with their basic wage in order to bring the total up to R18.00 per week; while women workers were offered only R12.00. The employers immediately agreed. On the following day, 6 February, the issue was decided. The employers' offer was typed out and a copy given to every worker. Plainclothes policemen were present in force at the factory-gate meeting. With policemen standing immediately behind the union officials, the workers proved 'quite receptive' to the offer that was put (*ibid.*, p. 36). They accepted the proposal and went back to work. The TWIU was accorded recognition at the Smith & Nephews plant.

Care should be taken not to criticise South African trade unionists *in general* for being cautious or even timid by the standards of trade unionism in Western Europe, North America or Australia. 'Ordinary' trade-union activities are tolerated by the state in South Africa only to a very limited extent. For this very reason, the workers *en masse* may often be able to act more freely than the legally hemmed-in union apparatus. If the union, in such a situation, insists on representing the workers, it can only limit their struggle. It is where the workers are divided or hesitant that union leadership is important from the workers' point of view. Even where the union is unable to lead - as was the case in the Durban strikes - it may still be able to support or encourage the workers indirectly. But the role of the unions is a tactical question which needs to be considered in every situation. The decisive question is what the workers stand to gain by using 'wildcat' tactics, and what would be accomplished if the union intervenes. Such accomplishments might be immediate (e.g. wage increases) or of a long-term nature (e.g. recognition of the workers' organisations). In two of the three cases reported by the IIE the answer to this question is clear. There is no indication that the workers gained anything as a result of the intervention by union officials. In the case of the Smith & Nephews strike recognition of the TWIU was gained as a result of the African workers' strike.

Looking at the Durban strikes as a whole, it is clear that for a time an abnormal situation prevailed. By the sheer size of the strike movement, the workers gained a certain immunity from police reaction. Completely independently of any trade union the workers were making unprecedented advances in terms of wage increases and concessions from employers and the state. Their action was equally independent of the state machinery for wage determination. By their firm yet disciplined action the workers compelled the respect of the public in general and of white workers in particular. In this situation it could not have been impossible for the registered unions to have given unobtrusive but vital support to the strikes. Meeting facilities could have been made available (as was done in the case of the CTM strike); facilities could have been offered for workers to duplicate material; the principles of working-class organisation could have been discussed informally with the strikers under phenomenally favourable conditions.

Only to a very limited extent did the unions rise to the challenge. In general they played no role at all. Even during this historical upheaval, even though many of their own members were involved, the leaders of the registered unions remained anchored in 'defensive passivity'. They had forgone an important opportunity of associating themselves with the movement of the African workers and gaining the confidence of the latter through the decisive medium of action; they continued to stand aloof from the mainstream of the South African labour movement.

Conclusions

The Durban strikes were characterised, from the African workers' point of view, by their unprecedented success. Not only were mass reprisals avoided; wage increases and other gains were achieved in the great majority of cases. Nor were the effects of the strikes confined to those factories where strikes actually took place. Wage increases were also granted by employers who feared that their workers might follow the example of the strikers. The repercussions of the strike wave set in motion by the Durban strikes were felt from one end of the country to the other. This was reflected by the sharp rate of increase of African industrial wages from 1973 onwards (see Table 7.10).

Table 7.10 *Average annual earnings of African industrial workers, 1970-5*

1970	R619	1973	R860 (+ 17.81%)
1971	R667 (+ 7.75%)	1974	R1,053 (+ 22.44%)
1972	R730 (+ 9.45%)	1975	R1,271 (+ 20.70%)

Source: *South African Statistics*, 1976.

Not only employers but also the state was forced to make concessions. The Minister of Labour, Viljoen, continued to maintain that African trade unions would not be recognised but promised to amend the Bantu Labour (Settlement of Disputes) Act. Even more significant from the workers' point of view was the reluctance or inability of the police to act decisively against them. It must have been clear to the workers, as the IIE puts it, 'that the police were, in the last resort, on the side of the employers' (1974, p. 44). Yet the police acted with restraint, apparently on orders from above. Employers were entitled to dismiss strikers and the police were entitled to arrest workers in their thousands on any number of charges, ranging from illegal striking to holding meetings without a permit or creating a public disturbance. Yet to have done so, as the IIE puts it, 'would almost certainly have created a very dangerous situation' (*ibid.*, p. 43).

A clear example was provided by the Hammarsdale general strike, where 7,000 workers, having struck illegally, proceeded to hold an illegal mass meeting in the presence of the police. Although they were chanting and waving sticks, which may be regarded as 'dangerous weapons' in South Africa, the police did not attempt to intervene. Two groups of workers broke away from the main body and marched towards the factories. The police headed them off but no arrests were made. On another occasion armed police did attack a procession of about a thousand municipal workers who were carrying sticks and marching through the streets of Durban: 106 of them were arrested and convicted of causing a public disturbance. Their sentence, however, was R30, or thirty days' imprisonment, of which R25 or twenty-five days was suspended. Also, a group of 150 building workers moving from site to site in the centre of the city was arrested, but received very light sentences. On another occasion when the police stopped marching strikers they did no more than ask them to surrender their sticks – and promised to return the sticks after the march was over. Clearly, the authorities considered discretion the better part of valour, a most unusual situation in South Africa. Apart from the fear of provoking even broader layers of workers into action, a further object was undoubtedly to limit as far as possible the disruption suffered by employers. The workers had to be got back to work even at the cost of concessions. The light sentences that the arrested men were given made it possible for them to return to work immediately. The alternative was to 'teach them a lesson'. This might have meant bringing much of industry to a standstill and causing serious unrest.

Even more significant are the tactical conclusions that the workers themselves had drawn. A leading feature of the strikes was the distrust shown by workers towards employers and the state. This was reflected in their extreme reluctance to appoint representatives or to announce their actions in advance. Clearly, the workers expected that their leaders would be victimised, despite all assurances that employers might give, and that their plans would be frustrated if employers were told too much about them. Organisationally, the mass meeting was extensively used. As far as the outside world was concerned, the workers' organisation was informal and their action was spontaneous. Under conditions where strikes are illegal and the police form a serious threat, such a tactic was entirely consistent and, moreover, extremely effective.

These tactics gave the strike movement a highly democratic nature. Being obliged to remain anonymous within the ranks of the mass meeting, the workers' leaders were subject to direct control by those whom they were leading. The ultimate democratic safeguard, the power of immediate recall over all elected representatives, was present in the fullest sense. Conditions of legality would make it *possible* for workers' leaders to separate themselves from the mass and thus make possible the growth of a bureaucracy. Liberal support for African trade-union rights is not unconnected with this possibility. An important factor in the development of African working-class organisation, therefore, is the extent to which the implications of 'spontaneous' organisation are realised by the workers and their leaders, and the principles of democratic control are extended to the open unions in the future.

The IIE has the following to say in connection with the leadership and tactics of the strikes (1974, pp. 6, 38):

> in the absence of any workers' organisations which might have called the strikes, organised them, and managed the negotiations, it is very difficult to find out what actually happened. The strikes either came about through some quite complicated underground organisation (of which there is no evidence), or else they came about as a result of a large number of independent decisions by unofficial leaders and influential workers in different factories. .. Sometimes workers seem to have had informal meetings outside the gates before work, at which the decision to strike was immediately taken. In other instances, workers simply stopped work in one part of the factory, and the strike spread. In either case the result was a mass meeting of workers, either in or just outside the factory. Demands do not seem to have been clearly formulated. In some instances the mass meetings called on employers to speak to them. In other cases they seem to have left the initiative to the employer. Demands usually emerged in these confrontations with management, with the workers taking up whichever initial cry appeared to them to be most attractive. Employers were barracked, jeered at, and disbelieved, but never threatened with violence. However, by this stage employers had usually called in the police.

Maree finds this inadequate: 'The most sad omission of the "Durban Strikes"', he writes, 'is a study of the leadership and the organisational patterns that most probably existed during the strikes' (1976, p. 99). Undeniably, the work would have gained a great deal in value if closer attention had been paid to the way in which decisions were taken and experiences were digested. The IIE, on the other hand, sees working-class organisation as an instrument of 'stable industrial peace' (*ibid.*, pp. 107 ff.). The methods evolved by the Durban strikers had nothing in common with this. The workers turned their backs on 'industrial peace' and struggled for change with all the might at their disposal. From the liberal point of view the Durban strikes were uncontrollable and alarming. The workers' tactics prepared the ground for future confrontations and needed to be opposed. The offhand and faintly contemptuous manner in which the IIE deals with these tactics is thus entirely consistent. A serious and conscientious study by this organisation was not to be expected.

Maree goes on to criticise the way in which the IIE disproves the 'agitator theory' (1976, pp. 99–100):

> Although there certainly is value in disproving the agitator theory it has the immense disadvantage that it is defensive. It is an approach that implicitly accepts the ideology of the elite, i.e. the government and the employers. The authors could have taken a more aggressive stance by refusing to use this ideological framework, but to look at strikes from the point of view of the workers instead. If they had done this, they would not have conceded that the term agitators is even applicable to workers ... industrialists fly in experts from overseas to tell them how to utilise and control their labour force more efficiently, but these experts are not called agitators even though they are telling the employers how to behave in their own best interests. But when workers consult outsiders how they as workers should behave in their best interests these outsiders are branded as agitators. By taking a defensive attitude and proving that there were no 'agitators' the authors of 'Durban Strikes' played into the hands of the workers' opponents.

Again, while Maree's remarks are apt, it is doubtful whether the IIE can be expected to benefit from them. The IIE is inspired by the vision of an industrial economy where African workers 'will begin to co-operate wholeheartedly in its development' (1974, p. 180). Is it not likely that, from this standpoint, workers' leaders and advisers who advocate class struggle might indeed be seen as 'agitators' in the worst sense of the word?

The Durban strikes consisted of a mass movement of the African working class, supported by sections of Indian workers. It arose from the conditions that are common to the African working class. It was preceded by widespread discussion and agreement at the level of the shop floor and the compound. There is no evidence that the strikes were centrally organised or led. The theory put forward by many employers and the state, that the strikes were caused by a small number of individuals who succeeded in intimidating the vast majority of workers, has no foundation in reality. Thus the following incident was reported by an employers' organisation in an attempt to prove, and not to disprove, the 'agitator theory':[3]

The police were called to one relatively small firm, in large
numbers, and the officer in charge told the assembled workers
'With us there is no danger of intimidation. Anybody who wants
to go to work can go into the factory.' And, said our informant,
'nobody moved'.

Senior police officers, too, effectively discounted the theory of the
state: 'So far,' a senior police officer was (on 18 January) reported to
have said, 'we have no evidence to indicate that there is anything
organised' (IIE, 1974, p. 15). A fortnight later, when the strikes were at
their height, the Port Natal Divisional Commander of police was more
emphatic still: 'There was still no definite proof that agitators were
behind the stoppages,' he declared. 'Had there been we would have
taken action' (*ibid.*, p. 90).

Two further features of the strike movement should be noted.
The workers tended to strike at the factory, as opposed to staying at
home. The strikes were thus 'concentrated and highly visible' (*ibid.*,
p. 100), and took on a demonstrative character. Workers at neighbouring
factories could observe the mass meetings and note the progress of the
strikes. This was undoubtedly a more potent means of spreading the
strike call than any verbal or written propaganda could have been.
Related to this was a form of 'flying picket system' which seems to
have developed in some cases. The IIE describes this as follows (*ibid.*,
p. 20):

Many bands of municipal workers marched through the streets of
the city centre, and there were eye-witness reports of minor cases
of intimidation. One group stopped a refuse-removal truck and
chased the African workers on it. Crowds are also reported to
have threatened to burn down the City Engineer's labour office
if the African clerks there did not stop working.

Similarly, a group of about 150 building workers is reported to have
gone round from site to site. In industries like these, where the workers
are scattered over different places of work, it is clear that different
tactics are called for than in cases where the entire work-force is concentrated in a single plant. In a factory the problem of organisation can
be solved by spontaneous discussion or calling a mass meeting. Where
the workers are dispersed, this is impossible; nor can they be reached
by demonstrative strikes at the plant. The only alternative is to take
the strike to them. This must inevitably involve some form of 'flying
picket', i.e. groups of strikers going round informing other workers of
the strike and persuading them to join it. At the same time, this tactic

sets an important precedent. It may equally be put to use when the attempt is made to transform a plant-based strike into a general strike.

If the decision-making method developed by the Durban strikers was one of the most democratic ever to have emerged in South Africa, the workers also attempted to enforce the decisions that were reached. Legally, this amounted to the criminal offence of inciting or attempting to incite a strike. Opportunities for discussing strategy and tactics were limited. Under the prevailing conditions a strike would be most likely to succeed where a majority of workers, on the basis of experience, are tending towards the conclusion that the time has come to act. Towards any dissident minority, unorthodox or peremptory methods of persuasion might of necessity have to be used. The IIE observes that, very likely, strike-breakers were occasionally threatened with violence. What 'intimidation' took place, however, was 'intimidation of a small minority by the great majority of workers' (*ibid.*, p. 94) – a very different proposition from that of the employers.

The African workers of Durban thus developed their own rudimentary system of democratic centralism in order to conduct their struggle successfully. This system proved remarkably effective, combining general consensus and support with a certain measure of discipline. Employers and the state were unable to repress the movement that ensued; they were forced to come to terms with it. At the same time, they fought every inch of the way, making use of every available device to strengthen their own position and undermine that of the workers. The strategy urged on its members by the Durban Chamber of Commerce, for example, was as follows (*ibid.*, pp. 40–1):

1. Notify the Department of Labour (Telephone number 28371).
2. Advise your workers that you will consider their demands on condition that they return to work.
3. Advise the workers that there will be no pay for the time they are on strike.
4. If you consider that your present rates of pay are fully justifiable, stand by these and in no circumstances move from that stand.
5. If you feel that an increase in minimum wage is necessary determine this increase and tell them of your decision. Thereafter stand by your decision.
6. Do not attempt to bargain as this will only encourage the Bantu to escalate his demands. Action must be positive, definite and final.

7. Grant increases of a definite amount in preference to percentages on earnings. Percentages are not easily understood by the Bantu and across-the-board increases are a greater benefit to the lowest paid workers.

8. Do everything possible to avoid violence but if this should arise, call the police immediately.

9. Stoppages to date have been mainly good natured and the tactful police action has contributed greatly to this. Make every effort to keep it this way.

In practice, employers tended to call in the police regardless of whether violence had arisen. They tended to negotiate with the police at their side, presumably hoping to intimidate the workers. This could be seen from the beginning of the strikes, though of course the tactic has been used for generations.

If the workers stood firm despite all the 'positiveness' shown by the employer, the tactic of 'negotiation by sacking' very often followed. The IIE explains (*ibid*., p. 42):

> They [the employers] informed the workers that they were all dismissed, but could apply for reinstatement at the new rates, or else they gave them a deadline after which all workers who had not returned to work would be dismissed. In most cases this seems to have been a negotiating ploy, and most of the workers who were dismissed in this way were eventually taken back.

Known activists can be eliminated by this means. In some cases the sacking of workers' leaders can give rise to fresh disputes and strikes.

In most cases the strikers won concessions, though often considerably less than their demands. Thus they tended to go back to work with a sense of victory and of their own strength, but on the other hand with continued dissatisfaction and a sense of having been cheated. This mood would provide a fertile climate for continued industrial unrest.

Yet the struggle of the African workers could not remain confined to struggles at plant level concerned with specifically industrial issues. It could only be a question of time before the forms of struggle developed at Durban would be used in support of political demands. In this sense the Durban strikes amounted to a preliminary skirmish, an announcement of struggles to come and a rough indication of the form in which those struggles would take place. Most of the strikes, according to the IIE, were 'demonstration strikes'. They 'did not develop into a major trial of strength between the two sides' (*ibid*., p. 43). Yet the movement initiated by the Durban strikes could culminate only in a decisive confrontation. Either the workers would make increasing headway in satisfying their outstanding demands - an intolerable prospect for employers and the state - or the latter would succeed in forcing the movement to a halt. In practice, this struggle would turn out to be lengthy, with neither side inclined to precipitate a major battle prematurely.

Chapter 8

From Durban to Soweto

In that the grievances of the African working class in Durban were not peculiar to Durban, it was inherently unlikely that the strikes would remain confined to Durban. In fact, they rapidly began spreading to other parts of the country. At the same time, no wave of strikes as intense and concerted as the Durban strikes took place for another three years. One reason for this has already been noted. The Durban strikes put pressure on employers throughout the country and prompted a general tendency for the wages of African workers to be increased more rapidly than before. In this sense the Durban strikes took the entire African working class forward and alleviated its immediate necessity to struggle.

Another factor was the growing unemployment among African workers as conditions of recession set in. The estimated numbers of African workers for whom the economy could provide no fixed employment are shown in Table 8.1. From the workers' point of view the worsening scarcity of jobs increased the danger of being sacked for striking and being replaced by work-seekers from the reserves or from the streets. Even relatively skilled workers enjoyed less security than before. Thus, while the causes of industrial unrest were in no sense exhausted by the Durban strikes – on the contrary, the pressure of inflation was growing steadily worse – the struggle was partly muted. Yet in all major centres striking continued sporadically on much the same pattern as in Durban. At the end of 1974 a journalist concluded (*Cape Times*, 3 January 1975):

> Perhaps the most negative aspects of the year were this failure
> to halt inflation and restore some stability to the relationship
> between prices and incomes, and the failure to provide a

collective bargaining mechanism for African workers to improve their position, as without one they will inevitably continue to resort to striking when dissatisfaction boils over.

Table 8.1 *African unemployment (estimated), 1970–6*

1970	1,019,000	1974	1,484,000
1971	1,127,000	1975	1,723,000
1972	1,315,000	1976	1,995,000

Source: SACTU (1977, p. 5).

While the extent of the strikes diminished in 1974 and 1975, industrial unrest continued at levels that were unprecedented in comparison with the previous ten or twenty years (see Table 8.2). The main difference that set in after March 1973 was precisely that striking became more sporadic. This helped to restore the confidence of the capitalist class. Workers on strike in a single factory can be treated with greater impunity than might be considered advisable in the case of a massive wave of struggle. If a strike is isolated, it may be possible for the employer to replace the entire work-force; when thousands of workers are involved, this possibility will be excluded. Thus from 1973 to June 1976 a war of attrition was waged between African workers and employers, on the surface subdued and scarcely reported in the press, in reality harsh and irreconcilable. On the militance of the workers and their readiness to struggle, the setbacks that they suffered in this period had no noticeable effect.

Table 8.2 *Strikes by African workers, 1973–5*

Year	Total stoppages	Workers involved	Man-days lost	Wages lost
1973	370	98,029	229,137	R368,523
1974	384	58,975	98,396	R244,189
1975	276	23,295	18,720	R47,282

Source: *South African Statistics*, 1976.

A survey conducted in Cape Town by Janet Graaff from November 1975 to February 1976 provides us with valuable insight into the conditions and attitudes of the African working class during this period. 211 African workers were interviewed of whom half were entitled to remain in Cape Town in terms of section 10 of the Bantu (Urban Areas) Act; 40 per cent were working on a yearly contract, and 10 per cent were working illegally. The survey made it quite clear that low wages remained a focal point of conflict. The average earnings of the men interviewed was R26 per week: 50 per cent, however, earned less than R25, and 75 per cent less than R30 per week (Graaff, 1976, p. 86). Of the workers who specified their grievances at work, 77 per cent expressed dissatisfaction with their wages, and 43 per cent complained about unwarranted deductions from their wages and arbitrary action by management: *'Irrespective of industry, of job category, and of legal status,'* Graaff concludes, *'the overriding grievance concerns low wages'* (*ibid.*, p. 88).

This raises the question of what means of settling their grievances were available to the workers: 39 per cent of the workers who specified their grievances stated that relations with their foreman and/or their manager were unsatisfactory and that their negotiating institutions were ineffective. The inadequacy of the negotiating institutions – in practice, works committees and liaison committees – was demonstrated even more concretely by the fact that the majority of workers took their grievances direct to the management or foremen, even where a committee existed.[1] What, then, do the workers think should be done to improve the situation? Significantly enough, scarcely any of the workers believed in individual action. Of those who gave definite replies to this question, the majority thought in terms of a factory-based organisation of African workers only. A minority – some 15 per cent of all respondents – thought in terms of wider organisation. Of these, 40 per cent meant an African trade union, and 20 per cent meant that Africans should join coloured trade unions. Of the workers who advocated factory-based organisation, 43 per cent were in favour of works committees, and 6 per cent in favour of liaison committees. The remaining 51 per cent, Graaff reports, 'responded to the effect that *workers should act as a unified group*, approach management as a unified group, and negotiate with management as a unified group' (*ibid.*, p. 91).

This confirms the lessons of the Durban strikes. Above all else, African workers are faced with the problem of wages that are totally unsatisfactory. They have no formal instruments by which this problem can be solved; they are left to their own devices in the struggle for improvement. Trade unions are relatively unknown to the African workers of Cape Town; liaison committees and works committees are regarded with a measure of suspicion. As in Durban, the mass meeting was the tactic that lay most readily to hand.

Significant differences existed in certain respects between migrant workers and workers born in Cape Town. In general, the latter were more advanced in terms of skills, social awareness and understanding of the need for wider organisation. A further correlation with conditions at Durban was the attitude towards coloured workers. In Durban, African and Indian workers had had the recent experience of struggling side by side; in Cape Town, coloured and African workers had yet to go through this experience. Allowance should be made for this important difference. 44 per cent of the African workers interviewed had had little or no contact with coloured workers. Of these, 65 per cent stated that they would not help coloured workers to improve their work situation, and 54 per cent expected no help from coloured workers in return. Among those who had had some contact with coloured workers, on the other hand, the attitudes were more or less reversed. Even at this stage, therefore, a basis existed - as in Durban - for common action by coloured and African workers. In the struggles of 1976 this basis would be built upon and greatly strengthened. Without any sign of division or hesitation, large masses of coloured and African workers would go on strike in support of the struggle in Soweto.

The Nautilus strike

The nature of the struggles of the mid-1970s can best be understood by examining a number of strikes that have been reported in some detail. One of these took place at Nautilus Marine, a firm of ship repairers in the Cape Town docks. During June 1974 the 286 African workers employed there unanimously decided to form a works committee. A provisional committee was elected and the employers were asked to call a statutory meeting at which the election could formally be confirmed. After first refusing, the employers eventually called this meeting on 27 June 1974. Also present was Mr Lambrecht, the Bantu Labour Officer. According to the account of one worker, the following took place at the meeting (Nautilus, 1976, p. 60):

> the management asked the workers whether they wanted a Works Committee, the workers thereupon all raised their hands to show their approval. Management then asked the 12 people who had

already been informally elected to come forward and asked if
the workers chose these people as their representatives. Again
the workers indicated their approval.

At this point the employers made it clear that they wanted a liaison
committee elected and not a works committee. They declared that
they would not allow a works committee to be formed. The workers,
however, rejected the liaison committee out of hand. Not one man
would agree to serve on it. The meeting then broke up.

In the period that followed relations between management and
workers deteriorated further. A peitition calling for a works committee,
signed by all the African workers, was handed to the employers, but
without effect. In mid-August an incident took place that proved to be
decisive. An African sand-blaster named Maqula, who had been working
at Nautilus for nineteen years, was dismissed on the grounds that he
had been 'criticising the firm' or 'giving the firm a bad name'. The
workers then decided that the time had come to act. There was no
African trade union in Cape Town which they could approach. They
turned for support to the Western Province Workers' Advice Bureau.
The response of the Advice Bureau was to instruct a firm of lawyers
with a view to enforcing the workers' rights in terms of the Bantu
Labour Relations Regulation Act. A letter was written by the lawyers
to Nautilus Marine requesting that a statutory meeting be held in
order to elect a works committee. The reaction of the firm was to send
one of its managers to the lawyer's office to return the letter and tell
the lawyer to 'keep his nose out of the private affairs of Nautilus'
(*ibid*., p. 617). At this stage the workers decided to take matters into
their own hands. The *South African Labour Bulletin* gives the following
account of the events that followed (*ibid*., pp. 61-2):

> They [the workers] turned up one morning at work and simply
> refused to get into their overalls. They were approached by
> management who enquired why they were not getting dressed
> for work. The workers' unanimous response was that they wanted
> to know why Mr Maqula had been dismissed. Management said
> that he had been giving the firm a bad name. The workers then
> asked whether it was not the case that Mr Maqula had been
> working for Nautilus over the last 19 years. Management affirmed
> this. Then the workers asked when was it that Mr Maqula had
> commenced giving the firm a bad name; management could give
> no reply to this. The workers then made two demands: the first
> was that . . . Mr Maqula should be reinstated and the second was

that they should be allowed to elect a Works Committee. The work stoppage lasted only three hours. In that time management completely capitulated; they sent a car to fetch Mr Maqula from the township, he was reinstated with a public apology and presented with a new overall. In addition to that, management conceded that a registered Works Committee could be formed and that such a Works Committee could be affiliated to the Workers' Advice Bureau.

This sudden retreat on the part of the employers, however, proved to be no more than a ruse. The Nautilus works committee was formed in September 1974. At one of its first meetings with the employers on 20 September the committee put forward the following demands (*ibid.*, pp. 62–3):

1. Six months' unpaid leave for migrant workers to return to the reserves [this amounted to the restitution of a former practice].
2. A minimum wage of R35.00 per week.
3. Removal of three African foremen ('boss-boys') from the restroom used by the other workers.

The works committee said that the foremen in question were working against the interests of their fellow-workers, carrying stories to management and urging management to turn down the workers' wage claim. Clearly, the workers had decided to isolate these men. A heated dispute developed between the committee and the employers over the issue of the foremen. The committee could gain no satisfaction. As a result the workers decided to work no more overtime, night shifts or week-ends.

The employers reacted by calling in the police. On the pretext of investigating the death of one of the workers, railway policemen took away all works committee members to the railway police headquarters in Cape Town. The men were detained in separate cells all day. Then they were questioned individually by policemen and Special Branch members under the command of a certain Major van Heerden. They were questioned not so much about the death that was allegedly being investigated but about the works committee itself. The police, the *South African Labour Bulletin* reports, 'wanted to know where the workers got the idea to form a Works Committee and how they formed it. They also questioned them about training courses that were run on Saturday afternoons at Athlone by the Workers' Advice Bureau' (*ibid.*, pp. 63–4).

The workers' response was to repeat their two basic demands for six months' unpaid leave and R35.00 per week. Major van Heerden told them that Nautilus Marine was situated on railway property and therefore, in future, they should come to him if they had any disagreement with their employers. He told them to stop creating trouble and to stay away from the Advice Bureau. The workers replied that the railway police had done nothing to help them in the past, while the Advice Bureau had tried to help them. According to one worker, Major van Heerden then told them that they would be prosecuted if they repeated 'what they had done'.

It thus became clear that the employers at Nautilus Marine were not prepared to tolerate an assertive and independent attitude on the part of African workers. Like many South African employers, they were genuinely aggrieved at any support the workers might enjoy, even in the matter of enforcing their legal rights. In such a situation, one might say, the whole object of employing unfree labour is destroyed. Relations at Nautilus now became strained to breaking point. On Monday, 30 September the employers resorted to sacking workers. Ten African workers, including several works committee members, were dismissed. The next morning the workers attempted to repeat the tactic that had previously been successful. They held a meeting with management and demanded to know why the ten men had been expelled. They also pointed out that the works committee had not been informed, and no complaints against any of the men had been brought to the attention of the works committee. Management apparently gave a somewhat contradictory account. One argument was that the workers had been laid off for economic reasons. It was added, according to another account, that the employers 'wished to employ new workers who would not listen to certain "agitators" among the workers' (*ibid.*, p. 65). A third worker said that the employers were 'not prepared to give reasons for the dismissal of the 10 workers but that they threatened to carry on dismissing 10 workers daily if the workers continued to be difficult and "cheeky"' (*ibid.*). The workers demanded that the men be reinstated. The employers refused. The workers then walked out on strike.

The following morning, 2 October, the strikers returned to Nautilus and presented the employers with a list of their demands. These included (*ibid.*, pp. 65–6):

1. The reinstatement of the sacked workers.
2. No further victimisation of workers.

3. Management must be prepared to negotiate with the Works Committee and not call in the police whenever there was disagreement.
4. A minimum wage of R35.00 per week.

The railway police were once again present and watching the developments. The strikers were led into a large hall where the coloured workers could not see them. A certain Mr Nel, on behalf of the employers, told the works committee that because of the lack of obedience on the part of the workers, the management had decided to terminate the services of all [African] workers' (*ibid*., p. 66). The strikers were told to return the next day to collect their pay. If they wanted to reapply for work at Nautilus, they were told, each applicant would be considered individually. On 3 October the workers returned for their wages and found they had not been paid for the last day they had worked. They were also not given their holiday pay. When they protested they were told by the police to leave. In the pay packets were slips of paper which men who wanted to reapply for employment had to fill in. It was accepted by the strikers that the contract workers among them should reapply, since in their case dismissal would mean expulsion to the reserves. When on 4 October the contract workers presented themselves, however, Nautilus refused to take them back.

The attitude of Nautilus Marine was made clear beyond all doubt by a member of the management, Mr Williams. In a telephone conversation with the Advice Bureau he said that there used to be harmony at Nautilus but that, on account of the Advice Bureau, a new element had crept into the situation. The strike, in his view, was due completely to the National Union of South African Students or to the Wages Commission of the Students' Representative Council of the University of Cape Town. Williams often repeated that 'there were nasty things going on' and that he 'did not know what it was all about' (*ibid*., p. 67). He also said that the workers had been getting too much money, and as a result of this they no longer wanted to work all the time. Management as well as certain workers, he alleged, had been threatened by the works committee. The chairman of the works committee had allegedly told the employers that the workers knew where they lived. Finally, Williams said, about fifty to sixty of the African workers 'whom they really wanted' had been taken back. For the rest, the work-force had been augmented with coloured workers.

What Williams did not disclose was that the strikers had been blacklisted. This was discovered by twelve Nautilus workers who managed to find work at Trident Marine, another dockyard firm. On their second day at their new work, Special Branch policemen arrived and spoke to their employers. The employers then told the twelve men that they could not employ them because they had been at Nautilus. Also, at Globe Engineering, a worker was sacked after two days when it was learned that he had come from Nautilus. At African Oxygen, the *South African Labour Bulletin* reports, 'a young worker had the experience of starting work on Wednesday the 9th of October, 1974, at 7.30 a.m., but at 10 a.m. management called him and told him that he was dismissed because management had no right to employ him since he came from Nautilus' (*ibid.*, pp. 68-9).

The former vice-chairman of the Nautilus works committee, a worker named Ndingane, and two other ex-Nautilus workers – who had been among those sacked from Trident Marine – managed to find work at Murray & Stewart. Shortly after being employed they were, once again, dismissed. A foreman who went to plead their cause came back and said that 'there was nothing he could do because they were Nautilus workers who were responsible for a strike' (*ibid.*, p. 69).

The cause of the struggle at Nautilus Marine, the *South African Labour Bulletin* concludes, was the unwillingness of the employers to accept the spokesmen chosen by the workers and pay heed to the workers' complaints. Fundamental to this, however, was the fact that the African workers at Nautilus were no longer behaving in the way that 'cheap docile labour' is expected to behave. From the employers' point of view this must have constituted an intolerable state of affairs. In such a situation the workers' deputies were marked for reprisals the moment they presented themselves. In this way the lack of legal protection of works committee members was once again exposed, and the importance of secrecy and informality in the organisation of the African working class was once again made clear.

In the final analysis support from the rank and file is all that can safeguard working-class leadership in a situation of open conflict. At Nautilus such support was given to the hilt; and yet the workers' action ended in defeat. The reason must be sought in the isolated nature of the strike and the relatively small number of African workers that Nautilus employed. During the Durban strikes employers were unable to dismiss thousands of workers at once; at Nautilus mass dismissal was apparently regarded as the lesser of two evils. For the Nautilus workers and for other workers in smaller plants, the conclusion to be drawn from this is clear. If plant-based organisation is inadequate to stand up to the employer, then organisation must be built on a broader basis. In the first place workers can turn to other factories in the same area - especially in the same industry - and make common cause with the workers employed there. In the case of the Nautilus workers, this would have meant discussing and organising with the workers at other dockyard firms. In this situation the blacklisting of Nautilus strikers should be regarded not simply as a vindictive gesture but as a tactically necessary precaution on the part of the employers in the Cape Town docks and the police responsible for guarding law and order there.

Blacklisting, however, can be effective only to a point. Contact between workers at different factories - as at Hammarsdale - may also take place undetected by employers and the police. Through experience, the need for broader organisation was becoming more obvious to African workers as industrial struggles continued. If the Nautilus workers had been supported by all other workers in the Cape Town docks, including the coloured workers; and if their dismissal would have led to a general strike in the docks, then it is almost certain that their demands would have been substantially conceded. On the basis of experiences such as these, the mid-1970s provided a fertile climate for the resurgence of African trade unionism.

The Conac strike

Apart from wage demands, the issue of workers' representation has been one of the most explosive in South African industry during recent years. Demands by workers for the election of a works committee instead of a liaison committee, or for the recognition of their union, have led to numerous disputes. The Nautilus struggle was only one example of this. At the Swiss-owned firm of Conac Engineering in Pietermaritzburg a different type of conflict arose in September 1975. In this dispute two outside parties intervened: on the one hand, the Department of Labour; on the other hand, an unregistered trade union. The struggle, in other words, extended itself beyond the classical triangle of workers, employers and the police. As at Nautilus, the employers relied on the forces of the state. In this connection the auxiliary role played by the nominally impartial Department of Labour is especially instructive. But the workers had also attempted to break out of their isolation and join forces with other workers. By means of the union they attempted to place themselves in a stronger position *vis-à-vis* their previously all-powerful employers. The role played byby the union is thus crucial and deserves the closest study.

About 110 African workers were employed at Conac Engineering. A liaison committee had been in existence since 1973. Racially segregated factory committees had also been instituted by the employers in respect of white and coloured employees. An industrial agreement of the Iron, Steel and Metallurgical Industries Industrial Council applied to Conac Engineering, including its African workers. In terms of this agreement overtime work was limited to ten hours per week unless a special exemption was granted by the Council. At Conac, however, workers were required to work as much as thirty-eight hours overtime per week. Such overtime was moreover compulsory, also for non-African workers. From time to time workers were dismissed for not working overtime. Among the African workers this led to great dissatisfaction. At the same time, they found the liaison committee – which was convened not more than once every two months – completely ineffectual as an instrument for changing the situation.

Relations in the factory, the *South African Labour Bulletin* writes, 'were such that African workers had no control over their working lives' (Conac, 1976, p. 82). Under these circumstances some African workers from Conac approached the Metal and Allied Workers' Union (MAWU) in July 1975. Within a few weeks about a quarter of the African workers had joined the union. In October, following more dismissals of men who had refused to work overtime, the workers instructed the liaison committee to inform management that they would not be working overtime on the coming Saturday. The reaction of the employers was to forbid the liaison committee to hold any further communication with the workers.

On the Saturday in question the majority of African workers boycotted overtime work. Also, on Monday 11 October the majority refused to work overtime. As at Nautilus, lack of docility among the African workers was incomprehensible and intolerable to the employers. The following morning the African workers were intercepted at the factory gate. The manager came to address them. He said that the conflict had been caused by 'agitators' and called on the men to divide into two groups: those who would accept the existing overtime arrangements, and those who would not accept them. Sixty workers joined the second group. They were told to wait outside the gate, where they would be paid off. The workers, however, regarded their dismissal as illegal and refused to accept their pay-off wages under any circumstances. MAWU officials were then called in. It was decided that three elected liaison committee members, who were among the dismissed men,

283

should go to the Department of Labour. They should report a lock-out at Conac Engineering and demand implementation of the legal procedure for the settlement of disputes.

At the Department of Labour the three liaison committee members met with what the *South African Labour Bulletin* terms an 'astonishing reception'. They were stopped by an official who read the inscription on their overalls and told them: 'You're from Conac, go away from here, you are drunk!' (*ibid*., p.84). From this stage onwards the struggle between the sacked workers and the employers was fought out mainly by proxy, with MAWU representing the workers and the Department of Labour representing the employers.

The union officials next took the liaison committee members to consult with an attorney. The officials telephoned the manager of Conac, who refused to negotiate and said that the workers were dismissed. The attorney then telephoned the divisional inspector of labour and asked him to investigate the lock-out. In legal terms, it should be noted, the situation seemed quite clear. The workers had been locked out within the definition of the Industrial Conciliation Act for refusing to submit to allegedly illegal practices. The reply by the inspector was thus remarkable. He denied that there was either a lock-out or a dispute at Conac Engineering. However, he said, his inspectors were investigating a possible strike. As for the liaison committee members, he declared them to be 'agitators' (*ibid*., p. 85).

MAWU encountered even greater hostility on the part of the Department of Labour. Returning to the factory, the liaison committee members found that Department of Labour officials, accompanied by Special Branch agents, were trying to persuade the locked-out workers to return to work on the employers' terms. The workers' response was that all negotiations should be conducted with the union. The officials replied that the union was unable to help, since they were from outside the factory and had nothing to do with the problems in the factory. The workers retorted that this argument applied to the Department of Labour as well. They also said that they would return to work only on condition that all were re-employed. The following morning they returned to the factory and were told by Department of Labour officials that they were dismissed and should collect their wages. Special Branch agents were once again present and 'closely followed' an attempt by the workers to discuss with union officials (*ibid*., p. 86). All the locked-out workers then left, refusing to accept their wages.

The strategy of the union was to continue exploring the official channels. Affidavits and schedules were drawn up, showing the amount of excess overtime that the Conac workers had worked. These were delivered to the Department of Labour, which referred the matter to the industrial council. In the meantime the manager of Conac issued a statement that there were 'trouble makers' operating, and that 'this time they have chosen my factory' (*ibid.*). The industrial council inspector proved to be no more co-operative. When asked by the union's attorney whether overtime exemptions had been granted to Conac Engineering, he alleged that he was prevented by the secrecy clause in the Industrial Conciliation Act from disclosing the requested information.[2] Several months later it transpired that this inspector had not yet begun investigating the alleged violation of the industrial agreement by Conac Engineering.

At this stage the Department of Bantu Administration and Development also entered the fray. The locked-out workers from Conac approached the Department to apply for work, and once again got an 'astonishing reception'. First they were told that unless they accepted re-employment at Conac - presumably on the employers' terms - they would be endorsed out of the urban area. A more senior official then appeared, saying that the men were free to seek work elsewhere in Pietermaritzburg and would not be endorsed out. The most likely explanation, according to the *South African Labour Bulletin*, is that the new workers taken on by Conac Engineering were unfamiliar with the work. Apparently they required extensive training, and this at a time when the employers were trying to maximise production. Very possibly the employers were eager to get the locked-out workers back, and had asked the Department of Bantu Administration and Development to arrange this. The Department, on the other hand, did not want the locked-out workers to be re-employed because they were members of MAWU. This might account for the contradictory attitudes encountered by the workers.

By the end of the year no action had yet been taken by either the Department of Labour or the industrial council in relation to the complaints of the Conac workers. The senior state prosecutor had declined to prosecute Conac for illegally locking out the workers. In December an apparent breakthrough occurred when a meeting with the labour inspector was arranged by the union's attorney. The aim was to discuss the possibility of action in terms of section 24 of the Bantu Labour Relations Regulation Act, which prohibits the victimisation of workers' statutory representatives. With the attorney went members of the Conac liaison committee as well as a MAWU official who was to act as interpreter. The meeting served little other purpose, however, than to emphasise the attitude of the state towards African trade unionism. At the office of the inspector the following took place (*ibid.*, p. 89):

> Mr Stock [the inspector] ordered him [the MAWU official] to leave the room and did not call in any other interpreter. The worker representatives were thus excluded from discussion.
> Mr Stock explained to the attorney that it was the policy of his department not to be of any assistance to those industrial workers who were members of unregistered Trade Unions. He said that the Union officials were all 'sea-lawyers', and out to cause trouble. He then said that the Bantu Labour official for Pietermaritzburg, Mr Smith, was performing a competent job in maintaining close contact with workers, and maintaining good relations between workers and management.

From the point of view of the Conac workers, therefore, the legal and official channels led nowhere. From these experiences the *South African Labour Bulletin* concludes that 'It is obvious to workers that the State and employer-sponsored works and liaison Committee system is hopelessly inadequate to mediate this structural conflict between employers and employees' (*ibid.*, p. 90). It ends by expressing the fear that continued collaboration between the Department of Labour and employers will strengthen the tendency 'towards open conflict between employers and workers in the form of work stoppages and lock-out situations' (*ibid.*) The meaning of 'mediation' in this context is not explained. Struggle on the part of the workers is implicitly opposed. In particular, no comment is given on the strategy followed by the union. Yet from the working-class point of view this question is vitally important. A definite function of the legal and administrative system in South Africa is to arm employers against the advance of the workers. The MAWU officials, however, confined themselves completely to the remedies offered by this system in their attempt to further the interests of the workers at Conac Engineering. A totally contradictory situation thus arose, of which the outcome was predictable.

The shortcoming of MAWU in this situation, it is submitted, was precisely its inability to fulfil the basic function of a workers' union: that is, to counterpose the *independent* power of the workers to that of the employers, embodied in this case by the state machinery. This is not to deny the importance of using whatever limited opportunities the state machinery may offer to protect the workers' interests. It is only to point out the inevitable inadequacy, from the workers' point of view, of these opportunities in themselves. In any event, as the Durban strikes once again indicated, workers' interests tend to be recognised, and concessions tend to be made, only when demands are supported by *adequate force*: that is, in general, by widespread strikes or the threat of widespread strikes. Obviously it was impossible for MAWU to organise action along these lines. Certain functions of industrial organisation in South Africa can only be carried out in a secret, informal way. The question remains what tactics a legal trade union in South Africa could follow that would not interfere with incipient tendencies among the workers at rank-and-file level to carry on the struggle independently. Or to take the question one step further: if open trade unions in South Africa cannot fully carry out the tasks of industrial organisation at present, to what extent can they assist the workers in doing so themselves?

Only a general approach to the question will be attempted here. Industrial union is a necessary development from the African workers' point of view. Trade-union organisation could be an important means to this end. It goes without saying that every trade union will attempt to build up an organisational apparatus to carry on the activities of the union in the most efficient way possible. It is equally self-evident, however, that in the last resort 'industrial union' means not so much the union apparatus but rather the actual degree of union among the workers in the industry concerned. No union apparatus can operate effectively under any circumstances except as a conscious instrument of the workers on whom it depends. Should officials act independently, the main strength of working-class organisation – the strength arising from united action – is lost. Union officials, acting independently, do not necessarily confront employers as representatives of a powerful organisation capable of paralysing the industry. The demands that they put forward will not necessarily be demands for which large sections of workers will be prepared to struggle. On the contrary, the officials will be mere individuals who might possibly find support among the workers or 'make a nuisance of themselves'. This applies regardless of the intentions of the union officials concerned or the policies which they as individuals support.

In the case of the dispute at Conac Engineering it appears that the MAWU officials were guided by legal procedures and legal advice rather than by discussion with the rank and file. After the initial meeting little consultation with the workers appears to have taken place. Several mass meetings were held by the workers during the first few days of the lock-out at which they were presumably concerned with the question of what was to be done. No mention is made of what was contributed to these meetings by union officials, nor, in the case of one or two meetings, whether they were present. Certainly there is no suggestion that the MAWU tactic in this struggle was hammered out step by step with the full understanding and agreement of the workers. On the contrary, it was concluded by the Wednesday that 'All further procedures would have to be channelled through the unions' attorney' (*ibid.*, p. 87). The effect was to exclude the workers from direct participation in the struggle. The MAWU officials confronted the employers and the state as individuals, and they were treated accordingly. The power of the union remained a potential power. If to the workers the burning question was how to harness this power, then from the MAWU officials they received no answer.

Again, it does not follow that such legal possibilities of advancing the workers' interests as may nominally exist should have been ignored. It follows, rather, that sufficient pressure should have been put on employers and the state to compel them to give effect to the workers' legal rights and if possible to safeguard the ground thus gained. From the workers' point of view the crucial task, apart from negotiating with state officials, was to persuade the workers in other factories to support them, if needs be by coming out on strike. The important lesson of the Durban strikes could hardly have been forgotten: when workers take action in sufficient numbers and on a sufficiently broad front, it becomes impossible for employers and the state to defeat them.

Under prevailing conditions in South Africa, it should be repeated, it is impossible for union officials to carry out this task in full. Given the network of police informers, activities along these lines by union officials are likely to be nipped in the bud. A second feature of the Durban strikes, however, was precisely the great success enjoyed by the unofficial or 'invisible' leadership which the workers had developed among themselves. Through informal links of this nature, it is quite possible that workers in one factory could be mobilised in support of workers in another factory, and that contact could be preserved in readiness for future action. Informal organisation, in other words, can be extended from one factory to encompass other factories, and ultimately entire industries or cities. In the case of the Hammarsdale general strike it was seen how organisation along these lines could spring into existence at a moment's notice. There is no reason for doubting that many African workers understand the importance of such a development very well.

It is in the light of developments of this nature that the role of the

African trade unions should be considered. On the one hand, union activity could have an important mobilising effect among unorganised workers. It could provide the initial impulse, as well as the ongoing stimulation, out of which powerful organisation of the working class could grow. On the other hand, for this to happen, the initiative should never be taken from the workers' hands. Officials would have to ensure that 'organisation' is never regarded as meaning inactivity on the part of the workers, and passively entrusting their interests to the union. Organisers would have to explain the laws relating to trade-union activity in South Africa, making clear what the union can do and what it cannot do. Above all they would have to make clear the limitations of trade-union organisation and the need for the workers to continue discussing among themselves. In this way union officials could do much to ensure that union intervention does not inhibit but, on the contrary, encourages informal organisation among the rank and file on as broad a basis as possible. From the workers' point of view such informal organisation is not a substitute for trade unions; it is a necessary extension of the narrow legal scope remaining for formal organisation.

The Heinemann strike

Another reported dispute took place at Heinemann Electric during the early part of 1976. Heinemann Electric is situated near Johannesburg and employed about 600 African workers. In October 1975 MAWU started to organise the workers at this factory. Over 500 African workers joined. The employers, apparently in an attempt to combat the union, decided to form a liaison committee. The workers responded in no uncertain manner to make their wishes clear. On 20 February 1976 representatives of MAWU handed the following petition to Heinemann (*FM*, 2 April 1976): 'We the workers of Heinemann Electric wish to state that we are members of the Metal and Allied Workers' Union (Transvaal) and that we reject works and liaison committees. We want the union to represent us and not a works or liaison committee.' The petition was signed by 484 workers. The employers, however, ignored this advice and proceeded to hold elections for the liaison committee. The response of the workers was to boycott the elections; only twenty-seven votes were cast. Fresh elections were held by the employers; this time not a single worker voted. Undeterred, the employers held elections yet again. On this occasion three workers voted. The employers were thus forced to take MAWU seriously. On the other hand, they had no intention of dealing with the union. They dismissed their defeat in the liaison committee elections by claiming that MAWU had 'interfered' with the workers and persuaded them not to vote. A director of Heinemann stated that trade unions 'have no interest in the factory'. The company was only prepared to negotiate with registered trade unions. As far as MAWU was concerned, the personnel manager of the parent company, Barlow Rand, was very definite: 'In no way are we prepared to see the union as the mouthpiece of the workers' (*FM*, 9 April 1976).

Since the great majority of workers had demanded precisely this, it is clear that the employers at Heinemann Electric had decided on a course of direct confrontation. Such a confrontation was soon provoked when at the end of March twenty workers were dismissed, including two MAWU shop stewards. The remainder of the African workers refused to start work the next morning, demanding reinstatement of the workers dismissed. The employers responded by calling in the police and sacking the entire African work-force. On the following day, 29 March, the workers returned to the factory gate and repeatedly requested a meeting with management. This request was turned down. At ten o'clock the police ordered the workers to disperse within half an hour. At half past ten, when the meeting was actually in the process of dispersing, the police carried out a baton charge. As it happened, the incident received some publicity. The employers and the police found few apologists. The *Financial Mail*, looking at the matter from the liberal point of view, asked whether employers like Heinemann 'think they can indefinitely resist [African] workers' demands for trade union rights by mass sackings?' If so, it commented, 'they are set on a disastrously stupid course' (2 April 1976). Also, Buthelezi uttered a warning, in almost prophetic terms, to employers and the state: 'Whether this is a result of the Whites' war psychosis is difficult to tell, but it is doubly alarming at the present time when any spark such as this could light a powder keg in South Africa' (*ibid*.). As a matter of historical fact, it was not the Heinemann strike but a school students' demonstration in Soweto a few months later that proved to be that spark.

The Heinemann strike underlined yet again the relatively exposed position of workers struggling in a single factory. It re-emphasised the continued preparedness of the African workers to struggle despite all the formidable obstacles with which they are confronted. It also showed again that harsh employment policies are not limited to the Afrikaans-speaking petite-bourgoisie; identical policies may be imposed by big employers and foreign corporations.[3]

Finally, the question was once more posed of the relationship between the formal and informal organisation of the workers. At Heinemann it was the union that provided the initial impulse for the workers to organise themselves. Next to the union, however, the mass meeting was an essential organ for carrying on the struggle. Out of the mass meeting informal 'sub-committees' could have been created for the purpose of developing links with other factories, planning strategy and tactics and carrying out the many further tasks which the union in its exposed position is unable to perform.

The Armourplate strike

The Soweto uprising and the events that followed confirmed the main lesson of the Durban strikes. In a general-strike situation the workers are in a strong position compared with an isolated strike. In the political general strikes of August and September 1976 the African workers' movement reached dramatic new heights which far overshadowed the determined but isolated factory-based strikes of the previous three years. For a few brief days the power of united working-class action was unmistakably asserted. As yet, however, the organisation and political preparation for continuing such action was lacking; the means of generalising the conclusions to be drawn from the experience of the African working class during this period had yet to be created. Side by side with the general strikes, isolated strikes continued to break out on much the same pattern as before. Yet despite the stifling curbs on discussion and organised contact among the African working class, the movement did not remain static. Partly through the force of example, partly through the pressure of events, and partly no doubt through clandestine discussion, the strategy and tactics of the workers tended slowly but surely to develop.

An illustration of this process is provided by the strike at Armourplate Safety Glass on the Rand during September 1976. Two significant features characterised this strike. In the first place the struggle was carried beyond the factory itself. In the second place the Glass and Allied Workers' Union (GAWU), an unregistered trade union, broke important new ground in supporting the strike without leading the workers into the tortuous and hostile maze of bureaucratic channels as had happened to the Conac workers. Although in themselves these two developments were insufficient to change the outcome of the struggle, it was another indication that the workers' movement was ready to leave the stage of isolated strikes and that, when conditions call another general strike wave into existence, this will happen on the basis of far greater experience and strategical maturity among the workers than had been the case in Durban in 1973.

Armourplate is an affiliate of the British Pilkington group. Prior to July 1976 it employed 205 African workers, three-quarters of whom belonged to GAWU. There was also a works committee in existence. Armourplate, it appears, had begun to suffer the effects of the recession. The workers had been put on a four-day week. At the end of July three men were discharged because there was no more work for them. Such was the mood among the workers that these dismissals provoked a confrontation. The four-day week, the works committee said, had been accepted on condition that there would be no dismissals. This was denied by the employers, but the denial was rejected. The workers gave Armourplate thirty days to reinstate the dismissed men, failing which a strike would be called in terms of the Bantu Labour Relations Regulation Act.

As the deadline approached, the works committee asked GAWU to mediate. The employers, however, on two separate occasions refused to meet negotiators from the union. To negotiate with the union, Mr Breakspear (of management) explained, would be 'a great disservice to the works committee' (*FM*, 10 September 1976). When reminded that the works committee itself had asked GAWU to intervene, Breakspear gave a different reason for his refusal to negotiate. He was, he said, 'not prepared to have trade unions or anyone else brought in at this stage. The workers are not trying to negotiate, they are demanding' (*ibid.*).

On 3 September the deadline expired and on 6 September the strike began officially. As far as it is possible to tell, this was the first occasion in South African history that African workers legally went on strike. The legal status of the strike, however, proved to be insignificant in the events that followed. The far-reaching powers of employers to take counter-measures against striking workers proved to be virtually unaffected by the technical question of whether a strike is legal or illegal. From the outset the employers made their position clear and threw all their forces into the attack. At the propaganda level, the works committee was accused of having called the strike. In effect, this was the 'agitator theory' in a slightly different form. It implied that the mass of workers were opposed or indifferent to the strike, and only the efforts of the works committee were bringing it about. In reality, however, the opposite was the case. Not only did the works committee advise against the strike, but also GAWU had warned the workers about the danger of going on strike under conditions of recession. The fact that the strike nevertheless took place can only be ascribed to the determination of the workers to resist the attack on their security and to see their work-mates reinstated.

The tactics which the employers subsequently used were the well-known tactics of 'negotiation by sacking' and calling in the police. Even though the strike had been called in accordance with legal procedures, the employers refused to acknowledge it as a strike. The workers, they alleged, had resigned. Again, though there was no question of an illegal strike, strikers were called in for questioning by the security police. Under these conditions of pressure and intimidation, the employers attempted to break the strike by 're-engaging' individual strikers and recruiting new workers to take the place of the intransigent majority of strikers. There can be no doubt that this process was designed to eliminate known leaders among the workers. All strikers were invited to 'rejoin' but to this invitation Mr Breakspear added: 'As a result of the recession in the motor components industry, we are not able to re-employ the 205 workers we had previously' (*FM*, 24 September 1976). By this time, it is interesting to note, it was no longer the works committee that was allegedly responsible for the strike; Breakspear had reached the conclusion that the strike had been 'instigated from outside'. The state played its customary role in the Armourplate dispute. The security police intervened. Also the Department of Labour, though it accepted at first that the strikers had been dismissed, later changed its mind. The strikers then learned that, as far as the Department was concerned, they had 'deserted' from their jobs (*ibid.*).

Early in October the police once again struck. Twenty-seven workers, while peacefully picketing the factory, were arrested in terms of the Riotous Assemblies Act. All were convicted and sentenced to fines of R50.00, or seventy-five days in prison. All these events, however, failed to change the strikers' minds or make them submit to the employers' terms. Thus three men returned to the factory to collect their wages; they were asked to rejoin, but refused. Approximately two weeks after the beginning of the strike, only thirty-five new workers had been found. It can be inferred that the employers had some difficulty in replacing the more skilled workers, but that this was not serious enough - given the need to reduce production - to bring about major concessions.

The struggle of the Armourplate workers became generalised only to a limited extent. Nevertheless, because every step in this direction is vitally important, the way in which it happened should be carefully examined. Fundamentally, it was the accumulation of capital itself that created the conditions for ripples of the Armourplate strike to be transmitted elsewhere. Armourplate is one of a number of factories owned by the Pilkington group. A second factory, Pilkington Glass, is situated in Springs. At the beginning of the strike it was reported that the workers at Pilkington Glass were 'very unhappy' about the situation and it was feared that the strike might spread to them (*FM*, 10 September 1976). When these workers were subsequently called on to help fill the places of the strikers, they refused. Instead they collected food and money for the strikers. GAWU, too, supported the strikers within the limits imposed by the state. In particular, it raised the money to pay the arrested pickets' fines. Other unregistered unions also contributed money. Even two coloured workers from Port Elizabeth, who had been transferred to train the new workers, were indignant when they discovered the position at Armourplate and demanded to be returned. In Britain, workers at Pilkington and the General and Municipal Workers' Union gave financial support to the strikers at Armourplate in South Africa.

All these expressions of solidarity were insufficient to change the outcome of the struggle. Workers elsewhere were confronted with the strike mainly through coincidence or extraneous causes. Although the strikers undoubtedly discussed their problems with other workers and raised the question of strategy and tactics, no record exists of what was done in this regard. Ironically enough, it was the employers who brought the strike to the notice of the workers at Pilkington Glass and the men from Port Elizabeth. Under certain conditions workers who learn of a strike indirectly or by coincidence may respond with indifference or be impotent to act. Such were conditions in South Africa in 1976, however, that the workers at Pilkington Glass and several unregistered unions responded to the strike with a limited but definite show of support.

As for the workers themselves, though they were unable to win reinstatement, they emerged from the struggle not without gains. They had refused to submit to pressure and they had kept their ranks unbroken under difficult conditions. Above all, their struggle had been carried beyond the factory itself, and important experience had been gained of the role that a trade union could play. GAWU reports (1977, pp. 69–70):

> The men were really well united in their determination. Most
> attended a meeting of strikers held each weekday and night. They

were pleased that the action they took was completely legal and although their expectations from such legal action were rudely shattered they believed that they had done the right thing. They said that even should they lose the struggle they felt they had taught management a lesson which they would not easily forget. They believed that things would thus be better for Black workers in the future. They were proud to be able to give Black workers in general an example of what unity can do. When they learned that the answer to the Union's request for mediation would take almost two weeks for reply they said they had suffered for so long why not a further two weeks. They were particularly encouraged by the support received from their own Union, the other Unions locally and Urban Training Project. Support from glass and other workers overseas also meant a great deal to them.

By the time of the Armourplate strike the new wave of unrest sparked off by the Soweto uprising had swept across the country. For a time all attention was focused on the struggle led by the school students that was daily erupting on the streets. Industrial struggle by the African workers, already held back by the pressures of recession, for a time receded further to the background. Yet the significance of industrial struggle remained as great as ever. While they are deprived of political organisation, workers must tend to struggle on the shop-floor. In the course of this struggle, in outline, the basic tactics of future political struggle are likely to be created. From this point of view the period from 1973 to 1976 was significant. The struggle that broke out anew in Durban spread steadily across the country, penetrating into areas and factories that had previously been peaceful. With it, the methods of struggle used by employers as well as workers became increasingly generalised. Among growing masses of African workers the tactics of wildcat striking and the workings of the political system were being driven home by the lessons of experience. In the wake of this movement followed organisation; factory committees sprang up throughout the country, and the unregistered trade-union movement rapidly expanded. It could only be a question of time and changing conditions before the weapons developed by the workers in this struggle would be turned to political ends.

For a time the movement of the African school students cut across this development. The social climate in South Africa was dramatically changed by the political struggles of 1976. The working class was fortified and hardened by the experiences of this period. In the relative lull that followed the workers were left to resume the development that had started with the Durban strikes. The task that continued to face them was that of consciously rebuilding the unity and concertedness of action that had emerged spontaneously in Durban.

Chapter 9

Soweto

The Soweto uprising of June 1976 did not take South Africa completely by surprise. It had been preceded by years of industrial unrest. From the late 1960s onwards there had been heightened political activity among university students. Intelligent observers, whatever their political position, could detect in this course of events all the signs of an impending outburst. A mood of new, uncompromising radicalism was permeating every section of the black population. Events in Mozambique and Angola made the prospect of social change seem all the more immediate and increased the tension among the people in the townships and factories: 'In trains, buses, taxis, hospitals and schools,' reported two African journalists in March 1976, 'there is talk of nothing but the new developments.' A shop-sweeper in Germiston declared: 'I have been suffering for a long time. Would war change all that? If it would, then I welcome it.' Even an African businessman reflected this radical mood: 'We have no sympathy for the present Government. We welcome any kind of change so long as there won't be any discrimination. Even if Russia or Cuba were involved, we would not be perturbed' (*Cape Times*, 27 March 1976). And Chief Gatsha Buthelezi, at the end of April, uneasily declared: 'I am not a revolutionary, but I see a revolution coming' (*Die Burger*, 1 May 1976).

The school students' demonstration in Soweto on 16 June 1976 was the outcome of several weeks of protest against compulsory instruction in Afrikaans. On 17 May 1,600 students had walked out of Orlando West Junior Secondary School. In the days that followed they were joined by the students of several other schools. On 8 June a police car was set on fire at Naledi High School and policemen were stoned. Tear-gas was used against the students. A committee of students from several schools in Soweto planned a mass meeting at Orlando West Stadium for 16 June.

297

Before seven o'clock on the morning of 16 June more than 15,000 students had massed together to march to Orlando Stadium. Their posters were made out of exercise-book covers and old cardboard boxes and carried the following slogans: 'Down with Afrikaans'; 'Afrikaans is a tribal language'; 'Blacks are not dustbins'; 'Afrikaans is oppressors' language'. Singing and cheering, they made their way towards the stadium. As they passed other schools they called on the students to join them. Outside Orlando West Junior Secondary School they were confronted by a line of heavily armed police. The policemen carried sub-machine guns. They also had loudhailers, but did not address the students. The students continued singing and shouted that they did not want the police. Tear-gas canisters were then thrown by the police. The students held their ground. According to pro-government sources and certain witnesses, stones were flung at the police at this point. According to other reports, stoning only began after the police had opened fire. The first blood flowed when a policeman drew his pistol and shot down a schoolboy standing just in front of him. More shots were fired. The first to die was 13-year-old Hector Petersen. From the pathologist's report it appeared that he was shot from behind.

According to eye-witnesses absolute chaos now broke out. The students fought back with stones. News of the shooting raced through Soweto. Barricades were thrown up and vehicles set alight. In particular, buildings were attacked: government offices, liquor stores, churches and shops. Homes, however, were not damaged. New slogans were being shouted: 'Less liquor, better education'; 'We want more schools and less beer halls'.

More battles developed with the police, who were beginning to shoot indiscriminately. According to one witness, the students seemed oblivious of the danger. Even the police were disconcerted by the implacable hostility with which they were confronted. One white policeman recounted (*Rapport*, 20 June 1976): 'What I remember most about that first day is the vehemence, the hatred of which they are capable. This isn't only since yesterday. It's been in them since childhood. Nobody has ever sworn at me like that.' Black policemen reportedly shook their heads and muttered: 'It is bad, very bad' (*ibid.*).

To the workers returning to Soweto on the evening of 16 June the situation came as a surprise. At Inhlazane station thousands of men and women poured from the trains and found themselves confronted by the security police. No attempt was made to explain the situation to them. A huge crowd gathered. The police threw tear-gas and carried out a baton charge. The workers responded by hurling bricks and stones at the police. In this way, by the evening of 16 June, numbers of workers were joining the students and youths on the streets.

The uprising immediately began to spread as small groups of students slipped though the police cordon around Soweto to carry the news to other African townships. On 17 June school students took to the streets in Kagiso, Alexandra and Tembisa. The struggle took the same form as in Soweto. Government buildings, vehicles, beer halls, shops and banks were attacked by the demonstrators. Barricades were put up. In Alexandra a new slogan reflected the shifting focus of the struggle: 'Why kill kids for Afrikaans.' From the student grievance of Afrikaans instruction, general anger and shock at the methods used by the state was coming to the fore. Indeed, it soon became accepted on all sides that the Afrikaans language issue was no more than the final straw, the detonator of the explosion. The government, characteristically, acknowledged no genuine and serious grievances among the population that might have accounted for the massive outburst of anger. 'Agitators' were seen as the only possible cause. The uprising, according to Prime Minister Vorster, was 'obviously not a spontaneous eruption, but a purposeful attempt to polarise people in which various organisations played a role' (*Star IAW*, 19 June 1976). The police colonel Swanepoel who led the riot police in Soweto was even more definite on this. Certain signs given by the leaders of the demonstrations, he said, were 'proof that Communists were behind the riots' (*Cape Times*, 18 September 1976).

The policy of the state was never in any doubt. Meetings and demonstrations were broken up by force. Any attempt at resistance was met with greater force. After three days of fighting between police and unarmed demonstrators, the police themselves recorded that ninety-seven people had been killed and more than a thousand injured. Even the pro-government press admitted, however, that 'many more than one hundred had been killed' (*Rapport*, 20 June 1976). By 24 June 908 people had been arrested. There is evidence that those arrested met with extreme cruelty and intimidation at the hands of the police. The following testimony, for example, was given to the Cillie Commission[1] by a journalist, Mr Nonyane, who spent the night of 17 June outside the Orlando police station (*Cape Times*, 25 September 1976):

Mr Nonyane described how he heard people screaming in the charge office. He saw a group of 20 students being beaten by Black policemen outside the charge office in the middle of the night. The students were led into the courtyard and made to hop for 20 minutes while police hit them with batons and rubber hoses all over their bodies . . . . Mr Nonyane said bodies of people killed in the rioting were laid out outside the police station and the pile continued to grow during the night. In the early hours of the morning the students were again brought out, forced to hop for another 20 minutes and then told by policemen to load corpses into a mortuary van. As they did so the van attendant kicked and assaulted them, Mr Nonyane said.

It was against this background that the Assistant Commissioner of Police for the Witwatersrand, Brigadier J. F. Visser, declared (*Star IAW*, 19 June 1976): 'My patience is at an end. I have the support from above that I wanted. From now on we will use tougher methods.' This was not an idle threat. A few months later senior officers provided the following details of police activity to the Cillie Commission (SRR, 1976, pp. 84–7):

	Rounds fired	Killed by police	Injured by police
Soweto	16,000+	172	1,439
East Rand	17,000+	20	53
Cape Peninsula	–	92	387

By the beginning of December, according to official figures, 386 people had been killed and 1,500 injured. In reality casualties were almost certainly much higher. On one particular night, for example, seventy deaths were reported at two Cape hospitals; for the whole city that night the official death figure was nine.

The first waves of struggle continued for approximately three months. During this period it spread to many parts of the country. It developed from student demands to general demands, and it spread from students to workers. There were other things behind the struggle besides the Afrikaans language issue, the *Star* wrote on 18 June: 'There was the frustration over housing and the absence of street lighting . . . . There was anger over inadequate and expensive transport, the bad roads and unfeeling bureaucracy. These . . . were some of the "agitators" eating into the soul of Soweto, making it one of the world's most volatile communities.'

The same, of course, can be said of the African community in general. By 18 June the rebellion had spread to the University of Zululand in Natal, to the townships of Tokosa and Daveyton near Benoni, to Natalspruit and Katlehong near Germiston and to Vosloorus near Boksburg. On 21 June it broke out at Atteridgeville, Mabapone and Mamelodi near Pretoria. During the next few days it spread to Ga-Rankuwe, north-west of Pretoria, to Lowveld and Lekozi near Nelspruit in the Eastern Transvaal, and to Lynnville on the Far East Rand. By 25 June the two state mortuaries in Johannesburg were full. A relative lull set in, which lasted till 19 July. Then a new wave of unrest began among the African youth. Schools now formed the main target of attack. More than fifty schools were burned down in the Transvaal, the Orange Free State and Natal.

In August the struggle escalated sharply. On 11 August serious unrest for the first time broke out among school students in the Cape Peninsula. Struggle continued in the weeks that followed, involving much killing of young people by the police, culminating in clashes in the centre of Cape Town from 1 to 3 September. Unrest also broke out in Port Elizabeth and in various Cape country towns such as Oudtshoorn, George, Wellington, Stellenbosch, Riversdale and Paarl. Most of the people involved in this struggle were classified as 'coloured'. The ambiguous position in which the law has placed this category of South Africans was being clarified in practice. Coloured students and workers were expressing their grievances in the same way that the Africans were doing, and they were encountering the same reaction from the state. In the coloured areas of Bonteheuwel and Ravensmead battles were fought between the police and demonstrators similar to the battles of Soweto and Alexandra.

The escalation of the struggle was reflected in the mass arrest of black leaders during August. Over the weekend of 14 and 15 August, more than sixty prominent Africans were arrested, including thirty-nine members of the Black Parents' Association in Soweto. By the end of the month there were more than 800 people in detention, seventy-seven of whom were being held in terms of section 10 of the Internal Security Act. Many detainees, according to the Minister of Police, Mr J. T. Kruger, were being held because by their influence they were capable of worsening the unrest.

At the same time, the police were resorting to ever harsher methods in their effort to crush the protests and resistance. Demonstrators were being attacked and shot down in an increasingly deliberate way. School students were being attacked in their schools on little or no provocation and systematically beaten up or killed. Thus, on 4 August, police opened fire on students marching from Soweto to Johannesburg behind the banner 'We are not fighting, don't shoot'. Three students were killed and nine wounded.

The police resorted to violence only when they were confident that they would win. Thus at Tembisa near Boksburg on 17 June, the police allowed an illegal march by students to be held. 'Under the circumstances police action could have led to violence,' the officer in charge told the Cillie Commission. 'I believe we made the right decision because the marchers later dispersed and went home' (*Cape Times*, 2 October 1976). In general, however, the police could act with impunity against the unarmed youths. Their policy was to provoke violence or allow it to develop, then crush it with greater violence in order to drive home the lesson of their superior military strength. The district commander of police for the East Rand, Brigadier J. Wiese, considered that the police would have been justified in using 'far more violence' in his area – not in the interests of peace and order, but because more than R2 million of damage to property had been caused by the insurgents.

In September a Cape Town newspaper published a number of excerpts from press files giving a vivid idea of the nature of the struggle, the methods of the police and the way in which broad sections of the black population were being drawn irresistibly into conflict with the state. The following are only a few of the hundreds of clashes that took place (*Cape Times*, 24 September 1976):

> *The Argus, August 24*: A report of the closing of the Bonteheuwel High School after a placard demonstration quoted a senior police officer on the scene as saying: 'The pupils are apparently unhappy that they were dispersed by teargas and rubber pipes. They object to being hit by the police.' . . . .
>
> *The Cape Times, September 2*: Mrs J. Naidoo said that she was in a crowd near the disturbances . . . when the police charged. She could not run with her two children aged 4 and 5, and assumed that the police would realize she was not a trouble-maker. She was attacked with batons while trying to protect her children, she said, and had to receive 12 stitches in the head. She added: 'The police clubbed down two old women. One of them must have been in her sixties and was carrying a white cane.' Mrs Naidoo said the police only stopped hitting her when the crowd realized there were babies with her and started converging on the police.
>
> *The Cape Times, September 2*: 'They were just hitting indiscriminately,' said Mr Fafant Abrahams, 28. 'I was waiting to catch my bus to work when about 20 children came screaming down the

road with two riot police at their heels. One of them stopped, lashed out at me with his baton and knocked me to the ground.' He was treated by a doctor for a lacerated scalp and was off work for three days . . . .

The Cape Times, September 4: . . . A Cape Times reporter described a police entry into Alexander Sinton High School after cars had been stoned in the area. He said police threw teargas canisters into class rooms and beat children as they rushed out. Shotgun blasts reverberated through the quadrangle and screaming children ran in all directions.

The Cape Times, September 8: A report . . . gave a description of events on the Grand Parade and police dispersal of a crowd of youths: 'Several youths fell to the ground where they were beaten by batonwielding police. Three girls in their teens were carried bleeding to a panel van. . . . As the injured girls were being lifted into the van, railway police charged at the group around the vehicle and clubbed them.' . . .

The Cape Times, September 9: A report said that Mr Donald Davids, 21, was on his way home from a prayer meeting in Bonteheuwel when he was shot by riot police who were clashing with rioters on an open field in front of his house. He was given emergency treatment at Groote Schuur Hospital for gunshot wounds in the abdomen . . . .

The Cape Times, September 10. Mr Banudey Dajee, 37, a Retreat shopkeeper . . was shot dead by police near his own shop. His father said: 'Police were shooting at looters all over and there was a lot of confusion.'

The Argus, September 11: A news report said that Salie Noordien, 13, of Manenberg, was shot in the head with birdshot when he went to fetch bread for neighbours. Police were hiding in a shop that had been broken into and they fired on a group of skollies . . . hitting Salie, who was taken to Groote Schuur Hospital under police guard. Two weeks previously a young cousin of the Noordien family was shot dead.

On the Witwatersrand renewed struggle broke out in mid-September. The headmaster of a high school in Soweto, Mr G. J. Tabane, gives the following account of how the police dealt with students who were singing in the school grounds behind locked gates (*Cape Times*, 18 September 1976):

> But the police blasted it [the gate] open . . . . When three vans
> drove in with heavily armed Black and White policemen, the
> pupils began scattering in different directions . . . . That's when
> the firing started. Some of the pupils were wounded by shotgun
> pellets. There was a great deal of confusion as the pupils screamed
> in pain. It was ugly, I have never witnessed anything like that before.

A list of similar incidents could be extended almost indefinitely. These
were the events with which thousands of workers were confronted
in the streets where they lived. The people being killed, wounded or
detained were their children, relatives, friends or neighbours. Inevitably
the terrific use of violence by the state intimidated many people. At
very least it impressed on them the merciless nature of the struggle in
which they were caught up and the need for caution. On the other
hand, the methods of the state inevitably awakened widespread bitter-
ness and anger, and brought political awareness to many who had
previously been apathetic.[2] Under these conditions opposition to the
state continued to mount up. The presence of the police could at most
prevent opposition from being manifested. Wherever police control
was lifted, rebellion tended to break into the open. This was the keynote of the mass movement in South Africa during the second half of
1976.

The strikes

During August and September the African and coloured working class
massively took strike action on two separate occasions, thereby transforming the struggle against the state which up to that point had been
dominated by the students. This once again raised the question, in a
more concrete form, of the relationship between the black proletariat
and other sections of the population. The black population consists
of a (predominantly urban) proletariat, flanked on the one side by a
dwindling agrarian population and on the other side by an even smaller
middle class. Because of education and social status, the middle class
is able to exercise an influence out of all proportion to its numbers.
Yet any significant movement of the black population must depend
very largely on the urban working class. Conversely, any movement
that fails to gain the support of important sections of workers will
be inconclusive; it will leave the nerve-centres of the country - the
centres of urban production - in the hands of the capitalist class and
the state.

304

Clearly, workers can be mobilised most effectively on the basis of their own demands and interests; and the demands of the mass of the workers will be demands for the most far-reaching transformation of society. On the other hand, precisely because of their material destitution, the African workers encounter the most severe difficulties in producing a national leadership to co-ordinate their struggle. Given the severe restrictions on communication in South Africa, any leadership directly rooted among the workers is almost by definition confined to the local or clandestine level. At the same time, more and more students, intellectuals and middle-class people are being driven into active struggle against the state. Among the educated classes, in general, the tradition of political organisation is more strongly developed than among the workers. It is thus possible and even likely that any emergent working-class movement will be dominated for a time by radical groups or individuals from the middle classes and the intelligentsia.

The relationship between the proletarian mass and a non-proletarian leadership, however, is inherently one of conflict. In general it will only endure until the workers have developed an adequate leadership of their own. In this process there are different courses open to the middle-class elements within the movement. On the one hand, they may be integrated fully into the movement, abandoning any self-interest they might have and subjecting themselves to the discipline and interests of the workers. On the other hand, they may try to impose their own ideas and methods on the workers. This will bring them into conflict with the growing consciousness and self-assertion of the workers; in the end they must split off or be expelled. These are the general tendencies that were reflected, if only to a limited extent, in the events of August and September.

During June and July it was the most volatile section of the African population, the youth and young intellectuals, that gave furious expression to the tension and anger of the African people in general. Intensely committed and regardless of personal danger, they surged far ahead of the steady, dogged struggle of the workers in the factories. An all-absorbing effort of this nature can only endure for a time, or it must be transformed and reconstructed on more durable foundations. The question that arises is how far the African students' movement succeeded in developing itself. Organisationally, the movement reached its highest level in Soweto. A Students' Representative Council (SSRC) was formed, a body on which broad masses of students could be represented, decisions could be taken by the movement as a whole and action could be co-ordinated. A similar development in the workers' movement, while it would take longer to come about, could have momentous consequences. A body representing the mass of workers in any given area, capable of co-ordinating the action of workers in hundreds of factories or entire industries, could become not only a mighty organ of struggle but an organ of social power. Development in this direction, which is already implicit in the industrial struggles of the workers, was thus foreshadowed even more concretely by the example of the SSRC.

The relationship between students and workers among the African people of South Africa is relatively close. For many years it has been state policy to admit Africans to the cities only for the purpose of selling their labour-power. By definition, the African population in the cities is basically a working-class population and African students in the cities are mainly workers' children. The majority, moreover, themselves have no other prospect before them than wage labour, often beginning at a very early age. The events of June and July forced the students to reassess their attitude towards their elders and reconsider their relation- ship with the adult workers. 'The kids say we are irrelevant, that we have been talking to the authorities since 1912 but with no result', an adult intellectual explained (*FM*, 3 September 1976). Experience, however, proved that the students for all their courage and determi- nation did not have the power to enforce their demands or put the state in danger. As long as the struggle remained confined to students, it could be suppressed without seriously straining the economy. At the same time, the state left no stone unturned to isolate the students from, and discredit them with, the remainder of the black population. For the students, broadening their struggle to encompass the adult workers thus became strategically essential. In their close relationships with parents, family and neighbours the means of doing this lay readily to hand.

From the beginning African workers found themselves involved in the uprising that had broken out around them. At first such involve- ment was accidental or individual, for example through demonstrations near their homes or their factories being closed as a result of fighting in the area. There are many indications, however, that the workers spontaneously sympathised with a struggle which could only be inter- preted as being a struggle against the state. Thus a journalist who entered Alexandra on 18 June together with a group of workers de- scribes how they gave the clenched-fist salute when meeting a group of demonstrators. One of them pointed to the burning township and said: 'If you go down there you will see what black power means'

(*De Volkskrant*, 19 June 1976). On the same day at Vosloorus on the East Rand, workers waiting for their buses in the early morning became angry at the delay which the road blocks and security checks were causing. When the buses finally arrived, the workers stoned them and set them on fire. A police mortuary van was also attacked and destroyed. During the fighting in the streets of Cape Town on 7 September, a white policeman who injured himself was loudly jeered and whistled at by watching construction workers. Also, the nurses at Tygerberg Hospital, where many victims of the police were taken, were said to be 'rebellious'. Leaflets were circulating among the coloured staff. On one day 120 nurses stayed away from work. Nurses thronged together in the hospital grounds; some of them threw boxes at passing motor-cars.

From these and other indications it can be seen that the militance of the youth found an immediate echo among the adult workers. From their side the students broadened their programme to reflect the demands of the black population in general and the workers in particular. Thus on 23 August the students of Langa High School in the Cape put forward the following demands: the release of detained students and all other detainees, regardless of colour; equal pay for equal work; free education. On 1 September African students demonstrating in the streets of Cape Town carried placards denouncing job reservation and the pass laws. Other slogans demanded equal education, an end to apartheid, and release of the prisoners on Robben Island. The uprising was no longer a student uprising only. It was developing into a general rebellion of the masses in the towns and cities. The students played a leading and spectacular part but the ultimate power rested with the workers.

On 4 August the students of Soweto for the first time tried to organise a strike. Judging by reports, little preparation appears to have gone into this. The action was aimed at preventing the workers from going to work rather than organising them. A section of the railway line from Soweto to Johannesburg was torn up; buses taking workers to the cities were stoned and jeered at by students. These tactics apparently did little to convince workers of the need to strike. Before the month was out, however, more systematic efforts began to be undertaken.

At this point it should be made clear that 'to organise' in this context does not mean to manipulate or induce artificially events that would otherwise not have happened. In South Africa it is all but impossible to 'organise' strikes in this sense. The state has the power and the determination to nip such efforts in the bud. Among African workers striking is only feasible where discontent over common grievances has become general. Through informal discussion the thought must have crystallised that the time had come to act. At this stage the call to strike may find a considerable response. Certain further conditions, however, must be present. The call to strike must link up with the workers' own understanding of the situation. It must be uttered by people with whom they are familiar or in whom they have confidence. In practice, the call to strike can most readily be sounded by the spokesmen of the workers themselves. It can also be communicated, however, by 'outside' individuals and organisations that have gained the confidence of the workers.

Strikes under these conditions will tend to have a spontaneous, *ad hoc* character. To 'organise' a strike means to co-ordinate the unco-ordinated action that is spontaneously taking place. It will mean giving the signal for the workers to lay down their tools; it will mean preparing a strategy and gathering resources in advance to deal with the counter-measures and the numerous difficulties that can be expected. To be most effective a strike must be built on the conscious participation of at least a majority of workers. Daily mass meetings are a means of bringing this about. To organise a strike, therefore, is to introduce the conclusions of working-class struggle in general into the struggle being fought by a specific group of workers. It means to translate these conclusions into a concrete plan of action, discussing this plan with the workers and together with the workers carrying it out.

In Soweto in August 1976 there is no doubt that large numbers of workers found themselves in a situation of conflict with the state. Quite apart from long-standing grievances such as the pass laws, poverty, insecurity, and the constant irritants of racial discrimination, there was now a situation where children – often their own children – were being killed and the police were invading the townships, making them unsafe. The workers' indignation was reaching a level where they were prepared to take action. The situation was more complex, however, than with a dispute within a single factory. In the factory the issues and demands are relatively simple and the workers are constantly in touch with one another. In Soweto in 1976 nothing less than the role of the police and the entire policy of the state were at issue. Literally hundreds of thousands of workers were involved, among whom no organs of communication existed nor any organisation that was capable of co-ordinating the movement towards a strike.

In this situation two crucial questions arise: who is to decide when the strike should begin, and how is the call to be communicated to the workers? On 4 August a first attempt was made to resolve these questions in practice. The students took the initiative in sounding the call to strike. The method they chose of communicating it was to intercept the workers on their way to work and try to dissuade or prevent them from going any further. This attempt was unsuccessful. When a few weeks later a second attempt was made, some of the previously unsuccessful tactics were repeated. Significant new elements were present, however, which led to completely different results.

The Soweto general strike of 23 to 25 August reflected a conscious orientation of the students towards the African working class. T. Mashinini, leader of the SSRC, declared that the students had gone as far as they could; it had now become important to strike at the industrial structure of South Africa. Over the preceding week-end, pamphlets in the name of the ANC calling for a three-day general strike were distributed throughout Soweto. The focus of the action was the repressive measures that the state and the police had taken. One demand was for a meeting with the Prime Minister and the Minister of Police. The reaction of the government and employers, as well as a sizeable section of liberals, was unambiguously hostile. The effort at organising the strike was regarded – not only by the government but also, for example, by the South African Institute of Race Relations – as mere intimidation.

From the early hours of Monday 23 August armed police were patrolling the streets of Soweto in force. Crowds of students picketing the railway stations were fired upon. Anti-strike leaflets were spread. Despite this, the strike reached massive proportions. Johannesburg employers in general reported an absenteee rate of approximately 80 per cent. A survey revealed that in Langlaagte and Industria up to 90 per cent of the African work-force were absent on the first day of the strike. In the case of one large department store, only 2.5 per cent of its workers came to work (*FM*, 27 August 1976). Bus services to Soweto were curtailed and several trains were cancelled 'because nobody was using them' (*Die Burger*, 24 August 1976). On Tuesday 24 August more workers came to work but on Wednesday 25 August the strike had once again expanded.

The general reaction of employers was to take such reprisals as they could. In most cases strikers were not paid. In the steel and engineering industries workers who were thought to have stayed away out of sympathy with the strike were threatened with dismissal: 'We cannot subsidise subversion', explained the head of an employers' organisation (*FM*, 27 August). The president of the Transvaal Chamber of Industries declared that some employers might use the occasion to dismiss workers 'who have given them trouble in the past'. Many employers would also reconsider their dependence on African workers, and might make more use of coloured workers or machines. Apart from withholding wages, however, there was little that employers could do. They were rendered virtually impotent by the sheer dimensions of the strike. A sense of this impotence and of disquiet was reflected by at least one personnel officer, who admitted: 'The biggest percentage of absentees has been among manual labourers. I can't help wondering whether this is not some sort of show of strength, rather than the result of intimidation' (*ibid*.). Senator A. Scheepers, president of the Garment Workers' Union, pointed out the importance of the workers' action in even more hostile terms (*Star IAW*, 28 August 1976): 'In this week alone three months profit has been swallowed up . . . . If the unrest continues we will have unemployment because factories will go insolvent.'

The police, on the other hand, were enabled to strike heavy blows at the students and the workers of Soweto. Some of the youth persisted with the tactics that had been followed on 4 August. Several instances of threats and reprisals against strike-breakers were reported in the press. One such incident was the burning of some rooms in the Mzimhlope Hostel, where many hundreds of Zulu migrant workers were housed. In the ordinary course of events a conflict of this nature could have been settled and mistakes corrected through discussion of the aims and methods of the struggle. In this particular case, however, the state intervened with a plan of action that had previously been prepared. Of course, the existence of such a plan is officially denied; yet the evidence points overwhelmingly at this.

On 15 August members of the Black Parents' Association had applied to the Supreme Court for an interdict against two members of the Urban Bantu Council who, they alleged, had threatened to burn down their houses and were seeking the aid of hostel leaders to help suppress the unrest. According to one affidavit, a meeting was held in the house of the unofficial 'mayor' of Soweto at which, in the presence of a police sergeant, it was decided that students who accosted workers should be killed. The police sergeant took note of the discussion and allegedly assured the meeting of police co-operation. Subsequent developments corroborate these charges. By Sunday, 22 August a major-general of the South African Police was confidently predicting a reaction against those who were trying to organise the strike. On

Tuesday morning, as if to drive the message home, the *World* published a statement by a colonel of police urging workers to thrash any students who attempted to stop them from going to work.

On Tuesday afternoon this strategy was carried into practice. Approximately a thousand men from the Mzimhlope Hostel began attacking houses and residents in the vicinity. Over the next few days fighting between migrant workers and residents, particularly students, became widespread. By Thursday, 26 August twenty-one deaths had been officially confirmed. Eleven people were said to have died in the clashes between hostel-dwellers and residents, while the police admitted to 'possibly' having killed the remaining ten; 107 people had been injured. Police casualties amounted to one officer who was hit in the ribs by a stone. By Monday, 30 August the death toll had risen to forty.

According to all available evidence, the rampage by the Mzimhlope workers was inspired and led by the police. Very soon after the fighting began, grave questions were raised in the press. On Friday, 27 August the *Financial Mail* observed:

> Nor is it clear what caused Wednesday's 'backlash' on the part of the Zulu hostel dwellers. . . . Some Soweto residents are suspicious about the 'backlash' however. 'The gangs seem very well organised and they have chosen the houses they have burnt very carefully', said one.

The *Star*, in a leading article on Thursday, 26 August, conceded that 'individual policemen may have been urging on groups of Zulus to deal with the "troublemakers" '. Other reports were even more explicit. Several reports were published of policemen urging migrant workers not to damage houses, since these were the property of the state, but to confine their attacks to people. The official explanation, that the police 'were forced to shoot to protect law-abiding people from gangs of intimidators' (*Star IAW*, 28 August), is contradicted by many eye-witness reports. Reporters of the *Star*, for instance, 'saw police standing by in three hippo armoured vehicles, vans and cars near the [Mzimhlope] hostel, watching the mob. They did nothing to protect the residents'. Another reporter wrote (*ibid.*):

> Men carrying butchers' knives, pangas, tomahawks, intshumentshu [sharpened spikes], kieries and stones started chasing people around . . . . What amazed me was that as they assaulted people, heavily armed police stood by and did nothing to protect the residents. The hostel-dwellers, swinging their weapons wildly, shouted: 'we will kill these people'.

From press reports two factors emerge suggesting why the police singled out the men of Mzimhlope Hostel to lead the attack on the students and the local population in general. The Mzimhlope Hostel is described as 'a strong Inkatha constituency' (*FM*, 27 August). The basic conflict, according to some observers, lay between the 'Black Consciousness movement and traditional supporters of Chief Gatsha Buthelezi and the Inkatha ka Zulu cultural movement' (*ibid*.). A pro-government newspaper on 26 August published a cartoon of the fighting with the caption: 'What would Gatsha Buthelezi say if he saw Zulu Inkatha putting Black Power in its place?' (*Die Volksblad*). In fact, Buthelezi replied on that same day. He called on the hostel-dwellers to stop fighting. The following day he visited Soweto. His conclusions were that the hostel-dwellers had been intimidated, that they had organised to protect themselves, and that the police had then intervened, transporting the men to different parts of Soweto and urging them to retaliate against the local people.

It will be noted that Buthelezi's appeal was made only two days after the fighting had begun, and a day after the strike had ended. It can safely be assumed that the leaders of Inkatha had no wish to be associated with a police-led rampage by a thousand men against an immensely popular strike. The mere existence of Inkatha, however, undoubtedly helped to make possible the organisation of a backlash. A second factor was the burning down of part of the Mzimhlope Hostel. Many hostel-dwellers, it was reported, kept their savings in their rooms. The destruction of their scanty possessions is bound to have enraged the workers. This may well have been the deciding factor for the police in selecting the Mzimhlope Hostel as their base of operations.

Nevertheless, from the point of view of employers and the state, the bloody anti-strike campaign of 23 to 27 August ended in defeat. The strike in Soweto went ahead as planned. Despite all the killing and divisions that were caused, the militance and the strike fever of the workers and the youth were not to be suppressed. On the contrary, divisions were rapidly bridged and militance increased. The mood of Soweto in this period is vividly captured in the description by Mkele (*FM*, 3 September 1976):

> There is an attempt to create division among us, but there is a
> lot of unity in Soweto and other areas. Attitudes hardened
> as a result of the shooting, and the adult population has come
> now to identify with the children. The longer the situation goes

on, the harder the attitude of the Black population is going to be. They are going to be completely solid. The children have got the situation very well organised. They are organising themselves, and they have their own Soweto Students' Representative Council. Obviously the impetus came from SASO and the BPC, and the SA Students' Movement which was formed. The children tell their parents when they must stay at home. You'd be amazed to hear 12-year-olds saying: 'Daddy, on Monday, Tuesday and Wednesday, you are staying away from work. Just to ensure that you do, will you please see to it that your car stays in the yard.' No teacher or principal dares order the students around any more. One principal started telling the kids off. They heard him out and then told him: 'You know, we've always known you were a sell-out.' They beat him up and kicked him around, and then put him in his car and told him he must not come back. Then they told the assistant principal, 'Hey, you are now the principal.' When the 'mayor' of Soweto held a meeting to report back on his talks with the government, he could only do so with the express permission of the students. Three young girls at the meeting wanted to know from him: 'Who authorised you to go to Pretoria? On whose behalf were you talking?'

In mid-September this mood of militance and defiance once again erupted in a strike that was even more massive than the general strike of August. The balance of power between the workers and the youth on the one hand, and employers and the police on the other, had shifted. The anti-strike campaign in September was relatively feeble. No weapon could be found as potent or divisive as the use made of the hostel-dwellers in August. In any event this weapon had been blunted, while the issues became more clearly defined. The strike took on the character of a massive demonstration, with employers and the state looking on. Most important of all, the strike found an echo in Cape Town, where it was massively supported by the coloured working class. The September general strike became the most important instance of common action by African and coloured workers in the history of South Africa.

The strike was preceded by the spreading of leaflets throughout Soweto by the SSRC. The leaflets appeared in Zulu, English and Sesotho, and called on workers to stay at home on 13, 14 and 15 September. Among the grievances put forward were the following: the killing of children by the police; detention without trial; the docking of wages of workers who had gone on strike before; the attacks on demonstrators by some hostel-dwellers. For the hostel-dwellers there was now a special slogan: hostel people do not fight. Nurses were exempted from the strike. The leaflets further called on people to keep off the streets and said that the strike should be as peaceful as possible. According to an employers' spokesman, the emphasis in the leaflets had changed from being anti-government to being anti-business. 'typically communist' (*FM*, 17 September 1976).

The response of the workers was massive. According to the *Financial Mail* the strike was 'largely successful' (*ibid*.). It was joined by approximately half a million workers on the Reef. The average rate of participation, according to the *Financial Mail*, appeared to be over 50 per cent. In the steel and engineering industries, according to employers, the absentee rate ranged from 28 to 60 per cent. At the Main Tin Plant of the Metal Box Company in Industria, only fifteen out of 250 African workers came to work. Of the 600 African workers employed by by Premier Milling, some 200 were absent on Monday, 360 on Tuesday and 300 on Wednesday. At Advance Laundries approximately half the African workers stayed away. At the different branches of the OK Bazaars and Checkers department stores and supermarkets absenteeism ranged from 50 to 70 per cent. Witwatersrand University was 'very seriously affected'. Various employers admitted that they were unable to cope, or able to cope in the short term only, as a result of the workers' action. In the steel and engineering industries some companies reported 'quite serious production losses' (*ibid*.).

Employers took such counter-measures as they could. Their most obvious tactic was once again to dock the pay of absent workers. One employers' spokesman explained that 'after discussions with the police, his organisation initially took the view that management should not dock pay and so put up the backs of the employees, driving them into the opposition camp. Now, however, it was necessary to drive them back to work' (*ibid*.). There also appears to have been some confusion. A spokesman for the Transvaal Chamber of Industries said that lock-outs against striking workers were being contemplated by some employers for the future. The Federated Chamber of Industries, on the other hand, was 'completely unaware of any lock-out plans' (*Star IAW*, 18 September). Dismissals were once again threatened, though probably only a small fraction of the strikers could have been sacked without causing serious disruption.

On the eve of the strike the police launched a massive raid on Alexandra township. Over 800 people were arrested. The raid, however, had no noticeable effect. Beyond this there was little the police could do. 'Train and bus services,' it was reported, 'appeared to be running normally and there was no sign of intimidation of those going to work' (*ibid.*). The police chief in charge of riot control stated that on Wednesday 15 September no incidents whatever were reported in Soweto between 7 a.m. and 4 p.m. Even a pro-government newspaper, to which the terms 'striking' and 'intimidation' are synonymous, was forced to content itself with the report that on Tuesday, for the second consecutive day, thousands of black workers did not arrive at work (*Die Burger*, 15 September). From all accounts the strike was solidly supported by African workers all along the Reef. A spokesman for the Metal Box company believed that 'there was much less coercion of workers this time, and more acquiescence on their part in the stay-away' (*FM*, 17 September). This finding, while couched in the special terminology of employers and the state, unmistakably reflected the rising tide of militance among the workers and working-class youth in the cities.

In particular, it should be noted that there was no hint of a 'back-lash' among the hostel-dwellers in September. Only a few weeks earlier official spokesmen had been stressing the dedication of these workers to law and order and their rejection of the militant youth. Now they were supporting the strike. The *Financial Mail* (17 September) published an unconfirmed report that 'Zulu hostel workers were offended by criticism by other Blacks that they were opposed to the stay-away on August 23, 24 and 25, and have played an active role in promoting this week's strike.' The *World* (15 September) quoted a Soweto student who excitedly declared: 'The hostels are now on our side.'

It should also be noted that, under South African conditions, strike-breaking need not mean opposition to a strike. Of the workers who went to work during the September strike, some undoubtedly did so out of loyalty to their employers or failure to see the necessity of striking. Out of five strike-breakers interviewed by the *Star*, however, not one reflected this attitude. Sheer economic necessity was the only concrete reason that emerged. A woman employed in a restaurant explained the dilemma in which a substantial section of the unfree working class, earning low wages and without job security, is caught (*Star IAW*, 18 September): 'It hurts to stand here and make money while others stay in Soweto. Some of the brothers in Soweto need the money as much as I do. But I have five children and no husband – what can I do?' This attitude was undoubtedly shared by many other strike-breakers. Poverty and the threat of dismissal or arrest are part of the tremendous pressure to which all African strikers are subject. Support for the strike, we may conclude, was by no means inflated through 'intimidation'. On the contrary, support for the strike was inhibited by the power of employers and the state – held back, to use the official terminology, by official intimidation.

Events in Cape Town followed the same pattern as on the Reef. Strike action in support of the struggle in Soweto had for some time been hanging in the air. During the first two days of the general strike in Soweto thousands of leaflets were distributed in the coloured and African areas of Cape Town. The *Financial Mail* reports (17 September):

> In view of the fact that the strike was conceived amid great confusion – countless pamphlets gave conflicting instructions and confusing dates – the stay-away appeared to be remarkably effective. On Tuesday a counter-campaign against the strike, in which thousands of pamphlets were dropped from an official helicopter, warned workers of dire economic consequences if they stayed away. The pamphlet called on workers not to jeopardize their jobs to further the objectives of a few [anonymous] people.

In one case three men were arrested for producing and distributing a leaflet in Athlone on 13 September. The leaflet stated that a strike by the workers would take place which would prove that the South African economy depends on blacks alone. The men were charged in terms of the Terrorism Act; thus they faced a minimum sentence of five years' imprisonment and a maximum sentence of death. They were, however, acquitted.

The following is the text of one leaflet that has been widely publicised:

STRIKE

The racists do not spare the bullets. Their guns try to cut down our march for freedom. But the march to freedom must not end. Reject all concessions that the racists grant us. Concessions are crumbs. We want freedom not crumbs. Reject the CRC, Indian Council, the homelands, the management committees. All black people suffer alike. Get rid of apartheid. Ban all apartheid places such as Three Arts, Nico Malan, stadiums, etc.

STRIKE! STRIKE! STRIKE!

WEDNESDAY 15th THURSDAY 16th

Do not go to work or school. Nobody must be in the streets.

316

You will go to work at your risk. If you strike you will hit the
system where it hurts. Take this home. Spread the word.

FREEDOM COMES WITH SACRIFICE
WE SHALL OVERCOME!

An anti-strike leaflet was published in reply, stating that 'the march
to "freedom" is a march to hunger and to a jobless society'. It informed
workers that 'if you strike you strike a blow at yourself and your
family'. These are the conflicting arguments with which the workers of
Cape Town were confronted. The conclusion that they reached is clear
from their response - a conclusion in which experience was no doubt
the deciding factor. While the pro-government press loyally proclaimed
on Thursday morning that the strike had failed in Cape Town, police
patrols in the major coloured and African townships estimated an 80
per cent boycott. The strike was particularly strongly supported among
the women workers. According to employers, the turnout in industry
was approximately 50 per cent. In shops it ranged from 60 to 100 per
cent. On the other hand, in the clothing industry - the major industry
of Cape Town - attendance ranged from 10 to 15 per cent. In this
industry some nine-tenths of the workers are women. The docks, too,
were seriously hit. Only 20 per cent of the stevedores reported for
work on Wednesday. Ship-repairing companies also reported substantial
stay-aways. Many construction sites in the centre of town were deserted.
As in Soweto, there were no reports of intimidation. The centre of
town was unusually quiet and deserted. In townships like Manenberg
and Bonteheuwel, police patrols 'reported an almost sepulchral atmosphere' (*FM*, 17 September).

As in Johannesburg, employers in Cape Town threatened workers
with the weapon of dismissal. Attempts were made to deepen the
division between strikers and strike-breakers with special rewards for
the latter. In one print shop the fifteen workers (out of thirty-one) who
came to work were each presented with R10.00 and a personal letter
from the employer: 'How can one disappoint a man like that?' a senior
worker asked. 'We are now more loyal still to the company and will
definitely not stay away from work or pay attention to the intimidation
campaign.' This worker further announced his intention of framing
his employer's letter and hanging it on his wall. Such statements were
treated as front-page news by the pro-government press (*Die Burger*,
16 September).

The general strategy of the capitalist class was reflected in an editorial
published in the *Star* on Thursday 16 September. The familiar tactic of

isolating and eliminating militant workers is here adapted to the general-strike situation, and the equally familiar conclusion is drawn that, besides repressing strike campaigns, it is equally important that concessions should be made on the employers' terms. This significant policy statement deserves to be quoted in full.

STRIKES: EMPLOYERS HAVE TWO DUTIES

The Soweto 'stay-away' has created an awkward dilemma for many thoughtful employers. During the earlier disturbances and strikes they paid their workers, even though they did not come to work. Those employers believed workers exposed themselves to very real danger if they ignored that first strike call, and should therefore not suffer through involuntary absence. But as the strikes grow almost into something like 'a way of life', the backlash has set in and more employers are beginning to say: enough is enough. In the sense that the strikes are essentially political and are not normal – let alone legal – domestic industrial disputes, there is some justification for the policy of 'no work, no pay'. It is tough, and certainly unfair on the genuine cases of workers terrified to expose themselves and their families to violence if they defy the strike calls. But the truth is that if workers do not favour the strike, yet know they will be paid anyway, there is no incentive for organised resistance to intimidators. And if employers continue to pay, they are virtually financing the strike themselves. But employers do have two important moral obligations, one to their loyal workers and the other to themselves. The first is to the 30 to 40 per cent who have been coming to work anyway. There can only be contempt for the companies that sent home those who came to work, and docked half their pay. Nor can one admire the insensitivity of businessmen who take the loyalty of their staff for granted and pay them the usual rate for defying the strike movement. Workers who have taken undoubted risks deserve a bonus, some extra recognition, and if they do not get it can hardly be blamed for losing heart. Employers also have an obligation to recognise that the strike has its roots in the battle to achieve a better life for urban Blacks. Employers are caught in the crossfire of this battle and if they simply sit tight with their heads down, they may become prime casualties as the conflict grows.

Read back to front, this argument reveals its meaning. On the one hand, the strikes are recognised as a reflection of 'the battle to achieve a better life for urban Blacks'. Employers as a class may be eliminated if this battle develops unchecked. But how to check it? It is taken for granted that the strike movement must be fought. It is then assumed that large numbers of workers, described as 'loyal', are more or less indifferent to 'the battle to achieve a better life' in which the strikes are rooted. Of these workers it is now demanded that they offer 'organised resistance' to the strike movement, presumably after the example of the Mzimhlope hostel-dwellers. Employers should pay them to do this. What, then, of 'the battle to achieve a better life'? Implicitly it is assumed that employers and the state, in their own time and on their own terms, must be left to attend to this.

Conclusions

By September unrest among the youth in Soweto and elsewhere had become endemic. Political struggle was no longer to be rooted out. In the months that followed, the movement of the school students continued developing throughout the country, though in a more sporadic manner. According to all the laws of common sense, unarmed students cannot indefinitely continue defying armed police. Yet this is precisely what appeared to be happening as month after month, in one town after another, struggle flared up once again. By the middle of 1977 a massive campaign against the Bantu education system had built up, involving a boycott of classes by some 300,000 African students and the resignation of hundreds of African teachers in Soweto.

This development not only shows the intense determination to change society by which the student movement was impelled. It also shows the degree of support that the students enjoyed from the black population in general and working-class parents in particular. No isolated student movement could have kept up its momentum for so long in the face of furious suppression by the state. Significantly, the struggle was almost entirely a struggle of the urban population. The movement of the African and coloured youth cannot be understood except in the context of the movement of the urban proletarian masses.

As in theory, so in practice the middle classes played little part in the struggle except as spokesmen – in essence temporary spokesmen – for the workers. The relative inactivity of the rural population can be explained by its scattered, diffuse nature and its lack of political coherence except on a limited, local level. A leading part, on the other hand, was played by the students and the youth. This in itself is not surprising. The youth and intellectuals in general form a volatile, sensitive section of society, quick to respond to and amplify any tremors or movement among the masses of the people. At the same time, the movement of the youth and intellectuals, in itself, is relatively insignificant. They occupy no key position in the economy and can cause little damage by abandoning their normal role. A student movement can only acquire significance by linking up with those sections of the population on whom society depends.

In the Soweto period this link was established only to a limited extent. Approaches to the workers were made on an *ad hoc* basis and were mainly concerned with a single, particular action. There is no evidence of more fundamental fusion in the form of a joint programme of joint bodies such as the SSRC. No use was made of the structures developed at factory level by the workers in the preceding period. No attempt was made, even under the exceptionally favourable conditions of an incipient general strike, at linking up these structures into a broader organisation. It goes without saying that most work in this direction would have had to take place underground, just as the strikes themselves were clandestine or semi-clandestine. The students, however, tended to take their action to the streets, to mobilise by example rather than by organisation, to conduct propaganda by the deed rather than by analysis and discussion. In a revolutionary situation methods of this nature may have results. In South Africa in 1976 the effect was to bypass the beginnings of working-class organisation and create an ephemeral movement that disappeared as quickly as it came. The strikes of August and September, it can be concluded, arose from the spontaneous indignation of the workers as much as from the organising efforts of the students. In the absence of proper organisation, the strikes ended leaving little behind except a wealth of new experience.

A significant form of action developed by the students in this process was the mass picketing of bus and railway stations. Picketing, as we have seen, is mainly illegal in South Africa and requires an extremely careful approach. At the best of times it is no simple matter. In general, in order to succeed pickets should be composed of striking workers or operate under the auspices of organisations whose authority is recognised by the workers. The strike must be seen as a matter of the workers themselves. Suspicious non-strikers can more easily be persuaded by their work-mates than by strangers whose identity and interest in the matter have first to be explained. From this it does not follow that students should be excluded from the picket line; but here, as elsewhere in the labour movement, students can best play a role by acting under the guidance of the workers and on terms that are acceptable to the workers whom they are addressing. Student pickets have the function of assisting the workers or workers' organisations that have called the strike. To appear on the scene and attempt to enforce decisions that were taken behind the workers' backs, however much the workers might be in sympathy with them, is tactically and politically incorrect.

From all accounts it appears that the students of Soweto paid insufficient regard to these considerations. In effect an ultimatum was presented to the workers which, in the eyes of many workers, the students had no right to present. The bold initiative taken by the students was thus weakened by the tactics that were followed. The success of the strikes was achieved despite, not because of, these tactics.

The tensions created by the students' approach was exacerbated by the methods used in some cases against workers who crossed the picket lines. A number of violent clashes were reported and reprisals against strike-breakers extended to measures such as the burning of rooms at the Mzimhlope Hostel. In the general atmosphere of Soweto at this time, given the absence of coherent organisation and strategy, conflicts of this nature were to some extent inevitable. Equally inevitable, however, were the consequences. Violence by pickets against strike-breakers may well form part and parcel of a strike. Strike-breaking had been severely dealt with, for example, in the early strikes by the white miners on the Reef. In some cases the homes of strike-breakers were ransacked and their furniture burned on the streets. Another device was the 'scab cage', in which strike-breakers were paraded through the streets to the jeers and derision of the working-class population. Violence of this nature, however, is characterised by the fact that it is used by the mass of striking workers against a minority of strike-breakers. In the case of the Soweto students, violence was used *on behalf of* a majority of striking workers. To many workers, the position must have been unclear.

It may thus be concluded that, quite apart from outside pressures, picketing in Soweto was complicated by the nature of the pickets themselves. First, the pickets were held by students acting independently of the workers. Second, the pickets mainly attempted to stop the workers from going to work, as opposed to persuading them of the correctness of the strike. The success of one particular strike, as opposed to clarity in the minds of the workers, appears to have been the students' overriding aim. To a certain extent the students thus found themselves struggling *against* the workers rather than organising *with* them. Conditions in Soweto at this stage undoubtedly presented many opportunities of building links with militant, politically minded workers. As it is, tensions were created which the police could transform into a bloody conflict between different sections of the Soweto working class.

These problems can be seen as a direct result of the absence of a broadly based, authoritative organisation among the working class, and hence the absence of a coherent strategy for conducting a general strike. A further consequence was the tendency for mistakes to be repeated. An example of this was the struggle that erupted at Christmas between migrant workers and residents in the African areas of Cape Town. As in Soweto four months earlier, students attempted to enforce their plan of action without having clarified the issue beforehand and built up sufficient support among the working class. The result was, once again, that the police could transform the tensions that arose into a pogrom against the youth and residents in general. The task of a workers' organisation under these conditions would have been to analyse the experience of the movement from day to day, to draw the practical conclusions and explain these to broader layers of workers. The lessons of the August general strike would undoubtedly have formed an important subject of discussion; no effort could have been spared to prevent similar disasters in future. In this way the experience of each separate section of workers would have been digested and generalised throughout the working class as a whole. It would also have been communicated to the students and other groups associated with the workers' movement.

As it is, the lack of adequate organisation foredoomed the entire struggle to the level of protest and rebellion. The highest form of organisation that developed was the SSRC, in itself an important and significant body, yet a body on which the workers of Soweto were not represented, even though every important issue depended very largely on them. Significant also was the distribution of pamphlets in the name of the ANC, which still carried a certain authority. At the same time, a call to action, no matter how authoritative or effective, can never take the place of careful, conscientious preparation and leadership of that action. The call to action, in other words, is not the same as leadership and organisation.

This organisational weakness is reflected in the fact that no further major strikes took place in the period that followed. The period from June to September can be characterised as a period of mass struggle, with all that the term connotes in South Africa: a movement based on the urban working class, dominated in the short term, supported in the long term by other militant sections of the people. The dominant role of the students in this period was reflected in numerous features of the struggle, for example in the tendency to take to the streets as opposed to building up strength in the factories. Conversely, the power of the workers was subtly but increasingly asserted. The students at an early stage recognised that only the workers could take the struggle further. The programme of the students' grievances was almost immediately broadened to incorporate working-class demands. Most significant of all were the objects selected for attack by the mass movement as a whole. Not only objects and institutions owned by whites or symbolical of the state were destroyed; everything alien to the working class became the accepted target of the movement as a whole. Property in general came under attack from a movement that depended in the final analysis on the propertyless workers. Vehicles, churches, banks, shops and business premises were treated in the same way as government offices and buildings. A blow at property is a blow at the property-owner. In this way the movement was steadily developing into a conflict between the propertyless masses and the property-owners supported by the state. What belonged to the workers themselves was not damaged. This expresses the basic relationship of forces in South Africa in a more consistent way than the superficial appearance of the conflict as a struggle between blacks and whites. The racial theory fails to explain why parts of the black community joined hands with the state on certain crucial issues, and why they were opposed to the workers and working-class youth in the struggles of 1976.

The period of social struggle initiated by the Soweto uprising can thus be characterised, on the one hand, as a development towards unity in action between the black working class and other sections of the black population, in particular the youth. As events showed, the growth of such unity is by no means a simple process. Common aims, as well as programmatical and tactical differences, must be consciously realised before common action can take place on a solid basis. From the point of view of the black workers the strikes amounted to a flexing of their muscles. From the solid foundations of industrial experience and action a great leap was suddenly taken to the highest form of struggle, the political general strike. The workers proved themselves capable of making this historical transition. The precedent, however, has yet to be worked out at the level of organisation. The gap between strikes at factory level and strikes at the national level had been bridged once. What remained was to fill in and eliminate this gap. This must involve a process of conscious preparation, of discussion and study of the issues involved by every section of the working-class. A point must be reached where the workers will be as much in command of a general strike as of a factory-based industrial dispute.

From every point of view the question of working-class organisation is thus posed as the decisive factor in the situation. Compared with the close, systematic organisation of employers and the state, the workers and the youth were in a state of incoherence. There is no possibility of the black working class enforcing its demands in the face of state opposition until it has built up the necessary organisation. This must involve not only industrial organisation, ensuring unity at the level of the shop-floor, but also political organisation, involving common perspective, a common strategy and programme which at least the most active groups of workers will support. On the one hand, therefore, organisation is a means of overcoming the divisions that have been created between different sections of workers. More fundamentally, it is the instrument for asserting the historical potential and power of the working class in practice.

Chapter 10

State reaction

The transition from the relative quiet of the 1960s to the industrial and political turmoil of the 1970s put the South African state under mounting pressure. The nature of the period that was opening up was made clear to many observers by the Durban strikes. During the parliamentary session of 1973 an uneasy awareness was revealed on both sides of the House. The Minister of Transport agreed with an Opposition speaker that the 'facts of reality' were 'compelling people to take up standpoints which were unthinkable a year ago'. The Leader of the Opposition reacted to the Durban strikes as follows (IIE, 1974, p.117):

> Now, as the Honourable . . . Prime Minister knows, these strikes
> were virtually all illegal, yet so far as I know no steps were taken
> to prosecute either the strikers or those who organised the
> strikes. I think we all realise that a new era in industrial relations
> in South Africa has been rung in as a result of what has happened.

What were the characteristics of this new era? The state was being faced with mass opposition on an increasing scale. The economy was beginning to flag. South Africa was being surrounded by a ring of hostile states. Moderates, attempting to mediate between the masses and the state, found themselves astride a chasm that was yawning wider. But it was the organisations looked towards by the masses that faced the greatest challenge of all. On the one hand, their task was to translate the growing pressure for social change into a viable strategy and programme. On the other hand, they were confronted with the hardening resistance of the state. To the black masses of South Africa the prospect of major victories was appearing on the horizon. Retreats in this period would only be tactical retreats. Continued submission was fast becoming unthinkable. Always some section of the masses, in particular the workers and the youth, would move into action again. Employers and the state were being driven on to the defensive. There was no real prospect, at least for the time being, of bringing the mass movement to a halt, of driving the youth and the workers back into the confines of law and order for any length of time. On the contrary, law and order had to be adapted to accommodate the new situation. The anti-liberal government was forced to introduce liberal reforms in a grudging and piecemeal way. In this process it was shown how reforms can complement repression, how relentless oppression of the masses can go hand in hand with conciliatory gestures to the petite-bourgeoisie. It was also shown that the state serves the interests of the capitalist class in general, not only of one section of that class. State policy continued to embody a compromise between the narrow demands of the white middle class and the interests of big business. As pressure grows and options dwindle, the state may become unable to maintain this balance. It may be forced to withdraw into one camp or the other. By the mid-1970s this stage had not yet been reached. Despite all doubt and criticism, the farmers as well as the mining corporations could remain in business, their faith in 'South Africa' still alive, their confidence in the government's ability to handle future crises not yet critically shaken.

Since 1948 the state apparatus has been controlled by the National Party. The state bureaucracy has become increasingly staffed by National Party members and supporters. Pressures on the state have tended to find their echo in the forums of the National Party. As tensions mounted in the mid-1970s and the demands on the state grew more pressing, the contradictions within the National Party likewise became sharper. The Afrikaner bourgeoisie and liberal intellectuals, like their English-speaking counterparts, increasingly came to the conclusion that the traditional state policy could not be maintained without considerable adjustment. In the interest of social stability it was essential that the burdens of the black middle classes should be eased. Opposed to this spirit of relative compromise were the fears and insecurity of the mass of voters supporting the National Party. They, too, were growing aware that some form of social change was impending. They had no independent alternative to advance. The diehard position of the Herstigte Nasionale Party appeared less feasible than ever and, in the mid-1970s, commanded less support than ever. Under these conditions the white masses continued to follow the lead that they were given, but with growing reluctance and misgivings.

These contradictory pressures were clearly manifested in the policy of the National Party, in particular from 1973 onwards. On the one hand, the growing insistence on some form of liberalisation could not be ignored. International as well as internal confidence in the trading and investment potential of South Africa was at stake. With the rise of the 'verligte' tendency inside the National Party, internal party stability also became a problem. On the other hand, the party leaders were faced with the fears and prejudices among their followers which they themselves in previous years had done so much to inculcate. At all costs the impression had to be avoided that the interests of the white workers and petite-bourgeoisie were being compromised or betrayed: 'The moment we [use black workers] in a manner which undermines the feeling of security of the White worker,' one Nationalist Member of Parliament argued in 1973, 'we can forget that the government, or any other government for that matter, will be able to allow this evolutionary process to take a proper course' (IIE, 1974, p. 113). While the government was forced in the direction of 'liberal' policies, therefore, it was unable to move in a straight line.

To the 'liberal' capitalists and their supporters, both inside and outside the country, this position was far from satisfactory. The government, in their view, was pandering too much to the white masses and neglecting more important matters. In 1975 the *Star* saw the tasks of the Nationalist leadership as follows (26 June):

There must be few people today who would like to be in
Mr Vorster's shoes. On the one hand he must contend with a
militant Marxist-Maoist Mozambique. On the other hand he
faces the beginnings of a very definite White backlash in places
like Middelburg and Gezina. All of which is taking place against
a background of rising expectations – and increasing frustration
– among South Africa's Black people. . . . Caught as he is on the
horns of this unpleasant dilemma, there is only one way out
for Mr Vorster. South Africa must become an enlightened
capitalist state which offers equal opportunities and an effective
say in government to all its people. It must convince its Black
and Brown citizens that it offers them as much dignity,
opportunity and prosperity as Mozambique offers its people.

From the point of view of the international bourgeoisie this advice might be absolutely sound. From the point of view of the Nationalist leaders to whom it is addressed it begs the question of how the transformation of South Africa into an 'enlightened capitalist state' is to be achieved. One obvious task was to prepare the Nationalist rank and file for the necessary changes in policy. Indeed, as events accelerated, increasingly serious efforts were made by Nationalist leaders and ideologists to re-educate the Afrikaner masses and build up support for the basic ideas of 'liberal' capitalism. Thus in November 1975 the mass Afrikaans-language weekly *Rapport* announced that only two possibilities existed in South Africa: 'either a settlement between black and white in our part of the world, or violent revolution'. A year later Dawie, the influential Nationalist columnist, was insistently exhorting his readers to understand the true meaning of separate development: 'If there are peoples or sections of peoples in South Africa with no convincing prospect of full citizenship in their own states,' he wrote, 'such a prospect must be offered to them in a common state structure with the whites.' He argued that the problem of South Africa is a 'freedom problem' and went on to explain: 'It is a problem [located] in the hearts of South Africans, especially of the governing party. If it is not solved there, it will disastrously undermine our ability to resist' (*Die Burger*, 6 November 1976).

The contradictions within the National Party, however, could not be disposed of by argument alone. The debate within the party reached acrimonious proportions. The Minister of Water Affairs accused the editor of the Nationalist daily, *Die Transvaler*, of disloyalty to the Prime Minister. The Minister was also unable to find much difference between *Rapport* and the liberal *Sunday Times*. This remark is most perceptive; indeed, verligtedom and liberalism have their roots in the same circles of big business and high finance, where language differences are unimportant. All the suspicion and hostility of the Nationalist rank and file towards these alien forces is echoed in the Minister's remark. It was these divergent forces that the government was trying to harness. Its policy became increasingly ambiguous and contradictory. Towards investors and liberal critics it presented itself as a champion of pragmatism and orderly reform. Towards the electorate it presented itself as an unyielding defender of the status quo. This contradiction will become more clear if we examine the two main trends of National Party policy in turn.

The Prime Minister reacted to the Durban strikes as follows (IIE, 1974, pp. 105–6):

> I want to say at once that the events there contain a lesson for
> us all. We would be foolish if we did not all benefit from the

lessons to be learned from that situation. It is most certainly my intention, as far as my responsibility extends, to benefit from them. Employers, whoever they may be, should not only see in their workers a unit producing for them so many hours of service a day. They should also see them as human beings with souls.

The lessons learned by the government from the Durban strikes were reflected in the amendment of the Bantu Labour (Settlement of Disputes) Act which Parliament immediately enacted. When the strikes began the works committee system was virtually a dead letter. No effort had been made by the state or by employers to get it off the ground. For more than a decade there had been little pressure from the workers to bring about any such effort. At the beginning of 1973 only eighteen statutory works committees existed in the whole of South Africa, with 118 non-statutory committees (SRR, 1973, p. 276). The Durban strikes provided a twofold stimulus to employers and the state: in the first place, to activate the committee system as a means of subduing the labour unrest; and second, to streamline the system in order to make it more acceptable to the workers.

In April 1973 the Minister of Labour published a draft Bill and called for representations. In essence, the draft Bill provided for the creation, besides works committees, of 'liaison committees'. Liaison committees would consist of representatives of the employer as well as representatives of the workers. Most of the existing non-statutory committees could then be recognised and the new system would receive a flying start. The reactions of employers' organisations to the draft Bill were generally favourable. The Federated Chamber of Industries regarded the Bill as 'a modest step in the right direction'. The Steel and Engineering Industries Federation of South Africa 'by and large [went] along with the Bill'. The Associated Chambers of Commerce 'supported the proposals in principle but nevertheless felt that a *de facto* situation would arise where African trade unions would emerge' (*ibid.*, p. 277). The Durban Chamber of Commerce likewise saw the Bill as a 'step in the right direction' but noted that no structure was created for negotiation. It added the following significant remark, reflecting its own experience (*ibid.*, p. 278):

It seems that the proposed Liaison Committee on which both employer and employee are represented is an essential feature to ensure that employees will negotiate, and the Chamber believes that this type of committee should be established in at least the larger undertakings as a forum for negotiation.

TUCSA, on the other hand, condemned the draft Bill and feared that it would give rise to 'unparalleled chaos and industrial unrest'. It called instead for an amendment to the Industrial Conciliation Act that would enable African workers to join the registered unions. This call was supported by the Institute of Race Relations. In the final version of the Bill this proposal was ignored, while that of the Durban Chamber of Commerce was very largely followed. At the same time, the Act of 1953 was renamed the Bantu Labour Relations Regulation Act.

Under the new rules the liaison committee became the primary form of industrial organisation for the African working class. Such a committee may be established by the employer and his employees in respect of the establishment where the latter are employed. Not less than half its members must be elected by the workers. The remainder must be designated by the employer. The chairman need not be a member of the committee. He may be appointed either by the employer or by the committee. The function of a liaison committee was defined as follows (section 7(2)):

> to consider matters which are of mutual interest to the employer
> and his employees and to make to the employer such recommen-
> dations concerning conditions of employment of such employees
> or any other matter affecting their interests as the committee
> may at any time deem expedient.

A works committee could only be elected in respect of an establishment or part of an establishment where no liaison committee exists and where more than twenty African workers are employed. The functions of a works committee were the following (section 7A(10)):

> to communicate the wishes, aspirations and requirements of the
> employees in the establishment or section of an establishment
> in respect of which it has been elected, to their employer and
> to represent the said employees in any negotiations with their
> employer concerning their conditions of employment or any
> other matter affecting their interests.

The Act also provided for the establishment of 'co-ordinating works committees', consisting of the chairmen and secretaries of the works committees representing two or more sections of the same establishment. The co-ordinating works committee, too, had the function of representing the workers in negotiations with their employer. It may appear, therefore, as if the distinction between works committees and trade unions has been blurred. Works committees have the legal capacity to negotiate with employers, a role that is normally fulfilled by trade unions. However, works committees are confined to a single factory or plant, and hence are immeasurably weaker than a union would be. It will also be noted that no obligation rests on the employer to negotiate with a works committee. Negotiations, moreover, are confined in advance to secondary issues. Wages and conditions of employment are determined in the first place by industrial councils or wage boards, in which works committees play no role. The furthest the Act went in allowing African workers to take part in the official process of collective bargaining·was the provision that Regional Bantu Labour Committees may co-opt at least one member of a liaison committee, works committee, or co-ordinating works committee. An African worker so co-opted may attend industrial council meetings without, however, having the right to vote.

In the event of a labour dispute the regional committee, inspector or Bantu labour officer concerned is required to 'consult' with the liaison committee, works committee or co-ordinating works committee (if any) in respect of the establishment where the dispute is taking place. Victimisation of works or liaison committee members is forbidden. In practice, however, employers are more or less free to dismiss committee members as long as other reasons are advanced. In that case victimisation is all but impossible to prove.

Despite their technical right to negotiate, therefore, works committees can in no way take the place that trade unions have traditionally taken within the workers' movement. In practice, only unofficial plant-level bargaining falls within their reach. As for the more fundamental problems experienced by black workers, neither works committees nor liaison committees have the remotest possibility of coming to grips with these.

The practical distinction between works and liaison committees is limited. None the less, works committees, due to the absence of employers' representatives, are relatively independent and hence, potentially, an instrument with which workers can confront their employer. To this extent they are also a training ground not only for the workers' representatives but also for the workers themselves in learning to control their representatives and call them to account. The conclusion of the Durban Chamber of Commerce that liaison committees are preferable from the employers' point of view is correct. This view has been borne out by a survey of 326 large companies conducted by the University of the Orange Free State in 1974. In 39.7 per cent of cases it was found that productivity had increased since the setting up of a liaison committee. In 82.6 per cent of cases grievances had been reduced and in 97.4 per cent of cases communication was said to have improved; 82.2 per cent of the employers were satisfied with their liaison committees and with the results they had produced (SRR, 1975, p. 212). Most significant of all – and this the Survey of Race Relations fails to mention – in 91 per cent of cases the liaison committee had been set up on the initiative of the employer (*South African Labour Bulletin*, May–June 1976, p. 24). Most of the employers in question regarded liaison committees as ' "anti-polarisation" device[s] conferring benefits such as better guidance by management and prompt solutions of problems'. In 81.9 per cent of cases the workers had had no say in choosing the chairman of the committee. Only in 16.6 per cent of cases could candidates for the committee be nominated freely by the workers without restrictions as to age or seniority. By establishing a liaison committee, employers moreover forestall the establishment of a works committee by the workers. The issues at stake in the choice of a works or liaison committee, therefore, may be limited in themselves. Yet such was the tension between employers and African workers that the workers' insistence on forming a works committee as opposed to a liaison committee was sometimes enough to spark off a bitter struggle.

How does a liaison committee function in practice? Valuable information on this point emerged in the case of S. *v*. T. Colgien Mbali, heard in the Durban Regional Court in January 1974. The liaison committee was at Pinetex, a textile factory belonging to the Frame Group. According to A. Frame, on behalf of management, the establishment of the liaison committee had been 'the desire of management and request of some of the workers'. The constitution of the committee could only be amended subject to the approval of management, 'because we must have some veto otherwise at this particular stage it may get out of control'.[1] Frame himself was the chairman of the committee; the alternative of an elected chairman had not been mentioned to the workers. In the absence of Frame the administrative manager 'automatically' took the chair. The committee had the function of making recommendations. Some concrete problems were solved by the committee but 'wages and important things aren't. They have to go higher.' If the workers demanded higher wages and management refused, then it would be 'up to management' how the problem is solved. In one case where management had disagreed with a recommendation by the committee, they had organised a ballot among the workers which reversed the decision of the committee. The 'final say is with management'. In the words of Mr Frame, 'the most important thing to remember is that we are still managing the factories, we are still the bosses'. Frame disapproved of trade unions for African workers. Two workers employed by Pinetex admitted to spying on their fellow-workers at the request of management. One spy was paid R10.00 per week for reporting anything 'wrong' in the factory, the other received nothing besides his normal wage because management had convinced him that it was his 'duty' to spy. Both spies were to be used as state witnesses in the subsequent court case.

If employers in general preferred liaison committees, a minority of employers saw works committees as being more credible and hence a more effective means of preserving industrial peace. Out of thirty-four firms with works committees, according to a survey of June 1974, management had taken the initiative for establishing the committee in 44 per cent of cases. In general, given the oppressed condition of the African working class, almost superhuman resistance on their part is needed to prevent management from carrying out its wishes. It is likely that African workers seldom saw compelling reasons for struggling against the creation of a committee by their employer. The result of the unprecedented zeal among employers and state officials for estab-lishing committees was a spectacular rise in the number of committees. Statutory works committees increased from eighteen prior to the strikes to 207 at the end of 1974, and 239 in May 1975. Liaison committees increased from the original 118 non-statutory committees at the end of 1972 to 773 at the end of 1973, 1,482 at the end of 1974, and 1,751 in May 1975. By the end of 1975 there were 287 works committees, 2,042 liaison committees, and five co-ordinating works committees (SRR, 1976, p. 319).

A further reform brought about by Act No. 70 of 1973 was the extension to African workers of a technical right to strike. The wide-spread determination among African workers to strike in support of their demands, and the manifest inability of employers and the state to prevent them, made a mockery of the absolute prohibition on strikes contained in the Act of 1953. This prohibition was accordingly lifted. Instead, strikes by African workers were prohibited under the following circumstances (section 18):

(a) during the currency of any order in terms of the Industrial
Conciliation Act dealing with the matter giving rise to
the strike;

(b) if any other wage regulating measure that has been in force
for less than a year contains a provision in respect of the
matter giving rise to the dispute;

(c) if the workers are employed by a local authority or in the
provision of light, power, water, sanitation, passenger transport
or a fire extinguishing service.

The following procedure was laid down for a legal strike:

(1) the matter must be referred to the works or liaison committee,
if any, and such committee must be unable to resolve the
dispute;

(2) a report on the dispute by the employer or the workers must
be submitted to the Bantu Labour officer;

(3) a period of 30 days must elapse from the date of the report.

Striking in disregard of these provisions remains a criminal offence.
It is also an offence for workers to take sympathetic action in support
of other workers. In practice, the concession of a right to strike has
made little or no difference from the African workers' point of view.
It has certainly failed to channel their energies into legal forms of
protest. The first legal strike by African workers – the Armourplate
strike – was dealt with in the same way as an illegal strike. In 1973 the
police were called to the scene of 321 strikes and labour disputes;
353 African workers were arrested in the course of these disputes
(SRR, 1974, pp. 325-6). In 1974, according to the Minister of Labour,
police intervention was called for in sixty-nine strikes and 841 workers
were arrested (SRR, 1975, pp. 210-11). According to the Minister of
Police, on the other hand, the police were called in to forty-seven
labour disputes, twenty-eight work stoppages and 113 strikes during
the first six months of 1974 alone (SRR, 1974, p. 326). In 1975, to
revert to the computation of the Minister of Labour, police intervention took place in sixty-one strikes and 493 workers were arrested
(SRR, 1976, p. 317). Bearing in mind the number of strikes in 1973
compared with 1974 and 1975, we must conclude that the right to
strike made little difference in practice. From the point of view of the
African workers, hemmed in with the same restrictions on their freedom
to organise and move, the struggle continued in much the same way
as before.

In the final analysis, therefore, the significance of the reforms was
symptomatic rather than substantial. With these measures the government resigned itself to the impossibility of enforcing an absolute
prohibition on strikes by African workers any longer. On the other

hand, by encouraging the formation of a new type of factory committee partly nominated by employers, independent working-class
organisation was pushed even further into the background. Although
widely criticised by liberals as being inadequate, the new committee
system reflected the essence of liberal policy. Effective control over
the African working class by non-violent and voluntary means is the
main aim of liberal policy. In the liaison committee, the state and
the majority of employers thought they had discovered an instrument
to this end. A further reform was the repeal of the Masters and Servants
legislation and the penal provisions of the Bantu Labour Act. This
happened in the following way (SRR, 1974, p. 337):

> These Acts had received very critical attention in the United
> States where miners and dockworkers tried in August [1974]
> to prevent a ship from discharging South African coal in
> Mobile, Alabama, on the grounds that it constituted a
> contravention of section 307 of the United States Tariff Act of
> 1930, which prohibits the importation of goods produced by
> indentured labour under the threat of penal sanctions. The
> United Mineworkers Union of America argued that SA coal
> imports were a threat to the jobs of 8,000 union members in
> Alabama, and that Black labour conditions in SA enabled
> operators to produce SA coal cheaply enough to compete with
> US coal. The Star's US Bureau reported that the repeal of the
> penal provisions of this complex of masters and servants laws
> had removed the grounds for a joint court action brought by the
> Attorney-General of Alabama and the United Mineworkers Union,
> designed to prevent power companies in the American South from
> importing SA coal.

Also in other areas the government began to make more conciliatory
gestures towards the black population. The Deputy Minister of Bantu
Administration and Development conceded in May 1973 that the
urban African population would remain for generations to come. He
said that approximately 77 per cent of Africans on the Reef (including
mineworkers) were settled on a family basis. Steps should be taken to
make them as contented as possible. The Deputy Minister therefore
invited suggestions for easing the impact of the pass laws. Certain
government departments, including the post office and the railways,
were already allowing African workers to advance to more skilled jobs.

In particular a campaign was launched against so-called 'petty
apartheid'. During 1973 the municipalities of a number of major cities

began to abolish segregation in parks, libraries and other public places where segregation had never been imposed by Parliament. The government did not interfere. The Prime Minister commented that the government would 'constantly keep an eye on the position and, should city councils' intended steps cause friction or disturb the peace, the government will not hesitate to intervene and rectify the situation' (SRR, 1974, p. 153). However, no friction or disturbances broke out. The government, thus reassured, began to take similar measures of its own. New regulations were announced by the Secretary for Justice in August 1974, in terms of which certain foreign black visitors could make use of hotels on the same basis as whites. Black South Africans, on the other hand, remained subject to the same restrictions as before. In 1975 the government undertook to narrow the wage gap as soon as possible. Job reservation was relaxed in the building industry and in certain other areas, including government service. The training of African workers was encouraged by the state. In Windhoek, apartheid signboards were taken down from all public buildings on the eve of the Turnhalle constitutional conference. In January 1975 the luxurious Nico Malan opera house and theatre complex in Cape Town was opened to all races. A month later the dining saloons on the no less luxurious *Drakensberg Express* and *Blue Train* were opened to all races. In 1976 apartheid notices in post offices were removed (although for 'practical reasons', a number of separate counters remained). As for sport, congresses of the National Party agreed in September 1976 that the question of racial mixing should be left to the clubs concerned and to sports administrators, with a minimum of state interference. It was even suggested by the Minister of the Interior, Mulder, that the term, 'separate development' (itself the official successor to 'apartheid') should be changed to 'plural democracy' (SRR, 1976, p. 5).

The training of African workers now became encouraged by the state. The reason for this change of policy was the shortage of skilled labour that had gradually built up during the boom years of the 1960s and early 1970s. During this period it became impossible to replenish the supply of skilled labour out of the free working class alone. In 1973 the *Department of Labour Manpower Survey* (relating to the situation in April 1971) revealed a 'shortage' of 95,655 white and coloured workers. A survey by the Steel and Engineering Industries Federation of South Africa, relating to June 1974, showed that overtime in the basic metal and engineering industries 'had hit the limit of human endurance and in many factories the shortage of skilled labour was critical' (SRR, 1974, p. 257). During 1974 some 3,500 'white' jobs on the railways alone were filled by African workers. Under these conditions the government decided to assist employers in making more thorough use of the massive supply of African labour-power.

In April 1973 the Deputy Minister of Bantu Administration and Development announced that the government would provide training for African workers in those categories of work which, by law, they were allowed to do in 'white' areas. Two types of training were envisaged: pre-service training, in which African school students would be taught industrial skills as part of their school curriculum; and in-service training. The latter would take place at special training centres in industrial areas to serve employers with common training needs. In addition, the government would allow tax concessions to employers who ran their own training programmes for African workers. Such training programmes had to be officially approved. Furthermore, eight departmental training centres were envisaged. By day, school students would be put through these centres. Adult factory workers would be offered after-hours training.

By 1975 three training centres were in operation: at Sebokeng (Vereeniging) and at Orlando and Molapo (Soweto). The remaining centres were planned to open during 1976 and 1977 at Germiston, Pretoria, Pietermaritzburg, Durban, Port Elizabeth, Kempton Park and Springs. The tax concessions offered to employers enabled them to recover at least 82c of every R1 they spent on training programmes.

The training of African building workers has been regulated since 1951 by the Bantu Building Workers Act. In 1976, with the enactment of the Bantu Employees In-Service Training Act, the training of African industrial workers was placed in a legal framework. The Act provided that public training centres could be established by two or more employers, subject to conditions imposed by the Minister of Bantu Education as to the nature and content of the training. Such centres would have exclusive rights as far as the public training of African workers is concerned. No person could henceforth provide training for the employees of any other person except at a centre approved by the Secretary of Bantu Education. Levies may be imposed by the Minister on employers in the area of a public training centre to pay for the expenses of the centre. Employers may also apply to the Secretary of Bantu Education for the recognition of training schemes for their own workers. Recognition may be granted subject to such conditions as the Secretary deems fit. Where a training scheme is functioning in an 'economic development area', as proclaimed by the

Minister, the employer may receive a 'grant-in-aid' from the state. Co-ordination of this entire training system was placed in the hands of a council established by the Minister. This council must consist of six state officials, plus approved nominees from the Trade Union Council of South Africa, the South African Confederation of Labour, and a number of employers' organisations.

Besides the departmental training centres, eleven state trade schools for Africans were functioning in 1973, as well as six trade sections attached to other schools. By 1975 the number of trade schools had grown to fifteen, and three more were due to open in 1976. A small but increasing number of Africans were thus joining the ranks of skilled labour every year. In addition, many more African workers were employed in 'semi-skilled' or operative work. In 1971 1,011,200 African workers fell into this category.[2] Together with the development of South African industry, the skills and knowledge of the working class, including the African workers, were inevitably on the increase. The training of workers, however, is determined by the requirements of the capitalist class. One example is provided by the Dutch-owned firm of Hebox Textiles in Hammarsdale, where 1,200 African workers are employed. The training scheme at Hebox is 'based largely on accounting information, which isolates the areas of highest profit significance in the production process. The workers at these key points are then trained' (*FM*, 29 August 1975). Training serves to turn workers into more effective instruments for the production of commodities and profits. Also in this field reform has no purpose other than strengthening the position of the capitalist class.

Considered as instruments of social change from the working-class point of view, the reforms of the mid-1970s were thus limited and ineffectual. State policy was increasingly reflecting the pressure of the international capitalist class. In July 1977 the Nationalist columnist Dawie arrived at the identical conclusion that the Progressive Party had written in its programme in 1959 (*Die Burger*, 23 July 1977):

> Enable a strong, healthy middle class to develop, people who
> share in the good things of life, who have an interest in maintaining
> the economic structure and nothing to gain from struggle and
> conflict. If there are measures and practices left over from the
> past which obstruct this aim, now is the time to review them with
> a very critical eye.

The suggestion that a black middle class does not already exist is, of course, incorrect; but the intention is clear. The writer is calling for the encouragement and appeasement of the black middle classes in order to induce them to support the existing property relations. In fact, an increasing measure of appeasement and encouragement was manifested in state policy during the 1970s. Numerous changes have been made to relieve the African petite-bourgeoisie of some of the burdens of racial oppression and increase their stake in the capitalist system. An example of this was the extension of the rights of urban Africans announced by the Minister of Bantu Affairs and Development in May 1975 (*Argus*, 2 May 1975):

> The reintroduction of house ownership in urban townships as
> it had existed until the end of 1967 and giving qualified Africans
> the right to buy occupational rights of houses on land belonging
> to a local authority. With immediate effect, African medical
> practitioners and other professional Africans would be allowed
> to have their own consulting rooms or offices in African urban
> residential areas. . . . Trading rights of African traders in urban
> African residential areas would be brought as closely as possible
> into line with the procedure followed in the case of White traders
> in regard to the annual renewal of trading licenses. With due regard
> to certain local circumstances, African traders would also be
> permitted to trade in a larger range of commodities than at
> present and to establish more than one type of business on the
> same premises. Partnerships would be allowed. . . . Building
> ownership, as in the case of houses, would again become possible
> for African traders in urban African residential areas.

Similarly, following a meeting between members of the government and members of the CRC in August 1976, certain reforms in the interest of the 'coloured' middle classes were announced. Included among these were the following (SRR, 1976, p. 17):

(a) General industrial areas of towns should have no group character, being open to Coloured and Indian as well as White industrialists.

(b) In the larger towns and cities, Coloured and Indian businessmen would be allowed more freedom to trade outside their own group areas.

(c) Prominent Coloured people would serve on committees to be established to help plan Coloured residential areas, housing, and the handling of the squatter problem. . . .

(e) The Department of Prisons would revise the rank structure and training for Coloured personnel. . . .

(g) At scientific and art conferences there need be no separation in regard to meals, refreshments, and similar facilities.

These measures, the leader of the Labour Party commented, 'offered no real political changes, and would benefit only the more affluent sections of the community' (*ibid*., pp. 17–18). Precisely the same can be said of the easing of racial segregation in general. The basis of state policy, the reserve system and the provision of 'cheap docile labour', remained entirely unaffected. This, indeed, was predictable. The main object of liberalisation, as far as the state is concerned, is to remove unnecessary irritants and harness all possible forces in support of the capitalist system. The aim would be totally defeated by any significant improvement in the position of the African working class on whose continued destitution the wealth of the capitalist class depends.

In this way, too, the systematic nature of South African social relations is demonstrated once again. The essence of 'liberal' policy is gradually being implemented by an avowedly anti-liberal government. This can only be explained by the fact that the state and the 'liberals' have the same fundamental goal: protecting and advancing the capitalist economy and the interests of employers as a class. Not only in appeasing black middle classes but also in repressing the workers' struggle employers and the state are at one. In September 1976, for example, the Minister of Police urged businessmen to form their own organisations to protect their premises against civil unrest. In Cape Town the Minister told representatives of organised industry and commerce that 'far-reaching legislation granting civil and criminal indemnity to businessmen and private individuals who killed or maimed others in the course of protecting their property from rioters and looters would be introduced in Parliament if necessary' (SRR, 1976, p. 97). What is proposed here is nothing less than an open, armed alliance between employers and the state for defending capitalist property and, with it, the existing social order.

Yet the National Party experiences peculiar problems in carrying out its task. For reasons of 'history and ideology', the liberal critic complains, it is 'not equipped to respond in a creative way to the crisis' (*Cape Times*, 6 November 1976). The Nationalist government is dependent on the votes of the white petite-bourgeoisie and workers. It must balance between objective capitalist interests and the fears and demands of the white masses. Capitalist interests call for certain reforms in the system; the white masses are suspicious of reform in general and, for want of alternatives, cling to the status quo. Significant reforms would spur the black workers on to press home their demands. The South African state, compelled to repress the struggle of the workers and constrained in its ability to offer reforms to the middle classes, thus takes on an especially harsh and inflexible character.

Throughout the struggles of the mid-1970s the two contradictory faces of South African state policy remained uneasily joined together. Thus even while Vorster exhorted all and sundry to learn the lessons of the Durban strikes, his Minister of Labour expressed a very different view (IIE, 1974, p. 103): 'Will the inciters, the people who are behind these agitators, then pay the higher wages which are being demanded by the Bantu? Of course not, for the objective of these inciters is in fact to cause chaos in South Africa.' Another Nationalist Member of Parliament denied even more categorically that the workers' demands were worthy of being considered, let alone that there were lessons to be learned (*ibid.*, p. 114): 'It was not the Bantu workers so much who asked for and expressed the need for higher wages; this was done by people from outside, the agitators to whom I referred. Our Bantu workers are basically contented.'

The right wing of the National Party tended to overestimate the organisation of the workers' movement. From this point of view the strikes were planned deliberately 'to bring about a change in the social order' or, what is regarded as meaning much the same, 'to bring about general chaos in South Africa' (*ibid.*, p. 104). In this reaction it is not difficult to discover the extravagant fear of the petit-bourgeois threatened with the loss of his precarious position. At the same time, it was impossible for even the strongest opponent of chaos and agitation to put down the Durban strikes by force. Direct repression was ruled out by the form that the workers' movement took (which may also account very largely for the moderate tones of the Prime Minister). The Soweto uprising, on the other hand, at first took the form of demonstrations by school students which could easily be dealt with by the police. Under these conditions the state did not hesitate to practise the most ruthless repression. Nor did the 'liberal' Nationalists question this repression to any significant extent. On the contrary, even the 'liberal' Nationalist press gave unconditional support to the police.

This once again demonstrates the methodical nature of capitalist policy in South Africa. Reform and repression are two sides of one coin, to be used as conditions may demand. When faced with a serious challenge, liberals both inside and outside the National Party tend to fall back, verbally protesting their concern, on the right wing and the police. By closing ranks with the right wing, liberals inside the National

Party try to strengthen their position. Even by the late 1970s they had
no ready alternative to hand. The road to a liberal party had not yet
been prepared. Only in a much more extreme crisis can we imagine the
bourgeois wing of the National Party abandoning the Nationalist rank
and file and entering an open political alliance with other sections of
the South African capitalist class.

Faced with the upheavals of the mid-1970s, the overriding aim of the
state was to maintain control. The net result was intensified mass
repression, both in the legislative sphere and in the field of administrative action. Vigorous measures were taken to snuff out the beginnings
of radical ferment among white students and intellectuals in 1972 and
1973. A parliamentary commission was appointed in 1972, headed by
A. L. Schlebusch, to investigate four organisations to the left of the
parliamentary opposition: the South African Institute of Race Relations,
the Christian Institute, the University Christian Movement, and the
National Union of South African Students (NUSAS). In February
1973, at the height of the Durban strikes, the Schlebusch Commission
brought out two interim reports. One report recommended that a
permanent parliamentary commission on internal security be set up
to continue the work that it had begun. The other report recommended,
'in a spirit of urgency', that action be taken against eight NUSAS
leaders who were said to be responsible for radical tendencies within
the organisation. As a result of this report, all eight individuals were
banned. These were followed by banning orders on eight leaders of
SASO.

The significance of these events was not confined to the organisations
concerned. In the atmosphere of growing tension that was settling over
South Africa each new restrictive measure curbed the freedom of the
labour movement even further. The student demonstrations in central
Cape Town during June 1972 had attracted a certain amount of public
interest and support. The result was the Gatherings and Demonstrations
Act by which all open-air gatherings and demonstrations in central
Cape Town (apart from religious, official or authorised gatherings) were
prohibited. A further result of the unrest of the early 1970s was the
Riotous Assemblies Amendment Act of 1974. Introducing the Bill in
Parliament, the Deputy Minister of Justice explained that the power
of magistrates to prohibit meetings was too limited. The existing Act
'sometimes required exact compliance with elaborate formalities at
a time of emergency'. Thus effective action was impeded and offenders
were given the opportunity of obtaining an acquittal on technical

grounds. Moreover, the existing Act only applied to public gatherings in certain public places in the open air. The term 'public gathering' was accordingly replaced by the word 'gathering', which was defined as 'any gathering, concourse or procession of any number of persons'. Any gathering could now be prohibited, and a magistrate could now do so even without reference to the Minister. Attending a prohibited gathering was also made a criminal offence. A police officer dispersing a prohibited gathering no longer needed to warn those present that force would be used if they failed to disperse, nor need he repeat the order to disperse. Greater power of prohibiting meetings was thus vested in the lower bureaucracy; and the right of the police to use force against those who defy prohibitions must henceforth be taken for granted.

A further result of the attack on NUSAS was the Affected Organisations Act. This Act empowered the State President, if he is 'satisfied that politics are being engaged in' by an organisation in conjunction with persons or organisations abroad, to declare such an organisation an 'affected organisation' (section 2). Obtaining money from abroad on behalf of an affected organisation was prohibited. The state can confiscate money by alleging that it is being dealt with in contravention of the above provisions. The onus is thus placed on a party with an interest in the money to prove that such is not the case. NUSAS was the first organisation to be declared an affected organisation. However, the Act is a threat to every form of organised opposition in South Africa. The sources of financial support for political opposition in South Africa are limited. Sympathetic organisations abroad are the most obvious alternative. This applies in particular to trade unions that are affiliated to international trade-union organisations. The only means of avoiding the dangers of the Affected Organisations Act is to abstain from every form of activity that the state might regard as 'political'. An African trade union must refrain, therefore, from taking a stand on issues such as the pass laws and a host of other matters that are of vital importance to its members, or it must take the risk of having its funds confiscated. To working-class organisation in South Africa, yet another means of development has been cut off.

Also the 'hostility clause' was amended. It now no longer applies to 'Bantu and Europeans' only but instead lays down a much broader prohibition: 'Any person who utters words or performs any other act with intent to cause, encourage or foment feelings of hostility between different population groups of the Republic shall be guilty of an offence.'[3]

During this period the state was becoming increasingly concerned about the pressure on foreign investors to refrain from investing in South Africa or to withdraw their existing investments. In April 1973 the Minister of Foreign Affairs addressed Parliament about 'the political implications – please note, political implications – of this campaign for increased wages for non-White workers in South Africa in the case of foreign companies operating here in our country' (SRR, 1973, p. 185). The Minister claimed that the government was fully in favour of improved conditions for these workers. At the same time, he made it clear that the campaign for better wages was viewed with serious misgivings by the state (*ibid.*, pp. 185-6):

> As honourable members will perhaps know, several pressure
> groups and the United States have over a period of years waged
> such a campaign against us. Now this phenomenon has also
> raised its head in Great Britain and, according to reports received
> this weekend, in West Germany as well.

Why should a campaign, the aims of which the government claims to agree with, be seen as a campaign 'against us'? The answer can only be found in the contradiction between the demand for better wages and the requirements of the capitalist system in South Africa. Especially in a period of recession capitalist investment demands reduced costs as a means of restoring profitability; higher wages mean higher costs from the employers' point of view.

The importance of foreign investment to the South African economy is recognised in the most emphatic terms by South African employers as well as by the state. It is also understood very well that such investment takes place under conditions of employment that stand in the sharpest contrast to those of Western Europe. The demand for equal (or even improved) conditions in South Africa exposes the contradiction. Investors in South Africa will not or cannot comply with this demand. Were they to do so, the main reason for investing in South Africa would diminish or disappear.

The reply of the investors generally is to try and justify their activities in South Africa notwithstanding the system of apartheid. A common argument is to point at the destitution of the African workers as a reason for perpetuating their destitution. H. F. Oppenheimer, chairman of the Anglo-American Corporation, and S. M. Motsuenyane, president of the National African Federated Chamber of Commerce, are only two of the great many businessmen who argue that foreign investment means jobs for African workers. Work under any conditions, it is assumed, is better than no work at all. In addition to this bland self-justification, 'liberal' employers in South Africa are quick to agree that the wages and working conditions of their workers should really be improved. The impression is constantly given that change is just around the corner. Thus J. de Necker, chairman of Randbank, warned about the 'immense pressures' being brought to bear on South Africa's foreign trading partners. It was necessary 'to put our house in order as quickly as possible in order to limit our vulnerability against that day when foreign investors and banks would be forced against their will to cease conducting business with us' (SRR, 1974, p. 223).

Given the prospect of continuing economic instability, however, significant reform in South Africa is excluded for at least the foreseeable future. Employers are concerned to increase their profits rather than their wage bills. The improvements that African workers can expect can be no more than marginal and subject at all times to the interests of the capitalist class. Statements of intention like that of de Necker are unlikely to have any effect in the absence of considerable pressure.

Within South Africa and also abroad, as the Minister of Foreign Affairs observed, such pressure was growing in the mid-1970s. In March 1973 a British newspaper, the *Guardian*, commenced a series of articles on the employment practices of British companies in South Africa, exposing the extremely low wages that were paid in many cases and provoking considerable repercussions. In February 1974 the International Confederation of Free Trade Unions launched a campaign to prepare for an eventual economic boycott of South Africa. In the period that followed, the campaign within the labour movement internationally to build up support for the black workers in South Africa and enforce economic sanctions gained in strength with every passing year.

Throughout all these developments the concern of the South African state was to maintain South Africa as an attractive area of investment. Internally, it could and did take all possible measures to ensure maximum profitability and suppress labour unrest. There was relatively little it could do, however, to protect foreign investors against pressure in their own countries. Against this background section 2 of the General Law Amendment Act of 1974 was enacted. It laid down that 'except with the permission of the Minister of Economic Affairs, no person shall in compliance with any order, direction or letters of request issued or emanating from outside the Republic, furnish any information as to any business, whether carried on in or outside the Republic'.

In practice, such permission is refused by the Minister in cases where the business concerned is South African-owned to the extent of 50 per cent or more. Although the Minister of Foreign Affairs had claimed in 1973 that 'We do of course have nothing to hide in this regard' (SRR, 1973, p. 185), close check is kept on the flow of information concerning employment practices in South Africa. In this way foreign investors were provided with a certain alibi for keeping their employment practices in South Africa secret. The Ford Motor Company, for example, decided to publish no annual report on employee conditions in South Africa in 1975 'because its counsel in SA warned that this might violate the law' (SRR, 1975, p. 153). The British (Labour) government relaxed the requirements of the 'guidelines' it had published for British companies operating in South Africa. Only companies that owned more than 50 per cent of their South African subsidiaries would be required to disclose details about the employment conditions of their black employees in South Africa. Companies with a minority shareholding were thus exempted from applying to the Minister for permission to furnish the required information.

A survey of 141 British companies with subsidiaries in South Africa, published in 1976, revealed that the vast majority were unwilling or unable to provide information about conditions of employment in South Africa. 'Difficulties posed by South African legislation' was the reason given by some for their refusal to answer questions (SRR, 1976, p. 269). Far stronger reasons for refusing, however, appeared from the information that *was* obtained. After years of pressure from the unions, exposure in the press and official employment 'guidelines', more than 2,000 African workers employed by three British companies were still paid wages below the poverty datum line. The average minimum wage was approximately R110 per month for a forty-five-hour working week – that is, about R98 per month for a forty-hour week, or 30 per cent less than the household subsistence level. Notwithstanding all statements of intention, employment conditions in South Africa – regardless of the nationality of the employer – remained fundamentally unchanged.

From the point of view of working-class organisation, room for open activity became more and more limited as the state took more and more rigorous measures against all forms of organised opposition. In 1974 a new Publications Act was passed which began with the following remarkable provision: 'In the application of this Act the constant endeavour of the population of the Republic of South Africa to uphold a Christian view of life shall be recognized.' It is not so much anti-Christian publications, however, that the Act is primarily aimed at. Like its predecessor it is used very largely to prohibit publications that are ideologically or politically offensive to the state itself.

The Act provides for the creation of a directorate of publications, which in turn is empowered to set up committees. A list is compiled by the Minister of the Interior of persons eligible for membership of the committees. The operative provisions of the Act in relation to publications are contained in sections 8 and 9. Section 9 lays down that a committee may declare every edition of any publication which is published periodically in the Republic to be undesirable, if in its opinion any edition is undesirable and every subsequent edition is likely to be undesirable. The distribution and possession of an undesirable publication may be prohibited. 'Undesirable' is defined in extremely wide terms; in the final analysis it is left to the discretion of the committees. In particular, a publication will be deemed undesirable if it is 'harmful to the relations between any sections of the inhabitants of the Republic', or if it is 'prejudicial to the safety of the State, the general welfare or the peace and good order'. To produce, distribute or possess an undesirable publication, where this has been prohibited, is a criminal offence. The Minister may authorise the entry and searching of any premises and the seizure of any publications or objects. The requirement for the exercise of these powers is 'reasonable grounds' for suspecting that the publications or objects in question are undesirable. Also, the importation of publications may be prohibited if a committee is of the opinion that such publications are undesirable or likely to be undesirable.

A major weakness of the previous Publications Control Act, from the point of view of the state, had been the right of appeal to the Supreme Court against decisions by the Publications Control Board. Several of its decisions had been reversed as a result. This weakness has now been eliminated. The right of appeal to the Supreme Court has been abolished. In its place is a right of appeal to a Publications Appeal Board, appointed by the state. Thus one bureaucratic organ has the task of judging the actions of another, a situation which from the official point of view is eminently favourable. No loophole remains whereby any publication which is deemed undesirable by the handpicked appointees of the state can legally be published, circulated or possessed. Any publication by any organisation is only permitted subject to the approval of the state; any publication which challenges the state in a serious or consistent way is earmarked for prohibition.

Prohibition thus piled on prohibition as tensions mounted in the 1970s and opposition against the state was forced into ever-increasing new forms. In May 1976 the Internal Security Commission Act was passed by Parliament. This Act gave effect to the recommendation of the Schlebusch Commission that a permanent commission be set up to continue the work that it had begun. The Commission is appointed by the State President and has the function of investigating 'matters which, in the opinion of the State President, affect internal security and which are referred to it by the State President'. The content of any report by the Commission need not be made known, even in Parliament, if the Prime Minister after consultation with the Leader of the Opposition is of the opinion that it is not in the public interest to do so. The Commission, or a committee created by the Commission, has the same powers of summoning witnesses and procuring evidence as does the Supreme Court of South Africa.

The most drastic measure against political opposition to emerge from the upheavals of the mid-1970s was the Internal Security Amendment Act. By a strange irony this most oppressive of laws was promulgated on 16 June 1976, the day that the school students of Soweto rose up against oppression. Introducing the Bill in the Assembly in May, the Minister of Justice had made it clear that the aim was to broaden the restrictive provisions of the Suppression of Communism Act. South Africa must expect, the Minister said, that its enemies will intensify their underground activities, and must be prepared for this, especially on the university campuses and in the field of labour. The often-repeated complaint against the Suppression of Communism Act, that even avowed anti-communists were dealt with under its provisions, was finally taken to heart. All communists are underminers, but not all underminers are communists, the Minister explained. This should be reflected in the law. The accent would accordingly be shifted, to show that the act was concerned not only with subversion by communists but with subversion in general. In particular, the Minister was aware of the dangers, from the point of view of the state, of working-class organisation. Also in the field of labour, the Minister repeated, South Africa must in times of danger expect subversive activities to increase. A centrally controlled plan of action was already in operation, he claimed, to organise and mobilise workers into a power to be used by underground politicians for their own purposes: 'The labour field,' the Minister concluded, 'is an area which is exceptionally sensitive to unrest and large-scale agitation, and much groundwork has already been done there' (*Die Burger*, 8 May 1976). The Minister thus left no doubt that training and organising workers was viewed with the gravest suspicion. Where these activities exceeded the limits which the state considered acceptable, the Act would be invoked.

The Act amended the Suppression of Communism Act by renaming it the Internal Security Act. It gave additional powers to the state to prohibit organisations and to act against individuals. In addition to his existing powers, the State President was now authorised to declare unlawful any organisation if he is 'satisfied' that it 'engages in activities which endanger or are calculated to endanger the security of the State or the maintenance of public order' (section 2(2)). Similarly, persons may be prohibited from attending gatherings or subjected to orders of restriction ('banning orders') if the Minister of Justice is satisfied that they are engaging in activities of this kind. Alternatively, such a person may be detained in custody subject to such conditions and for such time as the Minister may determine. Prior to being detained in terms of this provision, a person may be arrested by any member of the South African police without warrant, and kept in custody for up to seven days until the notice of detention can be served.

The Attorney General may prohibit the release on bail of a person charged with a political offence 'if he considers it necessary in the interests of the safety of the State or the maintenance of the public order' (section 12A). State witnesses *and prospective state witnesses* may be arrested and detained under warrant issued by the Attorney General. Nobody other than certain state officials may have access to a person detained under this provision except on conditions determined by the state. The only protection enjoyed by such a person is a weekly visit by a magistrate. Presently, when we consider the practical implementation of the security laws, we shall see how inadequate this is and how completely political detainees are exposed to torture and death at the hands of the police.

The Internal Security Act, together with the Terrorism Act, comes as near as is legally possible to giving the state an unqualified power to deal as it wishes with political opponents. If this had been the *de facto* position even prior to 1976, the legal position was now brought into line. The Internal Security Act has sanctified the arbitrary use of state power and made its practical exercise even simpler than before. It has asserted for all the world to know the determination of the state to crush all serious opposition. It must serve as an encouragement to police interrogators, and a dire warning to all would-be opponents. The powers of repression with which every organisation of the working class is threatened have grown more menacing than ever before.

The implementation of the law

The ultimate basis of the capitalist system in South Africa is the movement of African workers from the reserves and the townships to the places of work through the corridors created by the official labour bureaux (see Table 10.1). Control over this enormous flow of people became increasingly rigorous. Table 10.2 shows the number of prosecutions which took place for breaches of the applicable laws and regulations.

Table 10.1 *Africans registered at local and district labour bureaux, 1972-5*

1972	3,070,657	1974	3,773,179
1973	3,437,686	1975	4,098,975

Source: SRR (1973, pp. 213-14; 1974, pp. 244-5; 1975, p. 167; 1976, p. 284).

Table 10.2 *Pass law prosecutions, 1972-5*

	1972-3	*1973-4*	*1974-5*
Curfew regulations	131,464	95,219	66,320
Registration and submission of documents	203,492	194,187	143,862
Bantu (Urban Areas) Consolidation Act (not specified above)	148,703	166,179	150,713
Bantu Administration Act (not specified above)	15,472	20,335	25,519
	499,131	475,920	386,414

Source: SRR (1974, p. 171; 1976, p. 207).

The decline in the number of prosecutions, however, is deceptive. It reflects no relaxation in the enforcement of the pass laws; on the contrary, it masks an *increasing* number of Africans arrested in terms of the pass laws and sent to 'aid centres' instead of being sent to trial. Aid centres were first provided for by law in 1964. In June 1971 the Deputy Minister of Bantu Administration and Development announced that aid centres would finally be established in practice. The aim was to 'reduce the burden on the technical offender and to divert the majority of these offenders away from the courts and the prisons' (SRR, 1971, p. 143). Instead of being sent to prison, Africans referred to an aid centre would be given the choice between accepting a specific job or being deported to a reserve. Aid centres could therefore function as 'a source of cheap labour for employers who could not attract workers by normal means' (*ibid.*, p. 144). Table 10.3 shows the numbers of Africans arrested under the pass laws who were diverted through this channel. Of those referred to the aid centres and not prosecuted, many were deported to the reserves. In 1974 this was the fate of 18,467 people; in 1975, 61,242. The aid centres were partially replacing the courts as organs for dealing with Africans who had broken the pass laws. The decline in pass law prosecutions thus reflects no relaxation in the application of these laws. On the contrary, it reflects a more relentless and efficient system than ever for dealing with African workers who fail to use the official channels for disposing of their labour-power.

Table 10.3 *Africans arrested and referred to aid centres, 1972-5*

	Total number referred to aid centres	Of these, number not subsequently prosecuted
1972	93,067	17,867
1973	138,980	44,387
1974	165,555	51,383
1975	221,537	204,193

Source: SRR (1973, p. 136; 1974, p. 173; 1975, p. 100; 1976, p. 209).

A second key element in the South African system of industrial relations is formed by the numerous restrictions on the freedom of working-class organisation. Between 1973 and October 1977 no organisation was formally prohibited. To gain an idea of the actual obstacles to working-class organisation, we must examine the use made by the state of other means of repressing opposition, in particular the power to prohibit publications, to restrict individuals and to bring individuals to court for their organisational activities.

We have already noted the huge mass of printed material that had been prohibited before 1973. Since that year, and especially since the introduction of the new Publications Act, the prohibition of publications has continued at an ever-increasing tempo (see Table 10.4).

State reaction

In 1975 the power to declare undesirable all subsequent editions of a periodical was used in forty-five cases. In the case of seventy-eight periodicals possession was declared illegal. In the great majority of cases publications and objects to be prohibited were submitted to the censor not by members of the public but by customs officials and the police. During the first five months of 1976 possession of a further 148 publications was prohibited. Fifty-one of these were prohibited as being indecent or obscene, and eighty-three as being prejudicial to the safety of the state.

Table 10.4 *Prohibitions of published material, 1973–5*

	Publications and objects	Films
1973	889	129
1974	1,059	127
1975	1,381	110

Source: SRR (1974, p. 72; 1975, p. 47; 1976, p. 147).

The banning or, in more serious cases, the detention of individuals, remained the favourite weapon of the state against political opponents. On 20 July 1973, according to the *Government Gazette*, 200 persons (171 black and twenty-nine white) were subject to orders of restriction. At the time of the outbreak of the Soweto uprising, 128 banning orders were in force. From this stage onwards the number of bannings once again increased. In particular, a concerted attack was launched on the African trade-union movement. The previous major onslaught by the state in the early 1960s had beheaded the movement and all but brought it to a halt. With the resurgence of the African unions after 1973, a renewed attack became inevitable. The first warning shots were fired during 1974, when three trade-union officials in Durban – H. Cheadle, D. Davis and D. Hemson – were banned. A more extensive attack, however, came in November 1976 (SRR, 1976, pp. 103–4):

By 18 November five people associated with the trade union movement had been banned. Eric and Jean Tyacke and Loet Douwes Dekker of the Johannesburg based Urban Training Project, as well as Mr Sipho Kubekha and Mr Gavin Anderson of the Metal and Allied Workers' Union, were all served with five year banning orders. Miss Jeanette Curtis, archivist at the SA Institute of Race

352

Relations in Johannesburg and formerly connected with the
Industrial Aid Society, was served with a banning order on
18 November. On the same day banning orders were served in
Durban on Mr John Copelyn, secretary of the Trade Union
Advisory and Co-ordinating Council (TUACC); Mrs Jeanette
Murphy, assistant secretary of TUACC; Mr Mike Murphy, part-
time acting secretary of the Black Transport and General Workers'
Union; Mr Charles Simkins, former research officer for the Institute
for Industrial Education; Mr Chris Albertyn, of the Textile Workers'
Union; Miss Pat Horn, literacy teacher; Mr Alpheus Mthetwa,
secretary of the Metal and Allied Workers' Union and Mr Mfundise
Ndlovu of the same union. In Cape Town the following people
were issued with banning orders: Mr Graeme Bloch, member of
the Cape Town SRC and president of the Students for Social
Democracy Movement; Miss Debbie Budlender, an economics
honours student and member of the university's wages and
economics commission; Mr Willie Hofmeyer, also of the wages
commission; Miss Judy Favish, a literacy worker for the Western
Province Workers' Advice Bureau; Mr Elijah Loza; Miss Wilma van
Blerk of the Food and Canning Workers' Union in the Western
Cape, Miss Mary Simons, a UCT lecturer; Miss Tanya Simons, a
librarian at UCT; Mr Jeremy Baskin, of the wages commission;
Mr John Frankish, a UCT medical student; Mr Gideon Cohen,
associated with the wages commission, and Mr Jack Lewis.
Mr Eric Abraham, local correspondent for various overseas
newspapers, was placed under 12-hour house arrest.

John Frankish had also been associated with the UCT wages commission
and the Western Province Workers' Advice Bureau. Elijah Loza, who
later lost his life in police custody, had previously been an activist of
the South African Congress of Trade Unions. It was these events that
provoked the international trade-union movement to call for a week of
protest action in January 1977. While this particular week of action
was organised on a limited scale and thus had limited results, it was the
beginning of a broader campaign that would lead to increasingly more
concrete acts of support by trade unionists in Europe and elsewhere
with the African trade-union movement in South Africa.

The number of persons detained in terms of the security laws
remains uncertain because the state does not regard it as being in the
public interest to reveal this information. During the last three months
of 1974 it became known that between forty and fifty members of the

Black Consciousness movement had been arrested. In March 1975 it was disclosed by the Attorney General of the Transvaal that besides the thirteen then on trial, twenty-six of the arrested persons were still in detention. In April 1976 the Minister of Justice stated that 'about fifty' people had been detained in connection with the alleged recruitment of guerilla fighters in South Africa. Then followed the Soweto uprising and the mass detention of all potential leadership – designed, as the Minister of Justice put it, 'to remove potential troublemakers from the scene' (SRR, 1976, p. 112). On 20 October the Minister stated that 374 people were in detention in terms of security legislation. Of these, 123 were being held in terms of section 10 of the Internal Security Act and 217 were being interrogated in terms of section 6 of the Terrorism Act. At that stage twenty-five people had been held in detention for more than ten months; in November 1976 Z. W. Nkondo was released after having spent 384 days in solitary confinement.

Of the political detainees, those whose activities can to some extent be proved are brought to trial and sentenced. At the end of 1973, 262 persons were serving prison sentences in terms of the Sabotage Act, seventy-two in terms of the Terrorism Act, and ten in terms of the Unlawful Organisations Act. During the following two years a considerable number of people convicted of sabotage during the early 1960s were released from prison upon the expiry of their sentences. Many of these were served with banning orders or redetained following their release.

A significant tendency is revealed by the political trials of the 1970s. In contrast to the 1960s, few people were alleged to have committed sabotage. The majority were now charged with various forms of organisational activity, often of having conspired with unlawful organisations abroad, in most cases the African National Congress. A considerable number had been active in the Black Consciousness movement (see Table 10.5). During 1976 at least three more people were convicted in terms of the Suppression of Communism Act, twenty-three in terms of the Terrorism Act, and two under other security laws. At least 1,122 people were convicted on charges arising from the unrest since June of that year. Of these, 662 were under 18 years of age; and 705 were sentenced to corporal punishment. In Grahamstown in January 1977 thirty-one school students were convicted in terms of the Terrorism Act on account of their activities during the uprising. All of them were sentenced to five years' imprisonment. In February 1977 at Pretoria, three school students were sentenced to five, six and seven years' imprisonment respectively. In the

Table 10.5 *Convictions in terms of 'security' laws, 1973–5*

	Sabotage	Terrorism/Suppression of Communism	Other
July–December 1973	–	17	9
1974	1	13	–
1975	–	8	1

Source: SRR (1974, p. 90; 1975, p. 57; 1976, p. 110).

same month, two youths at Parys were each sentenced to five years' imprisonment. At Port Elizabeth seven young men were sentenced to terms of imprisonment ranging from seven to fifteen years. During the first eleven months of 1977, 401 persons were brought before court in ninety-five separate trials in terms of the various security laws. Of these 144 were convicted and sentenced to a total of 898 years in prison (an average of more than six years each). Forty-five trials took place in terms of the Terrorism Act and thirty-eight in terms of the Sabotage Act. In all ninety-five trials the accused were specifically charged with furthering the aims of prohibited organisations; in the overwhelming majority of cases the organisation in question was the African National Congress. In December 1977 a further fifty-nine trials in terms of the security laws were proceeding (*Cape Times*, 10 December 1977). This massive spate of trials reflects, as clearly as any confrontation on the streets, the wave of struggle waged by the masses and the efforts by the state to crush it.

The forms of state action described above were taken in accordance with the letter of the law.[4] We now come to illegal forms of action against opponents of the state. The mobilisation of migrant workers by the police against the young militants of Soweto has already been described. Constant dangers faced by opponents of the state include acts of terrorism and intimidation by mysterious assailants who almost invariably remain unidentified and unapprehended. The following are only a few of the unsolved incidents over the past years (*Star IAW*, 14 January 1978):

The Reverend Theo Kotze, the recently banned Cape Director of the Christian Institute, has on many occasions been the victim of intimidatory attacks. In 1972 shots were fired and bombs were thrown at his home. The Christian Institute has also been a target for terrorists. On one occasion sticks of dynamite were found outside the door of the institute. On another the doors were set alight after inflammable paint thinner had been poured on them. In October 1976 the Most Reverend Denis Hurley, Durban's Catholic Archbishop, had paraffin bombs thrown at his home. In February 1976 bricks were thrown through windows at the home of leading Trade Unionist, Mr Edgar Ward. A series of threatening phone calls had been made prior to the incident. In June 1976 five 0.635 mm bullets were fired at Mr Donald Wood's home in East London. Slogans were also painted onto a wall at his house. Earlier his wife had been threatened. In January 1975 former NUSAS leader Mr Chris Wood had his car gutted after a petrol bomb was thrown through one of the windows. The Rev. Basil Moore, of the University Christian Movement . . . found his children's pet cat skinned on the step of their Johannesburg home. His children's plastic swimming pool had also been slashed. A parcel bomb exploded in the office of the banned Durban attorney, Mr Mewa Ramgobin, slightly injuring him. Mr Geoffrey Budlender, then president of the SRC, Cape Town, was lucky to escape with his life when petrol bombs gutted his home. Dr Tim Wilson, son-in-law of the late Bram Fischer, had his car smashed. The newly born baby of Dr Francis Wilson, senior lecturer in economics at UCT, received a card with a death threat scrawled over it. In December, 1975, the multiracial Lutheran Synod Meeting at Thlabane Township near Rustenburg was disrupted when tear gas bombs were thrown into the hall where it was being held. 17 clergymen were injured in the attack.

In the African townships extra-legal violence in the interests of law and order has been developed into a system. The Makgotla, or pseudo-traditional vigilante groups, operate with legal recognition and the approval of the state. The methods used by the Makgotla, however, are frequently illegal. Public floggings of alleged criminals are common; on occasion the victim is thrashed to death. The Makgotla are generally feared and despised by the African population. Support for the system appears to be limited to the state and the Makgotla themselves. While the Makgotla appear to involve themselves mainly in cases of alleged theft and other petty criminal offences, their heavy dependence on the state is charged with political significance. Like the Soweto migrant workers in August 1976, the Makgotla could also be used for political purposes. The most probable reason why this did not happen on a

a large scale during the unrest of the recent period is the isolation of
the Makgotla among the population. To set them in action at a time
of mass struggle would be to invite their destruction. Only where the
police have the upper hand, or in a decisive confrontation between
the masses and the forces of the state, are the Makgotla likely to be
thrown into the struggle.

Most notorious of all supra-legal practices used by the state, however, is the torture and killing of detainees by the security police in
the course of interrogation. This reveals the completely relentless
attitude of the state towards serious political opponents. While torture
is illegal, and is therefore denied by the Ministers concerned, there can
be no doubt that torture is commonly practised by the security police.
Organised opposition to the state is turned into a deadly dangerous
business which cannot be undertaken lightly. Once undertaken, it can
only be maintained on the basis of absolute political conviction and
a strong sense of responsibility. By the very harshness of its methods,
the state thus hardens and tempers the quality of its opponents. This
is not, as many reformist critics apparently believe, mere brutality on
the part of the police. The bitter and irreconcilable form that the
struggle takes on in practice is a true reflection of the bitter and irreconcilable contradictions between the capitalist class and the mass of
the workers which lie at the root of the struggle. Police torture is an
inherent consequence of the social system prevailing in South Africa.

As social conflict became more intense from 1973 onwards, the
evidence of torture and killing by the police became increasingly
abundant. The observer sent by the International Commission of
Jurists to the 'Black Consciousness trial' in 1975, for example, had the
following to report (Morand, 1975):

All the accused complain about the conditions of detention to
which they have been subjected. They complain first of
impermissible moral pressures. The power given to the police to
detain for an unlimited period a person accused of violation of
the Terrorism Act has been systematically used to obtain
confessions. Most of the accused complain of having been
insulted on numerous occasions. They also complain of being
struck by police officers. One of the accused stated moreover
that in the course of a particularly severe interrogation on
November 26, he was thrown into the air by two police officers
and left to fall heavily on the cement floor. Since then, he says,
he has suffered from pains in the lumbar and pelvic regions, and

from permanent headaches. He also states that his head was struck against the floor several times. Both his physical and mental health had been severely endangered. In February 1975, for the first time in his life, he had an epileptic fit. The most common torture described by the accused is called the 'imaginary chair'. It consists in compelling the detainees to remain for several hours in a sitting position, but without any kind of support. Sometimes nails are scattered around the prisoner so as to remove any temptation he may have to fall. Frequently the prisoner is told that he will be beaten if he does not succeed in maintaining the sitting posture. Several prisoners claim that they have in fact been beaten for not having been able to maintain this position. Certain defendants also complain of various threats of physical attacks. One of them was a threat to the detainee to drive a six-inch nail into his penis, a police officer having boasted that he had practised this operation with success upon a Jew.

Another accused person, Vincent Selanto, told the Johannesburg magistrates court about his interrogation by the security police in March 1975. He described how he had been assaulted and how his head had been pushed into the water of a toilet, whereupon he had promised to tell the truth. A witness named Michael Gumede, giving evidence in the trial of the 'Pietermaritzburg Ten', told the court how he had been assaulted and tortured by the police following his detention in November 1975. One of the accused, Anthony Xaba, testified that while being held in the same police station he had heard Gumede crying out and asking for mercy. When he finally agreed to give evidence, Gumede was released but warned to stick to his statement, or he would be re-arrested. In the same trial Colonel J. G. Dreyer, Divisional Head of Natal Inland Security, admitted that it was possible that one of the accused, Harry Gwala, had been interrogated continuously for two days and nights. In his view, however, detainees were humanely treated.

The list of allegations of cruelty and torture by the police could be extended almost indefinitely. A case of special relevance to the present study is that of Stephen Dlamini, president of the South African Congress of Trade Unions. Dlamini, a man of over 60 years of age, was detained by the security police in March 1976. His detention lasted for more than six months. After his release he made an affidavit as to the treatment that he had received. In this affidavit Dlamini describes how he was made to stand on his toes with gravel in his shoes for long periods of time. When he fell down he was picked up and his head was knocked against the wall. For a period of four days and three nights he was not allowed to wash, he was given water only once and allowed to go to the toilet twice. Different teams of interrogators relieved one another, each one using different methods. Dlamini was constantly shouted at and told to talk. He was hit about the head and kicked below the belt. He was made to run on the spot. His arm was twisted. The question he was constantly asked was why Mdluli had visited him.

The name of Mdluli brings us on to an even grimmer side of the activities of the police. Mdluli, like the Imam Haroun before him, was one of those who met a violent death while being interrogated by the police. So strong was the circumstantial evidence of torture by the police in this case that the Attorney General for Natal took the unique step of indicting four security police officers on a charge of culpable homicide. Inevitably, all four were acquitted through lack of evidence against them. No one except the accused and their colleagues had had access to Mdluli and could testify as to his death. Neither the accused nor their colleagues were willing to state under oath that the accused had been responsible. The result of the trial was unsatisfactory even to the judge. While acquitting the four men the judge 'admitted [that] he could not account for Mdluli's violent death within 24 hours of being arrested. He has asked for a new investigation.' The judge also 'urged that the matter not be left in its existing highly unsatisfactory condition' and called for the punishment of police officers, irrespective of rank, if it is established that Mdluli's death was caused by their unlawful action (*Cape Times*, 30 October 1976).

Such an attitude is contradictory and futile. The security branch itself was able to dismiss all allegations of torture made against them with the bland assertion that no security policeman has ever been convicted in a court of law for ill-treating a detainee. The *Cape Times* observes (16 July 1977):

> The claim is true. All policemen found guilty of ill-treating
> their prisoners have been members of other branches of the SAP.
> Yet the very circumstances under which the security police
> detain uncharged, unconvicted people incommunicado and
> indefinitely, subject them to solitary confinement and interrogate
> them for long periods during which they have no access to legal
> representation or independent medical supervision, make it
> almost impossible to prove, or disprove, the use of torture as an
> interrogation technique. No matter what the rules and standing
> orders, the system is open to abuse by individuals if not by the
> branch as a whole.

Notwithstanding this assessment, a very general reaction among the 'liberal' opposition in South Africa is to call for an 'independent judicial inquiry' into the deaths of detainees. The Minister of Justice, replying to this demand, pointed out that in matters of this nature a judicial inquiry takes place as a matter of course, following the post-mortem examination. Whether the inquiry takes the form of an inquest or of a judicial commission makes no substantial difference. The evidence available to the presiding officer will in both cases be the same; it will be the testimony, first and foremost, of the security police themselves. The crux of the matter lies in what the *Cape Times* terms 'the very circumstances' in which political detainees are held, completely isolated from the outside world, subject only to the mercy of the police. So uncompromising is the social struggle in South Africa that the state is convinced - and the *Cape Times* cannot deny it - that no lesser methods will suffice to maintain the existing order. To call for yet further inquiries into the conduct of the police is, in the circumstances, nothing but an evasion.

Despite all appeals, therefore, and despite all accusations and exposures in the press, the security police are going about their business. Ten detainees were officially admitted to have died in police custody during 1976, and a further twelve during the first nine months of 1977. The attitude of the state is in no doubt. The Minister of Police has gone on record as saying that the death of Steve Biko, under particularly notorious circumstances, left him cold. A Nationalist Member of Parliament only regretted that he himself did not have the opportunity to kill Biko. With statements like these still fresh in our memory, it is impossible to sustain the belief that extra-legal violence by the state against political opponents is merely an unfortunate aberration that can be corrected by inquiring into the matter and punishing a few culprits who will somehow be exposed. The reality of the matter is only too clearly that the struggle in South Africa between the state and the masses is an unrelenting, irreconcilable struggle in which no quarter is given or taken and no compromise is possible - either at the abstract level of conflicting analyses and demands, or at the most concrete level of all, the encounter between the political detainee and his interrogator.

The superficial reaction by reformist critics to the question of torture by the police once again recalls the contradictory nature of the policies that the capitalist class and the state find it necessary to pursue. On the one hand, certain limited criticisms of the existing society are indulged in, and certain concessions are offered to the black petite-bourgeoisie. On the other hand, demands by the masses cannot be conceded and must, in the final analysis, be suppressed. Where such demands are brought forward in an organised way, the organisation must be destroyed before it can gain significant support. In order to win support from the petite-bourgeoisie, however, the bourgeoisie must have relatively clean hands. To expect black leaders to ally themselves with undisguised oppression is to ask them to renounce all credibility that they might have among the masses, and hence to render them useless as instruments of pacification. From this point of view the all too obvious bestiality of the police must be deplored; the condonation of such bestiality by government leaders is a tactical disaster.

In order to stem the tide of revolt, on the other hand, the state machinery must be kept intact. The authority of the state must be maintained, even when the state is manifestly opposed to all demo- cratic demands. Only the state itself can be appealed to. To call on forces outside the state would be to call for revolution. Unhappily and filled with misgivings, the liberal bourgeoisie is entirely dependent on the state. No less filled with misgivings and no less dependent on the state are the conservative white middle classes. Concessions to their black rivals cannot be postponed indefinitely; yet these would swamp them in a tide of rising wages and competition. The state has continued to balance between these pressures while struggling against the threat of revolution as the stormy events of the 1970s unfolded. Throughout all the lulls and upsurges in the struggle, these were the internal tensions to which the rulers of South Africa are subject, and by which they must sooner or later be torn into bitterly warring camps.

Repression in South Africa reached a new climax on 19 October 1977 when seventeen organisations of the Black Consciousness move- ment, three news publications and one religious group were banned. The prohibited organisations were the following: the Association for the Educational and Cultural Advancement of the African People of South Africa; the Black Parents' Association; the Black People's Con- vention; the Black Women's Federation; the Border Youth Organisation; the Christian Institute of Southern Africa; the Eastern Province Youth Organisation; the Medupe Writers' Association; the Natal Youth Organ- isation; the National Youth Organisation; the South African Students' Movement; the South African Students' Organisation; the Soweto Students' Representative Council; the Black Community Programmes Ltd; the Transvaal Youth Organisation; the Union of Black Journalists; and the Zimele Trust Fund. The prohibited newspapers were the *World*, the *Weekend World*, and *Pro Veritate*.

State reaction

Even at this stage, however, it was incorrect to say that the government had chosen the road of 'irrational flight into the Afrikaner Nationalist laager, mouthing defiance at black South Africa and the world community', and plunged into 'war psychosis and white tribal hysteria' (*Cape Times*, 21 October 1977). The difference between the government and the 'liberal' opposition remained a difference of degree. The government had formed a different estimate of what 'black South Africa and the world community' would tolerate. It assumed that the world bourgeoisie would continue its dealings with South Africa under virtually any conditions short of revolution. It believed that the 'moderate blacks' would not be entirely displeased at having their radical opponents removed. 'Who can believe', the *Cape Times* demanded to know, 'that the Afrikaner Nationalist minority can hold down the black masses forever?' (*ibid.*). It is doubtful whether the government itself believed this. More likely it believed that the remaining, extremely conservative black leaders would be capable of holding the masses in check for as long as the state suppressed all alternatives. Should this estimate prove wrong, the government will no doubt adapt its tactics in keeping with the requirements of capitalist policy. The collapse of the existing state is unlikely to be the result of mere blunders on the part of the government, as liberals seem to fear. It is likely to be the result of forces superior to those of the state being mobilised against it.

Even at a time when, in liberal eyes, the state was plunging headlong down a path of fatal confrontation, therefore, the government had by no means abandoned its ambivalent position. Even while practising brutal repression, the government was at pains to stress its liberal intentions. The following explanation by the Minister of Justice for the bannings of 19 October might ring hollow and grotesque; none the less it makes clear the government's desire to continue enjoying support from the international bourgeoisie (*Cape Times*, 22 October 1977):

The reaction overseas concerns me very much, and I'm very
sorry about any tarnishing of the image of this country. This,
of course, is a thing that was in my mind for a long time. I knew
that there was an unpleasant act I had to take, but I was trying
to weigh it up against how it would go down overseas. Eventually,
I had to make an agonizing choice between my country's
reputation overseas and the peace and welfare of the
people in my land. And, given that choice, I say without any
hesitation I have no doubt I have done the right thing.

I chose to try and stop the unrest in my country.

To conclude that the National Party stands for repression and the 'liberal' opposition for reform would therefore be misleading. Not only the position of the National Party but also that of the liberal opposition is ambiguous. The ambiguity of the National Party was unwittingly but clearly reflected by the Nationalist organ, *Die Burger*, in its defence of South African intervention in the Angolan civil war: 'There are people,' it wrote, 'who seek a contradiction between South Africa's politics of relaxation in Africa and her resolute attitude towards the civil war in Angola. . . . Such a view confuses a policy of peace and relaxation with laxity and appeasement which history teaches us ends in disaster' (5 December 1975). In the distinction between 'laxity' and 'relaxation' the entire ambivalence of the National Party is reflected. In response to 'verligte' pressures, 'relaxation' is approved of; in response to 'verkrampte' pressures and terror of the black masses, 'laxity' is condemned. What precisely is the nature of this distinction? 'Relaxation', it is submitted, means minimum concessions on the terms laid down by the state. 'Laxity' means concessions exceeding this minimum, in which an element of initiative is surrendered to the masses. This distinction sheds light on state policy during the present period. Those forms of change and political organisation which can be accommodated within the framework of state control are permitted or even encouraged. Organisations that reject state control are suppressed. Repression may thus be seen as a *necessary condition* for any acts of liberalisation by the state. For at least the foreseeable future, a policy of *limited* reform, limited precisely by the framework of mass repression, remains the most likely course for the government to follow.

In the period following Soweto attempts by the state to adapt itself to the changing balance of forces became more purposeful and urgent. On the one hand, new institutions had to be created in which the support of larger sections of the black middle classes could be captured – a policy insisted on by the capitalist class internationally. On the other hand, means had to be found of disarming the white masses in their attempts to maintain the status quo. At the same time, the worsening economic crisis made it essential that the power of organised labour to defend the workers' living standards be limited still further. This applied first and foremost to the emergent African trade unions, but, increasingly, to the registered unions as well. Faced with these tasks, the state was required to shift from its traditional policy of racial domination to a policy corresponding more closely to the reality of the situation – a policy of undisguised class domination. And it needed in the first place to prepare its followers for this change, and if not to win their support, then at least to disarm them politically.

In May 1977 an official commission of inquiry under the chairmanship of the 'verligte' Professor N. Wiehahn was appointed to investigate all aspects of labour legislation and to recommend amendments. This step was welcomed by the 'liberal' opposition in Parliament: 'The fact that Prof. Nic Wiehahn is to be the chairman,' declared Dr Boraine of the PRP, 'suggests that this commission will be radical in its findings and recommendations because his own public statements indicate an awareness that urgent and drastic changes need to be made' (*Cape Times*, 13 May 1977).

Nor were these expectations entirely disappointed when two years later, in May 1979, the Wiehahn Commission released its first report. The majority – consisting of employers' representatives, academics and registered trade-union officials – made it clear that their aim was the 'promotion of industrial peace' within the 'free market economy' (Wiehahn Commission report, paras 1.19.1, 1.19.5). It recognised that 'black trade unions are subject neither to the protective and stabilising elements of the system [laid down by the Industrial Conciliation Act] nor to its essential discipline and control; they in fact enjoy greater freedom than registered unions' (para. 3.35.5). To prohibit black unions, however, was not feasible: 'a prohibition would undoubtedly have the effect of driving Black trade unionism underground and uniting Black workers not only against the authorities but, more important, also against the system of free enterprise in South Africa. It would certainly add fuel to the flames of radicalism on the part of those who wish to overthrow the system' (para. 3.36.6).

The Commission accordingly recommended measures for the encapsulation of African trade unions by means of registration and state control. These measures would apply to the existing registered trade unions as well. The 'closed shop' would be abolished, the prohibition of political activities would be strengthened, and section 77 of the Industrial Conciliation Act, providing for job reservation, would be repealed. In this way a system was designed by which the working class *as a whole* could be subjected to increasing discipline and state control in accordance with the needs of the capitalist class. From the capitalist point of view it was vital that the leaders of the independent African unions should lead the organised African workers – the vanguard of the working class – into this trap. The key question would be the ability of these leaders to stand firm.

The increasing uniformity in the conditions of white and black workers was thus extended to the level of organisation, thereby strengthening the basis for working-class unity. To combat this obvious danger the state sought means of enforcing new divisions among the mass of workers. Almost simultaneously with the Wiehahn Commission, the commission of inquiry led by Riekert into the conditions of urban Africans brought out its report. The measures it proposed were aimed at streamlining the system of influx control and, at the same time, using it more effectively as an instrument of division. The *Financial Mail* explains the essence of its recommendations (11 May 1979):

> Differential treatment of blacks with Section 10 permanent
> urban residence rights and 'illegal' people from outside the
> urban areas will not only be retained, but reinforced. Thus,
> says Riekert, 'the most important advantage of the black
> community development act will be the fact that it strengthens
> the position of established black communities in the white areas
> and will afford them new and much wider opportunities for
> decision-making', through community councils.

In terms of the Riekert proposals, workers from the reserves will only be allowed to enter the cities if '(1) there is a firm offer of employment; (2) approved housing is available; and (3) suitable workers are not available from the ranks of the urban unemployed' (*ibid.*). Restrictions on black businessmen are to be eased further, and trading and industrial areas open to capitalists of all races are to be established. Not only the black middle classes but a settled and relatively protected black 'aristocracy of labour' is to be encouraged; the full burden of oppression and exploitation is to fall on the shoulders of the migrant masses. In theory, in every factory and mine the workers will be split into two camps, desperately competing for the dwindling number of jobs, while the unemployed masses trapped in the reserves will enable the capitalist class to drive down wages ever lower. The organisations formed by the workers, in theory, will be under perfect state control, while a growing layer of petite-bourgeoisie will be drawn into harmonious and profitable collaboration with the capitalist class. In propositions of this nature state policy and the measures demanded by 'liberal' big business were increasingly merging.

At the political level, the state was preparing to cope with opposition among the white workers. Its essential task was to free the Executive from parliamentary control. In 1977 proposals were published for the amendment of the constitution in such a way that decisive power in matters of national importance would rest with the State President. The State President would be, in practice, the leader of the National Party. Separate 'parliaments' would be created for the white, coloured and Indian sections of the population. The African masses would have to make do with the Bantustans, supplemented by urban local authorities. A minority of coloured and Indian 'ministers' would be involved in the national executive, the Cabinet Council, over which the State President would preside. The Senate would be abolished.

By this means two birds would be killed with one stone. The leaders of the National Party would be given a relatively free hand in dealing with the crisis, and conservative coloured and Indian leaders would be implicated even more deeply in maintaining the existing order. A further wedge would be driven between the coloured and African people. For lack of support in the coloured and Indian communities the constitutional proposals could not be immediately implemented. The National Party fought and won the 1977 parliamentary elections on the basis of these proposals, thus preparing white public opinion for the changes that were impending. The conflicts and contradictions within the National Party, however, had by no means been resolved. The resignation of Vorster as Prime Minister, the 'Muldergate' scandal and the election of the 'verkrampte' Treurnicht as party leader in the Transvaal still lay in the future. A decisive struggle between the 'verligte' and 'verkrampte' elements in the leadership would have to be fought out before a more open alignment of forces along class lines could emerge.

Even the changes proposed in the late 1970s, however, could not substantially improve the position of the masses; indeed, it was never the intention that they should. From the point of view of the black middle classes, concessions were being offered on a somewhat less limited and more lucrative scale than before. From the point of view of the mass of workers, poverty was becoming worse and state oppression more irreconcilable than ever. The great and significant change to emerge from the crisis and upheavals of the mid-1970s was that conflict of a class nature, polarising the whole of society, became increasingly sharp and less ambiguous. This would have important implications as far as the relationship between the state and the white workers is concerned. Nor could it leave unaffected the relationship between the black middle classes and the mass of the proletariat.

Chapter 11

Liberal reaction

The struggles of the workers in the 1970s provided the basis for a growth of radicalism among the black population in general. The Durban strikes opened the eyes of conservatives and radicals alike to the potential power of the African working class. In the eyes of growing numbers of workers and intellectuals ideas of defeatism and conciliation were undermined more and more as events unfolded. The result was an increasing polarisation among the black population between the advocates of moderation and the new generation of radicals, who were drawn towards the alternative, hardly defined as yet, of uncompromising struggle against the state.

A key question in this process was the struggle for leadership of the African working class that developed during the 1970s. On the one hand, 'liberal' employers and politicians were begging the workers to be patient and trying to gain their support for a policy of limited reform. 'Moderate' black leaders, 'moderate' black trade unions and 'moderate' political organisations were the vehicles by which these ideas were transmitted. On the other hand, efforts were made – fiercely combated by the state – to develop the militance of the African workers into a conscious struggle for power, with the aim of transforming South African society. The essential guideline for such a development, a clear and viable programme, existed only in the most embryonic form. Among the majority of the people there was little clarity as to the precise demands to be fought for, let alone the strategy and tactics by which to achieve them. Differences of opinion and factionalism flourished, while the struggle itself proceeded in a disjointed, pragmatical, but completely determined way. The general mobilisation of the African working class remained a question of the future; yet its answer was steadily becoming clearer.

Liberal reaction

Moves towards a non-racial liberal party

The 1970s saw the decline and fall of that anachronistic carbon copy
of the National Party, the United Party. Successive splits to left and
right led, on the one hand, to the further reinforcement of the National
Party and, on the other, to the growth of the Progressive Party into
the official parliamentary opposition. In July 1975 a major split-off
from the United Party merged with the Progressives to form the Progressive Reform Party. In 1977 the United Party finally collapsed. Six
right-wing MPs were expelled from the caucus in January and formed
themselves into the South African Party as a halfway stage to joining
the National Party. In September four liberal MPs joined the PRP,
which thereupon changed its name to the Progressive Federal Party
(PFP). In Parliament the polarisation between bourgeois and petit-
bourgeois interests, as opposed to divisions along lines of language,
now became predominant. The National Party, as yet united, formed
an invincible bloc on the right. The PFP, although outnumbered by
more than six to one, confidently mounted opposition. In the semi-
war climate of the late 1970s it had less chance than ever of gaining
much further support, let alone majority support, from the white
electorate. Yet it remained the authentic mouthpiece of the ultimate
power within South African capitalism – the international bourgeoisie.

The following assessment of conditions in South Africa at the
beginning of 1977 was made from the point of view of the American
capitalist class (*Business Week*, 14 February 1977):

> Like a thunderstorm over the veld, profound changes are
> sweeping the vast sub-continent of Southern Africa . . . . The
> result, almost inevitably, will be black-dominated governments
> in Rhodesia and South-West Africa within the next two years
> and an expanding political role for blacks over a somewhat
> longer period in South Africa's complex society. . . . The United
> States has a great deal at stake [in Southern Africa] . . . . The
> way to assure continued access to the raw materials and the
> sea lanes, the Ford Administration concluded last year, is to
> support demands for racial equality in hopes that black
> governments that come to power will be friendly to the United
> States. Such a policy should also pay dividends in improved
> relations with the rest of black Africa, a potential market of
> 200 million persons and an important source of basic
> commodities.

With the change of a few words, these were also the hopes and beliefs of the South African 'liberal' bourgeoisie. American business corporations, in the view of President Carter and the American ambassador to the United Nations, Mr Andrew Young, have a 'constructive role to play in Southern Africa's evolution toward racial equality' (*ibid.*). The director of the Graduate School of Business at the University of Cape Town, Professor Feldberg, echoed this idea (*Rand Daily Mail*, 15 December 1976):

> The policy of separate development has for decades been sowing
> the seeds for the destruction of the free enterprise system. . . .
> Today, as in the past, South Africa needs business leaders with
> vision. Men who can see beyond the narrow confines of their own
> business. Fortunately our corporate statesmen are now taking a
> strong and positive position on our racial problems. . . . Thinking
> businessmen [however] should not merely be reacting to South
> Africa's current problems and taking suitable action, but should
> rather be looking at the problems of the future and taking
> positive steps to help create an environment in which all South
> Africans can live in peace and harmony.

Several organisations of employers have shown what this means in practice. Following a meeting with the American Secretary of State in March 1977, eleven major American companies in South Africa came forward with a programme for internal company reform. The corresponding political demands were put by the Secretary of State himself in a speech four months later. He warned the South African government that its relations with the USA would deteriorate 'if it failed to make rapid progress to end racial discrimination and to bring about the full political participation of all citizens' (*Cape Times*, 2 July 1977). Similarly, in response to the Soweto uprising, the Transvaal Chamber of Industries (TCI) submitted a 'blue-print for change' to the Prime Minister in August 1976. In this memorandum the traditional 'liberal' demand for lifting restraints on the employment of 'cheap docile labour' was repeated. The 'mature, family-oriented Black in the cities', it was argued, is 'more interested in his pay packet than in politics'; and it was necessary, the memorandum warned, 'to prevent a weakening of this middle-class attitude by frustration and indignity' (*Star IAW*, 21 August 1976).

In October 1976 the Associated Chambers of Commerce (Assocom) called for 'a powerful united front among business leaders to press the Government to speed ahead with sweeping racial reform' (*Star IAW*,

23 October 1976). In a motion passed by its annual congress a programme of 'initial action points' was put forward (*ibid.*):

> Recognition of the need for all races inside the urban areas.
> Permission to own property for all racial groups in their own parts
> of the urban zones.
> Relaxation of restrictions on Black businessmen in their own areas.
> Setting aside mixed trading areas in which all races may trade freely.
> Relaxation of all racial restrictions on jobs in White-owned
> businesses.
> Facilitate the establishment of restaurants for all races in White
> central business districts.

'It is both unsound and dangerous,' the proposer of the motion said,
'for Blacks to be moulded in a single strata [*sic*] of their own without
a real middle class.' The executive director of the Afrikaanse Handelsinstituut was the first to welcome these proposals.

A few months later Assocom revealed more of the 'sweeping racial
reforms' which it had in mind. Giving evidence to the Cillie Commission,
it stressed 'the importance of economic growth to social stability and
the need to meet the legitimate aspirations of blacks in order to promote
such growth' (*Star IAW*, 19 February 1977). To this end the following
recommendations were made (*ibid.*):

> Steps towards the ultimate orderly freedom of movement of
> blacks. Legislation to allow individual firms to decide for
> themselves on the employment of individuals without reference
> to race.
> Opportunities for workers of all races to negotiate with employers
> on a similar basis as that existing for whites.

Assocom furthermore called for the following 'specific restraints' on
the employment of African workers to be ended, thereby revealing the
interest of employers in the matter (*ibid.*):

> Restrictions resulting from the Environment Planning Act which
> precluded commerce and industry from absorbing the natural
> growth of the labour force as they wish.
> The legal provision which effectively allows trade unions to place
> ratio limitations on the employment of blacks.
> Job reservation legislation.
> Influx control and restrictions on freedom of movement which
> inhibit the use of black labour where most needed.

Another major initiative was launched by 'liberal' employers in November 1976. More than a hundred leading businessmen met in Johannesburg to set up an organisation known as the Urban Foundation. Its aim was to 'improve the quality of life in urban black communities'. Matters that would be given attention included the improvement of housing, education, community and recreational activities, and employment opportunities. The Foundation furthermore set itself the task of encouraging blacks 'to adopt free-enterprise values' (*Star IAW*, 4 December 1976). A liberal journalist explained (*Cape Times* 4 December 1976): 'Businessmen were called on to show the generous, enlightened and concerned side of capitalism as an effective counter to communism.'

It will be noted that the traditional rationalisation of its own existence by liberalism in South Africa – the defence of democracy and human rights against an intolerant government – bears only a passing relation to the above-mentioned proposals and demands. On the other hand, the link with the concrete function of liberalism in South Africa, the stabilisation of the capitalist system, is immediate and clear. We need only look at the function ascribed by Assocom to its own proposals for reform. The 'specific restraints' that are mentioned above, it said, not only have a direct effect on the employment of black workers, but they also give rise to 'frustration and deep resentment, and a lack of commitment to the system overall'. The latter aspect, Assocom concludes, 'has extremely serious implications and is, if anything, more important than the direct effects' (*Star IAW*, 19 February 1977).

In the approach of the Urban Foundation, too, concern for the preservation of the capitalist order unmistakably predominates over concern with social change. State policy is not challenged at all. On the contrary, as the *Star* pointed out on 1 December 1976, all the priorities of the Urban Foundation 'are areas in which the Government itself has already agreed that movement is necessary. There is nothing in the businessmen's programme that clashes with State policy.' Indeed, as the director of the Urban Foundation (a former judge) pointed out, the work of the Foundation 'will always be supplementary to that of the State'. Only through extensive involvement by the private sector to supplement state efforts, he believed, 'can a peaceful future be assured' (*Cape Times*, 16 April 1977).

From the point of view of the 'liberal' bourgeoisie, reform thus serves a twofold function. On the one hand, it is a political expedient that has been made necessary by the upsurge of the masses. In this sense reform is the lesser of two evils, the alternative being increasing strife and social instability. On the other hand, 'liberal' employers are irked by the numerous restrictions by which the use of 'cheap docile labour' is hemmed in. In so far as these restrictions serve mainly to place small employers (especially farmers) in a more competitive position, the multinationals find them superfluous and a nuisance. To this extent 'liberal' employers find themselves in opposition to state policy, something that is given great emphasis by the 'liberals' themselves. The political significance of doing so is clear: the greater the conflict is made to appear between 'liberals' and the state, the more credible liberalism will appear as an alternative to the existing policy of the state.

While the public image of the 'liberal' movement is reformist, therefore, its devotion to law and order was never in any doubt. Its anxiety for the preservation of South African capitalism, even in its most oppressive aspects, became more pronounced as the crisis deepened. Thus the TCI, in its 'blue-print for change', went so far as to argue that influx control was in the interest of blacks as well as whites. The recognition of African trade unions was not mentioned. The response of the 'left-liberal' *Daily Dispatch* to the first hint of mass struggle in East London was to publish a front-page editorial in English, Afrikaans and Xhosa appealing to 'all the people of our area' for 'peace'. It argued (*Cape Times*, 21 August 1976):

> Violence creates more violence, and too many innocent people will suffer, so let non-violence be our aim. You know well where your newspaper, The Daily Dispatch, stands on public issues. We fight for your rights, the rights of everyone of you – but this fight must be a fight with words, not with weapons.

– and more in the same paternalistic vein. In reality, of course, weapons and violence were overwhelmingly the monopoly of the state. There was no chance whatsoever that the police would be guided by appeals from the liberal press. The only conceivable effect could be to persuade the black masses to refrain from struggling and submit to law and order. In the *Cape Times* critical support for the state was declared even more explicitly: 'Where there is unrest, law and order must be restored as a matter of priority, as all will agree. But this is not enough.' And in the same issue (4 December 1976), to remove any shadow of doubt: 'Reasonable citizens of all persuasions will instinctively support the authorities in all reasonable steps to maintain order as a first priority. But an equally important priority is government by consent.'

Preserving the existing capitalist order, therefore, is the aim of 'liberal' policy. Suppressing unrest is one means to this end; reform and concession are others. This was also the attitude of the PFP. The manifesto of the new party, the *Star* wrote on 6 September 1977, 'stresses that the Progfeds intend to take a tough line on law and order, and recognizes that "instant change" is not possible. It must come gradually, in a phased and orderly manner.' Like its predecessors, the PFP rejected universal suffrage and called for a qualified franchise. It continued the traditional 'liberal' policy of unequivocally supporting the existing social order while equivocally calling for changes within it.

Together with 'liberal' ideas, the PFP inherited the 'liberal' function of 'building bridges' between 'moderate whites' and 'moderate blacks'. A major repository of 'moderate blacks' was discovered, not surprisingly, in the reserve bureaucracies. These were assiduously cultivated. In August 1973 the Transvaal Congress of the United Party was addressed by leading functionaries of the Gazankulu reserve, the CRC and the SAIC. Since that time repeated meetings have taken place between reserve leaders and the United Party, the Progressive Party and the successors of the latter. An especially outstanding part in the process of building bridges has been played by Buthelezi. The significance of the Kwazulu leader has lain in his ambitious efforts to build up a mass following and cultivate foreign connections. Prior to 1973, Buthelezi had confined his political activity to statements of intention. In the aftermath of the Durban strikes it became imperative to build up an organisation. The word of 'opposition within the system' finally became flesh. The new organisation was called Inkatha. It was described as a 'national cultural liberation movement'. One of its leaders describes its origin as follows (*Reality*, July 1977):

> Inkatha had started in Dr Nycmbesi's house in 1974 while a
> public meeting was being organised to receive Chief Gatsha
> Buthelezi and introduce members of his government to the
> Soweto public. The organizers of the meeting felt they would
> like to establish something more permanent and asked Chief
> Buthelezi for a name. He suggested the name Inkatha be revived.
> . . . In 1974 the revived Inkatha was officially launched. . . . Now
> in 1977 [the membership] is 100,400 with funds of R136,000.

Inkatha was first and foremost a Zulu organisation based on the Kwazulu Bantustan and the policy of 'separate development'. Its primary aim was 'to foster the spirit of unity among the people of Kwazulu throughout Southern Africa and between them and all their

African brothers in Southern Africa, and to keep alive and foster the traditions of the people' (Temkin, 1976, p. 396). Like the state, Inkatha – notwithstanding all words to the contrary – in practice encouraged Zulu-speakers to regard themselves not as South Africans but as Zulu, and to 'unite' with other South Africans as a separate Zulu bloc. This is fully in keeping with Buthelezi's own position: 'The homelands system,' his biographer explains, 'demands sectionalism. Buthelezi is a Zulu leader before he is an African or a black leader' (*ibid.*, p. 278).

Membership of Inkatha was originally limited to Zulu above the age of 18, though by 1977 non-Zulu were also being admitted. Despite this gesture the Soweto student leaders – many of whom were Zulu-speakers themselves – dismissed Inkatha as a divisive ethnic organisation.

The central committee of Inkatha is elected for a five-year period. The current president is Gatsha Buthelezi. During its term of office the leadership may not be publicly criticised by members. Criticism may only be uttered internally. Predictably, the programme of 'national cultural liberation' is vague in the extreme. As Welsh (1976) observes, there are 'traditionalists, labour leaders, young students and intellectuals, businessmen, all of whom are actual or potential sources of opposition that will be difficult to contain and reconcile within the ranks of the movement'. 'Culture' is defined in all-embracing terms. Democratic aims and principles are professed. According to a pro-government newspaper, Buthelezi's vision of majority rule is 'partly intended to disarm radical revolutionary elements in Black politics who saw him as a sell-out. "He must show that when it comes to talk, he is at least as fiery as they are"' (Temkin, 1976, p. 342). This assessment is undoubtedly correct.

In more concrete terms, Inkatha is pledged to non-violence. Support for capitalism is reflected in its aim to 'protect, encourage and promote trade, commerce, industry, agriculture and conservation of natural resources by all means in the interests of the people' (*ibid.*, p. 396). Nationalisation of the basic means of production is not referred to in this context as an anti-capitalist organisation could not have omitted to do. A leader of Inkatha confirms: 'We don't want communism, that is certain' (*Reality*, July 1977). Recruitment into the organisation appears to be based on verbal condemnation of the government and calls for unity, interspersed with appeals to racial sentiment. This approach, while bound to find some echo among the African population, can only be described as opportunist. Inkatha's contribution to the political development of Zulu-speaking workers appears from the following extract of an interview with Dr Nyembesi, one of the founders of the organisation (*ibid.*):

> *Question*: If as you say you believe in slow consensus among
> people at grass roots level, without having any clear policy, what
> do you say when you recruit people?
> *Answer*: You have a fine leader in Buthelezi. You must support
> him. You must work for the Zulu first and then attract all for the
> good of the black community.

Even more clearly describing the lack of internal democracy was
the General Secretary of Inkatha: 'After mobilizing the people the
INKATHA leaders will work out a clear-cut and well-graduated programme of positive action' (*Reality*, September 1975).

Inkatha can thus be seen as a basically conservative and undemocratic
organisation. To what extent did it succeed in involving urban workers
in the politics of Kwazulu and the cult of Buthelezi? In practice, its
political weakness was reflected in its lack of power to convince. The
membership is largely middle-aged: 'Half the people,' according to a
leading member, 'have not come forward to join the united front. A
barrier is the feeling that one cannot have anything to do with people
who operate within the system.' Indeed, to the youth in particular,
the 'fine leader' Buthelezi is in the final analysis nothing more than
'a homeland leader who works in the system' (*Reality*, July 1977).

Following the Soweto uprising, the calls from the liberal bourgeoisie
for an alliance with 'moderate blacks' became more insistent than ever.
The urban masses were stirring into motion. The existing instruments
of law and order might fail to stem the tide. How did Inkatha rise to
the occasion? 'Feeling that a national movement was necessary,' we are
told, 'Inkatha launched the Black United Front at the Jan Smuts
Holiday Inn on 8th October 1976' (*ibid.*). SASO and the BPC were
invited to join in setting up the BUF but refused to 'sit down with
homeland leaders'. Apart from Buthelezi and Inkatha, the BUF was
supported by Professor H. Ntsanwisi, head of Gazankulu, C. Phatudi,
head of Lebowa, and members of the Urban Bantu Council of Soweto.
According to its chairman, the BUF was 'one and the same thing' as
Inkatha. According to the BPC it was the creation of 'a bunch of
political clowns and opportunists' (*Sunday Times* (London), 5 December 1976).

The liberal approaches following Soweto were well received by
Inkatha. In January 1977 Inkatha formally offered an alliance to the
PRP. It proposed calling this alliance a 'People's Movement for Radical
Peaceful Change' (*Rand Daily Mail*, 14 January 1977). The leader of

the PRP, Eglin, expressed enthusiasm for the plan. The National Chairman of the PRP, Swart, was empowered to negotiate with Inkatha. A Progressive MP, Enthoven, called for 'similar meetings' with 'similar bodies, opinion-makers and leaders'. Regular consultation with Inkatha and other black organisations, he said, 'is not only desirable, but essential in order to promote understanding and maintain and create bridges between South Africans of various races' (*Cape Times*, 17 January 1977). The chairman of the BUF explained: 'Inkatha talks to the PRP because this is the only white political party who want to talk to us' (*Reality*, July 1977). It seemed as if a non-racial liberal party was finally being formed. Predictably, the government press reacted in sombre tones to the first hints of contact between Inkatha and the PRP: 'These people,' *Die Vaderland* warned, 'are playing with fire.' According to two Nationalist MPs, the proposal of a multi-racial alliance amounted to 'propagation of racial polarisation' (*Rand Daily Mail*, 16 December 1976).

The significance of Inkatha's undemocratic structure was shown in the course of these developments. Long after the plan for an alliance with the PRP had been launched, indeed a week after Swart had been appointed to negotiate with Inkatha, it was announced that Buthelezi was seeking a mandate from the members of Inkatha for this plan. The membership was presented with a *fait accompli*. There appears to have been good reason for this mode of operation. 'Black radicals', we are told, were 'furious' at what Buthelezi was doing (*World*, 23 January 1977). Any opposition among the members of Inkatha was thus circumvented by circumventing the membership itself. In this connection Buthelezi explained his own conception of organisational democracy: 'I feel it is dangerous for a Black political leader to go forward on his own ideas alone. He must be sure that the Black people support them' (*ibid.*). Such support may also be obtained, apparently, after the event. A greater contrast with the democracy of the mass meeting cannot be imagined.

Since these initial contacts little more has been heard of the 'People's Movement for Radical Peaceful Change'. One reason may be the hostility of the government, persuading the parties to bide their time. In the months that followed, however, the PRP was making its bid to capture the remaining bourgeois elements out of the disintegrating United Party. For this purpose it needed to put its most 'moderate' face forward. By the time that the merger had been completed the immediate pressures of the Soweto period had eased. No general strike had taken place for some months and student resistance had grown sporadic. The immediate necessity for a non-racial liberal party had receded into the background once again. On the other hand, certain foundations for such a party had been laid, to build on gradually in the period that followed or to make use of in a future crisis.

Buthelezi may be regarded as an ideal 'moderate black leader' from the point of view of the liberal bourgeoisie. He addresses himself to the black population in general, not only to the Zulu-speaking section, in essentially racial terms. By means of abstract 'fiery talk' a certain audience can be gained, thus creating the appearance of popular support. Buthelezi represents the ambitions of precisely that conservative section of the black middle classes that the liberals are trying to cultivate. Buthelezi himself is perfectly frank about this (*FM*, 10 December 1976): 'The encouragement of a middle-class in Black society to stabilise society will fail if that middle-class is expected to be a buffer between a minority of haves and a majority of have-nots.' Instead of a purely nominal role, the black middle class must gain a real interest in South African capitalism if it is to be expected to defend the system. Industrialists, Buthelezi says, must 'consult Blacks on a level which leads to a joint strategy'. He does not 'want to hear about the benefits of a free enterprise system which is closed to the Blacks in South Africa'. On the contrary (*ibid.*):

> Blacks should be admitted to all the country's universities and
> technical universities and technical colleges; to all the professions
> and trades; they must be allowed to own property whenever they
> have the money to buy that property; they must be free to
> develop their business wherever they have the ability to do so.
> Outside these freedoms there is no free enterprise in South Africa.

Essentially, Buthelezi thus has no programme other than the programme of the liberal bourgeoisie. His role is, on the one hand, to reconcile this programme with the policy of 'separate development', and on the other hand to win support for this programme among the masses. The 'independence' of the reserves, Buthelezi argues, 'should not be conditional on the breaking up of the integrated economy which is the life-blood of all the peoples of South Africa' (Buthelezi, 1974, pp. 11–12). Buthelezi, like other 'liberals', is trying to strike a road to the liberals in the National Party. He defines his strategy as one of 'meaningful dialogue', which, he declares, 'can begin on the basis of the homelands policy'. (*ibid.*, p. 10). The aim is not to prevent the fragmentation of South Africa and its people but to participate in such fragmentation. 'Dialogue,' Buthelezi says, 'implies that South

Africa as we all know it should not be broken up into a series of independent states by unilateral decisions of the White group only. Even on the basis of the homelands concept, we need to work out every detail jointly: this means by leaders of both Black and White' (*ibid.*, p. 11). Besides voicing the demands of the conservative petite-bourgeoisie in general, Buthelezi thus serves as spokesman for the reserve bureaucracy in particular.

The PFP, too, has accepted the 'homelands' policy as the basis for meaningful dialogue. Its manifesto accepts that 'some of what has happened under National Party rule cannot be undone, but can be comfortably accommodated in a federal system' (*IAW Star*, 6 September 1977). Practically speaking it is the reserve bureaucracies who will refuse to surrender the privileges that they presently enjoy that would have to be 'accommodated' in this way. Or as Buthelezi puts it, 'if we accept that the economy of South Africa belongs to all, let us also accept that the emergence of independent homelands is not contradictory to the idea of all the states, White or Black, being associated on certain matters of general concern' (Buthelezi, 1974, p. 12). Through the policy of 'meaningful dialogue', Buthelezi promises, 'all the pressures on South Africa would abate or even cease altogether' (*ibid.*, p. 10). It is 'urgently necessary for us to move in the directions which I have indicated if the homelands policy is to be accorded any credibility within this country or abroad' (*ibid.*, p. 20). This position he describes as 'our attempts as Black people to bend over backwards, in our attempts to meet our White countrymen who wield power over us' (*ibid.*, p. 21).

Buthelezi's role has been recognised not only by the PFP but also by the bourgeoisie abroad. When visiting the USA in November 1976, Buthelezi was acclaimed as 'leader of South Africa's 18 million blacks' by the mayor of Washington, D.C. (who was described as standing 'close to Carter') (*World*, 12 November 1976). In February 1977 Buthelezi again went on a private lecture tour of the United States. He was offered 'black American aid for the realisation of full freedom and self-determination for the Zulu nation and the black people' in South Africa (*Star IAW*, 19 February 1977). In March Buthelezi was back in Ulundi to deliver a noteworthy plea in support of foreign investment in South Africa to the Kwazulu legislature (*Star IAW*, 26 March 1977):

> It is true that for a century and a half investors have had great
> rewards from their investments here – based largely on the
> exploitation of blacks. But looking at the question impartially,

the other side of the exploitation coin was economic progress. Even through that exploitation there was progress, even for the victims of that exploitation.

The question of foreign investment in South Africa, as Buthelezi himself indicates, is not an academic one. A mounting campaign has been waged over many years by opponents of state policy to end all foreign investment in the country. The bourgeoisie both in South Africa and abroad, on the other hand, feel that investment should be left to continue as the investors themselves see fit. Buthelezi comes out unmistakably in support of the bourgeois position. This is unacceptable to opponents of apartheid, as Buthelezi would discover to his cost. In September 1977 he was invited to address a symposium at the Indian university of Durban-Westville on 'possible alternatives for peaceful coexistence in South Africa'. Students picketed the meeting, carrying placards with slogans such as 'Gatsha, is there an alternative to total liberation?', 'Puppets on a string' and 'What's in this pseudo-liberal nonsense?' Inkatha representatives 'in full regalia' were greeted with boos and jeers. Buthelezi and the other Inkatha representatives had to beat an ignominious retreat to the rector's office. Buthelezi's reaction was furious. He 'reminded' Indians of the riots of 1949 when many Indians were killed by Zulu: 'I don't want to be responsible for sparking off another Indo-Zulu riot,' he said, 'but I cannot allow myself to be insulted in this way.' Buthelezi pledged never to return to the Durban-Westville campus 'under any circumstances' (*Star IAW*, 24 September 1977).

A course similar to that of Buthelezi and Inkatha has been followed by the Labour Party in the Coloured Persons' Representative Council. In elections to the CRC in 1975 the Labour Party increased its number of members from twenty-six to thirty-one, thus giving it an absolute majority. More significant, however, was the massive and growing extent to which the elections were boycotted by the voters (see Table 11.1).

As social tensions mounted in the mid-1970s, the Labour Party veered more erratically than ever between verbal defiance of the state and practical compliance with state policy. In August and again in September 1974 Labour delegations took part in discussions with the government. The main demand on both occasions was the granting of full parliamentary rights to coloured people. This demand was rejected by the government. The leader of the Labour Party, Leon, thereupon drew the following conclusion: 'I am not interested in further window-dressing talks with the Prime Minister .... We now have no alternative but to go to those people whose arms are open to us – the Black people of South Africa' (SRR, 1974, pp. 18–19). This boldness, however, was soon to evaporate. Having gained an absolute majority in the CRC in the elections of 1975, Leon announced that the Labour Party 'would now call upon the Prime Minister to scrap the CRC and to give full parliamentary representation to the Coloured people' (SRR, 1975, p. 14). Once again, therefore, the mass of the people were ignored. In practice the Labour Party continued with the same tactics which, after the experience of previous years, had been so categorically renounced. In October 1975 Leon and his executive once again met with the Prime Minister. Twenty-seven questions as to the government's intentions were submitted by the Labour Party leaders. These the Prime Minister refused to answer. In the face of constant rebuffs of this nature the Labour Party leaders were forced to make retaliatory gestures. In the same month it was decided that Leon, in his capacity as chairman of the executive of the CRC, should refuse to appropriate the budget moneys. The Minister thereupon revoked his appointment and replaced him with Mrs A. Jansen, a government nominee.

Table 11.1 *Participation in CRC elections, 1969 and 1975*

	1969	1975
Estimated number of persons qualified to register as voters	802,500	900,000
Number of voters registered	637,587	521,357
Percentage of voters registered	79.5	58.0
Number of voters cast	300,666	251,631
Percentage of qualified persons participating	37.5	28.0

Source: SRR (1975, pp. 13–14).

Just as the Labour Party's defiance of the state consisted very largely of gestures, so its turn to 'the Black people of South Africa' was little more than a gesture towards the Black Consciousness movement. This proved no more fruitful than its gestures against the state. In April 1973 the youth organisation of the Labour Party had been allowed to become non-racial. This had been urged by youths who supported Black Consciousness. The Soweto uprising, however, put an end to any hopes the Labour Party leaders might have had of gaining mass support among the black population. Social divisions were deepened and the bureaucracy, even half-hearted bureaucrats such as the Labour Party leaders, found themselves even more isolated than before. The youth, as the Institute of Race Relations put it, 'tended to reject their elders in the Labour Party' (SRR, 1976, p. 15). Leon himself confirmed this: 'Already these kids are against anybody who works within the system. . . . The time will come when Coloured leaders will not be able to control their people' (*ibid.*). He appealed to the government to hold talks with coloured leaders who could use their influence to calm the situation.

This attitude reflects very clearly the concern of the bureaucrat faced with the threat of revolutionary upheaval. Like Buthelezi, Leon sees his function as that of 'controlling the people' at a time of struggle against the state. Like Buthelezi and Inkatha, the Labour Party leaders stood in a relationship of conflict with their people. Also in other respects the position of the Labour Party resembled that of Inkatha. The Labour Party, too, had embarked on a course of support for the liberal bourgeoisie. At the Labour Party conference of January 1976 Leon was given a free hand 'to continue his association with the Progressive Reform Party and to bring about a convention of all national leaders in South Africa' (*ibid.*, p. 14). In August 1976 the Labour Party called on the government 'to form immediately a coalition government of all white parties in . . . Parliament, to be followed by a multi-racial national convention'. This convention would have the task of formulating 'a new non-racial, democratic constitution for the country' (*ibid.*, p. 15).

Officials from the reserves were not the only 'moderate blacks' to whom the liberals built bridges. Another leading 'moderate' was Percy Qoboza, editor of the *World*, who leaped into prominence in December 1976 when he was held for questioning in a pre-dawn raid by the police. Liberals were outraged. Mr Qoboza, the *Rand Daily Mail* wrote in a leading article on 15 December, is 'undoubtedly one of the most important black men in South Africa today'. He was 'well-known and respected internationally', being 'outspoken but also outstandingly level-headed'. 'If moderate black leaders are treated in this manner,' the *Rand Daily Mail* demanded to know, 'what hopes can there be of Black men in general believing in peaceful solutions to the problems of our country?'

In an interview shortly before his arrest, Qoboza shed more light on the nature of his 'level-headedness'. 'That South Africa will be transformed,' he said, 'I have no doubt. The only thing that gives me sleepless nights is whether the change will come by evolution or by revolution' (*Star IAW*, 24 December 1976). Liberal employers in his view have a 'decisive' role to play. In respect of the Urban Foundation he put forward the following position (*ibid.*):

> There has been a lot of comment among our people about the motives of the business community – whether it is a reaction to fear generated by the happenings of June 16, or a practical demonstration that the social conscience of the business sector has at last been awakened. I don't care what the motives are, I see this as a positive step by the business community, who must of necessity develop a social conscience and responsibility towards the people who have kept the wheels of industry rolling, sometimes under the most appalling conditions. I welcome their involvement in this field. I believe they can play a decisive and admirable role in accelerating the pace of change and in influencing the Government to move faster than it has been doing.

Qoboza, too, supported the demand for a 'national convention of people representing all shades of opinion'. He shared the liberal attitude of deference to the state. The ball, he said, is 'entirely in Mr Vorster's court. He, more than anyone else, can decide how the change will come'. Also, towards liberals in the National Party, Qoboza was conciliatory. The National Party, he said (*ibid.*):

> rode on the back of the tiger of racism. And now, in trying to get off the tiger's back, it's obvious they are faced with the danger of being eaten up. If Mr Vorster is sincere in climbing off the back of that tiger, all he has to do is call to us, and I believe we still have the goodwill to help him get off without his necessarily ending up in the tiger's stomach.

The Prime Minister, as we know, was not yet ready at this stage to accept Mr Qoboza's offer. On 19 October 1977 Qoboza was among those arrested and the *World* was one of the newspapers that was banned. Overnight Qoboza achieved world fame. His reputation as an opponent of the state was enhanced immeasurably. In January 1978, while still in detention, he was honoured by the International Federation of Newspaper Publishers – an organisation, according to the *Star*, which is 'the voice of international newspaper proprietors, capitalists and businessmen who have the ear of premiers and presidents around the world' (23 January 1978). Upon his release in March 1978 Qoboza revealed that he had been well treated in detention and had not been interrogated. Together with certain other detainees he had been visited in prison by the Minister of Justice. Qoboza relates (*Star IAW*, 11 March 1978):

> He [the Minister] asked me if I would do anything to undermine law and order if I was released. I told him that in my entire life I had never done anything to undermine law and order. Then he asked me if I would do anything personally that would make other people break the law. I told him I had never done anything to encourage people to break the law. The ultimate solution to our country's problems . . . must be decided around the conference table.

Immediately on his release Qoboza was appointed editor of the *Post*, the most influential remaining newspaper aimed at the black community.

The growing rapport between black and white 'liberals' has not been confined to the level of abstract ideals. Agreements have been reached which in effect lay down the basic programme for a non-racial liberal party. Towards the end of 1973, for example, a conference on 'federalism' was convened by the liberal newspaper editor Donald Woods. Present at the conference were several reserve leaders, the Progressive Party and other liberal organisations. To this audience Chief Gatsha Buthelezi outlined his ideas for a 'Federal Union of Autonomous States of Southern Africa'. A further point in the programme of 'liberalism' was thus articulated. 'Federalism' is an alternative to the qualified franchise, a means of evading the prospect of mass rule in South Africa in much the same way that the government is doing, except that the formal trappings of racism are to be removed. The conference further confirmed the commitment of the 'liberal' reserve leaders to the capitalist system. Whites would be welcomed not only as people in the enlarged, consolidated 'homelands', Chief Mangope added subsequently, but also 'for the sake of their know-how and their capital' (SRR, 1974, p. 183). His fellow Bantustan leaders, Buthelezi and Phatudi, agreed.

In September 1975 an important meeting took place between the leaders of the PRP, the Kwazulu, Gazankulu, Lebowa and Quaqua reserves, the Labour Party and the South African Indian Council. A joint declaration was signed, once again calling for a national convention to decide on the future of South Africa. The full text read as follows (SRR, 1975, pp. 8-9):

> We, the leaders of organisations and statutory bodies which have been separated from one another by the laws of our country, declare that we will work together for peaceful change in South

Africa. Because we share a common ideal for our Fatherland, South Africa, and are in agreement on the fundamental issues relating to the future of our country, we have decided to create the necessary machinery in order to:

(i)   examine and articulate our agreement on these fundamental issues;

(ii) consult at regular intervals during the next year;

(iii) keep lines of communication open so that immediate consultation between us will take place if the circumstances render it necessary.

We realise that plans for the future of our country will have to be the outcome of frank discussion and exchange of views between representatives of the various sections of our wider South African community, and to be successful must have broad national assent. We accordingly declare our intention of working towards the holding of a convention as representative as possible of all who are South Africans, for the purpose of obtaining a mandate from the people for the constitutional and other proposals which will emanate from the initiative we have taken today.

We are agreed that apartheid or, as it is called, separate development, does not offer a solution and that any constitutional system must embody a Bill of Rights safeguarding the rights of both individuals and groups. We accept that in one united South Africa, territory and not race must form the basis of government which should not be racially exclusive.

A letter was sent to the Prime Minister urging him to call a national convention. The same leaders met again on several occasions. A recognisable political bloc, consisting of white and black 'liberals', was coming into existence. Its aims were reformist but largely unspecified. Its most concrete demand was the demand for a national convention.

In the final analysis the 'moderate blacks' and the 'liberal' wing of the reserve bureaucracy may thus be regarded as appendages of the 'liberal' bourgeoisie. Concretely their function is to popularise the ideas of liberalism among the black population. Demagogy and opportunism are indispensable methods in the performance of such a role. Merely to support the PFP would be politically suicidal. Some attempt must be made to link up with the growing radical currents among the people. Some criticism of state policy must be uttered, though this must remain within the limits of non-violence, constitutional reform and the ideology of capitalism. For all these reasons the liberals and moderates failed to win powerful mass support. Even prominent 'radicals' such as Leon and Buthelezi are widely regarded as 'government stooges' and are rejected. The middle-aged membership of Inkatha, the Labour Party's 'overwhelming' election victory in 1975 when it was supported by less than 15 per cent of the people qualified to vote – all this speaks volumes for their isolation from the mass movement of the 1970s.[1] It is fitting to leave the final word to a working-class supporter of the Labour Party who wrote the following in a letter to the press (*Die Burger*, 4 December 1976):

> The party is directionless . . . and also confused because of the double-talk by the leaders. One moment Mr Curry [deputy leader of the Labour Party] tells his supporters and his caucus to reject the Cabinet Council, and the next he apparently pleads with the caucus to accept it, because if Dr Bergins serves in the Cabinet Council he would be a big threat to the Labour Party, according to Mr Curry . . . . I have never heard such double-talk, let alone indecisiveness. First the Labour Party had to get rid of its leader at the time, Mr M. D. Arendse, because he was going to talk to the Prime Minister. Today the leaders are wearing out a trail (*loop 'n stofpad*) to the Prime Minister's office. Nominated members of the CRC were looked down upon and they were rejected by the Labour Party. Today Mr Curry welcomes them in his party. Management committees were an instrument of separate development and had to be rejected. Today the management committees are loaded with Labour members. . . . It is only government supporters who serve on the Executive of the CRC, it was said. The Labour Party will never serve on it because then we would sell out our people. Today four Labour members are on it . . . . The policy of the Labour Party is quite healthy but the party lacks sober and purposeful leadership.

Vacillation and contradiction, however, are inherent in the position of leaders that enforce an unpopular policy while at the same time appealing for popular support. The anti-government ideas of Inkatha and the Labour Party, as verbally proclaimed, and the strategy followed by their leaders, stand in irreconcilable opposition. Yet Inkatha and the Labour Party were the most radical organisations of their kind. Among the masses of the workers and youth the more conservative groupings were viewed with still greater suspicion or disdain.

Liberalism and the trade unions

The right wing of the black middle classes formed only one prong of the liberal assault on the workers. Other allies were found among the leadership of the trade unions, both registered and unregistered. Through these channels persistent attempts were made to turn the workers away from the struggle for power and confine them to reform within the framework of the capitalist system.

The attitude of the reserve bureaucracy towards the movement of the workers can be judged from the views of the 'radical' Buthelezi. In keeping with his general position Buthelezi denies the existence or at least the importance of class divisions within the African population (*Reality*, November 1975):

> The black struggle is not something that can be simplistically
> reduced to a struggle between patricians and plebeians, or between
> urbanites and peasants or between intellectuals and hoi-polloi. We
> have no such segmentations in our society except in theory, our
> colour levels us all up. . . . We have one struggle whether we are
> chiefs or commoners.

While liberal employers thus stress the importance of an African middle class, it is ironical that an important spokesman of this class should be at pains to deny its existence. Buthelezi's views, however, unmistakably reflect the right-wing middle-class position. On the question of trade unions he is at one with the capitalist class: 'Trade unions are not machinery for staging strikes, but for negotiation in order to avoid strikes' (*ibid*.). Similarly, Dladla, Kwazulu councillor for community affairs, supported trade-union rights for the citizens of Kwazulu within the framework of the existing registered unions.

The Durban strikes gave Buthelezi's Kwazulu government the opportunity to intervene directly in the African workers' struggle. In March 1973 strikers at the Alusaf refinery in Richards Bay called on the Kwazulu government to negotiate with their employers. Mr Dladla was delegated to perform this function. On behalf of the Kwazulu government he supported the workers in their demand for higher wages. Some very militant statements accompanied this intervention. Dladla advised the Alusaf strikers that if the situation forced them to go to jail, then they should do so. Chief Buthelezi deplored the fact that soldiers had been sent in to keep the aluminium smelter running, and hoped that the workers would 'continue to voice their feelings without fear' (IIE, 1974, p. 119). With the support of his government Dladla ordered that no more Zulus should be released to work at Alusaf until wages had been improved. From the workers' point of view this intervention, while encouraging and highly appreciated, took them little further. In the end they returned to work after accepting the increase of R2.00 per week which they had been offered at the outset.

The Soweto uprising presented the reserve bureaucracy with an even greater challenge to prove themselves in the struggle. Their general reaction was to call for 'an end to the rioting'. Chief Buthelezi suggested that a conference of leaders should be held to 'resolve the crisis' (SRR, 1976, p. 60). In the general strike of August 1976 Inkatha played the role of a strike-breaking force. Although its leaders may not have intended this to happen, Inkatha provided the police with ready forces to use against the students and workers of Soweto. The collaboration between policemen and members of Inkatha was no more than a reflection of the collaboration between the leaders of Inkatha and the state. In Durban the influence of Inkatha most likely played a major role in withholding the workers from following the example of Soweto.

There can thus be no doubt that the 'moderates' and the reserve leaders, in so far as they have any power over the urban working class, exert a conservative influence. Their influence, however, tends to be limited to those workers who are rurally orientated. Among urban workers in general interest in Bantustan politics is small. Liberals like Qoboza or Mkele, again, form a relatively isolated elite within the African population. In order to gain a real grip on the mass of African workers the ideas of liberalism would need a more effective vehicle. Of importance to the 'liberal' bourgeoisie, therefore, is the 'liberal' trade-union leadership.

The Progressive Party attitude towards African trade unionism was explained by Mrs Suzman in the aftermath of the Durban strikes (IIE, 1974, p. 111):

If the Honourable . . . Minister is worried about Africans using trade unions for political purposes, I want to point out that trade unions also prevent political disorder because the history of the world has surely shown over the years that political disorder largely follows economic grievances. If these can be prevented via orderly trade unionism and via orderly negotiations for wage rates and for conditions of work, the chances of political disorder are less. They are not greater as a result of trade unionism.

The TUCSA leadership has a similar point of view. 'The history of trade unionism throughout the world,' the general secretary of TUCSA wrote, 'has shown that if certain fundamental rights are denied to the workers, they will still establish their institutional forms to achieve these rights, despite any opposition towards granting them these rights. The Whites in South Africa did this after 1922, and the Blacks started again after 1973' (Coetzee, 1976, p. 186).

This explains why TUCSA decided in 1974 to allow the affiliation of African trade unions once again.[2] No importance was attached to the interests of the African workers or to the struggle for working-class unity. In no way did the leadership of TUCSA move against the pressure of the racist right wing in the registered trade unions. On the contrary, it merely moved with the tide. The growing strength of the African workers' movement, coupled with the growing weakness of the state, had completely undermined the position of the right wing. The changing balance of forces pushed not only the TUCSA leadership to the left, it affected the movement at every level. On the one hand, it remained a fact that free labour is non-economic in South Africa. Free workers live in constant fear of being made redundant. 'The rate for the job' merely remained a formula on paper. No attempt was made by the TUCSA leadership to solve the problem by this means. As long as the *existence* of 'cheap docile labour' was not challenged, but on the contrary taken for granted, racist attitudes among the free workers would inevitably persist.

On the other hand, doubts were arising even within the SACL as to the continued viability of the extreme right-wing position. In March 1975 the Federal Consultative Council of South African Railways and Harbours Staff Associations broke with the SACL. The reason was that 'In terms of its rules the FCC could not put matters on the Confederation Agenda unless all seven FCC unions agreed. The result was that some of the small conservative unions in the FCC were able to veto the introduction of issues such as African job advancement and worker representation' (SRR, 1975, pp. 208-9). In May 1976 the Footplate Staff Association, one of the railway unions previously affiliated to the SACL, joined with the (non-affiliated) Amalgamated Engineering Union to form a new trade-union co-ordinating body, the South African Central Labour Organisation (SACLO). A month later Grobler's own Artisan Staff Association broke with the SACL and joined SACLO. The membership of SACLO rose to 74,000 workers, while that of the SACL dropped to 173,000. The new co-ordinating body accepted that the growth of African trade unions was inevitable and that the existence of the urban black population could not be ignored. It wanted to maintain the living standards of white workers, but it also wanted to come to some *modus vivendi* with the African working class. Its membership, like that of TUCSA prior to 1974, was limited to registered trade unions.

Also within the ranks of TUCSA it appeared that support for the earlier position still existed. In September 1976 the 'mixed' Boiler-makers' Society (16,500 members) left TUCSA. Its secretary, Brouwer, declared that the union continued to support the recognition of African trade unions. The reason for leaving TUCSA was explained as follows (SRR, 1976, p. 316): 'We have thousands of Coloured and Asian workers whose jobs we have to protect. We can't do this at the same time as putting Africans into their union as proposed by TUCSA. We cannot allow African workers to move into their jobs.' The Boilermakers' Society decided to join SACLO. A 'coloured' union, the National Union of Furniture and Allied Workers, left TUCSA on similar grounds.

The reasoning adopted by these unions was similar to that of the SACL. Under *existing* conditions African workers can undercut non-Africans in the job market. A majority of African workers in a union could commit that union to accept lower wage rates and worse con-ditions of employment than the union at present commands. 'The rate for the job' is understood to mean a *lowering* of the wage rate to the level of migrant labour. TUCSA provided no convincing answers to these questions. In particular TUCSA was unable to show the workers how a rate for the job could be achieved that would draw up the wages of all workers to the level of free labour. A rate for the job in this sense requires a united stand by African and non-African workers. In a period of economic decline like the present it could only be achieved by the most uncompromising struggle.

The TUCSA leadership judged itself to be incapable of mounting a struggle of this nature. It confined itself to general statements of principle and intention. The result was an extremely contradictory situation in the registered trade-union movement. On the one hand, the dogmatic racism of the SACL was proving to be false. On the other hand, no answer was given by the 'liberal' leaders to the question of wage differentials that had nurtured racism to begin with. SACLO was the embodiment of this contradiction, subscribing to the racism of the SACL while at the same time retreating towards the liberalism of TUCSA. Until such time as 'the rate for the job' is developed into a concrete and viable strategy, it is difficult to see how the present fearful vacillation between the two horns of the dilemma can possibly be overcome: on the one hand, the effort to protect the existing standards of living on the basis of racism and capitalism; on the other

Liberal reaction

hand, the necessity of coming to terms with the giant of African labour.

If the TUCSA leadership put up only a formal and ineffectual alternative to the right wing of the registered trade-union movement, it adopted a hostile, conservative attitude towards everything on its left. The decision by the British Trades Union Council to give some support to SACTU evoked a furious reaction from the TUCSA leaders. SACTU, they declared, is no genuine workers' organisation. It has no official membership in South Africa, it is working abroad, and moreover it is a political instrument for introducing communism in South Africa. Even the banning of four trade-union officials in Natal in 1974 could evoke no positive action from the TUCSA leadership. It refused to send a representative to the protest meeting organised in Durban.[3] In 1976 the National Union of Motor Assembly and Rubber Workers expressed its serious doubts as to continued membership of TUCSA. Its general secretary, Sauls, stated that TUCSA was not doing enough to protect the interests of black workers and questioned the relevance of TUCSA in the existing situation. In 1979 Sauls would be among the founders of the Federation of South African Trade Unions (FOSATU), a new non-racial trade-union alliance.

The role of the TUCSA leadership can only be explained in the light of its relationship with the capitalist class. While isolated from the rank and file, the leadership showed great zeal in co-operating with employers. In December 1974 it devised a joint programme with the Institute for Personnel Management to train managers and workers in industrial relations. Managers and trade-union officials would 'sit together and study matters such as legislation, mutual problems and harmonious negotiation . . . . Mr Arthur Grobbelaar, general secretary of TUCSA, said that the mere fact that management was co-operating with labour in attempting to remove potential conflict showed that conflict could be avoided' (SRR, 1975, p. 207). In 1976, TUCSA assisted the capitalist class in setting up the Institute of Industrial Relations. The aim of the Institute is to avert industrial conflict by providing 'training' in industrial relations for workers and employers. Its guiding principle is that healthy industrial relations must recognise the existence of two parties, management and labour; conflict cannot be resolved by the unilateral action of either. The fact that South Africa was caught in the throes of a worsening economic recession, and that the demands of workers and employers were moving further and further apart, was ignored. Yet, 'recognising' two diverging standpoints does not provide a means of reconciling them; it is rather the prelude to deadlock or conflict. The fact that

390

the TUCSA leadership was determined to prevent all working-class struggle even under these conditions shows the gulf that separates it from the problems of the workers and the closeness of the ties that bind it to the capitalist class.

In keeping with this position was the attitude of the TUCSA leaders towards the struggles of the African working class. It was 'vital for industrial peace', said Steve Scheepers, vice-president of TUCSA, that African workers should be compensated for the rise in the cost of living. Also African unemployment, with its 'obvious threat of unrest' had to be 'avoided' (SRR, 1975, p. 208). This attitude, it may be noted, was shared by the SACL. Even the right wing now warned employers 'to maintain and supplement the buying power of Black wages or face labour unrest on a disturbing scale' (*ibid*., p. 209). Unfortunately, neither the TUCSA nor the SACL leaders – any more than the 'liberal' economists whom they were unconsciously echoing – told the government how, in a period of falling profits and production, these measures were to be carried out.

This is the general background against which TUCSA's efforts to organise African unions 'parallel' to registered unions should be seen. The hallmark of the 'parallel unions' is control by the officials of the registered unions. In the words of Grobbelaar, the running of the parallel unions, even after they have appointed their own staff and officials, 'should continue to be subject to the overall supervision of the registered union' (*FM*, 19 November 1976). Thus the parallel unions are characterised by manipulation and dubious practices. At least eleven parallel unions have been formed, though it appears that some of these exist on paper only. The largest parallel union, the National Union of Clothing Workers (23,000 members) provided a clear example. Not only major influence in the African trade-union movement but also financial advantage could be gained from controlling this union. A delegate of the NUCW to the TUCSA annual conference of 1976 declared that the union had been affiliated to TUCSA against the decision of its highest policy-making body. This decision, he said, had been unconstitutionally reversed by the executive. The pressure brought to bear on the NUCW executive by the leadership of the registered Garment Workers' Union to force it to affiliate to TUCSA had included the threat of eviction from its premises. Control over the NUCW on behalf of the TUCSA bureaucracy appears to be exercised by Senator A. Scheepers, once an activist of the GWU. During the executive elections of TUCSA, it was alleged, the general secretary of the NUCW 'runs to consult Senator Scheepers and then casts our votes'. Union members claim that Scheepers virtually vetoes NUCW decisions if she does not approve of them: 'She calls the executive in and lectures them like grade school children and then tells them to go back and reconsider. Usually they do' (*ibid*.).

These accusations are denied by Scheepers, though inadvertently the substance is conceded. The registered union still negotiates on behalf of the NUCW, despite a tutelage of some fifty years: 'To tell you the truth,' Senator Scheepers confesses, 'the African union's negotiation ability is still not up to standard' (*ibid*.).

Even stronger paternalism, if not downright contempt for the workers, is shown by Steve Scheepers, the TUCSA official 'responsible' for some other parallel unions. The nominal president of the African Leather Workers' Union, S. Lekeba, was reluctant to talk about the union: 'Please discuss it with Mr Scheepers.' Union 'members' deny having joined the union, though compulsory deductions are made from their wage packets. They say that no regular meetings take place, no shop stewards are elected and complaints are referred to coloured stewards of the registered trade union. Allegations of malpractice and intimidation of workers by union officials are rife. A number of union members interviewed had never heard of their supposed president, Lekeba.

Scheepers, predictably, denies everything and puts the blame for all problems on the workers' shoulders: 'Coloured shop stewards only take up complaints when Bantu shop stewards are too lazy to come in here, which happens often,' he says. 'But they're quickly here when their shop stewards' commission is paid out.' Scheepers is opposed to African workers being trained to negotiate on their own behalf. This, he said, could create racial friction. Therefore he personally negotiates on their behalf at industrial council meetings.

Another parallel 'union', the African Glass Workers' Union, is not even listed in TUCSA's trade-union directory. Scheepers insists, however, that the workers in this sector are organised: 'The Union existed in 1962 and I haven't dissolved it yet.' Asked for the name of the union's president, Scheepers claimed that he had 'retired' and added: 'I will have to get another one elected.' Another parallel 'union' is the African Tobacco Workers' Union. The secretary is supposed to be one Nicholas Hlongwane. Hlongwane, however, says that he is only an organiser and that the secretary of the registered union in fact 'runs' the parallel union. Independent African trade unionists, on the other hand, say that Hlongwane is only an office worker employed by the registered union. They say they have invited him to meetings 'but are always told he is busy making tea or fetching the post'. Hlongwane himself was afraid to discuss the union: 'We don't want to attract government attention. Please leave us alone' (*ibid.*).

From the standpoint of liberal strategy, therefore, the parallel unions have failed. This was shown by the TUCSA annual conference of 1976. Only five unregistered unions – those affiliated to TUCSA itself – were willing to attend the conference. Even the delegates of these unions were bitterly critical of TUCSA. They feared that TUCSA was not really prepared to support them. From the standpoint of working-class organisation, on the other hand, TUCSA's 'parallel-union' activities are totally destructive. The principle of working-class unity is being tarnished and compromised in the eyes of thousands of African trade unionists who have suffered manipulation and intimidation by registered union officials. Thus credence is lent to the idea that blacks should organise separately from whites. The *Financial Mail* dismisses 'parallelism' as 'paternalism', and warns (*ibid.*):

> The independent trade union movement is growing and it is
> unlikely that African workers will go along with parallelism much
> longer. The parallel union 'members' interviewed by the FM all
> expressed an eagerness to join a *bona fide* trade union. But they
> are suspicious of 'unions' in which they have no say.

The TUCSA leadership appears unable to comprehend this criticism. At the annual conference of 1975 it blamed an 'unnamed financial weekly' for 'conducting some sort of vendetta or campaign' against TUCSA. 'It is not known why such a campaign has been embarked on,' it was alleged, 'but quite possibly this is because the publication serves employer interests.' The point that the *Financial Mail* and the TUCSA leaders are serving the same 'employer interests' and that the TUCSA leadership is being criticised only for its ineptness appears to be lost on TUCSA. In this situation little confidence could be placed in the ability of the TUCSA leadership to control the African trade-union movement. Therefore, it was essential that liberals should be active in the independent African trade unions as well. Like the TUCSA bureaucracy their role is to supervise the African unions 'in order to ensure that they remain "responsible"' (*ibid.*). But they would do so in a less crude and more effective way.

The current liberal interest in the African trade unions was awakened by the upsurge of the African trade-union movement. 'By 1970, Black trade unions had almost disappeared,' M. A. du Toit records. 'The situation was dramatically changed by events, particularly the spate of strikes in Natal during 1973, and 20 Black trade unions, with a total membership of nearly 40,000, were in existence by July 1974' (1976, p. 165). The South African Institute of Race Relations compiled a list of twenty-four African trade unions in existence as at 31 August 1975 with a total membership of 59,440 (SRR, 1975, pp. 206-7). Of these unions – few of the parallel unions are included – seventeen were formed round about 1973. The new African unions were mainly centred upon two co-ordinating bodies. In Natal, the Trade Union Advisory and Co-ordinating Council organised the following independent unions:[4] National Union of Textile Workers, Metal and Allied Workers' Union, Chemical Workers' Industrial Union, Furniture and Timber Workers' Union, Transport and General Workers' Union. In Johannesburg, the Urban Training Project co-ordinated, on a looser basis, the following independent unions: Engineering and Allied Workers' Union, Transport and Allied Workers' Union, Sweet, Food and Allied Workers' Union, Laundry and Dry Cleaning Workers' Association, Building, Construction and Allied Workers' Union. In addition, the Urban Training Project (UTP) helped with the formation of two more African trade unions in 1975. These were the Commercial, Catering and Allied Workers' Union and the Glass and Allied Workers' Union. The UTP, as we shall see, is the principal body through which liberal influence is exerted in the African trade-union movement.[5] But it is by no means the only one.

The liberal foothold in the independent African trade unions was gained on the one hand through organised intervention, on the other hand through objective social processes that brought bourgeois elements into temporary contact with the workers. The upsurge of struggle among the black workers during the early 1970s brought with it the radicalisation of a section of students and intellectuals, white as well as black. Numbers of these were drawn towards the emerging organisations of black workers. Some learned to look at the problems of South Africa from the point of view of the workers and to place their skills at the disposal of the workers. Others failed to rise above the level of philanthropy. In this way a clear contradiction developed among radical intellectuals, between those attempting to steer the workers towards the spectre of orderly reform, and those striving for independent organisations that would struggle uncompromisingly for the interests of the workers. In this process, consciously or unconsciously, certain intellectuals were absorbed by the liberal camp.

The main conduit pipe of white intellectuals into the African workers' movement was the various 'service organisations' that were formed in the early 1970s. In general these organisations had strong connections with the liberal universities. A common aim was to educate and organise workers. They offered the African workers information as to their legal position and the functioning of the system of industrial relations, a complaints and advisory service, as well as certain material benefits. At the same time, they stimulated organisation in the factories and at trade-union level. The first organisation of this kind, the UTP, was started in 1971 and was formally constituted in 1973. It was followed in March 1973 by the Western Province Workers' Advice Bureau in Cape Town, in May 1973 by the Institute for Industrial Education in Durban, and in March 1974 by the Industrial Aid Society in Johannesburg.

White radicals in the trade-union field had little to do with their counterparts in the Black Consciousness movement. While in one sense the activities of black and white intellectuals were parallel, they were kept apart by the ideology of Black Consciousness. Ironically enough it was the white intellectuals who were able to approach the African workers more directly on the basis of working-class interests. The Black Consciousness movement, generally speaking, minimised these interests and approached black workers not as workers but as blacks. Black workers were to be incorporated into 'black' organisations, led and dominated by intellectuals, making little or no effort to fight for the specific demands of the workers. Such organisations could be no substitute for trade unions. Given its preoccupation with racial as opposed to class distinctions, the Black Consciousness movement left the field of working-class organisation almost entirely to others. The single ostensible trade union organised on the basis of black solidarity, BAWU, was a workers' organisation in name only.

Different tendencies developed in the methods and ideas of the 'service organisations'. The liberal tendency was most clearly embodied by the Urban Training Project. The UTP is described as 'a training institute for black trade union leaders' (CNV, 1977, p. 1). Its activities were said to be 'strictly a-political' (*ibid.*, p. 38). This, however, is incorrect; a definite political bias is shown by the UTP. The need for independent trade unions, for example, is explained in openly liberal terms by L. Douwes-Dekker, chairman of the UTP. Every negotiated settlement between workers and employers, he believes, must of necessity be less than the workers have demanded. Union leaders therefore have the function of persuading the workers to accept compromises. For this reason it is important that leaders should be elected, since workers will be less inclined to accept compromises when urged to do so by management. Applying these principles to the mining industry and the bloody suppression of worker unrest, Dekker pleads for a truce and for new institutions based on the alleged common interests of workers and employers. If no concession is made towards the sharing of decisions, he warns, the potential of revolution will become a reality (Coetzee, 1976, pp. 198–203).

These ideas do not differ from those of the PFP. Workers and employers, notwithstanding the enormous differences between their respective situations, are considered to be partners. Not struggle by the workers is needed but improved forms of communication with employers. Trade unions are not only the instrument for voicing workers' interests at the negotiating table, they have the no less important function of keeping the workers in check and suppressing demands that are unacceptable to employers. These ideas, the classical ideas of 'business unionism', are not being preached in the African trade-union movement by the UTP alone. It forms part of the broader debate on whether capitalism can meet the demands of the black population of South Africa. It is an argument that will finally be settled by practical experience alone. It will have to be proved to the workers that job security, freedom of movement and organisation and rising living standards can be gained by leaving it to union officials to bargain with employers. Should this strategy fail to produce the gains that are expected – and given the decline of the South African economy, it is difficult to see how failure can be avoided – militant struggle for all-out demands will increasingly stand forth as the only remaining alternative.

The 'liberal' bourgeoisie pursued its ends by different means. Certain basic demands were brought forward by the organisations of 'liberal' employers. The Progressive Party and its successors served as a political rallying-point for white liberals, translating the basic demands into a political strategy and programme. Sections of the African trade-union movement had been brought under liberal control, either directly or in the form of the 'parallel unions' organised by TUCSA. Finally and more tenuously at the present stage, bridges towards the 'black moderates' were busily being constructed in the shape of informal alliances with a number of black leaders. A full-blown 'liberal' party, representing all sections of the 'liberal' bourgeoisie and their followers, as yet belonged to the future.

The perspectives of the 'liberal' bourgeoisie in South Africa reflected those of the bourgeoisie abroad. This can be seen in the traditional orientation of South African liberals towards the Western governments, especially, since the decline of British imperialism, towards the USA. According to the columnist Gerald Shaw, 'South Africa's interests and America's' are at root identical. By this he means the following (*Cape Times*, 14 May 1977): '(1) The achievement of a peaceful transition to independence and majority rule in South-West Africa and Rhodesia; (2) The achievement of orderly change within South Africa itself.' The Carter administration, it is argued, is 'playing for big stakes in Africa'. It will not be a question of 'the Americans telling us how to run our internal affairs. It will be a question of the Americans telling us what kind of South Africa could be backed and supported as a respected member of the Western alliance.' The alternative is bleak: if the white population 'insists on retaining all the political power, there is no prospect of a lasting understanding with Washington. We would be on our own. And before long, we would be at war' (*ibid.*).

Drawing a balance-sheet of the prospects of the liberal opposition, Shaw remained moderately optimistic in the post-Soweto period. It must be acknowledged, he wrote, 'that the domestic situation is pretty bad – in terms of disturbed race relations and the state of the economy' (*Cape Times*, 6 November 1976). The burning of schools and business premises had caused a 'hardening of attitudes among some sections of the white community'. Another liability was the 'unhelpful response of the Nationalist Cabinet'. On the 'credit side', however, it is pointed out that 'the present generation of South African Black leaders are men who are prepared to negotiate'. This statement, it turns out, refers to 'the Buthelezis, the Mangopes, the Phatudis and their fellows' (who, it is admitted, have 'something of a credibility problem among young Blacks'). There are also 'many Whites, also, who prefer the path of negotiation to acquiescence in bloody violence' Despite the 'unhelpful response' of the government, it is said that 'our hopes must rest on a significant section of Nationalist Afrikaners coming to the realization that the maintenance of Afrikaner political hegemony is not essential for the survival of Afrikanerdom'. The 'strong and vigorous intellectual life' at Stellenbosch and Potchefstroom universities is seen as a hopeful sign (*ibid.*).

In this way the strategy of the 'liberal' bourgeoisie, as we have analysed it, is confirmed. The groping towards an alliance with 'Black leaders who are prepared to negotiate' and 'a significant section of Nationalist Afrikaners' is vividly described. The role of the unified party of liberals is explained as follows: 'There are peacemakers and creative spirits in all groups . . . . And it is on this group of people, ultimately, that our chances of staving off disaster will depend.' The role of these 'creative spirits' the writer immediately makes clear, must consist in the first place of exerting 'influence' on the existing government (*ibid.*).

These arguments illustrate, too, the fatal weakness of the 'liberal' movement in South Africa. The Shaws, the Suzmans, the Buthelezis and Qobozas have one decisive characteristic in common. All of them depend, in the final analysis, on the power of the state. The orderly change called for by the PFP, the non-violence preached by Buthelezi, Qoboza's devotion to law and order, all presuppose that the unfree masses must be disciplined by some force while racial discrimination is abolished in a 'peaceful' way. In so far as the present government cannot be conceived of as abolishing racial discrimination, it follows that the government must change the constitution in order to usher in a 'liberal' regime. The question immediately arises of why the government should take such a step, removing itself from power and threatening its supporters with ruin. 'Liberal' spokesmen tend to assume that the government will do so in response to pressure. What kind of pressure, however, would force the government to abdicate? As far as pressure from abroad is concerned, events have shown that political and economic sanctions will remain at the level of gestures for as long as South Africa remains a functioning component of the world capitalist system. More likely liberals have in mind the threat of revolution in South Africa itself when they speak of the pressure that would cause the government to dissolve itself into a national convention. The mass movement would have to advance to a point where the state is unable to maintain law and order by military force alone and needs new bases of support. It is only under these conditions that the Suzmans, the Buthelezis and Qobozas are likely to be offered power.

The role of the 'liberal' leaders is thus directly related to the struggle of the masses. This explains why, when mass struggle is at a low ebb, the forces of liberalism are mainly inert, whereas, conversely, during a period of mass struggle such as the 1970s the forces of liberalism are mobilised to keep pace with the approaching threat of revolution.

While superficially 'liberalism' and the mass movement may appear as alternative forms of opposition to the state, in reality they are opposites. In the final analysis the 'liberal' bourgeoisie is opposed not so much to the state but to the working class. This is not paradoxical in the least. The state is a capitalist state and 'liberalism' represents the ideas of the upper strata of the capitalist class. The difference between liberalism and the struggle of the masses is not one of 'degree';

it is absolute and irreconcilable. Liberalism finds its fulfilment in the preservation of the capitalist state, the mass movement in its abolition. It is an historical irony that liberal leaders can only rise to power on the crest of the mass movement, while at the same time their task is to fight this movement and suppress it. Their hour of greatest eminence is at the same time their hour of greatest peril.

South African 'liberalism' may be compared with a reserve army waiting behind government lines, nervously criticising the tactics of the front-line troops. It is in its interest to try and ensure that a break-through is averted. Its main tactic consists of appealing to the enemy forces to show moderation and restraint. It is unlikely that this tactic will succeed. Unless it is propped up by massive foreign intervention – and this is unlikely in the present situation – South African 'liberalism' is unlikely to survive for long the pressures of the mass movement by which it may be swept to power.

From the right-wing Nationalist point of view, liberalism is correctly identified as the prelude to disaster. This explains the apparently unreasoning hatred and suspicion with which even the mildest of liberal attitudes is looked at from this quarter. The lack of perspectives of capitalist policy in its traditional as well as its 'liberal' forms is symptomatic of the crisis of the capitalist system in South Africa during the present period.

Chapter 12

Organisation of the workers' movement

As the upheavals of the 1970s grew more violent, the lack of effective organisation among the mass of the workers and youth became increasingly evident. The contrast between the fiery determination of the masses and their lack of unified action was glaring. The limits of isolated skirmishing were reached with the school students' uprising of mid-1976. The state was geared to deal with struggles of this nature. The general strike of September 1976 represented a supreme exertion of the spontaneous and semi-spontaneous mass movement. To go beyond this point, national organisation would be needed, co-ordinating the activities of the workers and the youth in all the key centres of the country. The slogans and demands that were coming forward daily in the townships and the schools needed to be linked to a programme of struggle that would offer the masses a convincing perspective of social change. Only then could the workers be expected to submit to the demands of organised struggle for any length of time. At one level, therefore, the development of the mass movement in South Africa called for the development of *ideas*, of a conscious understanding of events, of the lessons of the past and the ways in which the demands of the movement could be realised. At the same time, it called for the development of *organisation* based on these ideas. Organisation lacking this conscious, systematic basis is ultimately doomed to disintegrate under the pressure of events.

The chief responsibility for organising the mass movement of the 1970s rested with the organisations that had historically gained influence among the masses. Amid efforts by the 'liberal' bourgeoisie to seize control of the mass movement, the future of the existing organisations depended on their ability to offer an alternative to liberalism. The slogan of 'armed struggle' was a clear reply to the

400

slogan of 'peaceful change'; but more than slogans was needed. On all the crucial issues with which the workers were faced, positions had to be taken up and convincingly explained. How to carry on armed struggle successfully, for example, had yet to be made clear against a background of past failure. The existing organisations, enjoying the attention of the workers, have the first opportunity of answering these questions. Future support, however, as opposed to support remaining from the past, will depend on the answers that are given. We must therefore examine the role played during the 1970s by the organisations that were orientated towards the masses.

The unregistered trade unions will not be considered in this context. Trade unions in South Africa are in no position to develop a revolutionary programme or to organise struggle on this basis. Even workers who see the need to organise often hesitate to join a union through fear of victimisation. In the minds of most workers effective struggle for social change is linked to illegality. Within the unregistered unions, under constant police surveillance and riddled with police informers, every step towards developing a more general programme of action is fraught with the greatest danger. Within the unregistered unions we cannot expect to find answers to the questions of programme and organisation with which the working class is faced. These questions can only be dealt with seriously at the level of secret or illegal organisation.

The Black Consciousness movement

During the 1970s the left wing of the Black Consciousness movement increasingly turned towards the masses. This led to growing conflict with the state and, in October 1977, to the prohibition of the organisations in which this development took place. At the same time, the ideas of Black Consciousness had little to offer the workers. Concentrating as they did on racial contradictions, these ideas lagged behind the degree of understanding that had already developed among the politically conscious workers. Many workers understood that the idea of struggle between black and white was an oversimplification. From the point of view of the workers' movement, the ideology of Black Consciousness represented no step forward but, rather, a step back. To the intellectuals involved in the Black Consciousness movement, on the other hand, these ideas were the start of an important development. They were brought face to face with the limitations of middle-class organisation in a situation where the black middle classes have no independent role to play. During and after the Soweto uprising the futility of continuing the struggle except by uniting with the workers became increasingly clear. In this process the implicit divergence between the left and right wings of the movement grew into an open division.

This development can be illustrated by comparing the Durban strikes of 1973 with the political general strikes of 1976. In the Durban strikes the Black Consciousness movement appears to have played no role whatsoever. The movement as a whole, even its left wing, appears to have had no perspective of working-class struggle and was caught unawares by the movement of the workers. By 1976 a peculiar amalgam between the ideas of Black Consciousness and an intuitive orientation towards the adult workers had emerged among the working-class youth of Soweto. On the one hand, the slogans of the Black Consciousness movement were repeated and student action showed some resemblance to the Black Consciousness tradition. On the other hand, the potential power of the working class was understood, and the school students consciously turned towards the workers.

The 1970s thus marked the radicalisation of the left wing of the movement. At the black universities in particular Black Consciousness caused an ongoing ferment. This gave rise to no coherent, mass-based movement and in itself presented no danger to the state; yet, from the police point of view, it amounted to a continuing irritant in an already unsettled situation. During 1974 this unrest became more serious. A confrontation developed in September when the executives of SASO and the BPC called public meetings in support of Frelimo. These meetings were prohibited, but in two cases – in Durban and at Turfloop – they nevertheless went ahead. At Currie's Fountain, Durban, the crowd of a few thousand people was surrounded by the police and attacked. At Turfloop also the police forcibly broke up the meeting. This led to further clashes and a mass picket of the local police station in October. Classes were boycotted and the university hall was occupied by students. The struggle resulted, as at the University of the Western Cape in 1973, in the appointment of a Commission of Inquiry to investigate the grievances of the students.

These events were followed by the arrest and detention of at least forty-seven Black Consciousness leaders. Thirty-three of these subsequently made statements to the police and were released. Of the remaining detainees, twelve were brought to trial in Pretoria at the end of January 1975. They were charged, in terms of the Terrorism Act, with conspiracy, with intent to endanger the maintenance of law and order, 'to transform the State by unconstitutional, revolutionary and/or violent means, to foster feelings of racial hatred and antipathy by Blacks towards the Whites and/or the State; to condition the Black population groups for violent revolution; to produce, publish or distribute subversive and anti-White utterances and publications; and to discourage foreign investment in the South African economy' (SRR, 1975, p. 60). In the case of some of the accused the charges were withdrawn or separate trials were ordered. The trial of the remaining nine was resumed in August 1975.

The trial of the 'SASO nine' became one of the longest in South African legal history. In January 1976 the state case was concluded. In November 1976 the case for the defence was closed. In December all nine of the accused were found guilty. As the *Star* pointed out in June 1976, 'there are no physical acts of terrorism or recruitment alleged in the 82 page indictment apart from charges of writings allegedly composed or distributed by the nine accused. Instead the charges relate to the September 1974 "Viva Frelimo" rallies, SASO and BPC documents and speeches and the theory of their Black Consciousness philosophy. . . . The trial has become recognised as the "Trial of Black Consciousness" rather than of the nine accused' (SRR, 1976, p. 181). The court found that neither SASO nor BPC 'had the characteristics of revolutionary groups' but were 'protest groups'. The accused were guilty, however, of 'conspiring to commit acts capable of endangering the maintenance of law and order, and thus contravening the Terrorism Act' (*Rand Daily Mail*, 16 December 1976).

If the trial of the 'SASO nine' made clear the commitment of many Black Consciousness militants to struggle against the existing social order, it also revealed their isolation at that stage from the mass of urban workers. At a time of widespread strikes and working-class unrest there were 'no physical acts of terrorism or recruitment', no involvement in the growing African trade-union movement, with which the State could charge them. There were only propagandist activities of the most general kind which could at most be marginal to the struggles that the workers were engaged in. The trial of the 'SASO nine' proved yet again that the state was not prepared to tolerate for long any organised opposition outside the framework of Parliament and the various bureaucratic institutions. At the same time, it showed the power of the spirit of revolt that was permeating every section of the black population, even its middle and upper layers, groping to find an effective means of expression.

Action against militants of every description increased as the economic and political crisis deepened. SASO was banned from the Turfloop campus in February 1975. The administrations of Gazankulu and Lebowa described the activities of SASO as 'unfortunate' (SRR, 1975, p. 264). More and more SASO activists were detained by the police. In the course of 1975 and 1976 the entire national executive of SASO was detained at one stage or another. In July 1976 the president, the vice-president and the general secretary of the BPC were detained.

Despite the increasing repression they encountered, the Black Consciousness militants persisted. The Soweto uprising of June 1976 and the events that followed involved them more closely in the struggle of the urban masses. Their influence was mainly exerted by means of two organisations, the South African Students' Movement (SASM) and the Black Parents' Association (BPA). The SASM has been described as a 'younger wing of SASO' organising the school students. At the same time, there are important social differences between black school students and black university students. The latter are drawn mainly from the upper and more affluent layers of the population. Among the school students, on the other hand, there is a much greater working-class element. This distinction may account very largely for the different mood and tactics of the school students compared with those of SASO.

The BPA was formed in the course of the struggle 'to help the victims of rioting and their families, and to try to substitute dialogue for violence and persuade pupils to return to their classes' (SRR, 1976, p. 26). The BPA was supported by the BPC, SASO, SASM, the YMCA YWCA, and the Housewives' League. Dr Manas Buthelezi became chairman. Another prominent member, Mkele, explained in graphic terms the relationship between the BPA and the school students of Soweto (*FM*, 3 September 1976): 'The students have confidence in the Black Parents' Association and are willing to talk through it . . . but they will sit behind us and tell us what to say.'

Little effort appears to have been made to organise the seething mass of workers in Soweto. BAWU appears to have played no role in the general strikes of August and September. Little can be said with any certainty about the influence of the ideas of Black Consciousness on the struggles of the youth and the workers in Soweto. Concretely, the ideas of Black Consciousness called for racial solidarity and uncompromising opposition to the state. Solidarity and uncompromising struggle, however, were equally called forth by the material situation itself. At the same time, social and political differences within the black population were sharpened, thus undermining the tendency towards solidarity based exclusively on race. While the exhortations of Black Consciousness militants undoubtedly encouraged the spontaneous movement of the youth, it is not clear what new perspectives, demands or direction they brought into the struggle.

The most important organ of struggle in Soweto was the Soweto Students' Representative Council. Again, apart from certain slogans, there was little about its actions that could be attributed to the ideas of Black Consciousness in particular. The demands that were raised and the tactics that were followed appear to have developed spontaneously in the heat of the battle itself. The ideas of Black Consciousness were undoubtedly a cohesive and motivating factor to the youth; yet these ideas had little to offer in the sense of strategy and tactics. Its major strategical premise, the unity of black people in opposition to white people, in practice proved to be false. Not only did the militant youth of Soweto encounter opposition among the black people, they also found support among whites both in South Africa and abroad. They were confronted with material interests that transcended racial barriers. Black Consciousness failed to explain these aspects of the struggle. Its strength lay not in its analysis of the events that were taking place, nor in its explanation of the course that should be followed. Its power was of a more transitory nature. It reflected the initial, spontaneous impressions among the youth of white domination and black suffering; it offered an added rationale for resistance. From this stage onwards its shortcomings were bound to become increasingly clear in practice.

More conservative sections of the African middle classes also subscribed, at least verbally, to the philosophy of Black Consciousness. Their numbers and social weight were insufficient, however, to determine the character of the movement as a whole. Essentially it was no more than the terminology of Black Consciousness that the left and the right wings of the movement had in common. The question of political dominance still had to be settled. Given the limited prospects of reform on a capitalist basis in South Africa, the conservatives were at a serious disadvantage.

To the capitalist class, an alliance was possible only with the right wing of the movement. The left wing stayed beyond their reach. Yet only the left wing had any real prospect of gaining mass support. The conservatives thus had a crucial role to play. Their function was to hold the radicals in check. The call for 'black solidarity' was the most effective means of doing so, of persuading revolutionary minded youth to adapt their pace to that of businessmen and preachers. This accounts for slogans of black advancement that are as vague as they are fiery. At the same time, the compromise could only be temporary. The two basic tendencies in the Black Consciousness movement were moving in opposite directions.

At the Black Renaissance Convention in December 1974 the conflict emerged into the open (SRR, 1975, p. 27):

> Homeland delegates were not generally welcomed. By majority vote, Blacks working within the separate development system were excluded from voting. 'Bantustans' were regarded as being tribally divisive. Delegates from the SA Students' Organisation (SASO) and the Black People's Convention (BPC) are stated to have interrupted proceedings continually and to have boycotted speeches by Dr Manas Buthelezi, Natal director of the Christian Institute, and Mrs Fatima Meer, a lecturer at the University of Natal. Father Smangaliso [Mkhatshwa, the organiser] told a Press reporter later that, strategically, the performance of SASO and BPC members had been a disaster. They alienated the more mature delegates, and arrogantly created the false impression that they were the sole custodians of the term Black. Nevertheless, they deserved admiration for the dogged determination that they brought to the convention.

The 'doctrinaire blacker-than-thouism' of the SASO and BPC spokesmen, Father Smangaliso Mkhatshwa warned, was 'a danger to Black solidarity and resurgence'. On the basis of the theory of Black Consciousness, this argument is unanswerable. In order to answer it the radicals needed to develop their analysis further. They needed to abandon the idea of a fundamentally united black people, welded together by common oppression, and to explain the nature of the political divisions that existed among blacks. By 1976 it appears that this stage was being reached. At the annual conference of SASO in June the outgoing president stated that the government 'was promoting the growth of an aspiring middle class amongst Blacks in order to preserve the *status quo* in the country'. Blacks, he said, 'should see their struggle not only in terms of colour interests, but also in terms of class interests' (SRR, 1976, p. 374).

Implicitly this is a rejection of the theory of Black Consciousness and the strategy of black solidarity. It implies a break with the purely middle-class elements professing the philosophy of Black Consciousness and a conscious turn towards the working class. There is no evidence, however, that the theory and practice of class struggle was explained systematically even among the radicals themselves. Still less does it appear that SASO assisted the workers to see their struggle in terms of class interests. The very phraseology of Black Consciousness could only obscure this insight. The ideological and political contradictions within the Black Consciousness movement remained very largely implicit. The old ideas had not yet been thoroughly criticised, and the new ideas were not yet fully understood, when the Soweto uprising broke out. The effect was to rule out any conscious choice among the masses between the divergent political directions that the Black Consciousness movement in reality represented.

By October 1977 the ambivalence of the movement had still not been resolved. This ambivalence was highlighted once again in the crisis sparked off by the death of Steve Biko. In September Biko – a founding member of SASO and honorary president of the BPC – had been detained by the police and killed. In the massive reaction following his death the different tendencies manifested themselves clearly. On the one hand, there was widespread concern and indignation among liberals both in South Africa and abroad. Influential liberals, such as the newspaper editor Woods, could claim Biko as a personal friend. His funeral, where the Bishop of Lesotho spoke, was attended by the diplomatic representatives of six Western states. Side by side with this reaction there was a response of a very different kind. Masses of young people travelled from Soweto, East London, and other centres to King William Town, where the funeral was held. They came in a spirit very different from that of the Western ambassadors or the Bishop of Lesotho. At the assembly point in Soweto, mourners had been attacked by the police 'for no apparent reason. Sjamboks were used. Shots were heard' (*Star IAW*, 26 September 1977). Along the route numerous road-blocks were encountered. Returning to East London, young people were involved in clashes with the police. Two policemen were stoned and killed. Vehicles were set on fire and buildings attacked. The contrast between the reactions to Steve Biko's death is significant and striking. It reflects, in the final analysis, the contrasting tendencies within the Black Consciousness movement itself, and their different orientation towards the outside world.

This crisis appeared to be the last straw as far as the state was concerned. On 19 October SASO, the BPC and SASM were declared illegal. Every other organisation that could conceivably further the ends of the radicals was likewise declared illegal. Included among these was the BPA, in which, as we have seen, students sat behind their elders and 'told them what to say'. The Black Allied Workers

Union (BAWU), the National African Federated Chambers of Commerce
(NAFCOC) and the Interdenominational African Ministers' Association
of South Africa (IDAMASA), on the other hand, were allowed to
continue in existence.

We have encountered the 'liberal' argument that declaring an organisation illegal is the least effective way of fighting it. Does this apply to
the Black Consciousness movement as well? It is submitted that it does
not. The strength of the left wing in the movement had lain very
largely in its ability to organise openly or semi-openly during a period
when little or no alternative existed for the masses. Even so they had
built up no organisation in the sense of a clearly defined programme,
strategy and tactics that was widely understood and accepted. They
remained essentially protest groups based among intellectuals. Their
links with the urban masses remained tenuous. The workers largely
remained onlookers to their struggle. After October 1977 SASO and
the BPC were no longer set aside from other aspiring mass organisations by the advantage of legality. As illegal organisations they have
no definite superiority over other illegal organisations. While a certain
continuity of action is to be expected, the main advantage of the
radical Black Consciousness organisations has been destroyed. Henceforth an underground Black Consciousness organisation can only exist
side by side with other illegal organisations on the basis of clear programmatical differences. In the absence of a working-class programme
and policy, the task of continuing the work of SASO or the BPC
underground can have little to recommend it to the urban masses. If
underground activity is to be engaged in, then turning to one of the
traditional organisations is a more logical step.

By the end of 1977, therefore, the opportunity of the Black Consciousness movement to become a mass organisation of the urban
working class had all but disappeared. From the workers' point of view
political organisation now meant a choice between underground organisation or joining a legal body linked to the state bureaucracy, such as
Inkatha. As far as the more experienced workers are concerned, the
the choice will not be difficult to make. Our task is to follow them in
this choice and examine the main alternatives that were available to
them once they had decided on underground organisation.

The South African Communist Party

Against the background of mass struggles the position of the SACP in the 1970s stood out more clearly than before. As an organisation it remained inactive throughout all the important battles that the workers fought. No evidence can be found of campaigns or activities developed by the SACP on the basis of its own demands or under its own colours. Members of the SACP appeared to work exclusively for the ANC and SACTU, and in no way distinguished themselves from the positions adopted by the leadership of these organisations. Thus there is little to judge the party on except its propaganda. This propaganda, presumably, reflects the ideas in which members of the party are educated. But even this, as we shall see, remained remarkably non-committal. It amounted to little more than opposition to apartheid and Western imperialism, and uncritical support for the ANC leadership.

In April 1977 the Central Committee of the SACP adopted a lengthy political report setting out the conclusions it had drawn from the events of the preceding period (*AC*, no. 3, 1977, pp. 21–50). In this document the contradictions contained in the programme of the SACP are repeated and compounded. The fundamental weakness of the party remains its confusion between race and class and its uncertainty as to the significance of class relationships. On the part of its opponents, the SACP has no difficulty in recognising theories which ignore the class basis of the world alignment of forces. It is able to distinguish between real liberation of the masses and 'liberation' of an elitist minority dependent on imperialist patronage, between revolutionary nationalism which leads to social emancipation and nationalism which serves a small class of exploiters. As to the class basis of the revolutionary nationalism which it espouses, however, the SACP remained ambiguous. The goals of revolutionary nationalism, as embodied by Frelimo and the MPLA, are described as (i) full economic independence, (ii) preventing the fruits of sacrifice being stolen by an indigenous exploiting class, and (iii) eventually achieving full emancipation within a framework of socialism. In relation to South Africa it is convincingly argued that the majority of the black middle classes can be won to the side of the mass movement. It is shown that these classes will benefit from the abolition of apartheid. It is emphatically repeated that the main content of the present phase of struggle is a so-called 'national democratic revolution' to destroy internal colonialism. 'Internal colonialism', we have seen, refers to racial oppression. No doubt is left: the struggle for socialism must not yet be launched in South Africa. Concretely, the SACP is calling for an alliance of the black workers, poor 'peasants' and the black middle classes in order to end apartheid.

What must be the nature of this alliance and the relationships within it? Precisely at this point, where clear and concrete guidelines are most needed, the SACP relapses into contradiction. On the one hand, it believes that the workers should be subordinated to an alliance of all classes. The SACP regards itself as the vanguard of the working class and the ANC as an organisation representing all classes of the black population. It is said to be in the best interests of the workers that the SACP should accept the leadership of the ANC. On the other hand, the SACP also says that the working class – hence, by implication, itself – should be dominant in the alliance of classes and supreme in the new state. There has thus been no improvement in the confusion of the SACP on the question of who should be leading whom since its programme of 1962. This fundamental ambiguity casts its shadow over all further conclusions that the SACP arrives at.

All the problems of the SACP are revealed in its contradictory position in respect of the ANC. On the one hand, it characterises the ANC as a movement of all classes and also the leading organisation of the South African revolution; on the other hand, it regards the working class as the leading force in the revolutionary alliance of classes. Either this means that the SACP must lead the revolution, or it means that the working class must be the leading force within the ANC; the ANC, in other words, should be a revolutionary proletarian party. The latter conclusion, however, would make it impossible for the SACP to present itself as vanguard of the working class. It would reduce its role to that of a fraction in the ANC, struggling to transform the ANC into a revolutionary proletarian organisation, drawing behind it other sections of the population whose interests run parallel to the interests of the workers. Neither of these alternatives is acceptable to the leaders of the SACP. In practice, a policy of uncritical support for the ANC has been followed. This policy, however, is contradicted rather than supported by the analysis of class relationships arrived at by the SACP itself.

At the *theoretical* level these contradictions arise from the attempt by the SACP to answer the question of leadership organisationally rather than politically. It starts from the existence of itself and the ANC, and ascribes a role to each. The result is a schema of organisational relations which is in conflict with the class relations that the SACP itself acknowledges in South African society. A political approach, on the other hand, must proceed from an analysis of class relationships, and define the roles of political organisations on this basis. From a working-class point of view the question is the following: how are the interests of the working class (as the leading force of the oppressed population) best served – by an alliance of classes in which the demands of the working class are paramount, or by an alliance of classes on a basis of parity, in which the demands of the workers are submerged in a programme of compromise with the demands of other classes? By a socialist organisation, or by an organisation pledged to postpone the socialist transformation of society?

As we have seen, the SACP reserves the socialist role for itself and ascribes a non-socialist function to the mass organisation. It attempts to evade the questions that this raises by dividing the revolution into stages. The working class, as leading force of the oppressed population, is expected to lead the struggle for non-socialist democracy and, having established this, to overthrow it once again in order to establish socialism. The 'first stage' must be led by the ANC, loyally supported by the SACP; the 'second stage' must be led, presumably, by the SACP, either in opposition to the ANC, or in coalition with an ANC that has, by some unspecified means, become 'socialist'. Significantly, the SACP states that it has no *immediate* political aims separate from those which it ascribes to the movement headed by the ANC. It is not explained what differences are anticipated beyond the immediate future.

The tasks that the SACP identifies in the post-Soweto period are consistent with its ambiguous position. The terms 'Marxist-Leninist' and 'revolutionary' are freely used, but as we have seen it is regarded as being Marxist-Leninist strategy to bring forward no concrete demands except those of the ANC (which are regarded as being non-socialist), and to offer no leadership to the working class at a time of massive working-class struggles. Significantly enough, in setting out the lessons it has learned from the Soweto struggle, this working-class party barely mentions the workers, except to declare that the black workers rallied to the call of *the youth*. The question immediately arises: what was the call of the SACP itself? Obviously, organisational goals in South Africa cannot be discussed in any detail. The general goals of the SACP, however, can be summarised as follows: maximum unity (between workers, youth, rural people, coloured people, Indians, Africans, women, radical whites and the black middle classes); strengthening of the armed struggle; strengthening of underground organisation; support from the international communist movement; the release of political prisoners. The purpose of all this activity, however, remains as ambiguous as ever. It is said that the movement is committed to destroying the framework of national oppression and also the foundations of economic inequality and exploitation. It is not clear what is meant by this. The destruction of economic exploitation would normally be taken to mean the destruction of capitalism and the building of socialist relations in its place. This, however, the SACP emphatically denies. It insists on the need for an intermediate stage of 'national democracy' in which, for an unspecified period, the state would delay the struggle for socialism until further unspecified conditions have matured. Fifteen years later, the confusion arising from its programme of 1962 had not yet been resolved. The absence of definite political perspectives is reflected in the slogans with which the report is concluded:

Long live the spirit of Soweto!
Long live our great South African Communist Party!
Long live the great African National Congress!
Long live liberation unity!
Long live proletarian internationalism!

If the SACP had failed to gain any greater clarity as to its programme and perspectives in the fifteen years following 1962, there were indications by the mid-1970s that a certain theoretical ferment was taking place among some party intellectuals. The discussion centred, not surprisingly, on the contradiction between the theory of class struggle of the SACP and its *de facto* nationalist position. We have seen that, by 1976, Slovo had relegated the theory of 'internal colonialism' to insignificance. In a series of articles in the *African Communist* the question is thrashed out at more length. Writer after writer returned to the question of 'nationalism' as if sensing the SACP's fundamental weakness on this question, attempting to develop an approach that could stand up to theoretical scrutiny and also, perhaps, lay the basis for a more consistent political position. On the other hand, none of the writers went so far as to challenge outright the ideas of the SACP leadership. Again and again they collided with the principal obstacle on the road to a consistent analysis of class struggle in South Africa, the theory of 'internal colonialism'. Attempts are made to circumvent this obstacle; no attempt is made to remove it. Thus the writers fail to make much progress in the direction of a clear and consistent analysis. In the end the articles amount to little more than a collective attempt at reconciling the ideas of the SACP leadership with Marxist theory, and possibly at persuading the leaders to shift to a position that can be more easily defended. If this was the intention, it appears to have ended in failure. The exiled leadership of the SACP was far removed from any form of rank-and-file control, from workers in factories demanding unambiguous answers to their questions. Judging from public statements by the party leadership at the end of 1977, it was decided to terminate the discussion.

The theory of 'internal colonialism' is defended by Molapo (*AC*, no. 3, 1976, pp. 82-93). His first task is to refute the idea that South Africa comprises a single state in which the mass of the people are struggling for equal democratic rights. According to Molapo, it is a struggle by the African people for their own (separate?) state power. Rather naively, he concedes that the great disadvantage of the 'one nation' thesis is that it obscures the alleged colonial nature of South African society. It is this flaw, he admits, that the 'two nations' thesis is deliberately intended to counter. It is, in other words, an attempt at evading the conclusion that the struggle in South Africa is a class struggle taking place within a single state. The advantage of the 'two nations' thesis, Molapo admits further, is to make the goals of national liberation struggle (as opposed to class struggle) more apparent. It amounts to support for the otherwise unsubstantiated programme of the 'national democratic state'.

The 'two nations' on which Molapo builds his case amount, in reality, to nothing more than the traditional 'white' and 'non-white' categories established by successive governments. In words, Molapo asserts the existence of class struggle in South Africa. In practice, the contradiction between the two racial categories is substituted for class struggle. At the same time, Molapo concedes that neither of the two 'nations' are nations in the fullest sense of the word. For this reason the 'two nations' thesis is said to need slight adjustment. What the nature of this adjustment might be Molapo does not mention. Similarly, it is conceded that the 'national class alliance' (giving rise to national struggle as opposed to class struggle) is possible only under certain circumstances. We are given to understand that these conditions are present in South Africa. What precisely they might be, however, is once again left unsaid.

Finally Molapo argues that the 'white national framework' has long ago performed its 'national democratic' tasks. Further democratic advance can only be achieved by the *African* South African nation. This entire line of reasoning, needless to say, is contradictory, garbled, and far removed from the Marxist analysis that it claims to be. Molapo's confusion as to the nature of the state is only one example of this. The idea of the state as a *racial* institution, of an 'African' state as opposed to a 'white' state, is fundamentally opposed to the Marxist theory of the state as a class institution. Molapo's essay, in short, assumes *a priori* the correctness of the theory of 'internal colonialism' and the

413

subordination of class struggle to the struggle between two nations in South Africa. He does nothing to place this theory on any firmer foundations; indeed, he exposes its weaknesses all the more clearly.

An attempt at correcting the grossest of Molapo's errors is made by Ngwanya (*AC*, no. 4, 1976, pp. 48–59). Ngwanya tacitly drops the 'two nations' thesis and defines the South African nation as the totality of all its people, black and white, who regard South Africa as their home-land. This nation has not yet emerged as a unity. It is kept divided by the system of apartheid. Ngwanya pays only lip-service to the theory of 'internal colonialism'. The coloniser and the colonised share the same country; at the same time, they form a single nation. It is the white ruling class, Ngwanya explains, that has imposed its will and ideas on the white group in general, and fears the unity of all the people. To Ngwanya, 'racial' and 'national' groups are synonymous. The South African nation is made up of different groups. In reality Ngwanya here strikes at the root of the 'internal colonialism' theory, by which the failure of the SACP to organise the workers as a class is justified. Having done so, however, he grows more cautious. The struggle of the African people (or group) as a whole, he now declares, is the driving-force of the South African revolution. At the same time, it forms part of the struggle against capitalism. Ngwanya thus relapses into the same ambiguity as the SACP programme. The solution of the racial question, he states, must involve placing the major means of production in public ownership. The revolution, however, must be a 'democratic' revolution. The vast majority of the black people, Ngwanya says, have been turned into working people. At the same time, he warns against any 'sectarian' development of the national liberation struggle. 'Sectarian' struggle in this context can only mean class struggle led by the working masses, as opposed to the 'national' struggle of workers dissolved into other 'objectively progressive elements'. Not only does the working class form the majority of the people, Ngwanya himself concedes, but the stronger its influence within the national movement, the stronger and more far-reaching will be the nature of the struggle. Yet non-sectarianism apparently consists of submerging this class struggle in a national struggle at the insistence, it seems, of a small minority of 'objectively progressive elements' who would be repelled by the open assertion of the demands of the working masses.

That this is a high price to pay for 'non-sectarianism' escapes Ngwanya's notice. At the same time, he questions implicitly the SACP theory of revolution in two stages. He concludes that the struggle will go on, even after liberation day. It is possible to interpret this as meaning that the revolution will not stop at the tasks of non-socialist 'national democracy' but will continue under the momentum of the aroused working class to finish off capitalism once and for all and place power in the hands of the workers. These questions are probed further by Langa (*AC*, no. 2, 1977, pp. 99–106). Langa recognises, on the one hand, the weakening of imperialism on a world scale and, on the other, the bourgeois nature of the states that have emerged in most of independent Africa. This 'neo-colonialism' he characterises as a defensive response to anti-imperialist struggle. Langa then identifies an analogous development in South Africa: the weakening of South African capitalism to a point where new forms of domination are required. Thus the theory of 'internal colonialism' is bypassed; Langa is free to address himself to the class contradictions involved. He identifies the need of capitalism in South Africa to increase the exploitation of the African working class, and to find new support in an alliance of the Bantustan administrators with the urban African petite-bourgeoisie. Under these circumstances, it is implicitly suggested, the notions contained in the programme of the SACP are no longer applicable. Langa refrains, however, from drawing any positive conclusions. Instead he ends by asking two questions. First, what political response is needed to the emergence of an African bourgeois and petit-bourgeois layer in opposition to the African masses? Second, do the *Freedom Charter* and the programme of the ANC adequately deal with this question, or should the primacy of the African working class be more accurately reflected?

It is possibly at this stage that the leadership of the SACP became alarmed at the course that the debate was taking. In an article that appeared at the beginning of 1978, apparently reflecting the leadership's point of view, issue is taken with the suggestion that the SACP is not revolutionary enough (*AC*, no. 1, 1978, pp. 19–31). As his adversaries the writer singles out a number of small left-wing groups in Britain and in particular the authors Callinicos and Rogers.[1] For present purposes, the criticism raised against their book as such is less important. More important are the ideas attributed to the authors against which the article is aimed. So dangerous are these ideas, according to the writer, that they would not only mislead but counter and disrupt the whole revolutionary movement in South Africa. As we shall see, these ideas are merely the logical answer to the questions that have been raised in the pages of the *African Communist* itself.

The focal point of the attack is the idea that the problems of South Africa can be solved by a revolutionary working class overthrowing the capitalist state and substituting for it a workers' state and a socialist system. This idea is reviled as being a straitjacket and a dogma. The main objections appear to be the following. First, if the proletariat is the only truly revolutionary class, it follows that other classes such as the petite-bourgeoisie are at best vacillating allies of the revolution and incapable of leading it. Second, the national struggle, in cutting across the lines of class struggle, would tend to obscure the real conflict. These conclusions are said to contradict the entire ideological basis of the SACP and also that of the South African revolutionary movement as a whole. Working-class theories of this nature, the author states, have been weeded out of South African thinking by decades of revolutionary experience. According to the author, the South African revolutionary movement is built on an opposite view, the view that the struggle for national liberation (led by the petite-bourgeoisie?) is truly revolutionary. This struggle is aimed at a transformation of society that would strike at the roots of South African capitalism.

The contrast that is drawn between 'working-class theories' and the theory of national liberation *in this sense* appears to be false. Striking at the roots of capitalism, on the face of it, is scarcely the 'opposite' of establishing a workers' state and building socialism. The contradiction can only lie in the meaning given by the SACP to 'striking at the roots of capitalism'. The programme of the SACP, it has been argued, fore-shadows a society in which the state will have the function of keeping the working class in check in order to prevent the transition from 'national democracy' to workers' (socialist) democracy. Fifteen years later, the idea of a socialist transformation of society except in the indefinite future is opposed with even greater vehemence. The reason for this can only lie in the importance that the SACP attaches to 'progressive' middle-class allies, who may not be called 'vacillating' or 'incapable of leading the revolution', but who appear to be bitterly hostile to socialism. It is significant that, in his eagerness to dismiss the possibility of working-class revolution in South Africa, the writer describes the working class as a *minority* of the black population that needs to win allies among the (unspecified) majority. According to the programme of the SACP, on the other hand, the workers had formed a majority of the African people as early as 1962. It is a profound lack of confidence in the power of the working class to lead the struggle, despite its formal assertion in the SACP programme, that finds ex-pression in these terms. This lack of confidence, perhaps, is the ultimate reason for the persistent search by the party leadership for progressive elements that will support the workers, on condition that the workers refrain from struggling for socialism.

A political position of this nature is obviously precarious and difficult to defend. The author accordingly devotes a considerable part of his energies to discrediting his opponents. Thus he attacks their sources of information, without, however, disputing the accuracy of the information itself. A remarkable diatribe is reserved for the authors Callinicos and Rogers. Their criticism of the SACP is depicted as an unwarranted intrusion by foreigners, from the sectarian ranks of British ultra-left Marxism, into the South African revolutionary movement. This intrusion, which the author likens to an explosive device being hurled into the movement's centre, is regarded as being deliberately subversive. It is seen as an attempt to sow divisions within a united movement or to undermine its leading cadres. What could be the motive for such a malicious attack? In criticising the SACP, the article concludes, the authors are allies of the US government.

Throughout most of the international labour movement, bald allegations of this nature would be regarded as scandalous and unjustifiable. At the end, somewhat lamely, the writer attempts to counter the impression of harsh intolerance that his outburst has created. He states that the SACP does not reject criticism provided it is well-meaning and responsible. The present criticism, however, is considered to be misguided and playing into the hands of the enemy. The present critics are unworthy in every sense. By this very profession of willingness to discuss, the writer shows a profound hostility to any genuine discussion of policy and programme. He stigmatises and dismisses the most obvious questions in advance as being counter-revolutionary and disruptive. The main taunts hurled at Callinicos and Rogers – their isolation, their insignificance, their lack of involvement in the South African revolution – are in themselves reasons for ignoring their criticism rather than becoming furious at it. Why should a SACP spokesman get angry at two unimportant critics, instead of ignoring them? The answer can only be that others in the South African revolutionary movement are tending towards similar 'working-class theories' which – as the article shows despite itself – cannot be refuted on the basis of Marxist theory or practice. The attack is aimed at the idea that the programme of the SACP is 'not revolutionary enough' and is holding back the revolution. The SACP is identified by the writer with the revolutionary movement as a whole. To question the ideas of the party leadership is to attack the unity of the entire movement. Under these conditions room for well-meaning and responsible criticism becomes limited indeed. To members of the SACP, who might have been inclined to take up Langa's questions, this article is clearly a warning.

Having sounded this warning, the writer is at pains to establish a basis for conciliation. The article begins and ends on a note of reasoned tolerance. The writer admits to shifts in the position of the party in the past[2] and holds out the possibility of further shifts in future. He speaks of a revolution to end colonial-style repression, which cannot succeed without expropriating the main heights of the economy, in which the working class is uniquely equipped to place itself at the head of all oppressed classes and groups. He sees this revolution as merely the first act in a continuing process of reconstructing the country on the basis of socialism. Here the writer expounds in essence the theory of permanent revolution. Presumably, left-wing members of the SACP are expected to be satisfied with this. Yet it is clear from what has gone before that the SACP expects the implementation of these perspectives to take the form of uncritical support for a 'non-socialist' ANC. Above all, the idea of a rapid transition to socialism, and the organisation of the workers on this basis, is totally rejected. The dispute, in reality, is no longer *whether* the transition to socialism will take the form of a single, continuous revolutionary process; it is shifted to the question of whether this process must be compressed into the shortest time span possible, or whether it has to be stretched out indefinitely.

The implications for the working class are clear. On the level of abstract propaganda, the SACP may speak of the working class placing itself at the head of all oppressed classes and groups. This bold perspective is far removed from the timid doubts to which the writer, by the logic of opposing the struggle for socialism and a workers' state, is eventually compelled to retreat: in fighting for class power, can the working-class 'minority' hope to win support from the 'majority' of the black population? In the final analysis, therefore, the SACP is a working-class party in name only. In terms of ideas and organisation it has nothing to offer the workers.

The African National Congress

The upsurge of mass struggle in South Africa made powerful demands on the ANC to give effective leadership. At this stage the ANC leaders had been in exile for nearly a generation. Among the masses in the factories and townships old experiences had long been digested and new conclusions drawn. The mass struggles of the 1970s took place independently of the ANC. This posed important and urgent questions to the exiled cadres. Among those who were not entirely committed to the theory of 'internal colonialism' the need could be seen for a clearer understanding of the struggle in South Africa and a more adequate response to the movement of the workers. Political development within the ANC was once again set into motion. At the same time, this development was inevitably affected by the distance between the leaders and the masses in the country whose day-to-day experience and awareness must determine all effective strategy. The ANC was influenced by the tactics and traditions that had grown up in the period of exile, by the reliance on diplomacy, alliances at state level and other forms of activity that are far removed from the struggles of the workers.

The separation between the exiled leaders and the masses in the country could be seen most clearly in the almost exclusive reliance that continued to be placed on the strategy of guerilla warfare. Preparations for guerilla war, combined with diplomatic activities, absorbed most of the energies of the ANC even while mass struggles swept the factories and streets. The tendency towards military struggle in the absence of working-class organisation was embodied most clearly by the SACP. The ANC, on the other hand, stood under ever-increasing pressure to develop a strategy and programme for co-ordinating the movement of the workers and the youth.

The conclusions drawn by the ANC leadership out of the first period of mass unrest were set forth by secretary-general Nzo in a speech reported in January 1975 (*Sechaba*, pp. 2–4). Apartheid is explained as a system of forced labour allocation and the means by which high growth rates are obtained. The theory of 'internal colonialism', as a peculiar system of social relations by which the tasks of the revolutionary movement are determined, is not found necessary to explain the situation in South Africa. The task of the liberation movement is defined as the dismantling of the state and its fundamental restructuring. As to the nature of the state, however, ambiguity persists. On the one hand, it is said that a white minority holds power. The white population is lumped together into a single ruling 'class'. The state, on this basis, must be regarded as a state of the 'white people' as a whole. In keeping with this view the white working class is considered a section of the enemy. On the other hand, the South African social system is regarded as a capitalist system. On this basis the state must be regarded as a capitalist state, and the ruling class cannot be defined in racial terms.

These two interpretations can only be reconciled if we regard South Africa as a complete historical anomaly, having as its leading feature a capitalist class existing in a capitalist system without holding ultimate state power in its hands. By regarding the state as an organ of the white people as a whole, Nzo is arguing that state power is shared between the capitalist class and other classes of the white community, including the white workers. This raises the question of how the white working class seized a portion of state power from the hands of the capitalist class and how they exercise that power. The only visible means by which the white workers can influence state policy is through their votes. It may be noted in passing that no party of labour exists. The party with the strongest electoral support among white workers, the National Party, does not pretend to be anything other than a capitalist party. Electing a number of capitalist politicians to Parliament, however, is a far cry from sharing state power. Parliamentary influence is thus mistaken for state power. According to this line of reasoning, revolution would be superfluous under conditions of bourgeois democracy. By gaining the right to vote and a certain standard of living workers join the 'ruling class', irrespective of all economic contradictions between them and the capitalist class. On this basis it would follow that the American state is not entirely a capitalist state because the workers share 'state power'. In capitalist countries where working-class parties form governments it might even be concluded that the state is no longer a capitalist state but has been transformed into a workers' state.

If this line of reasoning were consistently applied to South Africa, we would be left with the classical racial analysis of a struggle between racial blocs. Class analysis would be superfluous. If, in the case of whites, the conflicting interests of capital and labour can be accommodated, it would seem harmoniously, within a single state, there is no reason why this should not be possible in the case of blacks as well. There is no reason, on the face of it, why the white people's state should not be replaced by a state of the black people.

Nzo does not resolve these difficulties. However, the racial analysis is tacitly abandoned and it is the class analysis that is developed further. The character of the South African revolution, Nzo concludes, will be determined in the first place by the size, experience and consciousness of a black working class which is unique in Africa. A perspective of class is regarded as the vanguard force and the life-blood of the revolution. After 1973 other sections of the black population were seen as class is regarded as the vanguard force and the life-blood of the revolution. After 1973 other sections of the black population were seen as reinforcing the workers' movement; it was the black workers' strikes that shook the foundations of the economy and white rule. The youth were implicitly regarded as being mainly working-class youth; 'higher wages' was regarded as their primary demand.

These radical conclusions were strengthened by young militants who fled South Africa during the Soweto uprising and joined the ANC. According to Dlamini, former vice-president of SASO, the struggle is not really a racial struggle. People are more concerned about the socioeconomic structure. The ANC must provide an answer to this struggle. In contrast to Nzo, Dlamini regards white and black workers as fellow-workers employed by the same wealthy few. The higher wages paid to whites are a means of setting worker against worker, of making the white worker think that he is better than the black, and making the black worker hate the white instead of hating the exploiter. Class differences are recognised within the black population. Dlamini describes how one wealthy individual, Maponya, fled from Soweto during the uprising because he was afraid of the people. The people no longer identify their enemies by colour alone. They know who the enemy is, even if he has the same colour.

Within the ANC, the full implications of this analysis have yet to be made clear. If the working class constitutes the vanguard force of the revolution, it follows that the success of the struggle must depend first and foremost on the organisation of the workers, not merely in support of guerilla struggle but as vanguard force of the revolution. 'National liberation' means working-class revolution, and the reconstruction of the state must be based on the power of the organised working class.

The conclusion that the working class must be the vanguard force of the South African revolution thus has strategical as well as political implications. The ANC long ago concluded that the struggle for power can only be an armed struggle. As to the *form* that armed struggle must take in a struggle led and dominated by the urban working class, however, there is less clarity. With the Durban strikes and the Soweto uprising, with vast masses of workers and working-class youth spontaneously moving into action, this question became crucial. Yet the belief in guerilla warfare as basic strategy persists, without any definite analysis of the conditions for military operations and the prospects of military victory. This belief is encouraged by the SACP. On the other hand, the idea is emerging that an armed struggle led by the workers must depend on the political organisation of the working class. In the period since 1973 this idea has been increasingly juxtaposed to the idea of guerilla warfare. Thus in one and the same publication it is said that the youth must join *Umkhonto we sizwe* above all;

421

at the same time, it is said that the youth must organise in the factories, mines, townships, villages, schools and elsewhere (*Sechaba*, no. 3, 1976, p. 17). At a certain level of abstraction these tasks can be reconciled with one another. Through certain of its organs a movement may organise military struggle while through other organs it may organise the workers in the work-place. In this sense the task of young people would be to participate in all these different activities. Put in this general way, however, little clarity emerges as to the nature, perspectives and priorities of the struggle. Individuals or groups are presented with two alternatives: to leave the country and join *Umkhonto*, or to organise at home. Similarly, Nzo went no further in the speech already referred to. He said that political resistance does not have an exclusively armed nature and that many different forms of struggle are needed under South African conditions. The question of where to begin is not answered. What is actually a fundamental strategical question is left to each individual to work out for himself.

This ambivalence is present also in the ANC propaganda distributed underground in South Africa. In a leaflet published in December 1974 it is said that military struggle is only one side of the struggle. What the other side consists of is not mentioned. Workers, students and democrats are urged to meet secretly for the purpose of assisting the guerillas and doing unspecified political work – presumably calling on others to assist the guerillas as well. Implicitly, military struggle is regarded as being predominant. Not the working class but a guerilla army, it is suggested, will be the vanguard force of the revolution. In some underground publications by the ANC, on the other hand, more attention is paid to the political dimension of the struggle and less to the purely military aspect. In ANC leaflets distributed in March 1976 political preparation is given some emphasis. On the one hand, it is said that the people must be ready to answer the call of the ANC for armed guerilla action. On the other hand, it is said that the people must know for whom they are fighting. Secret political groups must be organised to study the goals and objectives of the struggle as outlined in the *Freedom Charter*. The following demands are raised: living wages; better working conditions; recognition of the independent black trade unions; rejection of the Bantustan system; free, compulsory and proper education; rejection of the pass laws and racial discrimination; and unconditional release of political prisoners.

Groups that are organised on the basis of these demands would have a clear orientation towards the working class. A second leaflet likewise refers to *Umkhonto we sizwe* as the armed spearhead of the struggle that will defeat the forces of the state. At the same time, 'everyone' is called on to become a 'freedom fighter'. Liberation cannot come unless the masses are involved in all forms of the struggle. Once again emphasis is placed on organising in the factories, townships, schools and elsewhere. In the ANC underground newsletter *Amandla* published in February 1976 no mention is made of guerilla struggle. The following organisational tasks are set out: build secret ANC cells to hold political discussions on the situation in the country and the ideas of the ANC; organise trade unions; organise protest meetings against the rising cost of living; speak out against Bantustans and Bantustan leaders; speak out against tribalism and racialism; preach the idea of a single, united South Africa; organise the youth against Bantu education; organise support for the People's Republics of Angola and Mozambique; oppose the war effort of the state; and organise units of the ANC wherever they do not exist. Activity along these lines means organisation among workers. The effect would be to mobilise workers and raise the perspective of a new society among them. Confusion is likely to arise, however, both as to the nature of this society and the form that the struggle as a whole must take. There is no clarity as to the ideas of the ANC around which workers must be organised. It is not explained why guerilla activities must take precedence over mass activities, or what are the prospects of *Umkhonto we sizwe* defeating the forces of the state.

One leaflet calls for the transfer of both political and economic power from the white racist minority to the black majority, and freedom and justice for all (*Sechaba*, no. 3, 1976, pp. 7–8). More explicitly, a leaflet distributed in July 1976 demanded sharing the country's wealth by taking over mines and monopoly industry for the benefit of the people. It called for sharing the land among those who work it, and power to the people (*Sechaba*, no. 1, 1977, p. 12). In itself, such propaganda does not provide sufficient theoretical basis for a workers' organisation that is capable of growth. It cannot take the place of a concrete programme based on the day-to-day experience of the workers. It does not explain enough about the aims of the struggle, or how to achieve these aims, for workers to develop a common sense of purpose. It cannot mobilise workers throughout the country as a coherent vanguard force. The nature and the aims of the struggle need to be discussed much more clearly before workers will be able to develop strategy and tactics corresponding to their own situation and yet forming part of a single concerted movement. To the workers themselves, these ideas are too vague to discuss on the shop floor except at the level of abstract speculation. Factory groups would be left in uncertainty as to whether they should send their members abroad for military training or whether they should organise towards specific tactical goals, for example common trade unions with coloured and Indian workers, equal pay for equal work, or token political strikes. These are only some of the urgent questions which face politically active workers. The pressure on the ANC to answer these questions, and to develop a programme of action for uniting the spontaneous struggles of the workers, may be expected to continue and increase.

Actions, however, speak louder than words. The activities of the ANC inside the country accompanying its propaganda can be expected to shed more light on its actual orientation. Being underground, these activities are largely unknown. Some idea as to their nature, however, can be gained from the trials of ANC activists that have taken place during the last few years. In dealing with this material proper caution should be observed. Court findings, not to mention charge sheets and the evidence of witnesses, cannot simply be taken at face-value. The records available at the time of writing are, moreover, extremely incomplete. Subject to this proviso, the impression emerges that the ANC in the mid-1970s was mainly engaged in distributing propaganda material, setting up cells for the purpose of recruiting guerilla fighters and engaging in acts of sabotage. These activities appear to have been resumed in the course of 1974. There is little evidence, on the other hand, of activity being organised on the basis of the working-class demands that are regularly raised in the propaganda.

The cases of persons charged with ANC activities can be divided into different categories. In a number of cases the main charge was the manufacture and distribution of illegal propaganda material.[3] In some of these cases the alleged activities by the accused were aimed at least partly at the workers. Thus Suttner was accused of inciting black workers to organise clandestinely in their factories. In the case of Mati, evidence was led that the accused brought ANC leaflets calling for a strike into the country and that these were distributed throughout South Africa.[4] For the rest, persons charged with ANC activities were almost exclusively charged with taking part in the organisation of military or sabotage operations. In a few cases individuals were charged with attempting to leave the country for the purpose of military training.[5] Other cases related to the possession of firearms or acts of sabotage.[6] Finally, in a large number of cases the accused were charged with recruiting people or taking them out of the country for the purpose of military training.[7]

Two especially outstanding trials of ANC supporters in the post-Soweto period have been the trial of the 'Pietermaritzburg ten' and that of the 'Pretoria twelve'. These cases related to major ANC networks and shed more light on the functioning of the ANC underground. In the case of the Pietermaritzburg ten the main charges were in connection with the establishment of an escape route for ANC recruits to Swaziland. Some forty-three people were said to have been recruited by the accused for military training abroad. According to a police witness, a detailed plan existed for landing trained revolutionaries on the coast, forming them into a sabotage force and overthrowing the government by force. The distribution of thousands of ANC leaflets by post was alleged. Other witnesses described how they had acted as couriers between some of the accused and contacts in Swaziland. A suitable place for crossing recruits into Swaziland was said to have been found. Various witnesses told how certain of the accused had attempted to form ANC cells or recruit them for military training. At least two trade-union organisers who had been involved with the accused were called to give evidence against them. One of these, H. Nxasana, said that in January 1974 he had heard of plans to revive the ANC by establishing three-man recruiting cells. Later in the year the message had been repeated, and it was added that SACTU should also be revived. Seven young men told how they had been taken across the border on 18 March 1976. They were told that they were going for military training. Thereupon they went to the Swaziland police. This was allegedly the second group of recruits that had been taken across the border. The third group, a week later, consisted of eight police decoys (including four white policemen with their faces blackened) who overpowered two of the accused, apparently on the Swaziland side of the border.

The defence case contradicted the state case in one important respect. According to the accused, the purpose of recruiting had been training in trade-union organisation and not military training. Gwala, a former SACTU organiser, testified that their recruiting was part of the revival of SACTU. Meyiwa, another of the accused, said that SACTU was still alive in the minds of African workers. He told the court that a network of twelve organisers was envisaged in Natal. Three of the other accused gave evidence of a similar nature.

The worst accusations, however, were levelled not at the accused but at the South African police. Witness after witness told how the police had extracted their evidence by torture and intimidation. Thus the state witness Nxasana was recalled by the defence to describe the torture that the police had inflicted on him during seventeen months of detention. He said that he could no longer separate his own evidence from that suggested to him by the police. Another state witness, F. Kunene, told how he had been forced to sign a statement that was written by the police. The torture inflicted on him had included whipping his fingers until all his fingernails were lost. When the police attempted to re-arrest him in the courtroom, the witness lay down on the floor and screamed that the police would kill him. The police subsequently charged him with perjury.

According to the magistrate who had visited the detainees in prison, two of them had complained of assault by the police. Since he had no power to investigate complaints, he had referred them to the station commander.

Nine of the accused were convicted on this evidence and five of them – Gwala, Nene, Meyiwa, Xaba and Mdlalose – were sentenced to life imprisonment. The judge remarked that these five men, who had previously served sentences on Robben Island, had shown themselves to be dedicated revolutionaries; he could see little or no prospect of 'reforming' them. The remaining accused were sentenced to terms of imprisonment ranging from seven to eighteen years.

The case of the Pretoria twelve has been described as the most important political trial in South Africa since Rivonia. The indictment consisted of seventy-nine charges relating to the establishment of an ANC underground network for recruiting persons, taking them out of the country and returning others together with arms and ammunition for purposes of sabotage. The trial opened on 10 May 1977. The main state witness, I. Rwaxa, said that he had recruited 260 people and made several trips with three of the accused to take them across the border. Under cross-examination, however, he said that he had been repeatedly assaulted by the police until he had made a confession dictated by the police and agreed to give false evidence. He asked the judge for an order protecting him from the police. This was refused. Numerous other state witnesses had similar experiences to relate. S. Legoro and T. Tseto had both been held for six months in solitary confinement before giving evidence. E. Tsimo had been held in solitary confinement since December 1976 and was tortured. A nephew of one of the accused had spent seven months in solitary confinement. A 14-year-old boy, who gave evidence of having been instructed in the use of firearms by one of the accused, had been held alone in the police cells for seven months. At least four state witnesses refused to testify. Three of these were jailed for six months each by the judge, Mr Justice Davidson.

Another state witness, N. Mosime, retracted his statement, which he said he had made after being assaulted by the police in Rustenburg police station. Yet another important state witness had been declared an habitual criminal. The remaining witnesses told how the accused had tried to recruit them for training abroad and spoke to them of sabotage. Evidence was given of stocks of prohibited literature of the ANC and the SACP being found, as well as firearms. At the close of the state case certain admissions by the accused were handed in. M. Sexwala admitted having left South Africa for purposes of training and being involved in an incident on 30 November 1976 when a hand grenade was exploded in a police Landrover. N. Tsiki admitted having left the country and taking part in a sabotage incident on the Pretoria–Pietersburg railway line in October 1976. Soon before the defence case was due to open the presiding judge died. At that stage the trial had lasted for nearly five months and 2,690 pages of evidence had been given. As a result, the accused were remanded in custody for a complete retrial beginning in January 1978. They had then been in custody for a year.

One object of the state in bringing political opponents to trial is undoubtedly to focus attention on the fact that these opponents had resorted to violent methods. From the state point of view such violence justifies the repression of political organisation among the black population in general. Even from the state point of view, however, the trials were having contradictory results. The effect was to focus attention not so much on violence by the accused as on violence used by the police against their helpless prisoners. In particular it was strongly suggested that the detention of state witnesses, supposedly for their own protection, in reality served to make possible unlimited intimidation by the police and the extraction of false declarations under torture. Solitary confinement and the prohibition of access to lawyers bear no visible relation to the protection of the witnesses from outside interference. It serves rather to prevent them from calling for help and places them under unbearable strain. The trials thus became increasingly embarrassing to the state. On the other hand, avoiding all trials in future and relying exclusively on detention by administrative order was likely to be even more embarrassing. This would be seen as an admission that political opponents are being arrested indiscriminately on the basis of mere suspicion.

These considerations appear to be the reason for a remarkable outburst by the Minister of Justice in May 1978 against what he called the 'deliberate undermining of our democratic legal system' (*Cape Times*, 13 May 1978). Such undermining consisted of 'delaying tactics in security cases, demonstrations in and near courts of law, intimidation of witnesses, the frequent appearance of certain advocates and lawyers in security proceedings, and the enormous sums of money that were available to defendants in these cases'. Most of these allegations were patently far-fetched, in particular the suggestion that detainees held incommunicado by the police, subject to indefinite solitary confinement, need yet further 'protection' against outside intimidation. The main thrust of the Minister's arguments appears to be aimed rather at the defence of accused by advocates who are not sufficiently concerned with protecting the state from embarrassment arising from the methods of the police. Obviously, the Minister cannot complain in so many words about advocates exposing torture by the police, next to which the alleged offences by the accused tend to pale into insignificance. Yet this seems to be what he is getting at: 'I am referring,' the Minister says, 'to those individuals who associate themselves with the case and aims of underminers to such an extent that it becomes questionable whether the trust vested in them as officials of the court is justified' (*ibid.*). During the parliamentary recess the Minister promised he would investigate these practices and determine what could be done to prevent them.

This emphasises yet again the irreconcilable nature of the conflict between the state and its opponents. From the state point of view it is purely and simply a question of destroying any means by which its opponents can resist, regardless of whether such means are legal or illegal. From the point of view of the workers' movement the task is thus reduced to that of organising a force superior to the forces of the state. In order to do so it is necessary to clarify the aims and methods of the struggle. Individuals or groups who are unclear as to these cannot be expected to function effectively in carrying out the work of the organisation. In the general demands of the *Freedom Charter* and the general slogan of armed struggle, the ANC has mapped out a course reflecting in general terms the struggle of the mass of workers. The task, therefore, is to concretise these general perspectives in such a way that individual activists will be able to make effective propaganda and put forward effective strategy and tactics in relation to the specific problems with which their fellow-workers are confronted every day. Only if the members are thoroughly versed in the concrete aims of the movement, in a consistent method of analysis and in the lessons of past experience, can they be expected to function as an organised body, playing a vital role in the daily struggles of the workers as opposed to simply carrying out instructions from above.

Towards the end of 1975 a simmering conflict within the leadership of the ANC broke into the open with the expulsion of the so-called 'group of eight'. This can be seen as a symptom of the ANC's movement away from the traditions of conservative nationalism and the strains arising from this. In an official ANC statement the 'group of eight' are described as racialist, 'ultra-black' and anti-communist (*Sechaba*, no. 2, 1976, pp. 40-3). They are accused moreover of disrupting the unity of the ANC. The occasion was not utilised, however, to make clear the political differences between the 'group of eight' and the remainder of the leadership. An important opportunity of educating the membership by contrasting the programme of the ANC with that of the 'group of eight' was missed. The ANC's own position remained ambiguous. This would be dramatically illustrated in November 1979 following reports of an amicable meeting between the ANC leadership and Chief Gatsha Buthelezi.

A more comprehensive statement was put out by the SACP in which the similarity was indicated between the ideas of the 'group of eight' and those of the PAC (*AC*, no. 2, 1976, pp. 22-4). The SACP criticises the concept of nationalism held by the 'group of eight', according to whom the South African struggle is no different from anti-colonial struggles in Africa, Asia or Latin America. In contrast, the SACP quotes the programme of the ANC to the effect that a large and well-developed working class is present in South Africa. Nationalism in South Africa, it is argued, cannot therefore mean the classical drive by an elitist group among the oppressed people to replace the foreign oppressor. The 'group of eight', according to the SACP, would like the ANC to retreat into vague patriotism, while in reality the course of the struggle has forced the ANC to reject and overcome this vagueness. For the rest the SACP concentrates on denying that non-Africans, and the SACP in particular, exert any undue influence within the ANC. It concludes by attacking 'wedge-driving' in general. Whatever the ideas of the 'group of eight', they stand condemned to the extent that they are different from those of the majority of leaders. Different ideas, it is suggested, must be enemy-inspired. Despite its greater length, therefore, the SACP statement goes little further than the terse ANC statement, and makes no attempt to explain the differences involved in any concrete terms. Against the ideas of the 'group of eight' the SACP has only its theory of 'national democratic revolution' to put, and this, as we have seen, is scarcely less ambiguous.

At the same time, the dispute raised the question of how the ideas of a revolutionary organisation are arrived at. The ANC states that it holds to the principle of democratic centralism. This principle implies that decisions are taken on the basis of the fullest possible discussion inside the organisation. Every member must have the opportunity of hearing all arguments on any given question and expressing his own views. Where necessary, organs of the organisation or even individual members must be able to publish their ideas and circulate these to the membership in general. Unless this process is allowed to take its course, the leadership, which carries the final responsibility for the correctness of every decision, will be unaware of what the members think. It will lack the benefit of proper consultation with the members and hence will be unable to take decisions corresponding to the mood of the organisation. Since it is the members that must carry out decisions, undemocratic procedures will weaken the organisation. Members will be confronted with decisions which they had no part in making, which they may or may not find correct. At the same time, centralism means that decisions, once taken, are binding on the members of the organisation. If it were otherwise, decisions would have no purpose. It is clear, however, that undemocratic decisions can be more disruptive under certain conditions than no decisions at all. If such decisions are enforced, resistance and divisions are created. If they are not enforced, they are reduced to empty formalities and the authority of the organisation is undermined. For the ANC, faced with the task of organising the mass of workers behind a programme that is generally supported and understood, putting the principle of democratic centralism into practice is therefore a vital task.

Given the nature of the South African state, there can be no question of open and general communication among the following of the ANC. Inevitably, a gap must exist between the leadership in exile and members in the country. This is clearly a problem by which the effectiveness of the organisation is reduced. In this situation the leadership is rendered all the more dependent on such forms of communication as do exist and on such discussion as can take place. Every nerve must be strained to link up with the mood, the problems and ideas of the workers in the townships; without this link the attempt at contributing to their struggle will be seriously weakened. On the other hand, there is the danger of adapting to the present situation, accepting the *de facto* isolation of the leadership and abandoning genuine democracy as being impracticable. Thus the statement that members have the right and duty to participate *at periodic intervals* in the review of work and the formulation of policy (*Sechaba*, no. 2, 1976, p. 43) is ambiguous. It might be taken as a reflection of the existing situation, or it might be

taken as a denial of the democratic-centralist principle that members
have the right to participate in formulating policy *at all times*. Similarly,
the National Executive Committee calls on members to regard an
attack on any of the leaders of the ANC as an attack on the organisation
itself (*Sechaba*, no. 1, 1977, p. 5). To insult the leadership, it is said,
is aimed at weakening the movement. Those who insult the leadership
are enemies. Taken at face-value, such a statement might mean a ban
on all criticism of the leadership. No distinction is drawn between
political criticism and insults or hostile attacks. Criticism, especially
criticism that is sharply formulated, may easily be regarded as insulting
by those at whom it is aimed. We are told, for example, that two
members of the 'group of eight' were suspended from NEC membership for six months in 1969. Even afterwards, it is said, they never
abandoned their subversive activities. The overwhelming majority of
ANC members, it is added, have been aware for almost a decade of
the activities of some members of the 'group of eight', of their arrogant
defiance of decisions and their clandestine attempts at discrediting the
organisation and its leadership. Under such conditions it would appear
to be not only the right but the responsibility of every member to
criticise the activities of the persons concerned, also - in fact, even
more so - if those persons belong to a leading body and are thus very
likely to damage the organisation with their mistakes. On the showing
of the leadership itself, strong criticism was justified against at least
two members of the NEC for a certain period of time. To have regarded
such criticism as the work of enemies, intent on weakening the movement by insulting the leadership, would clearly have been wrong. What
needs to be explained, side by side with warnings against disunity, is
the importance of criticism wherever it is needed, and of free discussion
to determine whether criticism is justified or not. Given the difficult
conditions under which the ANC must operate, the concrete question
is how internal discussion can be assisted and encouraged to take place
in the most effective way possible.

At the level of strategy, the meaning of 'armed struggle' continues
to remain unclear. Isolated acts of sabotage and the arming of small
groups of guerillas can be no more than a minor irritant to the state.
The central task arising out of the entire position of the ANC is an
armed uprising supported by the mass of workers in the key centres
of the country, and the political mobilisation that must precede any
decisive struggle. How to approach this task has yet to be concretely
explained. Even among young militants from Soweto who joined the
ANC 'armed struggle' appears to be understood as no more than an

alternative to non-violent methods. Yet in the final analysis the success or failure of the mass movement in South Africa will depend on the effectiveness with which armed insurrection is organised. This, in turn, will depend on the correctness of the analysis from which its aims and tactics are derived, and the extent to which these reflect the actual position of the workers who will form the backbone of the struggle.

The South African Congress of Trade Unions

Contrary to the tradition that political parties put forward political perspectives while trade unions confine themselves to economic questions, in the case of South Africa the clearest position on the nature of the social struggle has been developed within SACTU. Two general reasons can be found for this development. Since its formation SACTU has stood on the principle that the economic and political aspects of the workers' struggle in South Africa cannot be divorced. In addition, SACTU, unlike the ANC, is unambiguously an organisation of the working class. As such it is compelled to answer the question of what the role of the working class must be. On this question the constitution of SACTU took up the following position:

> The future of the people of South Africa is in the hands of its workers. Only the working class, in alliance with other progressive-minded sections of the community, can build a happy life for all South Africans, a life free from unemployment, insecurity and poverty, free from racial hatred and oppression, a life of vast opportunity for all people.

The Durban strikes and the struggles that followed recalled SACTU to renewed activity. An important development was the appearance in January 1977 of a two-monthly organ, *Workers' Unity*, aimed at the workers in South Africa. This marked a clear attempt to encourage working-class organisation on the basis of working-class interests. Developments in South Africa and the world were explained from a working-class point of view, revealing the relationship between the reality experienced by the workers and the capitalist system of which this reality forms part. The struggle in South Africa, SACTU concluded, is not against apartheid in itself but also against the whole system of class exploitation which underlies it. Apartheid serves the interests of the capitalist system in South Africa. The working class, growing in numbers and strength with every passing year, has become the driving-force of the approaching revolution. The power of the workers to stop production strikes at the root of the apartheid system. To carry the struggle forward, organisation of the workers is needed, especially at factory level. A strong network of organisation must be built up within and between the factories, secure from the police and capable of leading the workers forward with clear aims when the time arises. These are the general ideas with which SACTU approached the workers.

In July 1977 the following programme of demands was presented to all organisations of employers (*Workers' Unity*, July 1977):

1. Immediate recognition of the right of all workers to form and join trade unions of their own choice.
2. Abolition of the pass laws and the migratory labour system.
3. The unconditional right to strike for all workers in support of their demands.
4. A national minimum wage for all workers, regardless of race or sex, of R50 per week, indexed to inflation.
5. Abolition of all discrimination in the workplace on the grounds of sex or race, and an end to job reservation.
6. Free and compulsory education for all children, regardless of colour or creed, and extended training facilities for all workers; abolition of discrimination in education and training, including apprenticeships.
7. An eight-hour working day for all workers, with a total of 40 hours basic work per week.
8. No compulsory overtime work; a maximum of ten hours overtime per week; double rates for overtime during the week and two-and-a-half times the normal rate on weekends and public holidays.
9. Four weeks paid leave per year for every worker.
10. Twenty-one days sick leave per year with full pay for every worker, to be extended in cases of serious illness.
11. Full medical benefits for all workers and their families.
12. Unemployment pay and injury compensation for all workers at 100% of their current earnings.
13. The right for all workers to retire at 60 years of age on full pension.
14. The right for women workers to participate fully in all aspects of production, without discrimination.
15. Full political rights for all South Africans.

These demands, it was explained, represent only one step forward in the workers' struggle. The forces of the movement must be built by fighting for immediate improvements. In the process, however, the political consciousness of the workers must be raised. The aim of the workers' struggle is to make an end to the capitalist system. As outlined in the *Freedom Charter*, the mines, banks and monopoly industry must be taken into public ownership. The speaker who moved this demand at the Congress of the People in 1955 was quoted as saying that the workers will have to take over and run the factories, and the banks must be managed by a people's committee.

The strategy that SACTU advocates was explained more fully in September 1977. The struggle, it is said, is revolutionary. Every means, legal and illegal, must be used to build up the strength of the workers. For obvious reasons the foundations of the workers' movement in South Africa must be underground. The central aim at present is to strengthen these foundations. To this end groups of the most advanced workers must be secretly organised in every factory and area. The tasks of the groups are explained as follows (*Workers Unity*, September 1977): to discuss, explain and develop SACTU policy; to provide daily leadership to all the workers in the factories; to establish links with similar groups in other factories and areas; to maintain security against police informers; to draw in politically conscious workers, train them in the ideas and tasks of the workers' movement, and pass on to them the experience of the struggle; to guard against wrong influences spreading among the workers; to guide and influence the work of the open trade unions so that the errors of the leaders and officials can be corrected by the rank and file. An equally significant contribution by SACTU to the workers' struggle was its analysis of the economic crisis in South Africa and the perspective of working-class unity that this raises. In a policy statement published in January 1978 (*Looking Forward*), it is argued that the white workers, on the basis of job security, rising wages and the right to vote, have been used as political instruments for maintaining the capitalist system in South Africa. Their support has been bought out of the wealth that has flowed to employers and the state during the period of rapid industrial growth that has continued almost without interruption since the 1920s. The growth of industry, however, meant a massive growth of the African working class and at the same time an increasing dependence of the South African economy on the export of manufactured commodities. The world-wide recession of the mid-1970s, which led to the decline of world trade, thus brought South African capitalism into serious difficulties.

One result of the crisis has been a concerted effort by employers and the state to reduce wages and limit even further the limited trade-union rights that non-African workers, and white workers in particular, have enjoyed since 1924. Under these conditions, SACTU argued, the relationship between white workers and the ruling class will be seriously strained. This will threaten the entire social system with instability. At the same time, the government faces the need to make concessions to the black middle classes in order to win their support against the struggle of the workers. While these concessions are too little and too late, they are accompanied by attacks on the position of white workers. The government is thus assuming an increasingly dictatorial role not only in relation to the black population but also in relation to the white working class. More and more power is being concentrated in the hands of the executive, with the parliamentary influence of the white electorate being correspondingly diminished. Resistance by the white workers is becoming inevitable. Under prevailing conditions such resistance is likely to take on a right-wing character, at least for a certain period. Support for the crisis-ridden capitalist system, however, can offer them no lasting solution. The prevailing conditions are changing. Opposed to the deterioration of the capitalist economy stands the growing strength of the black workers' movement and its manifest ability to change society. What will be the nature of this movement and this change, seen from the white workers' point of view? SACTU calls for an orientation towards all workers, including white workers, on the basis of working-class interests and demands. Only on this basis is it possible that the confidence of sections of white workers could be won.

Workers' unity is thus seen as a *result* of the African workers' advance on the basis of a working-class programme, not as a *condition* for such advance. This conclusion was already foreshadowed by SACTU's constitution in 1955. It was also reached by the veteran trade-union leader, E. S. Sachs, who wrote the following in 1957 (p. 22):

Despite all difficulties, trade unionism among Africans is spreading and, when the 250,000 Africans who have had some contact with trade unionism become effectively organised, the division between Black and White in the trade union movement will largely disappear. Principle and morality are at a low level in South Africa, but power commands respect everywhere; and once the African workers have become strong, the European workers will seek their friendship and co-operation.

Any development of this nature will weaken the state even further. SACTU concludes that its efforts must be doubled and redoubled to build up the organisation which is needed to co-ordinate and lead the workers' struggle *in the places where the workers are*.

In these perspectives and demands the contradictions in the approach of the SACP and the ANC were resolved at the level of theory. The hesitation between class and racial analysis, between working-class and 'all-class' leadership of the struggle, is avoided. There is a consistent adherence to class analysis and to the conclusion that this leads to: the organisation of the working class, on a class basis, as vanguard force in the South African social struggle. What still remained was to put this conclusion into practice. The leadership of SACTU, like that of the ANC, finds itself in exile, and the special problems to which this gives rise have yet to be resolved. SACTU, no less than the ANC, owes the workers an answer to the question of what 'armed struggle' must mean if the forces of the state are to be defeated. SACTU had the inestimable advantage, however, of a consistent analysis and programme. The principle of *organisation in the places where the workers are* offers a basis on which further strategical conclusions can be reached. Groups of workers organised on this basis would be united by a common sense of purpose and a precise understanding of their role, without the confusion and divisions that arise from an unclear programme. Such political clarity and unity is essential in gaining the confidence of broader layers of workers. Building such groups, and gaining this confidence, was the task that SACTU had set itself.

By 1979, however, serious questions had arisen as to the course that the leadership of SACTU would follow. A document published in August 1979 (*The Workers' Movement and SACTU - a Struggle for Marxist Policies*) revealed that after a long struggle the editor of *Workers' Unity* had been removed and supporters of the position put forward in *Workers' Unity* had been excluded from further participation in discussion within SACTU. The authors of the document, identifying themselves with the position of *Workers' Unity*, conclude (pp. ii–iii):

> From the standpoint of the oppressed workers - the mass of the people of South Africa - it is possible to pose the basic issues of our liberation struggle in very stark and simple terms: Who will rule South Africa - the workers or the capitalists? Will our revolution against apartheid also bring an end to poverty and exploitation? Will our revolution be victorious like the Russian Revolution of October 1917, or will the workers be held back

from power and suffer a bloody defeat as in Spain in the 1930s
and Chile in 1973? . . . The political struggle in SACTU has boiled
down to this: Will SACTU be developed to play its part in
building a mass revolutionary working-class movement against
national oppression and capitalist exploitation? Regardless of
the outcome of this struggle in SACTU, the tasks remain for
every revolutionary to confront.

Workers' Unity appeared only twice in nine months following the
dismissal of its editor. Its main emphasis no longer fell on the issues
facing the workers in the country but on external solidarity work and
on support for the guerilla struggle.

In November 1979 there followed the *rapprochement* between the
leaders of the ANC and Gatsha Buthelezi – a move by the ANC leaders
that can only be interpreted as a move towards the right. Such a development was foreshadowed in the document mentioned above. It was
argued that the leadership of SACTU in the period of relative lull
following the Soweto struggles came under the sway of conservative
middle-class influences that were opposed to the independent movement of the workers. Action against a Marxist left wing is merely the
inevitable consequence of a turn towards the right.

For the section of the national liberation movement led by the
ANC, the 1970s thus ended on a deeply problematical note. A turn
towards the despised Buthelezi can only be explained by the absence
of other alternatives; little confidence, it would appear, was placed
in the outcome of the guerilla struggle or the mobilisation of the
masses. At the same time, any understanding with Buthelezi can only
be reached on a capitalist, anti-working-class basis.

From the point of view of the international capitalist class, Buthelezi
and Inkatha needed desperately to broaden their support beyond the
conservative, traditional-minded sections of the black population. An
alliance with a section of the ANC leadership is calculated, from this
point of view, to drive a wedge into the radical camp and win a certain
credibility among militant workers and youth. It would create a powerful bloc among the fragmented organisations of the black middle class
that might be able to struggle more effectively against left-wing and
Marxist tendencies among the workers than the state and the capitalist
class are capable of doing.

To the section of the working class looking towards the ANC and
SACTU for leadership, these events, while in one sense confusing and
demoralising, in another sense defined the tasks of the coming period

more clearly. It emphasised the seriousness with which the dangers posed by Buthelezi and Inkatha needed to be taken. It also emphasised the need for the greatest clarity as to programme and perspectives within the organisations of the workers themselves, to identify tendencies hostile to the workers' struggle and to find a way forward dictated by the interests of the masses.

Part IV

Conclusion

Part V

Conclusion

Chapter 13

Conclusion

This study has been concerned with the particular rather than the general. Specific aspects of the relationship between capital and labour have been dealt with in succession; much empirical detail has been included in order to present a concrete impression of South African society. In conclusion this approach needs to be reversed. The final task is to gain an understanding of the subject-matter *as a whole*. The processes that have been described must be abstracted from the level of conflicting events precisely in order to make them visible as processes and not as a series of incidents.

This study has proceeded from the standpoint that, essentially, wage labour is not individual but social in character. The performance of wage labour by one individual for another is part of the performance of social labour in general. The general conditions of social labour are socially determined. Every relationship between worker and employer is subject to conditions beyond the control of the parties to the contract of employment. Legal rules and collective bargaining are two important mechanisms by which social labour is regulated. Through these and other mechanisms the social nature of employment relations is unmistakably expressed.

Employment relations must therefore be studied from the standpoint of social relations as a whole. The individual employment relationship is a product, a reflection of social and historical developments. To understand his own position fully the individual worker (or employer) needs to understand the historical whole by which his function is determined and on which his existence as employer or worker depends. The study of economic and political conditions is not extraneous, it is essential to the study of industrial relations.

Notwithstanding its many peculiar features South African society is capitalist. European colonisation meant the imposition in South Africa of a capitalist market economy. Subsequent developments have taken place on the basis of this economy and subject to its laws. Nowhere is this made clearer than in the development of the labour market in South Africa. Farming, commerce, mining and industry were built on the foundations of the labour supply that European capital encountered in South Africa. Industrial capital did not develop gradually and organically out of agricultural surplus and commercial profit as in Europe. It was imported from Europe in the fully developed and concentrated form of finance capital. Its power was overwhelming. The Anglo-Boer War and the Union of 1910 merely set the political seal on the conquest of South Africa by finance capital. For an entire historical period the state identified its interests with those of finance capital, and British finance capital in particular. This state became the major instrument by which the interests of capital in South Africa were asserted.

Labour had largely been drawn from the defeated African peoples, who were in no position to bargain and were compelled to accept work on the terms on which it was offered. State policy has been aimed at preserving and perpetuating these relations between capital and labour. It has been aimed, essentially, at keeping the mass of the workers at the level of 'cheap docile labour'. On this basis the modern economy has been built. By means of the reserve system the working class has been fragmented, the employed have been separated from the unemployed, and the development of a stable urban proletariat has been held back, *but not prevented*. Rigorous forms of control have been needed to prevent the mass of workers from organising to throw off their disabilities. Channels by which the frustration and the energies of the unfree working class threatened to find political expression were sealed off. Even the upper layers of the black population were denied access to political power for fear of the role that the masses might thrust on them. The *class* oppression of the unfree mass of workers by capital took on the form of *racial* or *national* oppression by the state. Historically this system has served to repress every form of activity which might threaten the main pillar of capitalism in South Africa – the supply of 'cheap docile labour'.

This analysis is borne out by the development of state policy in South Africa. With the rise of industry and the growth of the urban working class *repression has been intensified*. The consistent refusal by the state to permit any change or reform by which its grip on the unfree workers might be threatened – a refusal that 'liberal' critics of the government treat as though it were mere 'stubbornness' – is fully in accordance with this analysis. And the history of appeals for reform by black and white 'liberals' alike – a history as long as it has been futile – tells its own unmistakable story.

Counterposed to the repression of the mass of workers is the relative freedom of a minority of workers, in particular the white, enfranchised workers. The result is a division of the working class into two camps, a division that the state has drawn in terms of race. As a policy, the maintenance of divisions in the working class is by no means unique to South Africa. In the Netherlands, for example, divisions between the social-democratic, Catholic and Protestant trade unions have been kept alive and used by employers during times of industrial unrest to disunite the workers. In South Africa, on the other hand, the division is not merely political or ideological. It has been given a *material* basis in the wage, political and social differentials that have been created or maintained. The line thus drawn through the working class is of vital importance to the survival of capitalism in South Africa. Economically the system depends on the fact that the mass of workers fall below the level of free labour. Politically, on the other hand, it depends precisely on the fact that a minority of workers fall above this level. On the basis of their relative advantage, the white workers have been reconciled to the system for an entire historical period.

Yet the relationship of white workers towards the capitalist class and the state is more contradictory than might appear at first. The tendency of market forces is to depress all wages to the lowest level at which labour-power can be bought. In South Africa 'economic' labour in this sense means unfree labour. Free labour must tend to be displaced; black workers must tend to replace white workers. The struggles by the white labour movement against this tendency met with historical defeat in the period 1907–22. Never for a moment did employers and the state lose command of the situation. The maintenance of the white workers' living standards thus cannot be explained simply in terms of the pressure exerted by the white working class itself. It must be explained first and foremost by the need of employers and the state to find a basis of support while carrying out their fundamental policy – the repression of the mass of workers. In return for their support, or at least their neutrality, non-African workers were offered limited trade-union rights, qualified job security and temporary exemption from attacks on their living standards. These benefits have been conferred in their fullest measure on white workers, thus creating the basis for a sense of racial exclusiveness and racialistic solidarity ('white nationalism'). This position has been legally enshrined since the period 1922–6.

The relationship between capital and white labour, however, while clothed in the trappings of nationalism, was essentially never more than an unstable compromise. The gap between the wage rates of free and unfree labour remained. This gap can only be maintained for as long as it serves the interests of the capitalist class and the state. At the same time, the existence of the wage gap is a source of fundamental insecurity to free labour. From the white workers' point of view the only solution lies in a policy of 'equal pay for equal work' *at the rates of free labour*. Although this demand has long existed on paper, the trade-union leadership has never attempted to enforce it. It is generally understood that employers will never consent to increase the wages of black workers to the level of free labour. For as long as employers have any control, 'equal pay for equal work' can only mean lowering white workers' wages to the level earned by blacks. Yet the idea of depriving employers of their power and enforcing a solution in the workers' interests is totally alien and repugnant to the leaders of the white workers in South Africa. Once this solution is excluded, protection on the basis of skin colour is the only remaining alternative. Yet such protection does not resolve the conflict of interest between capital and free labour. It merely perpetuates the conflict and postpones the confrontation. Under certain conditions employers will again be driven to terminate the 'status quo agreement', as the mining employers did in 1921. By the mid-1970s it appeared that these conditions were beginning to emerge.

South Africa has been severely affected by the world-wide economic recession. By the mid-1970s political and economic stability was something of the past. Increasingly the living standards of the white workers came under pressure. Free labour became a commodity which employers were less and less willing to afford. At the same time, the political support of the white working class was becoming inadequate from the point of view of employers and the state. The size and the militance of the black proletariat had reached dimensions where the traditional forms of domination had become inadequate. Increasingly it was felt that the black middle classes – or at least an influential section – had to be won to the side of the state as a means of holding the masses in check. This could only be achieved by relaxing the racist measures by which the black middle classes are at present alienated and embittered. Such a policy, however, would undermine the racial protection that the white working class and the white middle classes have grown accustomed to enjoy. It would reopen the wounds of 1922 and lead to renewed and bitter opposition. By the mid-1970s this perspective was beginning to emerge. Economically as well as politically, the basis for compromise between capital and white labour was beginning to wear thin.

This political dilemma reflected a division within the capitalist class itself.[1] The pressures of the 1970s had begun to undermine the 'national unity' of the owners of capital that had been so proudly symbolised by the Republic of 1961. During the post-Sharpeville years of sustained growth and increasing profits, co-operation and harmony could be maintained among the capitalist class. Sectional interests were largely submerged for as long as plentiful profits waited to be reaped. The onset of recession and dwindling markets, however, changed the situation. The law of the jungle began to reassert itself. Sectional differences re-emerged, and rapidly took on a political character. In particular, the ability of international finance capital and the national bourgeoisie to coexist peacefully in South Africa became strained. Out of their common lack of perspectives, conflicting political tendencies broke into the open.

As the wave of economic and political crisis mounted, international capital increasingly felt the need to follow a more 'liberal' policy in South Africa. The upper layers of the national bourgeoisie supported this demand. The lower strata, the small businessmen and farmers, on the other hand, felt themselves mortally threatened by any relaxation in the policy of national oppression. The basis for 'liberalism' in South Africa is the fact that many demands of the black middle classes can be accommodated within the capitalist system. Would such concessions, however, not prove to be the thin end of the wedge? Would it not lead the mass of workers to demand the same? Economically as well as politically, the spectre of reform spelled disaster to the white petite-bourgeoisie, whether in the form of wage increases, or in the form of competition from their black counterparts, who for so long had been banished to the fringes of economic activity. Strong opposition to liberalisation has therefore been mounted by the white middle classes. Inevitably it found a ready echo among white workers. Tensions thus developed between the state and its social basis. The parliamentary parties were divided. The United Party was torn apart. Inside the National Party, 'verligte' and 'verkrampte' tendencies emerged. Even the Progressive Federal Party, as it gathered new layers of support, started showing similar divisions between the avowed adherents of international capital and those who felt the need to compromise with the enfranchised masses.

The international bourgeoisie was thus placed in a dilemma. Should the South African state be allowed – in effect abandoned – to continue its traditional policies unchecked, despite the dangers this would mean to investment, trade and military interests? Or should a decisive change of policy take place, a break with the reactionary petite-bourgeoisie and an abandonment of the white working class as basis of support? Should everything be staked instead on an alliance with those 'moderate' black leaders who were likely to prove devoted servants of the capitalist class?

Thus far the world bourgeoisie, and with it the 'liberal' bourgeoisie in South Africa, have vacillated. They have made their reservations and intentions known, but have made no attempt to enforce them. They have no practical alternative to hand. Only when revolution is impending does it seem that international capital, by means of its 'liberal' agents, will be forced to make a decisive attempt at intervention. Buthelezi and Inkatha appear to have a crucial role in this, as rallying-point for the pro-capitalist right wing of the black middle classes. For the present, state policy can be expected to remain pragmatical, adapting itself to the conflicting pressures to which it is exposed. Limited concessions may be made to the black middle classes as an indication of things to come. But the repression of the mass of workers will undoubtedly continue. Tactical retreats will only take place within the framework of continuing mass oppression.

Yet sooner or later the contradictions of South African society will have to be resolved. The conflicts between different sections of the working class, between capital and free labour, between different layers of employers and, in the final analysis, between capital and labour in general, will subject South African society to strains that cannot be borne indefinitely. The fundamental question with which we are faced is therefore the question of how these conflicts are likely to be resolved. The most critical contradiction of South African society, it has been attempted to show, is that between capital and unfree labour. Around this relationship all other relationships revolve. The resolution of this conflict will create the conditions for the resolution of all other conflicts.

The precise outcome of the social struggles in South Africa cannot be foretold. The interplay between pressures and events is too complex to permit any absolute certainty as to what will happen. No supra-historical imperatives exist. Even the most careful analysis can turn out to be mistaken through the intervention of unknown or unforeseen factors. This, however, by no means implies a fatalistic attitude towards the future. An important function of social analysis is to try and grasp the nature of things to come. Yet every step in this direction should be duly qualified. It is a conditional prognosis and not a categorical assertion as to the course or courses that events are likely to take.

In preceding chapters different approaches have been noted to the question of how the conflict between capital and labour in South Africa is likely to be resolved. The 'liberal' approach in particular has been dealt with at some length. It has been attempted to show its fundamental weakness. 'Liberalism' presupposes the continued investment of capital in South Africa on a profitable basis. Indeed, it is aimed at creating conditions more profitable and more stable than at present by involving a section of the black middle classes in the administration of the system, and, in return, allowing it to share more fully in its profits.

The capitalist economy, however, continues to be based on the use of 'cheap docile labour'. 'Liberal' policy-makers conceive only of limited and partial reforms as far as the mass of workers are concerned. It is accepted that the existing instruments of social and political oppression cannot be entirely abolished but must be maintained at least in their essentials. To the mass of workers it is unlikely that policies of this nature would be acceptable. On the contrary, limited reform is likely to do no more than whet their appetite for change – a factor that the Nationalist government has been forced to take into account. A 'liberal' government would be likely to suffer the fate of all governments that offer too little and too late. It is likely to be swept aside by the very wave of popular pressure that it sets out to placate.

Would a *black* bourgeois regime be any more effective than a 'multi-racial' bourgeois regime after the model of Smith–Muzorewa in Rhodesia? Even a black regime, however, could not escape from the limitations to which capitalism in South Africa is subject. Oppressive policies and profitable production are inextricably woven together. Measures such as the pass laws which have been hated and opposed for generations do not become the more acceptable if passes are checked by black policemen instead of white, and a black civil servant is responsible for imprisoning offenders. Nor are black officials resented simply because of the fact that they collaborate with whites. It is the concrete forms of state policy, the specific measures imposed by black and white officialdom alike, that the mass of the workers suffer under and massively reject.

Certain questions thus arise to which a black bourgeois government in itself can offer no solution. Capital as such has no skin colour. Capital in South Africa leads a concrete existence. It is not a fictitious entity to which a different nature can be ascribed at will. If large-scale disinvestment is to be avoided, the present owners of capital in South Africa will demand to retain control or, at least, to be paid out in full the value of their investments. The black middle classes, to all intents and purposes, are incapable of expanding themselves into a national bourgeoisie that could take the place of the existing bourgeoisie in the productive process. Black managers could be scattered among white managers and black employers among white employers. Such a development, however, would have little effect on the condition of the masses. The nature of capital and the ownership of capital in South Africa are such that no attempt to make it 'black' is likely to be more than a transparent gesture.

The fundamental weakness of capitalism in South Africa is expressed in its dependence on 'cheap docile labour'. Without repressive measures this pillar cannot remain standing. 'Cheap docile labour' could only be dispensed with if capitalism in South Africa were to undergo an unimaginable transformation. Wages would have to be multiplied; profits and markets would have to expand astronomically; high walls of tariff protection would have to be built in order to eliminate foreign competition on the domestic market; at the same time, far greater access to foreign markets would have to be gained, even while producing at a far greater cost than before. These general conditions for capitalist democracy in South Africa contradict all laws of capitalist production. Even if the entire world economy were to be adapted in order to accommodate democratic reforms in South Africa, the very process of reform remains a vicious circle. Restructuring of the economy and massive capital injections are a basic condition for stability on a capitalist basis; but stability on a capitalist basis is equally a condition for massive capital investment. World capitalism has not yet resolved this impasse.

In practice, therefore, the precise meaning of 'black capitalism' is hazy. It may mean no more than the recruitment of black managers and employers out of the existing petite-bourgeoisie, as is already being done on a limited scale at present. The future of 'black capitalism' depends on the credibility and influence of this thin layer in relation to the mass of workers. The existing situation, however, can scarcely be reassuring to the proponents of 'black capitalism'. Over generations many black traders and professional people have built up a considerable store of mistrust and resentment among the working population. As money-lenders, creditors and employers they have established themselves as petty tyrants and exploiters in the eyes of many people. The attacks on black business property during the Soweto uprising are a significant reflection of this fact. Also politically, 'moderate blacks' have done much in the course of generations to destroy the credibility and prestige that they originally enjoyed. Even highly skilled moderates, such as Chief Gatsha Buthelezi, are contemptuously rejected by large sections of the black population, including most of the politically active youth. The conservative sections of the black middle classes, in short, are already compromised to a very large extent in the eyes of the very people whom they would be called on to control. How is it proposed to invest a black managerial class with political authority, other than authority depending on force of arms, hence on state repression essentially as at present?

In short, how is it proposed to prevent the black masses from continuing their struggle for complete emancipation? Even if a black pro-capitalist government were to be installed, the prospects remain fundamentally unchanged. For a limited period - perhaps no more than a few weeks - such a government might gain a breathing-space. The masses might wait and see if the government intends carrying out the changes that have been demanded for generations. They would wait with the keenest anticipation for the pass laws to be abolished, for the restrictions on organisation to be lifted, for differentials in wages and working conditions to be ended, for large-scale housing programmes and substantial wage increases that will raise their standard of living to that enjoyed by whites. When these improvements fail to materialise - as is almost inevitable in a period of political turbulence and world-wide economic decline - the disappointment and anger of the masses is likely to know no bounds. The same conflicts are likely to flare up as are taking place at present, but on a far more widespread scale, and a far greater level of intensity. How is 'black capitalism' supposed to make an end to this?

All these considerations suggest that no quick and easy way exists whereby the struggles of the black working class can be subdued indefinitely. The main conflict lies between the demands of the black workers on the one hand, and the structure of the existing society on the other. This conclusion as to the *nature* of the struggle, however, tells us little about its final outcome, and nothing about the course that developments in the foreseeable future may be expected to take. Certainly, as history has made clear, working-class victory is by no means inevitable in each and every struggle. Various conditions must be present before victory will be possible, let alone certain. In every struggle, victory and defeat are stark alternatives. To see the conflict between capital and labour in South Africa in its full perspective, it is necessary to consider the conditions for working-class victory on the one hand, and on the other hand the implications of working-class defeat.

'Chaos and anarchy' is often raised as a dire perspective for the future of South Africa. Such a perspective, however, is no less conditional than any other. Chaos and anarchy cannot develop as long as the present state retains its grip on society. Nor is chaos and anarchy possible if the bulk of the forces opposing the state are united around a single programme and succeed in gaining control of the country on the basis of this programme. Chaos is only conceivable if the existing state power breaks down but no coherent power emerges to complete the process and establish a new order. In such a situation, precisely because of the lack of an alternative, the capitalist state is likely to reconstitute itself and, sooner or later, reimpose the capitalist order. Counter-revolution would prevail, most likely involving bloodshed and repression on a scale that can scarcely be visualised at present. Popular resistance would have to be rooted out at a time when it is widespread; opponents of the capitalist order would have to be eliminated at a time when such opposition is rife. This, it has been seen in many counter-revolutionary situations, can mean the mass slaughter of working-class leaders and activists. This is the ultimate stage of chaos and anarchy that can be foreseen, before the peace of the grave is established, and the capitalist state is once again master of the situation.

In the conflict between capital and labour in South Africa counter-revolution is thus at all times a dread alternative to working-class success. Counter-revolution means the prolongation in one form or another of the existing social order. What remains to be considered are the conditions for a victory of the working class and the changes in the social structure that will be necessary if the demands of the workers are to prevail.

The crucial development in the present period has been the renewed movement of the masses. Economic decline has all but destroyed the basis for reform on any significant scale. Political upheaval, in particular since the Portuguese revolution of April 1974, has increased the strains and pressures to which South African society is subject. The Durban strikes of 1973 and the Soweto uprising of 1976 have been convulsive accelerations in a more general process of radicalisation among every layer of the black population.

A major question arising from these developments is the relationship between the struggle against apartheid and class struggle against the capitalist system. Apartheid is an integral part of capitalism in South Africa; the struggle against one aspect of this system cannot be separated from the struggle against the system as a whole. 'National oppression,' Legassick explains, 'is simply a *form* of social oppression, but a form which calls forth its own anti-thesis: "national liberation"' (1973, pp. 35-6). Above it has been attempted to show that the mass movement of the black people finds its driving-force in the demands and the power of the workers. The African population is predominantly a proletarian population; the struggle for national liberation is a struggle that the African workers, supported by sections of the middle classes and the rural population, must wage. The resolution of the conflict between capital and labour, and with it the national liberation of the African people, is thus in the final analysis a *single struggle* which hinges on the question of working-class organisation. On this question, above all, clarity is needed in the South African labour movement, a clarity that is being developed at present.

On a world scale the development of capitalism has meant the development of historical conflict between the classes of wage-earners and employers. Even during periods of economic boom the relative welfare of one section of the world proletariat has been accompanied by the destitution of another. Within capitalism every period of growth is but the prelude to decline. Wars and crises return, destroying much of what has been built up during the preceding period. Again and again situations arise where large numbers of workers become aware of the *inherent* nature of the conflict between themselves and their employers. Through organisation they discover their own nature as a class. They discover their central role in the productive process. They come to realise their own power to change society, to take charge of production and reorganise it on the basis of social need - a step that their employers are prevented from taking by the drive for profit and the pressures of competition. Again and again these ideas take root in the organisations of the working class. Again and again they stand forth as a hopeful alternative to the crises and inequality of capitalism. During periods of social crisis the struggle for and against these ideas can mount into a struggle for political power. The workers, potentially the rulers of modern society and potential builders of a new economic system, now face the task of realising this potential in practice. The organisations of the working class, having rallied the workers together in a long series of defensive struggles, now face the task of moving on to the offensive, against employers as a class and the capitalist system itself.

Many of those who would agree with this analysis in general, however, disagree when it comes to applying it in practice. Thus it is often argued that the theory and practice of working-class struggle cannot be applied in countries where the working class is small, and that this struggle can be taken to its conclusion in the advanced industrial countries alone. Also in these countries, however, other and more subtle reasons are advanced for postponing or abandoning the working-class struggle for socialism.[2] In the case of South Africa the SACP finds such a reason in racial oppression. The struggle against racial oppression, for 'national democracy', must be won *before* the struggle for socialism can begin. At the same time, it is conceded that racial discrimination (or 'internal colonialism') is a product of capitalism, and that racial discrimination cannot be attacked without striking at the roots of capitalism. The question is thus what is meant by 'striking at the roots of capitalism'. If the power of the capitalist class must be broken in order to make possible non-racial democracy, what will take its place? Who will have power in the post-revolutionary state – the working class as 'vanguard force' of the oppressed, or a coalition of the working class and organisations based on other classes? If the workers are the vanguard force, why do they need to share the power they have gained, and on what terms? What will be the relationship between the 'vanguard force' and other forces in the post-revolutionary state? If the problems of the working class under capitalism demand a socialist solution, what is to prevent the workers, having led the struggle against racialism and capitalism, from struggling to satisfy their demands in full, and carrying out the socialist transformation of society? If the forces bolstering South African capitalism have been defeated, who or what is to oppose the workers in this struggle?

These questions, all of which are begged by the equivocal position of the SACP, are vitally important to the workers of South Africa and the future of the labour movement. The SACP itself provides no open answer. To understand its position its programme must be examined carefully. On the one hand, it argues that socialism puts an end to the contradictions of capitalism by abolishing private ownership of the main means of production. At the same time it asserts, without further explanation, that in South Africa the struggle for socialism is not yet the order of the day. Although South Africa is a capitalist state, the SACP declares that the struggle must be aimed at 'national democracy', which is only a 'transitional phase' to socialism. The SACP is equally emphatic, however, that the workers and rural people must lead the struggle and stand at the head of the 'national democratic' state.

The contradiction between these ideas is highly significant and needs to be looked at more closely. A situation is described where the working class, supported by the rural masses, has become the dominant force in society. It has broken the power of the former ruling class. It is in the interest of the workers to carry through the complete transformation of society and advance to socialism by the shortest possible road. Yet, unaccountably, they fail to do so. The SACP asserts that they must postpone the completion of the revolution until an indefinite stage in the future. No indication is given of the conditions that would have to emerge before the workers may continue their advance. All that is clear is that the SACP believes that the struggle must be arrested at a certain point which is laid down in its programme.

The SACP regards itself as the vanguard party of the working class. The working class, in turn, is regarded as the leading force among the oppressed sections of the population. At the same time, the SACP subordinates itself and the working class to the leadership of the ANC. The ANC has its role no less definitely circumscribed: it is an alliance of all classes based on an 'all-class' programme. Thus the SACP, while claiming leadership of the leading force in society, at the same time defers to lesser social forces. It proposes to play a leading role *in name only*, while power is handed to other classes. In itself this makes clear that the SACP proposes to separate itself from the workers who must *in reality* form the vanguard of the struggle. On the other hand, however, the SACP expects the workers to follow its example and cease their forward movement at a certain stage. Yet the workers' very position impels them, as the SACP explains, to carry through the socialist transformation of society. How is the 'leadership' of the SACP to be maintained, and how can the leading force in society be restrained from accomplishing its task? Divisions among the workers are likely to exist; but the very defeat of the existing state presupposes a massive degree of unity built up in struggle. Goals will have been set; slogans will be current; a socialist understanding of the struggle will

Conclusion

be inculcated by socialists in the movement. In every struggle, as it develops, new horizons emerge out of rapidly changing conditions. As the struggle in South Africa unfolds it is likely that the *concrete* measures involved in the establishment of socialism will increasingly present themselves as immediate and urgent priorities in protecting the gains that have been made and furthering the interests of the people. The SACP cannot assume that mere verbal appeals will persuade the majority of workers to desist from carrying through these measures. In the final analysis, it has been argued, only the post-revolutionary state itself could be turned against the workers' movement if, under these conditions, their advance to socialism is to be prevented.

Even the state, however, is dependent on agents to carry out its will. Where would the post-revolutionary state find resources with which to subdue the very movement by which it has been placed in power? Which forces would be capable of restraining the leading force in society? Various possibilities exist on which the reasoning of the SACP might be based. The separation between the guerilla forces and the workers' movement has been noted. Would the guerillas be willing to serve as a counterweight to the workers and move to suppress their struggle? Even then, would they be capable of controlling a working class that is several million strong? The SACP appears to be less than confident of this. It acknowledges the working class struggling for socialism as the leading force in society. The forces capable of subduing the workers' movement would have to be sought externally. Foreign intervention would be needed to assist the 'national democratic state' in maintaining the non-socialist order. In this event 'national democracy' would amount to a state of military occupation.

These perspectives are in clear contradiction to the interests and the inner momentum of the workers' movement in South Africa. The goals that the movement will set itself must be of a very different nature. From the point of view of working-class organisation, the aim must be to establish a state that will serve as an organ of the mass movement in its advance to socialism by the straightest road possible, not as an organ for suppressing the movement. On this basis, what are the tasks of the workers' movement in South Africa?

To answer this question concretely would be to write the programme of the labour movement. On the one hand, such a programme is essential if clarity and purposeful organisation are to be achieved. On the other hand, a programme cannot be put together out of thin air. A programme capable of uniting the active sections of the working class must be based directly on the struggles in which the workers are involved and reflect the ideas of the workers themselves. It must explain the nature of these struggles and set out the measures that are needed to solve the problems by which the workers are confronted. Such a task falls beyond the scope of the present study. What needs to be attempted here is to identify the general conditions out of which the tasks of the workers' movement in South Africa emerge.

The ability of the workers' movement to transform society does not only depend on the numerical strength or weakness of the working class itself; it depends on the relationship of forces in society as a whole. In South Africa we need to consider, on the one hand, the strength of the working class in relation to other sections of the population. The concentration and cohesion of the urban proletariat, as well as its role in the key centres of production, place it in a uniquely powerful position. The middle classes and the rural population, in comparison, are diffuse and scattered. They play only a marginal role in the economic life of the country, while for their own part being largely dependent on industrial production. On the other hand, we need to consider the relative weakness of the capitalist class in South Africa, and its relative inability to develop the economy and meet the demands of the working population. This weakness arises from the nature of the world economy. Historically, the world market has been dominated by the bourgeoisie of the major industrial countries. For the rest of the world, there could be no existence on a capitalist basis except as colonies or appendages of the major industrial powers. Even in countries as enormous as India or as wealthy as South Africa, the national bourgeoisie has been unable to conquer enough of a market from their strong, established rivals to build prosperity at home.

Explicitly or implicitly, these general relationships are recognised by most of those who have seriously considered the matter. Legassick explains the implications (1973, p. 36):

'Self-determination', political independence [in the under-developed capitalist countries] does not remove national oppression and restore the 'interrupted' development of class struggle . . . *but does not even remove national oppression*. True self-determination is not in these conditions a bourgeois demand, for the bourgeoisie is not, on its own, 'national', as was that in Europe, but weak and tied to imperialism, concerned more with the interests of the trans-national bourgeoisie of which it is a minor part [than] with the 'nation' of which it finds itself a part. The consummation of nationhood, economically, culturally, and politically, falls

to others. In economic terms they must fulfil the tasks of
accumulation and socialization of production, in political terms
they must shape the institutions of the State, in cultural terms
they must create the national culture. . . . National Liberation
is not the prelude to, but the form of, social revolution.

The conclusion follows that significant social progress in a country
such as South Africa is impossible within the confines of the capitalist
economy. The working class is no isolated minority of the population
but the driving-force in the struggle for social change. The mass movement, even by gaining its *immediate* goals such as freedom of movement and full democratic rights, is likely to make the continued existence of capitalism in South Africa untenable. A vital question that
needs to be settled by the organisation of the South African working
class, therefore, is whether this struggle can possibly be arrested at the
stage of 'national democracy', in the manner demanded by the programme of the SACP, or whether it must continue, without interruption, until the power and control of the working people through their
elected organs, have been established over every social institution.

Above, reference has been made to the similar questions that
presented themselves in the Russian labour movement prior to 1917.
In concrete terms this debate could be reduced to the question of
whether the Russian revolution should have been arrested, for an
entire historical period, at the stage of the 'national democratic
revolution' of February 1917, or whether the workers' revolution of
October 1917 was justified and necessary. Trotsky's answer to this
question – given more than a decade in advance – is enlightening also
in relation to South Africa (1962 ed., pp. 57–62 *passim*):

Our liberal bourgeoisie comes forward as a counter-revolutionary
force even before the revolutionary climax. At each critical
moment, our intellectual democrats only demonstrate their
impotence. The peasantry as a whole represents an elemental
force in rebellion. It can be put at the service of the revolution
only by a force that takes state power into its hands. The
vanguard position of the working class in the revolution, the
direct connection established between it and the revolutionary
countryside, the attraction by which it brings the army under
its influence – all this impels it inevitably to power. The complete
victory of the revolution means the victory of the proletariat.
This in turn means the further uninterrupted character of the
revolution. . . . The very fact of the proletariat's representatives

entering the government, not as powerless hostages, but as the leading force, destroys the border line between maximum and minimum programme; that is to say, *it places collectivism on the order of the day*. . . . The proletariat, once having taken power, will fight for it to the very end. While one of the weapons in this struggle for the maintenance and consolidation of power will be agitation and organization, especially in the countryside, another will be a policy of collectivism. Collectivism will become not only the inevitable way forward from the position in which the party in power will find itself, but will also be a means of preserving this position with the support of the proletariat. . . . Our revolution, which is a bourgeois revolution with regard to the immediate tasks it grew out of, knows . . . of no bourgeois class capable of placing itself at the head of the popular masses by combining its own social weight and political experience with their revolutionary energy. The oppressed worker and peasant masses, left to their own resources, must take it upon themselves to create, in the hard school of implacable conflicts and cruel defeats, the necessary political and organizational preconditions for their triumph. No other road is open to them.

The differences between pre-revolutionary Russia and present-day South Africa are manifest. Above all the South African working class is much more powerful and developed, while the peasantry is insignificant. On the other hand, certain fundamental conditions are common to both situations. Capitalism exists in a relatively stunted form. The capitalist class cannot break through the limits on production imposed by the world market and is unable to develop society beyond a certain level. The masses of the people, however, are driven to advance beyond this level. Experience teaches them that their rulers are incapable of granting their demands. Their political consciousness increases, and their resolve to struggle grows. This increasingly forces the bourgeoisie to rely on dictatorial methods of rule to keep the masses in their place. In countries such as South Africa on the fringes of the Western industrial world, capitalist production implies authoritarian rule.

Only the organised labour movement has the power to defeat the state. In order to establish democracy the workers need to abolish capitalism and take charge of the basic means of production. This would consolidate their leadership of society as a whole. With these developments unfolding, abstract conceptions of 'stages' and a 'national democratic revolution' lose all significance and explanatory power.

Conclusion

Rather than following abstractions, the programme of the workers' movement should be guided by perspectives, by the concrete developments that can be foreseen. It should state in the clearest possible way the tasks that the mass of workers need to carry out in order to liberate themselves and thereby transform society. Without a programme of this nature, the workers' movement cannot rise to its task, and existing social relations will be permitted to continue.

In this sense the programme of the workers' movement is the key to the future of South Africa. It is the final and most concrete question arising from our study of the relationship between capital and labour in South Africa. If the national liberation struggle is the form that the struggle between capital and labour in South Africa has historically taken, then the programme of the national liberation struggle must essentially be a programme to mobilise the unfree working class. It must raise the demands that the workers will struggle for, and point out the forms of social change that will make possible the realisation of these demands.

The *Freedom Charter* contains the basic elements of such a programme. In addition to immediate democratic demands it calls for the nationalisation of the basic means of production as a means of returning the wealth of the country to the people. It also demands far-reaching democratic control, which is needed to ensure that the potential of the planned economy is realised. These measures cannot work miracles; but they *can* resolve the impasse that has been reached between workers and employers in South Africa and create new conditions under which further social development will be possible.

What remains to be clarified is the means by which this programme can be carried into practice. The idea of guerilla warfare has been dominant in the national liberation movement for nearly two decades. Guerilla warfare would undoubtedly put pressure on the state; it cannot, however, mobilise and direct the full power of the black population of South Africa, which is predominantly a population of urban workers and their families. To mobilise this power a strategy and a form of organisation based on the workers themselves will have to be developed. SACTU has already called for the formation of secret factory-based groups connected to one another and to the movement as a whole. What remains is to carry this perspective into practice and to organise groups of this nature into a national network. The question of armed struggle, in the sense of a struggle not confined to isolated groups but an insurrection of the masses, can be resolved only by an organisation of this truly democratic nature.

These general perspectives have been rendered a great deal more immediate by the struggles of recent years. The causes of the struggles have in no way been removed, nor is the South African state capable of removing them. All the elements are present for even greater conflicts in future. The workers' movement, which must always form the backbone of the mass movement, has gained a great deal of experience in the past few years. This experience, combined with the militance of the working-class youth, is the foundation on which the workers' organisations of the future will be built.

The more these perspectives take on flesh, the more frantic become the attempts by the capitalist class to divert the energies of the masses into less dangerous directions. The liberals' perennial call for a national convention is a pertinent example. Every plan of this nature, however, is utopian, in that it fails to come to grips with the basic cause of social conflict in South Africa: the dependence of capital on 'cheap docile labour'. This economic relationship inevitably calls forth political repression in one form or another. This is the crux of industrial relations as well as political relations in South Africa. No end to this struggle is conceivable that does not proceed from the complete liberation of the unfree working class. Such liberation, however, is beyond the capacity of capitalism in South Africa to sustain. Every plan for the stabilisation of capitalist society is in effect a proposal for continuing mass oppression in a different and (it is hoped) less explosive form. For this reason all 'reformism' must sooner or later meet with implacable rejection by the African working class.

In the coming years these contradictions are likely to come to a head. If the present situation of the black masses is intolerable, then economic recession is forcing employers and the state to make their burden greater still. The workers of South Africa will have to work harder in future in return for lower wages. Discipline in the form of police control will have to be intensified in order to make this possible. This is the practical meaning of the policy that employers in general, regardless of their attitude towards the black middle classes, are bent on as far as the working class is concerned. W. Pretorius, the general manager of Sanlam, was only stating a common attitude among employers when he declared (*FM*, 13 May 1977): 'Labour cost increases should be moderated. Workers should constantly be reminded of the need to temper standard-of-living expectations, and government should continue to clamp down on public service salaries.'

This is only the briefest outline of the emerging confrontation between capital and labour in South Africa. With every month the 'irresistible force' of economic crisis is grinding up harder against the 'immovable mass' of working-class resistance. The conflict will undoubtedly go through many stages. The struggle will ebb and flow, there will be temporary gains and setbacks on both sides. In the long run, however, even the staunchest supporter of capitalism in South Africa can scarcely believe that the country's beleaguered employers will prevail indefinitely against the forces that beset them from within and without, the inner sickness of economic crisis and the external pressure of a powerful working class that is being goaded beyond the limits of endurance. The coexistence of capital and labour in South Africa has entered a twilight period. In the struggles to come the capitalist class may grind itself to atoms and capitalists may disappear; but as long as industrial production continues, the workers will remain. Employers are totally dependent on their workers, who perform the labour and produce the profits by virtue of which employers as a class can exist. The workers, however, are dependent on their employers only while the latter are owners of the means of production. The process of social liberation outlined in the *Freedom Charter* would end this ownership. Only then would the struggle between capital and labour in South Africa be finally resolved. The words of the veteran trade unionist Bill Andrews, written in the aftermath of the crushing defeat inflicted on the white miners in 1922, are as fitting a conclusion to the present study as they were to the struggles of that time (Cope, n.d., p. 283):

> Writhing under the iron heel of a temporarily triumphant white
> terror, the workers may for a time lose heart, but sooner or
> later they will be forced by the very hopelessness of their
> position to again try conclusions with their taskmasters. With
> the experience which every attempt gives and the resultant
> improvement in organisation and discipline, there will come a
> time when success will crown their efforts. The workers only
> need to win once, and every check they receive in the colossal
> fight they are engaged in only serves as a further lesson, which
> when well learned brings them inevitably nearer to the day which
> at last shall emancipate them, and with them the whole human
> race.

Notes

1 The industrial revolution in South Africa

1 Although new names for these areas, such as 'Bantustans' or 'home-lands', have been coined from time to time, the original term 'reserve' is used here as it describes their essential function most accurately: they act as reserves of labour. Changes in terminology may obscure the fact that this function has never changed.

2 Some writers, such as van der Horst (1942, p. 300), believe that the 'contrary is surely the case. The reserves give their inhabitants *additional* bargaining power.' It was felt that the land in the reserves should give Africans an additional source of income. In other words, it was assumed that Africans with land, rather than those without land, are driven out in search of work. A more consistent view is referred to by van der Horst herself on pp. 200–1. See also F. Wilson, *Labour in the South African Gold Mines 1911–1969*, Cambridge, 1972, pp. 6–7; D. H. Houghton, 'Land Reform in the Bantu Areas and its Effect upon the Urban Labour Market, *South African Journal of Economics*, vol. 29, no. 3, September 1961, pp. 165–75.

3 In December 1975 and January 1976 African workers in the government-owned Post Office and on the railways were earning an average monthly wage of R89 and R78 respectively, compared with R115 in the manufacturing sector (*Financial Mail*, 4 June 1976).

4 Cited by Doxey (1961, p. 112). Du Toit considers the further possibility of guaranteeing 'a minimum existence for all' by means of a state subsidy but discovers the following objection: '[this approach] may harm capitalists principles and lean towards socialism, with the result that a larger percentage of the population will become work-shy' (M. A. du Toit, *South African Trade Unions*, Johannesburg, 1976, p. 105).

461

Notes to pages 38–66

2 Divisions in the working class

1 In the gold-mining industry, for example, the wages of white workers declined from 22.4 per cent of total revenue in 1946 to 19.4 per cent in 1969, while dividends over the same period increased from 13.2 to 19.2 per cent. The share of unfree labour dropped even more sharply from 13.5 to 8.8 per cent and taxes from 16.5 to 15.0 per cent (Wilson, 1972a, pp. 159–60).

2 See also D. Davis, 'African Trade Unions – Reformist or Revolutionary?', *African Communist*, no. 62, 3rd quarter, 1975. In the same vein Wilson suggests that 'exploitation' of the unfree miners is practised by the free miners; the mining companies merely find it 'profitable' to use the labour of the former (pp. 141–2). The IIE subscribes to this approach in both its pseudo-Marxist and purely impressionist forms (IIE, 1974, pp. 70, 152). Yet elsewhere in the same book a distinction *is* drawn between 'White manual workers' and 'the White middle classes' (p. 130). Confusion is thus complete.

3 Of the economically active population in 1970, 888,510 were included in these categories. Of these, 382,770 were employed in industry and transport (*South African Statistics*, 1974).

4 Hahlo (1969, p. 21). Africans in supervisory grades are in yet another position. They are more closely involved with management, and for this reason the labourers regard them as '"privileged" sell-outs' (*ibid.*, p. 30).

5 According to M. A. du Toit, it was the new coalition government that passed the Industrial Conciliation Act (1976, p. 14). In fact, it was passed some weeks before the Smuts government was dissolved. See *Government Gazette*, no. 1380, 31 March 1924; and *Government Gazette Extraordinary*, no. 1391, 9 May 1924.

6 For skilled African building workers the rates laid down in July 1973 ranged from 60c per hour (to be increased to 76c in accordance with increases in the consumer price index) in the case of the Cape Peninsula, down to 49c (62c) in respect of most rural areas (*Government Gazette*, no. 3977, 13 July 1973). For skilled non-African building workers, rates of 91c per hour for painters and 99½c for all other trades (subject to increase according to the consumer price index) were laid down in respect of the rural areas of the Western Cape at about the same time (*Government Gazette*, no. 3857, 13 April 1973).

7 By 1977, with the change of boom into slump, unemployment among white building artisans in the Transvaal had reached such proportions that the Department of Labour decided to withdraw all permits for blacks to do 'semi-artisan' work. As a result about 550 African workers were to be demoted or made redundant

(The *Star*, International Airmail Weekly, 12 February 1977).

3 Working-class organisation

1 *Report of the Transvaal Labour Commission*, 1904, Annex 1. By 'maximum average' wage is meant 'that the average daily wage for certain classes of Natives employed on piece-work was not to exceed [a given amount] per shift' (van der Horst, 1942, p. 193). The result is that 'if efficiency increases, wage-rates have to be cut' (*ibid.*, p. 209).
2 M. A. du Toit (1976, p. 116). From the fact that seventy-five trade-union officials had been listed under this Act by 1956, M. A. du Toit concludes that 'sufficient proof of communism in the unions had been found' (*ibid.*, p. 18).
3 G. M. E. Leistner, *Enkele Ekonomiese Aspekte van Bantoevolksver- huising en Trekarbeid in Suid-Afrika*, Pretoria 1968, p. 10. In the secondary and tertiary sectors, 64 per cent of the male African workers in the towns could be considered 'more or less settled' in 1960, and 36 per cent 'temporary' (*ibid.*, p. 9).
4 But not from membership of registered employers' organisations, thus making it clear that discrimination was aimed not against Africans as such but against Africans as workers.
5 The clearest evidence of the general situation will be found in the autobiography of Kadalie himself. Here, the comments that follow are justified many times over. One example will suffice. At an all-night session of the national council during the 1926 conference Kadalie relates, 'we pledged ourselves not to divulge [to Conference] the proceedings of our Council meeting'. The proceedings had been concerned with the transfer of the ICU headquarters from Cape Town to Johannesburg and the unconstitutional manoeuvrings of certain officials (Kadalie, 1970, p. 83).
6 In his autobiography Kadalie gives some semblance of consistency to his career by omitting all reference to his second leftward swing and his attempt to join the League Against Imperialism. He presents himself as a consistent anti-communist from the mid-1920s onwards who had harboured no pro-Soviet feelings at any stage of his career. At the same time, he glosses lightly over incidents such as his opposition to the pass-burning campaign of 1930 and makes no attempt to account for his Bloemfontein speech (see Kadalie, 1970, p. 202).

4 Legal regulation

1 'Prescribed area' means any area outside the 'Bantu areas' declared by the Minister, in terms of section 9 *bis*, to be a prescribed area. In practice, it refers to *urban* areas.

5 Political organisation

1 This is, of course, incorrect. The point is precisely that *not* all blacks are workers.

2 Limitations on time and space unfortunately preclude a full discussion of the history and ideas of the Unity Movement of South Africa. Essentially, however, the criticism developed below of the position of the South African Communist Party may be extended to the Unity Movement also. While several different political positions are put forward in the name of the Unity Movement, it is interesting to note that an extensive critique of the ANC by a veteran Unity Movement writer is concentrated entirely on the question of strategy and tactics ('collaboration' versus 'non-collaboration'), while the *political* content of the traditional ANC approach is nowhere seriously questioned. It is taken for granted that the aim of the struggle is 'the full franchise and full democratic rights'. See N. Makanda, *ANC – A History of Reformism*, Workers' Press, London, 23–27 January 1970. For a defence of this position, see UMSA, *The Revolutionary Road for South Africa*, Lusaka, 1969.

3 The UMSA, like SACTU, was never formally prohibited. In May 1950, in reaction to the Suppression of Communism Act, the Central Committee of the Communist Party of South Africa decided by majority vote, without consulting the membership, to dissolve the party. In 1953 a section of the former membership reorganised themselves into the South African Communist Party for the purpose of carrying on illegal work and participating in the (then) legal mass organisations (A. Lerumo, *Fifty Fighting Years*, London, 1971, pp. 91, 97). The abbreviation 'SACP' will be used to refer to both these organisations, which for practical purposes are one and the same. Thus Lerumo's book, published in 1971, ascribes a history of fifty years to 'the Communist Party', not a history of eighteen years.

4 We may note in passing that even the 'nationalistic' basis of the SACP stance is confused. It is not clear whether the South African population is made up of two 'nations' ('white' and 'non-white') or four ('white', 'African', 'coloured' and 'Indian') (PCP, pp. 24–5). For an attempt by the SACP in 1950 to reconcile this contradiction, see Gerhart (1978, p. 87n.).

6 Industrial organisation

1 Such measures imply splitting up the African industrial unions into separate unions for more and less skilled workers. The authors of *The Durban Strikes* (IIE) draw a similar conclusion but in less open terms. They endorse the view of van der Horst

that 'it is the function of Governments to govern and to provide
a framework to ensure that employers' and employees' actions
conform to the public interest' (*The Durban Strikes*, p. 190). The
crucial point is that in a capitalist state it is the employers who
determine very largely what is meant by 'the public interest'. Maree,
in an otherwise detailed discussion of the Durban strikes, fails to
deal with this fundamental issue (See J. Maree, 'Seeing Strikes in
Perspective', *South African Labour Bulletin*, vol. 2, nos 9–10,
May–June 1976).

7 The Durban strikes

1 It is true that the IIE devotes a chapter to the 'Political Economy
of Labour'. A detailed criticism of this chapter will not be
attempted here. Suffice it to note that the study is confined to
the classical liberal exercise of saving South African capitalism
from itself. The authors accept that reform must take place at
the expense of the white working class and 'property-owners'
in order to maintain 'saving' and 'growth' (i.e. profits) (p. 152).
They then look for 'some institutionalised way' of resolving the
conflict between capital and labour (p. 153) and see trade unionism
as an important means of preventing strikes and 'institutionalising
conflict' (p. 154). The chapter ends on the following note (p. 155):

> The solutions which we have suggested for some of South
> Africa's industrial and social problems necessarily involve
> redressing, to some extent, the great imbalance in the
> distribution of wealth and power between Black and White,
> and as such are perhaps not what, all other things being
> equal, the Whites would opt for. But all other things are far
> from being equal. To quote Deputy-Minister Heunis once
> more: 'Die blanke mag dalk selfs vind dat die beste belegging
> wat hy kan maak die belegging is wat 'n beter toekoms vir die
> nie-blanke verseker en 'n gesonde samelewing in Suid-Afrika
> behou.' ('The whites may even find that the best investment
> they can make is that investment that will ensure a better
> future for the non-white and retain a healthy community in
> South Africa.')

2 The IIE mentions two other registered unions, the Furniture and
Allied Workers' Industrial Union and the South African Tin
Workers' Union, which attempted to intervene but were rejected
by employers (IIE, 1974, pp. 44–5).
3 IIE (1974, p. 93). It should be explained that in the eyes of the
employers, this went to show 'how extraordinarily efficient the
intimidators were, to be able to exercise their control silently and
in the presence of the police' (*ibid*).

8 From Durban to Soweto

1 *Ibid*., pp. 89–90. Graaff finds it 'rather surprising' that *'four times as many works committee workers as others complain about the material conditions at work* . . . and furthermore twice as many works committee workers as others complain about the conditions of service'. This, she believes, suggests that works committees are not only ineffective but are 'possibly even a stumbling block in the processes of channelling and attending to grievances' (p. 90). It should also be considered, on the other hand, that a more critical spirit is likely to prevail among workers who have chosen works committees as opposed to liaison committees, and relations with employers are likely to be more strained.

2 See section 67, Industrial Conciliation Act, no. 28 of 1956, which authorises the disclosure of information by any industrial council official to any other person 'for the purpose of this Act'. According to the *South African Labour Bulletin* the prohibition relates to trade secrets only (Clarke, 1976, p. 8).

3 Heinemann Electric of New Jersey, USA, held a 30 per cent share in the Johannesburg company. The remainder was owned by the Barlow Rand corporation (*FM*, 2 April 1976).

9 Soweto

1 On 17 June 1976 the judge-president of the Transvaal, Mr Justice Cillie, was appointed as a one-man commission of inquiry to investigate the disturbances in Soweto.

2 Among those arrested for their part in the uprising were a well-known rugby player, a former beauty queen and the son of the Chief Minister of Bophuta Tswana (*Cape Times*, 9 October 1976; *Die Burger*, 6 November 1976; 4 December 1976).

10 State reaction

1 Quotations are from the report in the *South African Labour Bulletin*, May–June 1976. Mr Frame referred more than once to a meeting where management had been outvoted by the workers and abided by that decision. According to other evidence, however, no voting took place on the committee (*ibid*., p. 52).

2 *Department of Labour Manpower Survey*, no. 9, April 1971, as reproduced in Wolpe (1976, p. 231). 35,900 African workers were at that stage classified as 'skilled'.

3 Section 1, General Law Amendment Act, No. 94 of 1974. The penalty is a fine not exceeding R2,000, or imprisonment not exceeding two years, or both.

4 However, among the less visible forms of state action against political opponents is the interception and scrutiny of their mail

in terms of section 118 of the Post Office Act. According to
F. J. Theron, Deputy Postmaster-General, police requests for the
opening of mail in the interests of security are 'a fairly common
occurrence' (*Cape Times*, 11 February 1977).

11 Liberal reaction

1 In January 1978 the rapport between Inkatha and the Labour
   Party culminated in a formal alliance. Also involved in this alliance
   was a like-minded group from the South African Indian Council
   (*Star IAW*, 14 January 1978).
2 Grobbelaar, the general secretary, himself gives no other reason
   for this important decision (Coetzee, 1976, p. 183). It has been
   suggested that TUCSA's reasons for re-admitting African unions
   were not only political but also financial. The 1972–4 TUCSA
   annual reports showed a deficit of almost R16,000, while the
   affiliation of one African union alone, the National Union of
   Clothing Workers, brought in R7,200 (*FM*, 19 November 1976).
3 H. Bolton, a member of the TUCSA executive and secretary of
   the Garment Workers' Industrial Union (Natal), announced her
   union's withdrawal from TUCSA as a result of this incident. Later,
   however, it was announced that she had accepted TUCSA's reasons
   for not participating in the meeting (SRR, 1974, p. 320). For an
   account of how the decision to withdraw from TUCSA could be
   taken and reversed in the space of a single week, see R. E. Braverman,
   'African Trade Unions and the Liberation Struggle', *African
   Communist*, 1st qtr, 1975, p. 54).
4 *Review of African Political Economy*, September–December 1976,
   pp. 117–18. Considerable discrepancies exist as to the membership
   and other details of the unregistered trade unions. Thus, according
   to the South African Institute of Race Relations, the Transport
   and General Workers' Union in Durban was formed in 1975 and
   had 1,500 members as at 31 August 1975. According to the
   Review of African Political Economy, it had 18,000 members in
   July 1974.
5 The South African Institute of Race Relations served as
   distributing agent for trade-union literature produced by the
   UTP (SRR, 1975, p. 209).

12 Organisation of the workers' movement

1 A. Callinicos and J. Rogers, *Southern Africa after Soweto*,
   London, 1977.
2 Wrongly suggesting, however, that these shifts resulted from
   growing experience and understanding. The major shifts in the
   history of the party, those of 1928, 1935 and 1941, were dictated

by shifts in the position of the Communist International (see Roux, 1964, pp. 255–6).

3 See the cases of Suttner (*F*, November 1975, p. 3; January 1976, p. 6); Rabkin and Cronin (*F*, November 1976, p. 11); Maholobela (*F*, January 1977, p. 11); Mbala (*F*, May 1977, p. 14) Malatji and Zwane (*ibid*.); Gwamanda (*F*, July 1977, p. 2); Mati (*F*, January 1978, p. 6).

4 *F*, January 1978, p. 6.

5 Cf. the cases of Seloane and Ngalo (*F*, November 1975, p. 3); Tshabalala (*F*, May 1976, p. 12). In both cases the accused had been influenced by ANC broadcasts from Zambia urging people to volunteer for military training.

6 See the cases of Nkosi, Mothlante and Mose (*F*, March 1977, p. 13); Phala and others (the 'Springs six') (*F*, July 1977, p. 3; January 1978, p. 6); Liza (*F*, January 1978, p. 8); Motloung and Mahlangu (*F*, November 1977, p. 8; January 1978, p. 7).

7 See the cases of Maleka and Thathe (*F*, January 1977, p. 8); Ndebele and others (*ibid*.); Shubane and Ndzanga (*F*, July 1977, p. 2); Tinto (*F*, November 1977, p. 6); Zimu and others (*F*, January 1978, p. 6); Mdingi (*ibid*.); Qumbella and Huna (*ibid*., p. 7).

13 Conclusion

1 The argument that follows should not be confused with the Poulantzian theory of 'fractions of capital', as applied to South Africa by R. Davies, D. Kaplan, M. Morris and D. O'Meara, 'Class Struggle and the Periodization of the State in South Africa', *Review of African Political Economy*, no. 7, September–December 1976. For a critique of this theory, see S. Clarke, 'Capital, Fractions of Capital and the State: Neo-Marxist Analyses of the South African State', *Capital and Class*, no. 5, 1978.

2 The policies of the European social-democratic and communist parties may be consulted in this regard.

Bibliography

Books and brochures

African National Congress (no date), *Forward to Freedom*, Morogoro, Tanzania.

Agency for Industrial Mission (1976), *Another Blanket*, Horison, Transvaal.

Amnesty International (1978), *Political Imprisonment in South Africa*, London.

Attlee, C. R. (1937), *The Labour Party in Perspective*, London.

Austin, D. (1966), *Britain and South Africa*, Oxford.

Banks, J. A. (1974), *Trade Unionism*, London.

Benson, M. (1964), *On Trial for their Lives*, London.

Bernstein, H. (1978), *No. 46 – Steve Biko*, London.

Biko, S. (ed.) (1972b), *Black Viewpoint*, Durban.

Buthelezi, M. G. (1974), *White and Black Nationalism, Ethnicity and the Future of the Homelands*, Johannesburg.

Callinicos, A. and Rogers, J. (1977), *Southern Africa after Soweto*, London.

Carter, G. M. (1958), *The Politics of Inequality*, London.

Christelijk Nationaal Vakverbond (1977), *Delen of Nemen* (report on mission to South Africa).

Clegg, H. A. (1972), *The System of Industrial Relations in Great Britain*, Oxford.

Coetzee, J. A. G. (1976), *Industrial Relations in South Africa*, Cape Town.

Collins, P., Ensor, P., Hemson, D., Legassick, M. and Petersen, R. (1979), *The Workers' Movement and SACTU – A Struggle for Marxist Policies*, London.

Cope, R. K. (no date), *Comrade Bill*, Cape Town.

Counter Information Services (1977), *Black South Africa Explodes*, London.

Bibliography

Davidson, B., Slovo, J. and Wilkinson, A. R. (1976), *Southern Africa: The New Politics of Revolution*, Harmondsworth.
Davies, I. (1966), *African Trade Unions*, Harmondsworth.
D'Oliveira, J. (1977), *Vorster The Man*, Johannesburg.
Doxey, G. V. (1961), *The Industrial Colour Bar in South Africa*, Oxford.
Edelstein, M. L. (1972), *What Do Young Africans Think?*, Johannesburg.
Feit, E. (1971), *Urban Revolt in South Africa 1960-1964*, Evanston, Ill.
Forman, L. and Sachs, E. S. (1957), *The South African Treason Trial*, London.
Frankel, S. H. (1938), *Capital Investment in South Africa*, Oxford.
Galbraith, J. K. (1969), *The New Industrial State*, Harmondsworth.
Gerhart, G. M. (1978), *Black Power in South Africa*, Berkeley.
Gibson, J. T. R. (ed.) (1970), *Wille's Principles of South African Law*, 6th edn, Cape Town.
Gitlow, A. L. (1963), *Labor and Industrial Society*, Homewood, Ill.
Glass, Y. (no date), *Industrial Man in Southern Africa*, Johannesburg.
Gregory, T. (1962), *Ernest Oppenheimer and the Economic Development of South Africa*, Oxford.
Harmsen, G. and Reinalda, B. (1975), *Voor de bevrijding van de Arbeid*, Nijmegen.
Hellman, E. and Abrahams, L. (1949), *Handbook on Race Relations in South Africa*, Oxford.
Hepple, A. (1966), *South Africa, A Political and Economic History*, London.
Hepple, A. (1971), *South Africa: Workers under Apartheid*, London.
Hirson, B. (1979), *Year of Fire, Year of Ash*, London.
Hobson, J. A. (1938), *Imperialism, A Study*, London.
Horrell, M. (1961), *South African Trade Unionism*, Johannesburg.
Horrell, M. (1969), *South Africa's Workers*, Johannesburg.
Horst, S. T. van der (1942), *Native Labour in South Africa*, Oxford.
Horst, S. T. van der (1960), *The Economic Implications of Political Democracy*, Johannesburg.
Horwitz, R. (1967), *The Political Economy of South Africa*, London.
Houghton, D. H. (1973), *The South African Economy*, Oxford.
Hudson, W., Jacobs, G. F. and Biesheuvel, S. (1966), *Anatomy of South Africa*, Cape Town.
Hyman, R. (1971), *Marxism and the Sociology of Trade Unionism*, London.
Institute for Industrial Education (1974), *The Durban Strikes 1973*, Durban–Johannesburg.
International Defence and Aid Fund (1970), *South Africa: Trial by Torture*, London.

Johnstone, F. A. (1976), *Class, Race and Gold*, London.

Joubert, D. (1972), *Toe Witmense Arm Was*, Cape Town.

Kadalie, C. (1970), *My Life and the ICU*, London.

Kane-Berman, J. (1972), *Contract Labour in South-West Africa*, Johannesburg.

Karis, T. (1965), *The Treason Trial in South Africa*, Stanford.

Karis, T. and Carter, G. M. (eds.) (1972-7), *From Protest to Challenge*, 4 vols, Stanford.

Khoapa, B. (ed.) (1973), *Black Review 1972*, Durban.

Kiewiet, C. W. de (1937), *The Imperial Factor in South Africa*, Cambridge.

Kiewiet, C. W. de (1941), *A History of South Africa, Social and Economic*, Oxford.

Kleinschmidt, H. and McCarthy, M. (1974), *Arrest, Detention and Trials of Members and Supporters of SASO, BPC, BAWU, TECON*, Braamfontein.

Kock, A. de (1973), *Industrial Law of South Africa*, Cape Town.

Kohn, H. (1951), *The Idea of Nationalism*, New York.

Kooy, G. A., Albeda, W. A. and Kwant, R. C. (1969), *Apartheid en arbeidsbestel in Zuid-Afrika*, Bussum.

Kotze, D. A. (1975), *African Politics in South Africa 1964-1974*, London.

Kruger, D. W. (1960), *South African Parties and Policies*, London.

Kuper, L. (1965), *An African Bourgeoisie*, Yale.

Legassick, M. (1973), *Class and Nationalism in South African Protest: The South African Communist Party and the 'Native Republic' 1928-1934*, New York.

Legum, C. (1974), *African Contemporary Record, Annual Survey and Documents 1973-1974*, London.

Legum, C. and Legum, M. (1964), *South Africa: Crisis for the West*, London.

Leistner, G. M. E. (no date), *Ekonomiese Integrasie van Bantoe-arbeid*, Pretoria.

Leistner, G. M. E. (1968), *Enkele Ekonomiese Aspekte van Bantoe-volksverhuising en Trekarbeid in Suid-Afrika*, Pretoria.

Leistner, G. M. E. and Breytenbach, W. J. (1975), *The Black Worker of South Africa*, Pretoria.

Lenin, V. I. (1951 edn), *The Right of Nations to Self-Determination*, Moscow.

Lerumo, A. (1971), *Fifty Fighting Years*, London.

Mandela, N. (1963), *We Accuse*, London.

Manganyi, N. C. (1973), *Being Black in the World*, Johannesburg.

Marais, J. S. (1939), *The Cape Coloured People 1652-1937*, London.

Marquard, L. (1962), *The Peoples and Policies of South Africa*, Oxford.

Bibliography

Marx, K. (1974 edn), *Capital*, vol. I, London.
Marx–Engels, *Werke* (1974), Berlin.
Mathews, A. S. (1971), *Law, Order and Liberty in South Africa*, Cape Town.
Matthews, D. and Apthorpe, R. (1958), *Social Relations in Central African Industry*, Lusaka.
Merwe, H. W. van der and Welsh, D. (eds) (1972), *Student Perspectives on South Africa*, Cape Town.
Milton, J. R. L. and Fuller, N. M. (1971), *South African Criminal Law and Procedure*, Cape Town.
Ministers' Fraternal of Langa, Guguletu and Nyanga (no date), *Role of Riot Police in the Burnings and Killings, Nyanga, Cape Town, Christmas 1976.*
Mkele, N. (1961), *The African Middle Class*, Johannesburg.
Mnguni (pseudonym) (1953), *Three Hundred Years*, Lansdowne, Cape.
National Party of the Cape Province (1960), *Konstitusie*, Cape Town.
Neumark, S. D. (1957), *Economic Influences on the South African Frontier 1652–1836*, Stanford.
Nkondo, G. M. (ed.) (1976), *Turfloop Testimony*, Johannesburg.
Owen, K. (1964), *Summary of the Report of the Committee on Foreign Africans*, Johannesburg.
Paton, A. (1964), *Hofmeyr*, Oxford.
Pelzer, A. N. (ed.) (1963), *Verwoerd aan die Woord*, Johannesburg.
Rabie, J. (1960), *Die Evolusie van Nasionalisme*, Cape Town.
Rabie, J. (1964), *Referate Gelewer by die Volkskongres oor Kommunisme*, Pretoria.
Reynolds, L. G. (1974), *Labor Economics and Labor Relations*, Englewood Cliffs, N.J.
Robertson, J. (1971), *Liberalism in South Africa 1948–1963*, Oxford.
Roux, E. (1944), *S. P. Bunting, A Political Biography*, Cape Town.
Roux, E. (1964), *Time Longer Than Rope*, Wisconsin.
Sachs, A. (1973), *Justice in South Africa*, Brighton.
Sachs, B. (1961), *The Road From Sharpeville*, London.
Sachs, E. S. (1952), *The Choice Before South Africa*, London.
Sachs, E. S. (1957), *Rebels' Daughters*, London.
Sampson, A. (1958), *The Treason Cage*, London.
Schaeffer, M. and Heyne, J. F. (1968), *Nywerheidsreg in Suid-Afrika*, Pretoria.
Schlemmer, L. (1973), *Privilege, Prejudice and Parties*, Johannesburg.
Sills, L. (ed.) (1968), *International Encyclopedia of the Social Sciences*, New York.
Simons, H. J. and Simons, R. E. (1969), *Class and Colour in South Africa 1850–1950*, Harmondsworth.

South African Congress of Trade Unions (1977), *Economic Crisis in South Africa*, London.

South African Congress of Trade Unions (1978), *Looking Forward*, London.

South African Foundation (1962), *South Africa in the Sixties*.

South African Institute of Race Relations (annual), *A Survey of Race Relations in South Africa*, Johannesburg.

Spence, J. E. (1965), *Republic Under Pressure*, Oxford.

Strangwayes-Booth, J. (1976), *A Cricket in the Thorn Tree*, London.

Suid-Afrikaanse Buro vir Rasse-Aangeleenthede (1951), *Die Naturel in die Suid-Afrikaanse Nywerheidslewe*, Pretoria.

Temkin, B. (1976), *Gatsha Buthelezi*, Cape Town.

Thomas, W. H. (ed.) (1974), *Labour Perspectives on South Africa*, Cape Town.

Thompson, L. M. (1966), *Politics in the Republic of South Africa*, Boston–Toronto.

Toit, B. du (1978), *Ukubamba Amadolo*, London.

Toit, M. A. du (1976), *South African Trade Unions*, Johannesburg.

Trotsky, L. (1962 edn), *The Permanent Revolution and Results and Prospects*, London.

United Nations, Unit on Apartheid, (1969), *Repressive Legislation in the Republic of South Africa*, New York.

Unity Movement of South Africa (1969), *The Revolutionary Road for South Africa*, Lusaka.

Venter, A. J. (1974), *Coloured*, Cape Town.

Villiers, D. de (1970), *The Case for South Africa*, London.

Villiers, H. H. W. de (1964), *Rivonia*, Johannesburg.

Vyver, J. D. van der (1975), *Die Beskerming van die Menseregte in Suid-Afrika*, Cape Town.

Walker, E. A. (1957), *A History of South Africa*, London.

Walker, E. A. (ed.) (1963), *The Cambridge History of the British Empire*, vol. VIII, Cambridge.

Walker, I. L. and Weinbren, B. (1961), *2,000 Casualties*, Johannesburg.

Wilson, F. (1972a), *Labour in the South African Gold Mines 1911–1969*, Cambridge.

Wilson, F. (1972b), *Migrant Labour*, Johannesburg.

Wilson, M. and Thompson, L. M. (eds) (1969, 1971), *The Oxford History of South Africa*, 2 vols, Oxford.

Wolfson, J. G. E. (1976), *Turmoil at Turfloop*, Johannesburg.

Bibliography

Articles

Adam, H. (1973), 'The Rise of Black Consciousness in South Africa', *Race*, October 1973.

African National Congress (1976), 'Conspirators Expelled', *Sechaba*, no. 2, 1976.

Altman, J. R. (1976), 'Leadership Problems of Registered Trade Unions', *South African Labour Bulletin*, September 1976.

Bengu, S. M. (1975), 'The National Cultural Liberation Movement', *Reality*, September 1975.

Biko, S. (1972a), 'Black Consciousness and the Quest for True Humanity', *Reality*, March 1972.

'The Black Renaissance Convention', *Reality*, May 1975.

Braverman, R. E. (1975), 'African Trade Unions and the Liberation Struggle', *African Communist*, no. 1, 1975.

Budlender, G. M. (1975), 'Administrative Rule of African Workers', *Responsa Meridiana*, 1975.

Bundy, C. (1975), 'The Abolition of the Masters and Servants Act', *South African Labour Bulletin*, May–June 1975.

Clarke, S. (1978), 'Capital, "Fractions" of Capital and the State: Neo-Marxist Analyses of the South African State', *Capital and Class*, no. 5.

'Conac Engineering and the Department of Labour', *South African Labour Bulletin*, May–June 1976.

Davies, R., Kaplan, D., Morris, M. and O'Meara, D. (1976), 'Class Struggle and the Periodization of the State in South Africa', *Review of African Political Economy*, September–December 1976.

Davis, D. (1975), 'African Trade Unions – Reformist or Revolutionary?', *African Communist*, no. 62, 1975.

Douwes-Dekker, L., Hemson, D., Kane-Berman, J. S., Lever, J. and Schlemmer, L. (1975), 'Case Studies in African Labour Action in South Africa and Namibia', in Sandbrook, R. and Cohen, R. (eds) (1975), *The Development of an African Working Class*, London.

Dugard, J. (1974), 'The Political Trial, Some Special Considerations', *South African Law Journal*.

Duvenhage, B. (1957), 'Nie-Blanke Arbeid as Een van die Kernvraagstukke in ons Rasse-verhoudinge', *Journal of Racial Affairs*, October 1957.

February, V. (1976), 'From Ordinance Fifty Until the Erika Theron Commission', *African Perspectives*, no. 1, 1976.

Glass and Allied Workers Union (1977), 'Report on the Strike at Armourplate Safety Glass', *South African Labour Bulletin*, June–July 1977.

Graaff, J. (1976), 'Interviews with African Workers in Cape Town', *South African Labour Bulletin*, September 1976.

Hahlo, K. G. (1969), 'A European–African Worker Relationship in South Africa', *Race*, July 1969.

Hemson, D. (1978), 'Trade Unionism and the Struggle for Liberation in South Africa', *Capital and Class*, no. 6.

Horwood, O. P. F. (1962), 'Is Minimum Wage Legislation the Answer for South Africa?', *South African Journal of Economics*, June 1962.

Houghton, D. H. (1961), 'Land Reform in the Bantu Areas and its Effect upon the Urban Labour Market', *South African Journal of Economics*, September 1961.

Innes, D. and Plaut, M. (1977), 'Class Struggle and Economic Development in South Africa, The Inter-War Years', University of London, Institute of Commonwealth Studies, Discussion Paper.

Johns, S. (1973), 'Obstacles to Guerilla Warfare', *Journal of Modern African Studies*, 1973.

Johns, S. W. (1967), 'The Birth of Non-White Trade Unionism in South Africa', *Race*, October 1967.

Kachelhoffer, G. C. (1974), 'Die Wet op die Reëling van Bantoe-arbeidsverhoudinge', *Tydskrif vir Hedendaagse Romeins-Hollandse Reg*.

Kantor, B. S. and Kenny, H. F. (1976), 'The Poverty of Neo-Marxism: The Case of South Africa', *Journal of Southern African Studies*, October 1976.

Kessel, D. (1972), 'Non-White Wage Increases and Inflation in South Africa', *South African Journal of Economics*, December 1972.

Kingsley, S. F. (1950), 'Die Oorname van die Dienskontrakregistra-siestelsel deur Plaaslike Besture in die Transvaal', *Journal of Racial Affairs*, October 1950.

Langa, A. (1977), 'New Trends in African Nationalism', *African Communist*, no. 2, 1977.

Legassick, M. (1974), 'Legislation, Ideology and Economy in Post-1948 South Africa', *Journal of Southern African Studies*, October 1974.

Legassick, M. and Innes, D. (1977), 'Capital Restructuring and Apartheid, a Critique of Constructive Engagement', *African Affairs*, October 1977.

Leistner, G. M. E. (1967), 'Foreign Bantu Workers in South Africa', *South African Journal of Economics*, March 1967.

Leon, S. (1971), 'The Coloured People and the Labour Party of South Africa', *Reality*, May 1971.

Lewis, D. (1976), 'Registered Trade Unions and Western Cape Workers', *South African Labour Bulletin*, September 1976.

Leys, R. (1975), 'South African Gold Mining in 1974', *African Affairs*, April 1975.

Lipton, M. (1976), 'British Investment in South Africa: Is Constructive
Engagement Possible?', *South African Labour Bulletin*, October 1976.

Mackintosh, P. (1970), 'When Thieves Fall Out', *African Communist*,
no. 1, 1970.

Macrobert, J. M. J. (1976), 'Penal Sanctions Operating in the Sphere
of African Employment', *Responsa Meridiana*.

Mafeje, A. (1978), 'Soweto and its Aftermath', *Review of African
Political Economy*, 1978.

Maree, J. (1976), 'Seeing Strikes in Perspective', *South African Labour
Bulletin*, May–June 1976.

Merwe, P. F. S. J. van der (1971), 'Die Rol van Nie-Blanke Arbeid in
Blanke Suid-Afrika', *Journal of Racial Affairs*, October 1971.

Mhlongo, S. (1974), 'Black Workers' Strikes in South Africa', *New
Left Review*, January–February 1974.

Mhlongo, S. (1975), 'An Analysis of the Classes in South Africa',
Race and Class.

Mkhize, M. (1974), 'Thoughts on Race Consciousness', *African
Communist*, no. 3, 1974.

Molapo, B. (1976), 'On the National Question', *African Communist*,
no. 3, 1976.

Molteno, R. (1970), 'South African Election: An Analysis', *South
African Outlook*, July 1970.

Morand, C. A. (1975), 'Report to the International Commission of
Jurists on the Black Consciousness Trial', mimeo, Geneva.

Morris, M. and Kaplan, D. (1976), 'Labour Policy in a State
Corporation', *South African Labour Bulletin*, April 1976.

Morris, M. and Kaplan, D. (1976), 'Selby Msimang and Trade Union
Organisation in the 1920's', *Reality*, March 1977.

Morris, M. and Kaplan, D. (1976), 'Nautilus Marine: A Case Study of
Worker–Management Conflict', *South African Labour Bulletin*,
May–June 1976.

Ngcobo, R. P. (1975), 'Twenty Years of the Freedom Charter', *African
Communist*, no. 4, 1975.

Ngwenya, J. (1976), 'A Further Contribution on the National Question',
African Communist, no. 4, 1976.

Niekerk, B. van (1975), 'From Beyond the Grave', *South African Law
Journal*.

Nkosi, Z. (1977), 'The Lessons of Soweto', *African Communist*, no. 1,
1977.

Nolutshungu, S. C. (1972), 'The South African General Election of
1970', *African Review*.

O'Meara, D. (1978), 'Analysing Afrikaner Nationalism', *African Affairs*,
January 1978.

Rensburg, P. F. S. J. van (1965), 'Aspekte van Bantoe-arbeid in Blanke
Dorpsgebiede', *Journal of Racial Affairs*, October 1965.

Rhoodie, N. J. (1965), 'Sosiologiese Probleme wat gepaard gaan met die Gebruik van Bantoe-arbeid in Blanke Gebiede', *Journal of Racial Affairs*, October 1965.

Sisacho, D. S. (1976), 'Africanisation and Class Struggle', *African Communist*, no. 1, 1976.

Slovo, J. (1976), article in Davidson, B., Slovo, J. and Wilkinson, A. R. (1976), *Southern Africa: The New Politics of Revolution*, Harmondsworth.

South African Communist Party (1963), 'The Road to South African Freedom, Programme of the South African Communist Party', *African Communist*, January–March 1963.

South African Communist Party (1976), 'The Enemy Hidden Under the Same Colour', *African Communist*, no. 2, 1976.

South African Communist Party (1977), 'The Way Forward from Soweto', *African Communist*, no. 3, 1977.

Steenkamp, W. F. J. (1962), 'Bantu Wages in South Africa', *South African Journal of Economics*, June 1962.

Steenkamp, W. F. J. (1971), 'Labour Policies for Growth during the Seventies', *South African Journal of Economics*, June 1971.

Toit, D. du (1978), 'The White Workers in South Africa', *African Perspectives*, no. 2, 1978.

Toussaint (pseudonym) (1976), 'Black Bankers – Friends or Enemies of Liberation?', *African Communist*, no. 1, 1976.

Toussaint (pseudonym) (1978), 'Class and Nation in the South African Revolution', *African Communist*, no. 1, 1978.

Venter, F. (1975), 'Bantoeburgerskap en Tuislandburgerskap', *Tydskrif vir Hedendaagse Romeins-Hollandse Reg*.

Warwick, P. (1976), 'Black Industrial Protest on the Witwatersrand 1901–1902', *South African Labour Bulletin*, April 1976.

Webster, E. (1974), 'Background to the Supply and Control of Labour in the South African Gold Mines', *South African Labour Bulletin*, November 1974.

Welsh, D. (1976), 'Inkatha', *Reality*, March 1976.

Wentzel, J. (1977), 'Black United Front', *Reality*, July 1977.

Williams, M. (1975), 'An Analysis of South African Capitalism', *Bulletin of the Conference of Socialist Economists*, February 1975.

Wilson, F. (1975), 'Unresolved Issues in the South African Economy', *South African Journal of Economics*, December 1975.

Wolpe, H. (1972), 'Capitalism and Cheap Labour in South Africa', *Economy and Society*.

Wolpe, H. (1976), 'The "White Working Class" in South Africa', *Economy and Society*.

Zanzolo, A. (1963), 'The Theory of the South African Revolution', *African Communist*, January–March 1963.

Bibliography

Official publications

Government Gazette, Government Printer, Pretoria, periodical.
Report of the Commission of Inquiry into Labour Legislation, Government Printer, Pretoria, 1979.
Report of the Transvaal Labour Commission, His Majesty's Stationery Office, 1904.
South African Statistics, 1974, 1976, Government Printer, Pretoria.
Union Statistics for Fifty Years, Government Printer, Pretoria, 1960.

Name index

Abraham, Eric, 353
Adam, H., 166, 173, 174, 178
Albeda, W. A., *see* Kooy, Albeda and Kwant
Albertyn, Chris, 353
Altman, J. R., 221, 234
Anderson, Gavin, 352
Andrews, W. H., 96, 460
Attlee, Clement, 72
Austin, D., 162

Ballinger, Mrs, *see* Hodgson, Margaret
Ballinger, W. G., 113–15
Banks, J. A., 79
Baskin, Jeremy, 353
Batty, A. F., 102
Biesheuvel, S., *see* Hudson, Jacobs and Biesheuvel
Biko, Steve, 173–4, 175, 177, 178, 360, 407
Blerk, Wilma van, 353
Bloch, Graeme, 353
Bolton, H., 262
Bonner, P., 111–12
Botha, General Louis, 88, 89
Botha, Pik, 27
Breakspear, manager at Armour-plate Safety Glass, 292–3
Brouwer, B., secretary of Boiler-makers' Society, 389
Brown, Crawford, 101
Brown, Forrester, 101
Budlender, Debbie, 353

Budlender, Geoffrey, 356
Bunting, S. P., 90
Buthelezi, Chief Gatsha, 166, 168–70, 176, 240, 290, 297, 312, 373–9, 383, 385, 386–7, 429, 437–8, 446, 449
Buthelezi, Dr Manas, 404, 406

Callinicos, A. and Rogers, J., 415, 417
Carter, G. M., 151, 152
Carter, President J., 369
Centlivres, Chief Justice, 130
Chamberlain, Joseph, 44
Champion, A. W. G., ICU leader, 107, 109–10, 113–15
Cheadle, H., 352
Chitja, S., 229
Clarke, S., 283
Coetzee, J. A. G., 11, 48, 49, 52, 60, 81, 83, 95, 99, 105, 106, 111–12, 217, 219–20, 221, 226, 232, 233, 388, 396
Cohen, Gideon, 353
Cope, R. K., 35, 44, 50, 88, 94, 460
Copelyn, John, 353
Craddock, Sir John, 19
Cresswell, F. H. P., 59, 96
Cronjé, Dr F., 254
Curtis, Jeanette, 352

Davidson, Mr Justice, 426
Davies, R., 40, 89

Name index

Davis, D., 352
Dawie, journalist, 328, 329
Diedrichs, Dr N., 153
Dladla, B., member of Kwazulu
government, 386
Dlamini, Stephen, 358–9, 421
D'Oliveira, J., 131, 138
Dones, Charles, 100
Douwes-Dekker, Loet, 11, 352,
395–6; et al., 262
Doxey, G. V., 13–14, 20, 28, 29,
46, 51, 65
Dreyer, Colonel J. G., 358

Edelstein, M. L., 179
Eglin, C., leader of PRP, 159, 376
Enthoven, D., Progressive MP, 376

Favish, Judy, 353
Feit, E., 181–2, 205, 207
Feldberg, M., Professor, 369
Forman, L. and Sachs, E. S., 127,
145
Frame, A., 332–3
Frankel, S. H., 6
Frankish, John, 353

Gibson, J. T. R., 119
Gitlow, A. L., 71, 80, 83
Glass, Y., 4, 55–6
Graaff, Janet, 274–5
Grobbelaar, A., 255, 390–1
Grobler, C. P., 49, 83, 221, 226,
388
Gumede, Michael, 358
Gwala, Harry, 358, 425–6

Hahlo, K. G., 56
Harmsen, G. and Reinalda, B., 10,
11
Haroun, Imam, 359
Heerden, Major van, 278–9
Hemson, D., 352
Hepple, A., 58, 229
Hertzog, Dr A., 153
Hertzog, J. B. M., 151, 152
Hlongwane, J., 219
Hlongwane, Nicholas, 392–3
Hobson, J. A., 4, 73

Hodgson, Margaret (later Mrs Bal-
linger), 108
Hofmeyer, Willie, 353
Hofmeyr, Jan Hendrik, 18, 157
Horn, Pat, 353
Horrell, Muriel, 47, 115, 226–31
Horst, S. T. van der, 7, 19, 21, 33,
35, 38, 48, 60, 61–2, 63, 74
Horwitz, R., 25, 27
Houghton, D. H., 6, 17, 25, 26–7,
247–9
Hoxie, Professor, 80
Hudson, W., Jacobs, G. F. and
Biesheuvel, S., 145
Hurley, Denis, Archbishop of
Durban, 356
Hyman, R., 80, 81

Jabavu, A. M., 109
Jacobs, G. F., see Hudson, Jacobs
and Biesheuvel
Jansen, Mrs A., 380
Johns, S., 205, 207
Johns, S. W., 111
Johnstone, F. A., 20, 47, 51, 52–3
Joubert, D., 52, 63

Kadalie, Clements, 96, 102–3,
106–7, 108–16, 232
Kane-Berman, J., 77
Kaplan, D., see Morris and Kaplan
Karis, T., 128–9
Khoapa, Bennie A., 174
Kiewiet, C. W. de, 3–4, 5, 7, 10,
16, 17, 62, 91
Kingsley, S. F., 123
Koch, W. F., 222
Kock, A. de, 64, 214
Koka, D., 177
Kooy, G. A., Albeda, W. A. and
Kwant, R. C., 76
Kotane, Moses, 116
Kotze, D. A., 123, 165, 167, 168,
169, 170, 173, 176, 177, 179,
181
Kotze, Theo, 355
Koza, D., 149
Krause, F. E. T., 61
Kruger, D. W., 131, 155, 156, 158

480

Subject index

Page references in italics are to the tables